AQA PSYCHOLOGY

KAIRAYUKI MATSUNAGA

To Clementine with love

The roots of education are bitter, but the fruit is sweet.

(Aristotle, 384–322 BC)

AQA PSYCHOLOGY

AS and A-level Year 1

Sixth Edition

Michael W. Eysenck

LONDON AND NEW YORK

First edition published by Psychology Press 2000 as Eysenck, M. & Flanagan, C., *Psychology for AS Level*

Fifth edition published by Psychology Press 2012

Sixth edition published 2015
by Psychology Press

Published 2016 by Routledge
2 Park Square, Milton Park, Abingdon, Oxon OX14 4RN
711 Third Avenue, New York, NY 10017, USA

Routledge is an imprint of the Taylor & Francis Group, an informa business

British Library Cataloguing in Publication Data
A catalogue record for this book is available from the British Library

Library of Congress Cataloging-in-Publication Data
Eysenck, Michael W.
AQA psychology : AS and A-level year 1 / Michael W. Eysenck. —
Sixth edition.
pages cm
Includes bibliographical references and index.
1. Psychology—Examinations, questions, etc. I. Title.
BF78.E97 2015
150.76—dc23
2014048885

ISBN: 978-1-138-90209-1 (pbk)

Typeset in Goudy
by Apex CoVantage, LLC

Contents

About the Author

Michael W. Eysenck is one of the best-known psychologists in Europe. He is a Professorial Fellow at Roehampton University. He is also Emeritus Professor and Honorary Fellow at Royal Holloway, University of London. He is especially interested in cognitive psychology (about which he has written several books) and most of his research focuses on the role of cognitive factors in anxiety within normal and clinical populations.

He has published nearly 50 books. His previous textbooks published by Psychology Press include *Psychology for AS Level (5th Edn)* (2012), *Psychology for A2 Level* (2009), *A2 Psychology: Key Topics (2nd Edn)* (2006), *Cognitive Psychology: A Student's Handbook (7th Edn)* (with Mark Keane) (2015), *Memory (2nd Edn)* (with Alan Baddeley and Michael Anderson) (2015), *Simply Psychology (3rd Edn)* (2012), *Fundamentals of Psychology* (2009), *Fundamentals of Cognition (2nd Edn)* (2012), *Psychology: An International Perspective* (2004), *Perspectives on Psychology* (1994), and *Individual Differences: Normal and Abnormal* (1994). He has also written several articles on topics within the AS Psychology specification for the journal *Psychology Review*, and has given talks at numerous A-level conferences.

In his spare time, Michael Eysenck enjoys travelling, tennis, walking, croquet, and an occasional game of golf. He is a keen supporter of Manchester United Football Club.

The author and publisher are extremely grateful to Jo Wilcox, Evie Bentley and Craig Roberts for their help and expertise in updating this edition and the accompanying website.

AQA Psychology Companion Website

Web-based supplementary materials to accompany *AQA Psychology: AS and A-level Year 1*

The *AQA Psychology* companion website offers an array of supplementary materials for both students and teachers.

Student Resources include:

- Links to related websites and further reading.
- Flash cards to test definitions of key terms.
- A comprehensive chapter-by-chapter glossary of key terms used in the book.
- Discussion points.
- Interactive exercises.
- About the chapters: an introduction to the approach used and summary of the subject matter of each chapter.

Access to the Student Resources is freely available and free-of-charge.

Teacher Resources include:

- A PowerPoint presentation for each chapter, which can be used to support lectures.
- A testbank of multiple-choice questions.
- Exercises for use in the classroom.
- Weekly Teaching Plan.

Access to the Teacher Resources is restricted to teachers only by password protection. These Teacher Resources are free of charge to qualifying adopters.

Please visit www.psypress.com/cw/eysenck

Preparing for the Exam

1

Roz Brody, Evie Bentley, and Carol Benson

Studying psychology is both enjoyable and useful. Students of psychology not only gain knowledge that helps them understand themselves and others, they can also apply this knowledge to everyday life. So psychology can enable you to improve your memory, give you strategies for effective studying, and help you manage your stress and do well in your exams.

The study skills you need to be successful in exams are based on psychological principles involving learning and memory. So you should already be well placed to gain maximum advantage in the exam room! This chapter is divided into two sections that address your own study skills and the ways in which the AS exam will be assessed and marked.

This chapter is designed to take some of the stress out of the exam by giving you hints on how to study, and letting you know what the exam involves and what the examiners look for. You will probably return to this chapter as you work through the rest of the book.

This section will teach you how to develop your study skills, including increasing your motivation and improving reading skills using the SQ3R approach. There are also tips on how to manage your time to get the best results from your work. The next section of the chapter is on how to do well in the exam. In this section you will find out how to discover your own personal learning style, and how your performance in the exam will benefit from this knowledge. There is also information on what the examiners will be looking for, and how they award marks.

NOTE: At the start of each chapter there is a list of specification content. Check this list to see what you could be examined on.

HOW CAN I STUDY EFFECTIVELY?

Students of psychology should find it easy to develop good study skills because they are based on psychological principles. For example, study skills are designed to promote effective learning and remembering, and learning and memory are key areas within psychology. Study skills are also concerned with motivation and developing good work habits, and these also fall very much within psychology, although they are not part of your course. Most of what is involved in study skills is fairly obvious, so we will focus on detailed pieces of advice rather than on vague generalities (e.g. "work hard", "get focused").

Motivation

Most people find it hard to maintain a high level of motivation over long periods of time. We all know what happens. You start out with high ideals and work hard for the first few weeks. Then you have a bad week and/or lose your drive, and everything slips. What can you do to make yourself as motivated as possible? One psychological theory of motivation (Locke, 1968) suggested the following seven ways to set appropriate goals and maintain motivation:

1. You must set yourself a goal that is hard but achievable.
2. Once you have your goal, you need to commit yourself to it. Telling others about it can keep you motivated.

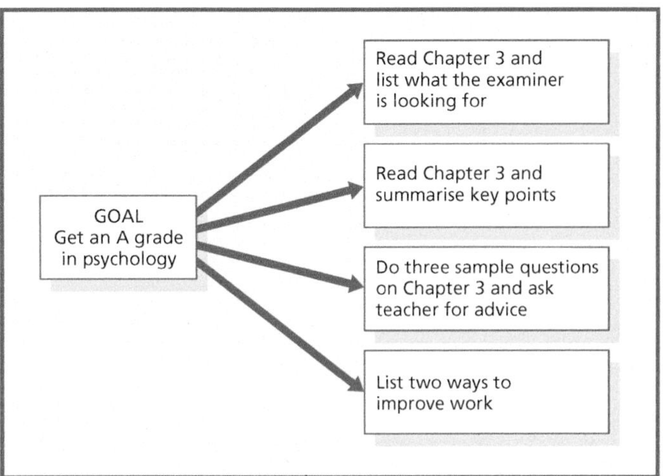

A major goal broken down into smaller goals.

3. You should focus on goals that can be achieved within a reasonable period of time (e.g. no more than a few weeks). Long-term goals like "I will get a grade A in my psychology exam" need to be broken down into a series of short-term goals (e.g. "I'll read and summarise the key points of Chapter 3 by Friday", "I'll do two timed answers on this chapter in the next week").
4. Set clear goals, and avoid vague goals.
5. Obtain feedback on your progress.
6. Once you have achieved your goal, move on to slightly harder goals.
7. Be honest about any setbacks and try to work out what went wrong, rather than simply saying it was bad luck. We can and do learn from our mistakes.

Your attempts to motivate yourself are only likely to be successful if you make use of all seven points. If you set yourself a very clear, medium-term goal, and obtain feedback, but the goal is impossible to achieve, then you are more likely to *reduce* rather than *increase* your level of motivation.

Reading skills

If you have ever turned over a few pages in a book and had no idea what you have just read, then this next section is for you. Studying psychology involves effective reading and being able to remember and use the information you have read. Morris (1979) described the **SQ3R** approach—Survey, Question, Read, Recite, Review, representing the five stages in effective reading—which has proved to be very useful. We will consider these five stages with respect to the task of reading a chapter.

KEY TERM

SQ3R: five strategies for effective reading: Survey, Question, Read, Recite, Review.

Survey

The Survey stage involves getting an overall view of the way in which the information in the chapter is organised. If there is a chapter summary, this will probably be the easiest way to achieve that goal. Otherwise, you could look through the chapter to find out what topics are discussed and how they are linked to each other.

Set a realistic goal.

Commit to achieving the goal.

Enjoy your achievement!

Question

The Question stage should be applied to fairly short parts of the chapter of no more than six pages. The essence of this stage is to get you to think about the questions you want answered by reading the text, such as "What does the S and Q in SQ3R stand for?"

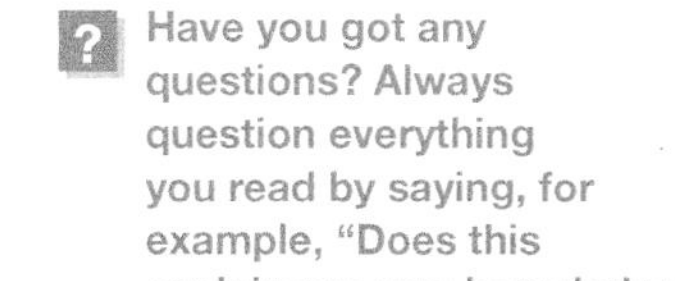

Have you got any questions? Always question everything you read by saying, for example, "Does this explain my own knowledge of the world?" or "Do I understand all the words?"

Read

While the Read stage obviously involves reading the text to answer your questions, it is also very important to integrate any new information with your pre-existing knowledge of the topic.

You might also want to use a highlighter pen to emphasise key points.

Recite

The Recite stage involves trying to remember all the key ideas that were contained in the part of the chapter you have been reading. Try explaining what you have just read to someone else. If you cannot remember some of the ideas, go back to the Read stage.

EXAM HINT

In order to succeed in exams, you must be able to recall the information you need. The Recite and Review stages of the SQ3R approach are designed to achieve precisely that.

Review

When you have read the entire chapter, you should Review the key ideas from the text and be able to combine the information from different parts of the chapter into a coherent structure. Producing a mind map of the key ideas can often help. If your mind seems a total blank you need to go back to the earlier stages in the reading process.

Time management

Studying effectively involves managing your time well. Often you may have good intentions at the start of the week, but as the time flies by you realise that the two or three essential pieces of work you were going to do haven't been tackled. And yet, when you know you will be extremely busy you often manage your time more effectively because you know that if you don't do the work now, there will be no time at the end of the week.

So what do you do with the 100 hours or more at your disposal each week? You probably only have some vague idea where most of the time goes. As time is such a valuable commodity, it is a good idea to make the most efficient use of it, as you will probably be surprised at how much time you tend to waste. Here are some suggestions on how to manage your time:

- Create a timetable of the times that are available and unavailable over a week. Now indicate which subjects you can study on different days, and how much time within each day you are going to spend on any subject.
- Decide what is, for you, a reasonable span of attention (possibly 30–40 minutes). Set aside a number of periods of time during the week for study. Make a commitment to yourself to use these periods for study.
- Note that the more of a habit studying becomes, the less effortful it will be, and the less resistant you will be to making a start.
- No one has limitless concentration. After initially high levels of concentration, the level decreases until the end is in sight. So make sure that the time you commit to studying is realistic. You can probably improve your level of concentration by including short (10-minute) rest periods. Remember to avoid distractions like the television in your study area (don't kid yourself that you can watch TV *and* study—reward yourself later with an hour slumped in front of the TV).
- During these study times, there will be a tendency to find other things to do (e.g. phoning a friend). This is where the hard part begins. You must try to be firm and say to yourself that this is time you have committed to studying, and that is what you are going to do. However, you will have time available later for other things. It is hard to do to start with, but it gets easier.

One motivational strategy is to reward yourself at regular intervals. For example, after you have read 10 pages or worked for an hour, have a cup of tea, go for a brief walk, or phone or text a friend. Make sure your rewards are for easily achievable goals—but not too easy!

Planning fallacy

Although you might have never heard of the **planning fallacy**, there is a good chance that you may have experienced it. Kahneman and Tversky (1979) defined the planning fallacy as "a tendency to hold a confident belief that one's own project will proceed as planned, even while knowing that the vast majority of similar projects have run late". In other words, we all kid ourselves that it will be easy despite knowing that, on previous occasions, we and other people have not managed to fulfil our planned intentions.

As we are psychologists, we might be interested to know if there is evidence to support this planning fallacy, and indeed there is. Buehler et al. (1994) found that, on average, students submitted a major piece of work 22 days later than they had predicted, even when they were specifically told that the purpose of the study was to examine the accuracy of people's predictions. Buehler et al. found that students were much better at predicting completion times for other students than for themselves. The reason for this is that they were more likely to use what is called "distributional" information (which comes from knowledge about similar tasks completed in the past) when making predictions about other students, whereas with themselves they tended to use "singular" information (related to the current task).

The testing effect

When students are revising for an exam, they often skim through their notes, discovering to their delight (or even surprise) that most of the material seems familiar. What this means is that they have reasonable recognition memory for the material. However, there is a large difference between *recognising* information as familiar and being able to produce it at will during an anxiety-inducing exam. To succeed in written exams, you must *recall* the information you need. As generations of students have discovered to their cost, good recognition memory for the information relevant to an exam is no guarantee at all that recall will be equally good.

KEY TERM

Planning fallacy: the false belief that a plan will be completed on time even though past experience suggests it won't.

This leads us neatly into the *testing effect*, which describes the best way to revise—by repeated testing rather than repeated study, the method used by many students. The testing effect was demonstrated by Roediger and Karpicke (2006). They gave students some text on a general scientific topic and asked them to memorise it, but they had to do this in a specific way.

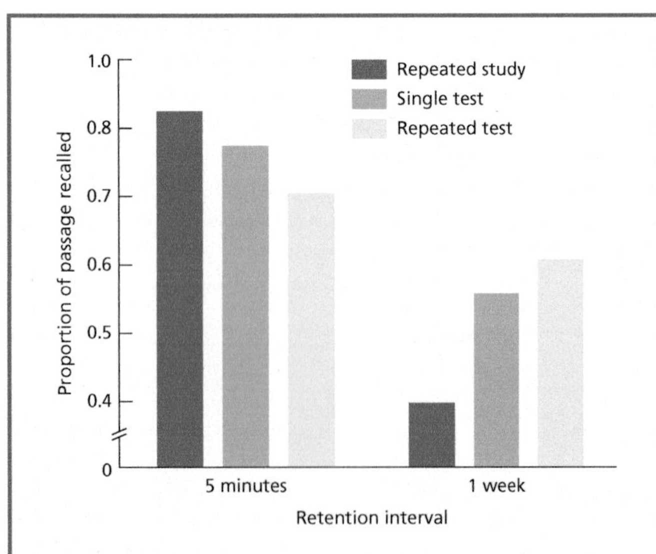

The results of Roediger and Karpicke's (2006) study on the testing effect.

- Group 1 (repeated study) were told to memorise the text by reading it through four times.
- Group 2 (single test) were told to memorise the text by reading it through three times and then trying to recall as much as they could (self test).
- Group 3 (repeated test) were told to memorise the text by reading it once and then giving themselves three self tests.

What did they find? Look at the graph on the left. It shows that repeated study works in the short term, but in the long term (after 1 week) repeated test proved a much more effective strategy. Most students "believe" in repeated study and in fact, in this experiment, the students in Group 1 (repeated *study* method) predicted they would do better than Group 3. In fact they did 50% worse than Group 3 (the repeated *test* method). So it would seem that repeated testing is better than repeated study.

How can we explain the testing effect? Bjork and Bjork (1992) argued that an excellent way to improve long-term memory is via effortful retrieval, as happened in the repeated test condition. "Effortful retrieval" means that your effort is focused on *recalling* the information rather than just repeatedly trying to remember it. The take-home message is that if you make the effort to recall information several times as you study it, this will make the information in question much more memorable in the long term.

? Why do many people fail to achieve work targets?

HOW CAN I DO WELL IN THE EXAM?

Very few students like exams, but there are a lot of strategies that you can use to make them less stressful, so that on the day of the exams you will be very keen to let the examiner know what you have learned about psychology.

Four key factors will help you do well in an exam:

1. Knowing how you learn.
2. Knowing what you will be examined on (*i.e. knowing the specification*).
3. Knowing how you will be assessed and what form the questions will take.
4. Knowing how to prepare for the exam and what to do in the examination room.

Knowing how you learn

Think about the strategies that work for you. Some students like summarising their notes onto cards. Others devise posters or put "post-its" around their room. Others find it much easier to learn information by discussing their ideas with a friend.

Try the quiz below to help you think about how you learn.

Look at the following questions and answer yes or no	YES	NO
1. I often see my notes in my head when I sit an exam.		
2. I can never seem to start my work.		
3. When I explain my ideas to someone else, they often become clearer to me.		
4. I find it easy to remember conversations word for word.		
5. If a friend phones me I'll stop working and chat for hours.		
6. I often say what I am writing down to myself.		
7. I find it easier to remember my notes when I highlight key points.		
8. I can remember my notes by repeating them over and over again to myself.		
9. I often look at my book, but nothing ever goes in.		
10. I like it when people ask me questions about psychology and I can explain things to them.		
11. I like using different coloured pens when making revision notes.		
12. I find it hard to work on my own.		
13. I can always find something else to do when I am meant to be studying.		
14. I can remember where things are on a page.		
15. I enjoy talking about psychology to my friends.		
16. I often hear my teacher's voice when I read through my notes.		

- If you answered yes to questions 1, 7, 11, and 14, you enjoy learning using a visual approach. Making posters, using "post-its" and coloured pens and highlighters will help you for the exam.
- If you answered yes to questions 2, 5, 9, and 13, you are easily distracted and find it hard to start work. You need to remove all distractions (e.g. mobile phone) and realise that it might take you 5–10 minutes to settle into doing the work. Focus on the task you have set yourself for a certain amount of time (e.g. 30 minutes) and then take a break.
- If you answered yes to questions 3, 10, 12, and 15, you enjoy learning in a social way. Working with a friend as you revise and discussing ideas will help you for the exam.
- If you answered yes to questions 4, 6, 8, and 16, you enjoy learning information using sound. Some students make recordings of the key points they need to remember, and then listen to them before they go to sleep.
- If you answered yes to a range of questions, you don't have a preferred method of learning information and may use a range of strategies to help you.

Knowing what you will be examined on

The AS Psychology exam is divided into *two* papers but it is essential to know which topics are assessed in each paper.

- Paper 1: Introductory topics
  - Social Influence
  - Memory
  - Attachment
- Paper 2: Psychology in context
  - Approaches to Psychology
  - Psychopathology
  - Research Methods

EXAM HINT

Read the specification—this will help you reduce the amount you need to revise!

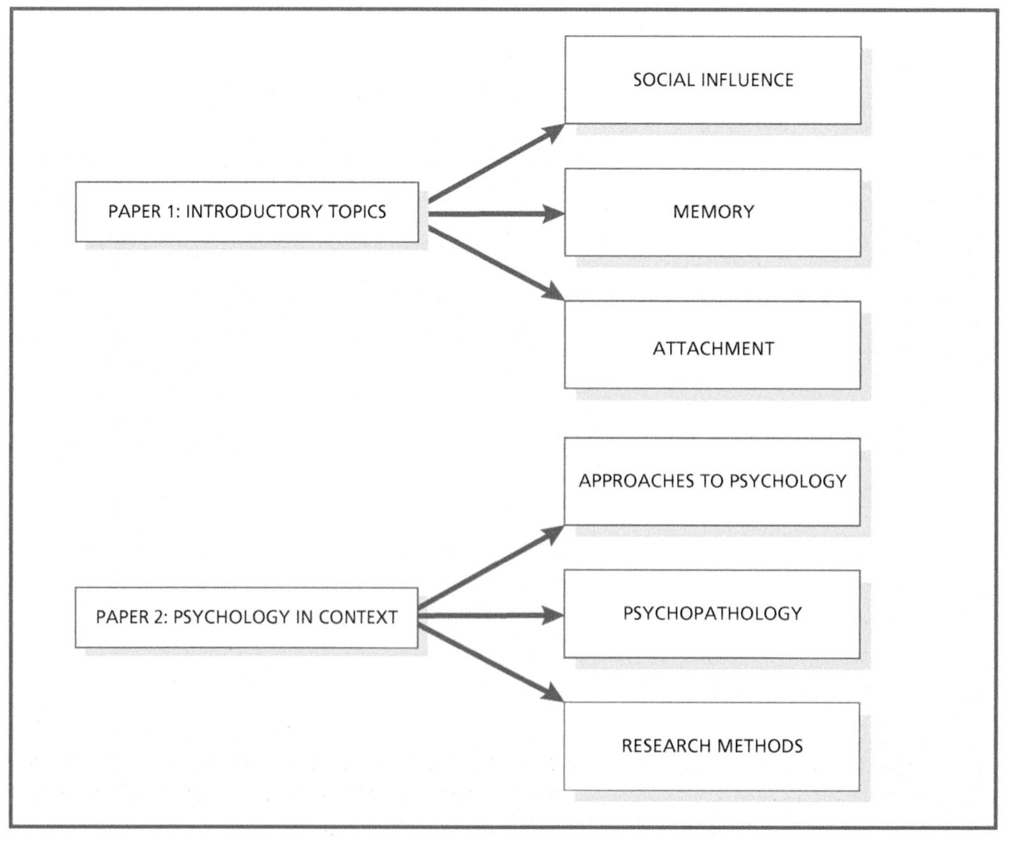

Each exam paper lasts 1 hour and 30 minutes and consists of a number of compulsory questions. Questions may be subdivided into more than one part.

There are a variety of question styles, which are described in detail below. All questions are based directly on the specification so make sure you know the specific terms in the specification.

Knowing how you will be assessed

There are two exams in AS Psychology and each lasts for 1 hour and 30 minutes. Each exam is worth 50% of the AS result.

There are three main assessment objectives in the exams. These are assessment objectives 1, 2, and 3, which are described in detail in the box below. Basically, AO1 is description, AO2 is applying knowledge, such as real life examples, sketched pie charts or graphs, and AO3 is evaluation.

EXAM HINT

You might want to return to this page as you read through the book so you get a better understanding of what the examiner is looking for as you progress through the course.

How you are assessed

AO1: Knowledge and understanding of scientific ideas, processes, techniques, and procedures.

AO2: Application of knowledge and understanding of scientific ideas, processes, techniques, and procedures:

- in a theoretical context
- in a practical context
- when handling qualitative data
- when handling quantitative data.

AO3: Analysis, interpretation and evaluation of scientific information, ideas and evidence, including in relation to issues, to:

- make judgements and reach conclusions
- develop and refine practical design and procedures.

In total on each exam there are 72 marks. In Paper 1 there are 72 marks in total which form 50% of AS level. Sections A, B, and C have 24 marks each. In Paper 2 there are another 72 marks, 24 each for sections D, E, and F.

In general you don't have to know what assessment objective a question is testing, you should just answer the question, as in the questions below:

Which TWO of the following are types of conformity? Shade TWO boxes only. (2 marks)

Authoritarian personality ☐

Agentic state ☐

Internalisation ☐

Compliance ☐

Briefly outline and evaluate normative social influence as an explanation of conformity. (4 marks)

Explain how social influence leads to social change. (6 marks)

It is important to understand what the actual wording of the question means. First, questions use the subject-specific vocabulary, but it is also essential that these terms are used in your answer to show your knowledge and understanding of psychology.

Here are some examples of words used in questions.
Describe: just do that! Describe whatever it is they are asking about, whether it is a theory, a research study or something else.
Evaluate: make a judgement using the evidence you know about.
Name: identify using a recognised psychological name or term.
What is meant by: give a clear definition.

Assessment objective 2: Application of knowledge

Questions that assess AO2 come in three forms:

1. You could be asked to "Discuss one or more explanations" of a theory, or "Explain" the findings or conclusion of a research study, or interpret details from stimulus material such as a description of research findings.
2. You could be asked questions based on methodology and an understanding of scientific ideas including research methods, theory and practical contexts, and qualitative and quantitative data, such as identifying an advantage of the research method used in a given example of a research study.
3. You could have a 12-mark question where you have to design a study to investigate a given situation, such as "gender differences in reading at age 7 years", and all of the marks would count as AO2 because you are applying your psychological knowledge here.

Strategies to improve your evaluation (AO3)

Kinds of AO3

One way to think about how you can improve your marks for AO3 questions is to consider how you can evaluate the research studies and theories you have studied. Focus on:

- *Application*. Can the research or theories be applied to everyday life? Does the research benefit humanity?
- *Methodology*. How was the research done? Can you comment on the validity, reliability or credibility of the research or information? What sampling technique was used, and can we generalise from this sample? Did the participants simply do what they thought the researcher wanted them to do? Could the researcher have been biased?
- *Culture/gender*. How universal are the findings? Do the findings have any relevance for non-Western societies and are the findings gender-specific?
- *Commentary*. Use evidence to support your answer. Consider the strengths and weaknesses of the evidence. Explore how psychologists have challenged different theories. Discuss how effective these challenges have been.

EXAM HINT

Avoid "common-sense" answers: you must convince the examiner that your answer is drawn from what you have learned, not from everyday knowledge.

AO3 trigger phrases

Don't expect the examiner to read your mind. Unless it is written down, they cannot know what you intended to say. Spell out the points to the examiners. Use phrases like:

- "This research on eyewitness testimony clearly has applications to everyday life where mistaken identity has led to the wrong person being imprisoned …"
- "One major problem with this research was that the sample was male and hence it is unclear whether these findings can be generalised to females …"
- "It is important to recognise the limitations of this definition in that what may be seen as normal in one culture (e.g. having three wives) might be seen as abnormal in other cultures."

EXAM HINT

When in doubt, try writing a sentence that starts "This suggests that …" or "Therefore, one can conclude …".

Constructing coherent arguments

Constructing coherent arguments takes practice. One way to construct your argument is by thinking about your conclusion, and then working backwards. For example, if you were given the question:

Discuss research into the effects of day care on children's social development. (12 marks)

Your conclusion might be that day care can have a beneficial effect on social development. Working backwards your answer would need to include:

- The evidence that might support your view.
- The strengths and weaknesses of this evidence.
- Other factors that need to be taken into consideration such as:
  - The type of day care being offered.
  - Individual differences.
  - The alternative care provided at home.

Making sure you have enough AO3

Some examiners suggest that answers to 8 or 12-mark questions can be broken down into two paragraphs. Using the knowledge that you can only get 4 or 6 marks for AO1 and that 4 or 6 marks are given for AO3 or a combination of AO2 and AO3, the first paragraph can be predominantly an AO1 response while the second paragraph would be AO2 and/or AO3. For example if you were given the question:

Discuss explanations of why people obey. (16 marks)

- *Paragraph 1* would describe one or more explanations for why people obey, such as the agentic state and/or buffers. In total this paragraph should be about 150 words.
- *Paragraph 2* would evaluate these explanations. This may involve research evidence that supports the explanations, or research evidence that challenges it, and comments about how the methodology could have been improved, and then your conclusion or judgement. This paragraph should again be 150 words.
- An alternative approach would be to use six paragraphs, each of about 50 words:
  - *Paragraph 1* Describe one explanation.
  - *Paragraph 2* Evaluate this explanation.
  - *Paragraph 3* Describe one explanation.
  - *Paragraph 4* Evaluate this explanation.
  - *Paragraph 5* Describe one explanation.
  - *Paragraph 6* Evaluate this explanation.

How the AS-level exams are marked

There are three types of question in each section of Paper 1 and Paper 2. These will be multiple choice questions, short answer questions, and some extended writing. Each section will count for 24 marks, so each paper will contain 72 marks in total, which will be 50% of the AS level total.

Examiners are given mark schemes to enable them to work out how many marks to award to an answer. Questions that are worth 2 or 3 marks tend to be marked in terms of a simple formula, such as:

- 1 mark for each strength and a further mark for explaining why it is a strength.
- 1 mark for a brief answer and a further 2 marks for elaboration.
- Up to 2 marks for factors and 2 further marks for elaboration of factors.

For questions worth 4 or more marks the mark schemes on this and the next page are either used singly or they are both used if the question involves both description and evaluation.

Description—knowledge and understanding: AO1			
4-mark question	6-mark question		
4 marks	6 marks	**Accurate and reasonably detailed**	Accurate and reasonably detailed description that demonstrates sound knowledge and understanding. There is appropriate selection of material to address the question.
3 marks	5–4 marks	**Less detailed but generally accurate**	Less detailed but generally accurate description that demonstrates relevant knowledge and understanding. There is some evidence of selection of material to address the question.
2 marks	3–2 marks	**Basic**	Basic description that demonstrates some relevant knowledge and understanding but lacks detail and may be muddled. There is little evidence of selection of material to address the question.
1 mark	1 mark	**Very brief/ flawed**	Very brief or flawed description that demonstrates very little knowledge or understanding. Selection of information is largely inappropriate.
0 marks	0 marks		No creditworthy material.

Application of Knowledge: AO2			
Level	6-mark	4-mark	
3	5–6		Relevant knowledge is clear and generally well detailed. Application to the subject matter is clear and effective and the answer is generally coherent with appropriate use of terminology.
2	3–4	3–4	Relevant knowledge is mostly clear and accurate.In general the material is used appropriately and effectively and is written coherently with few errors of clarity. Psychological terminology has mainly been used effectively.
1	1–2	1–2	Relevant knowledge is evident but not always explicitly related to the question. Links to the subject matter are not always effective. There is a lack of accuracy and detail and use of psychological terminology is absent or inappropriate.
	0	0	No relevant content.

Analysis, interpretation and evaluation: AO3		
4-mark question		
4 marks	**Effective evaluation**	Effective use of material to address the question and provide informed evaluation. Effective use of research evidence.Broad range of issues and/or evidence in reasonable depth, or a narrower range in greater depth. Clear expression of ideas, good range of specialist terms, few errors of grammar, punctuation, and spelling.
3 marks	**Reasonable evaluation**	Material is not always used effectively but produces a reasonable evaluation. Reasonable use of research evidence. A range of issues and/or evidence in limited depth, or a narrower range in greater depth. Reasonable expression of ideas, a range of specialist terms, some errors of grammar, punctuation, and spelling.
2 marks	**Basic evaluation**	The use of material provides only a basic evaluation. Basic use of research evidence. Superficial consideration of a restricted range of issues and/or evidence. Expression of ideas lacks clarity; some specialist terms used; errors of grammar, punctuation, and spelling detract from clarity.
1 mark	**Rudimentary evaluation**	The use of material provides only a rudimentary evaluation. Use of research evidence is just discernible or absent. Expression of ideas poor; few specialist terms used; errors of grammar, punctuation, and spelling often obscure the meaning.
0 marks		No creditworthy material.

EXAM HINT

The number of marks for each question is variable but you can judge how much to write by writing approximately 1 minute per mark on these short-answer questions. Be careful not to write too much or too little. Your answers may be correct but just lacking in detail/elaboration. Use research evidence and examples to increase the content.

Some ideas of how examiners use these mark schemes can be seen by looking at the following questions and examiners' comments.

Question: Describe one study of duration of short-term memory. (6 marks)

Candidate's answer: Peterson and Peterson did a study on the capacity of short-term memory. Participants were shown three-letter consonants, such as RTG. Then they were asked to recall them either after 3, 12, 15, or 18 seconds. The longer the interval, the worse their recall was.

Examiner's comment: The candidate has included some information, such as who did the study and what they did, but there is minimal detail. The findings have been treated rather briefly and certain other details were omitted (such as what the participants did while they were waiting to recall the digits). Therefore this answer would be described as "limited", close to "basic", and would get 3 out of 6 marks.

Question: "People who witness a crime want to be able to provide useful information to the police to help them catch the criminal." Outline and evaluate psychological research into the accuracy of eyewitness testimony. (12 marks)

Candidate's answer: Psychological research has investigated many areas of memory that are relevant to eyewitness testimony. The first area I will consider is Loftus's research on the way the language used in questioning the eyewitness will affect recall. In her experiment it was found that, if people were asked "About how fast were the cars going when they smashed into each other?", they estimated the cars' speed as being faster than if the word "hit" was used in the question. Questions that suggest a particular answer are known as leading questions.

Another line of evidence has looked at the effect of age of the witnesses on accuracy. Bronfenbrenner compared the memories of young children and older children and adults. They heard about an incident and 2 days later their memory of it was tested. Some of the participants had been given misleading information at the time of the incident. Bronfenbrenner found that in general there were few age differences except where there had been misleading information. The younger children were much more affected by this.

There are other factors which might reduce accuracy of eyewitness memory. Loftus showed that anxiety, especially when there was a physical threat such as a gun or knife at the incident, focused the eyewitness's attention on the weapon and not the culprit, and so their memory of the culprit was poor. This is called the weapon focus.

One criticism of this research is that these studies were laboratory experiments and so we cannot be sure the findings would be generalisable to everyday behaviour because of the artificial nature of the tasks. This criticism is supported by other studies, such as Valentine et al., which found no weapon effect on accuracy of eyewitnesses.

The evidence about age raises some real-life concerns. Adults such as jurors seem to readily accept children's testimony as they are seen as having no reason to lie, and also they seem confident. However, because of the reasons discussed above it is clear that children's testimony is as likely to be as, or more, flawed and inaccurate compared to adults'.

This is not to say that adults' memories are always correct. Several research studies, e.g. Brewer et al., have shown that older adults are as likely to have reconstructed memories as children, much more so than younger adults. Older adults also seem very suggestible, which makes their testimony less accurate. This could be explained by the young and the old being concerned to please the questioners and not wanting to cause trouble.

Examiner's comment: The candidate has presented a well-structured answer to the question, following a variation of the six-paragraph rule described on page 9. The AO1 material (description of psychological research) is accurate and generally detailed though the third paragraph lacks specific details of the research, so 5 out of 6 marks. The AO3 material (commentary on the research) displays depth—each point has been explained. The range is reasonable but not broad so again 4 out of 6 marks. This gives a total of 9 marks, which would be equivalent to a Grade B.

EXAM HINT

Remember: There is rarely a single right answer. Instead, obtaining high marks involves producing answers that are well-informed, well-constructed, well-argued, and in which the material used is well-selected so it is clearly related to the question.

So now you know what each unit is about and how you will be assessed. The last aspect of doing well in exams is to focus on exam technique.

Knowing how to prepare for the exam

Revise the topics you know you will be tested on:

- Make a glossary of key terms or concepts for each topic.
- Make sure you can describe and evaluate all theories, models, and research areas identified in the specification.

Methodology

Whenever you read about research ask yourself the following questions:

- What research method did they use?
- How did they select the sample?
- Was the sample biased in any way?
- Were there any other biases in the study?
- How were the data collected?
- How were the data analysed?
- What did they conclude from the study?
- What other conclusions could they have drawn?
- How ethical was the study?
- How could the study have been improved?

- Make sure you can apply your knowledge to real-life examples.
- Make sure you can evaluate, apply, and comment on psychological theories and research in terms of:
  - APPLICATION
  - METHODOLOGY
  - ETHICS
  - GENDER AND CULTURAL FACTORS
- Make sure you know how you will be assessed.

Proper preparation for the exam, and an understanding of how to gain marks, will increase your chances of getting a good grade.

In the examination room

- Read all the questions carefully BEFORE YOU START WRITING. Remember you have to answer all questions, so you need to plan your time wisely.
- Underline the key words in the question, so that if you are asked to describe the ***limitation*** of a certain method you don't describe its ***strength***.
- Before you start writing, quickly jot down the key points you want to include in your answer, so you don't forget your points as you start answering the question.
- Keep focused on the question set so that you don't fall into the trap of:
  - writing down everything you know about the topic, whether it is relevant or not;
  - repeating the same point over and over again;
  - drifting away from the question.
- In extended writing questions make sure each paragraph relates back to the question.
- Use the marks by the side of the question to help you plan your time. You should aim to spend approximately just over a minute per mark. If the question is worth 12 marks you need to spend three times as long answering this question as a 4-mark question.
- Be careful about how you express yourself:
  - Avoid making sweeping, inaccurate, ill-informed, or judgemental statements.
  - Avoid expressing personal opinions such as "I really don't like this study". Instead use phrases like "This study has been criticised for causing the participants stress".
  - Always back up your views with evidence.
  - Avoid one-word criticisms like "this study was unethical". Instead expand on your answer by stating why the study was unethical.
- And above all else, DON'T PANIC. Even if the examination questions aren't the ones you wanted, if you have prepared for the exam and understand how you can gain marks, you will be able to write an answer.

EXAM HINT

Remember that quantity doesn't equal quality. Stick to the point and organise your answer clearly so that the examiner can follow your argument.

Coping with stress in exams

If you know what to expect in an exam it removes the element of surprise and allows you to be prepared. This preparation will involve:

- organising your information;
- learning the information;
- understanding how the information can be used to answer questions in the exam.

But studying psychology also helps. Chapter 6 looks at stress management, so reading that before the exam will give you some ideas about how to lessen stress.

Here is some advice from that chapter:

- THINK POSITIVELY: This will increase your sense of control: "I can only do my best".
- AVOID DEFENCE MECHANISMS SUCH AS DENIAL: Recognise the feeling of stress and intellectualise your problem.
- RELAX: At intervals during the exam have a break and think positive thoughts unrelated to the exam.
- SOCIAL SUPPORT: Think about comforting people or things.
- PHYSICAL EXERCISE AND EMOTIONAL DISCHARGE: Go for a run before the exam, stretch your legs, find some means of discharging tension during the exam (that doesn't disturb anyone else).

Revision Questions

At the end of each chapter, and at the end of the book, you will find sample exam-style questions. These will give you an idea of the type of question you might be asked in the exam. You could also use them to practise writing answers under timed conditions and can then check your work against the sample answers we provide online.

What you need to know

The specifications for AS and A-level year 1 are the same for this topic, so you will need to cover everything in this chapter.

Social Influence will be examined in Paper 1 of the AS exam and Paper 1 of the A-level exam.

Social Influence

2

This chapter explores one very important topic in social psychology—social influence. What we say and how we behave are heavily influenced by other people. They possess useful knowledge about the world, and it is often sensible to heed what they say. In addition, we want to be liked by other people, and to fit into society. As a result, we sometimes hide what we really think, and behave in ways that will earn others' approval. All these issues relate to **social influence**, which can be defined as "the process whereby attitudes and behaviour are influenced by the real or implied presence of other people" (Hogg & Vaughan, 2005, p. 655).

This chapter examines two of the most common kinds of social influence: conformity and obedience to authority. **Conformity** can be defined as yielding to group pressures in terms of our expressed attitudes and/or behaviour. **Obedience to authority** involves behaving as instructed, usually in response to individual rather than group pressure. We will be considering factors that determine the extent of conformity and obedience to authority as well as explanations of these phenomena.

After that, we consider factors producing enhanced resistance to social influence. Some of these factors depend on the situation (e.g. social support) whereas others depend on the individual's disposition or personality (e.g. locus of control). This is followed by a section on factors determining whether and when minorities successfully influence majorities. The last section deals with the ways in which research on social influence (including minority influence) enhances our understanding of social change.

KEY TERMS

Social influence: how we are influenced by others, either by a group (majority influence), a small part of a group (minority influence) or an individual (e.g. obedience) to change our behaviour, thinking, and/or attitudes.

Conformity: changes in behaviour and/or attitudes occurring in response to group pressure.

Obedience to authority: behaving as instructed, usually in response to individual rather than group pressure, often in a hierarchy where the instructor is of higher status so the individual feels unable to resist or refuse to obey, though their private opinion is unlikely to change.

TYPES OF CONFORMITY

As we have seen, conformity can be defined as yielding to group pressures in terms of our expressed attitudes or behaviour. It is something we nearly all do some of the time. For example, if all your friends think a film is wonderful, you may pretend to agree rather than saying how boring you found it. Most of us probably conform much more often than we imagine.

Is conformity undesirable?

As you read through this section, you may find yourself thinking conformity is undesirable. That is often true. For example, Rodney King (a black man) was assaulted by four Los Angeles police officers. The assault was videotaped by a local resident, and shown in court. Even though the videotape indicated Rodney King was a victim of police brutality, the police officers were acquitted. Afterwards, Virginia Loya (one of the jurors) admitted she had changed her vote from guilty to not guilty because of pressures to conform to the views of other jury members.

However, conformity often leads to desirable behaviour. People live together and abide by social rules to facilitate their interactions—think of the rule that you must stop for a red traffic light! We also know other people possess useful knowledge about the world, and it is often sensible to heed what they say. In addition, most people want to be accepted by others.

Sherif's study

The first major study of conformity or majority influence was carried out by Muzafer Sherif (1935), who studied the **autokinetic effect**. If we look at a stationary spot of light in a darkened room, very small movements of the eyes make the light seem to move. Participants were tested one at a time, and then in small groups of three. They had to say how much the light moved and in what direction.

Each participant rapidly developed his/her own personal norm or standard. When three individuals with very different personal norms were put together into a group, they typically produced very similar judgements. Thus, a group norm rapidly replaced the personal norms of the group members, indicating the existence of social influence.

Sherif (1935) also used a condition in which individuals started the experiment in groups of three and were then tested on their own. Once again, a group norm developed within the group. When the group members were tested on their own, their judgements continued to reflect the group's influence.

Sherif's findings are not particularly surprising—the participants had no way of knowing what the "right" answer was, and so it made sense to take account of others' views. Solomon Asch (1951, 1956) wondered whether there would be conformity when the answer was *obvious* but the majority gave the wrong answer. If so, that would be surprising. Asch's notion that individuals are most likely to give way to pressure when several people are united against them reminds me of the old Spanish saying, "If three people call you an ass, put on a bridle!"

? Do some individuals and groups have more influence over you than others? If so, why do you think this might be the case?

? Which of these types of conformity (internalisation, identification, and compliance) involves a change of public behaviour but not private views?

Types of conformity: Internalisation, identification and compliance

Kelman (1958) argued it is important to distinguish between conformity in which individuals conform *publicly* but not *privately* and social influence in which their private beliefs change to agree with others. He outlined *three* different kinds of social influence within society as well as the laboratory:

1. **Internalisation** (genuine acceptance of group norms) occurs "when an individual accepts influence because the content of the induced behaviour—the ideas and actions of which it is composed—is intrinsically rewarding. He adopts the induced behaviour because it is congruent [consistent] with his value system" (Kelman, 1958, p. 53). Internalisation is involved when someone shows influence from other group members because he/she genuinely agrees with their views.

   Since the *content* of the message matters with internalisation, it is likely to be thoroughly processed. Internalisation is most likely to be found when the person or group providing the influence is credible and communicates what appears to be valuable information. Of importance, internalisation always involves private conformity and often also involves public conformity. Internalisation that occurs when a minority influences a majority is sometimes known as "conversion".
2. **Compliance** (or group acceptance) occurs "when an individual accepts influence because he hopes to achieve a favourable reaction from another person or group. He adopts the induced behaviour because . . . he expects to gain specific rewards or approval and avoid specific punishments or disapproval by conforming" (Kelman, 1958, p. 53). As the

KEY TERMS

Autokinetic effect: a visual illusion where a small spot of light in a darkened room appears to be moving when in fact it is stationary.

Internalisation: conformity behaviour where the individual has completely accepted the views of the majority.

Compliance: conforming to the majority view in order to be liked, or to avoid ridicule or social exclusion. Compliance occurs more readily with public behaviour than private behaviour, and is based on power.

influence is only *superficial*, compliance stops when there are no group pressures to conform. Compliance is most likely to be found when the person or group providing the influence is powerful and controlling. Of crucial importance, compliance involves conformity at a public but not at a private level—the individual's behaviour shows conformity but their private beliefs haven't changed. As we will see, Asch found extensive evidence for compliance in his studies in which participants conformed to the incorrect decisions of a unanimous group.

3. **Identification** (or group membership) occurs "when an individual accepts influence because he wants to establish or maintain a satisfying self-defining relationship to another person or a group" (Kelman, 1958, p. 53). Identification is found when someone shows influence with respect to the demands of a given role in society, conforming to what is *expected* of them. It is seen in the behaviour of nurses, traffic wardens and air hostesses regardless of how they may actually be feeling.

Norms are a set of rules established by the behaviour of a group of people. Conforming to group norms is a part of group membership. At a football game, different people are conforming to different norms—the home team has prescribed behaviours (clothes, songs, slogans), and so has the away team (such as unwritten "rules" for how to behave at an away match).

Later in the chapter, we consider a study involving a mock prison (the Stanford prison experiment). We have clear expectations concerning the roles of guards and prisoners in a prison—we expect guards to be tough and aggressive and prisoners to be quiet and submissive. As we will see, there is mixed evidence as to whether mock guards and prisoners behave as predicted on the basis that they identified with their assigned roles.

Kelman (1958) provided support for the distinctions among compliance, internalisation and identification. Black American students were presented with a message indicating it was important to maintain some private black colleges as all-black institutions to preserve black culture. This was a message initially opposed by most students.

In the compliance condition, the students were told the message came from a very powerful man who would withdraw funds from any college disagreeing with his position. In the internalisation condition, the same message was allegedly from a very credible source (a leading expert on the problems of minority groups). In the identification condition, the communicator was presented as a very attractive individual. He made it clear he was not only presenting his own opinions but that these opinions were supported by an overwhelming majority of black college students.

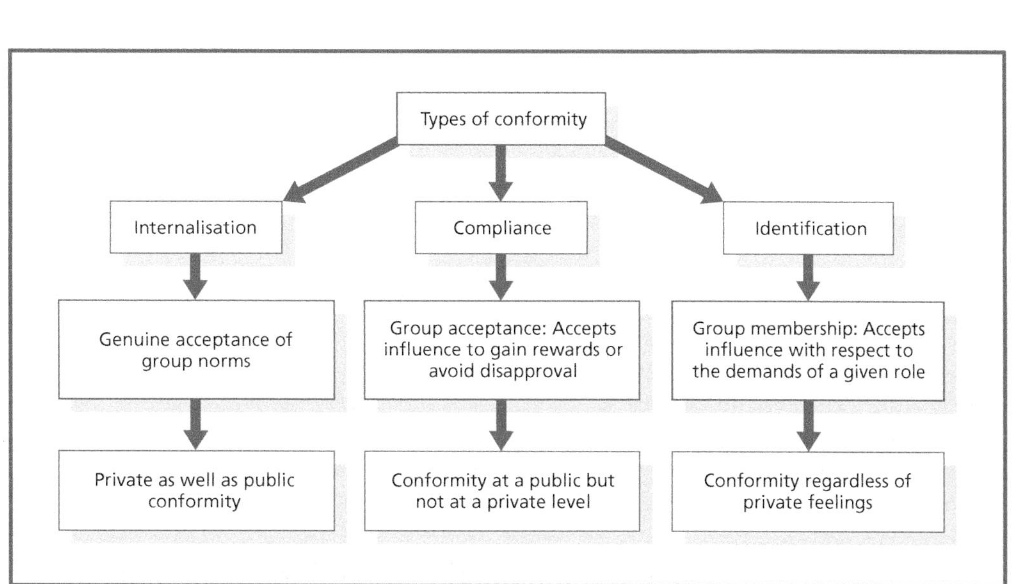

KEY TERM

Identification: conforming to the demands of a given role because of a desire to be like a particular person in that role.

After message presentation, participants completed a questionnaire concerning the relevant issues on three separate occasions. The first and second administrations of the questionnaire occurred immediately after the message. On the first administration, students were told their answers would be shown to the person delivering the message (public responding). On the second administration, students were told their answers were anonymous (private responding). The third administration of the questionnaire occurred 1–2 weeks after the message with private responding. There was no mention of the earlier message and the crucial questions were embedded in a much larger questionnaire containing questions about various attitudes. As a result, participants might well not have consciously thought back to the earlier message.

We will start with findings from the first two administrations of the questionnaire. In the compliance condition, students were significantly more influenced by the message with public than with private responding. Thus, their private views had changed less than their public ones as a result of exposure to the message. In contrast, in the internalisation condition, the views expressed were very similar with public and private responding. Thus, these participants had been influenced by the message privately *and* publicly. In the identification condition, students were influenced by the message with both public and private responding.

On the third administration of the questionnaire (private responding), participants in the compliance and internalisation conditions responded as they had done on the second (private responding) administration. In contrast, participants in the identification condition showed no influence of the earlier message—they did not consciously remember the earlier message which reduced their identification with other black college students as they completed the questionnaire.

Internalisation

What is of central importance with internalisation is that there is private conformity and generally public conformity as well. In what circumstances would we expect to find conformity due to internalisation? According to Kelman (1958), this is most likely to happen when the majority appears knowledgeable and members of the minority have little relevant knowledge to refute the majority position.

Earlier we discussed research showing evidence of conformity due to internalisation. Sherif (1935) studied people's judgements on the apparent movement of a light that was actually stationary. Individuals rapidly adjusted their judgements to conform to those of the other group members: this shows public conformity. When tested individually, their judgements typically remained similar to those they had given in the group situation. Since these judgements were given in the absence of any group, they indicate private conformity. Thus, the participants showed a mixture of public and private conformity suggestive of internalisation.

Why did internalisation occur in Sherif's (1935) research? The participants were in an ambiguous situation in which they lacked relevant knowledge or experience. As a result, their internal and external judgements were both strongly influenced by the majority.

Internalisation has often been found in cults. Monroney (2008), who had previously belonged to a cult, carried out research on six former cult members. All reported enormous pressure to conform to group influence in several ways. First, they were told to shed their previous self and adopt a new cult self. Second, they were expected to have little or no contact with family and friends. Third, they were rapidly enveloped in the culture of the cult: "All the participants, including myself, had instant friendships from other cult members. The cult became our family."

Monroney (2008) asked her six participants to rate on a scale of 0–10 how controlling the cult environment had been. Four of them gave a rating of 10. The powerful majority influence causes internalisation, as can be seen in the extreme forms of behaviour cult members engage in. For example, consider the Heaven's Gate cult in the United States. When its members were told to leave their physical bodies behind to find redemption in an extraterrestrial Kingdom of Heaven, 39 committed suicide.

In sum, several aspects of the situation jointly determine whether internalisation occurs:

- A knowledgeable majority.
- Minority members lacking relevant knowledge or experience.

- Situations in which minority members engage in thorough processing of the majority views.
- Situations (e.g. cults) in which strong attempts are made to prevent minority members from being exposed to views conflicting with those of the majority.

Compliance

Remember that compliance involves public conformity in the absence of private conformity. Asch's research on conformity (discussed later) provides strong evidence for compliance. Participants decided which of three lines was the same length as a given stimulus line. Participants tested on their own made the correct response over 99% of the time meaning they had no difficulty performing this task. The fact that participants when tested in a group situation with the entire group producing the same wrong answer conformed on about 35% of trials suggests conformity was due mostly to compliance.

Evidence of compliance in the Asch situation would involve finding that conformity is much less with public than with private responding. As predicted, conformity occurred on about 35% of trials with public responding but only 12.5% of trials with private responding. These findings don't indicate that all public responding in the Asch situation involves compliance. If that were the case, we might expect to find no private conformity at all.

We discuss Asch's research shortly. Accordingly, here we will simply identify some aspects of the Asch situation that determine whether conformity involves compliance:

- There is greater compliance when the group size is larger.
- Compliance is more likely when the accuracy of group performance is important.
- Compliance is more likely when individuals fear ridicule for disagreeing with the group.
- Compliance is more likely when individuals regard the majority as their ingroup rather than outgroup.

CASE STUDY: Groupthink

Conformity to group opinion has many important applications (e.g. in juries). The way individuals behave in these groups often matters a lot. Janis (1972) coined the term "groupthink" to describe how the thinking of people in these situations is often disastrously affected by conformity.

Janis was describing the "Bay of Pigs" disaster to his teenage daughter and she challenged him to explain why such experts could make such poor decisions. (The Bay of Pigs invasion of Cuba took place in 1961. President Kennedy and a group of government advisers made a series of bad decisions resulting in this extremely unsuccessful invasion—disastrous because ultimately the invasion resulted in the Cuban missile crisis and a threat of nuclear war.) Janis suggested that various factors increase conformity and result in bad decision making:

- Group factors. People in groups do not want to be ostracised, they want to be liked and therefore tend to do things to gain acceptance.
- Decisional stress. A group feels under pressure to reach a decision. To reduce this sense of pressure, group members try to reach the decision quickly and with little argument.
- Isolation. Groups often work in isolation, which means there are no challenges to the way members are thinking.
- Institutional factors. Often people appointed to higher positions are those who tend to conform, following the principle that a good soldier makes a good commander.

Identification

Identification is found when individuals perform roles in ways expected of them. What is a role? **Roles** are "patterns of behaviour that distinguish between different activities within a group" (Hogg & Vaughan, 2005, p. 303). Consider the brutal attacks by prison guards on prisoners in American prisons during the 1960s. This behaviour is an example of identification with a given role. Identification involves behaving in certain ways but it is not necessary for the individual to change his/her private views.

Why does identification with a given social role occur? There are two main reasons: (1) individuals with certain types of personality and beliefs may be attracted to that role; (2) individuals in a given social role respond to *expectations* concerning their behaviour held by other people and by themselves. In many cases, both reasons will apply.

KEY TERM

Roles: expectations, responsibilities, and forms of behaviour associated with a given position within a group.

Wearing a uniform may lead individuals to conform to an expected role. This is known as "identification".

In Zimbardo's Stanford prison experiment (discussed later), he selected psychologically healthy individuals to be mock guards and mock prisoners. As a result, the mock guards did not possess the personality characteristics (e.g. aggression; hostility) stereotypically associated with the role. Nevertheless, most of the participants (especially the mock guards) seemed to identify fully with the roles they had been assigned suggesting that identification with a role depends in large measure on the *situation*.

There are three further points. First, the extent to which identification occurs varies from person to person and from situation to situation. As is discussed later, an attempt to replicate the findings of the Stanford prison experiment failed because the participants failed to identify with their assigned roles (Reicher & Haslam, 2006).

Second, there can be significant problems associated with identifying with a given role. Consider **emotional labour** which "involves the expression of socially desirable emotions in interpersonal interactions" (Brotheridge, 2006, p. 139). Emotional labour is important in many jobs (e.g. nurses; social workers) and often involves faking one's emotional state. Workers who faked their emotions reported emotional exhaustion and a diminished sense of personal achievement (Brotheridge & Grandey, 2002).

Third, the extent to which identification is narrowly defined depends on the precise role in question. It could be argued that the role of prison guard is fairly narrowly defined. In contrast, consider the role of a friend—your friends probably vary enormously in how they think, feel and behave. Thus, the expectations associated with some roles are more rigid and clearly defined than other roles.

Asch's (1951) studies on conformity

? To what extent can we generalise about human behaviour from these studies?

Asch (1951) wanted to see whether a majority can influence a minority even when the situation is *unambiguous* and the correct answer is obvious. He aimed to find out whether conformity effects are present when it is apparently obvious that the majority have responded incorrectly. (See the box below.)

KEY RESEARCH STUDY

Asch's (1951) conformity study

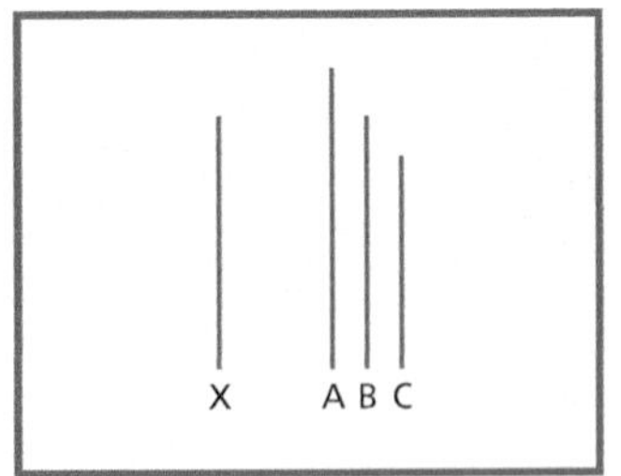

Asch set up a situation in which (in some of his experiments) seven people all sat looking at a display. In turn, they said out loud which of three lines A, B or C was the same length as a given stimulus line X (see illustration on the right). All but one of the participants were confederates of the experimenter—they behaved as the experimenter told them to behave beforehand.

On "critical" trials, the confederates gave the same wrong answer unanimously. The one genuine participant was the last (or last but one) to offer his/her opinion on each trial. The performance of participants exposed to such group pressure was compared to performance in a control condition with no confederates.

Findings

What did Asch (1951) find? On the critical trials on which all the confederates gave the same wrong answer, the genuine participants showed majority influence by also giving the same wrong answer on 37% of trials. We need to compare this figure against the error rate in the control condition (with no group), which was only 0.7%. Thus, participants answered correctly over 99% of the time without social pressure.

Many participants who gave wrong responses admitted they had yielded to majority influence because they didn't want to stand out. Individuals who gave only correct answers

KEY TERM

Emotional labour: the requirement of a role to express positive emotions (and suppress negative ones).

said they were confident in the accuracy of their own judgement or focused on performing the task as directed (i.e. striving to be accurate and correct).

The main conclusion is that conformity effects can be found even in an unambiguous situation in which the correct answer is obvious. Asch showed convincingly that group pressure to conform is much stronger than previously thought. However, the genuine participants actually gave the correct answer on two-thirds of the crucial trials. Thus, many people can successfully resist social influence.

Limitations

We will briefly discuss the main limitations with this study, some of which are discussed in more detail later. First, Asch's study was carried out in the United States in the late 1940s. At that time, conformity was high and "doing your own thing" was much less socially acceptable than in the 1960s and afterwards.

Second, Asch didn't really explain *why* there was so much conformity. He also failed to explain clearly *why* there were individual differences in the tendency to conform (we consider this issue later).

Third, Asch's research was limited in that the participants were all male college students. As a result, we cannot say from his findings whether the conformity he observed would have been obtained with different types of participants (e.g. older women).

Fourth, Asch's research raises important ethical issues. His participants didn't provide fully informed consent because they were misled about key aspects of the experimental procedures (e.g. the presence of confederates). In addition, they were placed in a difficult and embarrassing position—many became very anxious and distressed.

Fifth, even though this study by Asch (1951) is one of the most famous in the whole of social psychology, there was actually nothing very social about it because he used groups of strangers! Why this matters is discussed later.

EXAM HINT

Take note of the reasons why some people did NOT conform. In all, 25% of people never conformed in this study (i.e. they always gave the correct line length). The reasons why they did this are mentioned in the study—make sure you know these, so you can use them when discussing resistance to social influence, a topic that comes later in the chapter.

? Asch's participants weren't told the true nature of the study. Was this ethical?

Temporal, cultural and individual difference factors

The research discussed so far involved mostly American participants, many of whom were tested in the Asch situation in the late 1940s and early 1950s. Such findings wouldn't necessarily be obtained at other times and other cultures. Over the intervening decades, there have been considerable changes in views and behaviour in the United States and elsewhere. There are also large differences between cultures. In addition, **individual differences** in personality and other factors (e.g. education) help to determine conformity. In this section, we will discuss temporal, cultural and individual difference factors.

? Asch carried out his research in the United States. Why might the findings be different in other cultures?

Temporal factors

Perrin and Spencer (1980) repeated Asch's study in England in the late 1970s. They found very little evidence of conformity, and concluded the Asch effect was "a child of its time". However, the low level of conformity may have occurred because they used engineering students. These students had been trained in the importance of accurate measurement and so had more confidence than other people in their own opinions about the length of the lines.

Smith and Bond (1993, p. 124) reviewed studies using Asch's task in the United States concluding that, "Levels of conformity in general had steadily declined since Asch's studies in the early 1950s." However, even recent studies nearly all showed clear evidence of conformity. How can we explain this trend? The need for social approval decreased in the United States between the 1950s and the early 1980s (Twenge & Im, 2007). Individuals with a low need for social approval are less likely to pay much attention to the views of others.

Cultural factors

Bond and Smith (1996) reported a meta-analysis of cross-cultural studies of conformity using Asch's experimental design. The participants conformed on average on 31.2% of trials across these studies (slightly lower than Asch's figure). The highest figure was 58% wrong answers for Indian teachers in Fiji, and the lowest figure (apart from Perrin & Spencer, 1980) was 14% among Belgian students.

KEY TERM

Individual differences: the characteristics varying from one individual to another; intelligence and personality are major ways individuals differ.

When Asch's study was replicated, cross-cultural differences emerged.

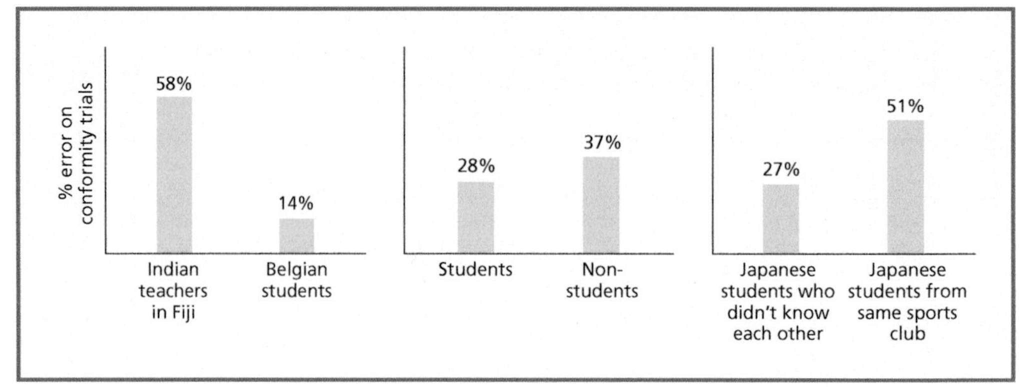

Social psychologists distinguish between individualistic and collectivistic cultures. **Individualistic cultures** (e.g. the United Kingdom and United States) emphasise the desirability of individuals being responsible for their own well-being and having a sense of personal identity. In contrast, **collectivistic cultures** emphasise group needs over individual ones, and value group identity and solidarity.

Kim and Markus (1999) found that a failure to show conformity is seen positively as *uniqueness* in individualistic cultures but negatively as *deviance* in collectivistic ones. Bond and Smith (1996) analysed numerous Asch-type studies in several countries. As expected, majority influence was greater in collectivistic cultures in Asia, Africa and elsewhere (37.1% of trials) than individualistic cultures in North America and Europe (25.3%). Thus, conformity is 50% greater in collectivistic cultures.

? What are some of the limitations of cross-cultural studies?

Individual differences

? Why do you think students were less likely to conform than non-students?

Some individuals conform more than others because of their biology or experience. Students made errors on 29% of crucial trials in the Asch task compared to 37% for non-students, perhaps because students are more independent in their thinking. Alternatively, their higher level of intelligence may make them more confident in their opinions.

Women sometimes show greater conformity than men (Eagly & Carli, 1981). Eagly (1978) suggested many studies are biased because they focus on "masculine" content, i.e. issues on which it is generally accepted that men are more knowledgeable. It would be expected that individuals who are very knowledgeable would be less open to influence.

De Young et al. (2002) consider the impact of various personality dimensions on conformity. Individuals high in conscientiousness and/or agreeableness were more conformist than low scorers.

? What does Asch's study tell us about nonconformity?

Conclusions

What conclusions should we draw from Asch's research? Asch (and many others) argued that his participants had a moral obligation to tell the truth. From that perspective, it is regrettable that 75% of the participants produced the wrong answer in response to group pressure at least once, and so exhibited mindless conformity. However, this argument is flawed for various reasons.

First, we mustn't overstate the amount of conformity. In fact, 25% of participants never conformed to the group's wrong answers, and nearly 70% defied the group on a majority of trials.

Second, many participants became aroused and somewhat distressed. Thus, they were aware of a strong conflict between producing the correct answer and their wish not to ignore the group.

Third, the participants were placed in a difficult dilemma. Many of their "errors" can be seen as expressing their respect for group cohesion and their desire to avoid ridicule. Most participants gave a mixture of correct and incorrect answers because this allowed them to show group solidarity *and* perceptual accuracy (Hodges & Geyer, 2006). Perhaps Asch's participants should be praised rather than criticised!

KEY TERMS

Individualistic cultures: cultures (mainly in Western societies) in which the emphasis is on personal responsibility, individual needs, and independence.

Collectivistic cultures: cultures (such as many in the Far East) in which the emphasis is on group solidarity and interdependence.

Group size, unanimity and task difficulty

We have discussed some key findings from Asch's (1951) enormously influential study. It is now time to discuss in detail key factors determining the amount of conformity observed in the Asch situation: group size; unanimity; and task difficulty.

Group size

Asch (1956) extended his original research. He manipulated various aspects of the situation to understand more fully the factors underlying conformity. He found majority influence increased as the number of confederates went up from 1 to 3, but there was no increase between 3 and 16 confederates.

Bond (2005) carried out a meta-analysis of Asch-type studies in which the majority was unanimous. When participants responded publicly (as in Asch's, 1951, study) so the other group members knew their answers, there was a weak positive relationship between group size and conformity. However, this conclusion was based on a smallish number of studies and very few studies used large group sizes. Conformity was similar with majority sizes of 3, 4, 5, 6, or 7 (but was greater with a majority of 8), which provides some support for Asch's conclusion that a majority of 3 produces as high levels of conformity as much larger majorities.

Bond (2005) discovered the findings were different when participants responded *privately* so the other group members were *unaware* of their responses. With private responding, there was a small *negative* relationship between group size and conformity.

How can we explain the effects of group size on conformity? It seems reasonable that the extent of any conformity effect would depend on the number of influence sources, and precisely this assumption forms an important part of the social influence model (Tanford & Penrod, 1984). What is more puzzling is why the effects of additional group members on conformity fairly rapidly seem to reach a plateau. Intuitively, we can see how this might work using an analogy suggested by Hogg and Vaughan (2005). If we start with a dark room, turning on a single light has a large effect. However, moving from, say, 8 lights to 9 lights has a much smaller effect.

What are the limitations of research on group size? First, approaches such as the social influence model say little about the *mechanisms* producing conformity. Second, conformity effects depend on *who* is in the majority group as well as *how many* are in that group. For example, a group of a given size produces substantially more conformity when it consists of ingroup members than when it consists of outgroup members (Abrams et al., 1990). Third, one possible reason why increasing group size has a smaller effect than might have been expected is that participants become more suspicious about the entire experiment when there are many other people holding unanimous opinions differing from their own. Fourth, more research is needed to clarify the different effects of group size on public and private conformity.

Unanimity

Asch (1956) investigated to see what would happen if the genuine participant had a supporter (a confederate who gave the correct answer on all trials and answered before the genuine participant). Participants with a supporter showed majority influence on only 5% of crucial trials—a dramatic reduction from the 37% found by Asch (1951) when there was no supporter.

There are at least two possible explanations for the reduced conformity observed when participants had a supporter. First, the supporter's responses might have provided useful information to each participant (e.g. "Here is information suggesting there is no problem with my eyesight!"). Second, the presence of a supporter might have reduced participants' need for social approval from the other members of the group by providing social support.

Asch (1956) decided between these two explanations by using a condition in which a confederate of the experimenter provided judgments even more incorrect than the majority. This was as effective as an accurate confederate in reducing conformity in spite of failing to provide useful information. There is less conformity in the presence of a supporter because participants feel less need for group social approval in the absence of group unanimity.

Allen and Levine (1971) asked participants to make visual and other judgements in a group setting. There were three conditions: (1) participants had no support; (2) participants had a valid supporter with normal vision; and (3) participants had an invalid supporter with very poor vision who wore very thick glasses.

There was very high conformity in the first condition (97% of critical trials) and a much lower level when there was a valid supporter (36%). The most interesting condition involved the invalid supporter, in which conformity was observed on 64% of critical trials. The lower conformity with a valid supporter than an invalid one occurred because the valid supporter provided much more useful information. The lower conformity with an invalid supporter than with no supporter occurred because breaking the group's uniformity reduced participants' need for social approval from other group members.

In sum, much of the typical conformity effect in the Asch situation depends on the group members displaying uniformity. When one group member breaks that uniformity, there are two main reasons why conformity is reduced. First, the dissenting group member can provide useful information concerning which response is correct (informational social influence—discussed shortly). Second, having the support of a group member provides participants with social support and reduces their reliance on the group for social approval (normative social influence—discussed shortly).

Allen and Levine (1971) showed conformity depends on *characteristics* of the supporter rather than simply on his/her *presence*. One limitation of research is that relevant characteristics of supporters have not been investigated systematically. However, educational attainment, race and sex all help to determine an individual's influence within a group (Melamed & Savage, 2013). We can see the importance of the supporter's characteristics if we take an extreme hypothetical example. Suppose the supporter was a young child and all the other group members were adults. Such a supporter would probably have minimal effects on conformity.

According to Baron et al. (1996), if a participant is told that a "counting the jelly beans" task is very important, he or she would be more likely to rely on, and be influenced by, the information provided by other group members.

Task difficulty

It is reasonable to expect that the amount of conformity observed in Asch-type situations would depend on task difficulty. More specifically, participants might well be more likely to conform if the task was very difficult and so they lacked confidence in their own opinions. Asch tested this prediction by using three lines differing less in length than in his original experiments. As predicted, participants exhibited more conformity when the line task was more difficult.

Baron et al. (1996) used a modified version of the Asch task in easy and difficult versions and the participants were instructed the task was important or unimportant. Baron et al. predicted participants would pay most attention to the other group members (and so exhibit the most conformity) when the task was difficult *and* important. The findings were as predicted.

Lucas et al. (2006) had students answer easy and hard problems in mathematics. There was more conformity with hard problems. This was especially the case with students who doubted their mathematical ability—those participants found the problems harder than those with more confidence in their mathematical ability.

What are the limitations of research in this area? Task difficulty depends on the skills and abilities of the participants as well as on the task itself but much research has not considered this. For example, a given problem in mathematics might prove a hard task for most people but not for a real expert.

Explanations for conformity: Informational social influence and normative social influence

? What is the difference between informational and normative social influence?

One of the most influential attempts to identify the factors responsible for conformity based on majority influence was that of Deutsch and Gerard (1955). They proposed two possible explanations:

- **Informational social influence**: This is "an influence to accept information obtained from another as *evidence* about reality" (Deutsch & Gerard, 1955, p. 629). It generally involves majority influence due to the perceived superior knowledge or judgment of others, as in Sherif's (1935) study. For example, several friends of yours might all have the same view (but different from yours) on a topic in psychology about which they know more than you. This form of social influence generally changes private as well as public opinion.

KEY TERM

Informational social influence: when someone conforms because others are thought to possess more knowledge.

- **Normative social influence**: This is "an influence to conform with the positive expectations of another" (Deutsch & Gerard, 1955, p. 629). It involves majority influence due to wanting to be liked by the other group members (i.e. social approval) and to avoid rejection. It undoubtedly played a major role in Asch's (1951, 1956) research. For example, when Asch (1956) had one confederate in a group of genuine participants give the wrong answer, the group laughed out loud. When the confederate continued to give wrong answers, he/she was rejected by the group. Many people are motivated to avoid such embarrassment. Normative social influence affects public opinions but is not likely to change private opinions.

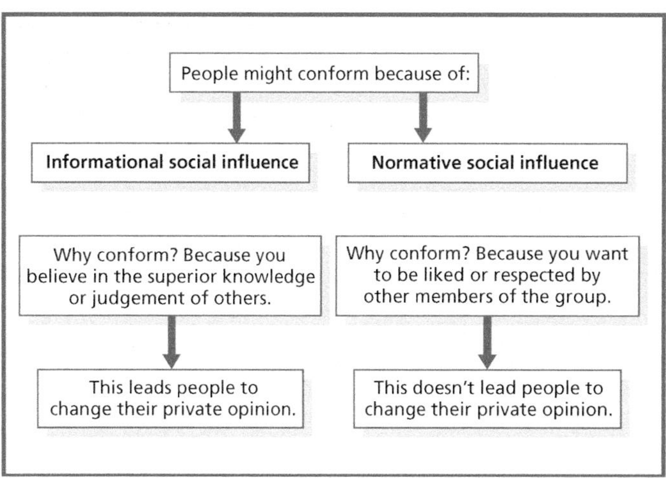

It is easy to imagine that Deutsch and Gerard (1955) believed that only one form of influence (but not both) would be operative at any given time. In fact, Deutsch and Gerard (1955, p. 629) argued that, "Commonly these two types of influence are found together." However, they predicted normative social influence would be especially important in the Asch-type situation when the correct answer was unambiguous.

Before proceeding, we will briefly consider a factor determining the extent of normative social influence. Suppose someone asked you to describe your best friend. Your description would probably include some indication of the groups to which he/she belongs (e.g. student at college; hockey team member). According to social identity theory (Tajfel & Turner, 1979), we all have **social identities** based on the different groups to which we belong. Our sense of ourselves is strongly influenced by our social identities. Having a positive social identity makes us feel good about ourselves and enhances our self-esteem.

Why are social identities important in influencing conformity? We feel positively about the groups to which we belong (ingroups) but negatively about many other groups (outgroups). This produces **ingroup bias** (the tendency to favour one's ingroup over outgroups). As a result, we are more influenced by group members (and thus exhibit conformity) when they belong to our ingroup.

Findings: Normative social influence

A useful starting point for understanding why participants often conform in the Asch situation is to ask them. That is what Asch (1951) did. Participants' self-reports focused on factors such as feeling self-conscious, fearing disapproval, and feeling anxious, suggesting normative social influence was at work. Self-reports provide interesting data but may not accurately identify why people conform.

We could explain the level of conformity found in Asch's basic situation by assuming the requirement to give judgements out loud maximised normative social influence. If so, conformity should be less if participants wrote down their judgements privately. Asch (1951) did precisely that, and conformity dropped to 12.5%—there is much less normative social influence when other group members are unaware of your judgements.

Bond (2005) compared studies in which participants responded publicly or privately (this study was discussed earlier). Conformity increased in line with increasing number of confederates with public responding. However, the *opposite* was found with private responding—the more confederates there were, the *less* private conformity there was! Thus, increased public conformity with increasing numbers of confederates is mainly due to normative social influence.

Deutsch and Gerard (1955) extended Asch's research. They used several conditions varying in the likely importance of normative social influence but with the same information about the judgements of other group members available to them. Thus, any group differences should depend mainly on differences in normative social influence. The main conditions were as follows:

1. *Face-to-face situation:* this was very similar to Asch's situation with three confederates and the genuine participant announcing his/her judgements publicly.
2. *Anonymous situation:* the genuine participant gave his/her judgements anonymously in an isolated cubicle by pressing a button, believing there were three other participants.

KEY TERMS

Normative social influence: when someone conforms in order to gain liking or respect from others.

Social identities: each of the groups with which we identify produces a social identity; our feelings about ourselves depend on how we feel about the groups with which we identify.

Ingroup bias: the tendency to view one's own group more favourably than other groups.

3. *Group situation:* this was like the anonymous situation except the experimenter said a reward would be given to the groups making the most accurate decisions.

Even the most independent of individuals can feel the need to conform under social pressure from peers.

What would we expect to find? Normative social influence (and so conformity) should be greatest in the third condition (social pressure to conform) and least in the second condition. That was precisely what Deutsch and Gerard (1955) found. They also used a variation of the anonymous situation in which participants wrote down their judgements on a sheet of paper and then threw them away. In this situation (designed to minimise normative social influence) participants conformed on only 5% of trials.

The effects of majority influence are much stronger when participants really care about the opinions of other group members. Abrams et al. (1990) argued their first-year psychology participants would show more conformity if the other group members were perceived as belonging to an ingroup (first-year psychology students from a nearby university) than if they were perceived as belonging to an outgroup (students of ancient history).

The above manipulation had a dramatic effect—there was conformity on 58% of trials in the presence of an ingroup compared to only 8% with an outgroup. Asch failed to realise he could have obtained much stronger majority influence if he had replaced groups of strangers with ingroup members.

Findings: Informational social influence

There is evidence from Asch-type studies that informational social influence can be an important factor. In a study discussed earlier, Allen and Levine (1971) provided the participants with a supporter who provided the correct answers even when the rest of the group did not. This supporter was either likely to provide useful information (because he had normal vision) or not likely to (because he had very poor vision). The participants exhibited less conformity with the former supporter than with the latter because he reduced the group's informal social influence to a greater extent.

So far we have focused on the Asch situation. Crutchfield (1955) devised a situation in which five individuals sat side by side in individual booths. They were shown slides containing multiple-choice questions and given the following instructions:

> *The slides call for various kinds of judgements – lengths of lines, areas of figures, logical completion of number series, vocabulary items, estimates of the opinions of others, expression of his own attitudes on issues . . .*

An important difference between the Crutchfield and Asch situations is that it was much harder for the participants to be confident of the correct answers in the Crutchfield situation. This was because many questions involved specialised knowledge. Thus, participants were far more likely to be seeking information than in the Asch situation, and so informational social influence should have been more important. Crutchfield (1955) found less intellectually effective participants showed more conformity because they were more affected by informational social influence.

Lucas et al. (2006) in a study discussed earlier found there was more conformity to the incorrect answers of others in the Asch situation with hard mathematical problems than with easy ones. This was especially the case with students who doubted their mathematical ability. It is reasonable to assume that informational social influence would be greatest when individuals were given hard problems and doubted their ability to solve them.

EVALUATION

- ⊕ Conformity generally depends on some mixture of normative social influence (involving emotional processes) and informational social influence (involving cognitive processes). Thus, Deutsch and Gerard (1955) successfully identified two key processes underlying conformity behaviour.

- ⊕ Some factors increasing or decreasing these types of social influence have been studied. Normative social influence is reduced when participants' judgements are anonymous and private, participants are permitted to throw away information about their judgements, or they have social support in the form a supporter or dissenter. Informational social influence is greater when the situation is ambiguous, accuracy is crucial, a supporter possesses valid information, and the participants doubt their knowledge or ability.

- ⊖ It is often not possible to decide whether the effects of any given factor on conformity behaviour are due to normative social influence, informational social influence, or some mixture. For example, conformity is markedly reduced if the genuine participant has one supporter. That supporter may provide social support (reducing the group's normative social influence) and/or useful information (reducing the group's informational influence). We have no easy way of telling which type of social influence is more important.

- ⊖ Deutsch and Gerard (1955) assumed that normative social influence would be extremely common, because it occurs whenever individuals seek social approval and acceptance. However, there is more to normative social influence than that. As discussed earlier, Abrams et al. (1990) found *seven* times as much conformity when the other group members belonged to one of the participants' ingroups rather than an outgroup. Thus, group belongingness is more powerful than simply the need for social approval.

- ⊖ It is possible to extend the above point concerning the importance of group belongingness. According to Reicher et al. (2012b, p. 358), "When a group is important to us, we see the world . . . from the perspective of its members. Their views are our views, their judgements are our judgements, their joys are our joys." Group belongingness means we are susceptible to strong normative social influence which often leads to enhanced informational social influence because of the respect we have for other group members. Thus, the distinction between these two types of social influence becomes blurred.

- ⊖ The extent of conformity behaviour depends on the situation in which an individual finds himself/herself *and* his/her personal characteristics. For example, highly intelligent and knowledgeable individuals are less affected by informational social influence than those of lesser intelligence and knowledge. In addition, individuals with a great need to be positively regarded by others will be more affected by normative social influence than those with a lesser need. Most research has focused on situational determinants of social influence, and as yet we lack a clear idea of how situational and personal factors *interact* to determine conformity.

Section Summary

Types of conformity

- Social influence involves an individual's attitudes and/or behaviour being affected by other people.
- Conformity can be undesirable. However, it is important to adhere to certain social rules and group cohesion requires much conformity to group norms.

- Kelman distinguished among compliance, internalisation, and identification. Compliance involves public conformity without internal agreement with other group members; internalisation involves public conformity plus internal agreement with others; and identification is conformity based on adhering to a given role in society.
- Conformity is most likely to take the form of internalisation when the majority is knowledgeable, when the minority members have no relevant knowledge, and when there is majority informational social influence.
- Situations producing internalisation include those in which minority members process thoroughly the majority's views and those in which minority members lack experience.
- Compliance to the majority occurs when the majority is large, there is normative social influence, and the accuracy of the group's performance is important.
- Individuals show compliance when they fear ridicule or regard the majority as their ingroup.
- Identification with a given role can occur because of the expectations associated with that role or because individuals with certain types of personality are attracted to that role.
- The extent to which identification occurs varies across individuals and situations. It can be very demanding to fulfil a given job role as is shown by the phenomenon of emotional labour.
- The extent to which identification is narrowly defined depends on the precise role in question.

Asch's studies on conformity

- Asch wanted to see whether conformity can be found when the majority produces the same incorrect answer.
- Asch found majority influence on about one-third of trials even when the correct response was obvious. Others have found the effects of majority influence can be even greater when the majority is an ingroup.
- Conformity in the Asch situation has decreased over the years, probably due in part to a general reduction in the need for social approval.
- Conformity in the Asch situation is 50% higher in collectivistic cultures than individualistic ones because group cohesion is more important in collectivistic cultures.
- The extent of conformity in the Asch situation depends on group size, unanimity, and task difficulty. More specifically, there is more conformity in larger groups than in smaller ones, when the majority is unanimous, and when the task is difficult and the answer non-obvious.

Explanations for conformity: Informational social influence and normative social influence

- Informational social influence generally changes private as well as public opinions whereas normative social influences affects only public opinions.
- There are various reasons for majority influence, including normative social influence and informational social influence.
  - Normative social influence: people conform to be liked or to avoid ridicule.
  - Normative social influence is greater when the majority is larger rather than small.
  - Normative social influence is greater when individuals feel an involvement with the majority (e.g. they form an ingroup).
  - Normative social influence is greater when the task is difficult and important.
  - Informational social influence: people conform to gain information or because they are uncertain what to do.
  - There is increased informational social influence when individuals perceive the majority to have superior knowledge.
  - There is increased informational social influence when the situation is ambiguous.
  - Normative and informational social influence are generally present together.

CONFORMITY TO SOCIAL ROLES

We have already discussed several reasons why individuals conform. There is another important reason based on **social roles**. Social roles are the parts we play every day as members of various social groups. Most days your social roles probably include those of friend and student. Social roles are associated with *expectations*—we expect someone playing the social role of friend to be supportive and encouraging and we expect a student to devote much time to studying and learning (hopefully!). The individual himself/herself has expectations as to what patterns of behaviour are appropriate in any given role and the other members of the social group also generally have similar expectations concerning that person's behaviour.

Changing our behaviour when in a given social role to fit our expectations and those of others is a fairly direct form of conformity. This form of conformity depends on **social norms**, which are the agreed standards of behaviour concerning the behaviour of someone occupying a given social role. Thus, for example, social norms tell us we should be lively and interactive at a party but quiet and serious in church.

One of the best-known studies designed to assess how social norms and social roles influence behaviour was the Stanford prison experiment (see Research Study). This study was based on the assumption that guards and prisoners in prisons occupy social roles with very clear social norms. We expect guards to be aggressive and even brutal whereas we expect prisoners to be submissive. These expectations reflect the rigid power structure within prisons – the guards have considerable power whereas the prisoners have little or none.

KEY RESEARCH STUDY

Stanford prison experiment (Haney et al., 1973)

Philip Zimbardo and his colleagues (Haney et al., 1973) studied the important issue of brutality in American prisons during the 1960s in the Stanford prison experiment, carried out in the basement of Stanford University's psychology department. Emotionally stable individuals acted as "guards" and "prisoners" in a mock prison. Zimbardo wanted to see whether hostility would be found in his mock prison. If hostility were found in spite of not using sadistic guards, this would suggest the power structure creates hostility.

What happened was so unpleasant and dangerous that the entire experiment was stopped 8 days early! Violence and rebellion broke out within 2 days. The prisoners ripped off their clothing and shouted and cursed at the guards. In return, the guards violently put down this rebellion by using fire extinguishers. One prisoner showed such severe symptoms of emotional disturbance (disorganised thinking and screaming) that he was released after only 1 day. Over time, the prisoners became more subdued and submissive. At the same time, the use of force, harassment, and aggression by the guards increased steadily, and their actions were clearly excessive reactions to the prisoners' submissive behaviour.

What conclusions can we draw? First, the study suggested that brutality and aggression in prisons are due mainly to the power structure rather than the aggressive and sadistic personalities of guards. Thus, the study seems to show conformity by identification. Years later, Haney and Zimbardo (2009, p. 807) drew the following conclusion from the

continued over

KEY TERMS

Social roles: the parts we play as members of social groups based on certain expectations about the behaviour that is appropriate.

Social norms: agreed standards of behaviour within a group (e.g. family; organisation) to which an individual is expected to conform.

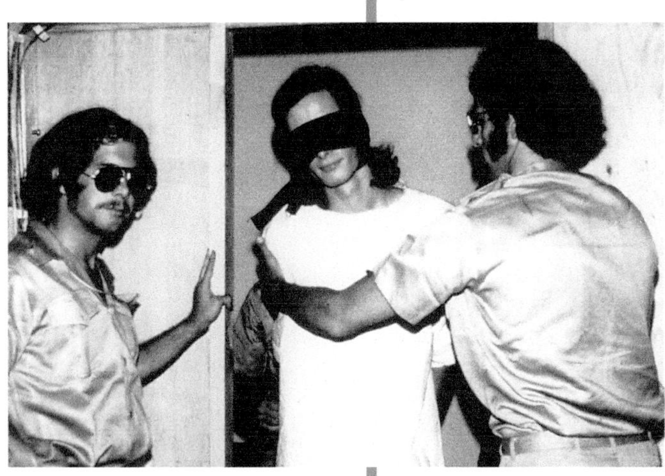

Some of the mock guards in Zimbardo's experiment became very aggressive during it, and four of the mock prisoners had to be released early.

Stanford prison experiment: "Certain very powerful social situations, settings, and structures can shape and transform the behaviour of the persons who enter them, suppress individual differences, and compromise deeply held values." In other words, Haney et al. (1973) argued that the behaviour they observed was due to the *situation* the participants were in rather than their personalities. However, real prison guards may be more sadistic than other people.

Second, the study showed how stereotypes about the kinds of behaviour expected of guards and prisoners influenced the participants' actions. According to Haney et al. (1973), guard aggression "was emitted [shown] simply as a 'natural' consequence of being in the uniform of a 'guard' and asserting the power inherent in that role". More generally, identification was shown by the guards and prisoners, who both conformed closely to expected forms of behaviour. In addition, most of the guards behaved in similar ways, and the same was true of the prisoners. This indicates a conformity effect, and may reflect the participants' need to be accepted by their fellow guards or prisoners.

Third, some findings could be interpreted in terms of deindividuation. **Deindividuation** is the decreased self-awareness that can occur in groups or crowds, especially when individuals are anonymous. It sometimes leads to aggressive behaviour. Evidence that deindividuation can increase violence was reported by Silke (2003). He studied 500 violent attacks carried out in Northern Ireland, 206 of them by offenders wearing disguises to mask their identities. Disguised offenders (who can be regarded as deindividuated) inflicted more serious physical injuries on their victims and were more likely to threaten victims after their initial attack.

There were some features in the Stanford prison experiment that could have led to deindividuation. All the guards wore a khaki uniform with dark glasses, whistles, and handcuffs. The dark glasses in particular may have increased feelings of anonymity and may have contributed to the levels of aggression shown by the guards. However, as we will see shortly, other theorists have different views of the processes occurring within groups.

Limitations

Various criticisms can be made of the Stanford prison experiment. First, and most important, Haney et al.'s (1973) argument that their findings favoured a **situational explanation** and showed a **dispositional explanation** (based on personality) was incorrect. This argument was developed further by Haney and Zimbardo (2009). There are several reasons why this argument (and the experiment itself) are flawed:

(1) They apparently assumed the findings would have been very similar if they had deliberately selected "guards" individuals with aggressive and sadistic personalities. Since they did not compare the effects of different personalities on behaviour in a mock prison they cannot know whether personality makes a difference.

(2) If the situation and adoption of the guard social role were all-important, we would have expected all the guards to behave in the same aggressive and brutal way. That was NOT the case. Zimbardo (1971, p. 154) pointed out that about a third of the guards "became tyrannical in their arbitrary use of power" with a single brutal guard who stood out. In contrast, other guards were friendly to the prisoners. These individual differences are inconsistent with a totally situational interpretation of the guards' behaviour.

(3) All the guards in the Stanford prison experiment were male. If the situation was all that mattered, we would expect to find as much brutality and violence if the study were repeated with only female guards. That seems improbable.

(4) The mock prison was very different from a real prison. For example, the participants knew they had not committed any crime and were free to leave. The artificial set-up may have produced effects due to **participant reactivity**, with the guards and prisoners merely play-acting. However, the physical abuse and harassment shown by the prison guards went far beyond play-acting.

KEY TERMS

Deindividuation: the loss of a sense of personal identity sometimes experienced by individuals in groups or crowds; it can lead to violent or aggressive behaviour especially when individuals are anonymous and so experience a loss of a sense of personal responsibility.

Situational explanation: deciding that people's actions are caused by the situation in which they find themselves rather than by their personality.

Dispositional explanation: deciding that other people's actions are caused by their internal characteristics or dispositions.

Participant reactivity: the situation in which an independent variable has an effect on participants merely because they know they are being observed.

(5) Some of the guards' hostility and aggression was due to following the experimenter's instructions rather than simply identifying with their social role. When Zimbardo briefed the guards, he told them:

> *You can create in the prisoners . . . a sense of fear to some degree, you can create a notion of arbitrariness that their life is totally controlled by us, by the system, you, me—and they'll have no privacy . . . they can do nothing, say nothing that we don't permit. We're going to take away their individuality. (Zimbardo, 1989)*

(6) Haney et al. (1973) claimed the guards had dreamt up most of the humiliations heaped on the prisoners (e.g. putting bags over their heads; binding prisoners together with chains; forcing them to use buckets instead of toilets). Carlo Prescott, a consultant for the study who had been a prisoner at San Quentin prison, pointed out that he had told the researchers about all these humiliations several months ahead of the study!

(7) There are various ethical issues. For example, the participants did not provide full informed consent because they did not know in detail what was going to happen. In addition, the prisoners were exposed to what most people would regard as an unacceptable amount of humiliation and distress.

CASE STUDY: Zimbardo's defence

Zimbardo pointed out that all of his participants had signed an informed consent form, which indicated that there would be an invasion of privacy, loss of some civil rights, and harassment. He also noted that day-long debriefing sessions were held with the participants, so they could understand the moral conflicts being studied. However, Zimbardo failed to protect his participants from physical and mental harm. It was entirely predictable the mock guards would attack the mock prisoners, because that is exactly what had happened in a pilot study Zimbardo carried out before the main study.

British study

Reicher and Haslam (2006) carried out a study for the BBC very similar to the Stanford prison experiment, using guards and prisoners selected to be well-adjusted. However, the findings were very different. The guards did not identify with their social role, whereas the prisoners increasingly identified with theirs. As a result, the guards were overcome by the prisoners. As Reicher and Haslam (2006, p. 30) concluded, "People do not automatically assume roles that are given to them in the manner suggested by the role account that is typically used to explain events in the SPE [Stanford prison experiment]."

Why did the findings differ so much? Participants in the BBC prison study knew their actions would be seen by millions of television viewers. As Zimbardo (2006) pointed out, this probably reduced the **mundane realism** of the experiment. This aspect of the study might have encouraged the guards to behave gently. However, this does not explain why the guards failed to become more aggressive over time as their awareness of being filmed diminished. Perhaps people are now more aware of the dangers of conforming to stereotyped views, in part because of the publicity given to the Stanford prison experiment.

How did Reicher and Haslam (2006) explain their findings? They argued that rather than identity being lost by individuals in groups (as assumed with the notion of deindividuation), what often happens is that individuals develop a shared social identity based on their common goals. In the case of the prisoners in the BBC study, this shared social

KEY TERM

Mundane realism: the use of an artificial situation closely resembling a natural situation.

identity was "the basis for effective leadership and organisation that allowed them to counteract stress, challenge authority, and promote social change" (Haslam & Reicher, 2012).

In sum, the BBC study shows us that a mock prison situation does *not* necessarily cause guards and prisoners to adopt their expected social role. Prisoners can develop a shared social identity allowing them to stand up for their rights rather than passively accepting the social role of being a typical prisoner.

ACTIVITY: A naturalistic observation of conformity

You could do a naturalistic observation of conformity in everyday life. This would comply with BPS Ethical Guidelines if you were careful to observe in a public place, and to respect your participants. How might you assess conformity to social norms? And how might you adjust your observation and data collection to reduce the chance of people feeling spied on, and in consequence becoming suspicious or agitated?

You could assess whether there is a relationship between how crowded a situation is and how often people conform to the social norm of clearing up their own litter. Write a directional or non-directional hypothesis to describe this relationship and justify your choice.

One way to do this might be to observe people in a fast food restaurant or in your school or college canteen. You could carry out your observation twice—once when it is very busy and again when it is fairly quiet. Avoid drawing attention to yourself by sitting chatting with a friend with a drink so you look very ordinary. You could have a magazine or newspaper on your table, and hidden in it a ready-drawn simple two-column grid—one column for conforming (people who clear away their own rubbish) and one for not conforming (people who leave their own rubbish). You would record no personal data at all, just ticks, and observe a set number of groups, perhaps the first twenty to leave in each session. At the end of each observation you would total each column and calculate the difference between them. You might expect to see a larger difference in one observation than the other. This would allow you to accept or reject your hypothesis.

When you have finished, reflect on your study. Did you encounter any unexpected difficulties? Was there anything that might have affected the validity of your data?

Section Summary

- The Stanford prison experiment provides some evidence that mock guards and prisoners adopt their expected social roles.
- There was some support for the notion that the violence often found in real prisons depends on the situation itself (e.g. the rigid power structure).
- Deindividuation may explain some of the aggressive behaviour observed by the guards in the Stanford prison experiment.
- A serious limitation with the Stanford prison experiment is that Zimbardo failed to show that dispositional factors (e.g. individual differences in personality) explain in part the behaviour observed in prisons.
- The Stanford prison experiment is flawed because of Zimbardo's excessive involvement in the actual conduct of the study.
- Some findings of the Stanford prison experiment have proved hard to replicate.
- The BBC prison study showed it is not inevitable that guards and prisoners adhere to fixed social roles. Shared social identity among the prisoners allowed them to avoid the passive social role associated with being a prisoner.

EXPLANATIONS FOR OBEDIENCE

This section is concerned with obedience to authority. What is obedience? According to Colman (2001 p. 501), it is "a form of social influence in which a person yields to explicit instructions or orders from an authority figure".

In nearly all societies, certain people are given power and authority over others. In our society, parents, teachers, and managers are invested with authority. Most of the time this doesn't cause any problems. If the doctor tells us to take some tablets three times a day, we accept he/she is the expert. However, the desirability of obeying authority is related to the *reasonableness* of their commands.

Obedience to authority resembles conformity as studied by Asch in some ways. However, there are several important differences (see the figure below).

Differences between obedience and conformity

OBEDIENCE	CONFORMITY
Occurs within a hierarchy. Actor feels the person above has the right to prescribe behaviour. Links one status to another. Emphasis is on power.	Regulate the behaviour among those of equal status. Emphasis is on acceptance
Behaviour adopted differs from behaviour of authority figure	Behaviour adopted is similar to that of peers
Prescription for action is explicit	Requirement of going along within the group is often implicit
Participants embrace obedience as an explanation for their behaviour	Participants deny conformity as an explanation for their behaviour

How does obedience differ from conformity?

Both obedience and conformity involve social pressure. In obedience, the pressure comes from behaving as you are instructed to do, whereas in conformity the pressure comes from group norms. A further distinction can be made in terms of the effects on private opinion. Obedience is more likely to involve public behaviour only.

Research on obedience to authority differs in three ways from research on conformity. First, the participants are ordered to behave in certain ways rather than being fairly free to decide what to do. Second, the participant is typically of lower status than the person issuing the orders, whereas in studies of conformity the participant is usually of equal status to the group members trying to influence him/her. Third, participants' behaviour in obedience studies is determined by social power, whereas in conformity studies it is influenced mostly by the need for acceptance.

An issue that interests psychologists is to work out how far most people are willing to go in their obedience to authority. What happens if we are asked by a person in authority to do something we think is wrong? What we should do is to refuse to obey. However, the lesson of history (e.g. Nazi Germany) seems to be that many ordinary people will do terrible things when ordered to.

Many people argue that only sadistic or psychopathic individuals would be so obedient to authority that they would be prepared to do appalling things to another human being. Other people argue that most of us would probably be prepared to treat someone else very badly if ordered to do so by an authority figure. The famous (many would say infamous!) research of Stanley Milgram (see the key research study below) addressed this issue.

Unquestioning obedience to authority may have catastrophic consequences. The picture shows survivors of the Auschwitz concentration camp at the end of the war in 1945, following a decade of persecution, imprisonment, and genocide.

Milgram's study is invariably described as an "experiment". Why might this be more correctly described as a "controlled observational study"?

KEY RESEARCH STUDY

Milgram (1963): Obedience to authority

Milgram (1963) wanted to see whether people would risk someone else's life if ordered to do so. His first study was conducted at the prestigious Yale University in the United States. In this study, he aimed to see whether he could set up a situation in which participants were more obedient to authority than was generally believed to be the case.

Forty male volunteers (a self-selected sample) took part in a controlled observational study, which they were deceived into thinking was a test of learning. The naive participant was always assigned the role of "teacher" and a middle-aged confederate, "Mr. Wallace", played the role of "learner". Mr. Wallace was said to have a heart condition. A word association test was the learning task, and the naive participant was instructed to deliver an electric shock to the learner for each incorrect answer.

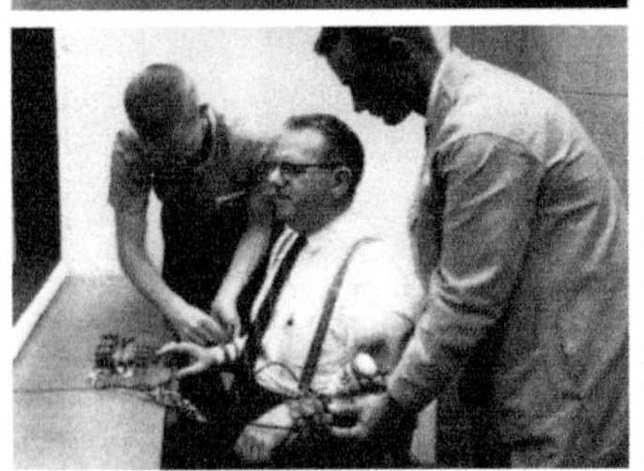

The photographs show the electric shock machine used in Milgram's classic experiment where 65% of the participants gave a potentially lethal shock to the "learner", shown in the bottom photograph. The photographs show the experimenter (in the overall) and the true participant, the "teacher".

If the teacher was unwilling to administer the shocks, the experimenter told him/her to continue. The teacher and learner were in separate rooms with no voice contact. The measure of obedience was the strength of the electric shock administered by the participants on a scale of 15 to 450 volts with 15-volt increments for each wrong answer. The participants understood that the highest levels of shock might be fatal, especially to a man with a heart condition. At 180 volts, the learner yelled, "I can't stand the pain", and by 270 volts the response had become an agonised scream. The participants didn't know until the end of the experiment that no shocks were actually administered. (The fact that no shocks were delivered shows psychologists are less sadistic than you may have started to believe!)

Would *you* have been willing to give the maximum (and potentially deadly) 450-volt shock? Milgram found everyone he asked denied they personally would do any such thing. He also found that 110 experts on human behaviour (e.g. psychiatrists) predicted no one would go to the 450-volt stage. In fact, 65% of the participants continued through to the highest level of 450 volts. This was hugely different from expert predictions!

This study is important for various reasons. First, Milgram studied a phenomenon of great societal relevance. Second, his findings were so strikingly unexpected that they showed psychologists' ideas about obedience to authority needed rethinking.

Limitations

There are several limitations with Milgram's (1963) study. First, the findings have poor generalisability. The study was carried out in a laboratory at a prestigious university and the findings might well have been less impressive in less prestigious surroundings. Generalisability was also reduced by the fact that all the participants were male. In fact, however, it turned out subsequently that obedience to authority is usually very similar in men and women.

Second, there may have been **experimenter bias**. Milgram was keen to show that people are very obedient to authority and this may have influenced how he set up his experiment. Support for this viewpoint is discussed later.

Third, Orne and Holland (1968) argued the research lacked mundane realism because the research set-up was in an artificial controlled environment. However, experimental realism can compensate for a lack of mundane realism, and it can be argued that is the case with this study.

Fourth, Milgram (1963) did not tell us what was different about the 35% of participants who refused to give the strongest electric shock. These individuals were less affected by the situational pressures involved than the other two-thirds of participants, but we do not know why.

KEY TERM

Experimenter bias: the effect that the experimenter's expectations have on the participants and therefore the results of the study.

Fifth, Milgram's research was very dubious ethically. Milgram totally failed to obtain informed consent from his participants, who simply did not know what would happen. In addition, the participants were not really free to leave the experiment—the experimenter urged them to continue when they indicated they wanted to stop. Milgram also failed to screen potential participants beforehand to ensure they were psychologically equipped to handle the pressures.

Milgram justified his research ethically by claiming all participants were fully debriefed afterwards about the purpose of the experiment and nearly all were pleased to have taken part. In fact, however, many participants were *not* debriefed or only told the real nature of the experiment weeks later. One participant reported: "I spent the night [after taking part in the study] in a cold sweat and nightmares because of the fear that I might have killed the man in the chair" (Nicholson, 2011, p. 746).

Milgram's initial hypothesis was that German obedience during the Second World War was a facet of German culture. He was going to compare how Americans behaved with how Germans behaved. However, he found to his astonishment that Americans were extremely obedient. Therefore, he concluded that obedience was in human nature, not just German nature.

Situational factors affecting obedience

What factors determine the extent to which individuals will show obedience to authority in Milgram's (1963) situation? Milgram (1974) addressed that issue by carrying out several variations on his original experiment. In general, he argued *situational* factors are of crucial importance. There are three main types of situational factors: (1) proximity of the participant to the learner; (2) location (the setting in which the study took place); and (3) the uniform of the experimenter.

Proximity

Milgram argued that obedience to authority could be increased by increasing the proximity or closeness of the participant to the learner. The basic idea was that participants would be more willing to administer severe electric shocks if the learner's plight was less obvious. There is an important distinction between physical proximity and psychological proximity. Physical proximity refers to the distance between the participant and learner whereas psychological proximity refers to how aware the participant is of the learner's position. We can see the importance of proximity across four situations used by Milgram (1974) (the percentage of totally obedient participants is in brackets):

- *Remote feedback:* The victim couldn't be heard or seen (66%).
- *Voice feedback:* The victim could be heard but not seen (62%).
- *Proximity:* The victim was only one metre away from the participant (40%).
- *Touch-proximity:* This was like the proximity condition except that the participant had to force the learner's hand onto the shock plate (30%).

In sum, *proximity* was an important factor influencing obedience to authority. There was less obedience when the participant was close to the learner and so was very aware of his distress. Reicher et al. (2012a) argued that the extent of obedience to authority in the Milgram situation depends very much on whether participants *identify* with the learner/victim or with

EXAM HINT

In this chapter, we look at how people resist pressures to obey. Possible factors include:

- Increasing the obviousness of the learner's distress by increasing his proximity to the participant
- Changing the experimental setting to make it more or less prestigious
- Changing the experimenter's uniform.

Use the later variations that Milgram conducted to support each factor. If possible memorise the % rates of obedience to show how much obedience dropped from the original 65%.

Reducing obedience to authority was achieved by:

increasing the obviousness of the learner's plight...		reducing the authority or influence of the experimenter...	
		at Yale University	65%
victim not seen or heard	66%	at a run-down office	48%
victim not seen but heard	62%	with experimenter sitting next to participant	65%
victim one metre away	40%	with experimenter giving orders via telephone	20.5%
victim's hand placed on shock plate	30%	when confederates of experimenter refused to give shocks	10%

the experimenter. The closer the proximity of the participant to the learner/victim, the greater the extent to which they identified with him and the lesser the extent to which they identified with the experimenter.

Location

Most of Milgram's research was carried out in an elegant Interaction Laboratory at Yale University. This prestigious location gave the experimenter social power as a legitimate authority figure. It may also have increased his apparent expertise and credibility as an experimenter. Milgram tested the importance of location by carrying out a study in a modest office in Bridgeport, Connecticut. From the participants' perspective, this study had nothing to do with Yale University but instead was carried out by an organisation called Research Associates of Bridgeport. In this setting, 47.5% of the participants exhibited total obedience which is somewhat less than the percentage showing total obedience under standard conditions (65%).

Reicher et al. (2012a) found that changing the location in this way reduced identification with the experimenter. They did this by having their participants read descriptions of Milgram's studies in the two different locations and asking them to indicate the extent to which they imagined Milgram's actual participants would have identified with the experimenter. It also led to a small increase in their identification with the learner/victim. Thus, the change of location reduced the authority and credibility of the experimenter.

Milgram also carried out a study in a basement at Yale University. This change of location was fairly modest in that the participants knew the study was associated with Yale University. As a result, it is perhaps unsurprising that this change of location had little effect on obedience.

In sum, research on the impact of location on obedience has probably shown only fairly modest effects because the locations selected have undermined the experimenter's authority to a rather limited extent. However, a more dramatic change of location (e.g. a slum dwelling) would probably greatly undermine the experimenter's authority and credibility and produce a large reduction in obedience.

? Why do you think that the setting in which the experiments took place made a difference?

Uniform

In nearly all Milgram's studies, the experimenter wore a white coat. This indicated to the participants that he possessed scientific expertise and this may have increased obedience to authority. Milgram investigated this issue in a study in which the experimenter was called away. An ordinary man who appeared to be another participant (but was actually a confederate of the experimenter) took over the experimenter's role and came up with the idea of increasing shock intensity every time the learner made a mistake. This had a dramatic effect on the participants' behaviour—only 20% exhibited total obedience. Note that the ordinary man differed in various ways from the typical experimenter in Milgram's other studies. He lacked the uniform of a scientist but he also lacked the scientific expertise and credibility of the typical experimenter.

The importance of uniform was shown in a field experiment by Bickman (1974) carried out on the streets of New York. Three male experimenters (one dressed in sports coat and tie; one dressed as a milkman; and one dressed in a guard's uniform that made him look like a police officer) gave one of three orders to pedestrians walking by:

1. Pointing to a bag on the street: "Pick up this bag for me."
2. Nodding in the direction of a confederate: "This fellow is overparked at the meter but doesn't have any change. Give him a dime."
3. Approaching a participant at a bus stop: "Don't you know you have to stand on the other side of the pole? This sign says 'No standing'."

Participants were more likely to obey the experimenter dressed as a guard than the milkman or civilian. These findings suggest obedience is related to the amount of perceived authority. However, what Bickman asked participants to do was much more trivial than what was expected of participants in Milgram's research and so his findings are only of partial relevance.

Obedience can be related to the amount of perceived authority.

Similar findings were reported by Bushman (1988) in a field experiment in which a woman ordered passers-by to give a nickel to a motorist who needed money for a parking meter. The woman was dressed in a uniform or as a business executive or she was dressed very casually (e.g. threadbare trousers and an old yellow T-shirt splattered with paint). Obedience was greatest when the woman wore a uniform (72%) but was only about 50% when she wore a business suit or was dressed casually.

In sum, people are more likely to be obedient when ordered to do something by someone wearing a uniform. This happens because wearing a uniform often confers legitimate authority on the individual—we are taught to do as we are told when ordered to do so by someone having the appropriate authority and legitimacy. Reicher et al. (2012a) developed this line of argument with respect to Milgram's research. They found participants (as imagined by other people who read descriptions of the studies) identified much more strongly with the experimenter when he wore a uniform than when he was casually dressed. This probably happened in part because of the uniform but also in part because he possessed genuine scientific expertise and thus authority.

Ethical research methods

One research method used by psychologists is "role play" to avoid ethical problems such as psychological harm (see page 362). Studies such as Milgram's could not be replicated today because of the anxiety caused to participants. An alternative is to ask people to act as if they are a participant in the study and see how they behave and feel. The limitation of this approach is that how participants behave and their reported feelings when role playing may differ from what would happen in a genuine experiment.

Criticisms of Milgram's research

Several criticisms have been made of Milgram's research. Some refer to the fact that his research was carried out at a given time (i.e. the 1960s and 1970s) and in a single culture (i.e. the United States). Critics have wondered whether the findings would vary at different times and in different cultures. Other major criticisms of Milgram's research approach concern the lack of internal validity and external validity, and the unethical nature of what he did. We will consider these criticisms now.

Milgram's findings: Limited by time and place?

In view of the ethical problems, it has not been possible in recent times to try to replicate Milgram's findings directly. However, Dambrun and Vatiné (2010) avoided the ethical problems. They put their French participants in an immersive video environment and told them the learner in the video was feigning discomfort and pain. Although this study took place 40 years after most of Milgram's experiments, the percentage of participants prepared to administer the strongest electric shock was comparable in both cases.

Burger (2009) carried out a Milgram-type study in 2006. However, he used various safeguards (e.g. the most intense electric shocks were not used; potential participants were screened to ensure they could handle the situation) to make the study ethically acceptable. The percentage of obedient participants was only slightly less than had been found by Milgram (1963).

Are Milgram's findings limited to the culture in which they were obtained? Relevant cross-cultural evidence was discussed by Smith and Bond (1993). Unfortunately, key aspects of the procedure varied across cultures, and so it is hard to interpret cross-cultural differences in obedience. However, the percentages of participants willing to give the most severe shock were very high in several countries: 80% or higher in studies carried out in Italy, Spain, Germany, Austria, and Holland, suggesting substantial obedience to authority. Blass (2012) reviewed studies using the Milgram situation and found only small and non-significant differences in obedience across cultures.

Validity of obedience research

? What is the difference between internal and external validity?

The validity of any research refers to the extent to which it satisfies certain standards. There are several types of validity. One is **internal validity**—the extent to which the experimental design did the job it was supposed to do. If the experimental set-up wasn't believable then the participants probably wouldn't behave as they would generally do in such situations. It is called *internal* validity because it concerns what goes on inside the experiment.

Another form of validity is **external validity**, the extent to which the results of a study can be applied to other situations and other individuals. It is called *external* validity because it concerns issues outside the study's specific context. We will consider both forms of validity in relation to obedience research.

CASE STUDY: Stanley Milgram's other research

Milgram's name is synonymous with obedience research. However, he carried out other studies. Tavris (1974) called him "a man with a thousand ideas". He wrote songs, including a musical, and devised light-shows and machines.

In relation to conformity, Milgram asked students to go up to someone on an underground train and say "Can I have your seat?" The students all recoiled in horror. Why were they so frightened? Milgram assumed the task would be easy. However, when he tried to say the actual words to a stranger on the underground he froze. He was overwhelmed by paralysing inhibition, and suggested this shows how social rules exert extremely strong pressure.

Internal validity

Did Milgram's participants *really* believe they were giving the "learner" electric shocks? Orne and Holland (1968) claimed Milgram's experiment lacked **experimental realism** because the participants may have found it hard to believe in the set-up. For example, they might have questioned why the experimenter wasn't giving the shocks himself—why employ someone else if there wasn't some kind of trickery?

However, in a replication of Milgram's experiment by Rosenhan (1969), nearly 70% of participants reported they believed the whole set-up. Coolican (1996) agrees with Milgram on the basis of film showing the participants in Milgram's studies were taking the situation very seriously and experienced real distress. We need to strike a balance here—Perry (2012) interviewed many people who had taken part in Milgram's research, several of whom claimed not to have really believed what they were told about it.

Orne and Holland (1968) also considered the issue of **demand characteristics**. Demand characteristics are those cues in an experiment "inviting" participants to behave in

KEY TERMS

Internal validity: the validity of an experiment in terms of the context in which it is carried out; concerns events within the experiment as distinct from external validity.

External validity: the validity of an experiment outside the research situation itself; the extent to which the findings of a research study are applicable to other situations, especially "everyday" situations.

Experimental realism: the use of an artificial situation in which participants become so involved they are fooled into thinking the set-up is real rather than artificial.

Demand characteristics: features of an experiment that help participants to work out what is expected of them and that lead them to behave in certain predictable ways.

certain predictable ways. One demand characteristic of any experiment is that participants should obey the experimenter's instructions. So, in Milgram's experiment, the reason the participants obeyed so completely was perhaps because this is how one should behave in an experiment.

? How can the concept of "demand characteristics" be used to explain the behaviour of the participants in Zimbardo's prison study?

Milgram's approach would also lack validity if the participants behaved as they did because they had entered into a social contract with the experimenter. In exchange for payment ($4.50; equivalent to about $35 today), participants might have felt they should obey the instructions they received—their behaviour showed obedience only within a contractual relationship. They were told they could leave and still be paid. However, the instructions "You must continue" made it quite difficult to leave.

External validity

External validity concerns the extent to which we can generalise a study's findings. The main challenge to external validity in Milgram's research is that it was carried out in laboratory situations, and so the findings might not generalise to the real world. However, consider the point made earlier that experiments are like real-life social situations.

Another way to answer the external validity criticism is by reference to the distinction between experimental and mundane realism (Carlsmith et al., 1976). Any research set-up resembling real life has mundane realism in so far as it appears real rather than artificial to the participants. Some experiments lack mundane realism. However, experimental realism can compensate for this when the way the experiment is conducted is so involving the participants believe it is real.

EXAM HINT

Notice how the terms experimental realism and mundane realism apply to an evaluation of Milgram's study. You could link these issues to internal and external validity, i.e. you should be able to assess how experimental realism questions internal validity and how mundane realism questions external validity.

Milgram claimed his research had both mundane realism and experimental realism. It had mundane realism because the demands of an authority figure are the same regardless of whether the setting is artificial or occurs more naturally outside the laboratory. It also had experimental realism because the experiment must have been highly involving and engaging for the participants to have behaved as they did.

Probably the best-known replication of obedience research is a real-life study by Hofling et al. (1966). In this study, 22 nurses were phoned by someone claiming to be "Dr Smith". The nurses were asked to check that a drug called Astroten was available. When the nurses did this, they saw on the bottle that the maximum dosage was 10 mg. When they reported back to Dr Smith, he told them to give 20 mg of the drug to a patient.

There were two good reasons why the nurses should have refused to obey. First, the dose was double the maximum safe dose. Second, the nurses didn't know Dr Smith, and were supposed to take instructions only from doctors they knew. However, the nurses' training had led them to obey instructions from doctors. There is a clear power structure in medical settings, with doctors in a more powerful position than nurses.

The nurses were more influenced by the power structure than the hospital regulations: all but one did as Dr Smith instructed. However, when asked what other nurses would have done in the same circumstances, they all predicted others would *not* have obeyed the instructions. Thus, the pressures to show obedience to authority are greater than most people imagine. This study raised important issues about hospital practices.

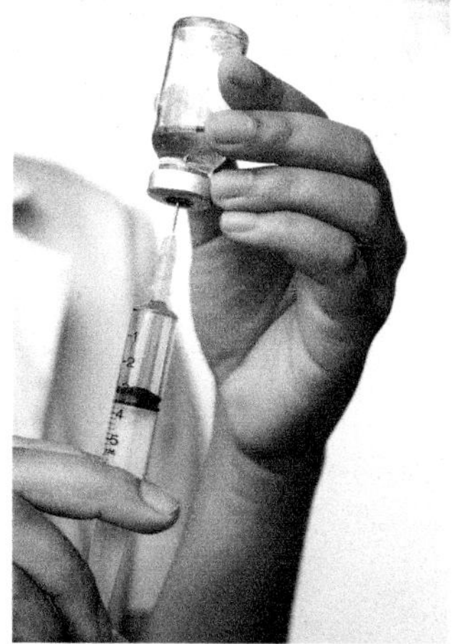

Hofling et al.'s (1966) study found that all but one of the nurses obeyed an unknown doctor's "dangerous" orders, even though they were only supposed to take instructions from doctors they knew. It is likely that the nurses were more influenced by the hierarchical power structure typical in their profession than by the hospital regulations.

Similar findings were reported by Lesar et al. (1997) in a study on actual medication errors in American hospitals. Nurses typically carried out doctors' orders even when they had good reasons for doubting the wisdom of those orders. Krackow and Blass (1995) compared nurses who carried out (or refused to carry out) inappropriate doctors' orders in real life. Compliant nurses were more likely to attribute responsibility for potential harm to the doctor rather than to themselves.

Rank and Jacobsen (1977) found only 11% of nurses obeyed a doctor's instructions to give too high a dose to patients when they talked to other nurses beforehand. Thus, social support can reduce obedience. This resembles Milgram's (1974) finding that obedience was much less when the genuine participants were accompanied by two confederates refusing to give electric shocks.

EXAM HINT

The issue of ethics is important in all psychological studies but ethics are particularly relevant to studies of conformity and obedience. In an exam, they can be useful in evaluating studies such as Asch, Milgram, Zimbardo's prison study, and Hofling et al. However, to make this an effective criticism, you need to make it clear in what way this is a limitation of the study—ethical issues do not challenge the results themselves, but do challenge the kind of research that has been undertaken.

ACTIVITY: An observational study of obedience

Design the procedure for an experimental study of obedience to authority in your school/college. Decide how you would operationalise "authority" as an independent variable. What would your experimental condition be? What would your control condition be? Ensure that any request that is made by this authority figure is reasonable and would be made in everyday life. Then decide how you would measure the amount of obedience and disobedience to see if there is a difference between the two conditions. What level of data would you obtain? Consider the ethical and methodological issues raised by the study. Would your teacher approve of your decisions?

? To what extent can the same criticisms be applied to Meeus and Raaijmakers' study as were raised against Milgram's original experiment?

? In what way does Meeus and Raaijmakers' study have greater validity than Milgram's study?

Meeus and Raaijmakers (1995) told participants they wanted to see how job applicants would handle stress in an interview. Each participant was given the role of interviewer, and the job applicants were actually confederates of the experimenter. The interviewer was told to create stress for the interviewee, and was given a set of negative statements to do this (e.g. "This job is too difficult for you"). Eventually the applicants pleaded with the interviewer to stop interrupting and then refused to answer any more questions.

In spite of the obvious distress caused to the job applicant, 22 of 24 participants (interviewers) delivered all 15 "stress remarks". They clearly felt stressed themselves but acted as if nothing was wrong. The study by Meeus and Raaijmakers (1995) shows once again the willingness of individuals to obey an authority figure even when both their stress and that of the recipient is obvious.

Explanations for obedience

? What are the main factors determining whether or not there is obedience to authority?

People may obey because the situation they find themselves in somehow puts pressure on them to be obedient. Alternatively, people may obey because obedience is a feature of human nature. We saw earlier that several situational factors influence the extent of obedience to authority, including the proximity of the learner/victim to the participant, the location in which the research takes place, and whether or not the person issuing orders is wearing a uniform. Below, we consider situational explanations for obedience. After that, we consider a dispositional explanation for obedience. Dispositional explanations emphasise the participant's disposition or personality and thus focus on individual differences in obedience.

Situational explanations

Several situational explanations for obedience to authority have been proposed. Here we will focus mostly on two of the most important ones. First, we discuss Milgram's explanation in terms of agentic state. Second, we discuss the notion that obedience to authority depends on legitimacy of authority.

Agentic state

Milgram (1974) argued strongly that obedience to authority depends mostly on situational factors. He identified three main features of the situation he used as being conducive to obedience:

1. Experience has taught us that authorities are generally trustworthy and legitimate, and so obedience to authority is often appropriate. For example, it would be disastrous if those involved in carrying out an emergency operation refused to obey the surgeon's orders!
2. The orders given by the experimenter moved gradually from the reasonable (small shocks) to the unreasonable (harmful shocks).
3. **Buffers**. These are aspects of the situation preventing the person from seeing the consequences of their actions. In Milgram's study, this occurred when the participants could not see the victim.

KEY TERM

Buffers: aspects of situations that protect people from having to confront the results of their actions.

According to Milgram (1974), the above situational aspects led to participants entering an **agentic state**. In this state, they became the instruments of an authority figure (i.e. the experimenter) and so ceased to act according to their conscience. Someone in the agentic state thinks, "I am not responsible, because I was ordered to do it." Milgram's view was that "Obedience is a natural response to the presence and instruction of an authority" (Reicher et al., 2012a, p. 320).

In essence, Milgram claimed we have an unfortunate tendency to do as we are told provided the person doing the telling is an authority figure. This contrasts with our everyday lives, where we are generally in the **autonomous state**, in which we are aware of the consequences of our actions and feel in control of our own behaviour.

Milgram (1974) claimed that the tendency to adopt the agentic state "is the fatal flaw nature has designed into us". This led him to stress the links between his findings and the horrors of Nazi Germany (discussed in detail later).

It appears some participants in the Milgram situation found themselves in an agentic state. Dambrun and Vatiné (2010) discovered that participants who gave the most electric shocks tended to hold the experimenter and the victim responsible for what happened rather than themselves. This refusal to accept personal responsibility is part of what is involved in the agentic state. In contrast, participants giving the fewest shocks accepted personal responsibility and did *not* hold the experimenter or victim responsible.

Milgram's notion of the agentic state provides a substantially oversimplified explanation of obedience to authority for various reasons. First, most participants in Milgram's studies were *not* in an agentic state. Most obedient participants experienced a strong *conflict* between the experimenter's demands and their own conscience. They seemed very tense and nervous, they perspired, they bit their lips, and they clenched and unclenched their fists. In addition, many argued strongly with the experimenter about what they were asked to do. Such behaviour indicates strongly they were *not* in an agentic state—they didn't surrender all personal responsibility.

Second, Milgram's views about the agentic state imply that participants in his studies felt controlled by the experimenter and virtually ignored the learner/victim's plight. That is disproved by the tension and conflict shown by most participants (point one above). In fact, participants were in conflict because they were aware of their different responsibilities to the experimenter and to the learner/victim. As Reicher et al. (2012a) found, the participants identified to some extent with the learner/victim in every condition used by Milgram. Thus, the victim's plight was *always* a factor in the participants' thinking.

Third, if the participants in Milgram's studies felt controlled by the experimenter, there should have been a very high level of obedience in every study. In fact, there were substantial variations in the percentage of fully obedient participants across studies. This variation is puzzling from the perspective of the notion of an agentic state. However, it is interesting to note that Milgram (1965) argued that it reflected "a potentially shifting set of alliances over the several experimental conditions". That is correct but not in line with the emphasis on an agentic state.

Fourth, many participants in Milgram's research claimed they had been fully obedient because they believed the experimenter was responsible for what happened. In many cases, this denial of personal responsibility may have been a convenient (rather than accurate) way of accounting for their behaviour.

Fifth, Milgram's focus on situational factors putting participants into an agentic state tends to neglect individual differences. How did some participants manage to avoid getting into an agentic state?

Legitimacy of authority

We have seen there is more obedience to authority when the authority figure appears to have legitimacy. For example, the experimenter in Milgram's studies was more likely to be perceived as a legitimate authority when he wore the uniform of a scientist and when the experiment took place in a laboratory at a prestigious university.

Some researchers (e.g. Blass & Schmitt, 2001) draw a distinction between social power based on harsh *external* influences (e.g. hierarchy-based legitimate power) and social power based on soft influences *within* the authority figure (e.g. expertise; credibility). Milgram

KEY TERMS

Agentic state: a state of feeling controlled by an authority figure, and therefore lacking a sense of personal responsibility.

Autonomous state: being aware of the consequences of our actions and therefore taking voluntary control of our behaviour.

Milgram found that participants were more likely to obey a figure they perceived as a legitimate authority (a scientist wearing a lab coat).

emphasised harsh influences (which is what the legitimacy of authority is all about), but soft influences are also important.

Blass and Schmitt (2001) presented participants with a 12-minute edited version of Milgram's documentary film, *Obedience*. Participants chose the best explanation for the strong obedience to authority shown in the film from the following choices based on various sources of power:

- *Legitimate:* experimenter's role as authority figure.
- *Expert:* experimenter's superior expertise and knowledge.
- *Coercive:* the power to punish the participant for non-compliance.
- *Informational:* the information conveyed to the participant was sufficient to produce obedience.
- *Reward:* the power to reward the participant for compliance.
- *Referent:* the power occurring because the participants would like to emulate the authority figure.

The sources of power most often chosen were in the order given above: legitimate power (a harsh influence) and expertise (a soft influence) were chosen most frequently, followed by coercive power (a harsh influence) and informational power (a soft influence).

What do these findings mean? First, they show Milgram was partially correct when explaining obedience to authority in terms of legitimate power. Second, they indicate that obedience to authority depends on at least two different sources of power. Third, they reveal the experimenter in the Milgram situation possessed several sources of power which jointly produced high levels of obedience.

What are the limitations with research focusing on the legitimacy of authority? First, such research often de-emphasises the role played by the learner/victim in determining how much obedience was shown. Second, the study by Blass and Schmitt (2001) involved people who had not actually taken part in any of Milgram's studies making judgements on the basis of a short film. The explanations for high levels of obedience in Milgram's studies by actual participants might have differed considerably from those of these non-participants. Third, there has been insufficient emphasis on individual differences—why were some participants less influenced than others by the legitimacy of authority?

Other situational factors

Burger (2011) identified five important situational factors not emphasised in the agentic state and legitimacy of authority explanations. First, the participants were in an entirely novel situation but assumed the experimenter had considerable experience with it. It is often hard to know how to behave in new situations, and so it was perhaps natural for most participants to do what the experienced experimenter told them to do.

Second, the participants in Milgram's research had very little time to think about their actions. More participants would probably have refused to continue with the experiment with additional time to think about their actions.

Third, the experimenter repeatedly told concerned participants he took full responsibility for what happened in the Milgram situation, which persuaded many of them to continue with the experiment. Tilker (1970) found there was much less obedience to authority when participants were told they (rather than the experimenter) were responsible for their actions.

Fourth, what was demanded of the participant increased slowly in 15-volt increments. This made it hard for participants to notice when the experimenter began to ask them to behave unreasonably. Think of the "foot-in-the-door" technique used by salespeople. They start with a minor request such as, "Can I ask you a few questions?" (getting their foot metaphorically in the door) and then gradually make larger requests. Before you know it, you have bought some item you can't afford!

Fifth, it was only when participants delivered the tenth shock (at 150 volts) that the learner first protested and demanded to be released. This had a major impact—more participants who refused to administer all the electric shocks stopped at this point than any other. More participants would probably have refused to obey the experimenter if the learner's anguish had been obvious earlier.

Burger (2011) argued that these factors undermine the notion that nearly everyone is willing to obey authority. His central point is that Milgram deliberately *biased* his situation to maximise obedience to authority by making it novel, depriving participants of thinking time, and so on.

? Why do you think situational explanations may be more common in some cultures than others?

EVALUATION

+ Numerous situational factors play a part in determining obedience to authority. Milgram (1974) found obedience to authority was least when the authority of the experimenter was reduced and the obviousness of the learner's plight was maximised. Some of these situational factors have powerful effects. For example, full obedience to authority was reduced from 65% in the standard condition to only 10% when the participant had confederates who rebelled against giving shocks.

+ Milgram's original findings are not limited by time or place. Similar findings have been obtained in numerous countries and in studies carried out many years later.

− The situational explanation based on the agentic state is oversimplified. It assumes that participants almost ignore the learner/victim and so experience little distress or conflict. These assumptions are incorrect.

− The situational explanation based on the legitimacy of authority is partially correct. However, it de-emphasises factors such as the expertise and credibility of the experimenter and pays insufficient regard to the concerns participants have for the learner/victim's suffering.

− As Burger (2011) argued, Milgram adopted a very biased approach when devising his experimental set-up. Factors such as the experimenter taking responsibility, denying the participants time to think, and only having the learner protest loudly some way into the experiment ensured there was high obedience.

− The fact that 35% of participants were not fully obedient in the standard Milgram situation indicates the situational pressures did not influence all participants similarly.

− Milgram exaggerated the links between his findings and Nazi Germany. For example, the values underlying Milgram's studies were the positive ones of increasing our understanding of human behaviour in contrast to the vile ideas prevalent in Nazi Germany. This issue is discussed more fully later.

Dispositional explanation

Adorno et al. (1950) argued that obedience to authority could be mostly explained in terms of personality or **disposition**. They said that some people have an **authoritarian personality** which makes them obedient and prejudiced. Such individuals have the following characteristics:

- Rigid beliefs in conventional values.
- General hostility towards other groups.
- Intolerance of ambiguity.
- Submissive attitude towards authority figures.

Why are authoritarian individuals so obedient? Adorno et al. (1950) claimed such individuals were treated harshly as children, causing them to have much hostility towards their

KEY TERMS

Disposition: an individual's basic character, temperament, or personality.

Authoritarian personality: identified by Adorno et al. as someone who is more likely to be obedient. These people tend to hold rigid beliefs, and to be hostile towards other groups and submissive to authority.

parents. This hostility remains unconscious, with the child seeming to idealise his/her parents. In later life, such children act submissively towards authority figures, and displace their hostility onto minority groups in the form of prejudice. These characteristics of the authoritarian personality make people especially likely to obey the orders of an authority figure.

Adorno et al. devised various questionnaires relating to their theory. The most important one was the **F (Fascism) Scale** which measures the attitudes of the authoritarian personality (look at the box below). Adorno et al. gave the test to 2000 people. Those scoring high on the F Scale also scored high on a scale measuring prejudice. This confirmed the validity of the scale.

Items from the F Scale devised by Adorno et al.

Indicate whether you hold slight, moderate, or strong support OR slight, moderate, or strong opposition to the following:

"Obedience and respect for authority are the most important virtues children should learn."

"Most of our social problems would be solved if we could somehow get rid of the immoral, crooked, and feeble-minded people."

"What the youth needs most is strict discipline, rugged determination, and the will to work for family and country."

"Familiarity breeds contempt."

"Sex crimes, such as rape and attacks on children, deserve more than mere imprisonment, such criminals ought to be publicly whipped."

Altemeyer (1981) came up with the similar notion of **right-wing authoritarianism**. This consists of authoritarian submission to authority, authoritarian aggression towards wrongdoers, and conventionalism (a belief there should be strict adherence to **social norms** and traditions).

Adorno et al. exaggerated the importance of a harsh environment in causing someone to develop the authoritarian personality. An alternative view is that genetic factors are important. McCourt et al. (1999) addressed this issue in a twin study. Identical twins share 100% of their genes whereas fraternal twins share only 50%. If individual differences in the authoritarian personality depend in part on genetic factors, identical twins should be more similar to each other than fraternal twins. That is exactly what has been found (McCourt et al., 1999). However, a harsh family environment may also influence the development of the authoritarian personality.

If authoritarianism is a disposition or personality factor, we would expect it to show *stability* over time. Ludeke and Krueger (2013) found there was a high degree of stability in authoritarianism over a 15-year period and this stability depended to a large extent on genetic factors.

EXAM HINT

If you are asked to explain why people don't obey, don't describe Milgram's study. You might use some of this to support an explanation but the study itself is not an explanation.

Findings

Milgram (1974) found high scorers on the F Scale gave stronger shocks than low scorers when ordered to do so by an authority figure, thus indicating that personality plays a part in determining obedience to authority. However, the fact that two-thirds of the participants in Milgram's experiments were fully obedient but far fewer people than that have an authoritarian personality means this approach provides only a partial explanation.

Other studies have produced similar findings. Miller (1975) studied obedience to an order that the participants should grasp live electric wires for 5 minutes while working on some problems in arithmetic. Those scoring high on the F Scale were more likely to obey this order.

Altemeyer (1981) used his own scale to assess right-wing authoritarianism. High scorers gave more intense electric shocks than did low scorers on a verbal learning task. Dambrun and Vatiné (2010) also studied individual differences in right-wing authoritarianism in a study discussed already. Those high in right-wing authoritarianism administered more shocks than low scorers.

Strong evidence of the importance of individual differences in personality in determining the extent of obedience to authority was reported by Haas (1966). Top management in a

KEY TERMS

F (Fascism) Scale: a test of tendencies towards fascism. High scorers are prejudiced and racist.

Right-wing authoritarianism: a personality type consisting of submissiveness towards authority figures, authoritarian aggression, and strict adherence to social norms.

Social norms: the explicit and implicit rules that specify what forms of behaviour, beliefs, and attitudes are acceptable within a given society.

company ordered lower-level management staff to indicate which one of their superiors should be fired. They were told their recommendation would serve as "the final basis for action". There was a fairly high correlation of +0.52 between hostility as a personality dimension (related to the authoritarian personality) and participants' degree of obedience.

EVALUATION

- ⊕ Individual differences in personality help to explain why only some participants show full obedience in the Milgram situation. In general, individuals displaying much hostility towards other groups (e.g. those with an authoritarian personality) are most likely to be fully obedient.
- ⊕ Research on the authoritarian personality clarifies why approximately one-third of participants in the standard Milgram situation were not fully obedient.
- ⊖ Milgram's experimental set-up provides a "strong" situation heavily biased towards making participants obedient. As a result, situational factors are very powerful and more important than personality and so the dispositional explanation is only of modest significance.
- ⊖ The percentages of participants showing total obedience varied substantially depending on the precise details of the situation. We cannot explain such variation in terms of individual differences in the authoritarian personality.
- ⊖ We might expect that individuals totally lacking an authoritarian personality would be disobedient from the outset in Milgram's situation. In fact, however, nearly everyone was willing to administer several electric shocks to the learner/victim.

Section Summary

Milgram's research

- Milgram's classic research showed that two-thirds of people were prepared to administer potentially fatal electric shocks to a man with a heart condition.
- The limitations in Milgram's research include possible experimenter bias, a lack of mundane realism, and serious ethical problems.
- Milgram had little to say about why 35% of his participants were not fully obedient.

Situational factors affecting obedience

- Milgram found that the extent of obedience was affected by proximity (physical and psychological), location, and uniform. All these factors led participants to identify more with the learner/victim and less with the experimenter.
- More recent research in several countries using the Milgram situation has produced similar findings.
- There are issues of internal validity (believability of the set-up) and of external validity (generalising to real life). The fact that many participants were obviously distressed suggests reasonable internal validity. Replication of Milgram's findings when nurses were ordered to obey unreasonable orders from doctors suggest good external validity.

Explanations for obedience

- Milgram argued that participants were put into an agentic state in which they became the instruments of an authority figure (the experimenter). This view is oversimplified. Most participants experienced conflict and distress, which indicate they had not surrendered all personal responsibility. In addition, they did not ignore the plight of the learner/victim.

- Milgram also argued that obedience to authority depends in part on its legitimacy. This is correct but the reality is more complex. Obedience to the experimenter depended on factors such as expertise and credibility as well as legitimacy.
- Other situational factors also help to explain Milgram's findings: the situation was novel for the participants; the participants had very little time for reflection; the experimenter said he took full responsibility; the electric shocks increased only slowly in intensity; and the learner/victim didn't protest and demand to be released until the tenth shock.

Dispositional explanation

- Individuals with an authoritarian personality are more likely than those lacking this type of personality to be fully obedient in the Milgram situation.
- Individual differences in personality explain some findings in the Milgram situation. However, situational factors are typically stronger in their effects than a disposition such as the authoritarian personality.

EXPLANATIONS OF RESISTANCE TO SOCIAL INFLUENCE, INCLUDING SOCIAL SUPPORT AND LOCUS OF CONTROL

So far we have focused on factors associated with social influence leading many people to exhibit conformity behaviour and obedience to authority. However, resistance to social influence has sometimes been found. Even in Milgram's original research, 35% of participants exhibited resistance to social influence or **independent behaviour** (resisting social pressure). In experiments in the Asch situation, independent behaviour was observed on about two-thirds of the critical trials.

Numerous factors produce increased resistance to social influence. We will initially focus on two of the most important: social support and locus of control. Social support is a *situational* explanation—there is more resistance to social influence in situations where social support is available. In contrast, locus of control is a *dispositional* explanation meaning it is concerned with individual differences in personality or temperament.

After that, we consider other important factors. These include identification, cultural factors, and whether or not the group is an ingroup or an outgroup.

Social support

? Can you think of an example where conformity and/or obedience are very useful or essential, and an example of where they should be challenged?

An important reason why individuals in the Asch and Milgram situations are susceptible to social influence is because they lack social support. There are several forms of **social support**. It can involve providing emotional support, informational support, tangible support (e.g. money) or companionship. We will consider the role of social support in studies on conformity and then those on obedience to authority. Before doing so, note that social support was very important in a famous real-world example of resistance to social influence—the American civil rights movement that transformed the status of blacks within American society. Of crucial importance was the mutual social support the dissenting minority members provided for each other in their legitimate battles with the majority. This example is discussed more fully later.

KEY TERMS

Independent behaviour: resisting the pressures to conform or to obey authority.

Social support: the supportive resources provided by other people; these resources can be emotional (e.g. affection), informational (e.g. advice or guidance), tangible (e.g. providing financial assistance) or can involve companionship (e.g. sense of belonging). Social support can be divided into perceived (an individual's subjective judgement of the assistance that is or might be provided) and received (specific supportive actions provided by others).

Conformity

Consider the Asch situation in which the participant is confronted by several other individuals all providing the same wrong answer. This produces a severe conflict between the individual's desire to be accepted by the group and his/her desire to show competence by making judgements based on the evidence of his/her own eyes. It follows that resisting pressures to conform involves reducing the desire for group acceptance and/or increasing the desire to make the correct judgements. We might assume the presence of social support in the form of at least one other member of the group consistently providing correct answers would increase the participant's ability to resist social pressure.

Asch obtained convincing evidence that social support increased resistance to social influence. When participants had no social support, they conformed to the group on up to 37% of trials. In contrast, they conformed on only 5% of trials when participants had one supporter (a confederate of the experimenter) who produced the correct answers when the rest of the group did not.

This resistance to social influence described above might have been due to reduced informational or normative social influence. Asch tested this in another study in which the supporter produced answers even more wrong than other group members. Participants in this condition conformed on only 5% of trials. In this case, social support reduced normative social influence more than informational social influences because the supporter wasn't providing useful information.

Levine et al. (1975) also studied the effects of social support in the form of a single supporter. This supporter produced answers that were correct or more wrong than those of the majority with visual items having a definite answer. As Asch had found, the presence of social support produced increased resistance to conformity regardless of whether the supporter's answers were very wrong or correct. Thus, we have evidence for reduced normative social influence.

Allen and Levine (1971) in a study discussed earlier focused on the validity of the social support provided in a conformity task involving visual judgements. In one condition, there was a valid supporter with normal eyesight, and in another condition there was an invalid supporter with apparently very poor eyesight. Participants showed much more resistance to social influence in the presence of the valid than of the invalid supporter (64% resistance vs 36%, respectively). However, there was more resistance with the invalid supporter than when there was no supporter (3% resistance). Participants' greater independence with the valid supporter than with the invalid one is due mostly to reduced informational social influence—the invalid supporter was a very suspect source of accurate information.

In sum, support has consistently been found to increase resistance to social influence. A key issue is whether social support reduces normative social or informational social influence. The available evidence suggests social support can increase resistance to social influence in both ways.

Obedience to authority

In the Milgram situation, it is much easier for participants to resist the experimenter's order if they have some social support because it diminishes the impact of the experimenter on the participant's behaviour. Milgram showed the importance of social support by finding total obedience was markedly reduced from 65% to only 10% when two confederates of the experimenter refused to administer electric shocks.

What happened in the above experiment is that one confederate refused to go on when the electric shock got to 150 volts and the second rebelled when the shock got to 210 volts. When the first confederate rebelled, 20% of participants refused to go on. When the second confederate rebelled, 60% of participants defied the experimenter by refusing to continue. Thus, strong social support in the form of two supportive confederates was required to produce large effects on resistance to social influence.

Why did social support reduce obedience to authority? As discussed later, Reicher et al. (2012a) argued that the social support provided by the confederates led the participants to identify more with the learner and less with the experimenter.

In the real world, individuals facing pressures to obey authority can often discuss what they should do with others which often makes it easier for them to resist such pressures. Remember the study by Rank and Jacobsen (1977) in which only 11% obeyed an unreasonable demand from a doctor when they had discussed the issue with other nurses.

In sum, social support reduces obedience to authority. Social support increases participants' tendency to identify with the learner or victim and also decreases their identification with the experimenter or teacher.

OVERALL EVALUATION

What are the limitations of research on social support? First, we must distinguish between *quantity* of social support (how many people?) and the *quality* of social support (how close emotionally are you to those providing social support?). Quality of social support is generally more important than quantity (Schaefer et al., 1981), but no relevant research has considered the effects of quality of social support on resistance to social influence—in every study, social support consisted of one or two strangers. Social support would probably be more effective if provided by someone emotionally close to the participant.

Second, there are important differences between men and women with respect to social support. Luckow et al. (1998) reviewed 26 studies on gender differences in seeking and using social support. Women sought social support more than men in 25 of these studies. Thus, social support should increase resistance to social influence more for women than men but this does not seem to have been investigated.

Third, the precise way social support is provided is probably important. For example, in Asch-type studies, social support has generally consisted of a confederate providing the correct answers when the rest of the group provided the same wrong answer. Participants' resistance to social influence might be greater if the confederate also smiled encouragingly at the participant and nodded when he/she produced the correct answer.

KEY TERM

Locus of control: a personality dimension concerned with perceptions about the factors controlling what happens to us.

Many of Hitler's followers' levels of obedience may have been determined by situational factors (following orders) rather than dispositional factors (following internal moral resistance). This woman is unable to conceal her misery as she dutifully salutes the triumphant Hitler.

Locus of control

It seems reasonable to argue there are individual differences in individuals' responses to situations such as those devised by Asch and by Milgram. If so, it is important to identify the characteristics of those individuals displaying resistance to social influence. However, Milgram (1974, p. 205) was sceptical about the importance of individual differences: "The social psychology of this century reveals a major lesson: often, it is not so much the kind of person a man is as the kind of situation in which he finds himself that determines how he will act."

We can distinguish between individuals who believe their behaviour is determined mainly by *external* factors (e.g. luck) and those believing it depends mainly on *internal* factors (e.g. their own ability and effort). We would expect those whose behaviour is most influenced by internal factors to be more resistant to social influence (external pressures) than those whose behaviour is strongly influenced by external factors.

Rotter (1966) devised a questionnaire assessing people's perceptions of control over personal outcomes, their generalised expectancies about the rewards they receive, and perceptions of control over entities such as governments. This questionnaire assessed **locus of control** (a personality dimension concerned with perceptions about the factors controlling our lives). This questionnaire indicates whether we perceive that what happens to us is under our own control (internal locus of control) or whether it is determined mainly by situational and relatively uncontrollable factors (external locus of control).

The most reasonable prediction is that individuals with internal locus of control are more likely to resist social influence. In addition, we might expect the differences in behaviour between internals and externals to be greater when the external pressures to conform or to obey are very strong—increasing external pressures should mostly affect externals who are very influenced by situational factors.

Can you think of a recent situation where you went against what you would have decided because of the "power of the situation"? This is an example of, in that instance, an external locus of control.

Conformity

Most evidence supports the prediction that those with internal locus of control will show less conformity than those with external locus of control. Shute (1975) studied the effects of peer pressure on attitudes to drugs. As predicted, participants with internal locus of control conformed less than those with external locus of control.

London and Lim (1964) found internals were more independent than externals on a conformity task. The most convincing evidence was reported by Avtgis (1998) in a meta-analysis of studies on the effects of locus of control on social influence and conformity. Those with internal locus of control showed a moderately strong tendency to show less social influence and majority influence than those with external locus of control.

However, some studies failed to find any relationship between locus of control and majority influence. Williams and Warchal (1981) identified individuals having low and high conformity scores on Asch-type tasks. The two groups did not differ significantly in locus of control. However, those showing little conformity were more assertive than those who conformed the most. Thus, assertiveness may be more important than locus of control in producing resistance to social influence.

Why is it that people high in self-esteem are more likely to resist orders to obey?

Other kinds of individual differences related to locus of control are also relevant. For example, individuals high in self-esteem have confidence in their own abilities and judgement and so their behaviour is influenced mostly by internal factors. As a result, individuals having high self-esteem tend to have internal locus of control (Judge et al., 2002). Those exhibiting resistance to social influence have higher self-esteem than conformers.

Kurosawa (1993) studied resistance to social influence in an Asch-type situation with low conformity pressure (two confederates) or high conformity pressure (four confederates). Self-esteem did not affect conformity in the low pressure situation. However, those high in self-esteem showed more resistance to social pressure than those low in self-esteem in the high pressure situation.

Obedience

Locus of control predicts the extent to which individuals will obey in the Milgram situation (Blass, 1991). Holland (1967) carried out three versions of the Milgram experiment: (1) a standard version; (2) a version in which participants were told there would be something "fishy" about the experiment; and (3) a version in which participants were told the actual shock levels would be one-tenth of what was indicated on the shock generator. Puzzlingly, the findings did *not* vary across these three versions. Overall, 37% of the internals were disobedient in that they didn't administer the strongest electric shocks, compared to only 23% of externals.

Miller (1975) carried out a study in which the participants were told by the experimenter to give themselves electric shocks by grasping live electric wires (!) and to perform other tasks. The experimenter seemed to have low or high bureaucratic authority. Participants with external locus of control were more obedient when told what to do by a high bureaucratic authority, whereas those with internal locus of control were unaffected by the experimenter's social status. These findings make sense given that externals are more influenced than internals by the situation and other people.

Real-world applications

We will briefly consider two ways internal locus of control is important in determining resistance to social influence in the real world. First, consider eccentrics, 130 of whom were studied by Weeks and James (1995). Most eccentrics clearly have an internal locus of control—they are non-conforming, they care little what others think of them, and they are opinionated and outspoken. These characteristics help eccentrics to challenge the established order and make creative contributions. Their achievements do *not* seem to be achieved at great personal cost, because most eccentrics are happy individuals.

Second, Oliner and Oliner (1988) studied 406 non-Jews who had (at considerable danger to themselves) rescued Jews from the Nazis during the Second World War, thus displaying a very high level of resistance to social influence. These individuals tended to be high in social responsibility and in characteristics indicative of internal locus of control.

In sum, both the real-world studies show the value to society of an internal locus of control. However, other factors are also involved. For example, eccentrics tend to be intelligent, which helps them make a substantial contribution. Those non-Jews who rescued Jews in the War tended to have strong relationships with other people (as is often the case with individuals with an internal locus of control). This fostered their motivation to help the victims of the Nazis. The role of social support in explaining resistance to social influence is discussed shortly.

EVALUATION

- ⊕ As predicted, individuals with an internal locus of control show more resistance to social influence than externals in the Milgram situation. Internals focus more than externals on internal factors and less on the situation.
- ⊕ Also as predicted, internals typically display more resistance than externals to social influence in the Asch situation. Internals (more than externals) focus on internal factors rather than external, situational ones.
- ⊕ There is some support (Miller, 1975) for the prediction that differences in resistance to social influence between internals and externals should be greater when situational pressures are greater than when they are weaker.
- ⊕ Other personality factors related to locus of control (e.g. self-esteem) also predict resistance to social influence.
- ⊕ Internal locus of control is associated with independent behaviour in eccentrics and those who rescued Jews victimised by the Nazis.
- ⊖ Locus of control has typically been assessed by the Rotter scale, which provides a very *general* measure. Such a general measure does not allow us to predict accurately individuals' behaviour in the *specific* Asch and Milgram situations.
- ⊖ The assumption that individuals whose behaviour is mainly controlled by internal factors will *always* show more resistance to social influence is dubious. For example, psychopaths (who are very aggressive and uncaring) would probably not only administer the maximum shock in the Milgram situation, but would enjoy doing so. Psychopaths in the Milgram situation would be driven by internal factors (e.g. desire to hurt others) and so their total obedience is completely inconsistent with the prediction that individuals with internal locus of control will resist social influence!
- ⊖ *Several* internal and external factors are involved in the Asch and Milgram situations. We could argue that resisting social influence involves a dominance of external

factors over internal factors (Sabini et al., 2001)—precisely the opposite to the usual assumption. In the Milgram situation, individuals resisting social influence may be strongly influenced by an external or situational factor (the suffering of others) but relatively unaffected by an internal factor (the disposition to obey authority). In the Asch situation, individuals unaffected by majority influence may be more influenced by an external or situational factor (the experimenter's instructions to give correct answers) than by an internal factor (the need not to look like a fool).

- It is often assumed that individuals' behaviour in the Asch and Milgram situations is caused to some extent by their cognitions (i.e. beliefs that their behaviour is determined mostly by internal or external factors). However, the evidence only indicates there is an *association* between beliefs and behaviour and so it is not clear that the beliefs have caused the behaviour. It is as likely that individuals' behaviour influences their beliefs about the factors determining their behaviour (Jo Wilcox, pers. com).

- The notion that internal and external factors are entirely separate is incorrect. For example, consider addicts. It is generally assumed they are driven by their internal cravings. However, their lives are very controlled by whatever it is that they crave. As Sabini et al. (2001, p. 8) pointed out, "The more internally controlled they [addicts] are, the more externally controlled they are." Thus, the distinction between internal and external factors does not have much meaning (Jo Wilcox, pers. com).

Cultural factors

Earlier in the chapter, we discussed research on cross-cultural differences in conformity, much of it based on the distinction between individualistic and collectivistic cultures. Individualistic cultures emphasise independence, personal responsibility, and each person's uniqueness. In contrast, collectivistic cultures emphasise interdependence, sharing of responsibility, and group membership.

The obvious prediction is that there should be less conformity in individualistic than collectivistic cultures because of the focus on independence and personal responsibility in individualistic cultures. As we saw earlier, more people show resistance to social influence in Asch-type studies in individualistic cultures than collectivistic ones (75% vs 63%, respectively; Bond & Smith, 1996).

Oh (2013) pointed out that nearly all previous cross-cultural research had focused only on compliance (public conformity). He considered cross-cultural differences in internalisation (private conformity). There were fewer cross-cultural differences in internalisation than compliance suggesting that most cross-cultural differences in conformity occur at a fairly superficial level.

Obedience to authority

We might expect there would be less obedience to authority in individualistic cultures than collectivistic ones. Those living in individualistic cultures emphasise personal responsibility and independence and so should be more likely to resist social influence in the Milgram situation. Relevant evidence was discussed by Blass (2012) in a review of Milgram-type studies. In American studies, 39% of participants showed some resistance to social influence compared to 34% for participants in other countries. Since America is often regarded as having an extremely individualistic culture, the findings are in the expected direction but were non-significant.

Why is there so little evidence that disobedience differs between individualistic and collectivistic cultures? Perhaps what matters is whether a culture is hierarchical or not—hierarchical cultures are ones emphasising status differences within society. There is probably more obedience to authority in hierarchical cultures because doing what you have been orderd to do by your superiors is an important part of such cultures.

Other factors: Conformity

? Why might engineering students be less likely to conform in studies such as Asch's than other students?

The importance of what group members think about the individual can be reduced in his/her mind if he/she regards the group as an outgroup of little relevance. As we saw earlier, conformity was shown on only 8% of trials in the Asch situation when the other group members were perceived as an outgroup (Abrams et al., 1990).

Individuals find it much easier to resist social influence if they have real confidence in the correctness of their own answers. Consider, for example, a study by Lucas et al. (2006) discussed earlier. Participants were given easy and hard problems in mathematics. They resisted social influence 92% of the time with easy problems but only 29% of the time with hard ones. With the hard problems, participants with high confidence in their mathematical ability resisted social influence on 39% of trials compared to only 20% for those lacking confidence in their mathematical ability.

Other factors: Obedience to authority

Reicher et al. (2012a) argued that the level of obedience shown in the Milgram situation depended on who participants identified with. If they identified mostly with the experimenter and the scientific community, they would be fully obedient. In contrast, they would be much more likely to be disobedient if they identified mostly with the learner and the general community.

Reicher et al. (2012a) tested the above predictions in a study in which participants were read short descriptions of 15 variants of Milgram's initial study. They indicated the extent to which each set-up would lead participants to identify with the experimenter or the learner. Identification with the learner was especially high in a few conditions including the following: (1) the participant is ordered to force the learner's hand onto the shock plate; (2) the learner is visible as well as audible; and (3) two confederates of the experimenter rebel and refuse to punish the learner. The key finding was a strong positive correlation of +.58 between identification with the learner and the level of disobedience.

In essence, Reicher et al. (2012a) emphasised the importance of focusing on the learner's plight. In this connection, it is interesting that the point at which most participants who failed to be totally obedient stopped obeying the experimenter was when the learner started to protest loudly. Before that point, participants could interpret silence from the learner as indicating he was coping with the electric shocks.

If participants in the Milgram situation are to show resistance to social influence, it is important they accept responsibility for what happens. Accepting personal responsibility is of major significance. For example, Dambrun and Vatiné (2010) found participants accepting personal responsibility administered fewer electric shocks than those who blamed the experimenter and/or the victim.

In the real world, the presence of highly respected role models refusing to obey authority can greatly increase the probability an individual will resist pressures to obey. Famous examples of such role models include Mahatma Gandhi and Martin Luther King (discussed later).

ACTIVITY: Resisting pressure

Does personal experience fit in with psychological explanations? You could try to test psychological models about resisting pressure. It could be interesting to ask a few participants each to draw up a table, with clear headings. The left-hand column could be for real examples of resisting pressure from their individual personal experiences, e.g. choosing not to go to the cinema with friends as they'd already seen the film. The right-hand column could be for their explanation of how they resisted the pressure to conform or join in. Each person should provide three or four examples.

This exercise could raise some ethical issues. Think about the kinds of ethical issues that would be raised and how to deal with them, and then write a briefing/consent form.

Section Summary

Social support

- Asch discovered that social support increased resistance to social influence. Indeed, there was conformity on only 5% of trials when social support was available.
- Social support increases resistance to social influence even when it consists of someone consistently producing answers more wrong than those of the rest of the group. This indicates that normative social influence was reduced.
- The increased resistance to social influence provided by social support is greater when the supporter possesses relevant skills than when he/she does not. This indicates informational social influence was reduced.
- In the Milgram situation, the presence of two confederates rebelling against giving electric shocks greatly increased the probability that participants would not be totally obedient.
- Social support in the form of two disobedient confederates was effective because it increased the tendency for participants to identify with the learner or victim.
- Social support in research with the Asch and Milgram situations has consisted of one or two supportive strangers. Social support would probably be more effective if provided by someone emotionally close to each participant.

Locus of control

- Individuals with internal locus of control believe their behaviour is determined mainly by internal factors whereas those with external locus of control believe their behaviour is mostly determined by external factors.
- Individuals with internal locus of control generally show more resistance to social influence than those with external locus of control in the Asch situation.
- Resistance to social influence in the Milgram situation is greater among those with internal locus of control than those with external locus of control.
- Eccentrics and non-Jews who rescued Jews from the Nazis are real-life examples of the value of internal locus of control.
- It is often assumed that individuals' cognitions (e.g. their belief that their behaviour is caused mostly by internal or external factors) influences their actual behaviour (e.g. resistance to social influence). However, it is as likely that their actual behaviour influences their beliefs.
- The distinction between internal and external factors is largely artificial and doesn't have much meaning.

Cultural factors

- Those living in individualistic cultures show more resistance to social influence in the Asch situation than those living in collectivistic cultures.
- The finding that those in individualistic cultures show less conformity is explicable on the basis that their cultures emphasise personal responsibility and independence.
- It is somewhat surprising that there is little difference in resistance to social influence in the Milgram situation between individualistic and collectivistic cultures. Perhaps such resistance is greater in non-hierarchical cultures than in hierarchical ones.

Other factors: Conformity

- There is much more resistance to social influence in the Asch situation when the other group members are perceived to belong to an outgroup.
- Individuals who are confident in their own ability are more likely to resist social influence.

Other factors: Obedience to authority

- Resistance to social influence in the Milgram situation is greater when participants identify with the learner/victim than when they identify with the experimenter.
- Participants accepting responsibility for what happens are more resistant to social influence.
- The presence of respected role models who refuse to obey authority increases resistance to social influence.

MINORITY INFLUENCE INCLUDING REFERENCE TO CONSISTENCY, COMMITMENT, AND FLEXIBILITY

So far we have focused on the powerful effects of majority influence on conformity behaviour. Most early research focused on majority influence in part because there are various reasons why we might expect **minority influence** (the beliefs and/or behaviour of a minority being accepted by the majority) to be less than majority influence. Many majorities are powerful and controlling, and can administer rewards and punishments. In contrast, minorities typically don't command much power and can't administer rewards and punishments to the majority. For these reasons, it used to be thought (incorrectly!) that minorities are merely the passive recipients of influence and rarely successfully engage in active persuasion.

In fact, minorities can have a strong influence provided they produce credible and convincing messages. Moscovici is probably the most influential theorist and researcher on minority influence. Accordingly, I will focus on his important theoretical contributions to our understanding of how minorities exert influence. First, however, I will consider some basic findings on minority influence.

Size of minority

Is a minority more influential when it consists of one person or when it consists of more than one person? Perhaps one person is more influential because the attention of the majority is focused on that person whereas attention is divided if the minority consists of several individuals. Alternatively, an individual on his/her own can be dismissed as eccentric or deluded more easily than a minority of two or more. Most of the evidence indicates that a minority of more than one is generally more influential than a minority of one (Moscovici & Nemeth, 1974).

Status

Members of minority groups are usually (but not always) of lower status than members of the majority group. That helps to explain why minorities typically find it harder than majorities to exert social influence. However, when the minority has higher status than the majority, its influence can be considerable. For example, consider a group in a classroom consisting of one teacher and perhaps 30 students. Most of the time, the teacher (having higher status) acts as a minority exerting great social influence over the substantial majority (i.e. the students).

There are numerous real-life examples in which one high-status individual (the leader) forms a minority of great influence. Tetlock et al. (1992) studied 10 cases in which an American President and his advisers were confronted by decision-making crises. Many of the decisions turned out to be disastrous. This was often the case in part because of a very powerful minority consisting of a strong leader (i.e. the President) and a few supporters.

More evidence of the importance of status was reported by Mannix and Neale (2005). Their key finding was that the views of the minority were more likely to be heard and accepted by the majority when the minority had the support of the leader of the majority.

KEY TERMS

Minority influence: the majority being influenced to accept the beliefs or behaviour of a minority.

Conversion: the influence of the minority on the majority. This is likely to affect private beliefs more than public behaviour.

Conversion theory

Moscovici (1980, 1985) argued that conversion occurs when the majority is influenced by the views of the minority. **Conversion** typically affects private beliefs more than public behaviour. Individuals within the majority might still appear to go along with the majority (perhaps for their own safety), but privately their opinions have changed. As we saw earlier, this is known as compliance.

According to Moscovici, majority influence typically occurs after relatively brief and superficial processing of the majority's views, whereas minority influence generally occurs after detailed and thorough processing of the minority's views. Moscovici (1985) argued that conversion is most likely to occur under certain conditions:

> What is the difference between compliance and conversion?

1. ***Consistency***: The minority must be consistent in their opinion.
2. ***Flexibility***: The minority mustn't appear to be rigid and dogmatic.
3. ***Commitment***: A committed minority will lead people to re-think their position and so produce conversion.
4. *Relevance*: The minority will be more successful if their views are in line with social trends.

On the face of it, consistency and flexibility are so different that it would hard for minority group members to use both at the same time. However, that is *not* the case. If consistency involves the mindless repetition of the same arguments in a dogmatic fashion, it is unlikely to exert influence on the majority. Minorities are much more likely to influence the majority if they express the same overall point of view consistently but show flexibility by varying the specific arguments they use to support that point of view.

Moscovici also suggested some behavioural styles minorities should have to exert an influence. These include being consistent in order to demonstrate certainty, convey an alternative view, disrupt the norm, and draw attention to their views. In addition, they should act on *principles* rather than just talking about them, and should make *sacrifices* to maintain the view they hold. It also helps if they are similar in age, class, and gender to those they want to persuade.

Successful minorities force the majority to *think* in new ways about an issue. They cause one to "examine one's own responses, one's own judgements, in order to confirm and validate them" (Moscovici, 1980, p. 215). More specifically, majorities "are motivated to consider the issue more carefully since there must be a reason why the minority takes the position it does and, further, is sufficiently confident to maintain it" (Nemeth, 2009).

There is a final factor. Moscovici argued that *distinctiveness* is an advantage for minorities. Thus, for example, a small minority of 18% is more distinctive than a large minority of 48%. As predicted, distinctive minorities have more influence on the majority than non-distinctive ones (Gardikiotis, 2011).

Findings

Moscovici et al. (1969) showed that a minority (especially if consistent) can influence a majority. There were four naive participants (the majority) and two confederates of the experimenter (the minority). All participants described the colours of blue slides. The minority described all slides as "green" (consistent condition) or two-thirds as "green" and one-third as "blue" (inconsistent condition). The participants showed minority influence (i.e. said "green") on 8.4% of trials with the consistent minority but only 1.25% of trials with the inconsistent minority.

> How do the results of this study compare with the studies that looked at majority influence?

Nemeth et al. (1974) confirmed that consistency is necessary for a minority to influence the majority. However, it isn't always sufficient. They essentially replicated Moscovici et al.'s study (1969) except their participants could respond with all the colours they saw in the slides rather than only a single colour. There were three main conditions:

1. The two confederates of the experimenter said "green" on 50% of the trials and "green-blue" on the other 50% in a random way.
2. As (1), except that the confederates said "green" to the brighter slides and "green-blue" to the duller ones, or vice versa.
3. The two confederates said "green" on every trial.

Nearly 21% of the majority's responses were influenced by the minority in condition 2, but the minority had no influence in conditions 1 and 3. The minority had no effect in condition 1 because it didn't respond consistently. The minority in condition 3 responded consistently, but its refusal to use more complex descriptions of the stimuli (e.g. "green-blue") made its behaviour seem rigid and unrealistic.

The above study is limited because it involved an artificial situation and thus lacks ecological validity. In addition, it differs from many real-life situations in that the decisions the participants were required to make were trivial and had no consequences.

KEY TERMS

Consistency: the extent to which the same opinions are expressed by all minority group members (inter-individual consistency) and over time (intra-individual consistency).

Flexibility: the ability to express a given point of view while varying the specific arguments used to support it.

Commitment: an individual's involvement in, and motivation for, a given viewpoint.

African Americans demonstrating for voting rights in front of the White House as police and others watch; sign reads "We demand the right to vote everywhere".

Why is it important for minority groups members to be consistent among themselves and over time? According to Moscovici, consistency leads the majority to attribute certainty and competence to the minority group members. Maass and Clark (1984) reviewed the evidence and found consistent minority groups were perceived as confident, certain, and competent.

Later we will consider the role of social influence in social change. One example of this is the civil rights movement in the United States in the 1960s. A major reason why this minority movement was so successful was that those involved showed enormous commitment over several years. This led the American majority to accept that those working in the civil rights movements had a very strong sense of the rightness of their position.

Message processing

According to Moscovici, minorities can make group members engage in more thorough processing than majorities. Supporting evidence was reported by Nemeth et al. (1990). Participants listened to word lists. The majority or the minority consistently drew attention to words belonging to certain categories. There was then a recall test for the words. There was much better recall when a minority had drawn attention to them, presumably because the words had been processed more thoroughly.

Further support for Moscovici's prediction was obtained by Martin et al. (2003). They gave participants two messages, the second arguing for the opposite position to the first. According to Moscovici, resistance to changing participants' opinions when given the second message should have been greater when the first message was endorsed by a minority because it should have been processed more thoroughly. That is what they found.

Public vs private influence

Wood et al. (1994) identified three conformity effects predicted by Moscovici's dual-process theory:

1. *Public influence*, in which the individual's behaviour in front of the group is influenced by others' views. This should occur mostly when majorities influence minorities.
2. *Direct private influence*, in which there is a change in the individual's private opinions about the issue being discussed. This should be found mainly when minorities influence majorities.
3. *Indirect private influence*, in which the individual's private opinions about related issues change. This should also be found mostly when majorities are influenced by minorities.

Wood et al. (1994) reviewed the relevant research. As predicted, majorities in most studies had more public influence than minorities. Also as predicted, minorities had more indirect private influence than majorities, especially when their opinions were consistent. However, majorities had more direct influence than minorities, which is contrary to Moscovici's theory.

Some of the clearest evidence that minority influence can be private but not public was reported by Nemeth and Wachtler (1974). They used a mock jury setting involving a personal injury case. The minority consisted of a confederate of the researchers. In public, the participants were totally uninfluenced by the confederate. However, their private views expressed on a post-experiment questionnaire were strongly influenced by the confederate.

Ingroups vs outgroups

David and Turner (1999) argued that minority influences will be found only when the minority is perceived as part of the ingroup. The participants were moderate feminists exposed to the minority views of extreme feminists. The views of the extreme feminists influenced the majority when the situation was set up as feminists vs non-feminists, because the extreme feminists were part of the ingroup. However, the views of the extreme feminists had little impact when there was a contrast between a moderate feminist majority and an outgroup of extreme feminists.

Nemeth (2009) discussed why social influence is greater from minorities consisting of ingroup members rather than outgroup members. She pointed out that the majority exhibits more discomfort and anger when the minority consists of ingroup members, and suggested these emotions lead majority members to assess their message more thoroughly.

EVALUATION

+ Minorities often influence majorities and several factors involved (e.g. consistency, commitment, and flexibility) have been identified.

+ The influence of minorities on majorities is mainly in the form of private rather than public agreement. The opposite pattern is found when majorities influence minorities.

– Moscovici exaggerated the differences in how majorities and minorities exert influence. As Smith and Mackie (2000, p. 371) pointed out, "Majorities are influential when their dissent offers a consensus, avoids contamination [i.e. obvious bias], and triggers private acceptance—the same processes by which all groups achieve influence."

– Moscovici did not attach sufficient importance to the *relationship* between the minority and majority. A minority regarded by the majority as part of the ingroup will typically exert more influence that a minority regarded as part of an outgroup (David & Turner, 1999).

– Majorities generally differ from minorities in several ways (e.g. power; status). Differences in the social influence exerted by majorities and minorities may depend on power or status rather than on their minority or majority position within the group. There are other differences between majorities and minorities. Majorities are perceived as the source of treatment, whereas minorities are seen as more distinctive than majorities and as the target of treatment (Seyranian et al., 2008).

– The great majority of studies have focused *either* on the influence of a minority on the majority *or* the influence of the majority on a minority. In fact, however, there are often simultaneous influences in both directions. Clark (1994) made use of the script of a film involving a jury's deliberation (*Twelve Angry Men*). Social influence was greater on participants exposed to arguments on both sides (minority and majority influence) than those exposed only to arguments from the minority.

Section Summary

- A minority consisting of one person generally exerts less social influence than a minority consisting of more than one person.
- Minorities have more social influence when they are of high status.
- According to Moscovici, minorities influence majorities through conversion, which affects private beliefs more than public behaviour.
- Conversion is most likely to occur when the minority is consistent, flexible, shows commitment, and has relevant views.
- Minorities will be more influential if they demonstrate certainty, convey an alternative view, disrupt the norm, and draw attention to their views.
- Messages from minorities are often processed more thoroughly than those from majorities.
- Research indicates that majorities typically have more public influence than minorities (compliance), whereas minorities have more private influence than majorities (conversion).
- Minority influence is generally greater when the minority is perceived as part of the ingroup rather than the outgroup. The majority exhibits more discomfort and anger

when the minority is part of the ingroup, and these emotions lead to more detailed processing of their message.

- Limitations of research on minority influence include:
  - the processes underlying social influence by minorities and by majorities are less different than assumed by Moscovici.
  - much research fails to take account of the fact that majorities are generally more powerful and have greater status than minorities.
  - there has been insufficient emphasis on simultaneous minority and majority influence.

KEY TERM

Social change: an alteration in the social structure of a society; minorities often try to produce social change to enhance the status of their group.

THE ROLE OF SOCIAL INFLUENCE PROCESSES IN SOCIAL CHANGE

? Minority influence is probably of more importance than majority influence in terms of social change. Can you think of an example where a minority of one changed the course of human history?

This section is devoted to social change. **Social change** refers to large-scale alterations in the social order within a society. I will start by focusing on ways social change has been produced by social influence. After that, I consider the effects minorities have had in producing social change via social influence.

Why is there extensive coverage of minority influence in social change? Most of the greatest social changes over the past several centuries occurred because of the efforts and commitment of relatively small numbers of people. Well-known examples of social change (or attempted social change) produced by minorities include the suffragette movement that led to women getting the vote in the UK, the civil rights movement in the United States that led to blacks being given equal rights with whites, and the activities of numerous terrorist groups around the world.

An important real-life example of a minority influencing a majority was the suffragette movement in the early years of the twentieth century. A relatively small group of suffragettes argued strongly for the initially unpopular view that women should be allowed to vote. The hard work of the suffragettes, combined with the justice of their case, finally led the majority to accept their point of view.

Social influence: Obedience

While reading this chapter, you may have found yourself worrying about the implications for society of research on obedience to authority. As a result of his research, Milgram (1974) became extremely pessimistic about the future: "The capacity for man to abandon his humanity, indeed the inevitability that he does so, as he merges his unique personality into the large institutional structures . . . is the fatal flaw nature has designed into us, and which in the long run gives our species only a modest chance for survival." In a similar vein, Milgram (1974) also referred to "the extreme willingness of adults to go to almost any lengths on the command of an authority".

The notion that evil behaviour (and an excessive willingness to obey authority) are not confined to a few psychopaths and other mentally ill individuals has been expressed by many other experts. For example, the philosopher Hannah Arendt argued that what was most horrifying about the Nazis was that they were "terrifyingly normal".

We might argue that Milgram's set-up was so artificial his findings don't have any real relevance to everyday life. However, that argument doesn't stand up to scrutiny. We saw that nurses in real-life situations will give patients too high doses of drugs if ordered to do so by a doctor (Hofling et al., 1966; Lesar et al., 1997). In addition, there is the Strip Search Prank Call Scam (Wolfson, 2005). Fast-food workers in the United States received phone calls from a prankster (not a researcher!) claiming to be a policeman. He persuaded many female workers to strip and sexually abuse other workers. This scam later formed the basis for a movie (*Compliance*).

For many people, the most compelling evidence that Milgram was right in assuming most people are willing to ignore their consciences in the face of authority comes from world history.

The horrors of Nazi Germany perhaps provide the most obvious example. However, the genocide in Rwanda, the mass murders in Stalin's Russia, and the torture and abuse at Abu Ghraib prison in Iraq are other striking cases of immoral behaviour and obedience to authority.

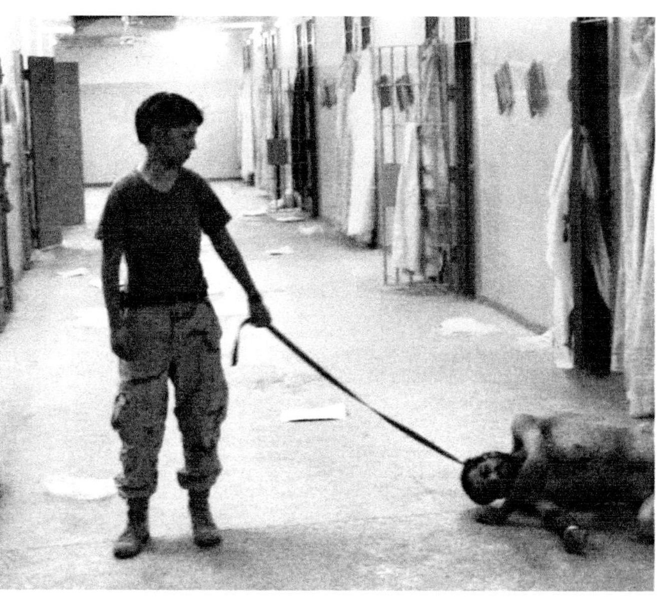

Events such as the torture carried out on prisoners in Abu Ghraib support Milgram's findings that most people are prepared to ignore their own conscience in the face of authority.

Nazi Germany

Milgram (1974) believed his findings had *direct* relevance to the horrifying social changes the Nazis imposed on Germany in the 1930s. Milgram's findings help us to understand how the Nazis changed German society. First, as discussed earlier, two sources of social power in the Milgram situation are legitimate power (based on authority) and coercive power (based on the threat of punishment). Both were important in Nazi Germany. The Nazis claimed legitimate power because millions of Germans had voted for them shortly before they seized power. They also had coercive power because opponents were treated harshly and were often killed.

Second, the Nazis imposed their appalling social changes on Germany through use of the foot-in-the-door technique—the demands imposed on German citizens gradually increased and so were harder to resist. Initially modest discrimination against the Jews increased systematically over time.

Third, the Nazi leaders generally accepted responsibility for the dreadful policies they imposed on Germany. Thus, ordinary Germans could argue they lacked personal responsibility for the changes occurring in Germany during the 1930s.

In fact, Milgram greatly exaggerated the similarities between his situation and Nazi Germany in several ways. First, he emphasised to his participants that the experiment had positive goals such as increasing our knowledge of human learning and memory. In contrast, the Nazis' goals were totally negative and abhorrent, including the systematic murder and eventual extermination of Jews, gypsies, and homosexuals.

Second, Milgram (1974) argued that people behaving in ethically unacceptable ways when obeying an authority figure do so because they have entered an agentic state in which they absolve themselves of all personal responsibility. That may well have been true of many Nazis working in concentration camps. However, it was certainly not true of the great majority of Milgram's participants, who showed obvious signs of tension, unease, and emotional turmoil.

Third, most Nazis who committed atrocities against the Jews did so without minute-by-minute surveillance. In contrast, the participants in Milgram's experiments were much more obedient when the experimenter could see what they were doing. Thus, Milgram's participants were much less enthusiastic about obeying authority than the Nazis.

CASE STUDY: War criminals

After the Second World War, the Allies tried many high-ranking Nazi officers. At his trial in Jerusalem in 1961, Adolf Eichmann argued he had only been obeying orders. He said he was not the "monster" the newspapers described but simply an ordinary person caught up in an extraordinary situation. Eichmann was described as having no violent anti-Jewish feelings (Arendt, 1963). The argument was that he was an autonomous individual who became agentic when he joined the SS and subscribed to the military code of obedience to those in authority.

Power structure

Obedience to authority is greater when the participant is of lesser status than the authority figure. In similar fashion, conformity is greater when the other group members are of higher status than the participant. An implication is that there will be more conformity and obedience to authority in hierarchical organisations or groups with large status differences than in non-hierarchical situations. It is no coincidence that many of the tragic situations that have occurred through undue obedience to authority (e.g. Nazi Germany; Abu Ghraib) have occurred in military groups having a very strong hierarchy.

CASE STUDY: The My Lai massacre

The My Lai massacre was one of the most controversial incidents in the Vietnam War. On 14 December 1969 almost 400 Vietnamese villagers were killed in under four hours. The following transcript is from a CBS News interview with a soldier who took part in the massacre.

Q. How many people did you round up?

A. Well, there was about forty, fifty people that we gathered in the center of the village. And we placed them in there, and it was like a little island, right there in the centre of the village, I'd say . . . And . . .

Q. What kind of people—men, women, children?

A. Men, women, children.

Q. Babies?

A. Babies. And we huddled them up. We made them squat down and Lieutenant Calley came over and said, "You know what to do with them, don't you?" And I said yes. So I took it for granted that he just wanted us to watch them. And he left, and came back about ten or fifteen minutes later and said, "How come you ain't killed them yet?" And I told him that I didn't think you wanted us to kill them, that you just wanted us to guard them. He said, "No. I want them dead." So—

Q. He told this to all of you, or to you particularly?

A. Well, I was facing him. So, but the other three, four guys heard it and so he stepped back about ten, fifteen feet, and he started shooting them. And he told me to start shooting. So I started shooting, I poured about four clips into the group.

Q. You fired four clips from your . . .

A. M-16.

Q. And that's about how many clips—I mean, how many—

A. I carried seventeen rounds to each clip.

Q. So you fired something like sixty-seven shots?

A. Right.

Q. And you killed how many? At that time?

A. Well, I fired them automatic, so you can't—You just spray the area on them and so you can't know how many you killed 'cause they were going fast. So I might have killed ten or fifteen of them.

Q. Men, women and children?

A. Men, women and children.

Q. And babies?

A. And babies.

William Calley stood trial for his involvement in this massacre. He claimed he was only obeying orders. Before the massacre, Calley showed no criminal tendencies and afterwards returned to a life of quiet respectability. His behaviour was that of a "normal" person. Kelman and Lawrence (1972) conducted a survey after the trial and found half the respondents said it was "normal, even desirable" to obey legitimate authority.

EXAM HINT

Exam questions are likely to ask you to *use* your knowledge of social influence research, i.e. research on conformity, obedience, and minority influence. You might be given an example of how people's opinions have changed in the last decade about environmental issues and asked to use your knowledge of social influence research to explain how this has happened. Or you could be asked how you might set about changing people's views on an important environmental matter, based on your knowledge of social influence research.

Social change produced by minorities

Research on minority influence is very relevant to understanding most major social changes in this country and around the world, and we will be discussing its relevance. However, two points need to be made here. First, minorities have achieved social change in numerous ways, and so we must avoid oversimplifications. Second, it is often hard to identify the main factors responsible for social change in the real world. For example, historians still argue over the precise reasons minorities such as the communists in Russia or the Nazis in Germany achieved power over the majority. This is the case because we simply have to consider what happened and so can't make use of the experimental method. We will consider two examples of minority influence in the real world: (1) terrorists; and (2) the American civil rights movement.

Terrorism

Terrorism represents one way minority influence can be used to achieve social change. As Kruglanski and Fishman (2006) pointed out, terrorism is a means to an end (e.g. overthrowing majority rule; putting an end to military occupation). According to the journalist Barbara Victor, terrorists are often motivated by a "fatal cocktail" involving religion, helpless deprivation, and nationalism.

Support for the notion of a fatal cocktail was reported by Kruglanski et al. (2009). They analysed video clips from farewell tapes of suicide terrorists, and interviews with captured terrorists and failed suicide terrorists. The terrorists' main motives for terrorism were nearly always based on an ideology or worldview involving religion and/or nationalism.

How much impact do terrorists have on majority opinion? Kruglanski et al. (2009) addressed this issue in a study on the inhabitants of 12 Arab countries, Pakistan, and Indonesia. The participants indicated their support (or otherwise) for terrorist attacks on Americans. Those endorsing individualistic goals (e.g. education; raising a family) were less supportive than those who endorsed collectivistic goals (e.g. defending one's nation or religion). Thus, majority members whose goals resembled those of the terrorists were more supportive of them.

Factors causing influence

What factors cause terrorists to have minority influence?

1. Most terrorist groups constantly put forward the same extreme views, and so have the advantage of consistency.
2. Terrorists exhibit high levels of commitment and sacrifice, perhaps most obviously in the case of suicide terrorists.
3. Many terrorist groups are pursuing goals seen as relevant and appropriate by the majority. For example, consider the second intifada (uprising) in Palestine. About 80% of the Palestine population supported the use of terrorist tactics (including suicide bombings) against the Israelis.
4. Many terrorist groups are very successful at drawing attention to their views by committing atrocities receiving massive publicity.
5. Terrorist groups often portray themselves as an ingroup representing the majority's interests and goals. As we have seen, terrorists in several Arab countries attract more support from those members of the population who share their emphasis on defending one's religion and nation.
6. Terrorists try to present themselves as principled individuals seeking to maintain religious values they claim are under attack.
7. Terrorist groups are typically distinctive in the sense that they represent a tiny minority. As we have seen, distinctive groups can have more influence than less distinctive ones.

American civil rights movement

The civil rights movement in the United States in the 1950s and 1960s produced massive beneficial social change for blacks within American society. This movement involved very large numbers of people engaged in various forms of civil disobedience. Here we will focus on only a few of the most important events.

One key event occurred on 1 December 1955, when a black woman called Rosa Parks refused to give up her seat on a bus in Montgomery, Alabama to a white person. She was arrested, which led to the Montgomery Bus Boycott in which primarily black citizens refused to use the local bus network. This boycott caused major financial problems for the bus companies involved, and led 1 year later to a ruling that declared segregated buses were unconstitutional.

Rosa Parks (1913–2005), whose refusal to move to the back of a bus triggered the bus boycott in Montgomery, Alabama.

The Greensboro sit-ins formed another landmark. These sit-ins were triggered by four black students who sat down at the "whites only" counter at the Woolworth's store in Greensboro, North Carolina on 1 February 1960. The next day, more than 20 black students joined in the sit-in. There was widespread publicity for these sit-ins, which subsequently spread across the South of the United States. The adverse publicity and loss of profit caused by the sit-ins led Woolworth's to stop their segregated policy in July 1960.

The final landmark event is the March on Washington for jobs and freedom on 28 August 1963. It was at a huge gathering connected to this march that Martin Luther King gave his famous "I have a dream" speech in which he emphasised the importance of racial harmony. This march played a significant role in the Civil Rights Act of 1964 that helped to eliminate racial discrimination in the United States.

Factors causing influence

Why was the minority (mostly black) involved in the civil rights movement so successful in achieving social change? Several factors were involved:

1. Those involved exhibited a very high level of commitment over a period of several years.
2. Those involved were willing to make sacrifices such as exposing themselves to abuse and to possible arrest. Their commitment and sacrifices convinced most Americans they believed strongly in the rightness of their position.
3. The civil rights campaigners were entirely consistent in the views they endorsed and the changes to society they wanted to achieve.
4. The civil rights movement attracted huge media attention. This led the white majority to think about the unequal position of blacks in American society.
5. It was very clear that those involved in civil rights were driven by principles (e.g. everyone is equal) that carried moral authority.
6. Martin Luther King was very successful at arguing that America should be a colour-blind society consisting of one large ingroup including blacks as well as whites. There is evidence (e.g. David & Turner, 1999; discussed earlier) that minorities have more influence when perceived as part of the ingroup including the majority. The fact that Martin Luther King was a Baptist minister and had qualifications from Boston University probably helped to make him more acceptable to the white majority.
7. There was a large increase in opportunities for tens of millions of Americans during the 1950s and early 1960s and much focus on individuals "doing their own thing". Thus, the civil rights movement was in tune with major social trends of that era.

Social change produced by minorities: Snowball effect and social cryptoamnesia

We have discussed historical important examples showing how minorities can sometimes be very successful in producing social change. Here we broaden out the discussion to focus on two general processes often associated with minority-triggered social change.

History teaches us that major social changes produced by minorities often take years or even decades. What often happens is that the number of people belonging to the minority seeking social change grows over time. This phenomenon resembles a snowball—as you roll a snowball through the snow it becomes larger and larger. Unsurprisingly, the way in which minorities advocating social change develop momentum and grow over the years is known as the **snowball effect** (van Avermaet, 1996).

How can we explain the snowball effect? Remember that minorities are usually better at changing the private opinions of majority members than their publicly expressed opinions. That makes it a little mysterious how the number of adherents to the minority group's opinion increases over time. We may be able to resolve this mystery with reference to social cryptoamnesia. **Social cryptoamnesia** is "the concealment of the origin in minority groups of some of today's well-accepted norms and values" (Vernet et al., 2009, p. 130). It permits social change to occur without the majority giving credit to the minority group responsible for that change. This makes social change more acceptable to most majority group members. Social cryptoamnesia also makes it easier to reduce conflict between the majority and minority.

Vernet et al. (2009) provide a good example of social cryptoamnesia. Initially, they found that all the Portuguese women in their sample had more favourable opinions about women's rights than about the feminist movement. This suggests they may have forgotten that it was

KEY TERMS

Snowball effect: the way in which a minority advocating social change grows in number over time.

Social cryptoamnesia: accepted social change in which the source of the minority influence instrumental in producing that change has been forgotten.

the feminist movement that was instrumental in securing women's rights. When the participants were reminded of the link between women's rights and the feminist movement, their ratings of the feminist movement became more favourable. Thus, social cryptoamnesia initially led the participants to undervalue the contribution of the feminist movement.

Conclusions

Minorities in many countries have successfully produced major social change. Each example is idiosyncratic in some ways. However, there are common themes. Most of the factors identified by Moscovici in his conversion theory are important. Consider the very different examples of terrorism and the civil rights movement. In both cases, minority influence involves consistency of views and actions, commitment to the cause, sacrifices to achieve goals, considerable public attention, a principled position, trying to establish themselves as an ingroup, and identifying with current social trends. The snowball effect and social cryptoamnesia help us to explain the factors involved in minorities producing social change.

The major limitation in trying to apply psychological research to social change is that we cannot establish cause and effect. This is so because all we have to rely on is the historical record. We do not know, for example, what would have happened in America if Martin Luther King had never existed. The Civil Rights Act was passed in the year after the Washington March at which he spoke, which suggests the latter helped to cause the former. However, there were other important changes, notably, the assassination of President Kennedy on 22 November 1963 and his replacement by President Johnson. Since Johnson was more motivated than Kennedy to eliminate segregation, the change of President may have played an important role.

Grounds for optimism

Many impressive examples of social change in society occurred due to the efforts of dissenters standing up for their beliefs. A good example is Mahatma Gandhi (1869–1948), who always advocated non-violent resistance. He led numerous campaigns in India to reduce poverty, to increase women's rights, and to achieve independence from Britain for India. In 1930, he led the 250-mile Dandi Salt March to protest against the salt tax imposed by Britain. He was a charismatic figure who gradually gained massive support for most of his campaigns.

Mahatma Gandhi (left) on the Dandi Salt March protest in 1930. He was an inspirational figure who promoted non-violent civil disobedience in his fight for independence for India.

What kind of person is willing to resist unjust authority? On the basis of research on social influence, we might expect individuals low in authoritarianism to be especially likely to stand up for their beliefs. Relevant evidence was reported by Mantell (1974), who found that young American men who were draft resisters during the Vietnam War mostly had very low scores on authoritarianism.

The importance of dissenting voices can be seen in research on obedience to authority and conformity. In Milgram's basic experiment, the participant decided whether to obey the authority figure on his/her own and about two-thirds of participants showed full obedience. There was markedly less full obedience to authority (10%) when participants were exposed to two dissenters who refused to give electric shocks.

In similar fashion, social support drastically reduces obedience to authority. For example, Rank and Jacobsen (1977) found only 11% of nurses obeyed a doctor's instructions to give too high a dose of medication to patients when they talked to other nurses beforehand.

In sum, as Milgram (1974) pointed out, "When an individual wishes to stand in opposition to authority, he [sic!] does best to find support for his position from others in his group. The mutual support provided by men for each other is the strongest bulwark against the excesses of authority."

Section Summary

Role of social influence processes in social change

- Nazi Germany resembled Milgram's situation in that legitimate and coercive power was used to produce obedience and the demands on individuals slowly became more unacceptable.
- Nazi Germany differed from Milgram's situation in that the Nazis' goals were abhorrent whereas those in Milgram's research were positive. In addition, there was much more denial of personal responsibility in Nazi Germany than Milgram's situation.
- History teaches us that there is generally more conformity and obedience to authority in hierarchical organisations with large status differences.

Role of minority influence in social change

- Terrorists are often motivated by a "fatal cocktail" involving religion, helpless deprivation, and nationalism.
- Social change produced by terrorists depends on most of the factors for minority influence identified by Moscovici. For example, they typically maintain a consistent position, and portray themselves as forming an ingroup fighting for principled ideas on behalf of the majority.
- Social change produced by civil rights campaigners in the United States also depended on the factors Moscovici claimed were required for minority influence. For example, they showed commitment by making many sacrifices and their actions were obviously based on moral principles that most people accepted.
- The fact that Martin Luther King was an educated man and a Baptist minister may have made him more acceptable to the white majority and thus reduced the notion of black activists as an outgroup.
- Social change often involves a snowball effect in which the supporters of the minority position gradually increase over time. The snowball effect may depend in part on social cryptoamnesia—it is easier for the majority to accept social change suggested by a minority if they forget its source.
- It is hard to establish cause and effect with social change because we have only the historical record available as evidence.

Further Reading

- The whole topic of social influence is discussed in detail in M.W. Eysenck (2013) *Simply psychology (3rd Edn)* (Hove, UK: Psychology Press).
- Major criticisms of Milgram's research on obedience to authority are discussed by J.M. Burger (2011) Alive and well after all these years. *The Psychologist, 24*, 654–657.
- Perry, G. (2012) *Behind the shock machine* (New York: New Press). Gail Perry identifies numerous problems and limitations with Milgram's research on obedience to authority.
- B.H. Hodges and A.L. Geyer (2006) A nonconformist account of the Asch experiments: Values, pragmatics, and moral dilemmas. *Personality and Social Psychology Review, 10*, 2–19. Hodges and Geyer show how Asch's conformity research has been misunderstood and misinterpreted.
- M.A. Hogg and G.M. Vaughan (2010) *Social psychology (6th Edn)* (Harlow, UK: Prentice Hall). Several chapters in this textbook contain comprehensive coverage of the topics discussed in this chapter.

EXAM HINT

Some examination questions require you to apply your knowledge. They start with a "stem" describing a scenario (as in question 1 on the next page). Whilst you probably have not seen the scenario before, if you have revised everything you will have the knowledge needed to answer the question. Just remember to apply your knowledge. You might briefly outline a theory or research study but then must use this to explain the scenario.

Revision Questions

The examination questions aim to sample the material in this whole chapter. For advice on how to answer such questions refer to Chapter 1, "How Can I Do Well in the Exam?".

1. The National Blood Service is always trying to recruit more people to become blood donors. They decide to consult a psychologist about how they might use psychological tactics to increase the number of donors.

   Using your knowledge of informational and normative social influence, suggest some possible strategies to encourage more people to become blood donors. (4 marks)

2. a. Identify **two** types of conformity and give examples of each. (4 marks)

   b. Outline and evaluate research into conformity. (16 marks)

3. a. Explain **one or more** reasons why people obey authority. (6 marks)

   b. Milgram conducted some well-known studies of obedience. Outline **one** other study of obedience. (4 marks)

   c. Milgram's studies on obedience were carried out in America in the 1960s and 1970s. Briefly discuss how this limits their value. (4 marks)

4. a. Explain what is meant by *locus of control*. (3 marks)

   b. Locus of control can be used to explain resistance to social influence. Outline **one** other explanation of resistance to social influence. (3 marks)

   c. Outline **one** study that has shown how people resist pressures to conform. (4 marks)

5. Discuss the role of minority influence in social change. (8 marks)

What you need to know

The specifications for AS and A-level year 1 are the same for this topic, so you will need to cover everything in this chapter.

Memory will be examined in Paper 1 of the AS exam and Paper 1 of the A-level exam.

Memory

3

You may think that in an ideal world we would remember every detail of things that happen, especially when they are important. However, if we remembered *everything* our memories would be very full. As a result, we would find it hard to think because of the enormous wealth of detail we would always be remembering. In fact, of course, we actually forget lots of things, many of them (alas!) things we didn't want to forget. What makes some things memorable and others forgettable?

This chapter explores one topic in cognitive psychology—human memory. How important is memory? Imagine if we were without it. We would not recognise anyone or anything as familiar. We would not be able to talk, read, or write, because we would remember nothing about language. In many ways we would be like newborn babies.

We use memory for numerous purposes—to keep track of conversations, to remember telephone numbers while we dial them, to write essays in exams, to make sense of what we read, and to recognise people's faces. There are many different kinds of memory, suggesting we have a number of memory systems. This chapter explores in detail the sub-divisions of human memory, factors that cause forgetting, and the accuracy of eyewitness testimony.

Learning and Memory

Memory is the process of retaining information for some time after it has been learned. Thus, there are close links between **learning** and **memory**. Something that is learned is lodged in memory, and we can only remember things learned in the past.

? Are learning and memory different? If so, what is the difference?

Memory and learning can most clearly be demonstrated by good performance on a memory test. For example, we could give someone a list of words for a specified period of time and then some time later ask them to recall the list. When learning and memorising the words in the list, there are three stages:

1. **Encoding:** When the person is given the list, they encode the words. They place the words in memory. "Encoding" means to put something into a code, in this case the code used to store it in memory—some kind of memory trace. For example, if you hear the word "chair", you might encode it in terms of your favourite chair you normally sit in at home. In other words, your encoding of the word "chair" involves converting or changing the word you hear into a meaningful form.

KEY TERMS

Learning: a relatively permanent change in behaviour, which is not due to maturation.

Memory: the mental processes involved in encoding, storage, and retrieval of information. Encoding depends on which sense provides the input; storage is the information being held in memory; retrieval involves accessing the stored information.

Encoding: involves the transfer of information into a code, leading to the creation of a memory trace, which can be registered in the memory store.

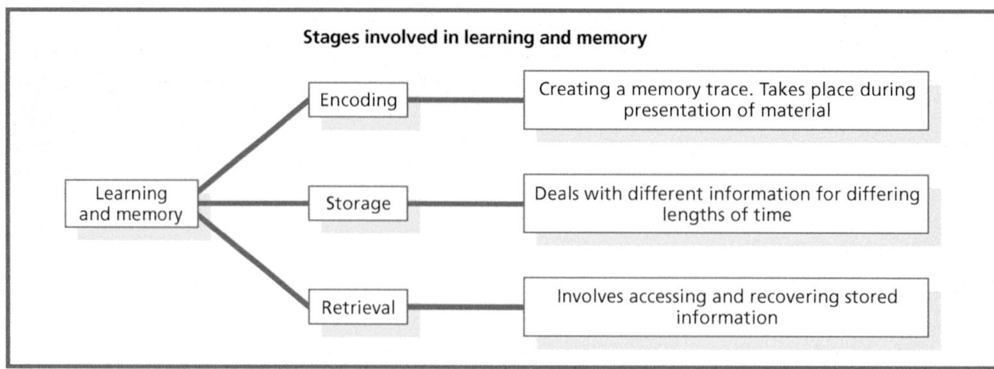

2. **Storage:** As a result of encoding, the information is stored within the memory system. As we will see, some information remains stored in memory for decades or even an entire lifetime.
3. **Retrieval:** Recovering stored information from the memory system. This involves recall or "remembering".

Psychologists interested in learning focus on encoding and storage. In contrast, those interested in memory concentrate most on retrieval. However, *all* these processes depend on each other—we only know an individual has learned something if they remember it, and memory depends on previous learning.

Testing memory

Psychologists use various methods to test recall or learning.

- Free recall. Give participants some words to learn and then ask them to recall the words in any order.
- Cued recall. After presenting the material to be learned, provide cues to help recall. For example, saying that some of the items are minerals.
- Recognition. Giving a list of words which includes some of those in the initial presentation. Participants are asked to identify those in the original list.
- Paired-associate learning. Participants are given word pairs to learn and then tested by presenting the first word in each pair and asking them to recall the second word.
- Nonsense syllables. Participants are asked to memorise meaningless sets of letters. These may be trigrams (three letters).

MULTI-STORE MODEL OF MEMORY

It is important to distinguish among three kinds of memory: sensory register; short-term memory and long-term memory. We will start with the **sensory register** which consists of various sensory stores. Environmental stimulation is initially processed within these sensory stores with one store for each of the sense modalities (e.g. vision; hearing). Information presented visually is initially held very briefly (for no more than 500 milliseconds) in **iconic memory** (visual sensory store), and auditory information is held for somewhat longer in **echoic memory** (auditory sensory store). Ioannides et al. (2003) found that information could be held for up to 5 seconds in the left hemisphere and 2 seconds in the right hemisphere. This difference probably reflects the dominance of the left hemisphere in language processing. Iconic and echoic memory are both severely limited in capacity—they can store only a few visual or auditory items.

There are sensory stores associated with each of the other senses (e.g. touch; taste). However, they are less important than iconic and echoic memory and have attracted much less research. In sum, the sensory register consists of several stores (one for each sensory modality) in which information is held for a very short period of time.

KEY TERMS

Storage: storing a memory for a period of time so that it can be used later.

Retrieval: the process of recovering information stored in long-term memory. If retrieval is successful, the individual remembers the information in question.

Sensory register: it consists of several sensory stores (one in each sense modality such as vision and hearing) each holding information very briefly when relevant stimuli are presented. Each sensory register has very limited capacity.

Iconic memory: a sensory store within the sensory register that holds visual information for approximately 500 milliseconds.

Echoic memory: a sensory store within the sensory register that holds auditory information for approximately 2 seconds.

Information in short-term memory typically lasts for only a short time (a few seconds). However, if it was very important to remember some information in short-term memory, you could probably maintain it for longer by repeatedly rehearsing it. In contrast, information in long-term memory can theoretically last forever or at least for a very long time.

Trying to remember a telephone number for a few seconds is an example of the use of **short-term memory**. This example illustrates two key features of short-term memory: very limited capacity and limited duration. **Long-term memory**, on the other hand, has unlimited capacity and lasts (potentially) forever. As an example, you might think of some of your most vivid childhood memories.

The model of memory put forward by Atkinson and Shiffrin (1968) is the most important theoretical approach based on the notion that there are three kinds of memory stores. This explains why their approach is known as the **multi-store model** of memory. Here are its crucial assumptions:

1. Human memory consists of three kinds of memory stores.
2. Information from the environment is initially received by the sensory stores within the sensory register. There is a sensory store for each sense modality—a store for what we see, one for what we hear, and so on. Information lasts for a very short period of time (fractions of a second, or a second or two) in these sensory stores.
3. Some information in the sensory stores is attended to (and processed further) within the short-term store. The short-term store has limited capacity—we can only keep about *seven* items in this store at any one time.
4. Some information processed in the short-term store is transferred to the long-term store. How does information get into the long-term store? There is a process of **rehearsal** in which information in the short-term store is repeatedly verbally to oneself to put it into the long-term store. The more something is rehearsed, the stronger the memory trace in long-term memory.
5. Information in the long-term store can often last for a very long time. As I have already mentioned, in some cases information in the long-term store remains there for our entire lifetime.
6. There are important differences between short-term and long-term memory in forgetting. When information is forgotten from the short-term store, it simply disappears from the memory system. In contrast, most information forgotten from the long-term store is still in the memory system but can't be accessed (e.g. because of interference from other information).

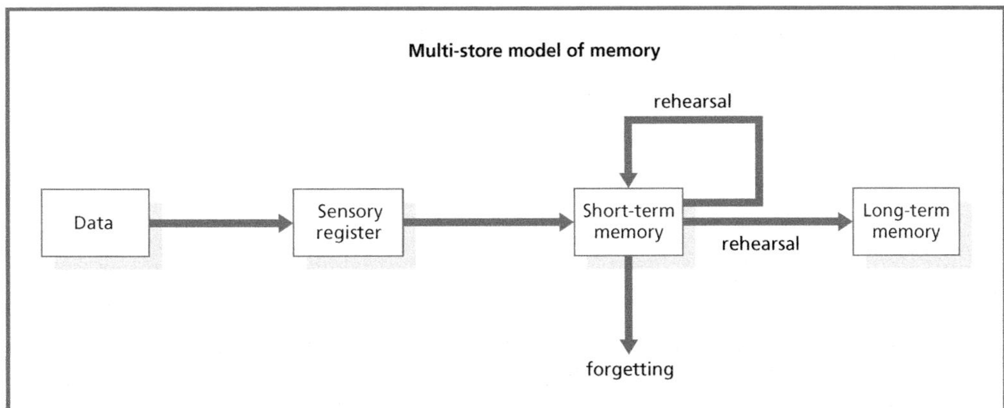

In what follows, we will be looking mainly at the short-term and long-term memory stores. However, we will start by considering the sensory stores within the sensory register.

Sensory register: visual and auditory sensory stores

Our sense organs are constantly bombarded with information. At this very moment, you are receiving visual information from this book, there is probably auditory information in the form of human voices or traffic noise, and you can feel something from that part of you in contact

EXAM HINT

If you have a question asking you to outline the main features of the multi-store model, you might find it useful to include a diagram in your answer IN ADDITION TO the written description. The diagram should be fully labelled and should include both structures and processes.

KEY TERMS

Short-term memory: a temporary place for storing information during which it receives limited processing (e.g. verbal rehearsal). Short-term memory has a very limited capacity and short duration, unless the information in it is maintained through rehearsal.

Long-term memory: a relatively permanent memory store with an unlimited capacity and duration, containing different components such as episodic (personal events), semantic (facts and information), and procedural (actions and skills) memory.

Multi-store model: a model in which memory is divided into three stores; sensory register, short-term memory, and long-term memory. This model has been highly influential but research has shown that memory is much more complex than assumed by the model.

Rehearsal: the verbal repetition of information (often words), which typically has the effect of increasing our long-term memory for the rehearsed information.

Even if we don't pay attention when we're spoken to, we are often able to repeat the last few things said. This is because that information is held for a few seconds in a sensory memory store.

with your chair. There is a separate sensory store for each type of information—iconic memory is used for visual information, echoic memory for auditory information, the haptic store concerned with touching and feeling, and so on. There has been most research on iconic memory, and so I will focus on it.

Sperling (1960) carried out the classic research on iconic memory He presented a visual array containing three rows of four letters each for 50 milliseconds (1/20 of a second). Participants could only report four or five letters when asked to provide full recall but claimed to have seen many more. Sperling assumed this happened because visual information had faded before most of it could be reported.

Sperling (1960) tested the above hypothesis by telling participants to recall only *part* of the information presented. Sperling's results supported his assumption—part recall was very good and suggested iconic memory held nine or ten items. Full recall was much lower because information in iconic memory decays within about 0.5 seconds and so all the items couldn't be recalled in time.

Why is iconic memory useful? The processes involved in visual perception *always* operate on information in iconic memory rather than directly on the visual environment. Iconic memory is also useful when watching movies. Movies are often presented at 24 frames per second with each frame differing slightly from the previous one. We perceive smooth rather than jerky motion because the iconic store allows us to integrate information from successive frames in a way that wouldn't be possible in its absence.

Short-term vs long-term memory: Brain damage

We all know certain kinds of information disappear rapidly from memory whereas others last for many years. Accordingly, you may think it is obvious there are separate short-term and long-term stores. I will shortly be discussing the main differences between these two stores. Before that, however, I want to discuss the strongest evidence for separate short-term and long-term memory stores. Strangely enough, it consists of research on brain-damaged patients. If short-term and long-term memory are really separate (and involve different brain areas), we might expect to find some brain-damaged patients with impaired long-term memory but intact short-term memory. Others should have impaired short-term memory but intact long-term memory.

In **amnesia**, a person loses much of their long-term memory. Amnesia is often due to an accident or chronic alcoholism. In spite of their brain damage, amnesic patients typically have intact short-term memory. This was shown convincingly by Spiers et al. (2001) in a review of 147 amnesic patients with serious long-term memory problems. *None* of these patients had a significant problem with short-term memory.

The opposite pattern (good long-term memory but poor short-term memory) has also been found occasionally. Consider KF, who suffered brain damage after a motorcycle accident. He had no problem with long-term learning and recall, but his digit span was greatly impaired (Shallice & Warrington, 1970).

Short-term memory, long-term memory, and the sensory register: Capacity, duration, and encoding

To prove the point that there are three types of memory store (or get as close to proof as we can), we need to start by listing all the likely differences among them. Since most of the evidence relates to the distinction between short-term and long-term memory, we will focus mostly on that.

KEY TERM

Amnesia: a severe loss of some kinds of long-term memory, usually as a result of brain damage.

When we have listed the differences, we can consider the relevant research evidence. Finally, we will evaluate that evidence. Here are possible (or probable!) differences among the memory stores:

1. *Coding:* Since words or other items in the short-term store are rehearsed or repeated in the short-term store, we might assume they are coded in terms of their sound (acoustic coding). In contrast, the information stored in long-term memory nearly always seems to be stored in terms of its meaning (semantic coding). Note, however, that we also store other kinds of information in long-term memory. For example, you know how to pronounce 'COMB' and 'YACHT' even though how they are pronounced can't be guessed from the spellings of these words. Thus, information about how to pronounce words is stored in long-term memory.

   The nature of coding within the sensory register is fairly straightforward: information in iconic memory is coded visually, information in echoic memory is coded acoustically, and so on. Thus, the type of coding varies from sensory store to sensory store depending on the sense modality for which it is specialised.
2. *Capacity:* The short-term store has very limited capacity. As mentioned already, its capacity was assumed to be about seven items. However, we will see later that its actual capacity is approximately four items. In contrast, the capacity of the long-term store is so large we are in no danger at all of filling it. What about the sensory register? It is hard to be precise. However, the capacity of iconic memory and echoic memory is very limited. It probably does not exceed 10 items in iconic memory and is probably less in echoic memory.
3. *Duration:* It is obvious from the names short-term memory store and long-term memory store that information has greater duration (i.e. lasts longer) in the long-term store than in the short-term store! As we will see, information in the short-term store, if not rehearsed, disappears within about 18–20 seconds. In contrast, elderly people can recognise the names of fellow students from 48 years previously (Bahrick et al., 1975). Thus, we have proof that long-term memory can last at least 50 years or so.

   What about the sensory register? As we have seen, information lasts in echoic memory for about 500 milliseconds (1/2 second) and for rather longer (perhaps a few seconds) in echoic memory.

EXAM HINT

The specification requires you to study the concepts of coding, capacity and duration. You may be set questions on each of these topics, including questions that ask you to explain the terms and, also, questions on research studies. For example.

- "Explain how psychologists have investigated the capacity of human memory. (4 marks)"
- "Explain how research has investigated duration in short-term human memory. (4 marks)"
- "Explain what research has shown about coding in human memory. (4 marks)"

Be prepared.

Now we will look at the evidence relating to these various assumptions about the short-term and long-term memory stores. After that, we will evaluate the multi-store model.

Short-term memory: Capacity

Psychologists have devised two main strategies to estimate the capacity of short-term memory: span measures and the recency effect in free recall.

? To what extent can we apply the findings of Jacobs to everyday life?

Span measures

In 1887, Joseph Jacobs used memory span as a measure of how much information can be stored in short-term memory. Jacobs presented his participants with a random sequence of digits or letters, and then asked them to repeat the items back in the same order. **Memory span** was the longest sequence of items recalled accurately at least 50% of the time. The average number of items recalled was between five and nine, and digits were recalled better (9.3 items) than letters (7.3 items).

Jacobs' approach was limited. First, his research lacked **mundane realism**, because his span tasks were not representative of everyday memory demands. Second, if we could only remember a few letters, we would be unable to remember the following sequence of 10 letters: P S Y C H O L O G Y! In fact, of course, we can remember that sequence because it's easy to organise the information in memory.

KEY TERMS

Memory span: an assessment of how much can be stored in short-term memory (STM) in the correct order at any time.

Mundane realism: the use of an artificial situation that closely resembles a natural situation.

Miller (1956) took account of the above point, and argued that the span of immediate memory is "seven, plus or minus two", whether the units are numbers, letters, or words. He claimed we should focus on **chunks** (integrated pieces or units of information). About seven chunks of information can be held in short-term memory at any time. The question of what constitutes a "chunk" depends on your personal experience. For example, "IBM" would be one chunk if you know about International Business Machines, but it would be three if you didn't.

Simon (1974) tested Miller's ideas on **chunking** by studying memory span for words, two-word phrases, and eight-word phrases. The number of words in the span increased from seven words to nine with two-word phrases and 22 with eight-word phrases. At the level of chunks, Simon argued that an entire phrase forms a single chunk. The number of chunks recalled varied less over conditions than the number of words—it fell from six or seven with unrelated words to four with two-word phrases and three with eight-word phrases. As with Jacobs' earlier research, the study by Simon (1974) lacks mundane realism in that the demands on the participants were very different from those of our everyday lives.

? Are there any problems with using letter or digit span as a measure of the capacity of short-term memory?

ACTIVITY: Chunking

Scientific method involves observing what occurs and seeing if there is a pattern. For example, you know that Miller found most people have an STM capacity of 7 plus or minus 2, which we call Miller's magic number. But you can test the idea that we can store far more than 9 items in STM by chunking them. This means we group similar things together in one category, for example: mug+spoon+teabag+sugar+milk. Ask whoever does the main shopping at home how they remember what's needed—do they chunk their list?

From such observations you could construct a prediction, called a hypothesis, and then test it. You could predict that people will recall more things, or recall them faster, if they chunk items rather than trying to remember them randomly.

You could try compiling and printing out a random shopping list for the supermarket, mixing up about 25 items from all around the store. Then make a second list of 25 different items but this time chunk them, i.e. group together similar items (like fresh vegetables; tinned goods; but don't use headings!). Test someone—not the main shopper—on the first list: give them 1 minute to read and learn, then 2 minutes to recall by writing items down. Then do the same for the second list. They will probably do better or faster on the second list, and you can explain why to them.

In science it is important to test the hypothesis, and find out whether it is correct or wrong. This is the way we increase scientific knowledge.

Cowan et al. (2005) argued that the capacity of short-term memory is often exaggerated. For example, people may recall some of the information from long-term memory rather than short-term memory and may also rehearse the information while it is being presented. Cowan et al. (2005) reduced the involvement of long-term memory and rehearsal by using the running memory task—a series of digits ended at an unpredictable point and participants then recalled the items from the end of the list. The average number of items recalled was 3.87, suggesting the true capacity of short-term memory is about four items. Subsequent research has confirmed that the capacity of short-term memory is about three or four chunks (Mathy & Feldman, 2012).

KEY TERMS

Chunks: integrated units of information.

Chunking: the process of combining individual items (e.g. letters; numbers) into larger, meaningful units.

Recency effect: better free recall of the last few items in a list with higher performance being due to the information being in the short-term store.

The recency effect

A familiar example of the **recency effect** is the observation that a pop group is only as good as their last hit song. People generally have a good memory for most-recent things (e.g. the movie they saw last). In relation to short-term memory, the recency effect can be measured using free recall—participants see a list of words or syllables, and immediately recall them in any order. The recency effect is demonstrated by the fact that the last two or three items in a list are usually much better remembered than items from the middle of the list. These last few items are well remembered because they are in the short-term store when the list presentation ends.

Glanzer and Cunitz (1966) introduced an interference task involving counting backwards by threes for 10 seconds between the end of the list and the start of recall. This eliminated the recency effect but had no effect on recall of the rest of the list. The two or three words at the end of the list were in a fragile state in short-term memory, and so were easily wiped out by counting backwards. In contrast, the other list items were in the long-term store and so were unaffected.

? If you were shown these ten words: cat, butter, car, house, carpet, tomato, beer, river, pool, tennis; and then asked to recall them immediately in any order, what words are likely to be best remembered?

ACTIVITY: Memory span

Read quickly through the following list of digits once. Cover the list and try to write the digits down in the correct order.

7 3 5 1 5 6 9 8 2 7 4

How many did you remember in the correct order? This is one way of measuring your memory span. Now try the following digits:

1 9 3 9 1 0 6 6 1 8 0 5 1 2 1 5

More digits, but if you recognised the "chunks" you should have remembered them all:

1939 Start of Second World War
1066 Battle of Hastings
1805 Battle of Trafalgar
1215 Signing of the Magna Carta

Did you find any recency effects when you tried to recall the list of digits? Try the test again (with different data) with this in mind.

Long-term memory: Capacity

As already mentioned, long-term memory has essentially unlimited capacity. Our ability to store information in long-term memory is surprisingly good. Konkle et al. (2010) presented participants with 2,912 pictures of scenes at 3 seconds per scene followed by a test of recognition memory. The scenes belonged to a total of 128 different general categories. Long-term memory for these scenes was very good. When participants chose between a previously presented scene and a new scene from a category not used during presentation, they were correct 96% of the time. Memory performance was above 75% even when the previously presented scene and the new scene both came from the same category.

Short-term memory: Duration

How long does information last in short-term memory? This is a crucial question. If information is lost rapidly from short-term memory, this must limit our ability to think about several things at once.

KEY RESEARCH STUDY

Peterson and Peterson (1959): Duration of short-term memory

Peterson and Peterson (1959) assessed the duration of short-term memory using what became known as the Brown–Peterson technique. They tested the hypothesis that information that is not rehearsed is lost rapidly from short-term memory. They used the experimental method under laboratory conditions to test this hypothesis.

On each trial, participants were presented with a trigram consisting of three consonants (e.g. BVM, CTG), which they knew they would be asked to recall in the correct order. Recall

continued over

Was the approach taken by Peterson and Peterson (1959) too artificial to tell us much about short-term forgetting in everyday life?

Why was information in short-term memory forgotten so quickly?

was required after a delay of 3, 6, 9, 12, 15, or 18 seconds. Thus, the length of the delay period was the independent variable.

The participants counted backwards in threes from a random three-digit number (e.g. 866, 863, 860, and so on) between the initial presentation of the trigram and the time when they were asked to recall it. This was done to prevent rehearsal of the trigram, because rehearsal would have improved performance by keeping information in short-term memory.

Recall had to be 100% accurate and in the correct order (serial recall) to be regarded as correct. Thus, the percentage correct serial recall was the dependent variable. The participants were tested repeatedly with the various time delays. Thus, the design involved repeated measures. The experimenters varied the time delay, and the effect of time delay on memory was assessed by the number of trigrams recalled.

Findings

What did Peterson and Peterson (1959) find? There was a rapid increase in forgetting from short-term memory as the time delay increased (see Figure). After 3 seconds, 80% of the trigrams were recalled, after 6 seconds 50% were recalled, and after 18 seconds fewer than 10% were recalled.

One conclusion is that information in short-term memory is fragile and easily forgotten. Another conclusion is that short-term memory is distinct from long-term memory in that forgetting is enormously faster from short-term memory.

Limitations

There are some criticisms of this study. First, Peterson and Peterson (1959) used very artificial stimuli (i.e. trigrams) essentially lacking in meaning. Thus, the study lacks mundane realism and external validity—short-term memory is likely to be better in everyday life than for consonant trigrams.

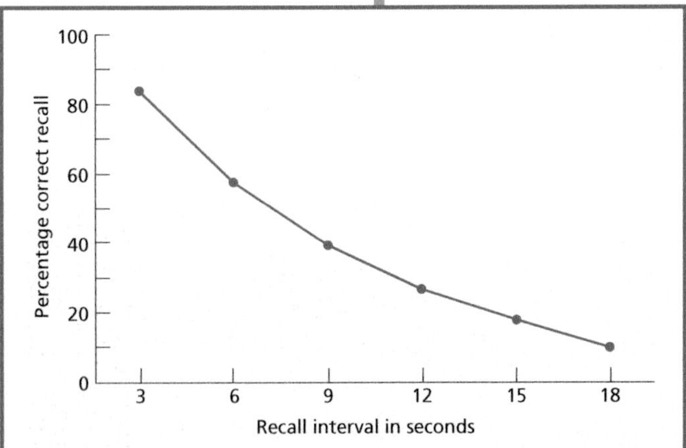

The graph shows a steady decline in short-term memory recall after longer retention intervals (from Peterson & Peterson, 1959).

Second, the participants were given many trials with different trigrams and may have become confused. Keppel and Underwood (1962) used the same task as Peterson and Peterson (1959) but observed *no* forgetting over time on the very first trial. Why was this? Forgetting is caused in part by proactive interference (disruption of current learning and memory by previous learning; see later in chapter), and only the first trigram presented is free from proactive interference.

Third, Peterson and Peterson (1959) only considered short-term memory duration for one type of stimulus. Their study did not provide information about the duration of short-term memory for other kinds of stimuli (e.g. pictures; melodies; smells). Evidence that the duration of short-term memory may be much longer for other types of material was reported by Nairne et al. (1999). When different words were presented on each trial, there was remarkably little forgetting over retention intervals up to 96 seconds! Nairne et al. pointed out that Peterson and Peterson used all the consonants *repeatedly* in their study and this may have created substantial interference.

Long-term memory: Duration

How can one assess how long a memory lasts? This is difficult. Even if you can't remember something, it is hard to prove it's not in memory somewhere but you simply can't bring it to mind. If you can remember something, it might be an *inaccurate* memory you have constructed.

KEY RESEARCH STUDY

Bahrick et al. (1975): Very-long-term memory (VLTM)

In spite of the problems involved, psychologists have successfully conducted research into "very-long-term memory" (VLTM). It is said the elderly don't lose their childhood memories, and many skills (e.g. riding a bicycle) are never forgotten.

Bahrick et al. (1975) studied the duration of very-long-term memory using photographs from high-school yearbooks (an annual publication where everyone's picture is shown with their name and other details). They used an opportunity sample of 392 American ex-high-school students aged 17 to 74. Age was the variable of interest in an independent groups design.

Participants' memory was tested in various ways:

(1) Free recall of the names of as many their former classmates as possible.
(2) A photo recognition test where they identified former classmates from 50 photos, only some of which showed their classmates.
(3) A name recognition test.
(4) A name and photo matching test.

Thus, there were four dependent variables (types of behaviour assessed) in this study.

Findings

There was 90% accuracy in face and name recognition even for those participants who had left high school 34 years previously. After 48 years, this declined to 80% for name recognition and 40% for face recognition. Thus, people do have genuine very-long-term memories. However, free recall was much less accurate: 60% accurate after 15 years and only 30% accurate after 48 years. Thus, very long-term memory is much better when suitable cues (e.g. photographs) are available.

Evaluation

Bahrick et al.'s research has high mundane realism. Asking participants to recall their classmates tests real-life memory. Thus, the research is more representative of natural behaviour and so has high external validity (i.e. the findings are likely to generalise to other situations).

Some memories never fade. Can you remember the names of your primary school classmates?

Classmates' faces are a very specific type of information. They might have emotional significance and there will have been much opportunity for rehearsal given the daily contact involved. The same is not true of other types of information and so the findings may be specific to this type of information. For example, wishful thinking plays a part in very-long-term memory for academic grades. Bahrick et al. (2008) found American ex-college students had reasonable recall of their academic grades over intervals of up to 54 years. However, the great majority of errors involved inflating the actual grade.

A serious limitation with the study is that there were different individuals in each age group. *Why* does that matter? An important reason why today's older adults have poorer memory than today's young adults is because on average they received less education—additional years of education enhance people's memories (Rönnlund et al., 2005). Thus, the finding that older adults in the study had poorer memory for their classmates than did younger adults has various possible explanations:

(1) It could be due to the greater length of time since they were at school.
(2) It could be due to the negative effects of age on memory ability.
(3) It could be due to the fact that older adults in Bahrick et al.'s study received less education than the younger ones and so had had poorer memory throughout their adult lives.

It is entirely possible all three factors were jointly responsible for the age difference in memory for classmates.

Coding in short-term vs long-term memory

When psychologists talk about coding, they refer to the way in which information is stored in memory. For example, coding can be in terms of acoustic (sound) or semantic (meaning) coding. The words "cap" and "can" are acoustically similar; "cap" and "hat" are semantically similar. We can remember words by the way they sound or by their meaning.

It seems short-term and long-term memory differ in the way information is coded. If you have to remember something for a short while (e.g. a phone number), you probably repeat it to yourself (rehearsal). People do this whether they *heard* the number or *saw* it, suggesting short-term memory may code information acoustically. Conrad (1964) studied this by comparing performance with acoustically and visually presented information. Participants were presented with six letters for 0.75 seconds each and asked to recall them in the same order. When the letters *sounded* alike (even though they were presented *visually*), errors were made in terms of sound confusions (for example, S being recalled instead of X). This showed short-term memory can involve **acoustic coding**.

Baddeley (1966) extended Conrad's research. He found that if participants recalled words from short-term memory, they didn't confuse words having the same meaning (e.g. "big" and "large"). However, they often confused words that sounded similar (e.g. remembering "cat" instead of "cap"). The opposite was true for long-term memory. This suggests short-term memory largely uses an acoustic code, whereas long-term memory depends mostly on **semantic coding** based on the meaning of words.

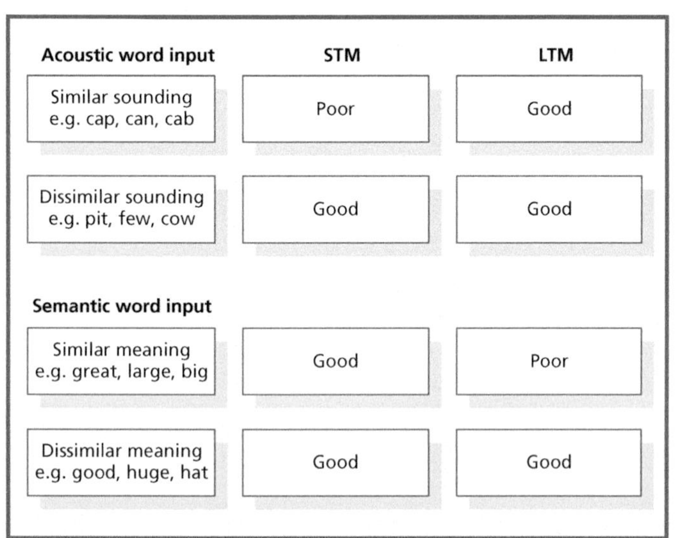

Schweppe et al. (2011) pointed out that short-term memory might be adversely affected when the to-be-learned items have *acoustic* similarity (i.e. they have similar sounds) or when they have *articulatory* similarity (i.e. they are pronounced using similar articulatory movements). Short-term memory was more affected by acoustic similarity, but articulatory similarity also sometimes had an effect.

Baddeley's (1966) approach was limited in that he didn't consider the possibility of **visual coding** existing in short-term memory. Posner (1969) found evidence that visual codes are used. For example, when "A" was followed by "A", people were faster to decide that it was the same letter than when "A" was followed by "a". The visual code for the second letter differed from that of the first letter when "A" was followed by "a" and that slowed people down.

EVALUATION

There is some validity in the notion that coding in short-term memory tends to involve rehearsal and acoustic coding. However, that is not the whole story. As we saw earlier, Simon (1974) found people can organise phrases into chunks in long-term memory—such chunking clearly involves semantic processing. In addition, encoding in short-term memory can involve visual coding (Posner, 1969) or articulatory coding (Schweppe et al., 2011).

There is also some validity in the notion that information in long-term memory is often encoded semantically. However, it can also be encoded in many other ways including acoustically, visually, or by taste or smell. If you don't believe me, then think of memories of someone's voice (acoustic encoding), the taste and smell of your favourite food or drink, or the feel of snow on your hands.

In sum, the types of information found in short-term memory and in long-term memory are much greater than used to be thought. Thus, we can't use coding differences as a way of showing clearly that there are separate short-term and long-term memory stores.

KEY TERMS

Acoustic coding: coding words in terms of their sound using information stored in long-term memory.

Semantic coding: coding or processing words in terms of their meaning based on information stored in long-term memory.

Visual coding: encoding letters or words in terms of their visual shape.

ACTIVITY: Semantic and acoustic recall

You could test the effects of semantic and acoustic recall by using Baddeley's (1966) word lists and asking for immediate or delayed recall. Construct four word lists:

Acoustically similar: man, cap, can, cab, mad, mat, map
Acoustically dissimilar: pit, few, cow, pen, sup, bar, day
Semantically similar: great, large, big, huge, broad, fat, high
Semantically dissimilar: good, safe, thin, deep, strong, foul, hot

Divide participants into two groups—immediate recall (short-term memory) and longer-term recall. Participants should be randomly allocated to conditions to ensure both groups of participants are equivalent.

For each group, which lists are they best at recalling and which lists do they perform least well on?

EXAM HINT

In an exam it is very important to be able to distinguish among the sensory register, STM and LTM. To make sure you can do this learn the table in the box below.

This is quite easy, as it's mainly common sense. The clue is to make sure you understand the terminology:

Capacity = How much does it hold?
Duration = How long can it hold information?
Coding = In what form is it "registered" in the memory store?

Features	Sensory register (echoic + iconic memory)	STM	LTM
Duration	Short (0.5–3 or 4 secs)	Short (seconds)	Long, potentially forever
Capacity	Up to 10 items	Limited by time and attention	Unlimited
Coding	Visual (iconic memory) Acoustic (echoic memory)	Acoustic (mostly)	Semantic (mostly)

EVALUATION OF THE MULTI-STORE MODEL

It is now time to draw up a balance sheet of the strengths and limitations of the multi-store model:

- (+) There is strong support for the basic distinction between short-term and long-term memory stores from studies on brain-damaged patients. Patients with amnesia have severe problems with long-term memory but not with short-term memory. In addition, some patients have problems with short-term memory but not with long-term memory (Shallice & Warrington, 1970).
- (+) The multi-store has been very influential. Many subsequent theories of memory used the multi-store model as their inspiration.
- (+) The capacity of the short-term and long-term memory stores is radically different. The capacity of the short-term store is between four and seven chunks. In contrast, there are no known limits on the capacity of the long-term store.

- (+) There are substantial differences in the duration of information in the three stores. Information stays in the sensory register for a fraction of a second or a few seconds. Unrehearsed information in short-term memory vanishes within about 20 seconds, whereas some information in long-term memory is still there 48 years after learning.

- (–) The model argues that the transfer of information from short-term to long-term memory is through *rehearsal*. However, in daily life most people devote very little time to rehearsal. Rehearsal may describe what happens when psychologists conduct experiments on word lists in laboratories but this isn't true to life.

- (–) It is assumed that information in the short-term store is coded in terms of its sound (acoustic coding) whereas information in the long-term store is encoded in terms of its meaning (semantic coding). I don't want to seem frivolous, but it seems to me like magic for information to change from sound to meaning as it proceeds along an arrow from the short-term to the long-term store!

- (–) Atkinson and Shiffrin (1968) argued that information is processed in short-term memory *before* proceeding to long-term memory. Matters can't be that simple. Suppose you use short-term memory to rehearse "IBM" as a single chunk. This is *only* possible after you have contacted long-term memory to work out the meaning of IBM! Most information in short-term memory *must* have made contact with information in long-term memory before being rehearsed.

- (–) The model is oversimplified in its assumption that there is a *single* long-memory store. In fact, as is discussed in the next section, there are at least *three* types of long-term memory store.

- (–) The model is oversimplified in its assumption that there is a *single* short-term store. Evidence there is more than one short-term store comes from work on the working memory model which is discussed later in the chapter.

Section Summary

What is memory?

- Learning and memory involve the retention of information, but the study of memory focuses on cognitive processes and retrieval.
- Memory tests assess learning.
- Psychologists distinguish among the sensory register, short-term memory, and long-term memory in terms of:
  - capacity;
  - duration;
  - coding.

Nature of the sensory register

- The sensory register is described as:
  - consisting of several memory stores (e.g. iconic memory; echoic memory);
  - each memory store within the sensory register has very limited capacity;
  - each memory store holds information very briefly;
  - coding is visual in the iconic store and acoustic in the echoic store.

Nature of short-term memory

- The short-term store is described as:
  - having limited capacity of between 4 and 7 chunks;
  - having limited duration;
  - using mainly acoustic coding.

- Capacity: Span measures indicate an STM capacity of about seven items but this can be increased by chunking. Capacity for STM can also be seen in the recency effect (higher recall for the last few items in a list).
- Duration: The Brown–Peterson technique reveals STM duration. If rehearsal is prevented, there is little recall beyond 18 seconds.
- Coding: This differs from long-term memory, which is more semantically coded.
- Evidence about different kinds of short-term memory comes from the study of brain-damaged individuals, which also supports a distinction between short-term and long-term memory.

Nature of long-term memory

- The long-term memory store is described as:
  - having an unlimited capacity;
  - lasting forever with some information;
  - using mainly semantic coding.
- Capacity: Unlike in STM, we never reach the upper limit of the LTM store capacity.
- Duration: Its duration has been shown in studies of VLTMs (very-long-term memories).
- Coding: This differs from long-term memory, which is more acoustically coded.

Multi-store model

- The multi-store model of memory supports the distinction between three separate stores and proposes that information is transferred from the short-term memory store to the long-term memory store by rehearsal.
- This model has been criticised in that:
  - Rehearsal is much less important in forming long-term memories than assumed within the model.
  - It is incorrect that information always goes into short-term memory before long-term memory.
  - The model is oversimplified in assuming there is only one short-term store and one long-term store.

TYPES OF LONG-TERM MEMORY

According to Atkinson and Shiffrin's (1968) multi-store model, there is only *one* long-term memory store. As soon as you start thinking about it, that seems unlikely. We have an enormous variety of information stored in long-term memory, including, for example, the knowledge that Keira Knightley is a film star, how to ride a bicycle, that we had fish and chips for lunch yesterday, and the meaning of the word "bling". Can all this knowledge really be stored within a *single* long-term memory store?

Cohen and Squire (1980) argued that long-term memory is divided into two memory systems: declarative memory and procedural memory. **Declarative memory** is concerned with "knowing that". For example, we know we had roast pork for Sunday lunch and that Paris is the capital of France. In contrast, **procedural memory** is concerned with "knowing how": we know how to play various sports, play the piano, and so on.

KEY TERMS

Declarative memory: long-term memory related to "knowing that"; it includes general knowledge and memory for personal experiences.

Procedural memory: long-term memory related to "knowing how"; it consists mostly of memory for motor skill and abilities.

ACTIVITY: Procedural and declarative memory

State whether the following involve procedural or declarative memory.

- Your name
- Driving a car
- The capital city of Japan
- The value of m^2 when $m = 6$
- Balancing on one leg

Think of some other examples of procedural and declarative memory.

If declarative memory and procedural memory belong to separate systems in different brain regions, some brain-damaged patients might suffer problems with only one of the two systems. This is exactly what has been found. There was a famous **case study** (detailed investigation of a single individual) involving HM. He received brain surgery because he suffered from frequent epileptic seizures. After the operation, his declarative memory was very poor—he couldn't remember most of the events and experiences he had had after the operation. However, his procedural memory was good. For example, he learned mirror drawing (tracing a figure seen only in mirror image) almost as rapidly as non-brain-damaged individuals.

CASE STUDY: The man who never got older

In the 1950s, a man known as "HM" (his actual name was Henry Molaison) sought medical help for his epileptic seizures. He had had to stop work because the seizures had become so frequent and severe, and they couldn't be controlled with drugs. In desperation, the surgeon removed the hippocampus from both brain hemispheres because this was the seat of his seizures. The operation did reduce his epilepsy but it also had a dramatic effect on his memory.

His personality and intellect remained the same, but his memory was severely affected. Some aspects of his memory were fairly intact: he could still talk and recall the skills he knew previously (semantic memory), he could form short-term memories, but was unable to form any new long-term declarative memories. For example, given the task of memorising a number he could recall it 15 minutes later but, after being distracted, he had no recollection. He could read the same magazine repeatedly without realising he had read it before.

HM moved house after his operation and had great difficulty learning his new route home. After 6 years he was finally able to find his way around the house. This shows he did have some memory capacity and, intellectually, he was quite "intact" so had some awareness of his predicament.

For many years, he reported that the year was 1953 (when he had his operation) and he was 27 years old. As time went on he realised this could not be true and he started to guess a more appropriate answer.

Spiers et al. (2001) reviewed 147 cases of amnesia (severe problems with long-term memory). They *all* had poor declarative memory, but *none* had any problems with procedural memory. The procedural skills the amnesic patients had acquired included learning to play the piano and mirror drawing. This is convincing evidence that declarative memory and procedural memory are separate forms of long-term memory.

? Which type of memory (procedural or declarative) is likely to be tested in a memory experiment?

So far we have seen that there is an important distinction between declarative memory and procedural memory. However, it is also important to distinguish between two types of declarative memory. This distinction is discussed fully below. Here we will simply note that some declarative memories refer to personal experiences (e.g. last summer's enjoyable holiday) whereas others refer to general knowledge (e.g. knowing that the Houses of Parliament are in London).

KEY TERMS

Case study: a detailed study of a single individual.

Episodic memory: a form of long-term memory concerned with personal experiences or episodes.

Explicit memory: long-term memory that involves the conscious recollection of information learned previously.

Episodic memory

One of the main forms of declarative memory is episodic memory. We use **episodic memory** to remember past events we have experienced. Episodic memories fulfil what are known as the www criteria—they contain information about *what* happened, *where* it happened, and *when* it happened. In the words of Tulving (2002, p. 5), episodic memory allows one "to re-experience … one's own previous experiences". Examples of episodic memory include remembering your first day at college or a party with your friends.

One of the most important features of episodic memory is that it involves explicit memory. **Explicit memory** is the conscious recollection of previously learned information.

You might imagine that episodic memory would resemble a video recorder providing us with accurate and detailed information about past events. As you have probably discovered, that is *not* the case. As Schacter and Addis (2007, p. 773) pointed out, "Episodic memory is … a fundamentally constructive, rather than reproductive process that is prone to various kinds of errors and illusions."

There is plentiful evidence for the constructive view of episodic memory. Later in the chapter, we consider research on eyewitness memory. Eyewitnesses often make mistakes when recalling what they saw at a crime event, for example, reconstructing the event's details based on "what must have been true". For example, we tend to assume that bank robbers are typically male, are in disguise, and have a getaway car, and eyewitnesses will sometimes mistakenly claim that these features were present even when they were not (Tuckey & Brewer, 2003 a, b).

We can explain the findings of Tuckey and Brewer (2003a, b) by assuming that we possess schemas or organised packets of knowledge that lead us to make certain expectations. Thus, for example, we have a "bank robbery schema" around which our recall of a bank robbery would be constructed. García-Bajos et al. (2012) focused on several aspects of the bank robbery **schema**, including the robber shouting, "Don't anyone move! Hands up!", eyewitnesses being frightened, the robber threatening to open the till, and the robber having his face covered. As predicted, eyewitness recall was better for actions forming part of the bank robbery schema than for those that did not.

Why is our episodic memory system so prone to error? Schacter and Addis (2007) identified three reasons. First, it would require an incredible amount of processing to produce a semi-permanent record of every experience. Second, we generally want to access the *gist* or essence of our past experiences with the trivial details omitted. If we rapidly accessed all the trivial details, we would "be unable to see the wood for the trees".

Third, Schacter and Addis (2007) argued that we use our episodic memory system to imagine possible future events and scenarios, which is useful when forming plans for the future. Imagining the future is only possible because episodic memory is flexible and constructive rather than inflexible like a video recorder.

Semantic memory

The other form of declarative memory is semantic memory. **Semantic memory** is, "an individual's store of knowledge about the world. The content of semantic memory is abstracted from actual experience and is … without reference to any specific experience" (Binder & Desai, 2011, p. 527). Here are some examples of semantic memory: (1) remembering that the First World War started in 1914; (2) remembering that Spanish is the language spoken in most of South America; and (3) remembering the rules of netball.

One of the important features of semantic memory is that it involves explicit memory. In other words, we typically show memory for general knowledge acquired previously by consciously recollecting it.

Much information stored in semantic memory consists of concepts. **Concepts** are mental representations of categories of objects. Thus, for example, "cat" is a concept, as is "daffodil" or "school". According to Rosch et al. (1976), many concepts are organised into hierarchies consisting of three levels. Superordinate categories (e.g. *item of furniture*) are at the top level of the hierarchy, basic-level categories (e.g. *chair*) are at the intermediate level, and subordinate categories (e.g. *easy chair*) are at the bottom level.

We do sometimes use superordinate categories (e.g. "That furniture is expensive") or subordinate categories (e.g. "I love my new iPhone"). However, there is generally a strong preference for using basic-level categories. Rosch et al. (1976) asked participants to name pictured objects. Basic-level categories were used 1,595 times during the course of the experiment, subordinate names 14 times, and superordinate names only once. We make most use of the basic level because it typically provides the best balance between informativeness and distinctiveness. Informativeness is lacking at the superordinate level (e.g. simply knowing an object

KEY TERMS

Schema: organised knowledge (e.g. about the world) stored in long-term memory.

Semantic memory: a form of long-term memory consisting of general knowledge about the world, concepts, language, and so on.

Concepts: mental representations of categories of objects or items.

is an item of furniture tells you little). Distinctiveness is lacking at the lowest level (e.g. most types of chairs possess very similar attributes or features).

Episodic memory vs semantic memory

We have seen that there are several important differences between episodic and semantic memory. There is additional support for the notion that they form separate memory systems based on research with brain-damaged patients. According to the separate-systems view, we might expect some patients to have relatively intact episodic memory but impaired semantic memory and other patients to show the opposite pattern. As we will see below, that is indeed the case.

Earlier we mentioned a study by Spiers et al. (2001) on 147 cases of amnesia. For present purposes, their most relevant finding was that episodic memory was impaired in every single case but many patients had much less severe problems with semantic memory. Amnesics sometimes show much greater forgetting of episodic than semantic memories formed before the onset of amnesia. For example, consider the amnesic KC. According to Tulving (2002, p. 13), "He cannot recollect any personally experienced events ..., whereas his semantic knowledge acquired before the critical accident is still reasonably intact ... . his general knowledge of the world is not greatly different from others' at his educational level."

Are there brain-damaged patients who have much more severe problems with semantic memory than with episodic memory? The short answer is "Yes". Patients with **semantic dementia** have severe loss of concept knowledge from semantic memory even though their episodic memory is reasonably intact. Such patients have damage to the anterior temporal lobe which is different to the brain areas most affected in amnesics (the hippocampus and related areas).

Episodic and semantic memory: Interdependence

So far we have implied that semantic and episodic memory are very different from each other. In fact, however, the two types of long-term memory are often interdependent. Suppose, for example, you thought about your most recent holiday and found yourself recalling lying in the sun on a beautiful sunny beach. This is clearly an example of episodic memory because you are remembering a personal experience. However, your memory includes concepts (e.g. sun; beach) that are stored in semantic memory.

Kan et al. (2009) gave participants the task of learning and remembering the prices of grocery items. On the face of it, this is purely an episodic memory task. However, when participants could use their knowledge of grocery prices on the task (semantic memory), their memory performance improved. Thus, memory performance reflected both episodic and semantic memory.

Procedural memory

We saw earlier that procedural memory is involved in learning how to play sports, how to play the piano, and in mirror drawing (drawing a figure reflected in a mirror). Another task that has been used to assess procedural memory is the pursuit rotor—this task involves manual tracking of a moving target.

We also saw earlier that amnesic patients typically have intact or nearly intact procedural memory in spite of often having severe problems with episodic and semantic memory. Many skills associated with car driving involve procedural memory. This was shown in a study by Anderson et al. (2007) on two severely amnesic patients. Their steering, speed control, safety errors, and driving with distraction were all comparable to those of healthy individuals.

One of the key features of procedural memory is that it involves implicit memory. **Implicit memory** does not require conscious recollection and so memory is typically demonstrated by the individual's behaviour. One of the most striking examples showing that procedural memory does not require conscious recollection is a study by Snyder et al. (2014) on college typists with an average of over 11 years of typing experience. The typists were presented with a blank keyboard and instructed to put in the letters in their correct locations. In spite of their huge relevant experience, they located only 57% of the letters correctly on average! Thus, they had excellent procedural memory in terms of the ability to type rapidly and accurately but this was accompanied by rather poor conscious recollection of the locations of the letters on the keyboard.

KEY TERMS

Semantic dementia: a condition caused by brain damage in which there is extensive loss of knowledge about the meanings of words and concepts.

Implicit memory: long-term memory that does not require conscious recollection.

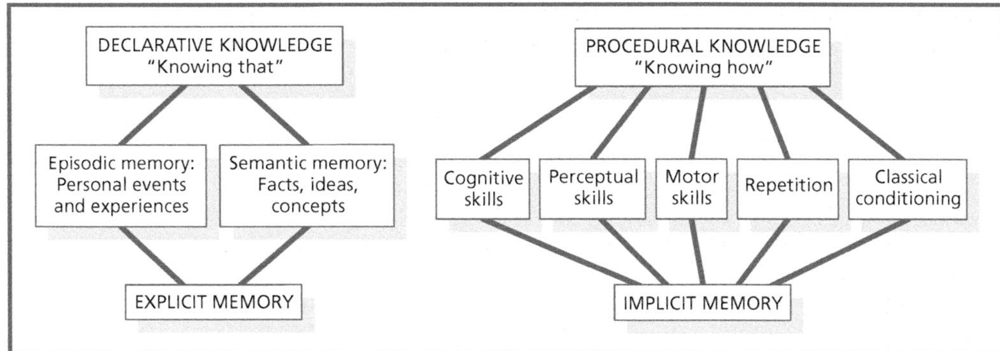

Explicit memory is memory based on conscious recollection whereas implicit memory is memory that does not involve conscious recollection.

Differences among episodic, semantic, and procedural memory

Episodic, semantic, and procedural memory are all important types of long-term memory. How do they differ from each other? First, they differ in terms of the involvement of conscious recollection. Conscious recollection is involved in episodic and semantic memory but it is not involved in procedural memory.

Second, and related to the first point, episodic and semantic memory are typically assessed by instructing people to produce memories by saying them or writing them down. In contrast, procedural memory is typically assessed by measuring their behaviour—for example, we know that someone possesses procedural memory for touch typing by seeing how rapidly and accurately they can type without looking. There is no need to ask them to describe the knowledge they possess.

Third, episodic, semantic, and procedural memories differ from each other in terms of *content*. Episodic memories refer to personal experiences and often contain what, where, and when information about specific events. In contrast, semantic memories typically refer to general knowledge the individual possesses which lack personal relevance, and procedural memories are typically motor and other skills the individuals has learned.

Fourth, an important difference concerns the effects of amnesia. Amnesia always impairs episodic memory. However, it very rarely impairs procedural memory and generally impairs semantic memory less than episodic memory. These findings mean that the brain structures damaged in amnesic patients (the hippocampus and related areas) are of great importance to episodic memory but of minimal or no relevance to procedural memory.

Section Summary

- Long-term memory can be divided into declarative memory which involves knowing that something is the case and procedural memory which involves knowing how to do something.
- Amnesic patients have severely impaired declarative memory but intact procedural memory.

Episodic memory

- Episodic is a type of declarative memory relating to personal experiences.
- Episodic memories contain information about what happened, where it happened, and when it happened.
- We have conscious recollection of episodic memories.
- Episodic memories typically convey the gist of our experiences rather than all the details.

Semantic memory

- Semantic memory is a form of declarative memory relating to general knowledge of the world.
- Unlike episodic memories, semantic memories lack personal relevance.

- We typically have conscious recollection of semantic memories.
- Much of semantic memory consists of concepts.

Episodic vs semantic memory

- Amnesic patients typically have severely impaired episodic memory but semantic memory is often less impaired.
- Patients with semantic dementia have impaired semantic memory (especially loss of information about concepts) but sometimes have almost intact episodic memory.
- Episodic and semantic memory are interdependent—many memories combine elements of episodic and semantic memory.

Procedural memory

- Procedural memory consists of information about various motor skills including how to play sports, play the piano, drive a car, and so on.
- Procedural memory is typically not associated with conscious recollection.

Differences among episodic, semantic, and procedural memory

- Conscious recollection is much more important with episodic and semantic memory than with procedural memory.
- We generally assess people's episodic and semantic memory by asking them to say or write down their memories; in contrast, procedural memory is typically assessed via their behaviour.
- The three types of long-term memory differ in terms of content: episodic memories consists of personal experiences, semantic memories consist of general knowledge, and procedural memories consist of various motor skills.
- Amnesia has different effects on the three types of long-term memory: it always has a severe impairing effect on episodic memory, little or no effect on procedural memory, and an intermediate impairing effect on semantic memory.

WORKING MEMORY MODEL

What is the usefulness of short-term memory in everyday life? Textbook writers sometimes argue it allows us to remember a telephone number for the few seconds taken to dial it. Nowadays, however, everyone has a mobile phone that stores numerous phone numbers.

In 1974, two British psychologists, Alan Baddeley and Graham Hitch, produced a convincing answer to the above question. They pointed out that we use short-term memory when working on a complex problem (e.g. in arithmetic) and need to keep track of where we have got to in the problem.

Suppose you were given the addition problem 13 + 18 + 24. You would add 13 and 18 and keep the answer (31) in short-term memory. You would then add 24 to 31 and produce the correct answer of 55. Baddeley and Hitch used the term working memory to refer to a system involving processing and short-term memory in combination, and theirs was a **working memory model**.

Baddeley and Hitch's (1974) working memory model differed from previous ideas about short-term memory in two main ways: (1) they emphasised its general usefulness in everyday life; (2) they argued (very reasonably) that rehearsal is only one of several processes occurring in short-term memory.

It is now time to consider in more detail the **working memory system** put forward by Baddeley and Hitch (1974) and developed by Baddeley (2001). It has *four* components, each having limited capacity:

- **Central executive**: A modality-free component, meaning it can process information from *any* sensory modality (e.g. visual; auditory). It is like attention.

KEY TERMS

Working memory model: the model of short-term memory proposed to replace the multi-store model. It consists of a central executive plus slave systems that deal with different sensory modalities.

Working memory system: the concept that short-term (or working) memory can be subdivided into other stores that handle different modalities (sound and visual data).

Central executive: the key component of working memory. It is a modality-free system (i.e. not visual or auditory) of limited capacity and is similar to "paying attention" to something.

- **Phonological loop** (originally called the articulatory loop): This is a temporary storage system holding verbal information in a phonological (speech-based) form. It is involved in verbal rehearsal and speech perception. The phonological loop consists of an articulatory process involving rehearsal and a phonological store that holds phonological information briefly.
- **Visuo-spatial sketchpad**: This is specialised for the rehearsal and temporary storage of visual and spatial information. It consists of an inner scribe that processes spatial and movement information and a visual cache that stores information about visual form and colour.
- **Episodic buffer**: This is a storage system that can briefly store integrated information from the visuo-spatial sketchpad and phonological loop. This component was added 25 years after the others and so it will be discussed a little later in the section.

? If you add up two items in your head—real-life mental arithmetic!—when out shopping, which parts of your working memory are you using?

How can we tell which component or components are being used when people perform a given task? According to the model, every component has limited capacity and is relatively independent of the other components in its functioning. Two predictions follow:

1. If two tasks use the *same* component, they cannot be performed together successfully.
2. If two tasks use *different* components, it should be possible to perform them as well together as separately.

Here is a simple example providing support for the second prediction. Your ability to make sense of the material in this book mainly involves focusing on visual information (using the visuo-spatial sketchpad) and attending to it (using the central executive). If you said "the" over and over again (using the phonological loop) while reading this book, it would have little effect on your comprehension. At any rate, that is what I would predict!

Here is an example of how the working memory system operates. Hitch and Baddeley (1976) asked participants to carry out a verbal reasoning task to decide whether each in a set of sentences provided a true or false description of the letter pair following it (e.g. A is followed by B: BA). At the same time, the participants performed a task where little thought or attention was involved (only using the phonological loop by saying 1 2 3 4 5 6 rapidly) or a task involving the central executive as well as the phonological or articulatory loop (remembering six random digits). As predicted, reasoning performance was slowed down by the additional task when it involved using the central executive but not when it involved only the phonological loop.

These findings are easy to explain within the working memory model. The reasoning task and saying 1–6 rapidly made use of different components of working memory, and so the two tasks didn't interfere with each other. It is less clear how the findings could be accounted for within the multi-store model. According to that model, even saying 1–6 rapidly should have used up the capacity of the short-term memory store. As a result, it should have been hard to carry out the reasoning task at the same time.

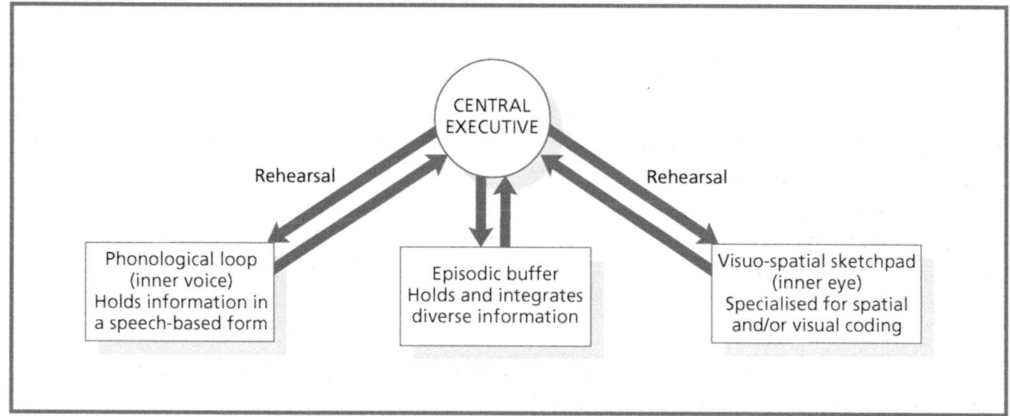

KEY TERMS

Phonological loop: a component of the working memory system concerned with speech perception and production.

Visuo-spatial sketchpad: a component within the working memory system designed for spatial and/or visual coding.

Episodic buffer: a component of working memory used to integrate and store briefly information from the phonological loop and the visuo-spatial sketchpad.

ACTIVITY: Processes in comprehension

You can investigate the processes involved in comprehension by using an approach similar to the one used by Hitch and Baddeley (1976). Select a fairly short text (250–300 words) that could be taken from a book or newspaper. There are three groups of participants assigned at random to the conditions. In the first condition, participants read the text and at the same time count backwards by threes, a task that involves the central executive and the phonological loop. In the second condition, participants read the text and at the same time say the numbers 1 2 3 4 5 6 rapidly over and over again, a task involving only the phonological loop. In the third condition, participants only read the text and do not perform a second task. A few seconds after the text has been read, participants in all three conditions are given the same comprehension test to assess how much information they have extracted from it. You should find that participants in the first condition have the lowest level of comprehension and that there is little difference between the second and third conditions. These findings would indicate the central executive (including attention) is important for comprehension, whereas the phonological loop is not. This experiment shows how the working memory approach can be used to assess the processes involved in comprehension.

Phonological loop

Verbal rehearsal (saying words over and over to oneself) is of central importance in the functioning of the phonological loop. Baddeley et al. (1975) studied the phonological loop. They asked participants to recall sets of five words immediately in the correct order. Participants' ability to do this was better with short words than with long ones. Further investigation of this **word-length effect** showed that participants could recall as many words as they could read out loud in 2 seconds. This suggests the capacity of the phonological or articulatory loop is determined by how long it takes to rehearse verbal information.

In sum, there is phonological (speech-based) coding in the phonological loop. Its capacity is approximately the amount of verbal information that can be read out loud in 2 seconds.

ACTIVITY: Mueller et al. (2003): Word-length effect

You can study the word-length effect for yourself. Write each of the words below on a separate piece of card and make two piles, one for each list. Then carry out the following experiment with five friends tested one at a time. Present four words at random from List A at one word per second to one friend and ask them to recall the words in the correct order. After that, do the same with List B. Next, present five words from List A and then five from List B. Keep going to work out the maximum number of words each friend can remember correctly in order from each list.

List A	List B
cult	advantage
dare	behaviour
fate	circumstance
guess	defiance
hint	fantasy
mood	interim
oath	misery
plea	narrowness
rush	occasion
truce	protocol
verb	ridicule
zeal	upheaval

The above words were taken from an article by Mueller et al. (2003). Their participants had an average span of 6.72 with List A words and of 5.09 with List B words. Mueller et al. found that the words in List A took an average of 418 milliseconds to say compared to 672 for those in List B. Thus, the number of items that can be stored in short-term memory depends in part on the time required to pronounce each one.

KEY TERM

Word-length effect: the finding that word span is greater for short words than for long words.

KEY RESEARCH STUDY

Robbins et al. (1996): Dual-task performance and working memory

Robbins et al. (1996) carried out an experiment to show how the working memory model works in practice. The participants consisted of 12 moderately good and very good chess players, who selected moves from various chess positions while performing a second task at the same time. This second task involved the central executive, the visuo-spatial sketchpad, the phonological loop, or none of the components of the working memory system (control condition). The independent variable manipulated by the researchers was the nature of the second task. Since all participants performed in all four conditions, it was a repeated measures design. The dependent variable (behavioural measure of interest) was the quality of the chess moves selected.

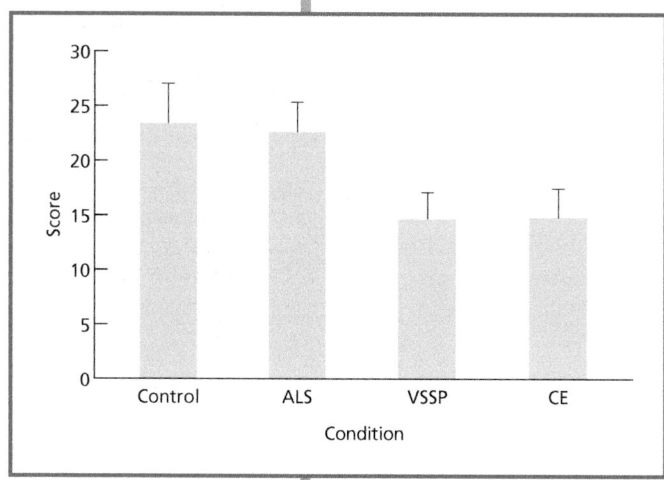

Quality of selected chess moves for participants with no secondary task (control), with a secondary task involving the phonological loop (ALS: articulatory suppression), with a secondary task involving the visuo-spatial sketchpad (VSSP), and with a secondary task involving the central executive (CE).

Findings

The findings are shown in the Figure. As can be seen, the quality of the moves selected was reduced when the second task involved the central executive or the visuo-spatial sketchpad. However, there was no negative effect when the second task involved the phonological loop.

What do these findings mean? They indicate that selecting good chess moves requires use of the central executive and the visuo-spatial sketchpad. We know this because chess performance suffered when these components weren't fully available. However, selecting good moves does *not* involve the phonological loop. We know this because chess performance did not suffer when this component was being used for the second task. Thus, this experiment shows the working memory model can be used to clarify which processes people use when performing complex tasks such as selecting chess moves.

According to Robbins et al. (1996), selecting good chess moves requires use of the central executive and the visuo-spatial sketchpad but not of the phonological loop.

Limitations

This is an important study because it shows clearly which components of the working memory system are and are not involved in playing chess. What are its limitations? First, it could be argued that outstanding chess players (e.g. grandmasters) have so much expertise that their chess performance wouldn't be affected by having to perform a second task at the same time. Thus, the findings may be limited to players below grandmaster standard.

Second, Robbins et al. (1996) were interested in the effects of the second task on chess performance. However, they also found that chess performance made performance worse on the second tasks involving the visuo-spatial sketchpad and the central executive. This complicates the interpretation of the findings.

Third, all the chess positions used were well into the game when several pieces had already been taken. It is possible that the involvement of the working memory system would differ early in the game when nearly all the pieces remain.

Baddeley and Hitch (1974) assumed the phonological loop is generally used when people remember visually presented words in the correct order. It follows that it should be harder to remember words having similar sounds than words having dissimilar sounds—there would be much confusion and interference among the words having similar sounds.

The above prediction was tested by Larsen et al. (2000). Here is one of their lists of words with similar sounds: FEE, HE, KNEE, LEE, ME, and SHE, and here is a list with dissimilar sounds: BAY, HOE, IT, ODD, SHY, and UP. As predicted, the ability to recall the words in order was 25% worse with the words having similar sounds. This is the **phonological similarity effect**. It indicates that speech-based rehearsal processes within the phonological loop were used in remembering these words.

Real world

What is the value of the phonological loop in everyday life? Children with a deficient phonological loop generally have problems with reading. For example, Gathercole and Baddeley (1990) discovered children with reading problems had an impaired memory span and found it difficult to decide whether words rhymed, suggesting they had a phonological loop deficit. The phonological loop is also useful when learning *new* words. In a study by Papagno et al. (1991), native Italian speakers learned pairs of Italian words and pairs of Italian–Russian words. In one condition, participants performed an articulatory suppression task (saying something meaningless over and over again) during the learning task. Articulatory suppression (which prevented use of the phonological loop on the learning task) greatly slowed down the learning of foreign vocabulary.

EVALUATION

More is known about the phonological loop than any other component of the working memory system. It is the component most resembling the short-term store in the multi-store model. However, there is a big difference—the phonological loop is merely one component out of four in the working memory model, whereas rehearsal is much more central within the multi-store model.

Visuo-spatial sketchpad

What is the capacity of the visuo-spatial sketchpad? Research suggests it can hold about four items. Vogel et al. (2001) presented a visual display of between 3 and 12 objects. After 900 milliseconds, a second display (identical to the first or with one object changed) was presented. Participants' ability to decide whether the two displays were identical was almost perfect with four objects. Performance declined progressively as the number of items in the display increased above four. Vogel et al. also found that performance declined only slightly when the retention interval was increased from 900 milliseconds to 4,900 milliseconds (nearly 5 seconds). This suggests that information can be held in the visuo-spatial sketchpad for several seconds.

The visuo-spatial sketchpad is used for the temporary storage and manipulation of visual patterns and spatial movement. Note that there are significant differences between visual and spatial processing. Consider individuals blind since birth. They can find their way around a familiar environment (e.g. their own living room) without knocking into the furniture—this is achieved by using spatial processing since they can't use visual processing.

The visuo-spatial sketchpad is used in many situations in everyday life, such as finding the route when walking, or playing computer games. Logie et al. (1989) used a complex computer game called Space Fortress, which involves manoeuvring a spaceship around a computer screen. Performance on Space Fortress was worse when participants performed an additional visuospatial task at the same time. Thus, the visuo-spatial sketchpad was needed for effective computer-game performance.

Spatial vs visual processing

What is the visuo-spatial sketchpad like? It might be a *single* system combining visual and spatial processing. Alternatively, there might be partially or completely separate visual and spatial systems. Klauer and Zhao (2004) tried to find out. They used two main tasks: (1) a spatial task involving memory for dot locations; and (2) a visual task involving memory for Chinese ideographs (symbols). Participants sometimes performed a second task at the same time as the main task. This second task involved spatial interference or visual interference.

What would we predict if there are separate spatial and visual components? First, the *spatial* interference task should disrupt performance more on the *spatial* main task than on the *visual* main task. Second, the visual interference task should disrupt performance more

KEY TERM

Phonological similarity effect: the finding that immediate recall of a word list in the correct order is impaired when the words sound similar to each other.

on the visual main task than on the spatial main task. As shown in the Figure, both predictions were confirmed. If the visuo-spatial sketchpad consisted of a single system, this pattern of results would not be expected.

Additional evidence supporting the notion of separate visual and spatial systems within the visuo-spatial sketchpad was reported by Smith and Jonides (1997) in an ingenious study. Two visual stimuli were presented together, followed by a probe stimulus. Participants decided whether the probe was in the same location as one of the initial stimuli (spatial task) or they decided whether it had the same form or shape (visual task).

Even though the stimuli were identical in the two tasks, there were clear differences in patterns of brain activation. There was more activity in the *right* hemisphere during the spatial task than the visual task. However, there was more activity in the *left* hemisphere during the visual task than the spatial one. These findings suggest there is a visual processing system based mainly in the left hemisphere and a spatial processing system based mostly in the right hemisphere.

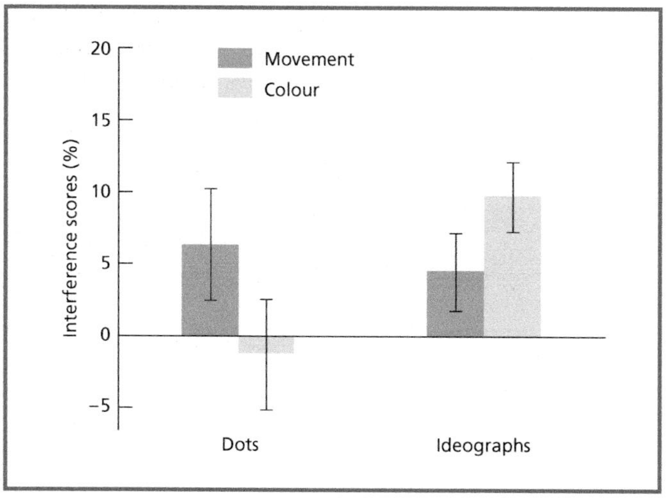

Amount of interference on a spatial task (dots) and a visual task (ideographs or symbols) as a function of secondary task (spatial: movement distribution vs visual: colour discrimination). From Klauer and Zhao (2004).

Gender difference

It has sometimes been argued that males are slightly better on average than females at spatial processing and navigation. This has been studied using tasks involving **mental rotation**. With such tasks, you have to imagine rotating a shape or object. In one of the most-used mental rotation tasks, participants are presented with a letter in its normal form or in reversed mirror-image form and have to decide which form it is in. The further from its upright form the letter is presented, the longer it takes participants to make the decision because mental rotation to the upright position takes longer (Cooper & Shepard, 1973).

Lippa et al. (2010) studied mental rotation in 53 countries. Males significantly outperformed females on mental rotation in every country, although the gender difference was often fairly small. One possible reason why males have slightly superior spatial ability is because they spend much more time than females playing video games. Spence et al. (2009) studied males and females who had rarely, if ever, played video games. The male and female participants reached the same level of performance on a video game following training.

EVALUATION

- (+) The visuo-spatial sketchpad is of major importance in our everyday lives.
- (+) We engage in visual and/or spatial processing most of the time and such processing involves the visuo-spatial sketchpad.
- (+) The systems involved in visual and spatial processing are different.
- (+) There are interesting gender differences in spatial processing within the visuo-spatial sketchpad.
- (–) We don't know much about the interconnections between visual and spatial processing—for example, how we combine visual and spatial information when walking.
- (–) We don't know much about the rehearsal processes used within the visuo-spatial sketchpad.
- (–) If we engage in complex visual or spatial processing, the central executive will be involved as well as the visuo-spatial sketchpad. However, we don't know how much complexity is needed before the visuo-spatial sketchpad is unable to cope on its own.

KEY TERM

Mental rotation: a type of task in which participants imagine rotating two- or three-dimensional objects in order to perform some task.

The central executive

The central executive, which resembles an attentional system, is the most important and versatile component of the working memory system. Indeed, it is so important that it is always used when we perform any complex task (e.g. understanding a psychology textbook; listening to a talk). In the original working memory model (Baddeley & Hitch, 1974), it was suggested that the central executive was *unitary*, meaning it functioned as a single unit. However, it is now clear that the central executive is more complex than that.

What is the central executive used for? One of the most influential suggestions stems from the research of Miyake et al. (2000), who gave their participants several tasks requiring the central executive. These tasks varied in terms of which of the following three functions they used:

The Stroop effect

RED

BLUE

RED

BLUE

1. *Inhibition function:* this is used when you need to prevent yourself from attending to task-irrelevant stimuli or responses. Thus, it reduces *distraction* effects. Consider the **Stroop task**, on which participants name the colours in which words are printed. In the most difficult condition, the words are conflicting colour words (e.g. the word BLUE printed in red). In this condition, performance is slowed down and there are often many errors. The inhibition function is needed to minimise the distraction effect created by the conflicting colour word.
2. *Shifting function:* this is used when you shift attention from one task to another. Suppose you are presented with a series of trials, on each of which two numbers are presented. In one condition there is task switching: on some trials you have to multiply the two numbers and on other trials you have to divide one by the other. In the other condition there are long blocks of trials on which you always multiply the two numbers and there are other long blocks of trials on which you divide one number by the other. Performance is slower in the task-switching condition, because attention has to be switched backwards and forwards between the tasks. Task switching involves the shifting function.
3. *Updating function:* this is used when you need to update the information you remember to take account of changes in the world. For example, motorists need to update their stored information when the speed limit changes from 30 mph to 20 mph or vice versa. In the laboratory, the updating function is required when participants are presented with members of various categories and have to keep track of the most recently presented member of each category.

KEY TERMS

Stroop task: a task that involves naming the colours in which words are printed. Performance is slowed when the words are conflicting colour words (e.g. the word RED printed in green).

Dysexecutive syndrome: a condition caused by brain damage (typically in the frontal lobes) in which there is severe impairment of the functioning of the central executive component of working memory.

Dysexecutive syndrome

We can understand the importance of the central executive by studying brain-damaged individuals whose central executive is impaired. Such individuals suffer from **dysexecutive syndrome**, which involves problems with planning, organising, monitoring behaviour, and initiating behaviour. They typically have damage within the frontal lobes, which occupy the front region of the brain and are involved in numerous complex cognitive processes. Individuals with dysexecutive syndrome typically have great problems in holding down a job and functioning adequately in everyday life.

The notion of a dysexecutive syndrome suggests that brain damage to the frontal lobes typically impairs *all* central executive functions. That is often the case with patients having widespread damage to the frontal lobes but isn't true of patients with more specific brain damage. Stuss and Alexander (2007) identified *three* different executive functions involving the frontal lobes: task setting (planning); monitoring (checking one's own performance, or "quality control"); and energisation (sustained attention or concentration).

Stuss and Alexander (2007) found many patients had major problems with only *one* of these central executive functions. Thus, rather than thinking in terms of a *single* global dysexecutive syndrome, we need to identify *three* more specific dysexecutive syndromes.

EVALUATION

- (+) The central executive is the most important component of working memory.
- (+) The central executive is involved in complex tasks such as selecting chess moves (Robbins et al., 1996) and verbal reasoning (Hitch & Baddeley, 1976).
- (+) We use the central executive whenever tasks involve attentional processes and/or planning, task shifting, organising, and monitoring.
- (+) Brain-damaged patients with dysexecutive syndrome show the problems encountered by anyone whose central executive is impaired.
- (–) A major issue is to work out the number and nature of functions carried out by the central executive. Miyake et al. (2000) and Stuss and Alexander (2007) argued there are three major functions. Unfortunately, however, their two lists of functions only overlap in part.

Episodic buffer

As mentioned earlier, the episodic buffer is used for the integration and brief storage of information from the other components and from long-term memory. As Baddeley (2012) pointed out, the function of the episodic buffer is suggested by its name. It is *episodic* because it holds integrated information (or chunks) about episodes or events in a multi-dimensional code combining visual, auditory, and other sources of information. It acts as a *buffer* between the other components of working memory and also links working memory to perception and long-term memory.

According to Baddeley (2012, p. 17), "The episodic buffer is an essentially passive structure on which bindings [integration of information] achieved elsewhere can be displayed." Baddeley suggested that the capacity of the episodic buffer is about four chunks (integrated units of information).

Why did Baddeley add the episodic buffer to the working memory model? The original version of the model was limited because its components were too *separate* in their functioning. One of the useful features of the episodic buffer is that it provides storage for verbal information from the phonological loop as well as for visual and spatial information from the visuo-spatial sketchpad.

Baddeley et al. (2009) studied the role of the episodic buffer. Participants were presented with sentences or random words. As expected, participants recalled many more words that had been presented in sentences. The advantage for words in sentences may reflect the capacity of the episodic buffer or it may be due to the ability of the central executive to integrate or chunk sentence information. Baddeley et al. decided between these two explanations by comparing what happened when the random words or sentences were presented on their own versus when they were accompanied by a second task requiring the central executive. The memory advantage for sentences over word lists remained even when the central executive was involved in processing the second task. Thus, it appeared that sentences are better recalled than random words mainly because of the use of the episodic buffer.

Coding and capacity

It is now time to compare the four components of the working memory system with each other. More specifically, we will consider coding (processing) and capacity for each component.

The nature of coding or processing is relatively specific for the phonological loop and the visuo-spatial sketchpad. As its name implies, the phonological loop is specialised for phonological (speech-based) processing based on the ways in which words are pronounced and the sounds of spoken words. In similar fashion, the visuo-spatial sketchpad is specialised for coding or processing that can be either visual or spatial in nature.

In contrast, coding or processing is much more general in the central executive and the episodic buffer. The central executive is an attention-like system and we can attend to and process an enormous range of types of information. Thus, we can use the central executive to code information about smell and taste as well as visual, spatial, or phonological information or information retrieved from long-term memory. The episodic buffer receives information from all the other three components of the working memory system as well as from long-term memory. Accordingly, coding in the episodic buffer is as diverse as that within the other components of working memory.

What about the capacity of the components of the working memory system? Crucially, all the components have limited capacity which means they can only process or store a relatively small amount of information. As we have seen, the capacity of the phonological loop is the amount of verbal material that can be rehearsed in about 2 seconds. The capacity of the visuo-spatial sketchpad is of the order of approximately four items, and the capacity of the episodic buffer is about four chunks or integrated units of information. Finally, the capacity of the central executive is limited by the constraints of attention—we can only attend to a very limited number of items at once (no more than about four) and this defines the capacity of the central executive.

How important is working memory?

Working memory is of fundamental importance in information processing and thinking. This has been shown in research stemming from the work of Daneman and Carpenter (1980), who argued that the essence of a working memory system is that it is used for storage and processing at the same time. They used a task in which participants read several sentences for comprehension (a processing task) and then recalled the final word of each sentence (storage task). The largest number of sentences from which a participant could recall all the final words more than 50% of the time was his/her **reading span**. This reading span was taken as a measure of working memory capacity.

Why did Daneman and Carpenter (1980) argue that reading span assessed working memory capacity? They assumed the processes involved in comprehending the sentences require a smaller proportion of the available working memory capacity of those with a large capacity. As a result, they have more capacity available for retaining the last words of the sentences.

Working memory capacity as measured by reading span is fairly closely associated with intelligence. For example, Conway et al. (2003) reviewed research on working memory capacity and general intelligence. The typical correlation was about +0.6, indicating that the two constructs (while by no means identical) are nevertheless similar. An important difference between those high and low in working memory capacity is that the former have much better attentional control. McVay and Kane (2012) found that individuals high in working memory capacity performed a task requiring sustained attention significantly better than low scorers. The main reason for this was that high scorers engaged in much less mind wandering (not attending to the task) than low scorers.

EXAM HINT

Evaluation questions will either ask you to describe a strength or limitation or to evaluate the model as a whole. Either way, it is quality rather than quantity that counts. Always *explain* your criticism. For example, don't just say "one weakness is that little is known about the working memory model". You should explain that this is because it hasn't been measured with precision and that the details of how the components work together are unclear. When writing an evaluation, you will gain more marks by explaining a few criticisms fully than by just listing a wide range of points.

KEY TERM

Reading span: the largest number of sentences read for comprehension from which an individual can recall all the final words more than 50% of the time; it is used as a measure of working memory capacity.

EVALUATION OF THE WORKING MEMORY MODEL

- (+) The working memory model is an advance on the account of short-term memory provided by the multi-store model because it is concerned with both active processing *and* the brief storage of information. As a result, it is relevant to activities such as mental arithmetic, verbal reasoning, and comprehension, as well as to traditional short-term memory tasks. Thus, it is much more than just a theory of memory.
- (+) The working memory model views verbal rehearsal as an *optional* process occurring within the phonological or articulatory loop. Information in working memory can be processed without involving rehearsal. This view is more realistic than the central importance of verbal rehearsal in the multi-store model.
- (+) Performance on tasks of any complexity depends on some combination of the four components of the working memory model, indicating they are particularly important parts of the human cognitive processing system. For example, we saw that choosing moves at chess depends very much on the central executive and visuo-spatial sketchpad (Robbins et al., 1996).
- (+) All components of the working memory model are important in everyday life. This is especially true of the central executive—brain-damaged individuals with dysexecutive syndrome have enormous difficulties in coping with other people and the environment. It is also noteworthy that working memory capacity correlates moderately highly with intelligence.
- (+) Knowledge of the functioning of the working memory system can benefit brain-damaged individuals. They can be taught how to make the best use of those components of the working memory system still functioning reasonably well.
- (−) The model is oversimplified. We can process and store briefly several kinds of information (e.g. those concerned with smell, touch, or taste) that are not considered at all within the model.
- (−) Relatively little is known about the central executive. It has limited capacity, but this capacity has not been measured with precision. It is argued that the central executive is "modality-free" (i.e. it does not rely on any specific way of receiving information, such as sound or vision) and is used in many different processing operations. However, the details of its functioning remain unclear.
- (−) It was originally proposed that the central executive was unitary in the sense that it "spoke with one voice". However, it now appears that it fulfils at least three functions (Miyake et al., 2000; Stuss & Alexander, 2007). As yet, the number and nature of its functions are unclear.
- (−) The four components of the working memory model *interact* with each other in the performance of many tasks. However, it is unclear *how* this happens in practice.
- (−) The model is concerned with memory. However, it tells us very little about long-term memory and how processing in the working memory system relates to the long-term storage of information. In this respect, the working memory model is less informative than the multi-store model.

Section Summary

Working memory model

- The working memory model consists of a central executive, a phonological loop, a visuo-spatial sketchpad, and an episodic buffer.
- Two tasks can be performed together without disruption if they use different components of working memory, but not if they use the same ones.
- The phonological loop is used when learning new words, the visuo-spatial sketchpad when finding a route or playing computer games, the central executive for complex thinking and reasoning, and the episodic buffer for integrating information from other components.
- Three of the functions of the central executive are as follows:
  - inhibition function: this is used to reduce distraction effects;
  - shifting function: this is used to shift attention from one task to another;
  - updating function: this is used to update the information in working memory.
- Working memory is of fundamental importance in information processing and thinking, and working memory capacity is closely associated with intelligence.
- The working memory model has been criticised in that:
  - It ignores the processing and storage of stimuli relating to the senses of smell and taste.
  - The number and nature of the functions of the central executive remain unclear.
  - We don't know in detail how the components of working memory interact with each other.
  - The model is concerned with memory but tells us very little about long-term memory.

EXPLANATIONS FOR FORGETTING

Human memory is very fallible and we often forget things we really wanted to remember (e.g. research findings in psychology). Note, however, that forgetting is often useful especially when we need to update information. For example, you no longer have any use for information such as last year's schedule of lessons or where your friends used to live. You may also be reassured to learn that having an almost perfect memory is much less advantageous than you might imagine.

Forgetting was first studied in detail by Hermann Ebbinghaus (1885/1913). His major discovery was that forgetting was very rapid over the first hour after learning but then slowed considerably. A Russian journalist Solomon Shereshevskii (often referred to as S) so impressed his editor with his ability to repeat anything said to him word for word that he was sent to the psychologist Alexander Luria. Luria discovered that S had exceptional imagery and that, "There was no limit either to the *capacity* of S's memory or to the *durability of the traces he retained*" (Luria, 1968).

Proactive interference: Long-term memory

One of the most important reasons why we forget is because of **proactive interference**. This involves memory impairment for something we have learned by other learning that had occurred previously. A good example of proactive interference dates back to Hugo Munsterberg in the nineteenth century. Munsterberg kept his pocket watch in one particular pocket. When he started to keep it in a different pocket, he often fumbled around in confusion when asked the time. Munsterberg had initially learned an association between the stimulus, "What time is it, Hugo?", and the response of removing the watch from his pocket. Later on, a different response was associated with that stimulus, which led to proactive interference.

Proactive interference has often been demonstrated using paired-associate learning (see Figure). Participants initially learn pairs of words on List 1 (e.g. Cat-Dirt). Then they learn different pairs of words on List 2 (e.g. Cat-Tree). Finally, they are given the first word (e.g. Cat-???) and are asked to recall the word paired with it on the second list. Memory performance tends to be poor because of interference from the initial associate (e.g. Dirt). Note that proactive

KEY TERM

Proactive interference: disruption of memory by previous learning (often of similar material).

Proactive interference			
Group	*Learn*	*Learn*	*Test*
Experimental	A–B (e.g. Cat–Dirt)	A–C (e.g. Cat–Tree)	A–C (e.g. Cat–Tree)
Control	–	A–C (e.g. Cat–Tree)	A–B (e.g. Cat–Tree)

Retroactive interference			
Group	*Learn*	*Learn*	*Test*
Experimental	A–B (e.g. Cat–Tree)	A–C (e.g. Cat–Dirt)	A–B (e.g. Cat–Tree)
Control	A–B (e.g. Cat–Tree)	–	A–B (e.g. Cat–Tree)

Note: for both proactive and retroactive interference, the experimental group exhibits interference. On the test, only the first word is supplied, and the participants must provide the second word.

Methods of testing for proactive and retroactive interference.

interference is maximal when two different responses are associated with the *same* stimulus (as with Munsterberg and the example in the Figure). In that condition, it is hardest to avoid confusion between the correct and incorrect responses.

Proactive interference is very common in everyday life. For example, suppose you have recently acquired a new iPhone. You may have found yourself occasionally misremembering how to carry out certain functions on it because of your memory for how you carried out those functions on your previous phone.

What causes proactive interference?

Jacoby et al. (2001) argued that proactive interference occurs because there is *competition* between two responses: the correct one and the incorrect one. As a result, there are two possible reasons why proactive interference occurs: (1) the incorrect response is very strong; or (2) the correct response is very weak. Jacoby et al. found proactive interference was due much more to the strength of the incorrect response than to the weakness of the correct response. Thus, a major cause of proactive interference is that it is hard to exclude incorrect responses from the retrieval process.

Can we reduce proactive interference?

Is there anything we can do to reduce the negative effects of proactive interference on long-term memory? Bäuml and Kliegl (2013) argued that proactive interference occurs in large measure because individuals' memory search is too broad and includes both relevant and irrelevant information.

It follows from the above argument that proactive interference should be greatly reduced if steps were taken to restrict people's memory search only to relevant items. Bäuml and Kliegl presented their participants with two lists of words and then tested their recall for the second list. In the crucial condition, participants spent their time between lists imagining their childhood home. This was done to make it easier for them to exclude words from the first list from the retrieval process while trying to recall those from the second list. As predicted, proactive interference was reduced by almost 40% in this condition compared to a control condition in which participants were not given any specific task to perform between the two lists.

Proactive interference: Short-term memory

How is information lost from short-term memory? Two main answers have been proposed. First, information may *decay* over time in the absence of rehearsal. Second, there may be *interference*. This interference could come from items on previous trials (proactive interference) or from information presented during the retention interval (retroactive interference—discussed shortly).

The classic study by Peterson and Peterson (1959; discussed earlier in the chapter) showed that there was almost complete forgetting of consonant trigrams from short-term memory after about 20 seconds. One of the limitations with this study was that participants were presented with a large number of consonant trigrams in the course of the study. As a result, proactive interference from consonant trigrams presented early in the experiment might have reduced short-term memory for trigrams presented later. As predicted on this account, Keppel and Underwood (1962) found no forgetting at all on the very first trial of the experiment in a study based on that of Peterson and Peterson (1959).

Berman et al. (2009) and Campoy (2012) compared the decay and interference accounts of forgetting in short-term memory. Decay effects were strong over short periods of time (up to about 3 seconds) but proactive interference effects were of greatest importance at longer time periods.

EVALUATION

There is strong evidence that proactive interference accounts for much forgetting from both short-term and long-term memory. Progress has been made in understanding the processes underlying proactive interference. We know that proactive interference occurs more because incorrect items are strong than because correct ones are weak. Accordingly, the best way to reduce proactive interference is by finding ways of restricting memory search so that it largely excludes items that could potentially cause proactive interference.

What are the limitations of theory and research on proactive interference? First, notions about interference explain why forgetting occurs but fail to explain why forgetting rate decreases over time.

Second, we need to know more about the reasons why and how various memory strategies (e.g. imagining your childhood home) reduce proactive interference.

Third, most studies of proactive interference in long-term memory have focused on episodic memory. It is likely (but has not been clearly established) that semantic memory is more resistant to proactive interference than is episodic memory (Solso, 1995).

Fourth, we can explain only some short-term and long-term forgetting in terms of proactive interference. Decay is also a factor in explaining short-term forgetting. As we will see, retroactive interference and absence of cues are other factors. It is also worth mentioning another factor briefly. Probably the most important reason why forgetting occurs most rapidly shortly after learning and progressively more slowly after that is because of consolidation. **Consolidation** is a physiological process that lasts for several hours and serves to fix information in long-term memory. Of crucial importance, memories are especially vulnerable to interference and forgetting when they are still being consolidated. Consolidation explains why it is that, "New memories are clear but fragile and old ones are faded but robust" (Wixted, 2004, p. 265).

Retroactive interference: Long-term memory

KEY TERMS

Consolidation: a physiological process involved in establishing long-term memories; this process lasts several hours or more and newly formed memories are fragile.

Retroactive interference: disruption of memory for previously learned information by other learning or processing occurring during the retention interval.

A major reason for forgetting is retroactive interference. **Retroactive interference** involves disruption of memory for something we have learned by other learning or processing that occurs during the period of time between the original learning and the memory test. Retroactive interference has often been studied using paired-associate learning (see Figure). Participants initially learn pairs of words on List 1 (e.g. Cat-Tree). After that, those in the experimental condition learn different pairs of words on List 2 (e.g. Cat-Dirt). Finally, they are tested for their ability to recall the paired associates from List 1 when given the first word (e.g. Cat-???). The requirement to learn a second list of paired associates after learning List 1 and before testing for recall of List 1 causes retroactive interference. This is especially the case when two different responses have been associated with the same stimulus (e.g. Cat-Tree and Cat-Dirt).

Retroactive interference is common in everyday life. Think of a friend you have known for several years. Try to form a clear visual image of what he/she looked like 5 years ago. I guess you found that hard to do because rich information about what they are like *now* interferes with your ability to remember what they *were* like. This is a common example of retroactive interference.

Anecdotal evidence that retroactive interference can be important in everyday life comes from travellers claiming that exposure to a foreign language reduces their ability to recall words in their own language. Misra et al. (2012) studied bilinguals whose native language was Chinese and second language was English. They named pictures in Chinese more slowly when they had previously named the same pictures in English. They were inhibiting second-language names when naming pictures in Chinese.

The next section of this chapter deals with eyewitness testimony and memory distortions by eyewitnesses. Of direct relevance here are studies in which eyewitnesses observe a crime or other incident and are then exposed to misleading information. This misleading information distorts eyewitnesses' memory for the incident. It does so by a process of retroactive interference given that this information is provided *after* the event to be remembered and *before* recall.

Suppose you become skilful at carrying out a task on one computer. After that, you become an expert at performing the same task on a different computer with different software. If you then go back to your first computer you might discover that you have forgotten how to carry out the task on that device. This is an example of retroactive interference.

What causes retroactive interference?

Lustig et al. (2004) argued that retroactive interference in paired-associate learning might occur for two reasons: (1) the correct response is hard to retrieve; or (2) the incorrect response is highly accessible. For example, if participants learn "bed-sheet" on List 1 and "bed-linen" on List 2, they may fail to produce "sheet" on the final test because its strength is weak or because the word "linen" is very strong. They found retroactive interference was due mainly to the strength of the incorrect response.

Retroactive interference is generally greatest when the new learning resembles previous learning. However, Dewar et al. (2007) found retroactive interference even when no new learning occurred during the retention interval. Participants learned a list of words and were then exposed to various tasks during the retention interval before list memory was assessed. There was significant retroactive interference even when the intervening task involved detecting differences between pictures or detecting tones.

Dewar et al. (2007) concluded that retroactive interference can occur in two ways: (1) expenditure of mental effort during the retention interval; or (2) learning of material similar to the original learning material. The first cause of retroactive interference probably occurs more often in everyday life.

Retroactive interference: Short-term memory

There is evidence that retroactive interference affects forgetting in short-term memory as well as in long-term memory. For example, Campoy (2011) presented participants with six-word lists having instructed them to recall only the first three words in the correct order. The second three words in each list were designed to produce retroactive interference. The key finding was that recall performance was worse when the last three interfering words were long than when they were short. Thus, long interfering words produced more retroactive interference than short words.

EVALUATION

There is convincing evidence that much forgetting from long-term memory occurs because of retroactive interference. We know that retroactive interference depends more on the strength of incorrect responses than that of correct ones. We also know that retroactive interference can occur because the interfering material is similar to the to-be-remembered material or because there is a substantial expenditure of mental effort during the retention interval.

What are the limitations of theory and research on retroactive interference? First, we need more research to identify strategies that would successfully reduce the extent of retroactive interference.

Second, it remains unclear why the forgetting rate from long-term memory decreases over time. As discussed earlier, this is probably mostly due to a physiological process known as consolidation and is not directly due to retroactive interference.

Third, there are several reasons for forgetting in short-term and long-term memory other than retroactive interference. Proactive interference and an absence of cues are two such factors discussed in this chapter.

Retrieval failure due to absence of cues

It is easy (but incorrect!) to assume that most forgetting occurs because the relevant information has been lost from long-term memory. In fact, however, it is very easy to show that forgetting often occurs simply because we lack the appropriate cues. For example, suppose you can't recall the name of the street in which a friend lives. If someone gave you a short list of possible street names, you would probably recognise the correct one. What we have here is a comparison between *recall* and *recognition memory* for the same information. Recognition memory is typically much better than recall because the to-be-remembered information is given to you as a cue in recognition memory but not in recall.

Tulving (1979) argued that forgetting typically occurs when there is a poor match of fit between the information contained in the memory trace and the cues available at retrieval. This is known as the **encoding specificity principle**. Evidence showing how forgetting can depend on the absence of cues is discussed in the Research Study by Tulving and Psotka (1971).

KEY RESEARCH STUDY

Tulving & Psotka (1971)

Aim

To investigate the effects of presence vs absence of retrieval cues on recall from long-term memory.

Method

Some participants learned six word lists divided into categories (e.g. four-footed animals; articles of furniture). Each list consisted of four words belonging to each of six categories with all of the words belonging to any given category presented in immediate succession. The participants recalled as many words as possible from each list after the presentation of each list. After they had learned their last list they tried to free recall all the words from all of the lists presented—this is recall without cues. Finally, the participants were given the names of all the categories from all of the lists they had seen and they tried again to recall as many words as possible—this is recall with cues.

Results

Overall recall across the six word lists was 50.4% when no retrieval cues were present. When category cues were present, however, mean recall was 70%. The adverse effects of an

KEY TERM

Encoding specificity principle: the notion that the ability to remember information depends on the amount of overlap between the information in the memory trace and that present in the cues available at the time of retrieval.

absence of cues were especially great if we consider only recall of words from the first list—70% of these words were recalled with cues compared to only 30% in the absence of cues.

Conclusion
The findings from this experiment show clearly that cues can greatly reduce forgetting from long-term memory.

Evaluation
There are some concerns with respect to ecological validity—it is rare in everyday life for learning and memory to involve categorised word lists. As a result, we cannot be sure that similar findings would have been obtained with other types of learning material. The findings certainly don't show that ALL forgetting from long-term memory is due to an absence of cues—after all, 30% of the words were not recalled even in the presence of cues.

Cues can take many forms. For example, Godden and Baddeley (1975) asked deep-sea divers to listen to 40 words on the beach or under 10 feet of water. They were then tested on their ability to recall these words in the same environment or the other one. Recall was much better when the environment was the same at test as at learning than when it was different (see Figure). Thus, the environment (e.g. beach vs under water) can provide a powerful cue.

So far we have focused on *external* cues (e.g. category names; test environment). However, cues can also be *internal* (e.g. mood state). In a study by Kenealy (1997), music was used to create a happy or sad mood state while participants engaged in learning. The next day there was a recall test for what had been learned and music was played again to create a happy or sad mood state. The key finding was that memory was better when the mood state was the *same* at learning and test than when it was different. Thus, internal mood state can act as a cue to enhance memory and decrease forgetting.

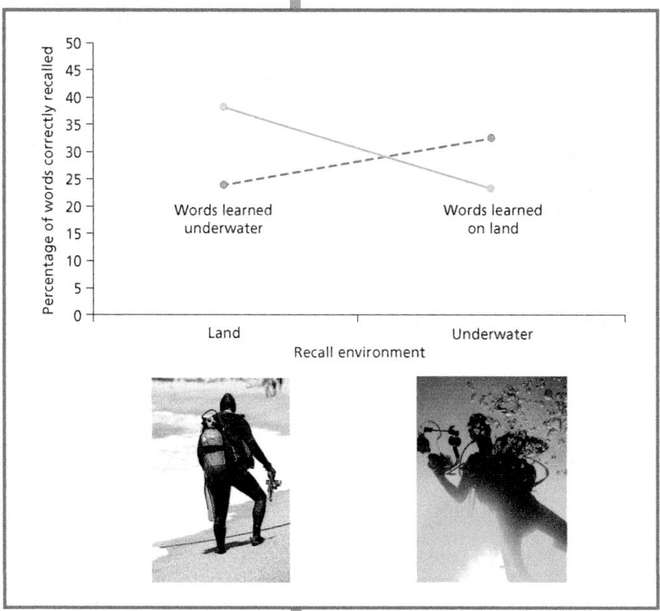

Words learned and tested in the same environment are better recalled than those items for which the environmental context varied between study and test. Data form Godden and Baddeley (1975).

EVALUATION

Memory is generally better (and so forgetting less) when cues present at retrieval contain information overlapping with that stored in long-term memory. Several kinds of cues (external and internal) have been shown to reduce forgetting. This general approach sheds light on why there is generally less forgetting with recognition memory than with recall—the cues provided on a recognition test are more powerful and relevant to stored information than are the cues provided on a recall test.

What are the limitations of this approach to forgetting? First, it is claimed that forgetting is reduced when there is much overlap between the information contained in cues and information stored in long-term memory. However, the extent of this overlap is rarely measured and, indeed, is very hard to assess accurately.

Second, the overlap between the cue and the correct response is NOT the only factor that matters. Goh and Lu (2012) presented word pairs such as park-GROVE and then observed how well the response word (e.g. GROVE) could be recalled given the cue (e.g. park). Cues were much more useful when the cue was *uniquely associated* with one response word rather than being associated with several response words. Thus, the effectiveness of a cue depends upon its *distinctiveness* as well as its *overlap* with stored information.

Third, some forgetting from long-term memory has nothing to do with the presence or absence of retrieval cues. There is accumulating evidence that many long-term memory traces (especially those relating to trivial memories) simply decay (mostly during sleep) (Hardt et al., 2013).

Section Summary

Proactive interference

- Proactive interference involves impairment of memory for something we have learned from other learning occurring previously.
- Proactive interference in long-term memory occurs because there is competition between the correct and incorrect responses.
- Proactive interference in long-term memory can be reduced if individuals restrict their memory search to relevant information.
- Proactive interference also occurs in short-term memory. However, decay may be more important than interference at very short intervals of time.
- Several other factors (e.g. retroactive interference; absence of cues; consolidation) are also important in explaining forgetting.

Retroactive interference

- Retroactive interference involves impairment of memory for something we have learned by other learning or processing occurring during the retention interval.
- Retroactive interference in long-term memory is found when eyewitnesses to an incident are subsequently exposed to misleading information about the incident.
- Retroactive interference depends more on the strength of incorrect responses than on the weakness of correct responses.
- Retroactive interference is greatest when what is learned during the retention interval resembles that involved in the initial learning.
- Retroactive interference is also found in short-term memory.
- Several factors other than retroactive interference are important in producing forgetting in short-term and long-term memory.

Retrieval failure due to absence of cues

- Much forgetting depends on an absence of cues rather than the disappearance of memory traces from long-term memory. However, many memory traces are removed by a process of decay.
- The main reason why recall is usually inferior to recognition memory is because it provides less effective cues.
- Cues leading to enhanced long-term memory can be external (e.g. words; environment) or internal (e.g. mood state).
- It is hard to assess the informational overlap between retrieval cues and information in memory traces.
- The effectiveness of any given cue depends on whether or not it is uniquely associated with the to-be-remembered information as well as on informational overlap.

EYEWITNESS TESTIMONY

KEY TERM

Eyewitness testimony: an account or evidence provided by people who witnessed an event such as a crime, reporting from their memory. Research suggests that this evidence may not be factually accurate.

In this section, we focus on a major practical application of human memory research— **eyewitness testimony**. Many people argue that we can safely rely on eyewitness testimony. Simons and Chabris (2011) found that 37% of Americans believe the testimony of a single confident witness should be sufficient to convict a criminal defendant. As we will see, however, eyewitnesses often make mistakes. Unfortunately, most jurors and judges underestimate problems with eyewitness testimony. Benton et al. (2006) found that judges disagreed with eyewitness experts on 60% of eyewitness issues, and jurors disagreed with the experts on 87% of them!

DNA tests can often establish that someone was *not* responsible for certain crimes. In the United States, 200 people have been shown to be innocent by DNA tests, and more than 75% of them had been found guilty on the basis of mistaken eyewitness identification. In 2011, DNA testing led to the release of Cornelius Dupree, 51, who had spent 30 years in prison for the alleged rape of a 26-year-old Dallas woman. He was convicted because he was identified as the culprit by the victim.

The accuracy of eyewitness testimony depends on various factors. For example, eyewitness memory is likely to be less accurate if eyewitnesses are presented with **misleading information**. It also seems reasonable to assume that very anxious eyewitnesses might find it more difficult to remember what they have witnessed. We will consider these (and other) factors in our subsequent discussion.

Eyewitness testimony has been found by psychologists to be extremely unreliable, yet jurors tend to find such testimony highly believable.

Misleading information: Leading questions

One reason eyewitness testimony is so unreliable is because the events witnessed are typically unexpected. As a result, eyewitnesses may not pay close attention to what is going on. A less obvious reason is that eyewitnesses' memories for an event are fragile, and so can easily be distorted and made inaccurate by the questions they are asked.

Eyewitnesses' memory can be distorted when they are asked **leading questions** sometime after the event they have seen. Here is an example of a leading question: "Don't you find studying boring?" The question suggests that you do find studying boring and so it is biased. Loftus and Zanni (1975) studied the effects of leading questions on eyewitness memory. Eyewitnesses watched a short movie of a car accident and then answered various questions. Some were asked, "Did you see a broken headlight?" whereas others were asked, "Did you see the broken headlight?" In fact, there was no broken headlight in the movie but the latter question implied there was. Only 7% of those asked about a broken headlight said they had seen it compared to 15% of those asked about the broken headlight.

Leading questions differ in terms of the extent to which they distort eyewitness memory. In a study by Sharman and Powell (2012), eyewitnesses viewed a DVD about an electrician called Eric who stole personal belongings from a client's house. Several minutes later they were asked various leading questions; some were closed (i.e. requiring a yes or no answer) and the others were open (i.e. requiring a fuller answer). Here are examples of the kinds of leading questions they used:

1. *Closed*:
   "Did the robber hold up the bank with a shotgun?"
2. *Closed specific*:
   "Did the robber hold up the bank with a shotgun that had a black barrel and a dark brown stock?"
3. *Open presumptive* (assuming the eyewitness had certain knowledge):
   "Tell me about the shotgun that the robber used to hold up the bank?"

Their recognition memory for information in the DVD was tested 1 week later. Closed specific and open presumptive leading questions significantly reduced memory accuracy but closed leading questions did not. Closed questions did not distort memory because they did not contain detailed specific information and because they did not require eyewitnesses to spend much time thinking about the answer.

KEY TERMS

Misleading information: incorrect information that may be given in good faith or deliberately (also known as misinformation); it is sometimes provided by those interrogating eyewitnesses and sometimes by co-witnesses.

Leading question: a question that suggests the desired answer.

Loftus and Palmer (1974) found that assessment of the speed of a videotaped car crash and recollection of whether there was broken glass present were affected by the verb used to ask the question. The verbs "hit" and "smash" have different implications as shown in (a) and (b).

KEY RESEARCH STUDY

Loftus and Palmer (1974): Effects of misleading information

Loftus and Palmer (1974) carried out two laboratory experiments. In the first one, participants saw a short film of a multiple-car accident. After viewing the film, they described what had happened and then answered specific questions. Some were asked, "About how fast were the cars going when they hit each other?" whereas for other participants the word "hit" was replaced by "smashed into", "collided", "bumped", or "contacted". In this experiment, the independent variable involved manipulating the verb used in the question. These were leading questions in that the verb implied that the cars were going relatively fast or slowly.

The dependent variable was the estimate of speed. Speed estimates were higher (40.8 mph) when the word "smashed" was used, lower with "collided" (39.3 mph), and lower still with "bumped" (38.1 mph) and "hit" (34.0 mph).

In the second laboratory experiment, participants watched a film of a multiple-car accident. Some were asked how fast the cars were going when they "smashed into" or "hit" each other. There was also a control condition in which there was no question about speed.

One week later, all participants were asked, "Did you see any glass?" There wasn't actually any glass in the film. However, 32% of those previously asked about speed using the verb "smashed" said they had seen broken glass (see Figure). In contrast, only 14% of the participants previously questioned with the verb "hit" said they had seen broken glass, and the figure was 12% for the control participants.

These experiments showed that our memory for events is so fragile it can be distorted by changing *one* word in *one* question! As we will see, this has had a major influence on the ways in which detectives question eyewitnesses. One limitation of these experiments is that they were laboratory-based and so were unlikely to engage the eyewitnesses emotionally. As a result, the eyewitnesses may not have done their utmost to produce accurate answers.

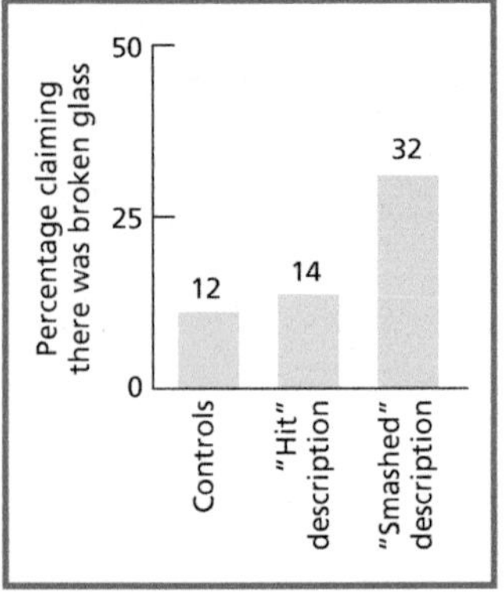

Results from Loftus and Palmer's (1974) study showing how the verb used in the initial description of a car accident affected recall of the incident after 1 week.

Misleading information: Post-event discussion

So far we have seen that misleading information in the form of leading questions can systematically distort eyewitness memory. In the real world, however, eyewitnesses are often exposed to misleading information from other witnesses (known as co-witnesses). Skagerberg and Wright (2008) asked 60 eyewitnesses to criminal events to complete a questionnaire. Their answers indicated that 58% of those who had witnessed a crime along with one or more co-witnesses had discussed it with at least one co-witness. General crime details and suspect details were the most common areas of discussion.

KEY RESEARCH STUDY

Gabbert et al. (2003): Influence of co-witnesses on eyewitness memory

Gabbert et al. (2003) carried out an experiment in which eyewitnesses (young and older adults) watched a short film of a girl stealing money from a wallet. They took part individually or in pairs. Those in pairs were led to believe that they were watching the same short film as their co-witness. In fact, however, each eyewitness saw a different perspective (as would typically be the case when eyewitnesses observe a crime). Of importance, only one eyewitness in each pair actually saw the crime being committed. Participants in the pair or co-witness condition discussed the event together. Finally, all the eyewitnesses individually completed a questionnaire relating to their memory of what they had seen.

What did Gabbert et al. (2003) find? A majority (71%) of eyewitnesses who had discussed the event with a co-witness mistakenly recalled information they had not witnessed but which had been mentioned during the post-event discussion when completing the questionnaire. Most worryingly, 60% of participants in the co-witness condition who had not actually witnessed the crime itself nevertheless claimed that she was guilty! The findings were very similar for younger and older adults.

This study shows that we need to take seriously the possibility that co-witnesses can produce distortions in what eyewitnesses report about an event. The main limitation of this study is that it is not entirely clear whether the distortions obtained reflect problems with memory or whether they reflect social pressure from the co-witness. This issue is discussed shortly.

EXAM HINT

With regard to eyewitness testimony, be ready to discuss several different essay questions:

- The accuracy of eyewitness testimony (EWT).
- The effects of anxiety on accuracy of EWT (see below).
- The effects of misleading information (leading questions and post-event discussion) on accuracy of EWT (see pages 104–105).
- The use of the cognitive interview to improve accuracy of EWT (see pages 109–111).

The tendency for eyewitness memory to be influenced by misleading information provided after the event is very strong. Eakin et al. (2003) showed participants slides of a maintenance man stealing money and a calculator. Eyewitness memory was impaired by misleading post-event information. More surprisingly, memory was impaired even when the eyewitnesses were warned immediately about the presence of misleading information and told to disregard it.

How worried should we be that eyewitnesses' memory can be distorted by information presented after observing a crime? Note that most research has focused on distortions for *minor* details (e.g. presence of broken glass) rather than *central* features. Dalton and Daneman (2006) presented eyewitnesses with misinformation about central (important) and minor (trivial) features. Memory distortions were much more common following misinformation about minor features. Thus, misinformation mostly distorts memory for trivial features rather than important ones.

Explanations

Why does misleading information distort eyewitnesses' memory? Perhaps eyewitnesses asked leading questions respond to social pressures (e.g. to please the experimenter). However, that seems unlikely. If that were the main reason, then eyewitnesses would presumably be less influenced by misleading information if offered money for being accurate in their recollections. In fact, Loftus (1979) found participants offered $25 for accurate memory were just as influenced by misleading information as those offered no reward. Misinformation acceptance is more likely (Loftus, 1992). Eyewitnesses "accept" misleading information presented to them after an event and subsequently regard it as forming part of their memory for that event.

Another explanation is based on **source misattribution** (Johnson et al., 1993). The basic idea is that a question may activate memories from various sources. The individual decides on the source of any activated memory on the basis of the information it contains. Source misattribution (remembering incorrectly the source of a memory) is likely when the memories from two sources (e.g. events) are rather similar.

Allen and Lindsay (1998) reported evidence of source misattribution. Eyewitnesses saw two slide shows describing two events with different people in different settings. However, some details in the two events were similar (e.g. a can of Pepsi vs a can of Coke). When the eyewitnesses recalled the first event, some details from the second event were mistakenly recalled.

Prull and Yockelson (2013) obtained a robust misinformation effect when a slide sequence was followed by a narrative containing misleading information. However, the misinformation effect was much smaller when participants focused specifically on the source of any

KEY TERM

Source misattribution: errors in long-term memory that occur when the rememberer is mistaken about the source or origin of a retrieved memory.

information they had retrieved. This finding suggests source misattribution is important in explaining the typical misinformation effect.

We turn now to explanations of distorted memories reported by eyewitnesses following post-event discussion with co-witnesses. It is probable that social influence (see Chapter 2) plays an important role. There is an important distinction between informational and normative social influence. Informational social influence occurs when the individual has the goal of providing an accurate account, whereas normative social influence occurs when he/she has the goal of gaining social approval.

Goodwin et al. (2013) carried out an experiment to decide which type of social influence was more important in affecting eyewitness memory. Participants watched a slideshow of a crime committed in a college bookshop with a co-witness. This co-witness was a confederate of the experimenter who deliberately provided misleading information in response to some questions about the event. Participants' memories for the crime were tested first in the presence of the co-witness (public report) and then individually (private report).

Goodwin et al.'s (2013) key finding was that misleading information provided by the co-witness (confederate) distorted eyewitnesses' public report but not their private report. The fact that distortions were no longer present in their private report suggests that eyewitnesses were subject to normative social influence rather than informational social influence. However, other evidence suggests that eyewitnesses are sometimes subject to informational social influence. In the study by Gabbert et al. (2003), for example, eyewitness responses on a questionnaire completed individually were influenced by misinformation provided by a co-witness. In sum, eyewitnesses' reported memories for an event are subject to social influence which is sometimes mostly informational and sometimes mostly normative.

Anxiety

Eyewitnesses (especially if they are also victims) are often very anxious and stressed during the witnessing of a crime because of the potential danger to themselves. Before discussing the effects of **anxiety** on eyewitness memory, consider two points:

1. Eyewitnesses remember attended aspects of the crime situation much better than non-attended aspects. Since the precise details of the crime situation determine what an eyewitness is likely to attend to, we must beware of simple generalisations.
2. While the threat or danger in which the eyewitness is placed is the main factor determining his/her level of anxiety, it is not the only one. Eyewitnesses with an anxious personality experience more anxiety in a given crime situation than those with a non-anxious personality.

Weapon focus

Eyewitnesses are especially likely to become anxious when observing a crime when the culprit has a weapon. We might assume that eyewitnesses exposed to a violent crime attend mainly to those aspects of the situation posing a *direct* threat. This assumption lies behind research on **weapon focus**—high levels of attention to (and good memory for) the criminal's weapon but *not* other information. Loftus (1979) discussed a study in which some participants overheard a hostile and aggressive argument between two people followed by one of them emerging holding a letter opener covered with blood.

Other participants overheard a harmless conversation between two people followed by one of them emerging holding a pen. When participants tried to identify the culprit from photographs, only 33% of those in the weapon condition did so compared to 49% in the other condition. This shows weapon focus.

Loftus et al. (1987) asked participants to watch one of two sequences:

1. A person pointing a gun at a cashier and receiving some cash.
2. A person passing a cheque to the cashier and receiving some cash.

KEY TERMS

Anxiety: a normal emotion similar to nervousness, worry, or apprehension, but if excessive it can interfere with everyday life and might then be judged an anxiety disorder.

Weapon focus: the finding that eyewitnesses pay so much attention to a weapon that they ignore other details and so can't remember them.

Eyewitnesses looked more at the gun than at the cheque (weapon focus). As a result, memory for details unrelated to the gun/cheque was poorer in the weapon condition.

We must be cautious about accepting findings on weapon focus at face value for two reasons. First, a weapon may attract attention because it is unusual (or unexpected) in most of the contexts in which it is seen by eyewitnesses. This led Pickel (2009) to predict that the weapon focus effect would be greater when the presence of a weapon is very unexpected. As predicted, there was a stronger weapon focus effect when a criminal carrying a folding knife was female, because it is more unexpected to see a woman with a knife. Also as predicted, the weapon focus effect was greater when a criminal with a knitting needle was male rather than female.

Second, most research is limited in that it is laboratory-based and so the findings may not generalise. Fawcett et al. (2013) addressed this issue in a meta-analysis based on numerous studies of weapon focus. Overall, there was a moderate effect on eyewitness memory of weapon focus. Of most importance, the size of this effect was similar regardless of whether the event occurred in the laboratory or the real world.

Eyewitness memory can be impaired by misleading post-event information. However, important information, such as the weapon used in a crime, is less likely to be distorted than trivial information.

Stress

Deffenbacher et al. (2004) carried out a **meta-analysis** combining findings from numerous studies on the effects of anxiety and stress on eyewitness memory. Average correct face identifications were 54% for low anxiety or stress conditions compared to 42% for high anxiety or stress conditions. In similar fashion, Deffenbacher et al. found in a second meta-analysis that the average recall of culprit details, crime scene details, and action of central characters was 64% in low anxiety or stress conditions compared to 52% in high anxiety or stress conditions. Thus, high anxiety or stress reduced eyewitnesses' identification accuracy and their ability to remember crime details.

Bothwell et al. (1987) showed the importance of **individual differences** in anxiety. They compared groups low and high in the personality dimension of neuroticism (high scorers are very anxious). When stress was *low*, 68% of those high in neuroticism and 50% of those low in neuroticism correctly identified the culprit. In contrast, when the stress level was *high*, only 32% of those high in neuroticism identified the culprit, much lower than the figure of 75% for those low in neuroticism. Thus, extremely anxious individuals (high neuroticism + high stress condition) had easily the worst memory.

KEY TERMS

Meta-analysis: a form of analysis in which the findings from several related studies are combined to form an overall estimate.

Individual differences: the characteristics that vary from one individual to another; intelligence and personality are major ways in which individuals differ.

"Well I know he was wearing tights."

Why does anxiety produce weapon focus?

An influential explanation of weapon focus is based on Easterbrook's (1959) hypothesis. According to this hypothesis, anxiety or stress causes a narrowing of attention on central or important stimuli which causes a reduction in people's ability to remember peripheral details. In other words, anxious or stressed individuals exhibit "tunnel vision", which makes sense when the situation is threatening or dangerous.

Yegiyan and Lang (2010) presented people with distressing pictures. As picture stressfulness increased, memory for the central details improved progressively. In contrast, memory for peripheral details was much worse with highly stressful pictures than moderately stressful ones. Thus, the findings supported Easterbrook's hypothesis.

EVALUATION

- (+) Weapon focus is an important phenomenon with eyewitness memory.
- (+) Stress and anxiety generally have negative effects on the memory of eyewitnesses.
- (+) Weapon focus is a reliable effect in the laboratory and in real life.
- (+) One reason for the weapon focus effect is that anxiety and stress create "tunnel vision".
- (−) The weapon focus effect may occur either because the weapon is dangerous or because it is unexpected in the current situation.
- (−) Individual differences in susceptibility to anxiety and stress are often overlooked.

Reconstructive nature of memory

An influential way of understanding the unreliability of eyewitness memory is based on the ideas of Bartlett (1932; see Chapter 5). He argued that memory does *not* simply involve remembering presented information. Our prior knowledge in the form of schemas (packets of knowledge) influences what we remember and how we remember it. According to Bartlett, what we remember depends on the information we were exposed to at the time of learning *and* our relevant schematic knowledge. The impact of schematic knowledge means that what we recall is sometimes in error—it is consistent with one of our schemas but does not correspond precisely to what we learned. Thus, we fill in the gaps in our memory on the basis of what we *think* might have happened.

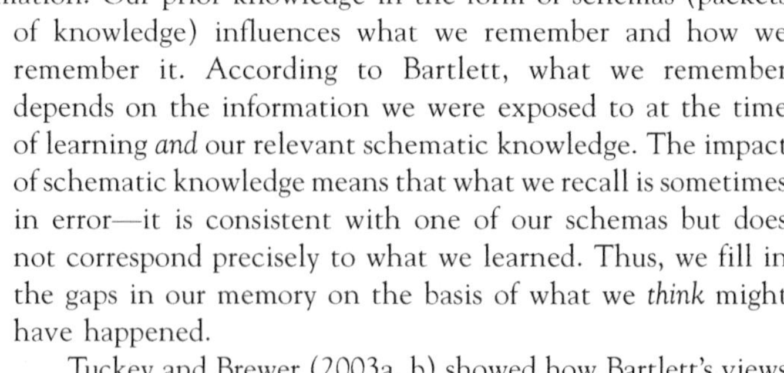

Tuckey and Brewer (2003a, b) showed how Bartlett's views could account for memory errors by eyewitnesses. Tuckey and Brewer (2003a) obtained information about people's bank robbery schema. It typically included the following aspects: robbers are male; they wear disguises; they wear dark clothes; they make demands for money; and they have a getaway car with a driver in it.

Can you imagine elderly ladies like these committing a robbery? Our stereotypical schemas may influence expectations of what a person is likely to wear, say, do, and so on.

Tuckey and Brewer (2003b) asked eyewitnesses to recall the details of a simulated crime. As predicted, eyewitnesses interpreted ambiguous information as being consistent with their crime schema. This led them to make memory errors based on information contained in the crime schema but not in the simulated crime.

Relevance of laboratory findings

Do laboratory findings on eyewitness testimony apply to the real world? Doubts have been raised because there are several important differences between eyewitnesses' typical laboratory experiences and when observing a real-life crime. First, eyewitnesses are much more likely to be the victims in real life than in the laboratory. Second, it is much less stressful and anxiety-provoking to watch a video of a violent crime than to experience a real-life violent crime. Third, in laboratory research, the consequences of an eyewitness making a mistake are trivial. In contrast, they can literally be a matter of life or death in an American court of law.

What is crucially important is whether the above differences have large effects on the accuracy of eyewitness memory. Evidence they may not was reported by Ihlebaek et al. (2003). They used a staged robbery involving two robbers armed with handguns. In the live condition, the eyewitnesses were ordered repeatedly to "Stay down!" A video taken during the live condition was presented to eyewitnesses in the video condition. Participants in both conditions exaggerated the duration of the event, and showed similar patterns in what was well and poorly remembered. However, eyewitnesses in the video condition recalled more information. These findings suggest the inaccuracies and distortions in eyewitness memory obtained under laboratory conditions *underestimate* eyewitnesses' memory deficiencies for real-life events and are not simply artificial errors.

Tollestrup et al. (1994) analysed police records on identifications by eyewitnesses to crimes involving fraud and robbery. Factors shown to be important in laboratory studies (e.g. weapon focus; poorer memory at longer time intervals) were also important in real-life crimes.

Limitations

Although most laboratory studies show eyewitness memory is unreliable and can be distorted, some studies show real-life recall can be very accurate. One such study was by Yuille and Cutshall (1986). They interviewed people who had witnessed a crime where one person was shot dead and another person seriously injured. These interviews (given 4 to 5 months later) were analysed, along with interviews given to the police immediately after the incident. The eyewitness accounts were generally accurate, and the accuracy and amount of information recalled didn't diminish over time. The eyewitnesses' accounts were also not distorted by leading questions.

? Why do people still believe eyewitnesses when we know memory is faulty?

Yuille and Cutshall (1986) concluded that laboratory studies such as those outlined above are not always generalisable to real life (i.e. Yuille and Cutshall's study has more **external validity**) and that more field research is needed. However, some caution is needed in interpreting their findings. First, only 13 out of 21 eyewitnesses agreed to be interviewed for research purposes and we do not know whether the memory performance of the eight missing eyewitnesses would have been similar to that of the 13 interviewed. Second, the 13 interviewed eyewitnesses among them made almost 200 memory errors relating mostly to the actions of those at the crime scene and to people descriptions.

There is another limitation with research on the effects of post-event information on eyewitness memory. It has typically been found that such information can distort memory of relatively minor details (e.g. broken glass; Dalton & Daneman, 2006). This may limit the practical importance of this line of research.

EXAM HINT

When discussing the reliability of eyewitness testimony it is better not to be too one-sided as research such as Yuille and Cutshall (1986) suggests real-life EWT can be reliable.

Improving the accuracy of eyewitness testimony including the use of the cognitive interview

Mistakes by eyewitnesses may occur because of what happens at the time of the crime or incident, or because of what happens afterwards. It follows from our previous discussion about misleading information that the questions (especially leading questions) asked during a police interview may distort an eyewitness's memory, and thus reduce its reliability.

KEY TERM

External validity: the validity of an experiment outside the research situation itself; the extent to which the findings of a research study are applicable to other situations, especially "everyday" situations.

What used to happen in the United Kingdom was that an eyewitness's account was often repeatedly interrupted. The interruptions made it hard for the eyewitness to focus fully on recalling the event, and thus reduced recall. As a result of psychological research, the Home Office issued guidelines recommending that police interviews should proceed from free recall (i.e. spontaneous reporting of what was remembered) to general open-ended questions, concluding with more specific questions. That reduces the chances of eyewitness memory being distorted by misleading information. However, psychologists have gone further and developed even more effective interview techniques.

Geiselman et al. (1985) argued that interview techniques should take account of basic characteristics of human memory:

? Have you had the experience of not being able to remember something until you found a clue to cue that memory, like running upstairs to get something and then being unable to remember what it was until you were back in the kitchen again? What was the memory cue in your own example?

- Memory traces are complex, and contain various features and/or kinds of information.
- The effectiveness of a retrieval cue depends on the extent to which the information it contains is *similar* to information stored in the memory trace. For example, if you wanted to remember the events of your early childhood, visiting where you lived as a child would probably provide good retrieval cues (the important role played by retrieval cues in remembering is discussed in the section on forgetting).
- Various retrieval cues may permit access to any given memory trace. For example, an eyewitness may remember additional information if they imagine themselves viewing the crime or incident from the perspective of another eyewitness who was also present.

Geiselman et al. (1985) used the above considerations to develop the basic **cognitive interview**, which is based on four general retrieval rules:

1. Mental reinstatement of the environment and any personal contact experienced during the crime.
2. Encouraging the reporting of every detail including fragmentary and apparently minor ones.
3. Describing the incident in several different orders.
4. Reporting the incident from different viewpoints, including those of other eyewitnesses.

Geiselman et al. (1985) compared the effectiveness of the basic cognitive interview and the standard police interview. The average number of correct statements was 41.1 using the basic cognitive interview compared to only 29.4 using the standard police interview.

Fisher et al. (1987) devised the enhanced cognitive interview. This is based on the following recommendations (Roy, 1991, p. 399):

> *Investigators should minimise distractions, induce the eyewitness to speak slowly, allow a pause between the response and next question, tailor language to suit the individual eyewitness, follow up with interpretive comment, try to reduce eyewitness anxiety, avoid judgmental and personal comments, and always review the eyewitness's description of events or people under investigation.*

Findings

Fisher et al. (1987) found the enhanced cognitive interview was more effective than the basic cognitive interview. Eyewitnesses produced an average of 57.5 correct statements when given the enhanced interview compared to 39.6 with the basic cognitive interview. However, there were 28% more incorrect statements with the enhanced interview. Fisher et al.'s findings were obtained under artificial laboratory conditions.

Fisher et al. (1990) trained detectives in the Robbery Division of Metro-Dade Police Department in Miami in the enhanced cognitive interview. Training produced an average increase of 46% in the number of pieces of information elicited from eyewitnesses at interview. Where confirmation was possible, over 90% of these pieces of information were shown to be accurate.

Memon et al. (2010) carried out a meta-analysis based on numerous studies in which they compared the effectiveness of the cognitive interview with that of the standard police interview. There was a large increase in the number of details recalled correctly by eyewitnesses with the

KEY TERM

Cognitive interview: an interview technique based on our knowledge about the way human memory works; paying attention, for example, to the use of retrieval cues.

cognitive interview (basic or enhanced) compared to the standard interview. The beneficial effects of the cognitive interview were reduced when the situation was highly arousing or when there was a long retention interval between the incident and the interview. However, the cognitive interview remained more effective than the standard interview even with high arousal and a long retention interval. The only negative effect on eyewitness performance of the cognitive interview was that there was a fairly small (but significant) increase in recall of incorrect details compared to the standard interview.

Does the cognitive interview reduce the negative effects of misleading information on eyewitness memory? Centofanti and Reece (2006) addressed that question. Eyewitnesses watched a video of a bank robbery followed by neutral or misleading information. Overall, 35% more correct details were recalled with the cognitive interview than with a structured interview. However, the negative effects of misleading information on eyewitness memory were as great with the cognitive interview as with the structured interview.

In Centofanti and Reece's (2006) study participants viewed a video of a bank robbery. They found that more correct details were recalled with the cognitive interview than with a structured interview.

Over the years, the police have typically used a shortened version of the cognitive interview in part because the entire cognitive interview can be very time-consuming. This shortened version typically focuses on mental reinstatement of the crime context and an attempt to recall every detail of the crime with reduced emphasis on eyewitnesses recalling the event in several different orders and from different perspectives. Colomb and Ginet (2012) found that eyewitness memory depended much more on mental reinstatement and reporting all the details than on altering the eyewitness's perspective and recall order.

EVALUATION

- (+) The cognitive interview has proved to be very successful in increasing the amount of information about crimes that can be obtained from eyewitnesses.
- (+) The enhanced cognitive interview is even more effective than the cognitive interview in enhancing eyewitness memory.
- (+) A shortened version of the cognitive interview with an emphasis on mental reinstatement and recalling every detail is very effective and much less time-consuming than the complete cognitive interview.
- (−) It is worrying that there is a small increase in the amount of incorrect information provided by witnesses when the cognitive interview is used.
- (−) The cognitive interview is generally less effective at enhancing recall when used at longer intervals of time after the crime or incident (Geiselman & Fisher, 1997). Thus, eyewitnesses should be interviewed as soon as possible after the crime or incident.
- (−) The cognitive interview doesn't reduce the negative effects of misleading information on eyewitness memory (Centofanti & Reece, 2006).

Additional factors

The cognitive interview includes many of the factors that improve the accuracy of eyewitness memory. However, other factors are also important, and we will consider two here. First, Perfect et al. (2008) compared recall when eyewitnesses closed their eyes or kept them open. Eyewitnesses recalled more visual and auditory details when their eyes were closed and there was no increase in false recall.

Why was this simple technique effective? In essence, it reduces cognitive load and reduces distraction from the immediate environment, thus allowing eyewitnesses to focus exclusively on their memory for the event (Vredeveldt et al., 2011).

Section Summary

Reliability of eyewitness testimony

- Eyewitness testimony is often inaccurate but is generally believed by jurors.

Factors affecting the accuracy of eyewitness testimony

- Misleading information presented before or after an incident can cause distorted memory.
- There is some evidence that misleading information has less of a negative impact with real-life crimes, and that memory distortions occur mainly to minor details rather than to information of central importance.
- High anxiety or stress leads to reduced ability of eyewitnesses to make accurate face identifications and to remember details of a crime.
- Most people possess a bank robbery schema. This can assist eyewitness memory, but can also cause eyewitnesses to make memory errors based on information consistent with that schema.

Relevance of laboratory findings

- Doubts have been expressed about the value of laboratory findings for eyewitness testimony in the real world. However, most factors found to be important in the laboratory are also important in the real world.
- If anything, eyewitness inaccuracies and distortions observed in the laboratory *underestimate* the memory problems experienced by eyewitnesses to real crimes.

Misleading information and the use of the cognitive interview

- The cognitive interview is used to enhance eyewitness memory. It involves mental recreation of the context at the time of the crime, reporting of all details, and recall in various orders and from different perspectives.
- The cognitive interview is an effective technique, but the enhanced cognitive interview (including minimising of distractions, avoidance of personal comments, and review of what the eyewitness says) is even more effective.
- The most important features of the cognitive interview are mental reinstatement and recall of all details no matter how apparently trivial.
- There are some limitations with the cognitive interview:
  - it produces an increase in the amount of incorrect information recalled compared to standard techniques;
  - it is less effective when used at long intervals after a crime;
  - its effectiveness is reduced when the situation is highly arousing.

You have reached the end of the chapter on memory which is an important topic within cognitive psychology. Cognitive psychology is an approach or perspective in psychology. The material in this chapter exemplifies how cognitive psychologists explain behaviour. They look at behaviour in terms of the way it can be explained by reference to mental (cognitive) processes (see Chapter 5). This is sometimes regarded as a rather "mechanistic" approach to the study of behaviour because it focuses on machine-like processes and can tend to minimise social or emotional factors.

Further Reading

- Most topics discussed in this chapter are dealt with in detail in M.W. Eysenck (2012) *Fundamentals of cognition (2nd Edn)* (Hove, UK: Psychology Press).
- The same is true of A. Baddeley, M.W. Eysenck, and M.C. Anderson (2015) *Memory (2nd Edn)* (Hove, UK: Psychology Press).
- There is a good account of the main factors influencing the accuracy of eyewitness testimony in G.L. Wells and E.A. Olson (2003) Eyewitness testimony. *Annual Review of Psychology*, *54*, 277–295.
- Reasons why eyewitness testimony is fallible are discussed by E.F. Loftus (2004) Memories of things unseen. *Current Directions in Psychological Science*, *13*, 145–147.

Revision Questions

The examination questions aim to sample the material in this whole chapter. For advice on how to answer such questions refer to Chapter 1, "How Can I Do Well in the Exam?".

1. a. Outline the main features of the multi-store model of memory. (6 marks)

   b. Explain **one** limitation of the multi-store model of memory. (4 marks)

2. a. Which two of the following statements describe features of short term memory? (2 marks)

   It has an unlimited capacity

   It has a capacity of seven +/− two items

   It has a duration of less than 1 second

   It has a duration of around 10 to 15 minutes

   It tends to encode information semantically

   It tends to encode information acoustically

   b. Which two of the following statements describe features of long term memory? (2 marks)

   It has an unlimited capacity

   It has a capacity of seven +/− two items

   It has a duration of less than 1 second

   It has a duration of around 10 to 15 minutes

   It tends to encode information semantically

   It tends to encode information acoustically

3. Describe and evaluate the working memory model of memory. (12 marks)

4. a. Explain **one** way that the accuracy of eyewitness testimony can be improved. (2 marks)

   b. Outline how psychologists have investigated the accuracy of eyewitness testimony. (4 marks)

   c. Explain why studies of eyewitness testimony have been criticised as lacking validity. (5 marks)

EXAM HINT

Some examination questions require you to apply your knowledge. They start with a "stem" describing a scenario (as in question 6 on this page). Whilst you probably have not seen the scenario before, if you have revised everything you will have the knowledge needed to answer the question. Just remember to apply your knowledge. You might briefly outline a theory or research study but then must use this to explain the scenario.

5. Discuss the use of the cognitive interview. (10 marks)
6. Tom is preparing to take his driving theory test. He needs to memorise all sorts of facts such as using headlights when you cannot see for more than 100m (328 feet) and you should allow at least a 2s gap between you and the vehicle in front on roads carrying faster-moving traffic.

   Which **two** words could be used to describe the type of long-term memory that Tom needs to use in order to learn these facts? (2 marks)

   procedural

   declarative

   episodic

   semantic

   implicit

   acoustic

What you need to know

The specifications for AS and A-level year 1 are the same for this topic, so you will need to cover everything in this chapter.

Attachment will be examined in Paper 1 of the AS exam and Paper 1 of the A-level exam.

Attachment

4

People develop attachments to all sorts of things—footwear, favourite restaurants, friends, lovers, and parents. You form attachments throughout your life, but among the most important ones are those formed early in development.

Attachment is like a piece of invisible string that binds individuals to permit healthy development. The tie is reciprocal—parents are as attached to their children as the children are to their parents. Attachment is a central topic in developmental psychology. In this chapter, we will consider how attachment develops and why it happens at all, as well as other related issues.

Next, we move on to the issue of the influence of early attachment on childhood and adult relationships. This is an important issue because the type and strength of attachments that children form early in life are predictive of their attachments many years later.

Finally, we move on to disruption of attachment, which happens when children are separated from their parent or caregiver. Such separation can involve deprivation and privation, and is found among children in institutional care.

What is attachment?

According to Shaffer (1993), an attachment is "a close emotional relationship between two persons, characterised by mutual affection and a desire to maintain promixity [closeness]". It is an emotional relationship experienced throughout the lifespan. When you are attached to someone, it makes you feel good to be in that person's company and also makes you feel anxious when they aren't there. You may also experience a longing to be reunited—this is the "desire to maintain proximity".

Maccoby (1980) identified *four* key behaviours associated with attachment:

There are certain behaviours that characterise attachment: distress on separation, pleasure when reunited, seeking out the attachment figure, and general orientation to each other.

- *Seeking proximity to primary caregiver*. The infant tries to stay close to its "attachment figure".
- *Distress on separation*. When caregiver and infant are separated, *both* experience feelings of distress.
- *Pleasure when reunited*. Obvious pleasure is shown when the child is reunited with his/her caregiver.
- *General orientation of behaviour towards primary caregiver*. The infant is aware of his/her caregiver at all times and may frequently make contact for reassurance.

In sum, attachment has a very strong emotional component. In addition, however, it also has a behavioural component (e.g. staying close to the other person). Finally, attachment has a cognitive component—for example, we have numerous happy memories of those to whom we are attached.

KEY TERM

Attachment: a strong, emotional bond between an infant and his or her caregiver(s) that is characterised by a desire to maintain proximity. Such bonds may be secure or insecure.

ACTIVITY: Observing attachment behaviours

If you know someone with an infant aged between 8 and 18 months, why not ask if you can carry out an observation to see if you can observe Maccoby's four attachment behaviours for yourself?

It is a good idea to do this at the infant's home, where he or she is most comfortable. The infant should not already be attached to you, so the child of a family friend or member of your extended family would be more suitable than your own sibling.

Put out some toys for the infant to play with. Help the parent or primary caregiver to check that the area is safe for the infant to play in alone. Ask the parent to start off by sitting in the room at a short distance away from the infant, and to allow the infant to play alone for a few minutes. He/she should not ignore the infant but should not initiate any interaction. Then the parent should move away to look at something else and/or leave the room for a minute, staying just outside the door in case the infant becomes distressed and needs to be reassured. Then he or she should return, allowing the infant to initiate any interaction.

Watch the infant closely throughout, looking for any of Maccoby's four attachment behaviours. You (or a second observer) might also look for attachment behaviours in the parent. Do you think your presence had any influence on the infant's behaviour? How do you think psychologists studying attachment might go about minimising this effect?

If you do not know any suitably aged children, you can carry out a similar observation using video clips by searching for key words such as "attachment" or "attachment behaviour" on YouTube. If you do this, bear in mind that the person holding the camera might have influenced the behaviour of the infant in some way.

CAREGIVER–INFANT INTERACTIONS IN HUMANS

The relationship between an infant and his/her caregiver is an important one. The main caregiver is generally the mother but in many cases it is the father or other family member. It is often argued that it is essential (or at least highly desirable) for successful emotional development for infants to experience a strong, close, and loving attachment with their caregiver.

Researchers have studied in detail the interactions that occur between infants and caregivers. For example, consider the approach adopted by Beebe et al. (2010). They used two video cameras to produce a split-screen view of a 10-minute interaction between mothers and infants. The subsequent data analyses focused on a second-by-second analysis of the interaction in three modalities (vision, sound, and touch). This remarkably detailed approach is known as **microanalysis**.

We will first of all consider the main developmental stages of attachment that infants go through in the first year or so of life. After that, we will focus on various aspects of caregiver–infant interactions and the relevance of such interactions for subsequent attachment behaviour.

KEY TERMS

Microanalysis: a very detailed analysis of the second-by-second interactions between infants and their mothers.

Longitudinal study: a study that lasts for an extended period of time so that changes in the participants can be observed.

Separation protest: the infant's behaviour when separated from the caregiver involving crying or holding out his/her arms; some insecurely attached infants show no protest when left by their attachment figures whereas securely attached infants do.

Schaffer's stages of attachment

The stage approach is a popular way to describe how children develop—to identify the ages at which certain typical changes occur for the first time (e.g. crawling; walking; talking). Schaffer and Emerson (1964) argued that infants go through *four* stages in their development of attachments to others (see box below). This theory was based on findings from their classic large-scale **longitudinal study** in which they followed 60 infants from a mainly working-class area of Glasgow over a period of 2 years. The infants were observed every 4 weeks until they were 12 months old and then again at 18 months. Attachment was measured in two ways:

- Using **separation protest** in seven everyday situations. The infant was left alone in a room, left with other people, left in his/her pram outside the house, left in his/her pram outside the

shops, left in his/her cot at night, put down after being held by an adult, or passed by while sitting in his/her cot or chair.
- Using **stranger anxiety**. Every visit started with the researcher approaching the infant and noting the point at which the infant started to whimper, thus showing anxiety.

Separation protest and stranger anxiety are signs that an attachment has been formed. Before the stage of specific attachments, infants show neither of these types of behaviour.

Stages of attachment identified by Schaffer

Asocial stage	Indiscriminate stage	Specific attachment	Multiple attachments
0–6 weeks	6 weeks–7 months	7–11 months	10–11 months
Smiling and crying not directed at any	Attention sought from different individuals	Strong attachment to one individual.	Strong attachments to two or more individuals

Schaffer and Emerson (1964) found that half the children showed their first specific attachment between 25 and 32 weeks (6–8 months). Fear of strangers occurred about a month later in all the children. In addition, the intensity of attachment peaked in the first month after attachment behaviour first appeared as assessed by the strength of separation protest. However, there were large individual differences. Intensely attached infants had mothers who responded rapidly to their demands (high responsiveness) and who offered the child the most interaction. In contrast, infants who were weakly attached had mothers who failed to interact.

Schaffer and Emerson (1964) found that in 39% of cases the person who usually fed, bathed, and changed the infant was not his/her primary attachment object. Thus, many of the mothers (and some of the fathers) were *not* the person who performed these tasks yet they were the main attachment object. Infants tended to form the strongest attachments with the adult who responded most accurately to their behaviour and needs. Adults who showed this quality were said to exhibit sensitive responsiveness.

Multiple attachments

Following the asocial, indiscriminate, and specific attachment stages, many infants became attached to one or more other people in addition to their initial specific attachment. The development of multiple attachments often occurred at about 10 or 11 months of age. By 18 months very few (13%) were attached to only one person and 32% had five or more attachments such as the father, grandparent, or older sibling. In 65% of the children, the first specific attachment was to the mother and in a further 30% the mother was the first joint object of attachment.

The multiple attachments formed by most infants vary in terms of their strength and importance to the infant. As is discussed later, there is typically a hierarchy of attachments—an infant may have formed three attachments but one may be stronger than either of the other two and one may be the weakest.

Schaffer and Emerson (1964) endorsed this notion of a hierarchy of attachment objects. Subsequently, however, Schaffer (1977, p. 100) somewhat modified his views: "Being attached to several people does not necessarily imply a shallower feeling toward each one, for an infant's capacity for attachment is not like a cake that has to be [divided]. Love, even in babies, has no limits."

Evaluation

Some criticisms can be made of the study by Schaffer and Emerson (1964). The data were collected *either* by direct observation *or* from the record kept by the others. Both methods are prone to bias and inaccuracy. Mothers recorded situations in which separation protest was shown and indicated the person to whom these protests were shown. Busy mothers may have

KEY TERM

Stranger anxiety: the distress experienced by a child when approached by a stranger.

produced these records some days after the events in question. However, such data would have been more accurate than the much longer time periods over which participants tried to remember in other studies. They would have had more external validity than data collected under laboratory conditions (e.g. the Strange Situation, which is discussed later).

The asocial stage (the stage at which infants' emotional reactions aren't directed at specific individuals) may be less asocial than Schaffer and Emerson (1964) assumed. Even very young infants typically respond to one special person in a unique way. Carpenter (1975) showed that 2-week-old babies could recognise their mother's face and voice. Infants looked at a face while hearing a voice. Sometimes the face and the voice belonged to the same person and sometimes they didn't. When they were presented with their mother's face but an unfamiliar voice or vice versa, most of the infants found this distressing and rapidly looked away from the face. Bushnell et al. (1989) presented 2-day-old babies with the faces of their mother and a female stranger until they had spent a total of 20 seconds focusing on one of the faces. Almost two-thirds of the babies preferred their mother's face over that of the stranger.

Another criticism of the study is that the infants in the study all came from Glasgow and most were from working-class families. These features of the study limit the extent to which we can generalise to other types of families in other areas. Finally, the sample size was only 60 which reduces the strength of the conclusions we can draw from the study.

Effective caregiver–infant interactions

Why do some infants have a secure attachment with their mothers whereas others do not? Ainsworth et al. (1978) put forward the **maternal sensitivity hypothesis,** according to which the sensitivity of the mother (or other caregiver) is of crucial importance. They identified four aspects of **maternal sensitivity**—alertness to infant signals; capacity to negotiate conflicting goals; promptness of response; and appropriateness of response.

De Wolff and van IJzendoorn (1997) carried out a **meta-analysis** based on the findings from many studies and obtained a correlation of +.24 between maternal sensitivity and security of infant attachment. This indicates a positive (but fairly weak) association. Most research on the maternal sensitivity hypothesis is correlational in nature and has involved finding associations between maternal sensitivity and secure attachment. As a result, it doesn't prove that differences in maternal sensitivity *cause* differences in security of attachment.

Clearer evidence can be obtained by looking at the effects of interventions designed to increase maternal sensitivity. Bakermans-Kranenburg et al. (2003) found across several studies that such interventions made infants more securely attached.

So far we have focused on the mother's role in determining the infant's attachment security. However, it is also important to consider the infant's role. Kagan (1984) put forward the **temperament hypothesis**, according to which the infant's temperament or personality influences its attachment to its mother. Since an infant's temperament depends in part on genetic factors, we might expect on the temperament hypothesis that identical twins (sharing 100% of their genes) would be more likely than fraternal twins (sharing 50% of their genes) to have the same attachment type. Bokhorst et al. (2003) found in a twin study that the role of genetic factors in accounting for individual differences in infant attachment type was negligible. Roisman and Fraley (2008) found in another twin study that genetic variation among children had no effect on infant attachment security or parenting quality.

If attachment type depends on infants' personality, we might expect that attachment type would be the same with their father as with their mother. However, this is only the

KEY TERMS

Maternal sensitivity hypothesis: the notion that individual differences in infant attachment are due mainly to the sensitivity (or otherwise) of the mother's interactions with her infant.

Maternal sensitivity: this involves the mother displaying various qualities in her interactions with her infant including alertness to infant signals and prompt and appropriate responding.

Meta-analysis: a form of analysis in which the data from several related studies are combined to provide an overall estimate.

Temperament hypothesis: the view that a child's temperament is responsible for the quality of attachment between the child and its caregiver.

case to a modest extent (De Wolff & van IJzendoorn, 1997). This suggests that an infant's attachment to its mother/father depends mainly on parental behaviour.

Co-ordination: Reciprocity and interactional synchrony

So far we have considered research in which the emphasis has been on what the mother contributes to infant–caregiver interactions or what the infant contributes. Many researchers have argued that what is more important is the extent to which the contributions made by the infant and by the caregiver are co-ordinated in a co-operative fashion to produce efficient and mutually satisfying communication. The essence of this approach was expressed by Beebe et al. (2010, p. 10):

> *Interaction [between mother and infant] is viewed as bi-directional, such that contingencies flow in both directions between mother and infant . . . both partners generate complexly organised behaviour that must be interfaced or co-ordinated.*

We can consider co-ordination of infant and caregiver interactions from various perspectives. Two major aspects of co-ordination are reciprocity and interactional synchrony. We will discuss them in turn.

Reciprocity

Reciprocity is "an interactive condition in which two individuals mutually respond to each other while performing activities together" (Apicella et al., 2013, p. 1). The essence of reciprocity is mutual exchange—ideally positive behaviour by the infant would be promptly followed by positive behaviour by the mother, and vice versa.

It might seem as if it should be a case of "more is better"—in other words, the mother–infant attachment should be most secure when there is plentiful reciprocal interaction. In fact, however, that is not entirely the case. Belsky et al. (1984) carried out a study in which they observed mother–infant interactions when each infant was 1, 3, and 9 months of age. At the age of 12 months, the infants' attachment to the mother was assessed using the Strange Situation (discussed later).

What did Belsky et al. (1984) find? Infants securely attached at 12 months had on average been involved in an *intermediate* level of reciprocal interaction with their mother when observed previously. As would be expected, infants who had been involved in a low level of reciprocal interaction with their mother tended to have insecure-resistant attachment. More surprisingly, infants who had been involved in the highest level of reciprocal interaction were also insecurely attached; however, they had insecure-avoidant attachment rather than insecure-resistant.

How can we explain Belsky et al.'s (1984) findings? An intermediate level of reciprocal interaction may provide an optimal level of stimulation for the infant. In contrast, a high level of reciprocal interaction is too stimulating for the infant and a low level is insufficiently stimulating.

Evidence of the negative effects of reciprocity failures was reported by Beebe et al. (2010) and discussed by Beebe and Steele (2013). They carried out a microanalysis of behaviour during mother–infant interactions when each infant was 4 months old. Then they used the Strange Situation (discussed later) to assess the infant's attachment at the age of 12 months.

Beebe et al. (2010) found some mothers sent out conflicting emotional signals when interacting with their infant. These conflicting signals represented a lack of reciprocity. Here are three examples:

1. The mothers would sometimes smile or show surprise immediately after their infant had indicated distress vocally and/or facially.
2. The mothers would sometimes fail to respond to their infant's increasing frequency of touching with increased touching of their own.
3. The mothers would sometimes respond to infant distress by gazing away from the infant's face.

KEY TERM

Reciprocity: a form of interaction between parent and infant involving mutual responsiveness.

What were the effects of these failures of reciprocity on the infants' attachment? Unsurprisingly, infants whose mothers exhibited these reciprocity failures tended to form a disorganised attachment (inconsistent and incoherent attachment behaviour).

In sum, reciprocity is an important aspect of infant–caregiver interactions. However, it is not the whole story. Such interactions involve three different sense modalities (vision; audition; touch) interacting in complex ways. We need to go beyond reciprocity to understand these complexities.

Interactional synchrony

Interactional synchrony is "a type of interaction between parent and child in which partners share a mutual focus, mirror each other's affect, exhibit a high degree of reciprocity, and are responsive to each other's cues" (Pasiak, 2011, p. 5). As that definition indicates, there is clear overlap between the notions of interactional synchrony and reciprocity. However, interactional synchrony is a richer and broader concept with more of an emphasis on emotional factors and less on behaviour. This goes some way to explaining why recent research has focused more on interactional synchrony than on reciprocity (Pasiak, 2011).

Trevarthen (1998) has carried out much research showing convincing evidence of interactional synchrony in mother–infant interactions. One of his key findings was that movements of the infant's hands, mouth, and eyes were often produced in rhythmical patterns with those of the mother. This was the case even when only the mother could speak.

Most research has focused on interactional synchrony between mother and infant. In a study discussed in more detail later, Mendonça et al. (2011) found that father–infant interactions showed comparable levels of interactional synchrony to mother–infant interactions.

If interactional synchrony is beneficial for infants and assists in the development of secure attachment, we would expect to find negative effects of disrupted interactional synchrony on infants. This issue was investigated by Murray and Trevarthen (1985) who instructed mothers to adopt a "frozen face" expression while interacting with their infants. The effects on the infants were as predicted. They exhibited much distress which manifested itself in crying and turning away from their mother. In addition, the infants tried to persuade their mother to become re-engaged in the interaction.

Does the level of interactional synchrony in infants predict subsequent infant–caregiver attachment? Most of the available evidence suggests the answer is "Yes". For example, consider a study by Isabella and Belsky (1991). They studied mother–infant interactions at 3 and 9 months of age and then mother–infant attachment was assessed using the Strange Situation (discussed later) at 12 months of age. There were two main findings. First, mother–infant interactions showing good interactional synchrony (well-timed, reciprocal, and mutually rewarding interactions) were followed by secure attachment. Second, mother–infant interactions in which the mother was minimally involved, unresponsive to their infant's behaviour, or intrusive and overstimulating were followed by insecure attachment.

EVALUATION

The notion of interactional synchrony goes beyond that of maternal sensitivity in two important ways. First, the notion of maternal sensitivity focuses primarily on the mother's contribution to infant–caregiver interactions whereas the emphasis with interactional synchrony is on both the infant and the caregiver. Second, research based on interactional synchrony has provided a very comprehensive and detailed account at a second-by-second level of interactions between caregiver and infant.

What are the limitations of research on interactional synchrony? First, most of the research has basically found that there is an association or correlation between the amount of interactional synchrony and infants' attachment type. Such evidence cannot provide definitive evidence as to whether interactional synchrony causes secure attachment, secure attachment causes interactional synchrony, or the causality goes in both directions.

KEY TERM

Interactional synchrony: a form of interaction between parent and infant involving mutual focus, reciprocal, and a mirroring of emotion.

Second, it would be an exaggeration to argue that *all* forms of interactional synchrony are beneficial. Synchronised parent–child interactions that involve negative emotions by both partners are maladaptive (Harrist & Waugh, 2002).

Third, the assessment of international synchrony in most studies involves the use of several measures which are only moderately correlated (e.g. Mendonça et al., 2011). As a result, it is often hard to know *which* components are most important for infants' development of secure attachment.

Fourth, researchers differ somewhat in their definitions of "interactional synchrony". It remains unclear which definition captures the essence of infant–caregiver interactions most successfully.

ACTIVITY: Theories of attachment

List all of the theories of attachment covered in this section. For each of them, suggest how the following questions would be answered: Why do attachments form? With whom are attachments formed? What is the major drawback of this explanation?

Role of the father

Most research on caregiver–infant attachment has focused on the mother as caregiver and so often de-emphasised the role of the father. However, there is increasing recognition that fathers often play a very significant role in the emotional development of their children (including their attachment behaviour).

One reason for the above change is that cultural expectations in several Western countries have moved in the direction of expecting fathers to play a greater role in bringing up children than was previously the case. Another reason is that the percentage of mothers working part- or full-time has increased considerably in recent decades and this has also led to fathers having a more active role.

A central issue is whether the father's role is similar to, or different from, that of the mother. As we will see, there are some important similarities as well as differences. We will start with what has often been claimed to be a major difference—mothers typically adopt a caregiver role to a greater extent than fathers, whereas fathers adopt a play-mate role more than mothers.

There is support for the above claimed difference in role between the parents. Fathers are more likely than mothers to foster risk-taking in their children by engaging them in physical play and enjoyable games (Paquette, 2004). Most infants prefer contact with their father when they are in a positive emotional state and wanting to play (Lamb, 1997). In contrast, most infants prefer contact with their mother when they are in distress and need comforting (Lamb, 1997). Note that the tendency for fathers to be much involved in physical play with their children is not true across all cultures. For example, fathers do not show this tendency in middle-class Indian families (Roopnarine et al., 1993).

The father's role in some Western countries differs from that of the mother in being more of a play-mate and less of a caregiver providing emotional support.

Paternal sensitivity

We saw earlier that maternal sensitivity is associated with the probability that infants are securely attached. If fathers play a significant role in their children's emotional development, we might expect to find that paternal sensitivity would also be associated with infant secure attachment. However, there are two reasons why we might expect paternal sensitivity to be less important than maternal sensitivity for infants' healthy emotional development. First, fathers in most families spend less time with their child than do mothers. Second, as discussed above, mothers are more likely than fathers to focus on the child's emotional needs.

Lucassen et al. (2011) reported a meta-analysis combining the findings from several studies. There was a mean correlation of +.12 between paternal sensitivity and infant–father attachment security. This association is weaker than the association between maternal sensitivity and security of infant–mother attachment and so suggests paternal sensitivity is less important than maternal sensitivity.

Lucassen et al. (2011) reported two additional findings. First, the size of the association between paternal sensitivity and infant–father attachment has not changed over time. This is perhaps surprising given the greater involvement of fathers in childcare in recent times. Second, the amount of stimulating play that fathers had with their children did not predict infant–father attachment. This finding is relevant given that we saw earlier that fathers spend more time than mothers playing with their children.

Several factors determine paternal sensitivity. For example in one large-scale study (NICHD Early Child Care Research Network, 2000), paternal sensitivity was greatest when fathers had non-traditional child-rearing beliefs, were older, and reported more marital intimacy.

Interactional synchrony

Earlier I mentioned a study by Mendonça et al. (2011) in which it was found that fathers had similar levels of interactional synchrony to mothers in their interactions with their infants. These findings were obtained when only one parent was present with the child. However, Mendonça et al. pointed out that in family life both parents and the child are often present together. Accordingly, they studied what happened when mothers interacted with their child in the presence of the father and when fathers interacted with their child with the mother present. The presence of the father reduced the mother's interactional synchrony only slightly whereas the mother's presence reduced the father's interactional synchrony to a much greater extent. Mendonça et al. argue that the presence of both parents causes traditional parenting roles to appear.

EVALUATION

There is evidence (mostly from Western cultures) that the father's role typically differs somewhat from the mother's. Fathers focus relatively more on play activities with their child whereas mothers focus more on caregiving and providing emotional support. However, parental sensitivity influences infant attachment to some extent, and fathers are comparable to mothers in interactional synchrony.

What are the limitations of research on the father's role? First, most evidence is correlational and so it is hard to be sure paternal sensitivity helps to *cause* secure infant attachment.

Second, numerous factors influence the father's role and the impact he has on his child's emotional development. These factors include the following: culture; father's beliefs; father's age; marital intimacy; and the amount of time father spends away from the home. The existence of so many factors means it is hard to make generalisations about the father's role and impact on the basis of studies that fail to investigate most of these factors.

ACTIVITY: A questionnaire investigating generational changes in child-rearing patterns

You could investigate changing patterns between generations in the roles of mothers and fathers in childcare.

Design a short questionnaire to find out about people's experiences of childcare before they started school. You could ask for their age, which gender provided child care, (male, female, or both), whether they were regularly cared for by anyone other than their parents, and whether they played mostly with male or female carers or both. You could ask some people aged up to 25 years to complete the questionnaire, then ask a similar number of people aged 35–55 years. You could then compare the two groups.

Important things to think about when designing your research:

- Closed multiple choice questions will make your questionnaire easy to complete and analyse but will need to be carefully planned. See pages 353–354 for advice on designing questionnaires.
- Attachment and care are sensitive issues that might cause distress to participants if researchers are not very careful about their questioning. Carefully consider any ethical issues that are relevant to this study, such as informed consent, privacy, and confidentiality. Write a short briefing at the top to fully explain the purpose of your research so that your participants can choose not to respond before starting. You should ask your teacher's approval for your questionnaire before distributing it.
- What size sample do you think you will need and what sampling technique could you most easily use? Are there any drawbacks to the technique you have chosen?
- Are there any drawbacks to using a questionnaire to study generational changes? Is there any way that you can minimise these problems?

Important things to consider when interpreting your findings:

- Are there any variables that might explain differences in your findings that you did not measure—for example, class, ethnicity, socio-economic status of parents?
- Can your study demonstrate broad changes in social roles or not?

Section Summary

- Schaffer and Emerson identified four stages of emotional development: asocial; indiscriminate; specific attachment; and multiple attachments.
- By 18 months of age, 87% of infants have multiple attachments, mostly to members of the family.
- According to the maternal sensitivity hypothesis, infants' secure attachment depends to a large extent on the mother's sensitivity.
- Maternal sensitivity includes alertness to infant signals and prompt and appropriate responding.
- According to the temperament hypothesis, the infant's temperament influences its attachment to its mother. There is only modest support for this hypothesis.
- Secure attachment in infants depends in part on co-operative co-ordination of infant–caregiver contributions when interacting.
- Reciprocity (mutual responsiveness and exchange) in infant–caregiver interactions appears to be important for secure attachment in infants.
- An intermediate level of reciprocity is optimal because it avoids over- or under-stimulation.
- Conflicting emotional signals sent out by the mother during infant–caregiver interactions are associated with disorganised attachment in the infant.
- Interactional synchrony between caregiver and infant involves mutual focus, affect, or emotion mirroring, high reciprocity, and responsiveness.
- The level of interactional synchrony predicts the infant's subsequent attachment.
- Most evidence finding an association between interactional synchrony and attachment security in infants is correlational and so cannot show the former causes the latter.
- The father's role in some Western countries differs from that of the mother in being more of a play-mate and less of a caregiver providing emotional support.
- Paternal sensitivity is positively associated with infant's secure attachment, but the association is weaker than that between maternal sensitivity and secure attachment.
- The father's role with respect to his infant depends on several factors including his beliefs, his age, the amount of time he spends at work, and marital intimacy.

ANIMAL STUDIES OF ATTACHMENT: LORENZ AND HARLOW

There is strong attachment between mothers and their children in many animal species. This is obviously advantageous in evolutionary terms—the newborn of most species are especially vulnerable and depend on attachment from one or both parents to maximise their chances of survival. Of course, this is especially the case with human infants.

We can distinguish between two different types of species. First, there are **precocial species**, which are species in which the newborn have the physical ability to move around. Second, there are **altricial species** in which the newborn are helpless and need prolonged parental care in order to survive. Several species of birds are precocial, whereas most species of mammals are altricial. In what follows, we will first consider an approach to attachment that focuses on precocial species and then discuss an approach focusing on an altricial species (monkeys).

Ethology: Lorenz

Ethologists study animals in their natural surroundings. One of the leading ethologists (Konrad Lorenz) studied various species of birds. He believed that their behaviour provided useful insights into the development of attachment. More specifically, he found the young of some bird species followed the first moving object they saw and continued to follow it after that regardless of whether it was their mother or Lorenz. Lorenz used the term **imprinting** to describe the birds' behaviour.

According to Lorenz, imprinting possesses two other key features:

1. There is a **critical period** in that imprinting is only possible during the first few hours after hatching.
2. It is irreversible in that a bird will remain imprinted to the same creature for its lifetime.

Lorenz hatched some goslings and arranged it so that he would be the first thing that they saw. From then on they followed him everywhere and showed no recognition of their actual mother. The goslings formed a picture (imprint) of the object they were to follow.

It is often argued that the notion of a critical period is too strong. It is more appropriate to describe it as a sensitive period (discussed more fully later). Thus, although imprinting is *less* likely to occur outside a given time window, it *can* nevertheless occur at other times. The idea of a sensitive period is that imprinting takes most easily at a certain time but may still happen at almost any time.

Bowlby was very influenced by the views of the ethologists. He argued that attachment behaviour in human infants can be explained to some extent in terms of imprinting and critical or sensitive periods. His views are discussed later in the chapter.

KEY TERMS

Precocial species: species in which the newborn are able to move around.

Altricial species: species in which the young are helpless when they are born and need a lot of parental care for months or even years.

Ethologists: researchers who study various animal species in their natural habitat or environment.

Imprinting: the tendency of the young of various species to follow the first moving object they see; this tendency has been claimed to occur only shortly after birth and to be irreversible.

Critical period: a biologically determined period of time during which an animal is exclusively receptive to certain changes.

Findings

Lorenz (1935) provided early support for the notion of imprinting. He took a large number of goose eggs and kept them until shortly before they were due to hatch. Half the goose eggs were placed under the goose mother and Lorenz kept the other eggs close to him. When the eggs were hatched, the newborn goslings that had been close to Lorenz followed him whereas the others followed the mother goose. Hess (1958) carried out a similar study on ducklings. He found that the effects were strongest when imprinting occurred between 13 and 17 hours after hatching. It was hard to show imprinting at time periods more than 32 hours.

Imprinting can influence sexual behaviour. For example, Immelmann (1972) arranged for zebra finches to be raised by Bengalese finches and vice versa. In later years, when the finches were given a free choice, they preferred to mate with the species on which they had been imprinted.

Do you think that there are problems with generalising from the behaviour of one species to another?

CASE STUDY: Amorous turkeys

Some psychologists were conducting research on the effects of hormones on turkeys. In one room there were 35 full-grown male turkeys. If you walked into the room, the turkeys fled to the furthest corner and if you walked towards them, the turkeys slid along the wall to maintain a maximum distance. This is fairly normal behaviour for wild turkeys. However, in another room, there was a group of turkeys who behaved in a very different manner. These turkeys greeted you by stopping dead in their tracks, fixing their eyes on you, spreading their tail into a full courtship fan, putting their heads down and ponderously walking towards you, all at the same time. Their intention was clearly one of mating. (Fortunately turkeys in mid-courtship are famously slow so it is easy to avoid their advances.)

What was the difference between these two groups? The first set were raised away from humans, whereas the second group had received an injection of the male hormone, testosterone, when they were younger. The hormone created an artificial sensitive period during which the turkeys imprinted on their companion at the time—a male experimenter. Subsequently, these turkeys showed little interest in female turkeys; however, they were aroused whenever they saw a male human—displaying their tail feathers and strutting their stuff.

It has been suggested that the reason this learning was so strong and apparently irreversible was because it took place at a time of high arousal—when hormones were administered. In real life, hormones may be involved as well. Perhaps, for these birds, a moving object creates a sense of pleasure and this pleasure triggers the production of endorphins, opiate-like biochemicals produced by the body, which in turn create a state of arousal optimal for learning.

(Adapted from Howard S. Hoffman, 1996, *Amorous turkeys and addicted ducklings: A search for the causes of social attachment*. Boston, MA: Author's Cooperative.)

Guiton (1966) found he could reverse imprinting in chickens. Guiton's chickens were initially imprinted on yellow rubber gloves. When the chickens matured, this early imprint acted as a mate template or pattern and the chickens tried to mate with the rubber gloves. This appears to support the claims made for imprinting. However, after the chickens had spent some time with their own species, they engaged in normal sexual behaviour with their own kind.

EVALUATION

- ➕ Imprinting often plays an important role in influencing attachment behaviour in several species of birds.
- ➕ Animal research on imprinting supports the notions of critical and sensitive periods.
- ➕ Lorenz's theoretical views had a strong influence on Harlow's theory of emotional development in humans (discussed later).
- ➖ Human infants are much more complex than young birds, and so the findings of ethologists have limited application to humans. Remember most birds belong to precocial species whereas humans belong to an altricial species.
- ➖ The findings from studies of imprinting in animals are very inconsistent (Bateson, 1979). This occurs because the existence or absence of imprinting depends on complex interactions between internal and external factors.

Harlow: Monkeys

The monkeys in Harlow's study appeared to be more attached to a cloth-covered artificial "mother" than to a wire version.

Some of the factors involved in attachment and bonding in monkeys were identified by Harlow (1959). He created 2 substitute monkey mothers. One was a "cloth mother" that was warm and soft to the touch, whereas the other "mother" was made of wire mesh. Infant monkeys separated from their real mothers shortly after birth greatly preferred the softer cloth mother to the wire mother. On average, they spent 18 hours a day cuddling against the cloth mother compared with under 2 hours a day against the other mother. This preference remained even when the infant monkeys could only obtain milk from the wire mother.

In other studies, Harlow showed that the baby monkeys were very strongly attached to the cloth mother. He created four "monster mothers", all of which were covered with cloth. One gave the infants blasts of air, the second shook so violently that the infants were often shaken off, the third contained a catapult that flung the infants away from it, and the fourth had a set of metal spikes which poked through the fabric from time to time. The baby monkeys became disturbed when they first experienced the unpleasant aspects of each monster mother. However, as soon as the monster mothers returned to normal, the baby monkeys almost immediately started cuddling them again.

Do infant monkeys have the same kind of attachment for cloth mothers as for their real mothers? According to Harlow (1958), the answer is "Yes": "Love for the real mother and love for the surrogate [substitute] mother appear to be very similar . . . the infant monkey's affection for the real mother is strong, but no stronger than that of the experimental monkey for the surrogate cloth mother, and the security that the infant gains from the presence of the real mother is no greater than the security it gains from a cloth surrogate."

Evidence for the above statement comes in another study carried by Harlow. Infant monkeys were placed in a strange environment containing several objects (e.g. boxes; cups) known to be of interest to monkeys. The monkeys explored their environment briefly and then returned to the safety and security of their cloth mother. This is very similar to what happens with human infants and their mother. When the cloth mother was not present, the monkey infants froze in a crouched position or ran rapidly from object to object crying and screeching.

? Why should one be cautious in using results from animal studies to explain human behaviour?

Preventing bonding

What happens when infant monkeys are prevented from bonding with their mother? Harlow and Harlow (1962) reported that there were far-reaching effects when baby monkeys were not allowed to see or interact with other monkeys for the first several months of life. When a number of monkeys isolated in this way were brought together, they behaved in various ways: many remained withdrawn and extremely fearful, whereas others became very aggressive. Some froze in strange postures, made meaningless repetitive movements, or simply stared into space.

Another effect of isolation was on the monkeys' sex lives. After a sexually experienced male monkey was placed in the same area as some previously isolated female monkeys, the male failed to make any of the females pregnant.

Harlow and Harlow (1962) also reported a few encouraging findings. Some negative effects on baby monkeys of being prevented from bonding with their mother were reduced when a substitute mother was present. There were also beneficial effects when isolated monkeys were put in the company of younger, normally reared monkeys. However, when isolated monkeys were placed with normally reared monkeys of the same age as themselves, they were unable to cope and hardly interacted with the normal monkeys.

Evidence that a lack of bonding or attachment with the mother at an early age need not have permanent effects was obtained by Melinda Novak (reported in Harlow and Mears, 1979). She studied monkeys isolated for the first 12 months of life. These monkeys were placed with normally reared monkeys less than one-third of their age so that the isolated monkeys wouldn't be frightened of them. Over a period of 2 years, there was a gradual disappearance of undesirable behaviour by the isolated monkeys and a slow increase in play and social contact.

In another experiment, four young monkeys were raised on their own without even a cloth or wire "mother". These monkeys spent the first few months of their lives huddled together, but gradually developed more independence and finally seemed to suffer no ill effects. These findings suggest that secure attachment based on infant–infant affectional bonds can be just as effective as secure attachment based on the mother–infant bond.

EVALUATION

+ Harlow found that monkeys are highly motivated to form a strong attachment with a mother-figure. This was shown in their continued cuddling of the "monster" mothers.

+ Harlow also found that strong attachment or bonding does *not* have to be with the mother—bonding with other infant monkeys can largely replace bonding with the mother.

+ Infant monkeys' attachment to a "mother" was influenced more by the comfort she provided (cloth preferred to wire) than by the provision of food (i.e. milk).

− We need to be cautious when generalising from infant monkeys to infant humans. Some of the apparent similarities across species may be misleading.

− Harlow's research on monkeys raises serious ethical issues. Many of the monkeys became emotionally disturbed and it is hard to justify this negative effect on their well-being.

− Monkeys are social animals who usually live in fairly large groups. As a result, monkeys reared in isolation were doubly deprived (they suffered social as well as maternal deprivation). This makes it hard to decide which factor was more important in explaining their abnormal behaviour.

Section Summary

- In precocial species (e.g. several bird species), the newborn can move around. In altricial species (e.g. monkeys; humans), in contrast, the newborn are helpless for some time.
- The ethologists (e.g. Lorenz) studied various precocial species.
- They argued that the young of some bird species followed the first moving object they saw and continued to follow it thereafter. This is known as imprinting.
- The ethologists claimed that imprinting was possible only during a critical period soon after birth. However, the evidence is more supportive of the notion of a sensitive

period—imprinting takes place most easily at a certain time but can happen at almost any time.
- The findings from studies of imprinting in animals are inconsistent.
- The notion of imprinting has more relevance to precocial species than to altricial ones (including humans).
- Harlow found that infant monkeys developed a strong attachment to a "cloth mother" that was warm and soft to the touch even when it didn't provide milk.
- Harlow claimed that infant monkeys' attachment to their cloth mother was similar to that shown by other infant monkeys for their real mothers.
- Infant monkeys who didn't see or interact with other monkeys for the first several months of life showed severe distress. These adverse effects were largely reversed when the monkeys later on had the opportunity to form infant–infant affectional bonds.

EXPLANATIONS OF ATTACHMENT: LEARNING THEORY AND BOWLBY'S MONOTROPIC THEORY

The great majority of infants (about 75% in many cultures) form **secure attachments** with their mother or principal caregiver. As we will see later, forming secure attachments is of great value in ensuring infants' happiness and healthy social development. There are more theories to explain how and why attachments are formed and maintained than you can shake a stick at. We will focus on two major theories: learning theory and Bowlby's theory.

Learning theory

The most basic principle of learning theory is that all behaviour has been learned (there is a general discussion of learning theory in Chapter 5). That means behaviour is not innate and does not depend on genetic factors. Learning theorists (also called "behaviourists") argued learning is the result of conditioning, which is a form of learning. According to learning theorists (or "behaviourists"), there are two main forms of conditioning—**classical conditioning** and **operant conditioning** (see the box). We will first consider traditional learning based on conditioning principles. After that, we will focus on a development of conditioning-based theories—social learning theory.

KEY TERMS

Secure attachment: the result of a strong positive bond between infant and caregiver, so that although the child shows distress at separation, he or she is easily comforted by the caregiver's return.

Classical conditioning: learning through association; a neutral stimulus becomes associated with a known stimulus–reflex response.

Operant conditioning: learning through reinforcement; a behaviour becomes more likely because the outcome is reinforced (rewarded). It involves learning contingent on the response.

Classical conditioning

- Unconditioned stimulus (US) e.g. food → causes → reflex response, e.g. salivation.
- Neutral stimulus (NS) e.g. bell → causes → no response.
- NS and US are paired in time (they co-occur).
- NS (e.g. bell) is now a conditioned stimulus (CS) → which produces → a conditioned response (CR) (a new stimulus–response link is learned, the bell causes salivation).

Operant conditioning

- A behaviour that has a positive effect is more likely to be repeated.
- Negative reinforcement (escape from aversive stimulus) is agreeable.
- Punishment is disagreeable.

Classical conditioning

How can infant attachment behaviour be explained by classical conditioning? The stimulus of food (an unconditioned stimulus) produces a sense of pleasure (an unconditioned response). The person providing the food (usually the mother) becomes *associated* with this pleasure. As a result, the provider of food becomes a conditioned stimulus that independently produces the unconditioned stimulus (pleasure). The food-giver thus becomes a source of pleasure to the infant. According to classical conditioning theory, this is the basis of the attachment bond.

What are the limitations of the classical conditioning account? First, it strongly implies that infants will form their major attachment with the mother or other food-giver. In fact, however, this was the case for only 61% of infants (Schaffer & Emerson, 1964).

Second, it is not clear why infants would form attachments with adults other than the food-giver. In fact, however, over 80% of infants have more than one strong attachment at the age of 18 months (Schaffer & Emerson, 1964).

Third, the attachments formed by infants are emotionally rich and complex. The classical conditioning account doesn't account for this richness and complexity nor for the great importance of attachment to infants.

? How do classical and operant conditioning differ?

Operant conditioning: Basic theory

According to the operant conditioning approach (e.g. Skinner, 1938), any response followed by **positive reinforcement** (reward such as food or praise) will be strengthened. All such responses are more likely to be produced in the future when the individual is in the same situation. Dollard and Miller (1950) put forward a simple account of the development of attachments based on operant conditioning. Their focus was on motivation, i.e. the forces driving behaviour:

- All humans possess various primary motives or drives, such as those of hunger, thirst, and sex. Stimuli satisfying these primary drives are **primary reinforcers**.
- A person will be "driven" to seek food to satisfy his/her hunger.
- Eating food results in drive reduction and is positively reinforcing or rewarding.
- According to the principles of operant conditioning, anything that is rewarded is likely to be repeated and so this behaviour is learned.
- The mother or other caregiver provides the food that reduces the drive, and so becomes a **secondary reinforcer**—he/she becomes a reinforcer by association with a primary reinforcer.
- From then on, the infant seeks to be with the person who has become a secondary reinforcer, because he/she is now a source of reward. The infant has become attached.

Mothers can also learn to be attached to their infants because of positive reinforcement. For example, mothers are rewarded when they make their child smile or stop crying.

Limitations

In the previous section, we discussed Harlow's research on infant monkeys. This research is of real relevance to human infants in spite of having been carried out on a different species. Harlow's research casts doubt on the learning theory approach. To test whether monkeys prefer the activity of feeding to bodily comfort, Harlow (1959) had very young rhesus monkeys taken from their mothers and placed in cages with two surrogate [substitute] mothers. One "mother" was made of wire and the other was covered in soft cloth. Milk was provided by the

EXAM HINT

The exam question will ask you about the learning theory of *attachment*. You will get very few marks for just describing classical and/or operant conditioning. Your descriptions must apply to attachment.

KEY TERMS

Positive reinforcement: a reward (e.g. food; money) that serves to increase the probability of any response produced shortly before it is presented.

Primary reinforcer: something that provides positive reinforcement because it serves to satisfy some basic drive; for example, food and drink are primary reinforcers because they satisfy our hunger and thirst drives, respectively.

Secondary reinforcer: a reinforcer that has no natural properties of reinforcement but, through association with a primary reinforcer, becomes a reinforcer, i.e. it is learned.

Although the wire mother on the left is where the baby monkey receives his food, he runs to the cloth mother for comfort when he is frightened by the teddy bear drummer (Harlow, 1959).

wire mother for some of the monkeys, whereas it was provided by the cloth mother for the others.

The key finding for present purposes was that the monkeys spent most of their time clinging to the cloth mother even when she didn't supply milk—this is NOT as predicted by learning theory. The reason was the cloth mother provided "contact comfort", which the monkeys regarded as more important than food. If the monkeys were frightened by a teddy-bear drummer, they ran to their cloth mother.

Learning theory is limited in other ways. First, it predicts all infants would be attached to the food-giver. However, Schaffer and Emerson (1964) found 39% of infants had their main attachment to an adult other than the one who mostly fed and looked after them.

Second, as mentioned earlier, this approach implies that infants would generally form only *one* strong attachment (i.e. with the food-giver). In fact, over 80% of infants at the age of 18 months have attached to more than one adult (Schaffer & Emerson, 1964).

Operant conditioning: Gewirtz

Gewirtz (e.g. 1991) put forward a more complex and realistic operant conditioning theory of infant attachment. He argued the mother is *always* a very important source of positive reinforcement or reward for her child, not just in the context of feeding. Mothers who are sensitive and responsive to their child monitor his/her behaviour carefully and use positive reinforcement to strengthen the attachment. For example, sensitive mothers provide reward to soothe the infant or to encourage him/her to respond to her.

There is much evidence (discussed later) that maternal sensitivity is associated with attachment—sensitive mothers are more likely than non-sensitive ones to have securely attached infants. It follows from Gewirtz's theory that aspects of maternal sensitivity that involve providing positive reinforcement when the infant really needs it should be most associated with infant attachment. That is what Dunst and Kassow (2008) found. These findings make sense—we would expect infants to be better adjusted if their mother is responsive to their needs.

What are the limitations of Gewirtz's theory? First, if securely attached infants are rewarded for interacting with their mother, it is not very clear why such infants often voluntarily separate themselves from their mother. Second, the theory focuses too much on the notion that attachment is merely a form of behaviour. In reality, attachment is a complex mixture of emotional, cognitive, and behavioural components. Third, it seems to assume infants' behaviour is dictated by the mother and the rewards or reinforcements she provides. In fact, infants make their own *active* contribution to interactions with the mother (see earlier discussion on reciprocity and interactional synchrony) and so are less passive than assumed by Gewirtz's theory.

Social learning theory

Social learning theory is a more sophisticated version of the learning theory approaches discussed so far (this theory is discussed in Chapter 5). Learning theory claims that learning takes place *directly* with no intervening mental process or processes. In other words, direct associations are formed between stimuli and responses. For example, a rat sees a lever and presses it to receive food reward.

Within social learning theory, on the other hand, it is argued that we also learn more *indirectly*. Much of what we learn is based on observing the behaviour of others (observational learning). Of most relevance here is vicarious reinforcement—we learn to produce a new behaviour by seeing someone else perform that behaviour and being reinforced or rewarded for performing it. According to social learning theorists, the kind of imitation involved in vicarious reinforcement is very important.

KEY TERM

Social learning theory: the view that behaviour can be explained in terms of direct and indirect reinforcement, through imitation, identification, and modelling.

Hay and Vespo (1988) used social learning theory to explain attachment. They suggested attachment occurs because parents "deliberately teach their children to love them and to understand human relationships" (p. 82). Some of the techniques involved are:

- *Modelling:* Learning based on observing and imitating a model's behaviour.
- *Direct instruction:* Providing reward or reinforcement when the child behaves in the required way.
- *Social facilitation:* Using the presence of others to encourage the child to understand positive relationships between people.

Some psychologists think of attachment behaviour as something that is learned because it is reinforced. Young children may learn about human relationships by imitating the affectionate behaviours of their parents.

Social learning theory emphasises the notion that infants' attachment to their mother or other caregiver involves learning certain responses (e.g. seeking closeness to the mother). All the techniques discussed by Hay and Vespo (1988) (i.e. modelling; direct instruction; and social facilitation) undoubtedly influence infants' attachment behaviour.

However, social learning theory focuses on only part of what is involved in attachment. For example, consider **oxytocin** (sometimes known as the "cuddle hormone"). Infants' attachment to their mother is greater when the mother has relatively high levels of oxytocin (Galbally et al., 2011). Such findings suggest we need to consider *internal* factors (e.g. mother's oxytocin level) as well as *external* ones (e.g. mother's behaviour; infant's behaviour) when understanding mother–infant attachment.

EVALUATION

- ➕ An infant's attachment to its mother probably occurs in part because he/she learns to associate food with the food-giver (classical conditioning). It also occurs in part because the mother rewards the infant and the infant rewards the mother (e.g. by smiling).
- ➕ There is some evidence (e.g. Hay & Vespo, 1988) that children can acquire attachment behaviour via social learning.
- ➕ It is likely that young children start to imitate aspects of the loving behaviour of their caregiver or caregivers as a result of observational learning.
- ➕ Research on social learning theory has practical applications. Parents or other caregivers need to be aware that their children use observation and imitation when developing attachments. Thus, it is very important for parents to act as positive role models.
- ➖ Harlow's evidence indicates that young monkeys preferred a cloth mother that didn't provide milk to a wire mother that did. This is the *opposite* of the prediction from learning theory, which claims infants form attachments to the person who feeds them. However, research on monkeys may not apply to humans. Against that, human infants often become attached to adults *not* involved in feeding or basic caregiving (Schaffer & Emerson, 1964).
- ➖ Learning theory is criticised for being **reductionist**, "reducing" the complexities of human behaviour to over-simple ideas such as stimulus, response, and reinforcement. These ideas are too simple to explain attachment.
- ➖ Social learning theory describes some processes involved in parent–child attachments. However, the strong emotional intensity of many parent–child attachments isn't really *explained* by social learning theorists.
- ➖ There is some evidence (discussed later) that genetic differences between infants help to explain why they differ in attachment type. However, genetic factors are ignored within the learning theory approach.

KEY TERMS

Oxytocin: this hormone promotes feelings of well-being and calm in mothers as part of the attachment process; it is sometimes referred to as the "cuddle hormone".

Reductionist: an argument or theory that reduces complex factors to a set of simple principles.

Bowlby's monotropic theory

John Bowlby (1907–1990) was a child psychoanalyst whose main interest was in the relationship between caregiver and child. He realised that Freud's views of the importance of maternal care could be combined with key ideas of the ethologists to produce a major new theory. As we saw in the previous section, ethologists study animals in their natural surroundings. In their attempts to understand attachment behaviour, they emphasised the notion of imprinting.

Bowlby's idea was that infants would show imprinting to their own mother, which would explain the strong attachment most infants have for their mother. This theory has had a profound effect on how psychologists think about attachment and infant development.

Attachment to only one person is called "monotropy" (leaning towards one thing). Bowlby (1953) claimed infants have a hierarchy of attachments, at the top of which is one central caregiver—this is the **monotropy hypothesis**. This one person is generally (but not invariably) the mother. Thus, the terms "maternal" and "mothering" don't have to refer to a woman. Bowlby (1969) said, "It is because of this marked tendency to monotropy that we are capable of deep feelings."

According to Bowlby, the special significance of monotropy is that it alone provides the experience of an intense emotional relationship that forms the basis of the internal working model—the schema the child has for forming future relationships (discussed later).

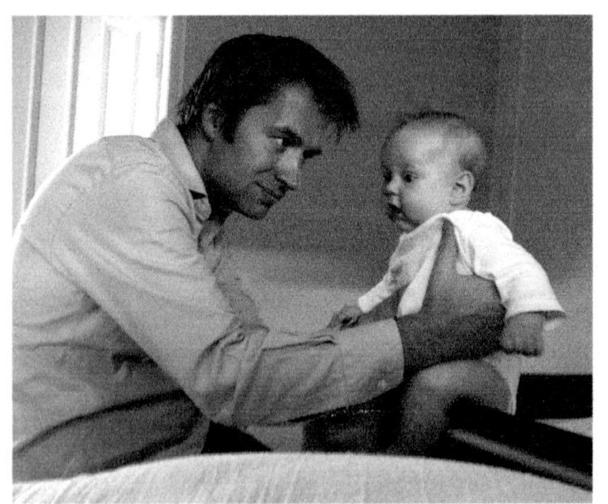

The attachment between a child and his or her caregiver (here Clementine and her father Simon) serves many important functions. According to Bowlby, it maintains proximity for safety, the caregiver acts as a secure base for exploration, and the attachment relationship acts as a template (pattern) for all future relationships.

Monotropy hypothesis

As we have just seen, Bowlby assumed with his monotropy hypothesis that infants form a single major attachment, although he accepted that they might also form less important attachments with other people. Bowlby also assumed that this single major attachment is typically (although not invariably) with the infant's mother.

Research by Schaffer and Emerson (1964), which was discussed earlier in the chapter, seems to cast some doubt on these assumptions. First, they found that infants' first major attachment was to the mother in only 65% of cases—that means the first major attachment for one-third of infants was NOT to the mother (typically it was to the father). Second, Schaffer and Emerson found 87% of 18-month-old infants had formed attachments to more than one person and 32% had at least five attachments.

What can we conclude from these findings? First, it seems as if there is more *flexibility* in terms of an infant's first major attachment than was assumed by Bowlby. Second, the fact that Bowlby accepted that infants might form a hierarchy of attachments allows us to reconcile his views reasonably well with the findings of Schaffer and Emerson (1964). In other words, Bowlby's monotropic theory allowed for multiple attachments provided that there was one especially important attachment. Third, in spite of what has just been said, Bowlby tended to emphasise the notion of a single major attachment whereas Schaffer and Emerson gave more emphasis to the notion of multiple attachments.

A fundamental principle of Bowlby's theory is that attachment is an innate and **adaptive** process for both infant and parent. Attachment behaviour has evolved and endured because it promotes survival. Attachment promotes survival in several ways:

1. *Safety*: Attachment results in a desire to maintain proximity and thus ensure safety. Both infant and caregiver experience anxious feelings when separated, which creates a proximity-seeking drive (striving to be close to the other person).
2. *Emotional relationships*: Attachment enables the infant to learn how to form and conduct healthy emotional relationships. Bowlby used the concept of the internal working model—a set of conscious and/or unconscious rules and expectations regarding our relationships with others— to explain how this happens.
3. *A secure base for exploration*: Attachment also provides a secure base for exploration, a process of fundamental importance for cognitive and social development. The child often returns periodically to "touch base" with its attachment figure. An insecurely attached child is less willing to wander. Exploration is very important for cognitive development, as was shown by Bus and van IJzendoorn (1988). They assessed the attachment types of children aged 2 years old. Three years later, the securely attached children showed more interest in written material than the insecurely attached children.

KEY TERMS

Monotropy hypothesis: the notion that infants have an innate tendency to form strong bonds with one caregiver, usually their mother.

Adaptive: the extent to which a behaviour increases the reproductive potential of an individual and survival of its genes.

Role of social releasers

According to Bowlby, attachment must be **innate** or the infant and parent might *not* show it. The infant and the mother/caregiver must both be actively involved for the attachment to be secure and lasting. Bowlby argued that the infant innately elicits caregiving from its mother-figure by means of social releasers. **Social releasers** are behaviours such as smiling or crying that encourage a response—humans are innately programmed to respond to these social releasers.

Most people feel uncomfortable when they hear an infant or adult crying, which helps to ensure someone will respond. It is a mechanism that maximises the chances of survival by keeping the caregiver close. These innate behaviours and innate responses are a fundamental part of the process of forming an attachment.

Bowlby's theoretical approach also provides an explanation for the notion (discussed later) that children separated from parent or caregiver show three successive stages of reaction (Robertson & Bowlby, 1952): protest; despair; and detachment. The protest stage increases the probability that the mother will find the infant. The following despair stage conserves energy and allows the defenceless infant to survive as long as possible in a dangerous environment.

The features of a baby face (here Clementine) are very appealing. They act as a "social releaser", a social stimulus that "releases" a desire to offer caregiving.

EXAM HINT

You need to know two explanations of attachment—learning theory and Bowlby's theory—and may be asked questions specifically on either of them. You may also be asked to "Outline ONE explanation of attachment. (6 marks)" and can then choose either explanation. Furthermore, you may be asked to "Outline ONE OR MORE explanations of attachment. (6 marks)", in which case you may do better to cover just one rather than trying to stuff both theories into your answer.

KEY RESEARCH STUDY

Bowlby's proposed phases in the development of attachment

Bowlby proposed that an infant is born with a set of behavioural systems that are ready to be activated, for example crying, sucking, and clinging (all called "social releasers"), and an ability to respond to the "stimuli that commonly emanate from a human being"—sounds, faces, and touch. Shortly thereafter other behaviours appear, which are equally innate though not present at birth, such as smiling and crawling. From these small beginnings, sophisticated systems soon develop.

In the table below, four phases in the development of attachments are described, with very approximate ages.

Phase 1 Birth–8 weeks	Orientation and signals towards people without discrimination of one special person	Infants behave in characteristic and friendly ways towards other people but their ability to discriminate between them is very limited, e.g. they may just recognise familiar voices
Phase 2 About 8/10 weeks–6 months	Orientation and signals directed towards one or more special people	Infants continue to be generally friendly but there is beginning to be a marked difference of behaviour towards one mother-figure or primary caregiver
Phase 3 6 months through to 1–2 years old	Maintenance of proximity to a special person by means of locomotion (movement) as well as signals to that person	The infant starts to follow his or her mother-figure, greet her (him) when she (he) returns, and use her (him) as a base from which to explore. The infant selects other people as subsidiary attachment figures. At the same time the infant's friendly responses to other people decrease and the infant treats strangers with increasing caution
Phase 4 Starts around the age of 2	Formation of a goal-correct partnership in which the child takes account of the caregiver's emotional goals	The child develops insight into the mother-figure's behaviour and this opens up a whole new relationship where the infant can consciously influence what she (or he) does. This is the beginning of a real partnership

Adapted from J. Bowlby (1969), *Attachment and love, Vol. 1: Attachment.* London: Hogarth.

KEY TERMS

Innate: inborn, a product of genetic factors.

Social releasers: a social behaviour or characteristic that elicits a caregiving reaction. Bowlby suggested that these were innate and critical in the process of forming attachments.

Klaus and Kennell suggested that prolonged skin-to-skin contact between baby and mother gave rise to greater bonding. However, recent research, including cross-cultural studies, indicates that other forms of attention also promote bonding.

Critical period

I mentioned earlier that Bowlby was influenced by the ethologists, who emphasised the concept of a critical period. In the case of biological characteristics, development must occur during a set period, otherwise it will not take place. Ethologists suggested this principle of a critical period might also apply to attachment. As we saw earlier, the ethologists obtained some support for this principle in studies on the following behaviour of various species of birds.

Bowlby's attempt to apply the notion of imprinting to attachment behaviour in human infants was based on the assumption that it had the following characteristics:

1. It occurs during a short critical period. If the infant is not exposed to a "mother" within a critical time window, imprinting won't take place.
2. It is irreversible—once imprinting to an object has occurred, it cannot be changed.
3. It has lasting outcomes. It results in the formation of a bond between the caregiver and its young and so has consequences in the short term for safety and food. It also affects the individual in the long term because it acts as a template or pattern for reproductive partners. Like attachment, this **bonding** process is desirable. It means the offspring are more likely to survive and so the parents' genes are passed on to the next generation.

Bowlby (1969) claimed that something like imprinting occurs in infants. He proposed that infants have an innate tendency to orient towards one individual (this is the monotropy hypothesis). This attachment is innate, and like all biological mechanisms should have a critical period for its development. Bowlby argued that this critical period ends at some point at about 3 or 4 years of age, after which it would be impossible to establish a powerful attachment to the caregiver.

The idea of a critical period is too strong. It would be more appropriate to describe it as a **sensitive period**. Thus, although imprinting is *less* likely to occur outside a given time window, it *can* occur at other times. The notion of a sensitive period is that imprinting takes place most easily at a certain time but may still happen at any time.

Klaus and Kennell (1976) argued there is a sensitive period immediately after birth in which bonding (part of attachment) can occur through skin-to-skin contact. They compared two groups of infants. One group had much more contact with their mother during the first 3 days of life. One month later, more bonding had occurred in the extended-contact group than the routine contact group. During feeding, the extended-contact mothers cuddled and comforted their babies more, and also maintained more eye contact with them.

Some later research failed to repeat the findings of Klaus and Kennell (1976). For example, Lozoff (1983) reported that mothers were no more affectionate towards their babies in cultures encouraging early bodily contact between mother and baby. However, there is some support for the skin-to-skin hypothesis. Bystrova et al. (2009) compared the effects of skin-to-skin contact for 25–120 minutes after birth, early suckling, and initial separation of mother and infant. Mother–infant interaction 1 year later was better in the skin-to-skin and suckling conditions than in the separation condition, suggesting there is a very early sensitive period for bonding.

In sum, the relationship between mother and baby develops and changes over time rather than being fixed shortly after birth. However, early bonding experiences may well be helpful.

KEY TERMS

Bonding: the process of forming close ties with another.

Sensitive period: the notion that imprinting is more likely to occur during a certain period of time rather than earlier or later.

Internal working model: a mental model of the world that enables individuals to predict, control, and manipulate their environment. The infant has many of them, some of which are related to relationships.

Internal working model

Bowlby argued that infants construct an **internal working model**—this consists of rules and expectations concerning their relationships with other people. According to Bowlby, this model influences their subsequent relationships including adult ones. We can obtain a clearer idea of the nature of internal working models in this quotation from Bowlby:

> *Each individual builds working models of the world and of himself in it, with the aid of which he perceives events, forecasts the future, and constructs his plans. In the working models of the world that anyone builds a key feature is his notion of who his attachment figures are, where they may be found, and how they may be expected to respond. Similarly, in the working model of the self that anyone builds a key feature is his notion of how acceptable or unacceptable he himself is in the eyes of his attachment figures. (Bowlby, 1973, p. 203)*

We can compare internal working models with schemas. Schemas are organised packets of knowledge; see Chapter 5). For example, you have schemas of what happens in a restaurant or when washing clothes. Internal working models resemble schemas in that both are cognitive structures that allow us to form various expectations. However, there is at least one major difference: motivational and emotional processes are much more important with internal working models than with schemas.

How are internal working models formed? According to Bowlby, these models start to be formed in infancy and are mostly influenced by the behaviour of close others. For example, consider infants who discover their crying behaviour typically produces a rapid loving response from their caregiver. This will lead them to feel that they are lovable and to develop positive expectations concerning others' behaviour. In contrast, infants who are rejected or ignored by their caregiver feel unlovable and develop negative expectations with respect to how others will behave.

Of most importance in the formation of an internal working model is the infant's primary attachment relationship. This is used as a template or pattern for future relationships. As we will see later, there is much evidence that the internal working models infants form early in life influence their subsequent attachments during childhood and adult relationships.

How consistent over time are internal working models? The inclusion of the word "working" implies that these models are works in progress and so they develop over time. However, if they changed substantially over time, infants and children would become confused as to the nature of their social world. In fact, infants typically develop stable internal working models unless they experience major life events or large changes within their family structure (Pietromonaco & Feldman Barrett, 2000).

Johnson et al. (2007) obtained experimental evidence supporting the existence of internal working models of attachment. They presented securely and insecurely attached infants with displays of responsive and unresponsive caregivers. They predicted that securely attached infants would expect the caregiver to be responsive and so would spend longer looking at the unexpected unresponsive caregiver. That is exactly what they found. Insecurely attached infants showed the opposite pattern because they expected the caregiver to be unresponsive.

EVALUATION

- (+) The notion that information about attachment figures and the self is stored in an organised way in internal working models is plausible.
- (+) Internal working models play a major role in influencing attachment behaviour at all ages (discussed in detail later).
- (+) Internal working models predict how individuals process attachment- relevant social information. Securely attached individuals process this information in a positively biased way where many insecurely attached individuals process the same information in a negatively biased way (Dykas & Cassidy, 2011).
- (−) We might expect any given individual would exhibit a similar attachment pattern with several other individuals. There is some support for that prediction. However, some children show different attachment types with their mother than with their

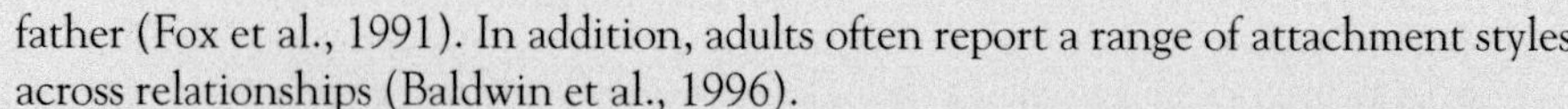

father (Fox et al., 1991). In addition, adults often report a range of attachment styles across relationships (Baldwin et al., 1996).

- It is often assumed that internal working models produce emotion but the causality could also go the other way—experiencing frequent positive or negative emotions might influence the nature of internal working models.
- The precise nature of internal working models is typically somewhat vague and has not been the subject of much research (Pietromonaco & Feldman Barrett, 2000).

EVALUATION OF BOWLBY'S THEORY

- Bowlby rightly emphasised the importance of attachment in infants and children. Indeed, nothing matters more for healthy infant development than having one or more secure attachments.
- Bowlby put forward the first ever systematic and comprehensive theory of attachment, and most subsequent theorists have used his main ideas.
- The notion that the infant's attachment to the caregiver is typically strong and robust has been shown to be correct.
- According to Bowlby, the infant's attachment to the mother is typically so strong and important that it persists even when he/she is maltreated by the mother. This is generally the case.
- Bowlby's theorising strongly influenced the development of the Strange Situation (discussed later), easily the most popular way of studying attachment behaviour in infants.
- Bowlby's claim that there is a critical period for the infant to form a strong attachment with its caregiver is partially correct.
- The notion that infants' initial internal working model formed on the basis of their primary attachment strongly influences their subsequent attachments has received support (discussed later).
- Most of the theory's assumptions are too strong and dogmatic. In other words, many of Bowlby's views are exaggerations.
- There is little support for the monotropy hypothesis with its emphasis on a *single* main attachment. Schaffer and Emerson (1964) found 31% of 18-month-old infants had five or more attachments. Most infants form two or more strong attachments at a relatively early age.
- Healthy psychological development is not always served by having only one primary attachment. It may be better to have a network of close attachments to sustain the needs of a growing infant (Thomas, 1998). This is certainly true in Caribbean countries. Even in European countries, infants probably benefit from the differences among their attachments. For example, fathers' style of play is more often physically stimulating and unpredictable whereas mothers are more likely to hold their infants, soothe them, attend to their needs, and read them stories (Parke, 1981). In Bowlby's defence, there is a *hierarchy* among an infant's attachments. For example, the Efe from the Democratic Republic of the Congo live in extended family groups. The

infants are looked after and even breastfed by different women but usually sleep with their own mother at night. By the age of 6 months, the infants still prefer their mothers (Tronick et al., 1992).

- Bowlby's view of attachment as a template (pattern) for future relationships leads us to expect any given child to form similar relationships with others. However, the similarities among a child's various relationships are quite low (Main & Weston, 1981). Howes et al. (1994) found parent–child relationships weren't always positively correlated with child–peer relationships. Even when there are positive correlations between the main attachment relationship and later relationships, other explanations are possible. Children who are appealing to their parents tend to be appealing to other people, so a child who does well in one relationship is likely to do well in others (Jacobson & Wille, 1986).

- There is very little direct evidence that infant attachment involves processes resembling imprinting, and it is preferable to focus on sensitive periods rather than critical periods. As we will see later, some children kept in isolation or severely deprived circumstances for the first several years of their lives nevertheless form strong attachments following adoption. Thus, it is NOT absolutely essential for children to form a strong attachment when very young.

Section Summary

- According to learning theorists, infant attachment behaviour can be explained in terms of classical and/or operant conditioning. The basic assumption is that the mother is rewarding for the infant because she provides a source of food.
- According to Gewirtz, securely attached infants are rewarded or reinforced by interacting with their mother.
- According to social learning theorists, infant attachment to the caregiver occurs through modelling, direct instruction, and social facilitation.
- The learning theory approach exaggerates the importance of food in infant attachment, and it is reductionist and oversimplified.
- Another limitation with learning theory is that it exaggerates the importance of behaviour in attachment and de-emphasises the strong emotional bond between infant and caregiver.
- According to Bowlby, attachment is an innate and adaptive process for both infant and parent. There is a critical period early in life during which bonding or attachment needs to take place. This resembles imprinting in some species of birds. In fact, it is preferable to think in terms of sensitive periods rather than critical periods.
- According to Bowlby's monotropy hypothesis, infants have a hierarchy of attachments at the top of which is one caregiver (typically the mother). In fact, many secure infants have strong attachments to two or more adults.
- An internal working model consists of rules and expectations concerning the infant's or child's relationships with other people.
- Internal working models resemble schemas except that motivational and emotional factors are more important with internal working models.
- In the formation of an internal working model, the infant's primary attachment is used as a template or pattern for future relationships.
- The notion of an internal working model is somewhat vague and it exaggerates the similarities in attachment type across children's relationships.

AINSWORTH'S "STRANGE SITUATION": TYPES OF ATTACHMENT

In order to understand the importance of infants' attachment behaviour, it is important to have a good method for assessing that behaviour. Several methods could be used. One approach would involve observational studies in which the experimenter simply observes the natural interactions between the infant and its caregiver (usually mother) in the home environment. However, the experimenter would have very little control over what happened—he/she wouldn't be in a position to manipulate aspects of the situation.

Mary Ainsworth was an American psychologist who spent some time in the 1950s working in London with John Bowlby at the Tavistock Clinic in London. This led her to adopt an approach to assessing infant attachment based in part on Bowlby's theoretical views (see the key research study below).

KEY RESEARCH STUDY

Ainsworth and Bell (1970): "Strange Situation" study

Mary Ainsworth devised the **Strange Situation** as a short but effective way of assessing the quality of an infant's attachment to its caregiver. Here we discuss the important study by Ainsworth and Bell (1970) on infants' attachments based on the Strange Situation. They aimed to investigate individual variation in infant attachments, especially differences between secure and insecure attachments. They hoped their method of assessing attachments (the Strange Situation test) would prove to be a reliable and valid measure of attachments.

The Strange Situation test lasts for just over 20 minutes and was used on American infants aged between 12 and 18 months. It takes place in the laboratory and the method used is controlled observation. The Strange Situation consists of *eight* stages or episodes as follows:

Stage	*People in the room*	*Procedure*
1 (30 seconds)	Mother or caregiver and infant plus researcher	Researcher brings the others into the room and rapidly leaves
2 (3 minutes)	Mother or caregiver and infant	Mother or caregiver sits; infant is free to explore
3 (3 minutes)	Stranger plus mother or caregiver and infant	Stranger comes in and after a while talks to mother or caregiver and then to the infant. Mother or caregiver leaves the room
4 (3 minutes)	Stranger and infant	Stranger keeps trying to talk to and play with the infant
5 (3 minutes)	Mother or caregiver and infant	Stranger leaves as mother or caregiver returns to the infant. At the end of this stage, the mother or caregiver leaves
6 (3 minutes)	Infant	Infant is alone in the room
7 (3 minutes)	Stranger and infant	Stranger returns and tries to interact with the infant
8 (3 minutes)	Mother or caregiver and infant	Mother or caregiver returns and interacts with the infant, and the stranger leaves

Several important findings were reported by Ainsworth and Bell (1970). There were considerable individual differences in behaviour and emotional response in the Strange Situation. Most infants displayed behaviour categorised as typical or secure attachment, while a few were insecure-resistant or insecure-avoidant.

KEY TERM

Strange Situation: an experimental procedure used to test the security of a child's attachment to a caregiver. The key features are what the child does when left by the caregiver and the child's behaviour at reunion as well as its responses to a stranger.

The securely attached infants were distressed when separated from the caregiver and sought contact and soothing on reunion. Insecure-resistant attachment was characterised by ambivalence (conflicting emotions) and inconsistency as the infants were very distressed at separation but resisted the caregiver on reunion. Insecure-avoidant attachment was characterised by detachment as the infants did not seek contact with the caregiver and showed little distress at separation.

Evaluation

The Strange Situation has been used numerous times in research. Indeed, it is easily the most popular method to assess infant attachment. It has the advantage of systematically placing the infant in various common situations in which its behaviour is carefully recorded.

Another advantage of the Strange Situation is that it is a straightforward method to use. In addition, numerous studies have reported similar findings to those of Ainsworth and Bell (1970); thus, their findings can readily be replicated. Finally, as we will see, the type of attachment behaviour displayed by infants in the Strange Situation predicts their future psychological adjustment.

What are the limitations of this study? First, the Strange Situation was developed in the United States and this study was carried out in that country. As a result, the Strange Situation may be culturally biased and the findings not applicable to other parts of the world. Attachment behaviour regarded as healthy in the United States may not be so regarded elsewhere in the world, and the same may be true of attachment behaviour regarded as unhealthy in the United States. This issue is discussed in detail in the section on cultural variations in attachment.

Second, the Strange Situation is artificial in ways that may distort behaviour. For example, some mothers or caregivers are likely to behave differently towards their child when they know they are being observed than they would do at home when alone with their child.

Third, the study was carried out in an unfamiliar playroom. As a result, the infants' behaviour may have been rather different to what it would have been in the comfort of their own home. This issue was addressed by Vaughn and Waters (1990) who compared the behaviour of 1-year-olds in the Strange Situation and at home. Securely attached infants in the Strange Situation had higher security and sociability scores based on their home behaviour than did insecurely attached infants. However, the differences in home behaviour between insecure-avoidant and insecure-resistant infants were small and non-significant.

Fourth, this study raises ethical issues. Many of the infants became distressed in the Strange Situation, which is clearly undesirable in many ways.

Fifth, as is discussed shortly, several researchers have disagreed with the notion that there are three types of attachment.

? What are the strengths of the controlled observation approach used by Ainsworth and Bell?

? Are there problems with using the Strange Situation in very different cultures?

EXAM HINT

This research is named on the specification, so you must learn how it was carried out, its findings, conclusions, and evaluation. It's not necessary to remember every tiny detail such as the exact timings in this study. However, you should be able to explain the key features of the study precisely. These would include:

- Features that make this a *controlled* observation, such as careful timing, sequencing, the controlled environment, and standardised procedure.
- The sequence of stages and the behaviours that the parent and stranger were asked to carry out.
- The attachment behaviours that the researchers would be looking for in the infant at each stage or transition.
- The findings and conclusions—specifically how behaviour patterns in the different stages were categorised into types.
- Evaluative points—make sure that you can fully explain (not just list) at least two strengths and two limitations.

How many types of attachment?

Ainsworth et al. (1978) reported the findings from several studies using the Strange Situation in the United States. They confirmed the notion put forward by Ainsworth and Bell (1970) that there are three main attachment types and provided a detailed account:

- *Secure attachment*: the infant is distressed by the caregiver's absence. However, he/she rapidly returns to a state of contentment after the caregiver's return, immediately seeking contact with the caregiver. There is a clear difference in the infant's reaction to the caregiver and to the stranger. Ainsworth et al. reported that 70% of American infants show secure attachment.
- *Insecure-resistant attachment*: the infant is insecure in the presence of the caregiver, and becomes very distressed when the caregiver leaves. He/she resists contact with the caregiver

Ainsworth and Bell proposed three attachment types. Main and Solomon proposed a fourth category, which they described as "disorganised attachment".

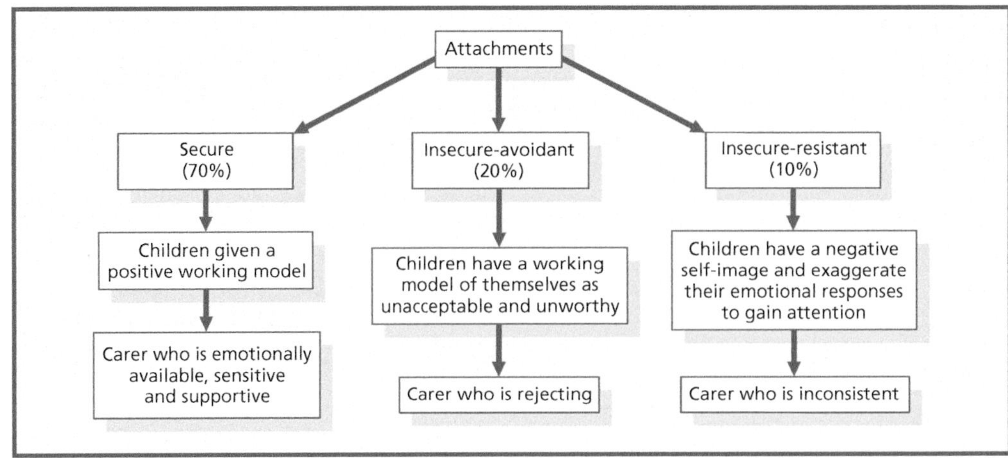

EXAM HINT

If you are asked to discuss different types of attachment in an exam question, you need to (a) describe secure, insecure-avoidant, and insecure-resistant attachment and (b) evaluate them. It is important to spend equal amounts of time on these two tasks—don't focus too much on the descriptions.

upon return, and is wary of the stranger. About 10% of American infants were found to be resistant.

- *Insecure-avoidant attachment*: the infant does not seek contact with the caregiver, and shows little distress when separated. The infant avoids contact with the caregiver upon return. The infant treats the stranger in a similar way to the caregiver, often avoiding him/her. About 20% of American infants were avoidant.

So far we have identified three main attachment types based mainly on research using the Strange Situation. However, this approach has its limitations. First, there is evidence for a fourth attachment type. Second, there are doubts as to whether it is a good idea to *pigeonhole* infants by categorising them as having a given attachment type.

Main and Solomon (1986) used the Strange Situation. As most researchers have done, they found evidence for secure attachment, insecure-avoidant attachment, and insecure-resistant attachment. In addition, however, a few infants displayed **disorganised attachment**—their behaviour was inconsistent and fitted none of the three main attachment types. Infants with disorganised attachment are more likely than other infants to have mothers who maltreat them or suffer from alcohol or drug problems (van IJzendoorn et al., 1999). Disorganised attachment is associated with subsequent aggressive behaviour and abnormality.

? Think back to the earlier section in this chapter on caregiver–infant interactions in humans. What factors determine infants' attachment style?

Placing infants into three categories based on attachment type is neat and tidy. However, it oversimplifies matters. Why is that? One reason is because infants *within* any given category differ in their attachment behaviour. For example, two children might both be classified as showing avoidant attachment, but one might display much more avoidant behaviour than the other. More generally, the boundary between just falling into an attachment category and just not falling into it is arbitrary.

We can take more account of **individual differences** in attachment by using *dimensions* (going from very low to very high) instead of categories. Fraley and Spieker (2003) identified *two* attachment dimensions:

1. *Avoidant/withdrawal vs proximity-seeking strategies:* This is concerned with the extent to which the child tries to maintain physical closeness to his/her mother.
2. *Angry and resistant strategies vs emotional confidence:* This is concerned with the child's emotional reactions to the attachment figure's behaviour.

As can be seen in the Figure, secure, insecure-resistant, and insecure-avoidant attachment all fit neatly into this two-dimensional framework. The dimensional approach is preferable to the categorical one of Ainsworth because it takes more account of small individual differences in attachment behaviour.

KEY TERMS

Disorganised attachment: a type of attachment in which the child's attachment behaviour is inconsistent and hard to classify.

Individual differences: the characteristics that vary from one individual to another; intelligence and personality are major ways in which individuals differ.

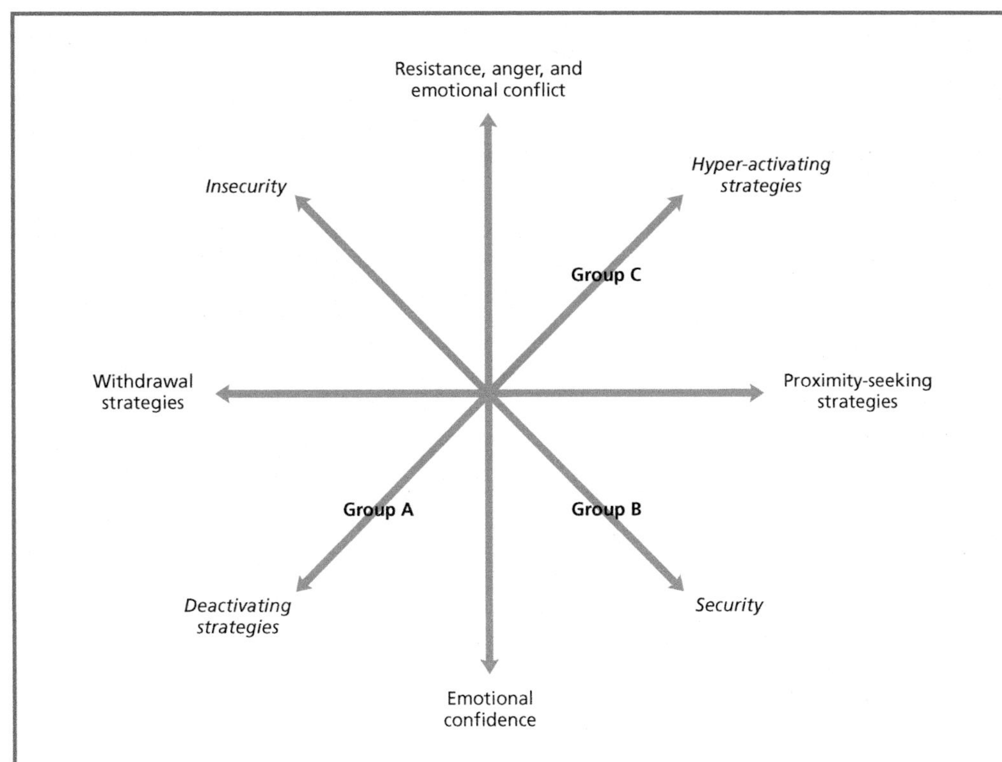

A two-dimensional model of individual differences in attachment. Group A has avoidant attachment, Group B has secure attachment, and Group C has resistant attachment. From Fraley and Spieker (2003).

Advantages and disadvantages of attachment types

Unsurprisingly, most of the evidence indicates that secure attachment is the preferred attachment type and it is linked to healthy emotional and social development. For example, Stams et al. (2002) found children securely attached to their mother at 12 months had superior social and cognitive development at the age of 7. Szewczyk-Sokolowski et al. (2005) found that securely attached preschool children were more accepted by their peers.

Fearon et al. (2010) carried out a meta-analysis of studies looking at the relationship between attachment type and aggressive or anti-social behaviour. Insecure-avoidant and insecure-resistant children were more likely than securely attached ones to have problems with aggression. However, the risk of problems with aggression was greatest in disorganised children lacking a consistent type of attachment.

One of the most thorough studies on the relationship between child attachment type and subsequent development was reported by Belsky and Fearon (2002). Attachment type was assessed at the age of 15 months and then five developmental outcomes were recorded at the age of 3. Infants categorised as securely attached had greater social competence, school readiness, expressive language (speaking), and receptive language (language comprehension) than insecurely attached ones. They also had fewer behaviour problems.

Are there any advantages associated with being insecurely attached (insecure-avoidant or insecure-resistant)? Ein-Dor et al. (2010) provided an interesting answer. They argued that insecure-resistant individuals are very vigilant to threats—this can be a substantial advantage in dangerous environments. As predicted, Ein-Dor and Perry (2014) found that insecure-resistant individuals were better than individuals with other attachment types at detecting deceit. Individuals who are insecure-avoidant focus more than others on self-preservation and are likely to be good at finding escape routes when danger looms.

In contrast, securely attached individuals may be so emotionally stable and non-anxious that they underestimate the seriousness of a threat to their well-being. The take-home message is that being insecurely attached is a disadvantage most of the time but may be advantageous when the situation is dangerous or threatening.

EVALUATION

- ⊕ There is reasonable consensus on the major attachment types.
- ⊕ The attachment types generally show reasonable consistency over time. For example, Wartner et al. (1994) found attachment classifications at 6 years were very similar to those at 12 months. That is valuable because it means we can use information about attachment types in infants to predict their future attachments and well-being (discussed more fully later).
- ⊕ Attachment type in infancy influences later emotional and social development. Elicker et al. (1992) found that social interactions at school could be predicted from behaviour in the Strange Situation several years earlier.
- ⊕ There is an understanding of the advantages and disadvantages of each of the main attachment types.
- ⊖ It is unresolved whether a categorical or dimensional approach provides a more adequate account of individual differences in attachment.
- ⊖ Sometimes there is very little consistency in individuals' attachment type. For example, Weinfield et al. (2004) carried out a longitudinal study on children considered to be at high risk at birth because of poverty. Attachment type was assessed at 12 and 18 months, and again at the age of 19. There was very little overall consistency in attachment type in this high-risk group. Reasons for this included changes in maternal life stress, family functioning during childhood, and child maltreatment.

Cultural variations in attachment

? Are attachment behaviours in different cultures broadly similar or very varied?

If attachment is an innate behaviour, we would expect attachment behaviours to be very similar around the world. On the other hand, mother–infant attachment behaviour may depend heavily on cultural expectations concerning what is regarded as appropriate. If so, we would expect large differences in attachment behaviour from culture to culture.

How do cultures differ from each other? There is an important distinction between **individualistic cultures** and **collectivistic cultures**. Individualistic cultures are ones in which individuals take responsibility for their own lives and the emphasis is on independence. Examples of individualistic cultures are the UK and the USA. In contrast, collectivistic cultures are ones in which the group is more important than the individual and the emphasis is on interdependence. Examples of collectivistic cultures are Japan, China, and Israel.

What differences in attachment might we expect to find in the two kinds of cultures? Here is one example. Consider infants' exploratory behaviour in the Strange Situation (discussed above). Mothers in individualistic cultures might regard such behaviour as indicating their child is securely attached and so is starting to become independent. Mothers in collectivistic cultures might be less positive about their child's exploratory behaviour because it suggests a weakening of interdependence (and so security) between mother and child.

Rothbaum et al. (2007) found American and Japanese mothers both felt positively about their child's exploratory behaviour. However, as predicted, the perceived association between exploratory behaviour and secure attachment was greater for American mothers (from an individualistic culture) than Japanese mothers (from a collectivistic culture).

KEY RESEARCH STUDY

Cross-cultural study by van IJzendoorn and Kroonenberg (1988)

Van IJzendoorn and Kroonenberg (1988) studied cultural variations in attachment types through a meta-analysis of research (combining findings from many studies) on attachment behaviour in several countries. They compared only the findings of observational studies using the Strange Situation to draw inferences about its external validity as a measure of attachment in other populations and other settings.

Van IJzendoorn and Kroonenberg (1988) compared the findings from 32 studies that had used the Strange Situation to measure attachment and to classify the attachment relationship between mother and infant. None of the children was older than 24 months of age. Research from eight different countries was compared, including Western cultures (USA, Great Britain, Germany, Sweden, and the Netherlands) and non-Western cultures (Japan, China, Israel). Van IJzendoorn and Kroonenberg researched various databases for studies on attachment.

Considerable consistency in the overall distribution of attachment types was found across all cultures studied. Secure attachment was the most common type of attachment in all eight countries. However, significant differences were found in the distributions of insecure attachments. In Western cultures, the dominant insecure type is avoidant. In contrast, the dominant insecure type in non-Western cultures is resistant, with China being the only exception (insecure-avoidant and insecure-resistant were equally common). A key finding was that the variation in attachment type *within* cultures was one and a half times as great as variation *between* cultures.

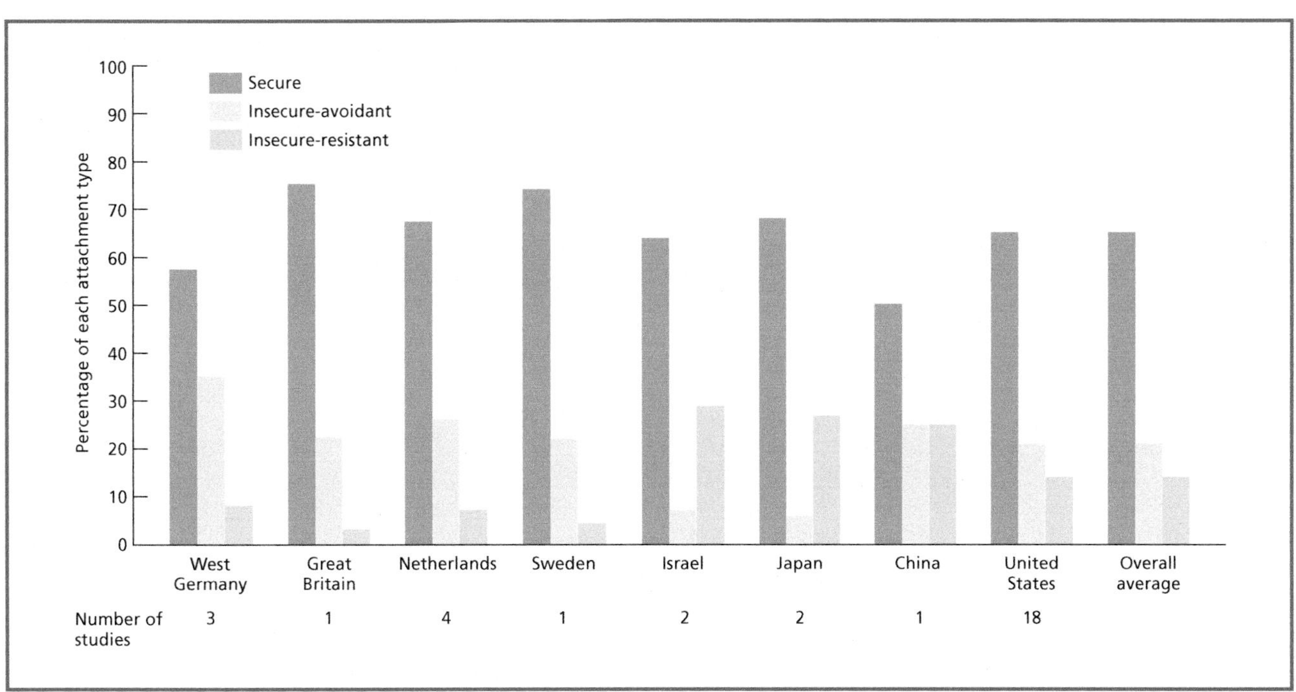

Infant behaviour in the Strange Situation, from studies in different cultures. (Data from van IJzendoorn & Kroonenberg, 1988.)

EVALUATION

- ➕ Van IJzendoorn and Kroonenberg reported a thorough meta-analysis to consider numerous findings on cultural variations using the Strange Situation.
- ➕ Their findings indicate it is wrong to think of any given culture as consisting of the same practices. The notion there is a *single* British or American culture is a gross oversimplification. In fact, there are several sub-cultures within most large countries differing considerably in their child-rearing practices.

+ The findings of van IJzendoorn and Kroonenberg suggest that the idea of focusing on cultural variations in attachment lacks validity.

− The study doesn't tell us *why* patterns of attachment vary so much *within* cultures. Perhaps variations in child-rearing practices are important. However, the study didn't provide any concrete evidence to support this speculation.

− It is very hard to know whether participants in the different countries were comparable. For example, the researchers failed to show that the percentage of middle-class mothers was the same in all eight countries. This limits the conclusions that can validly be drawn.

− The Strange Situation was created and tested in the United States, so it may be culturally biased (ethnocentric). In other words, the Strange Situation may reflect the norms and values of American culture. Thus, the Strange Situation lacks external validity, meaning the findings and insights based on it may be less meaningful than used to be thought. The research discussed by van IJzendoorn and Kroonenberg (1988) involves an **imposed etic**—the use of a technique developed in one culture to study another culture.

− The various findings were based exclusively on children aged no more than 24 months. Thus, the study is uninformative about children's attachments from the third year of life onwards.

? Thinking of your own experiences, what sub-culture(s) do you belong to? Do you know of any ideas about childcare that are specific to your sub-culture? What about your classmates?

EXAM HINT

You may be asked an essay question on this topic. For example, in the AS level you might be asked to "Describe and evaluate cultural variations in attachment" for 8, 10, or 12 marks.

At AS Level you should consider a more or less equal quantity of description and evaluation. The description could focus on the findings from studies of cultural variations. The evaluation is likely to focus on the weaknesses of the research methods used in the studies described.

At A Level, essay questions might be up to 16 marks. Here, you would be expected to evaluate in more depth than at AS level—perhaps around two-thirds of what you write should be analysis, commentary, and evaluation. Your evaluation might include an analysis of how the different strengths and weaknesses of research methods used in the studies might have affected the validity and reliability of their findings.

Sometimes the essay question will ask you to refer to a brief scenario in your discussion. In this case, you should aim to combine description of research, explanation of the scenario, and evaluation of theory or evidence in broadly equal proportions. Don't forget that at both AS and A Level, these longer questions are also looking for a clear and coherent paragraph structure, effective use of key terms, and good spelling, punctuation, and grammar.

Findings

Sagi et al. (1991) studied cultural variations in the Strange Situation in the United States, Israel, Japan, and Germany. The findings for the American infants were very similar to those reported by Ainsworth et al. (1978): 71% showed secure attachment, 12% showed resistant attachment, and 17% were avoidant. The Israeli infants behaved rather differently. Secure attachment was shown by 62% of the Israeli infants, 33% were resistant, and only 5% were avoidant. These infants lived on a kibbutz, which is a communal settlement in which children are looked after much of the time by adults not part of their family. However, since they mostly had a close relationship with their mothers, they tended not to be avoidant.

Sagi et al. (1991) found 49% of German infants had insecure-avoidant attachment compared to 0% in Japan. This reflects the emphasis on independence in Germany (an individualistic culture) versus the emphasis on interdependence in Japan (a collectivistic culture).

Japanese mothers practically never leave their infants alone with a stranger. However, in spite of the differences in child-rearing practices in Japan and in Israel, the Japanese infants showed similar attachment styles to the Israeli ones. Two-thirds (68%) had a secure attachment, 32% were insecure-resistant, and none was insecure-avoidant. It is not surprising that

KEY TERM

Imposed etic: the use of a technique developed in one culture to study another culture.

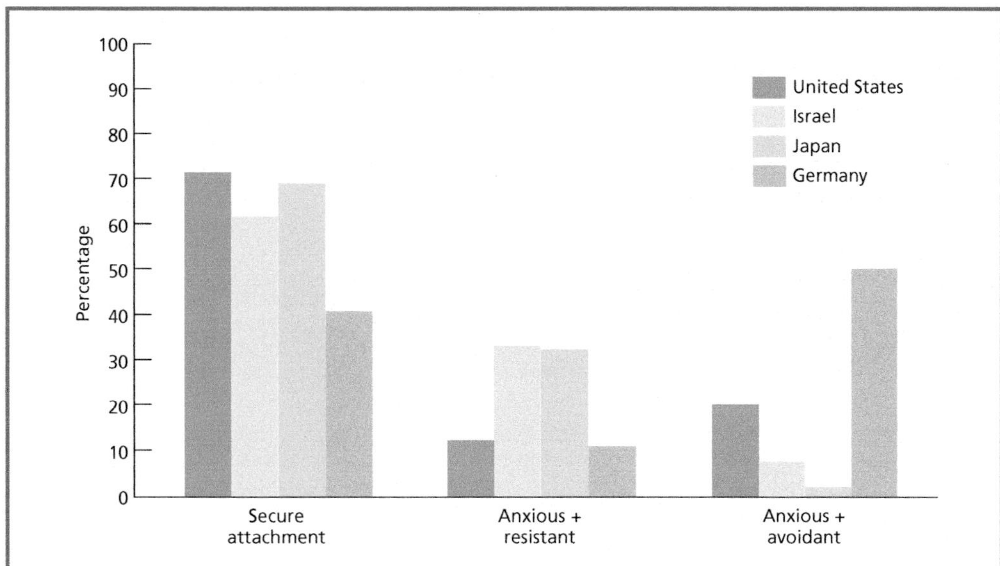

Children from different countries vary in their attachment types. The graph summarises research from Sagi et al. (1991) and Ainsworth and Bell (1970).

no Japanese infants treated a stranger similarly to their mother given that most had rarely if ever been on their own with a stranger.

Posada et al. (1995) carried out a study in seven countries (China, Colombia, Germany, Israel, Japan, Norway, and the USA). Most infants in every country were securely attached and showed clear evidence of regarding their mother as a secure base. However, the details of how secure-base behaviour was displayed varied across cultures.

Rothbaum et al. (2007) explored how American and Japanese mothers regard mother–child attachment. There were some important differences. For example, the mothers were asked how they would interpret it if their child called for its mother during naptime. American mothers regarded this behaviour negatively (e.g. the child was testing the limits of what it was allowed to do). In contrast, Japanese mothers regarded it positively as a sign of secure attachment. This difference reflects the greater emphasis on interdependence within collectivistic cultures.

Final thoughts

Rothbaum et al. (2000, p. 1101) argued as follows: "Assumptions . . . such as that children are the logical focus of attention and that behaviour in reunions best captures the dynamics of close relationships, are based in Western thought." These assumptions underlie most cross-cultural theory and research and are claimed to invalidate many findings. For example, the Strange Situation was devised by Western psychologists and may have limited relevance in other cultures.

Rothbaum et al. (2000) went on to contrast the Western notion of security or secure attachment with the Japanese word ***amae*** (a-mah-yeh), which means emotional dependence (literally "indulgent dependence"). Infants showing amae exhibit much clinging behaviour and need for attention. These forms of behaviour are regarded as indicating insecure attachment by Western psychologists but good adjustment in Japan.

Rothbaum et al. (2000) overstated the matter. It is true there are important differences in attachment behaviour between individualistic and collectivistic cultures. However, that doesn't necessarily mean that the entire notion of security or secure attachment has radically different meanings in different cultures. Of importance here is the study by Posada et al. (1995). They found ideas about the nature of security and a safe base were very similar across seven very different cultures.

In sum, it is likely that having infants securely attached to their mother is very advantageous in virtually all cultures. It is also likely to be true universally that children whose mothers or caregivers are sensitive to their needs are more likely to be securely attached than children whose mothers are less sensitive. These are deep and profound cross-cultural similarities. The precise forms of behaviour shown by securely attached children undoubtedly vary from culture to culture. However, these differences in behaviour are less important than the underlying similarities.

KEY TERM

Amae: a Japanese word referring to a positive form of attachment that involves emotional dependence, clinging, and attention-seeking behaviour. Such behaviour is regarded more negatively in Western countries.

Section Summary

- The "Strange Situation" provides a thorough assessment of infants' attachment type and is easily the most commonly used technique for measuring attachment.
- Ainsworth found using the Strange Situation that about 70% of infants show secure attachment, 20% avoidant attachment, and 10% resistant attachment.
- Research based on the Strange Situation has the following weaknesses:
  - it is culturally biased;
  - it is artificial because caregivers know they are being observed;
  - it involves an unfamiliar room rather than the infant's home; however, attachment behaviour is similar in both environments.
- There is an important distinction between secure and insecure attachment. Maltreated children are more likely than other children to be insecurely attached.
- Ainsworth argued that there are two forms of insecure attachment: insecure-avoidant and insecure-resistant. Insecure-avoidant children inhibit their attachment needs, whereas insecure-resistant children exaggerate their attachment needs.
- There is also a fourth attachment style: disorganised.
- Most children show consistency of attachment style over time.
- Secure attachment is associated with greater social competence and language skills.
- Individuals who are insecure-avoidant have the advantage of focusing on self-preservation and those who are insecure-resistant have the advantage of high vigilance in threatening situations.
- Considering attachment types within a two-dimensional framework (avoidant-withdrawal vs proximity-seeking, and angry and resistant strategies vs emotional confidence) permits a more fine-grained account of individual differences in attachment.
- Van IJzendoorn and Kroonenberg (1988) found that secure attachment was the most common type of infant attachment in eight different countries. The dominant insecure attachment type was avoidant in Western cultures but resistant in non-Western cultures.
- In spite of cultural differences in attachment, van IJzendoorn and Kroonenberg (1988) found that the variation in attachment types within cultures was greater than the variation between cultures.
- There are various weaknesses with the research of van IJzendoorn and Kroonenberg (1988):
  - It doesn't tell us why patterns of attachment vary so much within any given culture.
  - It is misleading to focus on cultures rather than sub-cultures. The research involved the Strange Situation test, which was created and tested in the United States and so may be culturally biased.
  - It considered only children aged no more than 24 months, and so tells us nothing about children's attachments at older ages.
- The Japanese regard amae (emotional dependence) as indicating that an infant is securely attached to its mother. In Western countries, however, such clinging behaviour is regarded as indicating insecure attachment.

KEY TERM

Maternal deprivation theory: Bowlby's view that separation from the primary caregiver leads to disruption and perhaps breaking of the attachment bond, with long-term adverse and possibly permanent effects on emotional development.

BOWLBY'S THEORY OF MATERNAL DEPRIVATION

Prior to the development of his theory of attachment, John Bowlby (1953) proposed the **maternal deprivation theory**, which focused on the effects of long-term disruption of attachment. According to this theory (often known as the maternal deprivation hypothesis), breaking the maternal bond with the child during the early years of its life is likely to have serious effects on its intellectual, social, and emotional development.

Bowlby (1953) also claimed that many of these negative effects could be permanent and irreversible. Contrary to popular belief, however, Bowlby argued that 25% (rather than 100%) of children suffer long-term damage from maternal deprivation involving long-term disruption of attachment (Di Dwyer, personal communication). Finally, Bowlby endorsed monotropy. This is the notion (discussed earlier) that human infants have an innate tendency to form strong bonds with one particular individual (typically the mother).

When Bowlby put forward his maternal deprivation theory in the early 1950s, it was regarded as revolutionary. Most professionals at that time felt that adequate physical provision was most important for healthy development. In spite of that, it was accepted by the early 1940s that children could suffer to some extent if they experienced long-term disruption of attachment with their mother. However, the full extent of such suffering hadn't been clearly established.

In the real world, circumstances such as divorce between parents or the death of a parent can disrupt the child's attachments or even prevent them from being formed. If attachment is critical to healthy psychological development, then Bowlby's theory would predict that any disruption to this process should result in the opposite effect—unhealthy psychological development. One way of determining the validity of Bowlby's theory is to consider the effects of such disruption.

In this section, we discuss the effects on the young child of being separated from one or more of the most important adults in his/her life. Most studies have focused on the long-term effects of disruption of attachment. However, we will first consider short-term effects.

Separation from the mother can have severe emotional effects on a child. The first stage of the child's response to the separation is known as protest: an intense period during which the child cries for much of the time.

Short-term effects of disruption

Even fairly brief disruption of attachment with a primary caregiver can have severe emotional effects on the child. Short-term disruption of attachment can be distinguished from long-term disruption of attachment. Short-term disruption of attachment (known as **separation**) involves distress when a child is separated for a fairly short time period from a person to whom there is an attachment bond. In contrast, long-term disruption of attachment (known as **deprivation**) occurs when a bond has been formed and is then broken for what are generally fairly long periods of time.

According to Bowlby's maternal deprivation theory, even short-term disruption of attachment with their primary caregiver can cause severe emotional effects to young children. In the early 1950s, this view was controversial, and the necessary evidence wasn't available. However, relevant evidence was published in 1952.

Robertson and Bowlby (1952) studied young children experiencing disruption of attachment with their mother for some time, often because she had gone into hospital. They observed *three* stages in the child's response, leading them to produce the protest–despair–detachment (PDD) model:

1. *Protest*, which is often very intense. The child cries often, and sometimes seems panic-stricken. Anger and fear are present.
2. *Despair*, involving a total loss of hope. The child is often apathetic, and shows little interest in its surroundings. The child often engages in self-comforting behaviour (e.g. thumb-sucking; rocking).
3. *Detachment*, during which the child seems less distressed. If the mother or caregiver re-appears during this stage, she is not responded to with any great interest.

It used to be thought children in the detachment stage had adjusted fairly well to short-term disruption of attachment. However, the calm behaviour shown by the child when its mother re-appears probably disguises its true feelings. Fortunately, most children re-establish an attachment to the mother over time.

KEY TERMS

Separation: the absence of the caregiver (e.g. due to work commitments, divorce, or hospitalisation) which usually causes great distress but not necessarily permanent bond disruption.

Deprivation: to lose something such as the care of an attachment figure for a long time.

How might the findings from the Robertson and Robertson study be applied to helping children in institutional care?

EVALUATION OF THE PDD MODEL

Is it inevitable that short-term disruption of attachment produces the various negative effects predicted by the PDD model? Robertson and Robertson (1971) suggested it isn't. They looked after several young children in their own home who had experienced short-term disruption of attachment with their mothers. They ensured the children became familiar with their new surroundings beforehand to minimise any distress. They also provided the children with a similar daily routine and discussed the children's mothers with them. This approach proved successful, with the children showing much less distress than most children experiencing short-term disruption of attachment.

The Robertsons also studied other children experiencing short-term disruption of attachment with their mothers who spent their time in a residential nursery. These children did not cope well—they received good physical care but lacked emotional care. The Robertsons said the nursery children experienced **bond disruption**, whereas the others did not because they were offered substitute mothering. Thus, short-term disruption of attachment need not lead to deprivation, but may do so if accompanied by bond disruption.

Barrett (1997) pointed out the lack of convincing evidence for the proposed sequence of protest, despair, and detachment. Of importance, the model doesn't consider individual differences. For example, a securely attached child may show little initial protest and cope relatively well, whereas an insecure-resistant child would be plunged more immediately into protest and despair.

Barrett (1997) also argued that the PDD model is flawed because it minimises the social competence of very young children. Thus, many young children have a greater ability to cope with short-term disruption of attachment than assumed by Robertson and Bowlby (1952).

EXAM HINT

Bowlby's maternal deprivation theory was proposed before his attachment theory. The two theories are two distinctly different things but it is easy to confuse them and end up writing about the maternal deprivation theory when asked about Bowlby's attachment theory. You would get no credit for this.

The maternal deprivation theory focuses on the negative effects of early separation on emotional development, whereas attachment theory is concerned with the positive effects of attachment on emotional development.

Maternal deprivation: Findings

We turn now to a consideration of research focusing on the long-term effects of disruption of attachment. In the context of the time, Bowlby's (1944) classic study of juvenile thieves had a major impact. He carried out his well-known study on clients from the child guidance clinic where he worked. He interviewed the children and their families, and gradually built up a record of their early life experiences. Some children had experienced "early and prolonged separation from their mothers", and some were emotionally maladjusted. In particular, he diagnosed the condition of affectionless psychopathy in some of the children, a disorder involving a lack of guilt and remorse. Could there be a link between this form of emotional maladjustment and early disruption of attachment?

Bowlby focused on children referred to the clinic because of stealing (these were the juvenile thieves). He compared them with control children referred to the clinic because of emotional problems but who hadn't committed any crimes. He found 32% of the thieves were affectionless psychopaths lacking a social conscience, whereas none of the control children was. Of the thieves diagnosed as affectionless psychopaths, 86% had experienced early disruption of attachment (even if only for a week before the age of 5). In contrast, only 17% of the thieves without affectionless psychopathy had suffered disruption of attachment in the form of maternal deprivation.

This study by Bowlby is important for various reasons. First, the findings seemed to show long-term disruption of attachment can have very severe effects, including a lack of emotional development (affectionless psychopathy). Second, Bowlby's results suggested that early long-term disruption of attachment could have long-lasting negative effects still present several years later. Third, the findings of this study led many other researchers to examine the relationship between children's early experience and their subsequent emotional development.

Bowlby (1951, 1953) supported his hypothesis with the research of Spitz (1945) and Goldfarb (1947). Spitz visited several very poor orphanages and other institutions in South America. Children in those orphanages received very little warmth or attention from the staff and had become apathetic. Many suffered from **anaclitic depression** (resigned helplessness and

KEY TERMS

Bond disruption: this occurs when a child is deprived of their main attachment object (in the short or long term) and receives no substitute emotional care.

Anaclitic depression: a severe form of depression in infants who experience prolonged separations from their mothers. The term "anaclitic" means "arising from emotional dependency on another".

loss of appetite). This was attributed to their lack of emotional care and long-term disruption of attachment with their mothers. Spitz and Wolf (1946) studied 100 apparently normal children who became seriously depressed after staying in hospital—the children generally recovered well only if the separation lasted less than 3 months.

Goldfarb (1947) compared two groups of infants who before fostering spent only the first few months or 3 years at a poor and inadequately staffed orphanage. Both groups were tested up to the age of 12. Those children who had spent 3 years at the orphanage did less well than the others on intelligence tests, were less socially mature, and more likely to be aggressive.

In the 1950s, orphanages in the UK gradually began to disappear and so research into the negative effects of living in such institutions was limited. Since then, however, there has been a new opportunity to study orphans—children from Romania. Findings on these children are discussed later.

Distinguishing among disruption of attachment, failure to form attachment (privation), and institutional care

Rutter (1972) pointed out that Bowlby assumed *all* experiences of disruption of attachment were the same. In fact, however, there are some very important differences. Children may experience short-term disruption of attachment, as in the Robertsons' studies, or they may have repeated and prolonged disruptions of attachment. Children may experience disruption of attachment with the mother without bond disruption, or they may have no adequate substitute care. Finally, children may experience a lack of attachment as a result of never having formed any close attachments.

Rutter (1972) argued there is a crucial difference between disruption of attachment and privation, a distinction *not* made by Bowlby. Disruption of attachment occurs when a child has formed an important attachment from which it is then separated. In contrast, **privation** (failure to form an attachment) occurs when a child has *never* formed a close relationship with anyone.

Many of Bowlby's juvenile delinquents had experienced several changes of home/principal caregiver during their early childhood. This indicated to Rutter (1981) that their later problems were due to failure to form attachment (privation) rather than disruption of attachment. Rutter argued that the effects of privation are much more severe and long-lasting than those of disruption of attachment. Research directly focusing on privation is discussed next.

As discussed earlier, it is hard to interpret the research of Spitz (1945) and Goldfarb (1947) based on children in orphanages and other institutions. The reason is that the experiences of these children differed in two important ways from those of most other children. First, these children had experienced privation. Second, these children had spent long periods of time in an institution, and the quality of most of these institutions was generally very poor. As a result, it is hard to know the relative importance of these factors. However, in recent decades there has been an increasing interest in studying the effects on children of living in an institution. Researchers in this area focus on institutional care—the negative effects on speed of social and/or cognitive development that occur when children are placed in institutions (e.g. hospitals; orphanages) for short or long periods of time. We will discuss studies on institutionalisation shortly.

KEY RESEARCH STUDY

Hodges and Tizard (1989): Effects of privation and institutional care

Hodges and Tizard (1989) studied the effects of privation but their study also tells us about the effects of institutional care. They investigated the permanence (or otherwise) of the effects of privation considering both emotional and social effects in adolescence. Sixty-five children taken into care and put into one institution before the age of 4 months formed an opportunity sample. This was a natural experiment using a matched pairs design, because

continued over

KEY TERM

Privation: an absence of attachments, as opposed to the loss of attachments, due to the lack of an appropriate attachment figure. Privation is likely to lead to permanent emotional damage.

? How does a natural experiment differ from a laboratory experiment?

? How might we account for the different patterns of behaviour shown by adopted children and children who returned to their families?

? How has the research of Hodges and Tizard added to our knowledge of the effects of deprivation?

EXAM HINT

When evaluating the strength of evidence for or against a particular theory such as Bowlby's Maternal Deprivation theory, it is important to look at the bigger picture and assess research studies using different methods where possible. The strengths and weaknesses of different studies can help you to decide which evidence should be given more weight. Case studies about extreme privation are memorable and can provide us with useful understanding of the complexities of attachment in unusual situations that can help to illuminate our understanding. But their reliability and explanatory value are also limited by these unique circumstances. For example, both Koluchová's case study and Hodges and Tizard's natural experiment help us to see that positive later experiences can help to overcome some of the effects of early privation, so the studies support each other, but Hodges and Tizard's study should be given more weight in your answer because it shows that the effects are broadly consistent within the groups and it provides a control condition for comparison.

the institutionalised children were compared with a control group raised at home. It was a longitudinal study (age on entering care to 16 years).

Each child had been looked after on average by 24 different caregivers by the age of 2. By the age of 4 years, 24 had been adopted, 15 restored to their natural home, and the rest remained in the institution. The children were assessed at ages 4, 8, and 16 on emotional and social competence through interview and self-report questionnaires.

Findings

What did Hodges and Tizard (1989) find? At the age of 4, the children hadn't formed attachments. By the age of 8, significant differences existed between the adopted and restored children. At the age of 8 and 16, most of the adopted children had formed close relationships with their caregiver. This was less true of the children who had returned to their own families, because their parents were often unsure they wanted their children back. However, negative social effects were evident in both the adopted and restored children at school—they were attention seeking and had difficulty in forming peer relationships.

At the age of 16, the family relationships of the adopted children were as good as those of families in which none of the children had been removed from the family home. However, children who had returned to their families showed little affection for their parents, and their parents weren't very affectionate towards them. Both groups of adolescents were less likely than adolescents in ordinary families to have a special friend or to regard other adolescents as sources of emotional support. Overall, however, the adopted children were better adjusted than would have been predicted by Bowlby.

Conclusions

What conclusions can we draw? The above findings show that some effects of privation (and institutionalisation) can be reversed, because the children could form attachments in spite of their privation (and experience of institutionalisation). However, some privation effects are long-lasting, as shown by the difficulties the institutionalised children faced at school. What seems to be especially important is for children who have been institutionalised to move to a loving environment. That was more likely to be the case for children who were adopted than those who returned to their own families.

Limitations

In spite of the strengths of this study, it has some limitations. First, the decision as to whether any given child should return to its own family or be adopted depended on complex issues to do with family dynamics and the child's wishes. As a result, it is hard to know precisely why adopted children suffered fewer long-term negative effects of institutionalisation than those restored to their families. Note that there would have needed to be *random* allocation of children to the adopted and returned-home groups to eliminate this limitation in the research.

Second, the interview and self-report data may provide a somewhat distorted perspective—perhaps some of the adolescents exaggerated or minimised the problems they were having with their lives.

Extreme privation

A few researchers have considered the effects of very extreme privation and isolation on children. The really surprising finding is the *resilience* of many of these children. Koluchová (1976) studied identical Czech twin boys (Andrei and Vanya) who had spent most of their first 7 years locked in a cellar. They had been treated very badly and were often beaten. They were barely able to talk and relied mainly on gestures rather than speech. The twins were fostered at about the age of 9 by a pair of loving sisters. By the time they were 14, their behaviour was essentially normal. By the age of 20, they were of above average intelligence and had excellent relationships with members of their foster family (Koluchová, 1991).

EVALUATION OF BOWLBY'S MATERNAL DEPRIVATION THEORY

- (+) Bowlby's theoretical approach (combined with his monotropic theory) correctly emphasised the great importance of infant–caregiver attachment.
- (+) Bowlby's theory made everyone aware of the potential damage that maternal deprivation could have on young children.
- (+) Maternal deprivation often has adverse short- and long-term effects on children.
- (−) The emotional problems shown by children in orphanages and other institutions may be due to the poor quality of those institutions rather than to disruption of attachment in the form of maternal deprivation.
- (−) Bowlby didn't distinguish clearly between disruption of attachment (the child is separated from a major attachment) and privation (the child has never had a close attachment).
- (−) Most adverse effects of maternal disruption of attachment and of privation can be reversed, and children are more resilient than Bowlby believed.
- (−) Even privation does not always have permanent effects. For most people, early experience is very much related to what happens later on. Bad experiences are often followed by more of the same. However, where severely bad experiences are followed by much better ones, the outcome is often good (e.g. the Czech twins).
- (−) Clearer evidence comes from Hodges and Tizard's (1989) longitudinal research that focused on privation. At one level, this study supports our conclusion that even privation can be recovered from by being given good subsequent care. However, Hodges and Tizard's research also suggests a rather different conclusion, which is that recovery is only possible within the context of a loving relationship. Hodges and Tizard found that those children who went on to have good relationships at home coped well at home but found relationships outside the home difficult. In some way, they lacked an adequate model for future relationships. This would seem to support Bowlby's attachment theory.
- (−) It is not always clear whether children have experienced disruption of attachment or privation. Suppose a child spends the first few months of its life with its biological parents and is then sent to an institution. Most children in that situation have probably experienced privation (never having had a loving attachment) but a few may have developed an attachment to their mother prior to going to the institution (disruption of attachment).

Romanian orphan studies: Effects of institutionalisation

We have already seen that children who spend long periods of time in institutional care often suffer considerably as a result. We have also seen that this is not invariably the case—in the study by Hodges and Tizard (1989), for example, reasonable recovery from institutional care occurred for those children adopted by a loving family.

In this section, we will consider the effects of institutionalisation. **Institutionalisation** involves children spending long periods of time in an institution such as an orphanage or hospital. Unsurprisingly, its effects are predominantly negative.

Our primary focus will be on fairly recent Romanian orphan studies. Before we discuss these studies, however, we will briefly consider whether there are very long-term effects of institutionalization. Sigal et al. (2003) addressed this issue in a study of middle-aged adults

KEY TERM

Institutionalisation: a wide range of negative effects (e.g. on attachment, social relationships, and development generally) when children spend long periods of time in an institution (e.g. orphanage).

placed in an institution at birth or early childhood. These adults were far more likely never to have married than a randomly selected control group (45% vs 17%), they reported fewer social contacts, and more psychological distress including depression.

Sigal et al. (2003) found that the very long-term effects were not limited to psychological factors. In addition, the adults who had been institutionalised were much more likely to suffer from various physical illnesses (e.g. migraine; stomach ulcers; and arthritis). Thus, adults institutionalised several decades earlier seem to suffer very long-term consequences psychologically and physically.

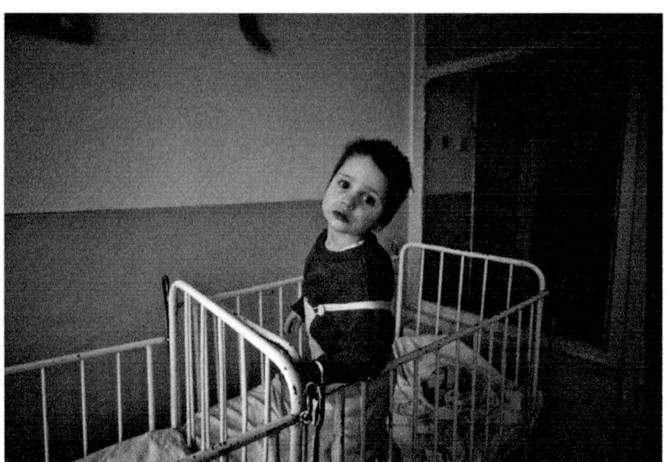

News reports in the 1980s highlighted deprivation in Romanian orphanages, with many children demonstrating anaclitic depression, having received basic sustenance but little human warmth or contact.

Romanian orphan studies

Much recent research has focused on Romanian children who spent their early lives in very poor institutions receiving very little attention or care and who thus experienced privation. Why are these Romanian orphan studies of major importance? These studies are of particular importance for various reasons. First, they are of high scientific quality. Second, they are longitudinal studies in which the children were followed up over a period of several years. Third, there was a very marked change between the conditions the orphans experienced in an institution and their subsequent lives after being adopted.

The study of these Romanian children provides information about the effects of institutionalisation. These children were subsequently adopted by caring British families and were tested several times up to the age of 15. Most of this research has been carried out by Michael Rutter and his colleagues in a very large longitudinal research project known as the English and Romanian Adoptee (ERA) Study.

Rutter and the ERA Study Team (1998) followed 111 Romanian orphans adopted in the UK before the age of 2. When the orphans arrived in the UK they were physically and mentally underdeveloped. By the age of 4, however, all had improved as a result of improved care. Those adopted the latest showed the slowest improvements educationally and in emotional development. However, reasonable recovery occurred given good subsequent care.

O'Connor et al. (2000) studied Romanian children exposed to very severe privation and neglect in Romania before being adopted by caring British families. They compared those children adopted between 24 and 42 months (late-placed adoptees) and those adopted between 6 and 24 months (early-placed adoptees). Both groups showed significant recovery from their ordeal in Romania. However, the late-placed adoptees had greater difficulty in achieving good cognitive and social development than early-placed adoptees.

Smyke et al. (2007) studied young children raised in institutions in Romania. Compared to young children of the same age raised at home by their parents, those in institutional care showed severe delays in cognitive development, poorer physical growth, and much inferior social competence. Smyke et al. considered the factors responsible for the low levels of cognitive development and social competence in the institutionalised children. Two factors are likely to be important:

1. The percentage of their lives these children had spent in an institution.
2. The quality of caregiving the children received (assessed by analysing videotapes of child–caregiver interaction).

What Smyke et al. (2007) found was that the institutionalised children's cognitive development and social competence depended far more on the quality of caregiving than on the percentage of their lives they had spent in an institution. Thus, being brought up in an institution doesn't inevitably cause major problems provided caregiver quality is high.

The outcomes varied very much from child to child (Rutter et al., 2010). Most children recovered almost totally from their institutionalisation but a minority did not. The marked recovery shown by a clear majority of the children reflects the loving care provided by most of the families adopting these children and the huge contrast between these loving families and their generally very negative experiences in Romanian orphanages.

ACTIVITY: Failure to form attachments (privation)

Attachments and the issue of day care are personal subjects and scientists must be sensitive when investigating them—researchers are obliged to consider possible psychological and physical risks to participants such as becoming upset, anxious, or stressed about their personal behaviour and/or history. Thus, questionnaires and surveys must be constructed sensitively and participants told they do not have to take part if they would prefer not to.

Find and print out a short piece about the Romanian orphans studied by Rutter and others, or one of the case studies of children who have failed to form attachments. Ask a few participants to read this and then say what they think were the four most important factors missing in these children's early lives. You could then look at your findings and see if there is much agreement, and get a snapshot of our cultural beliefs.

Deprivation-specific psychological patterns

Are the negative effects of institutionalisation very *similar* to the negative effects on children of experiencing *any* psychosocial stress and adversity? These negative effects include various emotional and behavioural problems. Alternatively, many negative effects of institutionalisation may be specific to institutional deprivation and *different* from the effects of other kinds of stressful environment (e.g. sexual abuse).

Kumsta et al. (2010) addressed the above issue as part of the ERA study. To their surprise, institutionalisation was *not* associated with the emotional and behavioural problems that typically follow psychosocial stress. Instead, the negative effects were mostly *specific* to institutionalisation. This led them to identify four **deprivation-specific patterns** associated with institutional deprivation that emerged by the age of 6 and were still present several years later in a minority of the children:

1. *Quasi-autism:* this pattern involves symptoms resembling those found in autism; these symptoms include social deficits and communication problems; poor understanding of the meanings of social contexts; and obsessive preoccupations (e.g. with watches; with the details of plumbing systems).
2. *Disinhibited attachment:* this pattern involves a lack of wariness of strangers; inappropriate affectionate behaviour; and a willingness to leave the caregiver to walk off with a stranger.
3. *Cognitive impairment:* this pattern involves a low IQ, and very general negative effects on cognition including poor performance on GCSEs.
4. *Inattention/overactivity:* this pattern involves problems with concentration and focusing on the task in hand.

Kumsta et al. (2010) pointed out that most children who had been institutionalised did *not* show the above deprivation-specific patterns. However, it is of concern that many previously institutionalised children show one or more of these patterns several years after being adopted.

EVALUATION

- (+) As mentioned earlier, research on the Romanian orphan children is important because it involves longitudinal studies of high scientific quality.
- (+) The research strengthens the argument that recovery even from severe privation is possible provided the children move to a loving environment.
- (+) The findings show that Bowlby's view that the effects of deprivation and privation are often irreversible was exaggerated.
- (−) It is not very clear why a minority of the children failed to recover following adoption.
- (−) More research is needed to establish precisely why some previously institutionalised children show deprivation-specific patterns years after adoption.

KEY TERM

Deprivation-specific patterns: negative patterns of behaviour often found in children who have been institutionalised but rarely in those who have suffered other forms of psychosocial stress.

Section Summary

- According to Robertson and Bowlby (1952), young children experiencing short-term disruption of attachment with their mother go through three stages: protest, despair, and detachment. There is no strong evidence for this sequence of stages, and this approach doesn't take account of individual differences among children.
- According to Bowlby's maternal deprivation theory, breaking the maternal bond with a young child (long-term disruption of attachment) often causes serious effects to its social, intellectual, and emotional development.
- Studies by Bowlby and others seem to indicate that long-term disruption of attachment in the form of maternal deprivation can produce negative effects that are still evident several years later.
- It is important to distinguish among disruption of attachment, privation (never having had a close attachment), and institutionalisation (adverse effects of living in an institution).
- Hodges and Tizard (1989) found that some of the negative effects of privation (lack of attachment) and institutional care can be reversed, with the children concerned forming strong attachments. What was most important was for children who had been institutionalised to move to a loving environment.
- There are various weaknesses with the maternal deprivation theory:
  - Bowlby failed to distinguish clearly between disruption of attachment and privation, in which the child has never formed a close relationship.
  - It is often unclear whether the adverse effects observed in children who have experienced privation or disruption of attachment are due to that or to poor quality care they receive afterwards.
  - The effects of privation and disruption of attachment are often more reversible than was assumed by Bowlby.
- Children brought up in institutions in Romania generally have poor social and cognitive skills. However, those who received a high quality of caregiving did much better than other institutionalised children.
- Over time since being adopted, most of the Romanian orphan children showed almost complete recovery due to the loving families who had adopted them.
- Romanian children brought up in British families sometimes suffer from one or more deprivation-specific patterns: quasi-autism; disinhibited attachment; cognitive impairment; and inattention/overactivity.
- Middle-aged adults who had been institutionalised in early childhood were found to have long-term negative psychological and physical effects.

INFLUENCE OF EARLY ATTACHMENT ON CHILDHOOD AND ADULT RELATIONSHIPS

As we saw earlier in the chapter, Bowlby argued in his monotropic theory that infants' initial major attachment (typically to the mother) has a substantial influence on childhood and adult relationships. There are various possible reasons why early attachment might influence childhood and adult relationships. However, what seems highly probable is that *memory* plays a key role. More specifically, information (much of it of an emotional nature) of their initial major attachment is stored in long-term memory and this is why this attachment has an impact on subsequent ones. Note, however, that internal working models are subject to change over time.

As we discussed earlier, infants and children form an internal working model which serves as the template for later attachments. Remember that an internal working model resembles a schema in that it is a structure in long-term memory that provides the basis for forming *expectations*. In the case of an internal working model, it includes a focus on how acceptable or unacceptable the infant is to other attachment figures. In essence, if your initial major attachment is a secure one, it leads you to expect future attachment figures to respond warmly and positively to you. In contrast, if your initial major attachment is insecure, it may lead you to have negative expectations concerning future attachment figures.

In order for an infant's internal working model to predict his/her childhood and adult relationships, it would be necessary for that model to remain fairly constant over time. Theorists differ with respect to how variable they believe the internal working model and attachment style to be. Fraley (2002) draws a distinction between the revisionist perspective and the prototype perspective. According to the revisionist perspective, early internal working models are typically revised and updated as a result of life's experiences with the result that adult internal working models can differ substantially from infant ones. This perspective allows for change in the pattern of attachment in relationships over time.

In contrast, it is assumed within the prototype perspective that, while there may be some changes, the essence of infant internal working models remains the same over time. According to this perspective, attachment patterns should be stable over the years. Bowlby's monotropic theory is closer to the prototype perspective than to the revisionist perspective.

Parenting is one of the most important relationships in adult life. A person's attachment to their own parents will influence their subsequent relationship with their own child.

Findings

How can we assess children's internal working models? One common method is to make use of the Strange Situation (discussed in detail earlier in the chapter). It is often assumed that the attachment type revealed by infants in this situation indicates the nature of their internal working model. Another common method is to use the Adult Attachment Interview (George et al., 1984) in which adults provide information retrospectively about their childhood experiences and their internal working models.

There is evidence that early attachment can predict subsequent attachment in childhood and adulthood relationships. One of the first studies was by Hazan and Shaver (1987). They classified their adult participants as secure, ambivalent (conflicting emotions), or avoidant attachment types based on their description of their childhood experiences.

Secure types described their adult love experiences as happy and trusting, and they accepted their partners regardless of any faults. Ambivalent types experienced love as involving obsession, desire for reciprocation, intensity, and jealousy, and worried that their partners might abandon them. Avoidant lovers typically feared intimacy, emotional highs and lows, and jealousy. They believed they didn't need to be loved to be happy. These findings suggest childhood attachment type influences adult romantic experiences.

Early attachment can predict subsequent attachment in adulthood, for example, securely attached children go on to have happy and trusting adult relationships. However, it has also been found that actual experiences of love can also influence attachment style.

A major problem with Hazan and Shaver's (1987) study is that the data concerning childhood attachments were collected several years later. As a result, what was recalled may have been inaccurate. Another issue is that Hazan and Shaver assumed that attachment type is *consistent* and determines the style of love. However, reality is more complex. In subsequent research, Shaver and Hazan (1993) found 22% of their adult sample changed their attachment style over a 12-month period, often as a result of relationship experiences. Thus, attachment style can influence style of love, but actual experiences of love can also influence attachment style.

Fraley (2002) reviewed the relevant evidence on attachment stability from infancy through to adulthood. He found across several studies that the mean correlation between early attachment and attachment later in childhood or adulthood was approximately +.40. This led Fraley (p. 135) to conclude: "There is a moderate degree of stability in attachment from infancy to adulthood, and the pattern of stability observed is better accounted for by a prototype-like process than a revisionist one."

It is important not to exaggerate the stability between early attachment and attachments and relationships many years later. As we saw earlier in the chapter, children who have suffered an absence of close attachments in childhood and been very poorly treated nevertheless often show much resilience. For example, Koluchová (1976) studied identical Czech twin boys (Andrei and Vanya) who had spent most of their first 7 years locked in a cellar. Following adoption, however, they developed excellent relationships with members of their foster family (Koluchová, 1991). In similar fashion, Romanian children who started life in institutions in Romania and were then adopted by English families often developed secure attachments (Rutter et al., 2010).

CASE STUDY: The Riley family

Jean Riley (54) and her husband Peter (58) adopted two children from Romania who are now aged 17 and 9. Cezarina, when they first saw her, was cross-eyed, filthy, and about 4 years behind in her physical development. First, Cezarina's physical problems had to be sorted out, but from then on she made good progress. However, Cezarina is "laid back" about things that seem important to Jean and Peter. Jean understands this attitude, though, because clearly examinations seem less important when a child has had to struggle to survive.

According to Jean, Cezarina is bright, but needs to have information repeated over and over again. She has also struggled to understand jokes and sarcasm, although this may be due to difficulties with learning the language. Jean sees Cezarina as naive and emotionally immature. Cezarina says herself that initially she was frustrated because she couldn't communicate. She sees herself as being different from other girls, although she likes the same things, such as fashion and pop music. Jean runs The Parent Network for the Institutionalised Child, a group for people who have adopted such children. Cezarina has partly recovered from her poor early experiences.

(Account based on an article in *Woman,* 21 September 1998.)

Further evidence that insecure attachment in childhood isn't necessarily associated with poor adult relationships was reported by McCarthy and Maughan (2010). They studied a high-risk sample of women all of whom reported negative parenting in childhood. Of those who reported insecure attachment in childhood, 28% nevertheless had good and satisfying adult relationships.

Most studies in this area are correlational and so cannot shed light on whether types of attachment in childhood and adulthood relationships are *caused* in part by early attachment. We could obtain somewhat stronger evidence by carrying out a longitudinal study over a period of years. Fraley et al. (2013) studied children from birth to 18 years of age. There was evidence that individual differences in adult attachment were associated with the quality of the caregiving environment and the internal working models constructed at that time. However, the association was relatively weak and means that several other factors were also involved.

Why is the association between children's internal working models and subsequent attachments relatively weak? There are various reasons. First, the security or otherwise of an adult's relationship attachments does not depend solely on his/her past history and experiences. Cohn et al. (1992) found the quality of the relationship in adult couples where one partner was securely attached and the other was not did not differ from that of couples where both were securely attached. Alexandrov et al. (2005) found that wives with an insecure working model of attachment reported greater relationship satisfaction if they were married to secure husbands than when they were married to insecure husbands.

Second, it is oversimplified in most cases to say that a given adult attachment pattern is always secure or insecure. Pierce and Lydon (2001) asked adults to keep a daily diary concerning their relationships. This revealed that there was greater variation in adult attachment patterns *within* individuals rather than *between* them.

Third, adult attachment styles depend on several factors in addition to the nature of early attachment. These factors include (but are not limited to) changes produced by the transition to parenthood, the number and nature of life events experienced, and (in some cases) counselling or treatment for mental disorder.

Case studies

Some of the studies described in this chapter are case studies. The advantage of such research is that it produces rich data that can be used by a researcher to develop new theoretical ideas.

However, we need to be very careful when interpreting the evidence from a case study. The greatest limitation is the typically low reliability. The findings that are obtained from one unusual or exceptional individual are unlikely to be repeated in detail when another individual is studied. Thus, it is often very hard to generalise from a single case study. Second, many case studies involve the use of lengthy, fairly unstructured interviews that may produce subjective information. Third, researchers generally only report some of the data they obtained from their interviews with the participant. They may be unduly selective in terms of what they choose to report or to omit.

EVALUATION

- (+) Most of the evidence has shown that early attachment predicts childhood and adult relationships.
- (+) The evidence supports Bowlby's assumption that early attachment has important consequences for subsequent emotional development.
- (−) An important issue is that we typically have only correlational evidence showing that an infant's internal working model formed when he/she was very young is associated with adult patterns of attachment. This need not mean there is a causal link—another possibility is that an individual's personality (which is fairly stable over time) influences his/her infant internal working model and his/her adult patterns of attachment.
- (−) Most studies have relied on retrospective reports from adults of their internal working models as children. These reports are sometimes biased—adults who currently have a positive internal working model process attachment-related information in a positively biased way, whereas those with a negative model process such information negatively (Dykas & Cassidy, 2011).
- (−) Bowlby's theorising about internal working models is somewhat vague and imprecise; it can be viewed "not as a fully worked-out theory, but as a promising conceptual framework to be filled in by others" (Bretherton & Munholland, 2008, p. 103).
- (−) Early attachment (and internal working model) are typically assessed using the Strange Situation. This is clearly limited because it involves the mother or caregiver. It is clearly possible that attachment type might be different if the Strange Situation involved the father.
- (−) The security/insecurity of adult relationships depends only to a modest extent on the individual's early attachment. It also depends on the security/insecurity of their partner, the life events they have experienced, and the transition to parenthood.

EXAM HINT

You could be asked an essay question such as "Outline and evaluate research into the influence of attachment on childhood and adult relationships" or "Discuss the effects of early institutionalisation" for 8, 12, or even 16 marks. Both of these questions require you to describe and to evaluate research.

When evaluating any research into attachments over time, you could consider a key distinction between two approaches to research. Researchers can either study adults or children *retrospectively,* asking them to recall experiences from early childhood and looking for correlational relationships between these experiences and their recent experiences; or they can study infants *longitudinally* as they grow up into adulthood, tracing their experiences as they occur. The second method is likely to produce more accurate and useful data, for three reasons. First, the longitudinal approach relies much less on very long-term memories, which are particularly subject to decay, interference and reconstruction. Second, because the study is done in real-time, some observational data can be collected, which may be less susceptible to social desirability effects than self-report data. Third, a control group consisting of children without adverse experiences can be selected for comparison with the children who have suffered from early adverse experiences: a natural experiment. This means that causal relationships can be suggested, rather than relying solely on correlation. Look out for studies using retrospective and longitudinal methods and compare their findings in your answer.

Section Summary

- According to Bowlby, children's initial major attachment leads to the construction of an internal working model that influences their subsequent relationships.
- An internal working model is a schema-like structure stored in long-term memory but subject to change.
- There is an association between early and later attachments, but the association is often relatively weak and based on correlational evidence.
- Reports of childhood attachment are often retrospective and so susceptible to bias and/or forgetting.
- The notion of an internal working model is somewhat imprecise and hard to test experimentally.
- An adult's romantic attachments depend on the partner's security/insecurity, the life events experienced, and the transition to parenthood.

Further Reading

- There is accessible and up-to-date coverage of the topics discussed in this chapter in L.E. Berk (2012) *Child development (9th Edn)* (New York: Pearson).
- All you might ever want to know about attachment is to be found in J. Mercer (2006) Attachment theory and its vicissitudes: Toward an updated theory. *Theory & Psychology*, *21*, 25–45.
- The effects of privation and what can be done to reverse those effects are discussed in M. Rutter, C. Beckett, J. Castle, J. Kreppner, S. Stevens, and E. Sonuga-Burke (2009) *Policy and practice implications from the English and Romanian Adoptees (ERA) Study: Forty-five key questions* (London: BAAF).

Revision Questions

1. a. Explain what is meant by "interactional synchrony". (2 marks)

   b. Outline findings from **two** research studies into the roles of fathers in attachment. (4 marks)

2. a. Outline **two** behaviours that are characteristic of a securely attached child. (2 marks)

   b. Outline **two** behaviours that are characteristic of a child described as "insecure-avoidant". (2 marks)

   c. Outline **two** behaviours that are characteristic of a child described as "insecure-resistant". (2 marks)

3. Describe and evaluate the use of the "Strange Situation" in attachment research. (8 marks)

4. Discuss what research has shown about cultural variations in attachment. (8 marks)

5. Sorina and Mikhael were born in Romania and later adopted by a British couple. Sorina was put into an orphanage when she was 5 months old. She was brought to live in the UK when she was 3. When she arrived she did not talk and was extremely small and under-developed for her age. She did improve with good care from her adoptive parents but still had some social and cognitive impairments when assessed at age 8. Mikhael had been in the orphanage from the age of 10 months to 2 years and 3 months. He was also underdeveloped and did not talk at first, but improved rapidly when he came to the UK. By age 8, his social and cognitive development was in the normal range.

   Discuss research that has studied the effects of institutionalisation on Romanian orphans. Refer to the experiences of Sorina and Mikhael to illustrate your answer. (16 marks)

6. Outline and evaluate research into the effects of early attachment on adult relationships. (12 marks)

EXAM HINT

See the Exam Hint on page 114 [end of Chapter 3] regarding questions that ask you to apply your knowledge.

What you need to know

If you are studying AS level, you will only need to cover the first four subjects on this list (Origins of psychology, Learning approaches, Cognitive approach, and Biological approach). If you are studying A-level, you will need to cover everything in this chapter.

Approaches in Psychology will be examined in Paper 2 of the AS exam and Paper 2 of the A-level exam.

Approaches to Psychology

As we have seen in the previous chapters in this book, there are several ways in which psychologists try to understand human (and animal) behaviour. This occurs in part because psychology is related to various other disciplines such as physiology, biology, neurology, sociology, medicine, and anthropology. We can think of psychology as representing the meeting point of these disciplines—this helps to explain both the complexity and the richness of contemporary psychology.

This chapter starts with a discussion of the origins of psychology. As we will see, these origins go back literally thousands of years. During most of that time, the approach taken towards psychology was philosophical—there was much systematic thinking about the causes of human behaviour but there was practically no experimental research. It was only in the middle of the nineteenth century that proper experimental studies were carried out by psychologists. What that means is that psychology as a science is under 200 years old.

All five approaches to psychology discussed in this chapter started in the late nineteenth century or during the twentieth century. Between them, they show how we can understand human behaviour from several different perspectives.

At the risk of oversimplification, these approaches are designed to answer different questions. Learning approaches focus on understanding the learning process in humans and other species with an emphasis on environmental influences. The cognitive approach focuses more broadly on all the internal mental processes involved in everyday life. The biological approach focuses on the relevance of genetic factors and our evolutionary past for understanding human behaviour. The psychodynamic approach focuses on the processes responsible for mental disorders and on ways in which these disorders can be treated successfully. Finally, humanistic psychology focuses on the factors that permit individuals to experience personal growth and lead fulfilled lives.

ORIGINS OF PSYCHOLOGY

The history of psychology spans a period of over 2000 years from the ancient Greeks through to the present day. Most advances in psychology have occurred over the past 150 years or so, but here we will very briefly consider a few of the earlier theoretical contributions of the great philosophers and thinkers.

Plato (427–347 BC) made it clear in his writings that he believed in the importance of individual differences. Plato compared memory with fixing impressions in wax and suggested that individuals differ in the receptivity of "the wax in their souls". He played a major role in developing the notion of "mental health" and believed the body and mind were both important factors in producing good mental health. The body needs gymnastic training, which finds an echo in today's numerous health clubs! In contrast, the mind needs training of the emotions through the arts and of the intellect through mathematics, philosophy, and science.

Aristotle (384–322 BC) was Plato's pupil and may have been the cleverest person who ever lived. He believed that some important differences between individuals are produced by heredity whereas others stem from habitual patterns of responding established early in life. Aristotle's acknowledgement of the combined influences of heredity and environment on individual differences in behaviour is very much in line with contemporary thinking (see section on the biological approach in this chapter).

One of the most influential of Aristotle's psychological theories was the notion that people, events, and things tend to be linked and remembered on the basis of three laws of association: contiguity or closeness; similarity; and contrast. For example, seeing Jane can make us think of Peter because we've previously seen Jane and Peter together (law of contiguity), or because Jane and Peter resemble each other (law of similarity), or because they're very different from each other (law of contrast). Of importance, Aristotle's law of contiguity (developed from earlier ideas of Plato) is very relevant to an understanding of classical conditioning (see section on the behaviourist approach in this chapter).

Wilhelm Wundt

Wilhelm Wundt (1832–1920) is assured of a permanent place in the history of psychology. The reason is that he established the world's first ever laboratory of psychology in Leipzig in 1879. The setting up of this laboratory played an important role in identifying psychology as an independent field of study. More specifically, setting up an experimental laboratory helped to separate psychology from its origins in philosophy. It led many people to describe Wundt as "the father of experimental psychology".

Wilhelm Wundt (seated) with colleagues in his psychological laboratory, the first of its kind.

Wundt's laboratory was also of importance because numerous psychologists who went to work there later became prominent in psychology. Examples include James Cattell, who became the first professor of psychology in the United States, Oswald Külpe (discussed below), and Charles Spearman, the English psychologist who developed an influential theory of intelligence.

In addition to his research, Wundt was a prolific writer who produced numerous long books about psychology. One of his central aims was to unite physiology and psychology. He started his book, *Principles of physiological psychology* (1874), by stating: "The present work shows by its title that it is an attempt to recognise that two sciences ... are concerned with one and the same subject matter, namely, human life" (p. 1).

Wundt (1874) put forward an influential theory of emotion called the tridimensional theory of feeling. According to this theory, all feelings or emotions can be placed within a three-dimensional framework with the three dimensions being as follows: pleasant–unpleasant; tense–relaxed; and excited–depressed. Thus, for example, anxiety is unpleasant + tense + excited. Similar dimensional models remain important to this day. For example, Barrett and Russell (1998) identified two dimensions of misery–pleasure and arousal–sleep. Misery–pleasure resembles pleasant–unpleasant and arousal–sleep is a combination of tense–relaxed and excited–depressed.

There is a massive contrast between Wundt's writings and the research carried out in his laboratory at Leipzig. Wundt wrote at length about numerous areas in psychology. However, his actual research was much narrower with an emphasis on simple sensory judgements (e.g. deciding on the relative brightness of two stimuli). He also contributed to the study of visual perception. For example, he invented the Wundt illusion in which two vertical parallel lines appear curved inwards.

Experimental methods

Most of the experiments conducted in Wundt's laboratory involved studying the behaviour of a *single* individual in detail. Often a second individual would then be tested to see whether the findings obtained from the first individual could be replicated (Popple & Levi, 2000). This approach is still used (especially with case studies of mentally disordered or brain-damaged individuals). However, the great majority of experiments involve comparing the performance of two or more groups of individuals. The advantage of this approach over Wundt's preferred method is that we can be more confident that the findings *generalise* to the population at large.

Wundt used various experimental approaches in his laboratory. One approach involved the use of reaction times. For example, Wundt asked participants to make the same response under two conditions: (1) the same stimulus was presented on each trial; and (2) one out of a number of possible stimuli was presented and the task was to respond as soon as the stimulus had been identified. Reaction times were often slightly longer in the second condition than the first, and this time difference was taken as an estimate of the time taken to identify a stimulus (Woodworth, 1938).

Wilhelm Wundt made clear the importance he attached to introspection (reporting one's conscious thoughts) as a method in the following quotation: "The distinguishing characteristics of mind are of a subjective sort: we know them only from the contents of our consciousness." He distinguished between *ordinary* introspection (in which individuals casually focused on their own thoughts) and *experimental* introspection. Experimental introspection required individuals to provide immediate reports of their conscious experience under carefully controlled conditions. He claimed that experimental introspection was much superior to ordinary introspection, in part because it produced findings that could be repeated or replicated.

EVALUATION

- (+) Wundt set up the world's first experimental laboratory in psychology and by so doing established psychology as an independent field of study.
- (+) Wundt facilitated the development of experimental psychology, the study of consciousness, aspects of cognitive psychology (e.g. perception), and emotion.
- (+) Wundt was a very prolific researcher and writer who published numerous books and articles totalling over 50,000 pages. That averages out at nearly one word every two minutes night and day throughout his life!
- (−) In spite of his productivity, Wundt failed to produce any theory or research finding of lasting importance. This led the American psychologist William James to write of Wundt that he aims "at being a Napoleon of the intellectual world. Unfortunately, he will have a Waterloo, for he is Napoleon without genius and with no central idea".
- (−) Wundt's research typically involved only one or two participants. This is a limited approach because we can't be confident that the findings generalise.
- (−) Wundt exaggerated the value of introspection. Most of cognitive psychology shows that we can study the mind effectively *without* focusing on the contents of consciousness. More generally, Wundt's attachment to introspection meant that he was sceptical about the possibility of studying reasoning and problem solving in the laboratory.

Introspection

We have seen that Wundt was very enthusiastic about introspection, and it is now time to consider this method in more detail. **Introspection** is the systematic investigation of one's own thoughts. On the face of it, it seems reasonable to study people's internal thoughts by asking them to say those thoughts out loud. Aristotle thought that introspection was the only way of studying thinking.

Two thousand years later there was still much enthusiasm for using introspection (as we have seen with Wundt). Oswald Külpe (1862–1915), who had carried out some of his early research with Wilhelm Wundt at Leipzig University, founded the Würzburg School. It was dedicated to the use of introspection. Participants focused on a complex stimulus (e.g. a logical problem), after which they reported their conscious thoughts during the task (often at some length). This revealed that people are consciously aware of sensations, feelings, images, conscious mental sets, and their own thoughts.

Note that there are some important differences between introspection as used by Wundt and by the Würzburg School. Wundt focused on immediate and typically short reports of an individual's conscious experience, where the Würzburg School obtained lengthy reports obtained some time after the relevant conscious experience.

Edward Titchener (1867–1927), who had studied with Wundt, used a form of introspection very similar to that used by members of the Würzburg School. In spite of that, there was a big controversy between them concerning imageless thoughts—thoughts containing meaning but lacking any form of imagery. Külpe argued that people sometimes have such thoughts whereas Titchener claimed that *all* thoughts have images. Sadly, this controversy couldn't be resolved.

Below we discuss behaviourism, an approach to psychology that started in America in the early years of the twentieth century. The behaviourists wanted to make psychology scientific and argued that introspection was basically unscientific. Accordingly, they said behaviourism would "never use the terms consciousness, mental states, mind, content, introspectively verifiable, and the like" (Watson, 1913, p. 165).

In spite of the problems with introspection already discussed (and others discussed below), it is still the case that it is often a useful technique to use. Ericsson and Simon (1980) argued that introspection is useful when two conditions are met:

1. Introspection should be obtained during task performance rather than afterwards to avoid memory problems.
2. It should be concerned only with information to which the individual is attending.

An example of the usefulness of introspection when the above conditions are met is research by Levy and Ransdell (1995). They asked writers to verbalise what they were doing as they wrote essays on computers. Their key finding was that writers had poor awareness of how they allotted their time—for example, they estimated they spent 30% of their time reviewing and revising but the actual figure was 5%!

Problems with introspection

We have already seen in the imageless thought controversy that the findings obtained through the use of introspection are often unclear. Another major problem was identified by the English scientist Francis Galton. According to him, the position of consciousness "appears to be that of a helpless spectator of but a minute fraction of automatic brain work".

Galton was writing in the nineteenth century, and there is now substantial evidence supporting his position. In a provocative article, Hassin (2013) proposed the "Yes It Can" principle. According to this principle, unconscious processes can perform the same high-level cognitive functions (e.g. goal pursuit; cognitive control; reasoning) as conscious processes. This may well be somewhat of an exaggeration. However, it is certainly true that unconscious processes can perform an impressive range of cognitive functions.

Another problem with introspection is that it is impossible to use it with any other species! As we will see, some of the most important research in psychology was carried out by Pavlov on dogs and by Skinner on rats and pigeons. It is no coincidence that Watson spent several years prior to his behaviourist manifesto in 1913 involved in animal research.

KEY TERM

Introspection: a careful examination and description of one's own inner mental thoughts and states.

EVALUATION

- (+) Introspection can provide useful information, especially if it relates to ongoing experience and concerns what the individual is currently attending to.
- (+) A form of introspection is still used in most research on visual perception—for example, it is hard to know how someone has perceived an ambiguous figure (e.g. the Wundt illusion discussed earlier) without asking them.
- (−) We are largely unaware of many of the processes influencing our thinking and decision making.
- (−) Our reports of our conscious experience may be distorted (deliberately or otherwise). For example, we may pretend to have more positive thoughts about someone else than is actually the case.
- (−) There is inevitably at least a short delay between having a conscious experience and reporting its existence. As a result, we may sometimes forget part of our conscious experience before reporting it.
- (−) We are generally consciously aware of the outcome of our cognitive processes rather than those processes themselves (Valentine, 1992). For example, what is the name of the first African American President of the United States? I imagine you rapidly thought of Barack Obama without any clear idea of how you produced the right answer.
- (−) As we have seen, it proved very difficult in practice to replicate findings involving introspection across different laboratories.

Emergence of psychology as a science

When and how did psychology emerge as a science? There is no simple answer to those questions. However, we can identify developments that contributed massively to its emergence. Boring (1950), who was a historian of psychology, argued that Gustav Fechner (1801–1887) was one of the key figures. According to Boring, "One may call him [Fechner] the 'founder' of experimental psychology or one may assign that title to Wundt" (p. 295). We have already discussed Wundt's contribution so we will turn to that of Fechner.

Fechner

Fechner was important because he (together with Ernst Weber, 1795–1878) introduced psychophysics into psychology. **Psychophysics** is concerned with the scientific study of the relationship between physical stimuli and the subjective sensations that are associated with them. The research carried out by Weber and then extended and developed by Fechner is of great historical importance because it represented the first proper experimental research in psychology.

Some of Fechner's research involved lifting weights. He was interested in finding out how small the difference could be between two weights while remaining just detectable (just noticeable difference). The just noticeable difference was less when both weights were relatively light than when they were both relatively heavy. Suppose someone could just tell the difference between a weight of 100 grams and one of 105 grams. The same person could just tell the difference between weights of 200 grams and 210 grams and those of 500 and 525 grams.

What the above findings show is that the just noticeable difference is a small, constant proportion of the weight of the lighter stimulus—in this case, 5%. Fechner obtained very similar findings when assessing just noticeable differences for visual brightness and sound intensity. The discovery that there are highly predictable relationships between the physical and psychological domains was of huge importance at the dawn of experimental psychology.

KEY TERM

Psychophysics: the study of the relationship between the psychological or subjective magnitude of sensations and the physical intensity of the stimuli producing those sensations.

Animal learning

In the United States, much of the earliest scientific research in psychology involved animals. One of the most important early American studies was carried out by Edward Thorndike (1874–1949) on cats. Hungry cats in closed cages could see a dish of food outside the cage. The cage doors opened when a pole inside the cage was hit. Initially, the cats thrashed about and clawed the sides of the cage. After some time, however, the cat hit the pole inside the cage and opened the door. On repeated trials, the cats gradually learned what was required. Eventually, they would hit the pole immediately and so gain access to the food.

Thorndike was unimpressed by the cats' performance. He referred to their apparently almost random behaviour as **trial-and-error learning**. This is rather unfair on the cats—there was a purely arbitrary relationship between the cats' behaviour (hitting the pole) and the desired consequence (the opening of the cage door). Thus, the cats had little alternative but to engage in more or less random behaviour initially.

What is of most importance about Thorndike's (1898) research is that it showed that behaviour can be modified by its consequences. It led Thorndike (1905) to propose the law of effect—responses in a given situation producing a satisfying state of affairs are strengthened and will tend to be produced again in the same situation. As we will see, the work of Skinner and others on operant conditioning was based on the law of effect.

Behaviourism

In the years following Thorndike's (1898) pioneering research, American psychologists started to move away from a reliance on introspection and towards a more scientific approach. It is often argued that psychology almost overnight became a science with the arrival of **behaviourism**. However, that exaggerates the speed of the change (Leahey, 1992). Nevertheless, the American behaviourist John Watson (1878–1958) played a key role in the change. In his incredibly influential article in 1913, he argued that, "Psychology as the behaviourist views it is a purely objective, experimental branch of natural science. Its theoretical goal is the prediction and control of behaviour. Introspection forms no essential part of its method."

What did the behaviourists decide to do having rejected introspection? Watson argued that psychology should be the study of behaviour because it is objective and observable. Watson focused on behaviour in part because of one of his key assumptions: "The behaviourist … recognises no dividing line between man and brute" (Watson, 1913, p. 158). You have no choice but to study behaviour in research on other species.

Watson's notion that behaviour is objective and observable is an exaggeration as was pointed out by Popper (1968). He said to his students at lectures, "Observe!", to which they replied, "Observe what?" The point is that no-one ever observes without some idea of what it is they are looking for.

Conclusions

Psychology emerged as a science in the latter half of the nineteenth century in Germany. While several leading German researchers played a part, Fechner and Wundt were the two who were most important. Subsequently, there were major developments in the United States in the early years of the twentieth century with the rise of behaviourism. Unmentioned so far (but discussed in detail shortly) was the research of the Russian physiologist Pavlov on learning in dogs which started in 1901. As we will see, Pavlov's research had a massive influence on behaviourism. Thus, developments in at least three different countries (Germany, United States, and Russia) all contributed substantially to the emergence of psychology as a science.

> **KEY TERMS**
>
> **Trial-and-error learning:** a type of learning in which the solution is reached by producing fairly random responses rather than by a process of thought.
>
> **Behaviourism:** an approach to psychology in which the emphasis was on observable stimuli and responses.
>
> **Learning:** a relatively permanent change in behaviour that is not due to maturation.

LEARNING APPROACHES

Compared to any other species, humans are extremely good at **learning**. In view of its obvious importance, the study of learning has always been of central importance to psychologists. Historically, the rise of behaviourism in the United States under John Watson (1913) was of major importance. Behaviourism was based on the assumption that psychology should study behaviour (and changes in behaviour with learning) rather than internal thoughts and feelings.

The behaviourists studied relatively simple forms of learning. For many years, they focused on classical conditioning and operant conditioning. When the limitations of these two forms of conditioning became clear, the behaviourists expanded their approach to develop social learning theory. All three approaches to learning are discussed in detail below.

Ivan Pavlov and his staff demonstrating classical conditioning on a dog.

Classical conditioning

The origins of behaviourism lie in Ivan Pavlov's (1849–1936) work as a physiologist. He was carrying out research into the digestive system and accidentally discovered a new form of learning by association. This is how it happened. When his experimental dogs were offered food, saliva production increased. He also noticed something particularly interesting—salivation started to increase as soon as the researcher opened the door to bring the dogs their food. The dogs naturally salivated when they smelled food (a reflex response) but they had now learned to salivate when the door was opened because that indicated that food would soon be arriving. The learning by association between the two stimuli (i.e. door opening; sight of food) is an example of **classical conditioning**.

Just to make the basic idea clear, here is another example. Imagine you visit your dentist. As you lie down on the reclining chair, you start to feel frightened. Why are you frightened *before* the dentist has caused you any pain? The sights and sounds of the dentist's surgery lead you to *expect* you are shortly going to be in pain. You have formed an association between the neutral stimuli of the surgery and the painful stimuli involved in drilling. In essence, the fear created by drilling in the past is now triggered by the neutral stimuli of the surgery.

KEY RESEARCH STUDY

Pavlov's research with dogs

Let's return to Pavlov and his dogs and focus on the research he carried out. Food in the mouth (or the sight of food) is an unconditioned stimulus (UCS) and salivation is an unconditioned response (UCR). No learning is needed for this stimulus–response (S–R) link, which is why both stimulus and response are described as "unconditioned".

In his experiments, Pavlov put dogs into a harness to limit their movement. Only the dog was in the experimental room in order to minimise any distracting stimuli. Pavlov wanted to measure the amount of salivation produced by dogs in response to food. However, this is not easily done when the saliva is in the dog's mouth. Accordingly, Pavlov performed a minor operation so that the dog's saliva flowed to the animal's cheek or chin, and trained dogs

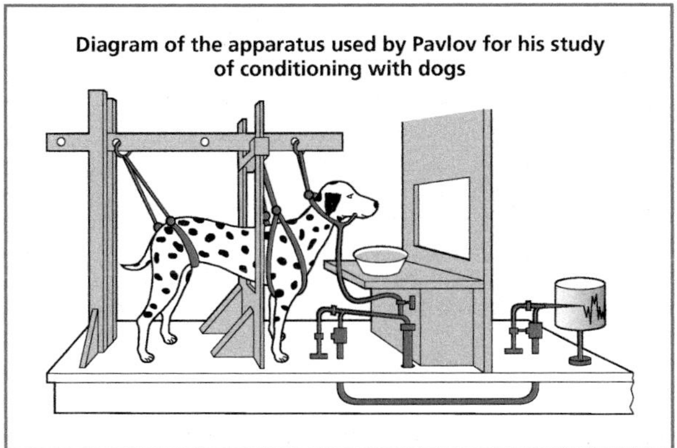

Diagram of the apparatus used by Pavlov for his study of conditioning with dogs

continued over

KEY TERM

Classical conditioning: a basic form of learning involving an association between two stimuli that are presented together repeatedly; as a result, the response initially elicited by the second stimulus is also elicited by the first stimulus presented on its own.

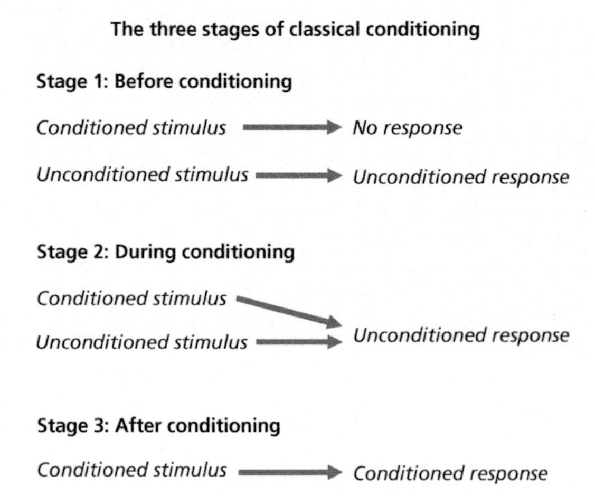

to salivate to other stimuli not naturally associated with salivation. In some of these experiments, he presented a tone just before food on several occasions so the tone signalled that food would be arriving shortly. Finally, he presented the same tone on its own without any food following. The dog salivated to the tone thus demonstrating classical conditioning.

What happens in classical conditioning? First, there is initially an unconditioned reflex, which is an unlearned connection between an **unconditioned stimulus** (e.g. sight of food) and an **unconditioned response** (e.g. salivation).

Second, a previously neutral stimulus (**conditioned stimulus**; e.g. tone) is presented with the unconditioned stimulus and the unconditioned response is produced

Third, after the conditioned and unconditioned stimuli have been presented together repeatedly, the animal or human produces a **conditioned response** (learned response to the conditioned stimulus; e.g. salivation) when the conditioned stimulus is presented *on its own*. When this happens, a conditioned reflex has been formed.

Pavlov carried out other studies that showed the existence of discrimination and generalisation. Suppose a given tone is paired with the sight of food. The dog learns to salivate to the tone. Then another tone is presented on its own. This tone produces a smaller amount of salivation than the first through *generalisation*. After that, the first tone is paired with food several more times but the second tone is never paired with food. Salivation to the first tone increases whereas that to the second tone decreases—the dog has learned to *discriminate* between the two tones.

There is another key feature of classical conditioning. When Pavlov presented the tone on its own several times, there was less and less salivation. Thus, the repeated presentation of the conditioned stimulus in the absence of the unconditioned stimulus stops the conditioned response. This is known as **extinction**.

What are the limitations of Pavlov's research? First, the experimental situation with its constraints on the dog's movement and absence of distraction was very artificial. Second, much animal learning (and even more human learning) does *not* involve classical conditioning as studied by Pavlov. Third, Pavlov used dogs in his research and there are problems in generalising to humans, in part because we possess language. For example, we can sometimes produce immediate extinction in humans by telling them the unconditioned stimulus won't be presented again (Davey, 1983).

KEY TERMS

Unconditioned stimulus: the stimulus that produces a previously well-established unconditioned response in an unconditioned reflex.

Unconditioned response: the previously well-established reaction (e.g. salivation) to a given unconditioned stimulus (e.g. food) in an unconditioned reflex.

Conditioned stimulus: a neutral stimulus that is paired with an unconditioned stimulus to produce classical conditioning.

Conditioned response: the new response (resembling the unconditioned response) produced as a result of classical conditioning.

Extinction: the elimination of a response in classical conditioning when it is not followed by the unconditioned stimulus.

Explanations

Classical conditioning occurs because the conditioned stimulus (e.g. a tone) allows the dog or other animal to *predict* the unconditioned stimulus (e.g. food). The tone provides a clear indication food is about to arrive. As a result, it produces an effect (salivation) similar to that produced by the food itself. Extinction occurs when the tone no longer predicts the arrival of food.

Ecological perspective

In most classical conditioning, the relationship between the conditioned and unconditioned stimuli is *arbitrary*. For example, consider Pavlov's research on dogs. There is no obvious reason for pairing a tone with the sight of food. What are the chances an animal living in the wild will often encounter the same arbitrary conditioned stimulus immediately before a given unconditioned stimulus? Slim or none.

What is going on? Domjan (2005) adopted an ecological approach, arguing that conditioning is fastest when learning is of most benefit to animals in their natural environment. For example, it is crucial to survival for animals (and humans) to learn rapidly to avoid poisonous foods. As predicted, rats needed only one learning trial

How does classical conditioning happen in the natural environment? Domjan (2005) argued that the conditioned and unconditioned stimuli are typically different features of the same object. He discussed findings from experiments on male Japanese quail in which the conditioned stimulus was the stuffed head of a female quail and the unconditioned stimulus was access to a live female. Classical conditioning was very strong—the male quail often grabbed the stuffed head and tried to copulate with it!

? Can you use classical conditioning to explain why some ex-smokers find it very difficult to resist the temptation to smoke when they drink a cup of tea or coffee?

Phobias and exposure therapy

The principles of classical conditioning have been applied to patients suffering from phobias (extreme fears of certain objects). Common examples include snake and spider phobia. According to the behaviourist account of phobias (discussed at length in Chapter 6), phobias develop through classical conditioning when the conditioned or phobic stimulus is associated with a painful or aversive stimulus causing fear. For example, someone might develop social phobia (fear of social situations) because on one occasion they experienced public humiliation.

There is some support for the classical conditioning account of the development of phobias (see Chapter 6). However, it is clear that several other factors are also involved. To the extent that phobias are acquired through classical conditioning, then presumably they can be eliminated through extinction. In other words, if the phobic or conditioning stimulus is presented repeatedly *without* any aversive consequences, the fear associated with that stimulus should gradually diminish. This line of thinking led to the development of exposure therapy. In exposure therapy, phobic individuals are exposed to the feared object or situation for lengthy periods of time until their anxiety level reduces. As is discussed in Chapter 6, exposure therapy has proved an effective form of treatment for phobias.

EVALUATION

- (+) All the phenomena of classical conditioning have been shown many times.
- (+) Classical conditioning often has important biological value (e.g. taste aversion). It allows animals to prepare themselves for the arrival of the unconditioned stimulus.
- (+) Exposure therapy, which has proved successful in the treatment of phobias, involves the process of extinction.
- (−) Much learning in non-human species doesn't involve classical conditioning. As we will see shortly, operant conditioning and modelling are also important.
- (−) Classical conditioning tells us practically nothing about numerous important aspects of human behaviour, including problem solving, reasoning, decision making, and language.
- (−) Most research on classical conditioning lacks ecological validity (applicability to everyday life) because the relationship between the conditioned and unconditioned stimuli is arbitrary.

Operant conditioning

Classical conditioning is undoubtedly important. However, it doesn't explain *all* learning. Another important form of learning was studied by Edward Thorndike (1898). In research discussed earlier in the chapter, he found that cats escaped increasingly rapidly from a cage when they received a food reward for so doing. These findings led Thorndike to state his "law of effect":

- Positive effects (rewards) lead to the *stamping in* of a behaviour.
- Negative effects (punishments) led to the *stamping out* of a behaviour.

This theory was developed by B. F. Skinner (1904–1990) into operant conditioning. **Operant conditioning** is learning that is controlled by its consequences (i.e. rewards or punishments).

KEY TERM

Operant conditioning: a basic form of learning in which the individual's behaviour is influenced by whether it is followed by reward or by punishment.

? How do classical and operant conditioning differ?

Thorndike's and Skinner's approaches were similar in that they both focused on the *effects* of behaviour in contrast to Pavlov's emphasis on the behaviours themselves.

KEY RESEARCH STUDY

Skinner's research

The essence of operant conditioning can be seen in Skinner's (1938) experiments with rats. A hungry rat was placed in a cage with a lever sticking out on one side. When the lever was pressed a pellet of food was delivered from a food dispenser. There was a cumulative recorder which recorded automatically each time the rat pressed this lever. It was possible to work out the frequency and speed of lever presses using this information.

At first the rat accidentally pressed the lever but it soon learned there was a link between lever pressing and food appearing. Skinner argued that the rat *operated* on the environment. The delivery of food provided reward and so increased the likelihood of a given behaviour.

In the basic experiment, rats were rewarded every time they pressed the lever (continuous reinforcement). Skinner also used other reinforcement schedules:

- *Fixed ratio*: Every *n*th (e.g. fifth) response is rewarded. Workers receiving extra money for achieving certain targets are on this schedule.
- *Variable ratio*: On average, every *n*th response is rewarded. However, the actual gap between two rewards varies considerably. This schedule is found in fishing and gambling.
- *Fixed interval*: The first response produced after a given interval of time (e.g. 60 seconds) is rewarded. Workers paid regularly every week are on this schedule—they receive a reward after a given interval of time but don't need to produce a specific response.
- *Variable interval*. On average, the first response produced after a given interval of time is rewarded but the actual interval varies. Self-employed workers whose customers make payments at irregular times are rewarded at variable intervals. However, they don't have to produce a specific response.

Skinner found that continuous reinforcement produced the lowest rate of responding. In contrast, the variable schedules (especially variable ratio) lead to very fast rates of responding because they created high levels of motivation. This helps to explain why gamblers find it hard to stop their addiction.

Skinner box for rats, showing chart recording of lever pressing

Skinner box for rats, showing chart recording of lever pressing. On the chart, each vertical line represents a single press on the lever.

Although gamblers have no idea when or if they will receive a payout, they continue to play. This is an example of the most successful reinforcement schedule—variable ratio reinforcement.

Types of reinforcement

When an animal performs a behaviour (or operates on the environment), there are four possible consequences:

- **Positive reinforcement** (e.g. receiving food) is pleasurable and so increases the likelihood of a behaviour occurring again.
- **Negative reinforcement** refers to the avoidance of an unpleasant stimulus. The result is also pleasurable (like positive reinforcement) and so increases the likelihood of behaviour. For

example, if the floor of the cage was electrified and pressing the lever stopped this, the rat would be more likely to press the lever.

- **Positive punishment** such as receiving an electric shock decreases the likelihood of a behaviour, e.g. if the rat received a shock every time it pressed the lever it would stop doing it.
- **Negative punishment** such as removing a pleasant stimulus decreases the likelihood of a behaviour, e.g. a teenager grounded for staying out late. The removal of a desirable option (going out) reduces the likelihood of staying out late.

EXAM HINT

It is easy to get confused between the different types of reinforcement and punishment. It can help to remember that "positive" refers to adding something to the situation, whereas "negative" refers to removing something from the situation.

A "reinforcer" is a change that makes the situation more pleasant, thus reinforcing the behaviour; whereas a "punishment" is a change that makes the situation less pleasant, thus discouraging the behaviour.

So, negative reinforcement involves removing an *unpleasant* stimulus to *reinforce* a behaviour; negative punishment involves removing a *pleasant* stimulus to *discourage* a behaviour.

Equipotentiality

Skinner assumed that virtually *any* response can be conditioned in *any* stimulus situation. This assumption is known as **equipotentiality**, but it is incorrect. In fact, animals' behaviour typically resembles their natural or instinctive behaviour. For example, it would be very hard (or impossible) to train an animal to run away from food to obtain a food reward.

Breland and Breland (1961) trained pigs to insert wooden coins into a piggy bank for reward. The pigs rapidly learned to do this. Much more interestingly, the pigs started to perform slower and slower until eventually they weren't getting enough to eat.

What had happened to the pigs? Over time, each pig started picking up the coin but then dropped it on the floor. The pig would "root it [turn it up with its snout], drop it again, root it along the way, pick it up, toss it in the air, drop, root it some again, and so on" (Breland & Breland, 1961, p. 683). The pig's behaviour increasingly reflected its natural food-getting behaviours. In the words of Breland and Breland, the pigs showed "instinctive drift" and this can't be explained easily in conditioning terms.

Moore (1973) obtained more evidence of instinctive behaviour. Pigeons pecked at keys for food or water reward. Birds pecking for food usually struck the key with an open beak and made sharp, vigorous pecks. When pecking for water, on the other hand, the pigeons had their beaks closed and there was a more sustained contact with the key.

Token economy

There are several real-world applications of operant conditioning. They include the training of circus animals, persuading people to work long hours in return for payment, and raising academic standards by praising students for performing well. Here we will briefly consider the token economy. What happens in a **token economy** is that individuals are given tokens (e.g. poker chips) in return for behaving in appropriate ways (e.g. maintaining personal hygiene). These tokens can then be exchanged for rewards. Token economies have been used with patients living in hospitals or other institutions. This is partly because the successful use of token economies requires detailed information about the individual's behaviour.

Silverman et al. (2004) used a token economy with cocaine users who had proved very hard to treat. Some patients were offered up to \$3,480 (about £2,000) in vouchers for remaining cocaine free over a 39-week period whereas other patients had no incentive. Of those given

KEY TERMS

Equipotentiality: the notion within operant conditioning that any response can be conditioned to any stimulus situation.

Token economy: a form of therapy based on operant conditioning in which desirable behaviour is rewarded with tokens that can subsequently be exchanged for rewards.

a high incentive, 45% remained abstinent from cocaine for at least 4 weeks compared to 0% of those with no incentive.

De Fulio et al. (2009) studied people with cocaine dependence given jobs involving data entry. Those in the token economy condition were rewarded for abstinence from cocaine with continuous employment on full pay. However, they suffered a temporary pay cut if they had cocaine in their urine samples. The control participants were given jobs regardless of whether they were drug-free. Over a 1-year period, the token economy participants had cocaine-free samples on 79% of occasions compared to only 51% for the controls.

The major limitation with token economies is that they often produce token (i.e. minimal) learning. Their beneficial effects can be greatly reduced when patients leave the token economy and find themselves in the much less structured environment outside the institution.

EVALUATION

- (+) Operant conditioning is often very effective. The behaviour of humans and other species can be controlled by clever use of reinforcement (e.g. the training of circus animals).
- (+) Operant conditioning (e.g. token economy) has reduced the symptoms of patients with mental disorders.
- (−) Skinner minimised the role of *internal* factors (e.g. goals; beliefs) in determining behaviour. As Bandura (1977a, p. 27) pointed out, "If actions were determined solely by external rewards and punishments, people would behave like weather vanes, constantly shifting in radically different directions to conform to the whims of others." In fact, we often pursue our long-term goals rather than being totally influenced by the immediate situation.
- (−) Operant conditioning is more about influencing people's *behaviour* than about *learning* in the broad sense. Suppose I offered you £1 every time you said, "The Earth is flat". You might (especially if short of money!) say it hundreds of times so the reward or reinforcement would have influenced your behaviour. However, I doubt whether it would affect your learning or knowledge so you actually believed the Earth was flat.
- (−) In real life, relatively little of our learning occurs because we perform rewarded responses as proposed by Skinner. Instead, we learn a huge amount simply by *observing* others' behaviour (discussed shortly).
- (−) Skinner's notion of equipotentiality is incorrect because it de-emphasises the importance of instinctive behaviour.

Social learning theory

Albert Bandura was one of the first psychologists to propose an alternative to the behaviourists' learning theory approach based on classical and operant conditioning. Bandura developed what is known as social learning theory. **Social learning theory** differs from traditional learning theory in various important ways. First, traditional learning theorists argued that behaviour is always learned through *direct* conditioning in which the individual learns through making certain responses. In contrast, Bandura argued that we often learn by *observing* what other people do rather than by actually engaging in behaviour. In the words of Bandura (1977b, p. 12):

> *Virtually all learning phenomena resulting from direct experience occur on a vicarious [second-hand] basis by observing other people's behaviour and its consequences for them. The capacity to learn by observation enables people to acquire large, integrated patterns of behaviour without having to form them gradually by tedious trial and error.*

KEY TERM

Social learning theory: the view that behaviour can be explained in terms of direct and indirect reinforcement through imitation, identification, and modelling.

Second, social learning differs from traditional learning theory in its emphasis on mental states. In order to imitate someone's behaviour there must be an intervening cognitive state (i.e. we perceive and interpret their behaviour), a notion that was rejected by most behaviourists.

Why is this form of learning so important to humans? One key reason is because it is typically much more *efficient* than classical and operant conditioning which involve actually experiencing a given situation. In the course of a single day, you can readily observe the behaviour of numerous people in hundreds of situations. In contrast, it would be very hard or impossible to put yourself in all those situations in a short period of time. It can also be safer to observe the fate of others who perform dangerous actions rather than performing the same actions yourself!

Bandura argued that, rather than only learning through directly engaging in a behaviour, we also learn by observing a behaviour. Observing the fate of others who perform dangerous actions can be much safer than performing those actions yourself!

Observational learning: Imitation, identification, and modelling

It is now time to go into more detail on social learning theory. Its main emphasis is on **modelling**, which involves learning based on observing and then imitating the actions of a model. There are three main forms of modelling. First, there is live modelling in which the model is physically present while being observed. Second, there is symbolic modelling in which real or fictional models are observed through the mass media. Third, there is modelling which involves the presentation of verbal descriptions or instructions.

One of the main features of modelling is **imitation**: observers often imitate or copy the actions they have observed being performed by another person.

There are four requirements for successful modelling:

1. *Attention*: the observer must attend to the model's actions.
2. *Memory*: information about the model's actions must be retained in memory.
3. *Actions*: stored information concerning the model's behaviour must be turned into appropriate actions resembling those of the observer.
4. *Motivation*: the observer must have sufficient incentive to imitate the observer's actions.

Imitation is a relatively simple form of learning. Identification (which resembles imitation in many ways) is a more complex form of learning. Bandura (1969, p. 255) defined **identification** within social learning theory as follows:

> *[It] is a continuous process in which new responses are acquired and existing repertoires of behaviour are modified as a function of both direct and vicarious experiences with a wide variety of actual or symbolic models, whose attitudes, values, and social responses are exemplified behaviourally, or in verbally coded forms.*

As the above quotation indicates, identification is broader than imitation (although they are fairly closed related). More specifically, there are two major differences between the concepts of imitation and identification. First, the extent to which a model is imitated depends on the extent to which the individual identifies with him/her. More specifically, we are more likely to imitate a model with whom we identify than one with whom we don't identify.

Second, imitation is often regarded as involving a fairly direct copy of the observed behaviour. In contrast, identification can involve numerous different forms of behaviour resembling and building on observed behaviour.

Vicarious reinforcement

Bandura (1977a, b) argued that a key factor associated with modelling is vicarious reinforcement. **Vicarious reinforcement** occurs when someone observes another person's behaviour being rewarded or punished. They are more likely to imitate that behaviour if it is rewarded rather than punished. Bandura (1977b) specified several mechanisms by which observers' behaviour is influenced by vicarious reinforcement:

1. *Motivational*: Vicarious reinforcement can motivate observers to imitate (or avoid imitating) the model's behaviour.

KEY TERMS

Modelling: a very common form of learning in which the learner observes and then imitates a model's actions; also known as observational learning.

Imitation: this involves someone imitating or copying the actions of a model whose behaviour has been observed.

Identification: according to Bandura, this resembles imitation in that it is based on modelling; however, it is more complex because it depends on the model's characteristics (e.g. perceived similarity to the individual) and the behaviour produced can extend beyond mere imitation.

Vicarious reinforcement: A situation in which the reinforcement or reward obtained by someone else has a reinforcing effect on one's own behaviour.

2. *Informative*: Vicarious reinforcement supplies information about the consequences of certain forms of behaviour.
3. *Influenceability*: Observers may become more affected by a given form of reinforcement after they see how the model responds to similar reinforcements.
4. *Emotional learning*: Vicarious reinforcement can generate emotional arousal or fear in observers.
5. *Modification of model status*: Vicarious reinforcement can lead observers to increase their assessment of the model's status if he/she is rewarded or to decrease it if he/she is punished.

Role of mediational processes

How does modelling within social learning theory differ from operant conditioning? At the risk of over-simplification, the emphasis within operant conditioning is on *response* learning—learning to respond appropriately in a given situation to receive reward or reinforcement. In contrast, the emphasis within social learning theory is on mediational processes—it is a more *cognitive* approach. Indeed, as Bandura developed his social learning theory he eventually changed its name to social cognitive theory.

What does this difference mean in practice? As Bandura (1999, p. 154) expressed it, "People are self-organising, proactive, self-reflecting, and self-regulating, not just reactive organisms shaped and shepherded by external events [as in the behaviourist approach]." In other words, Skinner assumed that our behaviour is at the mercy of the current situation, whereas Bandura argued that several mediational processes (e.g. attention; memory; motivation) all influence how we think and respond in any given situation.

The existence of vicarious reinforcement shows mediational processes play a role in determining behaviour. Consider what happens when an individual observes a model performing some action and then being punished for it. The individual learns the observed action but typically does not perform it. Thus, learning has occurred even when there is no direct impact of what has been learned on behaviour. We can explain this discrepancy between learning and behaviour in terms of mediational processes.

KEY RESEARCH STUDY

Modelling and the Bobo doll

Bandura (1965) carried out a study in which young children (average age = 51 months) watched a film in which an adult model behaved aggressively towards an inflatable Bobo doll. This doll is interesting to children partly because it has a weighted base

Adult "model" and children attack the Bobo doll.

causing it to bounce back when punched. In one condition, a second adult appeared towards the end of the film and gave the model some sweets and a soft drink for having put up a "championship performance" (reward condition). In a second condition, the second adult scolded and spanked the model for behaving aggressively (punishment condition). In a third condition, the model did not receive reward or punishment (control condition).

Children in the reward and control conditions imitated more of the model's aggressive actions than those in the punishment condition. Children in the punishment condition showed little evidence of modelling in their performance. However, they showed strong evidence of observational learning. When all the children were offered fruit juice and toys for showing what they had learned from the model, the amount of observational learning was as great for children in the punishment condition as for those in the other two conditions (see Figure).

What are the limitations of this study? First, much of the aggressive behaviour Bandura observed was play-fighting rather than real aggression. Second, the fact that the Bobo doll bounces back up when knocked down gives it novelty value. Children unfamiliar with the Bobo doll were five times as likely to imitate aggressive behaviour against it than those who had played with it before (Cumberbatch, 1990). Third, children are much less likely to imitate aggressive behaviour towards another child than towards the Bobo doll.

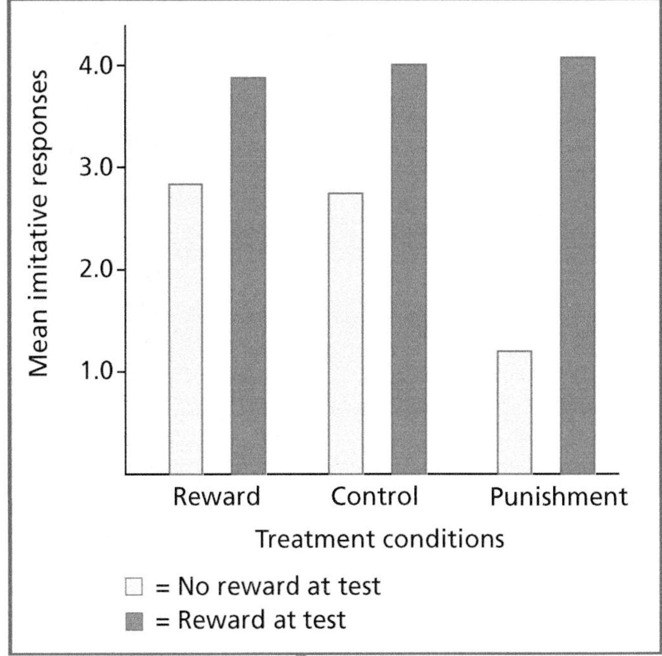

Imitation of aggressive behaviour by children as a function of the way an aggressive adult was treated (reward, control, punishment) and whether the children were or were not rewarded at the test for imitating the adult's aggressive behaviour. Data from Bandura (1965).

Findings

Numerous studies have provided support for social learning theory. For example, Mares and Woodard (2005) were interested in deciding whether the amount of time children spent watching television programmes with an emphasis on helping others would make their behaviour more positive. They carried out a meta-analysis combining the findings from 34 studies. Children tended to model or imitate the positive behaviour they had observed on television. In similar fashion, Paik and Comstock (1994) found in a meta-analysis on the effects of television violence that children who watched the most violent television tended to display more violent and anti-social behaviour than those watching less.

? Does this study have external validity? In other words, to what extent can we generalise the findings obtained in this study to real life?

We turn now to research on identification. Remember that according to Bandura the extent to which modelling occurs should depend on characteristics of the model. Brewer and Wann (1998) asked college students to watch a videotape of a model performing a puzzle task. There was more modelling of the model's behaviour when he was described as possessing social power (e.g. he was an expert) than when he was not.

? How important do you think observational learning is with respect to producing aggressive behaviour?

Further evidence supporting the notion that characteristics of the model influence the extent of modelling was reported by Bandura and Huston (1961). Young children showed more modelling behaviour when the model had previously behaved in a friendly way towards them compared to when the model had been rather cold and distant.

Observing a model perform an action that is rewarded or successful does *not* always lead to direct imitation of that action by the observer. Gergely et al. (2002) carried out a study in which infants of 14 months observed while an adult model turned on a table-mounted pressure-sensitive light using her forehead. In one condition, the model's hands were on the table and so the infants could see she had deliberately chosen to use her forehead rather than her hands to turn the light on. In this condition, 69% of the infants simply imitated the model.

The above findings support social learning theory. However, very different findings were obtained in a second condition in which the model pretended to be cold and so had her hands under the table wrapped in a blanket. This had a dramatic effect on the results. In this condition, only 21% of the infants copied the model's behaviour, choosing instead to use their hands to turn the light on. Thus, the extent to which individuals imitate a model's behaviour depends more than assumed by Bandura on their *interpretation* of the situation in which the behaviour is observed.

? What are some of the limitations of Bandura's research?

EVALUATION

- (+) Modelling occurs very often in children and adults but was largely ignored prior to Bandura's theories and research.
- (+) Phenomena such as vicarious reinforcement, imitation, and identification have all been demonstrated many times.
- (+) Social learning theory with its emphasis on mediational processes is a significant advance over the simpler conditioning theories that had preceded it.
- (−) Bandura (1999, p. 73) pointed out that, "Modelling is not simply a process of response mimicry as commonly believed." Instead, he argued that the observer's behaviour should "embody the same rule" as the model's behaviour. The problem with this argument is that it is rather vague, making it hard to decide whether both individuals' behaviour does or doesn't embody the same rule.
- (−) The processes underlying modelling and imitation can be much more complex than assumed by Bandura (e.g. Gergely et al., 2002)
- (−) Much behaviour can't easily be understood in terms of modelling. Consider, for example, young children's acquisition of language. They initially produce much shorter utterances than adults and rapidly move on to producing novel utterances. Neither of these aspects of children's language would be predicted on the basis of modelling.

EXAM HINT

Wundt, Pavlov, Skinner, and Bandura are all named on the specification. You might be asked an essay question such as "Discuss the contribution of Bandura's research to our understanding of human learning"; "Discuss criticisms of Wundt's introspective method made by behaviourists such as Skinner" or "Discuss the contribution of Pavlov's research on animals to our understanding of human behaviour". This means that you should know enough about each of these researchers to be able to discuss and compare them in depth. For example:

- The approach each individual proposed and the key assumptions, concepts and methods used in that approach.
- How each individual fits into the historical development of psychology: whose ideas or methods did they dispute? Who in turn disputed their ideas or methods?
- The details of their theories and of their research studies.

Whilst other researchers mentioned in this chapter—such as Fechner, Watson and Thorndike—are also important in the history of psychology, you will not be asked specifically about them as individuals.

Section summary

Classical conditioning

- Pavlov's research on dogs showed the existence of classical conditioning which involves learning via association between two stimuli (an unconditioned stimulus and a conditioned stimulus).
- Phenomena associated with classical conditioning include discrimination, generalisation and extinction.
- Classical conditioning occurs because the conditioned stimulus allows the dog or other animal to *predict* the arrival of the unconditioned stimulus.
- In most studies on classical conditioning, the relationship between the conditioned and unconditioned stimuli is arbitrary. In the natural environment, in contrast, the conditioned and unconditioned stimuli are typically different features of the same object.
- The principles of classical conditioning have been used to explain the development of phobias.

Operant conditioning

- Skinner carried out research on operant conditioning showing that hungry rats will press a lever repeatedly to obtain a food reward or positive reinforcement. A variable ratio schedule of reinforcement produced the fastest rate of responding.
- In addition to positive reinforcement, there is negative reinforcement, positive punishment, and negative punishment.
- Skinner's notion that virtually any response can be conditioned in almost any stimulus situation (equipotentiality) is incorrect.
- Operant conditioning led to the development of the token economy. This has proved moderately effective but sometimes has very limited effects when patients leave the token economy.
- Human behaviour is much less influenced by the immediate situation than assumed by Skinner.

Social learning theory

- According to social learning theory, most learning occurs through modelling rather than through direct conditioning.
- We can distinguish among live modelling, symbolic modelling, and modelling involving the presentation of verbal descriptions or instructions.
- The extent of modelling often depends on identification—the extent to which the individual identifies with the model.
- There is much evidence for vicarious reinforcement—behaviour is more likely to be imitated when it is rewarded rather than punished.
- The processes underlying modelling and imitation can involve more complex interpretations of the situation than assumed by Bandura.
- Much learning (e.g. language acquisition by children) does not depend very much on modelling.

COGNITIVE APPROACH

Cognitive psychology developed during the 1950s because of a growing dissatisfaction with the behaviourist approach. It is very hard to understand cognitive abilities such as language or problem solving from the behaviourist perspective because of its emphasis on observable behaviour. For example, what someone is thinking is generally not obvious from their behaviour. What is also needed is a focus on internal mental processes. That has been the particular focus of cognitive psychologists.

In essence, the behaviourists argued that people form links between stimuli and responses. In fairness to the behaviourists, however, it should be pointed out that some behaviourists (especially Tolman, 1932) argued that theorists should focus on internal processes mediating the effects of stimuli on responses. For example, he emphasised the notion of "cognitive map" (Tolman, 1948), according to which even rats store away integrated spatial representations of their environment. Cognitive psychologists developed such ideas, arguing that the internal processes occurring *between* stimulus and response are crucially important. These processes relate to attention, perception, thinking, reasoning, problem-solving, planning, learning, memory, and so on.

Tolman introduced the idea of "cognitive maps" as a result of his experiments involving rats and mazes; rats store store away integrated spatial representations of their environment—an example of an internal mental process.

Study of internal mental processes

It requires a certain amount of ingenuity to study internal mental processes since they aren't directly observable in behaviour. However, cognitive psychologists have become increasingly successful at doing precisely that. One of the most important reasons why this is the case is that cognitive psychologists have developed *four* major approaches to the study of human cognition:

1. *Experimental cognitive psychology*: this approach involves carrying out experiments on healthy individuals (often college students). Behavioural evidence (e.g. participants' level of performance) is used to shed light on internal cognitive processes.
2. *Cognitive neuropsychology*: this approach also involves carrying out experiments, but here the participants are brain-damaged patients. In spite of that, it is hoped the findings from such experiments will increase our understanding of cognition in healthy individuals.
3. *Cognitive neuroscience*: this approach also involves carrying out experiments (typically, though not always, on healthy individuals). This approach extends experimental cognitive psychology by using evidence from brain activity as well as from behaviour to understand internal mental processes.
4. *Computational cognitive science*: this approach involves developing computer models based in part on experimental findings to model or mimic some aspects of human internal mental processing and behaviour.

Is one of these approaches better than any of the others? The short answer is "No". Each approach has its own strengths and limitations. As a result, researchers increasingly use two or more of these approaches to shed as much light as possible on internal mental processes.

I will be discussing cognitive neuroscience and computational cognitive science later in this section of the chapter. Accordingly, we will focus on an example of how the experimental cognitive psychology and cognitive neuropsychology approaches can shed light on internal mental processes. The example concerns short-term memory (discussed in detail in Chapter 3).

How can we study an internal process such as short-term memory using behavioural evidence? First, we can assess its capacity by gradually increasing the amount of information participants are required to recall immediately in the correct order. The maximum amount of information that can be recalled correctly (memory span) provides an estimate of the capacity of short-term memory.

Second, we can assess how long people hold information in short-term memory by working out the longest retention interval at which recall performance remains high. Precisely this was done by Peterson and Peterson (1959), who discovered that forgetting occurred very rapidly from short-term memory.

Third, we can assess the extent to which short-term memory depends on verbal rehearsal of the to-be-remembered information. Suppose we present to-be-remembered words visually. If participants use verbal rehearsal, they should be affected by whether the words have similar or dissimilar sounds. As predicted, people have worse short-term memory when the words sound similar (and are thus easily confused) than when they sound dissimilar.

Fourth, suppose we argue short-term memory is a process that is different from long-term memory and thus involves different brain areas. That would imply that some brain-damaged patients should have intact short-term memory but very impaired long-term memory whereas others should show the opposite pattern. As is discussed in Chapter 3, both patterns have been observed by researchers within cognitive neuropsychology.

There are three take-home messages from our discussion of short-term memory. First, it is valuable to use several different experimental tasks to obtain an overall perspective on any given internal mental process. Second, it is valuable to use different major approaches (e.g. experimental cognitive psychology; cognitive neuropsychology) to enrich our understanding of human cognition. Third, it is valuable to base research on theoretical assumptions. For example, the assumption that people typically use verbal rehearsal on memory span tasks led directly to studies in which the similarity/dissimilarity of the sounds of the words was manipulated.

KEY TERM

Schema: organised knowledge (e.g. about the world) stored in long-term memory.

Role of schema

Bartlett (1932) emphasised the importance of schemas in learning and memory. A **schema** is a well-integrated packet of knowledge about the world, events, people, or actions. Schemas are stored in long-term memory, more specifically in that part of long-term memory known as semantic memory (see Chapter 2). Thus, they are internal structures. Bartlett's key insight (discussed shortly) is that what we remember is influenced by our schematic knowledge.

There are several kinds of schemas including scripts and frames. Scripts deal with knowledge about events and the consequences of events. In contrast, frames are knowledge structures referring to some aspect of the world (e.g. building) containing fixed structural information (e.g. has floors and walls) and slots for variable information (e.g. materials from which the building is constructed).

Bower et al. (1979) considered the kinds of information typically found in scripts. For example, they asked people to list 20 actions or events usually occurring during the course of a restaurant meal. There was much agreement on the actions associated with the restaurant script. At least 73% of the participants mentioned sitting down, looking at the menu, ordering, paying the bill, and leaving.

ACTIVITY: Schemas

In small groups, write your own schemas for the following:

- Catching a train
- Buying a newspaper
- Starting school

How easy was it to agree on a uniform pattern of events? Were any of the themes easier to agree on than the others? Why might this be?

Why is schematic knowledge useful? First, it allows us to form realistic expectations (e.g. of what happens in a restaurant). Thus, schemas make the world more predictable than would otherwise be the case because our expectations are generally confirmed.

Second, schemas play an important role in reading and listening because they allow us to fill in the gaps in what we are reading or hearing and so enhance our understanding. More specifically, they provide the basis for us to draw *inferences* as we read or listen.

Third, schemas assist us when viewing visual scenes. Palmer (1975) presented pictures of scenes (e.g. a *kitchen*) followed by a briefly presented object. Participants were better at identifying the object when it was appropriate to the scene (e.g. *loaf*) than when no scene was presented initially. Thus, activation of relevant schematic knowledge facilitated visual perception.

KEY RESEARCH STUDY

Bartlett (1932): *War of the Ghosts*

Bartlett (1932) had the ingenious idea of presenting people with stories producing a *conflict* between what was presented to them and their prior knowledge (schemas). Suppose people read a story taken from a different culture. Their prior knowledge might produce distortions in the remembered version of the story, making it more conventional and acceptable from their own cultural background.

In his study, Bartlett (1932) presented Cambridge University students with North American folk tales, of which the most famous was the *War of the Ghosts*:

> *One night two young men from Egulac went down to the river to hunt seals, and while they were there it became foggy and calm. Then they hear war-cries, and they thought: "Maybe this is a war-party." They escaped to the shore, and hid behind a log. Now canoes came up, and they heard the noise of paddles, and saw one canoe coming up to them. There were five men in the canoe, and they said, "What do you think? We wish to take you along. We are going up the river to make war on the people."*
>
> *One of the young men said: "I have no arrows."*
>
> *"Arrows are in the canoe", they said.*
>
> *"I will not go along. I might be killed. My relatives do not know where I have gone. But you", he said, turning to the other, "may go with them."*
>
> *So one of the young men went, but the other returned home. And the warriors went up the river to a town on the other side of Kalama.*
>
> *The people came down to the water, and they began to fight, and many were killed. But presently the young man heard one of the warriors said: "Quick, let us go home: that Indian has been hit."*

continued over

Now he thought: "Oh, they are ghosts."

He did not feel sick, but they said he had been shot.

So the canoes went back to Egulac, and the young man went ashore to his house, and made a fire. And he told everybody and said: "Behold I accompanied the ghosts, and we went to fight. Many of our fellows were killed, and many of those who attacked us were killed. They said I was hit, and I did not feel sick."

He told it all, and then he came quiet. When the sun rose he fell down. Something black came out of his mouth. His face became contorted. The people jumped up and cried. He was dead.

What did Bartlett find? The participants made numerous recall errors. Most of these errors conformed to their cultural expectations. He used the term **rationalisation** for this type of error.

EVALUATION

- (+) This study shows schematic information can systematically distort long-term memory.
- (+) The notion that what we learn and remember can be strongly influenced by our prior knowledge and expectations has been very influential.
- (−) Bartlett's (1932) approach was not very scientific: "I thought it best ... to try to influence the subjects' procedure as little as possible" (p. 78). As a result, there was deliberate guessing. Gauld and Stephenson (1967) found that instructions stressing the need for accurate recall eliminated almost half the errors in recall of *War of the Ghosts* usually obtained.
- (−) Bartlett's research has limited ecological validity in that it is unusual in everyday life to read articles or stories coming from a different culture.
- (−) The notion of a schema is somewhat vague and Bartlett failed to establish with any precision the schemas possessed by his participants.

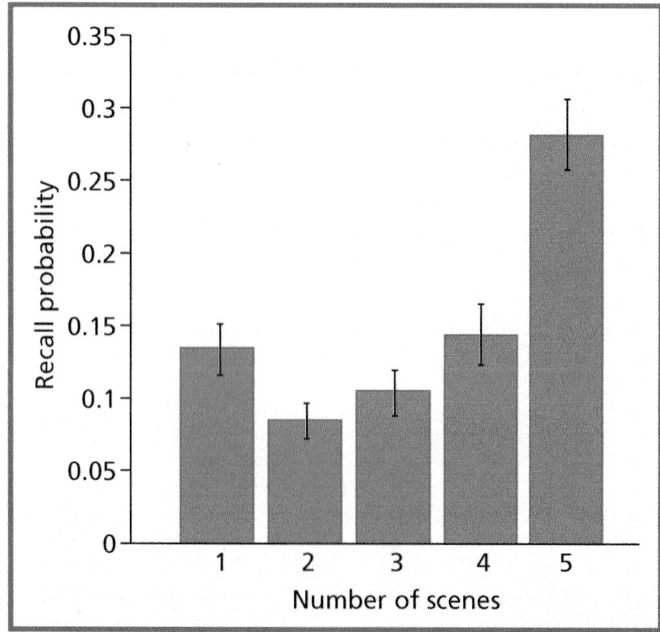

In Steyvers and Hemmer's (2012) experiment recall was highest for objects in the most schema-consistent category.

Findings

Bartlett reported that schemas caused numerous *errors* in memory, whereas Steyvers and Hemmer (2012) argued that schemas generally *enhance* memory in everyday life. They tested their ideas in a study in which participants were shown photographs representing five types of scene (e.g. *urban scene*; *kitchen*). The objects shown in each scene varied in their relevance to the schema. For example, *car*, *building*, and *street* are all very relevant to the schema for an urban scene.

What did Steyvers and Hemmer (2012) find? As can be seen in the Figure, recall was the highest for objects in the most schema-relevant category with recall tending to decrease as the degree of schema relevance decreased. This shows the beneficial effects schematic knowledge can have on long-term memory.

KEY TERM

Rationalisation: a term introduced by Bartlett to refer to the tendency in story recall to produce errors conforming to the rememberer's cultural expectations.

OVERALL EVALUATION

- (+) There is convincing evidence that schemas influence memory, visual perception, reading, and listening.
- (+) Some of the strongest evidence that schemas influence long-term memory comes from studies showing systematic distortions in recall for stories from a different culture.
- (−) There is no easy way to work out how much information is contained in a schema or the extent to which that information is integrated.
- (−) The conditions determining *when* a given schema will be activated are unclear. This makes it hard to test schema theory.
- (−) Some of the evidence (e.g. Steyvers and Hemmer, 2012) suggests that Bartlett exaggerated how much schemas distort memory. It would obviously be a major disadvantage if our long-term memory were constantly distorted by schemas!

Use of theoretical and computer models

Models play an important role in cognitive psychology. We can perhaps see this most easily by considering what would have happened if cognitive psychologists had decided *not* to put forward any models. That would make experimental research an almost random process—in the absence of theories and models, there would be little to guide researchers trying to decide which experimental topics are important and which are not.

Let's develop the argument in the previous paragraph. Experimental findings provide the basis for the construction (and subsequent revision) of models. However, the causality also goes the other way—models make various predictions, and so experiments are very often carried out to test these predictions. Thus, researchers advance our understanding of human cognition by constructing models to explain experimental findings and by conducting experiments to test the predictions of their models.

When we have an established model, we can use experimental findings to draw inferences about the underlying mental processes based on the assumptions of the model. If the experimental findings are consistently supportive of the model, we can use the model to explain these findings.

Cognitive psychologists have devised several kinds of models to explain and make inferences about mental processes. However, there is a very important distinction between theoretical models and computer models. **Theoretical models** are usually expressed in verbal terms and so their assumptions can be somewhat vague. In contrast, **computer models** are typically much more precise because they are expressed in the form of computer programs. The researcher needs to spell out explicitly all his/her theoretical assumptions when constructing a computer program because otherwise it will not be able to mimic human behaviour.

EXAM HINT

The specification requires you to understand how theoretical and computer models can be used to explain and make inferences about mental processes.

The word "inference" is used many times in this section and you may be asked to explain it in an examination, so it is important to understand it clearly. Inference is *the act of drawing a conclusion from evidence and reasoning*. In basic terms, this means that we use clues from observable behaviour, speech, etc., to build an explanation of what is really going on in peoples' unobservable minds. However, we don't just come up with a random explanation. Because inference goes *beyond* the observable evidence, it needs to be informed by a *theoretical model* that can make sense of and combine many different pieces of evidence into a coherent explanation. It is this ability to explain lots of evidence from different sources that provides the logic in the conclusion.

Alternatively, you might be asked to explain some evidence. For example, a question might ask you to explain some participant self-reports from a dual task experiment. To answer this question, you will need to apply your knowledge of a relevant theoretical model (i.e. the working memory model) to explain the underlying mental processes that can be inferred from the self-reports.

KEY TERMS

Theoretical models: models of human cognition typically expressed in verbal terms; the assumptions contained within such models may be imprecise.

Computational models: models of human cognition based on computer programs in which the underlying assumptions are spelled out with precision.

Theoretical models

There are thousands of theoretical models within cognitive psychology. Here we will focus on two theoretical models of memory discussed in detail in Chapter 3: the multi-store model and the working memory model. Most theoretical models are expressed in vague verbal statements which can make it hard to decide whether the evidence fits the theory. As Murphy (2011) pointed out, verbal theories provide theorists with undesirable "wiggle room".

Let's consider an example of a theoretical model having wiggle room: Baddeley and Hitch's (1974) working memory model (see Chapter 3). We know the central executive component of working memory is an attention-like system. However, the precise range of processing functions carried out by the central executive remains unclear.

In spite of that limitation with the working memory model, we can use behavioural measures to make *inferences* about the nature of the central executive. In essence, we start with theoretical assumptions of the model. For example, Baddeley and Hitch (1974) assumed that the central executive has limited capacity. As a result, we can't perform two tasks successfully at the same time if they both require use of the central executive.

We can use the above assumption to make predictions. Hitch and Baddeley (1976) assumed that the task of remembering six random digits would involve the central executive. They required participants to do that task at the same time as a verbal reasoning task—participants were presented with a sentence followed by two letters and decided whether the order of the letters matched the sentence (e.g. A precedes B: BA). Hitch and Baddeley assumed this verbal reasoning task would also involve the central executive. That led to the prediction that performance on the reasoning task should be slowed down by the simultaneous task of memorising six random digits. That is precisely what they found.

Let's analyse the above study in more detail. The researchers did not assess the central executive directly. Therefore, they had to draw *inferences* about the meaning of their findings based on their theoretical model—they *inferred* that memorising six random digits requires the central executive, they *inferred* that performing a verbal reasoning task requires the central executive, and they *inferred* that performance impairment on the verbal reasoning task when performed together with memorising six digits meant that the limited capacity of the central executive had been exceeded.

Note that any (or all) of the above inferences could have been incorrect. However, and this is the key point, making these inferences in the context of the assumptions of the working memory model allowed Hitch and Baddeley (1976) to explain their findings. This may sound like a risky strategy. However, there is plentiful other research supporting these inferences and literally hundreds of studies have established the working memory model firmly as an outstanding contribution to our understanding of human cognition (Baddeley, 2012).

It is perhaps natural to think that progress in our understanding of internal mental processes occurs only when we consistently obtain experimental support for a theoretical model. However, that is *not* correct. Some of the most important findings have been those that have convincingly disproved theoretical models. We will briefly consider an example based on the multi-store model of memory discussed in Chapter 3.

It was assumed within the multi-store model that we possess a single long-term memory. The obvious prediction from that assumption is that brain-damaged patients who have problems with long-term memory should have impaired long-term memory for *all* types of information. This assumption was disproved by research on amnesic patients whose episodic memory is extremely poor. However, Spiers et al. (2001) in a review of 147 amnesic patients found that none had any significant problems with procedural memory (e.g. skill memory). These findings showed the multi-store model was wrong and suggested strongly that the internal processes associated with those two types of long-term memory were very different.

EVALUATION

- (+) Theoretical models provide a valuable framework within which researchers can decide which experiments are most worthwhile.
- (+) Theoretical models (e.g. the working memory model) have contributed massively to our enhanced understanding of internal mental processes.
- (+) There has been much progress as theoretical models are replaced by superior ones. A major example is the replacement of the multi-store model with the working memory model.
- (−) Many theoretical models are expressed rather vaguely and this makes it hard to test them experimentally.
- (−) Theoretical models present an oversimplified view of reality. For example, the working memory is concerned only with processing in the visual and auditory modalities but it is obvious that we can also process information in other sense modalities (e.g. touch; taste; smell).
- (−) All theoretical models (even the most successful ones) have had some of their assumptions disproved by experimental findings.

Computer models

It is obviously desirable to avoid the theoretical vagueness often found with theoretical models. How can that be achieved? As indicated briefly above, one influential answer is to make use of the computational cognitive science approach. This approach involves constructing computer programs that simulate or mimic human cognitive processes. The crucial point is that a computer model "requires the researcher to be explicit about a theory in a way that a verbal theory does not" (Murphy, 2011, p. 300). Implementing a theory in a computer program is a good way to check it contains no hidden assumptions or imprecise terms. This often reveals that the theory makes predictions the theorists concerned had not realised! Alternatively, the computer program may not work because essential information has been omitted.

Findings

We will briefly consider one of the earliest and most influential computer models within cognitive psychology. Newell and Simon (1972) were interested in the processes involved in problem solving. This led them to develop a computer program called General Problem Solver which was designed to solve a wide range of problems. They started by asking people to solve problems while thinking aloud. They then used these verbal reports to decide what general strategy was used on each problem. Finally, Newell and Simon specified the problem-solving strategy in sufficient detail for it to be programmed in their General Problem Solver.

What were the key assumptions of the General Problem Solver? First, it was assumed that information processing is serial (one process at a time). Second, it was assumed that people possess limited short-term memory capacity which means they typically use fairly simple rules of thumb during problem solving. One example is known as hill climbing because it resembles a climber trying to reach the top of a mountain by constantly moving upwards. This strategy does not work very well in mountain ranges where climbers may need to go downwards some of the time to reach the summit. Third, they assumed that people retrieve relevant information from long-term memory during problem solving.

The performance of the General Problem Solver was generally similar to that of humans on several problems. This discovery was hugely influential because it suggested that we rely much more heavily than had previously been imagined on simple strategies such as hill climbing. However, what Newell and Simon (1972) also learned was that there were some minor differences between their computer model and human behaviour—the model was better than humans at remembering what had already happened on a problem but inferior at planning future moves. This led to the development of improved computer models of problem-solving behaviour.

EVALUATION

- ⊕ The greatest strength of computer models is the precision with which their assumptions are stated.
- ⊕ Computer models increasingly build upon the strengths of previous related models while eliminating their weaknesses.
- ⊕ The computer model General Problem Solver has been enormously influential because it revealed that humans often use very simple rules of thumb when trying to solve problems.
- ⊖ Many computer models are designed mainly to account for existing experimental data and don't make any *new* predictions.
- ⊖ Computer models typically de-emphasise motivational and emotional factors relevant to cognition. As the British psychologist Stuart Sutherland said jokingly, he would only believe computers are like humans if one tried to run away with his wife!
- ⊖ Computer models present an oversimplified view of human cognition.

Emergence of cognitive neuroscience

One of the most difficult problems faced by cognitive psychologists is trying to identify people's internal mental processes when they are engaged in performing a task. Of course, behaviour (accuracy and speed of responding) provides useful information about internal processes but such information is fairly indirect.

There are various ways we can try to obtain more direct evidence about internal mental processes. However, the most exciting and important development over the past 20 years or so has been the rise of cognitive neuroscience. **Cognitive neuroscience** involves using information about brain activity as well as behaviour to understand human cognition.

The most important technique used by cognitive neuroscientists is **functional magnetic resonance imaging (fMRI)** (see Chapter 6). It involves the use of an MRI scanner containing a very heavy magnet (weighing up to 11 tons). fMRI allows us to work out very precisely which brain areas are activated during performance of a task.

One of the limitations with most brain-imaging techniques is that they reveal only associations or correlations between patterns of brain activity and behaviour. For example, performance on reasoning tasks is typically associated with activity

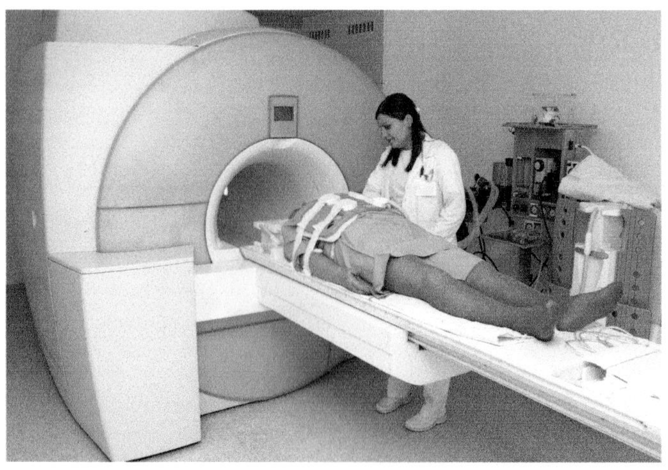

The magnetic resonanance imaging (MRI) scanner has proved an extremely valuable source of data in psychology.

KEY TERMS

Cognitive neuroscience: an approach that aims to understand human cognition by combining information from behaviour and the brain.

Functional magnetic resonance imaging (fMRI): a technique that provides detailed and accurate information concerning the brain areas activated during performance of a task.

within the prefrontal cortex. This is a purely correlational association and does not show that the brain regions activated are essential or required for task performance. For example, this brain activity might be caused by participants engaging in unnecessary monitoring of their performance or attending to non-task stimuli.

Findings

The cognitive neuroscience approach has become increasingly successful at shedding light on major theoretical controversies (there is further discussion of this point in Chapter 6). Here we will consider one example. There has been much controversy as to whether visual imagery resembles visual perception. Kosslyn (1994) argued that visual imagery involves mostly the same processes as visual perception. In contrast, Pylyshyn (2002) argued that visual imagery relies on relevant stored knowledge rather than visual images.

How can we decide between the above two theories given that most behavioural findings have provided inconclusive evidence? The early stages of visual processing involve areas located at the back of the brain within the occipital lobe. If visual imagery is very like visual perception, then we would expect these areas to be activated during a visual imagery task just as they are during visual perception. However, if visual imagery relies on stored knowledge, there is no reason why these areas would be activated during visual imagery. Kosslyn and Thompson (2003) carried out a meta-analysis based on numerous fMRI studies. Brain areas involved in early visual processing were generally activated provided that sensitive brain-imaging techniques were used.

Here is another example. Suppose we present listeners with degraded speech that is hard to understand. Wild et al. (2012) found with degraded speech that listeners rated it much clearer when the same sentence was presented visually at the same time (e.g. "His handwriting was very hard to read"). That finding is not at all surprising. However, there has been much controversy as to how to explain it. One possibility is that the visually presented sentence influences top-down processes—it allows listeners to predict and anticipate what is in the degraded speech. Another possibility is that the visually presented sentence influences bottom-up processes by enhancing early auditory processing of the degraded speech.

This controversy has proved very hard to resolve using behavioural data. Wild et al. (2012) adopted a cognitive neuroscience approach by assessing activity in brain areas associated with early auditory processing. There was more activity in these brain areas when a matching sentence was presented visually at the same time. Thus, an important reason why the matching sentence enhanced the perceptual clarity of the degraded speech was because it influenced bottom-up processes. This is the strongest evidence we have to support this theoretical viewpoint.

EVALUATION

- (+) Cognitive neuroscience has the advantage over experimental cognitive psychology of providing information about brain activity as well as behaviour.
- (+) Cognitive neuroscience provides us with very rich data concerning the brain areas associated with various internal mental processes (see Chapter 6 on Biopsychology).
- (+) As we have seen, cognitive neuroscience can contribute to the resolution of complex theoretical issues that had proved very hard to resolve using only behavioural data.
- (−) Cognitive neuroscience mostly provides only correlational data. For example, the finding that brain areas associated with early visual processing are often activated during visual imagery does not prove that these areas are causally involved in visual imagery.
- (−) It is proving very hard to identify patterns of brain activation corresponding to psychological processes (e.g. attention; planning).
- (−) Cognitive neuroscience suffers from most of the limitations of experimental cognitive psychology. For example, participants in fMRI studies (the most used technique) lie on their backs in claustrophobic and noisy conditions and have very restricted movement—this means there are problems with ecological validity (applicability to everyday life)!

OVERALL EVALUATION

- (+) The cognitive approach has led to the development of several major ways of studying human cognition. There has been substantial progress based on combinations of the four different approaches within cognitive psychology.
- (+) The cognitive approach is enormously flexible and can be applied to almost any aspect of human cognition.
- (+) Cognitive neuroscience provides very rich data and is increasingly resolving complex theoretical issues.
- (+) Theoretical models have clarified our understanding of human cognition and have been progressively improved over time.
- (+) Computer models have provided precise theoretical accounts of the various processes involved in human cognition.
- (−) One concern about the cognitive approach is that it depends mostly on laboratory research. As a result, its findings may not generalise to everyday life and so may lack **ecological validity**.
- (−) Cognitive neuroscientists typically assume that patterns of brain activation should relate fairly directly to psychological processes. As yet, it is unclear whether that assumption is correct.
- (−) Most research in cognitive neuroscience provides evidence of associations between brain activity and behaviour and doesn't prove the brain activity is causally necessary to produce the behaviour.
- (−) Many computer models don't make any new predictions.

Section Summary

Study of internal mental processes

- There are four major approaches within cognitive psychology:

  (i) Experimental cognitive psychology
  (ii) Cognitive neuropsychology
  (iii) Cognitive neuroscience
  (iv) Computational cognitive science

- All four approaches have different strengths and limitations and so the optimal strategy is to use all four approaches to study internal mental processes.
- Our understanding of short-term memory has been achieved by combining the experimental cognitive psychology and cognitive neuropsychology approaches.

Role of schema

- A schema is a well-integrated packet of knowledge about the world, events, people, or actions.
- Schemas allow us to form realistic expectations, to fill in the gaps while reading or listening, and can assist visual perception.
- Bartlett showed that there are systematic distortions due to schemas in people's memory for stories from a different culture.

KEY TERM

Ecological validity: the applicability (or otherwise) of the findings of laboratory and other research studies to everyday settings.

- Steyvers and Hemmer (2012) found with common types of visual scenes that schemas generally enhanced rather than distorted long-term memory.
- Schema theories are hard to test because we can't easily establish what information is contained in a schema nor do we know when any given schema will be activated.

Use of theoretical and computer models

- Theoretical models are typically expressed in verbal terms and are thus often somewhat vague.
- Theoretical models are a major factor in determining the kinds of experiments carried out by cognitive psychologists.
- Over time, most theoretical models are replaced by superior ones.
- Computer models are generally much more precise than theoretical models because they are expressed in the form of a computer program.
- Cognitive psychologists typically draw inferences about internal mental processes from experimental findings based on a theoretical model.
- Many computer models fail to make any new predictions.

Emergence of cognitive neuroscience

- Cognitive neuroscience provides useful information about brain activity as well as behaviour to enhance our understanding of human cognition.
- Cognitive neuroscience has proved very successful in resolving some major theoretical controversies.
- Cognitive neuroscience mostly provides only correlational data and fails to show that brain activity in any given area is essential or necessary for performance of a task.

BIOLOGICAL APPROACH

Caricature of Charles Darwin and his theory of natural selection, from 1871, showing him as an ape. He first published this concept of natural selection in The Origin of Species *(1859).*

It is now generally accepted that there are important links between psychology and biology (see Chapter 6). However, it was only after the publication of the book *The Origin of Species* by Charles Darwin that the relevance of biology to psychology began to be realised. Before its publication in 1859, people had assumed only human beings had minds, thus making us radically different from other species. The notion that human beings have evolved from other species meant this inflated view of the importance of the human species had to be re-assessed.

One of the main ways Darwin's thinking has influenced contemporary psychology is through the development of evolutionary psychology. **Evolutionary psychology** is built on the assumption that evolution has shaped our minds and behaviour as well as our bodies. As a result, much of our behaviour is adaptive, meaning it is well suited to the environments in which we find ourselves.

In this section, we will consider several ways in which psychology has benefitted from the biological approach. First, we discuss the relevance of evolution to understanding behaviour. Second, we consider the role played by genes in influencing behaviour. Third, we consider biological structures. Fourth, the focus shifts to the ways the study of neurochemistry has enhanced our understanding of behaviour.

KEY TERM

Evolutionary psychology: an approach to psychology based on the assumption that much human behaviour can be understood with reference to Darwin's theory of evolution.

Evolution and behaviour

Darwin's theory of evolution has had four major effects on psychology. First, psychologists began to develop theories of human psychology from the biological perspective. For example, Sigmund Freud's emphasis on the sex drive in humans would have been almost unthinkable before Darwin.

Second, an important lesson from Darwin's theory of evolution was that the study of non-human species could be of great value in understanding human behaviour. That helps to explain

The ability to wrestle with a mammoth went down well with the ladies.

why Pavlov's research on classical conditioning in dogs and Skinner's research on operant conditioning in rats and pigeons have had such a huge impact.

Third, Darwin argued that heredity is important in the development of a species and that offspring tend to resemble their parents. These ideas led psychologists to explore the role of heredity in influencing human behaviour. They also led to renewed interest in the issue of the relative importance of heredity and environment (the nature–nurture debate) in influencing human behaviour.

Fourth, Darwin focused on variation among the members of a species. According to his notion of survival of the fittest, evolution favours those members of a species best equipped to live in a given environment. These ideas led to an interest in individual differences and the study of intelligence and personality. The notion of survival is also important for a somewhat different reason. Humans have developed language, become more intelligent, are responsive to major environmental threats, and so on, in part because these developments have increased the chances of surviving and reproducing.

Several theories have been based on the assumption that much human behaviour can be explained in evolutionary terms. Here we will focus on evolutionary accounts of obsessive–compulsive disorder and specific phobia (these disorders are discussed in detail in Chapter 7 on Psychopathology).

Obsessive–compulsive disorder (OCD)

Obsessive–compulsive disorder (OCD) involves recurrent intrusive thoughts (obsessions) and repetitive behaviours (compulsions). What is puzzling about OCD is that most obsessions and compulsions revolve around contamination and predation (the preying of one animal on others) even though there are numerous other obsessions and compulsions from which OCD patients might suffer.

Szechtman and Woody (2004) argued that issues of hygiene and contamination and of predation were of huge importance in our evolutionary past (and remain so today in many parts of the world). As a result, humans developed a security motivation system designed to detect such potential dangers and prevent them from becoming life-threatening. That makes much sense because millions of our ancestors died because of unhygienic conditions or by being killed by wild animals. The security motivation system has an "easy-to-turn-on, hard-to-turn-off quality" because a single failure to be vigilant to life-threatening dangers can prove fatal. We all have a security motivation system, but OCD patients find it much harder than healthy individuals to turn it off.

Hinds et al. (2010) asked healthy participants to put their hands into a pile of soiled-looking nappies. This created a state of high activation indicating the involvement of the security motivation system. Of particular importance, activation remained high for several minutes after the removal of their hands from the nappies until the participants were allowed to wash their hands. This indicates that it can be hard to switch the security motivation system off.

Hinds et al. (2012) studied OCD patients with washing compulsions and healthy controls. Both groups were exposed to contamination (immersing a hand in a wet nappy). The intensity of activation of the security motivation system was comparable in both groups. However, as predicted, the OCD patients were less able than the controls to reduce this activation by hand washing.

Specific phobia

Specific phobia involves strong and irrational fear of a specific object or situation (see Chapter 7). There are numerous different specific phobias. However, phobias concerning spiders or snakes are especially common. This is puzzling given that millions of people have practically never seen any snakes or spiders! It is also noteworthy that people rarely develop specific phobias for potentially dangerous objects that have been invented only recently (e.g. cars).

Seligman (1970) argued we can understand the frequency of different specific phobias in evolutionary terms. He used the term **preparedness** to describe our tendency to develop fears most easily to objects (e.g. snakes; spiders) that posed real threats to humans earlier in our evolutionary past. In contrast, few people suffer from car phobia because there were no cars in our ancestral past.

KEY TERM

Preparedness: the notion that we develop fears more easily and rapidly for some objects (e.g. snakes) than for others (e.g. cars) because of our evolutionary past.

If humans are especially susceptible to snake and spider phobia for evolutionary reasons, we might expect they would be harder to treat than other specific phobias. However, that is *not* the case. Thus, snake and spider phobias may be less special than assumed by Seligman (1970). In addition, as pointed out in Chapter 7 (Psychopathology), numerous phobias such as *cherophobia* (fear of gaiety) or *triskaidekaphobia* (fear of the number 13) can't be explained in evolutionary terms.

EXAM HINT

Although the approaches section is primarily theoretical in content, when evaluating any approach you can comment on common issues in the methods favoured by that approach and illustrate these with examples of research studies.

The most significant problem with the methods used in the biological approach is a lack of causal evidence. Evolutionary explanations necessarily tend to be "post-hoc"—i.e they explain "after the fact", rather than making predictions in advance and then testing them. Genetic explanations have tended in the past to rely on correlational relationships between pairs of family members, although human genome research is improving the available evidence here. Neural and biochemical explanations sometimes rely on correlations between biological evidence and psychological experience in which it is impossible to say for certain which is the causal factor—for example in the treatment of depression with selective serotonin re-uptake inhibitors (SSRIs).

EVALUATION

+ "Evolutionary psychology may serve as the umbrella idea (i.e. an overarching scheme) so desperately needed in the social sciences" (de Waal, 2002, p. 187).

+ Evolutionary psychology has produced several original insights on many topics including explaining why OCD patients have certain obsessions and compulsions and why more people have spider phobia or snake phobia than other phobias.

− Evolutionary psychology needs to "put a little less evolution and a little more psychology into its explanations" (de Waal, 2002, p. 189). In other words, it needs to consider more fully the role of learning and culture in modifying the impact of evolution on our behaviour.

− The predictions of evolutionary psychology are often rather vague. For example, Pinker (1997, p. 42) argued as follows: "Our minds are designed to generate behaviour that would have been adaptive in our ancestral environment." However, we generally don't know precisely what would or would not have been adaptive in our evolutionary past.

− Evolutionary psychology seems to assume the behaviour of humans is relatively *rigid* and *inflexible* because of its evolutionary origins. In contrast, cognitive psychology (which has proved very successful) emphasises the enormous *flexibility* of human thinking and behaviour.

Genetic basis of behaviour

One of the great limitations of Darwin's theory was that it did not specify the *mechanisms* involved in inheritance. Thus, Darwin failed to answer the question, "How are characteristics passed on from one generation to the next?" We now know genes are of vital importance. The **gene** is the unit of hereditary transmission.

What is the nature of genes? In essence, **chromosomes** are strands of **deoxyribonucleic acid (DNA)** bearing the genes. Chromosomes occur in matched pairs, with humans having 23 pairs of chromosomes in each of their body cells. Each strand of DNA consists of a sequence of four nucleotide bases (adenine, thymine, guanine, and cytosine) arranged in a particular order and these strands essentially form the genetic code. The two strands of DNA forming each chromosome are coiled around each other in a double helix (i.e. spiral) pattern. These

KEY TERMS

Gene: the unit of hereditary transmission.

Chromosomes: strands of DNA bearing the genes.

Deoxyribonucleic acid (DNA): double-stranded coils of molecules of genetic material forming chromosomes.

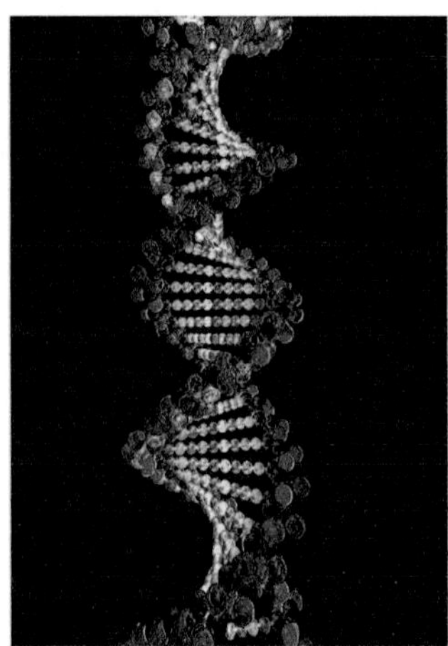

The two strands of DNA forming each chromosome are coiled around each other in a double helix pattern.

KEY TERMS

Meiosis: the process of forming gametes (sex cells); the chromosomes divide with one chromosome in each pair forming a separate gamete.

Gametes: sperm cells and egg cells formed by the process of meiosis.

Zygote: a fertilised egg cell.

Mitosis: this is a form of cell division in which the original nucleus divides into two nuclei with the same number of chromosomes as the original nucleus.

Monozygotic twins: identical twins derived from a single fertilised ovum (egg) and sharing 100% of their genes.

Dizygotic twins: fraternal twins derived from two fertilised ova (eggs) and sharing 50% of their genes.

Genotype: an individual's potential in the form of genes provided at the time of conception.

Phenotype: an individual's observable characteristics determined by his/her genotype plus environmental experiences.

Reduced penetrance: the finding that some individuals with a disease-causing genotype fail to develop the disease.

strands are bonded together, with guanine on one strand binding with cytosine on the other strand, and with adenine binding with thymine.

What happens during sexual reproduction? There is **meiosis**, which is a process of forming sperm cells and egg cells (known as **gametes**). More specifically, the chromosomes divide, with one chromosome of each pairing forming a separate gamete. When fertilisation occurs, a sperm cell and an egg cell combine to form a **zygote**, which is a fertilised egg cell. Meiosis is very important because it plays a major role in human genetic diversity.

What happens after the formation of a zygote is **mitosis**—this is a process in which the number of chromosomes doubles, followed by a division of the cell to create two cells, each of which has 23 pairs of chromosomes. Mitosis occurs repeatedly during the entire course of development and involves re-creating huge numbers of copies of the original zygote.

Of particular importance are the two sex chromosomes X and Y. Female mammals have two X chromosomes whereas male mammals have an X and a Y. During reproduction, the male contributes an X or a Y chromosome and the female always contributes an X chromosome. If the male contributes a Y chromosome the offspring will be male, whereas it will be female if the male contributes an X chromosome.

When we compare ourselves with other species, we discover some uncomfortable similarities. For example, human beings and chimpanzees share more than 98% of their DNA. More surprisingly, we share 70% of our genes with sea sponges (Srivastava et al., 2010) and they have almost 90% as many genes as us. Perhaps we should regard the apparently humble sponge with more respect!

Our knowledge of genetic transmission allows us to understand the extent of genetic similarity (or degree of relatedness) between family members. We know children share 50% of their genetic material with each of their parents, that siblings also share 50% of their genetic material, that the figure is 25% for grandparents and grandchildren, and that it is 12.5% for first cousins.

Of most importance, **monozygotic twins** (identical twins) have the same genetic make-up whereas **dizygotic twins** (fraternal twins) share only 50% of their genetic make-up. This is because identical twins come from the same fertilised egg whereas fraternal twins come from two different eggs. As we will see shortly, comparisons between monozygotic and dizygotic twins have proved extremely valuable in understanding the role played by genetic factors in many forms of behaviour.

Influence of genes on behaviour: Genotype and phenotype

It is important when considering genetic influences to distinguish between the genotype and the phenotype. The **genotype** is the genetic make-up of any given individual. The genotype corresponds to the genome, which is an organism's full genetic complement.

In contrast, the **phenotype** consists of an individual's observable or visible characteristics (e.g. intelligence; height; personality) that are determined jointly by his/her genotype plus the environment he/she has experienced throughout life. More generally, the phenotype consists of an organism's physical and psychological characteristics. As we will see shortly, genetic and environmental influences should not be seen as totally independent of each other—an individual's genotype often influences the environments chosen by him/her.

There are more differences between the genotype and the phenotype than you might imagine. For example, such differences have been found within the cerebral cortex. Hyde et al. (2009) studied the brains of 6-year-old children who received 15 months of instrumental musical training. This training produced significant changes in the primary auditory area and the primary motor area—thus, the phenotype in these brain areas differed from the genotype as a result of training.

Some of the differences between the genotype and phenotype can be explained on the basis that some genes have **reduced penetrance**, meaning that a disease-causing genotype does *not* lead to that disease in all individuals possessing that particular genotype. The classic example is phenylketonuria, a disease causing severe intellectual impairment. Individuals with the genotype for this disease invariably develop it if given a normal diet. However, individuals with the genotype who have a life-long diet with restricted phenylalanine typically manage to lead fairly healthy lives. Thus, whether the genotype for phenylketonuria leads to that disease depends on environmental factors.

Genes and behaviour

Below we consider the question of the extent to which genetic factors are important in determining individual differences in intelligence. It would be very valuable to be able to assess the genotype for intelligence directly. This is not currently possible but some progress has been made in identifying genes associated with high or low intelligence. However, we can assess the phenotype for intelligence by measuring an individual's level of intelligence. In similar fashion, we can gain some insight into the role of genetic factors in determining the existence of several mental disorders (see Chapter 6).

Family and twin studies

Why is knowledge of genetic relatedness within families of value to psychologists trying to understand human behaviour? The answer is straightforward. It allows us to shed some light on the nature–nurture controversy. Suppose we want to know the extent to which individual differences in intelligence are influenced by genetic factors. We could carry out a study assessing intelligence within a large number of families. We would use an intelligence test to assess each individual's intelligence quotient (IQ) as a measure of the phenotype. This is a measure of general intelligence: the average IQ in the population is 100 and most people have IQs between 85 and 115.

If genetic factors are of importance, we can make various predictions. Identical twins should resemble each other more in intelligence than fraternal twins. More generally, the greater the similarity in genetic make-up between family members, the more similar they should be with respect to intelligence.

Identical twins offer the opportunity to study the effects of nature and nurture. They are the same genetically so any differences in their behaviour should be due to the environment.

The degree of similarity in intelligence shown by pairs of twins is usually reported in the form of a correlation which is a measure of the strength of association between two measures. A correlation of +1.0 would mean both twins in a pair have exactly the same IQ whereas a correlation of 0.0 would indicate no relationship at all.

McCartney et al. (1990) considered the findings from numerous twin studies. The average correlation for identical twins was +.81 compared to +.59 for fraternal twins. Thus, identical twins are more alike in intelligence than fraternal twins, which suggests that genetic factors influence individual differences in intelligence. However, note that the environments may be more similar for identical than for fraternal twins and so the findings may be somewhat misleading. Note also that the correlation for identical twins is nothing like +1.00, and so we can be certain that environmental factors are important.

Bouchard and McGue (1981) used meta-analysis to assess the similarity of IQ between different pairs of relatives. As predicted, relatives having greater genetic similarity tended to be more similar in IQ. For example, the average correlation between siblings was +.47, whereas it was +.31 for half-siblings and +.15 for cousins.

It is important to note there are two kinds of genetic influence on intelligence. First, there is a *direct* genetic influence. Second, there is an *indirect* genetic influence on intelligence in which genetic factors help to determine the environments in which an individual finds himself/herself. For example, individuals of high genetic ability are far more likely to obtain A levels and go on to university than those of low genetic ability and this enhances their intellectual ability. As Dickens and Flynn (2001, p. 347) pointed out, "Higher IQ leads one into better environments causing still higher IQ, and so on."

? **What are the limitations of using twin studies to investigate the nature–nurture debate?**

A problem in interpreting the findings from twin studies is the possibility that identical twins tend to experience more similar environments than fraternal twins. If that is the case, the higher correlation for identical twins might be due to environmental factors rather than heredity. Identical twins spend more time together than fraternal twins and their parents are more likely to try to treat them exactly alike (Loehlin & Nichols, 1976).

We can address the above issue by studying the small number of identical twins separated in early life and then reared apart. Such twins are of special interest because they have the same heredity but grow up in a different environment. Bouchard et al. (1990) studied adult identical twin pairs separated at a mean age of 5 months. Even though these twin pairs had been separated in infancy, their IQs correlated +.75. The findings suggest genetic factors are important in determining individual differences in intelligence because the figure of +.75 is higher than that for fraternal twins brought up together (+.59). However, the finding that identical twins brought up apart are less similar in IQ than those brought up together (+.75 vs +.81) indicates that environmental factors are also important.

There has been a substantial amount of research on genetic factors in intelligence. However, genetic factors have been shown to be important with respect to numerous aspects of behaviour. Bouchard and McGue (2003) discussed some of this research. They identified very strong evidence that individual differences in personality depend in part on genetic factors. Even social attitudes (e.g. attitudes towards death penalty, abortion, and foreign aid) have been found to be determined to some extent by genetic factors.

We turn now to genetic influences on mental disorders. A key measure here is the **concordance rate**—the probability if one twin has a disorder that the other twin also has the same disorder. If genetic factors are important, the concordance rate should be higher for identical twins than for fraternal ones.

Several mental disorders are discussed in Chapter 7 (Psychopathology), and there is evidence from twin studies that all of them depend in part on genetic factors. For example, Loken et al. (2014) found in a meta-analysis that identical twins had a significantly higher concordance rate than fraternal twins for specific phobia, social phobia, and agoraphobia. McGuffin et al. (1996) found that identical twins had a higher concordance rate than fraternal twins for major depressive disorder, and Craddock and Jones (1999) found the same for bipolar disorder. Similar findings were reported in a meta-analysis by van Grootheest et al. (2005) for obsessive–compulsive disorder (OCD).

If genetic factors were totally responsible for any given mental disorder, then we would predict the concordance rate for identical twins would be 100%. In fact, concordance rates for identical twins for nearly all mental disorders are considerably lower than that. Thus, it is clear that environmental factors (e.g. life events) also play a very important role in determining mental disorders.

Nestadt et al. (2000) found in a family study that the concordance rate for OCD was greater for family members who were more closely related genetically. A potential problem here is that family members who are more closely related may share more similar environments (as well as heredity) than those who are less closely related.

Influence of biological structures on behaviour

Biological structures within the central nervous system are far more important than those anywhere else in the body in terms of their effects on behaviour (see Chapter 6). Our starting point for considering biological structures is the notion that the central nervous system is organised hierarchically (see Figure). The upper levels of the hierarchy are shown at the top of the figure; these levels developed most recently in evolutionary terms.

The top level of the hierarchy is the cerebral cortex, which is easily the most important biological structure in the brain. We differ from other mammalian species mostly with respect to the development of the cerebral cortex. Accordingly, we will focus mainly on the cerebral cortex but will also discuss other biological structures lower in the hierarchy.

KEY TERM

Concordance rate: in twin studies, the probability that if one twin has a given characteristic or disorder the other twin also has the same characteristic or disorder.

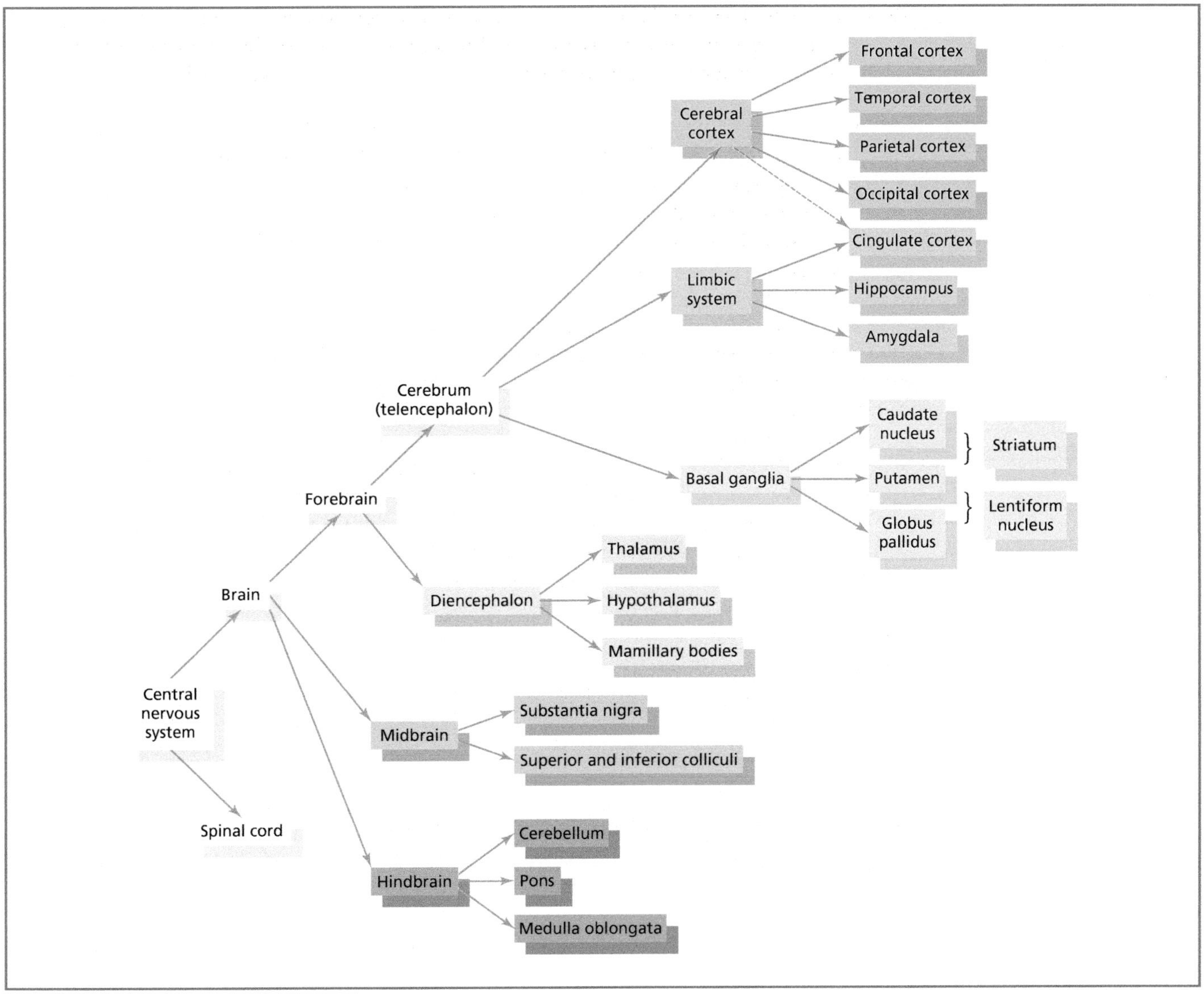

- Central nervous system
  - Brain
    - Forebrain
      - Cerebrum (telencephalon)
        - Cerebral cortex
          - Frontal cortex
          - Temporal cortex
          - Parietal cortex
          - Occipital cortex
          - Cingulate cortex
        - Limbic system
          - Cingulate cortex
          - Hippocampus
          - Amygdala
        - Basal ganglia
          - Caudate nucleus
          - Putamen
          - Globus pallidus
          - (Caudate nucleus, Putamen: Striatum)
          - (Putamen, Globus pallidus: Lentiform nucleus)
      - Diencephalon
        - Thalamus
        - Hypothalamus
        - Mamillary bodies
    - Midbrain
      - Substantia nigra
      - Superior and inferior colliculi
    - Hindbrain
      - Cerebellum
      - Pons
      - Medulla oblongata
  - Spinal cord

The central nervous system (CNS) is organized hierarchically. The upper levels of the hierarchy, corresponding to the upper branches of this diagram, are the newest structures from an evolutionary perspective.

Cerebral cortex

The cerebral cortex consists of two very thin (3 mm thick) folded sheets, one in each brain hemisphere. It is divided into four lobes (structurally distinct areas). These lobes are as follows (see Figure): the frontal lobes; the parietal lobes; the temporal lobes; and the occipital lobes.

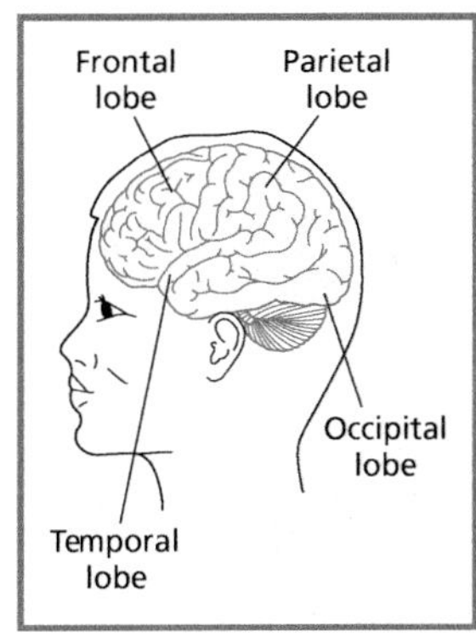

We can obtain some indication of the importance of the cerebral cortex for behaviour by considering individuals lacking it. Shewmon et al. (1999) studied four children born with a total or near-total absence of cerebral cortex. These children showed some evidence of musical discrimination (e.g. preferring some kinds of music to others) and an ability to recognise their mother. However, these very limited abilities represent a minute fraction of the cognitive abilities possessed by children with an intact cerebral cortex.

The four lobes of the cerebral cortex differ in what they do and their relevance for behaviour. How do we know which functions are associated with which areas within the cerebral cortex? Much of the evidence comes from brain-damaged patients. For example, patients who have suffered damage to a part of the limbic system known as the hippocampus have very severe problems with long-term memory (see Chapter 3).

Other evidence comes from the use of brain-imaging techniques. If certain brain areas are consistently activated when people are engaged in certain cognitive processes (e.g. attention) that is reasonable (but not conclusive) evidence that those cognitive processes involve those brain areas. It is perhaps natural to assume each brain region is specialised for a different function: this is **functional specialisation**. This assumption has been popular ever since the advent of phrenology about 200 years ago. **Phrenology** is the notion that individual differences in various mental faculties are revealed by bumps on the skull.

In spite of its popularity, the notion of functional specialisation is only partly correct. How do we know that? Key evidence comes from brain-imaging studies using functional magnetic resonance imaging (fMRI). If there is extensive functional specialisation, we would expect rather limited brain areas to be involved during the performance of any given task. In fact, what is typically found is that many brain areas are active simultaneously. (Note that there is a thorough discussion of functional specialisation in the brain in Chapter 6, Biopsychology.)

Sternberg (1995, p. 93) summarised the functions of the four lobes as follows: "Higher thought processes, such as abstract reasoning and motor processing, occur in the frontal lobe, somatosensory processing (sensations in the skin and muscles of the body) in the parietal lobe, auditory processing in the temporal lobe, and visual processing in the occipital lobe." These issues are discussed much more fully in Chapter 6.

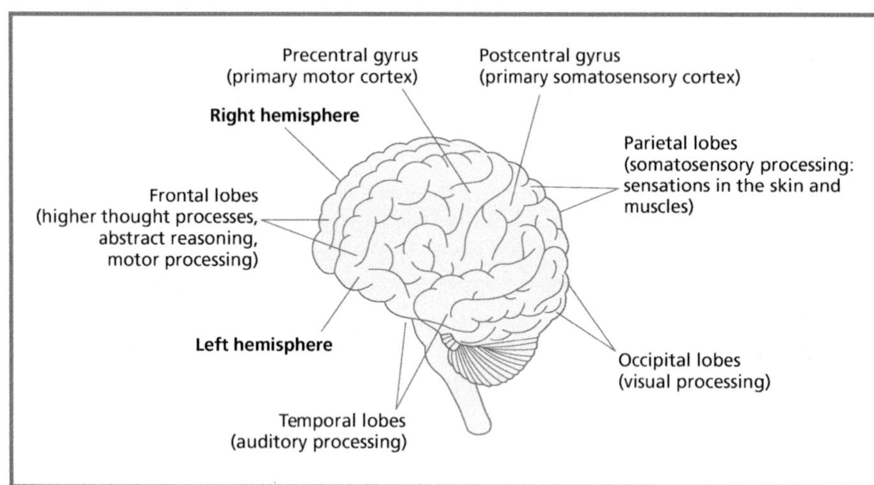

The frontal lobe (especially the area known as the prefrontal cortex) is of central importance with respect to most complex forms of thinking. Consider brain-damaged patients who have suffered damage to the frontal lobe. Such patients have **dysexecutive syndrome** meaning they have problems with planning, organising, monitoring their own behaviour, and initiating behaviour (see Chapter 3). In addition, for example, Duncan and Owen (2000) found the same areas within the prefrontal lobes were activated when very different complex tasks were performed.

The frontal lobes contain the primary motor cortex. This is involved in the planning and control of movements. Far more of the primary motor cortex is devoted to those parts of the body involved in making very precise movements (e.g. the fingers) than to those that do not (e.g. the toes).

The parietal lobe contains the primary somatosensory cortex. This area receives information from the various senses about temperature, pain, and pressure. Those parts of the body most represented in the primary motor cortex also tend to be well represented in the primary somatosensory cortex.

The temporal lobe is involved in auditory processing. The most important form of this processing is speech perception, which along with other aspects of language processing typically occurs mostly in the left hemisphere.

The occipital lobe (at the back of the head) plays a key role in vision, especially the early stages of visual processing. However, the temporal and parietal lobes are also involved. As much as 50% of the entire cerebral cortex is devoted to visual processing.

Limbic system

The limbic system consists of several structures including the hippocampus, the amygdala, and the cingulate cortex. We have already seen that the hippocampus plays a central role in long-term memory except with respect to memories for previous skill learning.

The amygdala is much involved in emotional processing of various kinds. The amygdala is strongly activated when people are confronted by emotional pictures or situations (Eysenck & Keane, 2015). Patients with a disease that destroys the amygdala have worse long-term memory impairment for emotional pictures (whether emotionally positive or negative) than for neutral pictures (Siebert et al., 2003).

KEY TERMS

Functional specialisation: the assumption that each brain area or region is specialised for a specific function (e.g. colour processing; face processing).

Phrenology: the notion that each mental faculty is located in a different part of the brain and can be assessed by feeling bumps on the head.

Dysexecutive syndrome: a condition in which damage to the frontal lobes causes widespread impairments to higher-level cognitive processes (e.g. planning; organising).

Finally, there is the cingulate cortex. This is involved in the detection of cognitive and emotional conflicts. There is much evidence that this area is activated when people have to make a decision between two or more options (Eysenck & Keane, 2015).

In sum, the limbic system "is involved in relating the organism to its present and past environment" (Ward, 2010, p. 28).

Basal ganglia

The basal ganglia assist in the regulation of motor activity and the programming of action. We can see the importance of the basal ganglia by considering research on patients with Parkinson's disease, a progressive neurological disorder involving damage to that area. Most research on skill learning (which requires making appropriate motor movements) indicates that Parkinson's patients have impaired performance (Foerde & Shohamy, 2011).

Forebrain

The forebrain contains the thalamus and hypothalamus. The thalamus acts as a relay station passing signals on to higher brain centres for all senses except smell. As is discussed later in the chapter, the hypothalamus is importantly involved in several functions. These include controlling hunger and thirst, sexual activity, and body temperature.

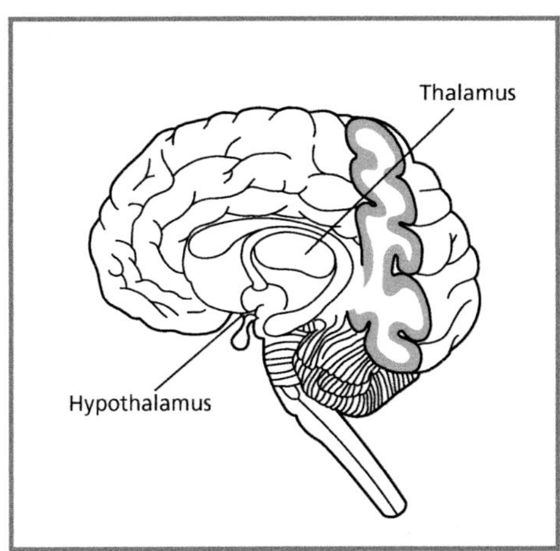

Midbrain

The midbrain is relatively smaller in mammals (including humans) than it is in reptiles, birds, or fish. Parts of it are used as routes for sensory information and other parts play a role in controlling arousal. Damage to one part of the midbrain (the substantia nigra) can lead to the onset of Parkinson's disease, in which there is increasing poor control of motor movements.

Hindbrain

Different areas within the hindbrain are involved in different processes. The medulla is involved in the control of breathing, salivation, and the regulation of the cardiovascular system. The medulla and the pons together are involved in controlling levels of arousal and are of relevance to consciousness. The cerebellum is involved in the control of balance and movement.

EVALUATION

The biological structures of the central nervous system all play an important role in regulating and controlling human behaviour. The development of cognitive neuroscience and sophisticated techniques for examining brain activity mean we have an increasing understanding of the roles played by different brain regions in determining behaviour. Part of this increased understanding has involved moving away from the notion of functional specialisation and towards the notion of brain networks involving several different brain areas.

What are the limitations of research in this area? First, brain-imaging data provide only correlational evidence and so cannot directly show whether any given brain area is necessary for a given cognitive process. Second, research on brain-damaged patients is important but has some problems. Suppose we find that damage to brain area X is associated with impaired attention. That might mean that area X is required for attention. Alternatively, damage to brain area X may simply prevent brain activity reaching brain area Y which is the one that is truly required. By analogy, a television set will not work if there is a loose wire in the plug, but discovering that is the case does not actually tell us much about how televisions work. Third, all biological structures within the central nervous system work in a co-ordinated and interactive fashion hard to examine in detail.

Influence of neurochemistry on behaviour

Neurochemistry is concerned with the study of chemical processes in the nervous system. More specifically, it deals with the effects of neurotransmitters and psychoactive drugs. **Neurotransmitters** are chemical substances that permit communication between neurons and **psychoactive drugs** are drugs that act on the nervous system and influence mental activity.

It has been claimed that the neurotransmitter dopamine (the "reward molecule") increases happiness and that a deficit in the neurotransmitter serotonin causes depression or sadness. One approach to studying these claims is to see if there is an association between individuals' levels of dopamine and serotonin and their happiness and depression levels. However, this would only be correlational evidence and would not allow us to conclude these neurotransmitters *cause* certain mood states.

More direct evidence concerning the influence of neurochemistry on behaviour can be obtained by administering psychoactive drugs or drugs designed to treat mental disorders that affect chemical processes. This would allow us to manipulate the levels of certain neurotransmitters to see whether these manipulations produced the predicted effects. We will briefly consider the evidence.

KEY TERMS

Neurochemistry: the study of chemical phenomena and processes that influence the nervous system and behaviour.

Neurotransmitters: chemical substances by which a neuron is able to communicate with another neuron.

Psychoactive drugs: drugs that operate primarily on the nervous system and influence mental and emotional states.

Cocaine

Cocaine comes from the leaves of the coca shrub which is found in countries such as Peru, Colombia, and Bolivia. It is a powerful drug having very strong rewarding or reinforcing properties. Cocaine influences people's behaviour by making them more talkative and energetic. Sigmund Freud, who often took cocaine, described "the exhilaration and lasting euphoria… You perceive an increase of self-control and possess more vitality and capacity for work" (1885/1950, p. 9).

What effects does cocaine have on brain chemistry? It blocks the re-uptake of the neurotransmitters dopamine, serotonin, and noradrenaline. That means cocaine prevents these neurotransmitters being re-absorbed by the neurons that released them and so increases their concentration in the synapses. Blocking the re-uptake of noradrenaline causes increased energy, blocking the re-uptake of serotonin increases confidence, and blocking the re-uptake of dopamine increases pleasure and can also increase dependency.

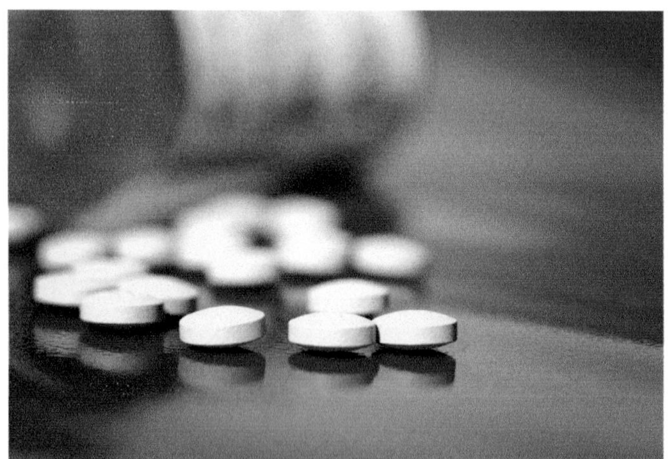

Drug therapy is used extensively in the treatment of depressive disorder. However, studies show that placebo pills also show beneficial effects, suggesting that expectations about the effectiveness of drug therapy plays a part in the treatment.

Drug therapy

Many forms of drug therapy for mental disorders involve the use of drugs designed to increase or decrease the levels of certain neurotransmitters. For example, it has been claimed obsessive–compulsive disorder (OCD) is associated with a deficiency of the neurotransmitter serotonin (see Chapter 7). Accordingly, this led to the development of drug therapy involving serotonin re-uptake inhibitors (SRIs) and selective serotonin re-uptake inhibitors (SSRIs) of which Prozac is probably the best known. Both classes of drugs are designed to increase the concentration of serotonin. As predicted, they are moderately effective in the treatment of OCD (Eddy et al., 2004).

As discussed in Chapter 7, the mechanisms underlying the effectiveness of SRIs and SSRIs in treating OCD are not as simple as the above account might suggest. It is not clear that OCD patients have low levels of serotonin and the drugs' effectiveness does not depend in any simple way on raising serotonin levels. In addition, brain functioning is very complex. Even if SRIs and SSRIs were shown to increase serotonin levels they undoubtedly have many other effects and increased serotonin levels would influence the levels of other neurotransmitters.

SRIs and SSRIs are also used extensively in the treatment of major depressive disorder. The rationale for using these drugs to treat depression is that depression is associated with low levels of serotonin and the drugs increase the concentration of serotonin—a similar logic to that used to justify the drugs' use with OCD. There is evidence that *blood* levels of serotonin are lower in individuals suffering from depression but it does not necessarily follow that *brain* levels of serotonin are also lower. In any case, reduced levels of serotonin in depressed patients might occur because low serotonin helps to cause depression but it could also occur because being depressed reduces serotonin levels.

There are also some doubts about whether the effectiveness of SRIs and SSRIs in the treatment of depression depends mostly on increased concentration levels of serotonin. For example, depressed patients given a placebo pill (an inactive substance) but led to expect it will reduce their level of depression often show beneficial effects—this is a **placebo effect** (Horder et al., 2011). That strongly suggests that some of the beneficial effects of SRIs and SSRIs are due to expectations about the drugs' effectiveness rather than simply their effects on brain neurochemistry.

Further doubts were raised by Angoa-Perez et al. (2014). They developed mice lacking the ability to produce serotonin in their brains. Unexpectedly, they did not exhibit depression-like symptoms. The mice were exposed to a stressful situation and then given SSRIs. Some responded positively to the drugs even though they could not produce any serotonin. While these findings are striking, the fact that the study involved mice means we need to be wary about generalising the findings to humans.

EVALUATION

- (+) It is indisputable that neurotransmitters have a substantial impact on our internal states and our behaviour.
- (+) There is evidence that mental disorders such as OCD and depression involve neurotransmitter abnormalities.
- (+) Successful therapy for several mental disorders including depression and OCD has often involved drugs that influence neurotransmitters in the brain.
- (−) The greatest problem with neurochemistry is that the workings of the brain are incredibly complex and interactive. Thus, for example, if we administer a drug designed to increase serotonin levels, it is likely to have widespread effects on other neurotransmitters and brain processes (Kringelbach & Berridge, 2009).
- (−) Even if OCD and depression are associated with low serotonin levels, that does not provide causal evidence proving low serotonin levels cause these disorders.
- (−) It has proved very hard to explain in detail precisely *why* and *how* any given drug exerts its effects on mental processes and behaviour.
- (−) The finding that there is a placebo effect in the treatment of depression suggests some of the beneficial effects of SRIs and SSRIs are due to expectations rather than changes to brain neurochemistry.

Section Summary

Evolution and behaviour

- Darwin's theory of evolution has had four major effects on psychology: (1) it led to biologically-influenced theories; (2) it led psychologists to argue that studying non-human species could be informative about the human species; (3) it led to an interest in heredity; and (4) it focused attention on individual differences.
- Mental disorders such as obsessive–compulsive disorder and specific phobias can be understood in evolutionary terms.

KEY TERM

Placebo effect: positive responses to an inactive substance or form of therapy based on the patient's beliefs that the substance or therapy will be effective, rather than on the actual make-up of the drug or therapy.

- Evolutionary psychology often de-emphasises the role of learning and culture in modifying the impact of evolution on human behaviour.
- Evolutionary psychologists sometimes exaggerate the rigidity and inflexibility of human behaviour.

Genetic basis of behaviour

- Genes are the units of hereditary transmission.
- Chromosomes are strands of DNA bearing the genes; they occur in matched pairs in humans.
- Our knowledge of genetic transmission allows us to understand the extent of genetic similarity between family members. Identical twins share 100% of their genetic material, fraternal twins share 50% of their genetic material, and children share 50% of their genetic material with each of their parents whereas the figure is 25% for grandparents and grandchildren.

Influence of genes on behaviour: Genotype and phenotype

- The genotype is an individual's genetic make-up whereas the phenotype consists of his/her observable physical and psychological characteristics.
- An individual's phenotype is determined jointly by his/her genotype and environmental experiences.
- Twin and family studies indicate that individual differences in intelligence depend importantly on genetic factors. Some of these genetic influences are indirect—individuals with high genetic ability generally put themselves in environments (e.g. sixth form colleges; university) that enhance their intellectual ability.
- Environmental factors are also very important in determining individual differences in intelligence.
- Twin studies have indicated that genetic factors influence individual differences in personality, social attitudes, and many mental disorders.

Influence of biological structures

- Biological structures within the central nervous system are arranged in a hierarchy with the cerebral cortex at the top.
- There is some functional specialisation within the cerebral cortex but networks consisting of several brain areas are very common.
- The four lobes of the cerebral cortex differ in their functions: the frontal lobes are involved in complex cognitive processing, the occipital lobe in visual processing, the temporal lobe in auditory processing, and the parietal lobe in somatosensory processing.
- The limbic system is involved in long-term memory and emotional processing. The basal ganglia are involved in the regulation of motor activity and the programming of action. The forebrain is used as a route for sensory information and it is also involved in controlling arousal. The hindbrain is involved in the control of breathing, salivation, arousal, and the control of balance.
- Brain imaging and the study of brain-damaged patients have limitations as methods for identifying the functions of different brain areas. It is hard to understand the complex interactions of different biological structures within the central nervous system.

Influence of neurochemistry

- In principle, we can understand the impact of various neurotransmitters on behaviour fairly directly by administering drugs.
- The very strong rewarding properties of cocaine occur because increased serotonin enhances confidence, increased dopamine increases pleasure, and increased noradrenaline increases energy.
- It has often been claimed that OCD and depression are characterised by low serotonin levels and that SRIs and SSRIs are effective because they increase serotonin levels.

- Any association between OCD or depression and low serotonin levels could be because the disorders cause reduced serotonin levels rather than the opposite direction of causality.
- It is not clear that the beneficial effects of SRIs and SSRIs on the symptoms of OCD and depression are due to increased serotonin levels.
- Brain neurochemistry is so complex (and the interactions among neurotransmitters so common) that it is very difficult to determine precisely the mechanisms by which drugs and neurotransmitters influence behaviour.

PSYCHODYNAMIC APPROACH

Note: the psychodynamic approach is on the A2 specification, but not the AS one.

The psychodynamic approach has been advocated by numerous theorists over the years. However, the first (and easily the most famous) theorist to propose a psychodynamic approach was the Austrian psychologist Sigmund Freud (1856–1939). The **psychodynamic approach** is based on the assumption that mental disorders have their origins in psychological factors rather than physical or biological ones. More specifically, unresolved unconscious conflicts are of central importance in triggering metal disorders. It follows that treatment for mental disorders should be psychological in nature—this led Freud to develop psychoanalysis as a method of treatment.

The term "psychodynamic" refers to a group of explanations designed to account for the *dynamics* of behaviour or the forces that motivate it. Freud's psychodynamic approach was called psychoanalysis and was based on his work as a psychiatrist in Vienna. He collected detailed information from his patients about their feelings and experiences, especially those relating to early childhood. Note that psychoanalysis also refers to a form of therapy for mental disorders based on Freud's explanations of human behaviour.

Sigmund Freud, 1856–1939

Psychodynamic theory explains human development in terms of an *interaction* between innate drives (e.g. the desire for pleasure) and early experience (the extent to which early desires were gratified). The idea is that individual differences in personality can be traced back to early conflicts between desire and experience. For example, a child may want to behave badly (e.g. steal sweets) but be in conflict because of the guilt experienced afterwards. Some conflicts remain with the adult, influencing his/her behaviour, and can cause mental disorders.

We will focus mostly on Freud's psychodynamic approach. Subsequent psychodynamic theorists were strongly influenced by Freud but developed and extended his approach. Freud strongly emphasised the importance of the patient's psychosexual development and traumatic experiences in early childhood. In contrast, many of those subsequently adopting the psychodynamic approach argued patients' current problems and difficulties are generally more important than their childhood (Eysenck, 1994). These current problems and difficulties generally revolve around interpersonal relationships.

KEY TERMS

Psychodynamic approach: an approach that regards the origin of mental disorders as psychological rather than physical, and suggests that mental illness arises out of unresolved unconscious conflicts.

Conscious: whatever it is we are attending to and/or thinking about at any moment is in the conscious mind.

Preconscious: this refers to the part of the mind containing ideas and information that can easily be accessed if they are relevant to the present situation.

Structure of personality

It seems as if most of the mind exists at the conscious level. The fact that you are generally consciously aware of why you have the emotions you do, and why you behave as you do, suggests our conscious mind has full access to all relevant information about ourselves. However, Freud's views were very different. He argued the conscious mind is like the tip of an iceberg, with most of the mind (as with an iceberg) out of sight.

Freud assumed there are *three* levels of the mind:

- The **conscious**—those thoughts currently the focus of attention—what we are thinking about at any moment.
- The **preconscious**—information and ideas that can be retrieved easily from memory and brought into consciousness.

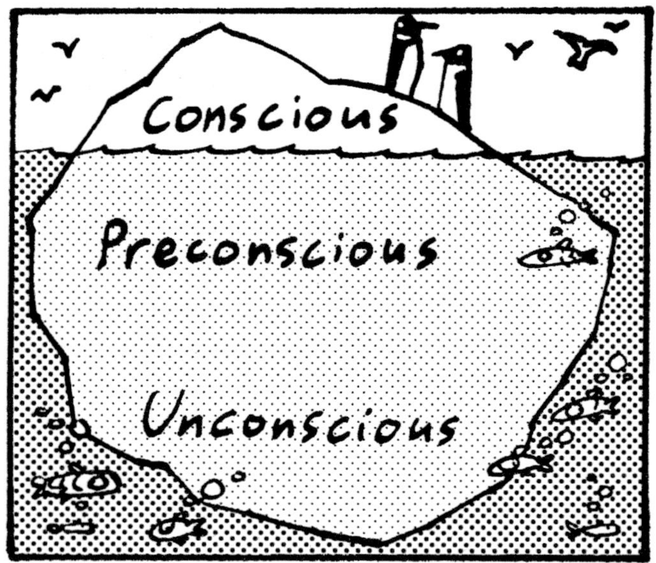

- The **unconscious**—this is the largest part of the mind, containing information almost impossible to bring into conscious awareness. Much of the information in the unconscious mind relates to very emotional experiences from our past (e.g. being bullied at school; being rejected by someone very important to us).

We have just seen that Freud assumed the mind exists at three different levels. He also assumed the mind is divided into *three* parts. In broad terms, Freud argued that the mind contains basic motivational forces (the id), a cognitive system used to perceive the world and for thinking and problem solving (the ego), and a conscience based on the values of family and of society generally (the superego). Let's consider each part in more detail.

1. **Id.** This contains basic motivational forces, especially innate sexual and aggressive instincts. The id follows the pleasure principle, with the emphasis being on *immediate* satisfaction. It is located in the unconscious mind. The sexual instinct is known as **libido.** While the libido is often referred to as the sexual instinct, it is actually much broader—it includes the motivational forces necessary for survival including eating and drinking. Freud regarded the libido as the central force of the id. However, as a result of the horrors of the First World War, he argued that humans possess a death instinct. This death instinct (**thanatos**) produces aggressive and self-destructive behaviour and operates in opposition to the sexual instinct.
2. **Ego.** This is the conscious, rational mind, and it develops during the first 2 years of life. It works on the **reality principle**, taking account of what is going on in the environment.
3. **Superego.** This develops at about the age of 5. It embodies the child's conscience and sense of right and wrong. It is formed when the child adopts the values of the same-sex parent (the process of **identification**). The superego is partly conscious and partly unconscious. It consists of the conscience and the ego-ideal. The conscience is formed as a result of the child being punished and it makes the child feel badly about behaving badly. The ego-ideal is formed through the use of reward—it makes the child feel proud after behaving well.

KEY TERMS

Unconscious: the huge collection of memories and experiences (especially emotionally upsetting ones); these memories are very hard to access.

Id: in Freudian theory, that part of the mind motivated by the pleasure principle and sexual instincts.

Libido: sexual desire; a major motivational force located within the id.

Thanatos: the death instinct, a major motivational force that causes aggressive and self-destructive behaviour.

Ego: the conscious, rational part of the mind, which is guided by the reality principle.

Reality principle: the drive on the part of the ego to accommodate to the demands of the environment.

Superego: in Freud's theory, the part of the mind that embodies one's conscience. It is formed through identification with the same-sex parent.

Identification: according to Freud, children's imitation of the beliefs and behaviour of the same-sexed parent.

EVALUATION

- ➕ All three components of Freud's theory (id, ego, and superego) are of major importance within human personality.
- ➕ Freud's notion that human personality consists of different aspects (e.g. the unconscious and conscious minds) allows us to explain how we can be both rational and irrational at the same time. In everyday life, we reveal these conflicts "when we say things like 'part of me wants to do it, but part of me is afraid to…'"(Jarvis, 2000).
- ➕ There is much evidence that unconscious processes influence our behaviour and Freud was the first psychologist to produce a theory emphasising the role of the unconscious.
- ➕ The notion that young children initially follow the pleasure principle but then increasingly follow the reality principle is plausible.
- ➖ It is hard to test Freud's theory. Imagine trying to design an experiment to show that human personality has only the three components identified by Freud!
- ➖ Freud argued that the ego is predominantly rational in its processing. In fact, however, the conscious mind is often irrational and relies on simple rules of thumb rather than deliberate thinking (Kahneman, 2011).
- ➖ Freud's theory does not take full account of the fact that humans are a social species.

Defence mechanisms

According to Freud, frequent *conflicts* among the id, ego, and superego cause the individual to experience anxiety. Most of these conflicts are between the id (which wants immediate satisfaction) and the superego (which wants the person to behave in line with society's rules). These conflicts force the ego to devote much time to trying to resolve them. The ego protects itself by using various **defence mechanisms** (strategies designed to reduce anxiety). However, they act more as a sticking plaster than as a way of sorting out an individual's problems. Some of the main defence mechanisms are as follows:

1. **Repression**. Keeping threatening thoughts out of consciousness, e.g. not remembering a potentially painful dental appointment.
2. **Denial**. Refusing to accept the existence or reality of a threatening event (e.g. patients suffering from life-threatening diseases often deny their lives are affected).
3. **Displacement**. Unconsciously moving impulses away from a threatening object and towards a less threatening object, e.g. someone made angry by their teacher may shout at their brother.
4. **Projection**. An individual may attribute their undesirable characteristics to others, e.g. someone who is unfriendly may accuse other people of being unfriendly.
5. **Intellectualisation**. Thinking about threatening events to remove the emotion from them (e.g. responding to a car ferry disaster by thinking about ways of improving ferry design).

Findings

There is some support for most of the defence mechanisms proposed by Freud. There has been much research on repression. The most relevant studies are those on clinical patients with recovered previously repressed memories of child abuse. Some of these recovered memories are not genuine but rather are due to the therapist's direct suggestions. However, many recovered memories are entirely genuine (Geraerts et al., 2007).

There has also been much research on displacement. Marcus-Newhall et al. (2000) reviewed studies concerned with displaced aggression (aggressive behaviour directed towards someone not responsible for making the individual angry). Displaced aggression was a moderately strong and replicable finding.

KEY TERMS

Defence mechanisms: strategies used by the ego to defend itself against anxiety.

Repression: a main ego defence mechanism suggested by Freud, where anxiety-causing memories are kept out of conscious memory to protect the individual. This is a type of motivated forgetting, and the repressed memories can sometimes be recalled during psychoanalysis.

Denial: failure to accept consciously threatening thoughts and events.

Displacement: one of the defence mechanisms identified by Freud in which impulses are unconsciously moved away from a very threatening object towards a non-threatening one.

Projection: attributing one's undesirable characteristics to others, as a means of coping with emotionally threatening information and protecting the ego.

Intellectualisation: excessive thinking about emotionally threatening events in order to minimise their emotional impact.

EVALUATION

- ➕ The notion that individuals use various defence mechanisms to protect themselves from anxiety is important.
- ➕ One of Freud's central ideas is that repression is used extensively to keep traumatic or very threatening memories in the unconscious. There is support for this idea although repression occurs less often than he assumed.
- ➖ A complete theory would specify the factors determining *which* defence mechanism will be selected in any given situation. Freud failed to do this.
- ➖ It is not clear that individuals use defence mechanisms as often as assumed by Freud.

Development: Psychosexual stages

One of Freud's key assumptions was that adult personality depends very much on childhood experiences. In his theory of development, Freud assumed all children go through *five* psychosexual stages:

1. *Oral stage* (occurs during the first 18 months of life). During this stage, the infant obtains satisfaction from eating, sucking, and other activities using the mouth.
2. *Anal stage* (between about 18 and 36 months of age). Toilet training takes place during this stage, which helps to explain why the anal region becomes so important.
3. *Phallic stage* (between 3 and 6 years of age). The genitals become a key source of satisfaction during this stage. At about the age of 5, boys acquire the **Oedipus complex**, in which they have sexual desires for their mother and therefore want to get rid of their father, who is a rival. They then also fear their father, who might realise what they are thinking. This complex is resolved by **identification** with their father, involving adopting many of their father's attitudes and developing a superego.

   So far as girls are concerned, Freud argued that girls come to recognise they do not have a penis and blame their mother for this. The girl's father now becomes her love-object and she substitutes her "penis envy" with a wish to have a child. This leads to ultimate identification with her same-sex parent. If you think Freud's ideas of what goes on in the phallic stage are very fanciful (and also remarkably male-centred), you're absolutely right!
4. *Latency stage* (from 6 years of age until the onset of puberty). During this stage, boys and girls spend very little time together.
5. *Genital stage* (from the onset of puberty and throughout adult life). During this stage, the main source of sexual pleasure is in the genitals and experiencing such pleasure with a partner.

Useful mnemonic

To help you remember Freud's stages of psychosexual development, the following mnemonic is made from the initial letter of each stage: Old Age Pensioners Love Greens!

KEY TERMS

Oedipus complex: Freud's explanation of how a boy resolves his love for his mother and feelings of rivalry towards his father by identifying with his father.

Fixation: in Freudian terms, spending a long time at a given stage of development because of over- or under-gratification.

Regression: in Freudian terms, returning to an earlier stage of development to cope with anxiety.

Development of adult personality and mental disorders

Freud coupled the theory of psychosexual stages with a theory of personality. If a child experiences severe problems or excessive pleasure at any stage of development, this leads to **fixation**, in which basic energy or libido becomes attached to that stage for many years. Later in life, adults who experience very stressful conditions often show **regression**, in which their behaviour becomes less mature, and more like that displayed during a psychosexual stage at which they fixated as children.

According to Freud, these processes of fixation and regression play important roles in determining adult personality. Some personality types are shown in the figure on page 205, along with descriptions and a link to the stage of psychosexual development at which fixation may have occurred.

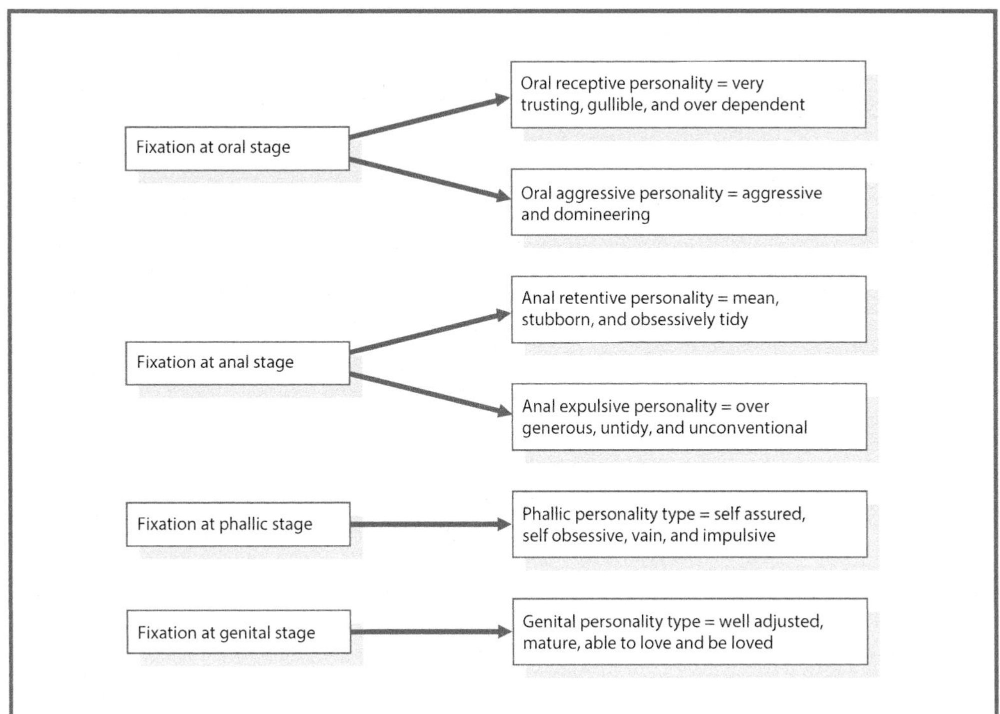

Freud suggested that adult personality types could be linked with fixations during each stage of development.

How did Freud explain the development of mental disorders? As just discussed, adults experiencing great difficulties show regression to a stage at which they had previously fixated. More serious mental disorders are associated with regression further back into childhood. Thus, for example, individuals with schizophrenia (involving a loss of contact with reality) regress to an earlier stage of their lives than those suffering from neuroses or anxiety disorders.

Findings

Freud assumed most adult mental disorders have their roots in childhood experiences or personality development in childhood. The evidence is mixed, but there is some support. Kendler et al. (1996) considered the role of childhood experiences. They studied adult female twins who had experienced parental loss through separation in childhood. These twins showed an above-average tendency to suffer from depression and alcoholism in adult life.

Caspi et al. (1996) considered the role of childhood personality in subsequent problems. They studied 3-year-olds, and then carried out a follow-up 18 years later. Children with an introverted personality at the age of 3 tended to be depressed at the age of 21. Children undercontrolled at the age of 3 were more likely to have developed anti-social personality disorder by the time they reached 21.

EVALUATION

- ⊕ Freud proposed the first systematic theory of the development of personality.
- ⊕ Freud played a major role in establishing developmental psychology with his emphasis on the notion that adult personality depends very much on childhood experiences.
- ⊖ Freud's stage-based theory suggests personality development occurs in a neater and tidier way than is actually the case.
- ⊖ Finding an association between having had a troubled childhood (or fixating at a given psychosexual stage) and adult mental disorder does not prove the troubled childhood helped to *cause* the adult mental disorder.

Research method: Case studies

Sigmund Freud claimed to be a scientist, but in practice he did not make use of the scientific method. Instead he used the case study method. The essence of a **case study** is that it involves studying a single individual in great depth. Case studies often produce interesting findings but the major problem is that we cannot safely *generalise* from a single individual to a larger sample or population.

CASE STUDY: Anna O

Freud's theory was largely based on the observations he made during consultations with patients. He suggested that his work was similar to that of an archaeologist, who digs away layers of earth before uncovering what he or she was seeking. In a similar way, the psychiatrist seeks to dig down to the unconscious and discover the key to the individual's personality dynamic.

"Anna O. was a girl of twenty-one, of a high degree of intelligence. Her illness first appeared while she was caring for her father, whom she tenderly loved, during the severe illness which led to his death. The patient had a severe paralysis of both right extremities, disturbance of eye-movements, an intense nausea when she attempted to take nourishment, and at one time for several weeks a loss of the power to drink, in spite of tormenting thirst. She occasionally became confused or delirious and mumbled several words to herself. If these same words were later repeated to her, when she was in a hypnotic state, she engaged in deeply sad, often poetically beautiful, day dreams, we might call them, which commonly took as their starting point the situation of a girl beside the sick-bed of her father. The patient jokingly called this treatment 'chimney sweeping'.

Dr. Breuer [Freud's colleague] soon hit upon the fact that through such cleansing of the soul more could be accomplished than a temporary removal of the constantly recurring mental 'clouds'.

During one session, the patient recalled an occasion when she was with her governess, and how that lady's little dog, that she abhorred, had drunk out of a glass. Out of respect for the conventions the patient had remained silent, but now under hypnosis she gave energetic expression to her restrained anger, and then drank a large quantity of water without trouble, and woke from hypnosis with the glass at her lips. The symptom thereupon vanished permanently.

Permit me to dwell for a moment on this experience. No one had ever cured an hysterical symptom by such means before, or had come so near understanding its cause. This would be a pregnant discovery if the expectation could be confirmed that still other, perhaps the majority of symptoms, originated in this way and could be removed by the same method.

Such was indeed the case, almost all the symptoms originated in exactly this way, as we were to discover. The patient's illness originated at the time when she was caring for her sick father, and her symptoms could only be regarded as memory symbols of his sickness and death. While she was seated by her father's sick bed, she was careful to betray nothing of her anxiety and her painful depression to the patient. When, later, she reproduced the same scene before the physician, the emotion which she had suppressed on the occurrence of the scene burst out with especial strength, as though it had been pent up all along.

In her normal state she was entirely ignorant of the pathogenic scenes and of their connection with her symptoms. She had forgotten those scenes. When the patient was hypnotized, it was possible, after considerable difficulty, to recall those scenes to her memory, and by this means of recall the symptoms were removed."

(Adapted from Sigmund Freud, 1910, The origin and development of psychoanalysis. *American Journal of Psychology, 21*, 181–218.)

The evidence that Freud himself reported to support his theoretical approach was very flimsy. It consisted of about a dozen case studies, none of which is at all convincing. For example, consider the famous case of Little Hans which was claimed to illustrate the development of the Oedipus complex and of specific phobias (extreme fear of objects; see Chapter 7). When Hans was 3 years old, he began to show much interest in his penis, which caused his mother to threaten to cut it off. When he was about 5, he saw a horse-drawn van tip over on its side. This caused him to develop a fear of horses and to refer to "black things around horses' mouths and the things in front of their eyes". As a result of his fear of horses, Hans was unwilling to leave the safety of his own home.

KEY TERM

Case study: an in-depth investigation of a single individual often involving collecting qualitative data.

Freud's diagnosis was that Little Hans suffered from an Oedipus complex. According to Freud, he was sexually attracted to his mother but was very frightened his father would punish him for this. The fear that Hans had for his father turned into a fear of horses, with Freud arguing that horses' black muzzles and blinkers resembled the moustache and glasses of Hans' father. The fact that Hans' fear of horses caused him to remain at home had the significant advantage that he could spend more time with his mother, to whom he was allegedly sexually attracted. Little Hans was treated by psychoanalysis and his phobia disappeared.

Most people are totally unconvinced by Freud's case history of Little Hans. There is very little evidence that Hans desired sexual contact with his mother or that he was very frightened of his father. Furthermore, the idea that Hans' great sexual excitement somehow turned into a state of high anxiety is fanciful. In addition, Freud had surprisingly little to do with the therapy—he was involved in one short therapeutic session with the rest of the treatment being delivered by Hans' father in consultation with Freud (Rolls, 2010).

? Freud developed most parts of his psychodynamic theory between the 1890s and the 1920s, from case studies of his patients. How might the strict social norms of Viennese middle class culture have given rise to such controversial ideas about childhood sexuality?

OVERALL EVALUATION

+ Freud is the most influential psychologist of all time. His ideas about the importance of the subconscious and unconscious mind have had a profound effect on human thinking and on the development of the psychodynamic approach.

+ Freud put forward the first systematic approach to abnormality focusing specifically on *psychological* factors as the cause of mental disorder and on psychological forms of treatment. Before Freud, most explanations of mental illness were based on physical causes or ideas (e.g. possession by evil spirits).

+ Freud essentially founded developmental psychology and proposed one of the first systematic theories of personality.

+ Psychoanalysis paved the way for later psychodynamic approaches. Freud focused very much on the individual and his/her personal conflicts dating back to childhood. Subsequent psychodynamic therapists put more emphasis on the patient's current social and relationship problems.

+ There is clear support for many of Freud's defence mechanisms.

+ Freud was right to emphasise the importance of the unconscious mind. However, the unconscious mind is less complex than Freud assumed.

− Freud was relatively uninterested in the *current* problems his clients were facing. Even if childhood experiences stored in the unconscious influence the development of mental disorders, this does not mean adult experiences can be ignored.

− Freud focused too much on sexual factors as the cause of mental disorders. Freud over-emphasised sex because he developed his theory at a time of great sexual repression, which caused sex to be repressed in many minds (Banyard & Hayes, 1994). Most modern psychodynamic therapists believe sexual problems are a *result* of poor relationships with others rather than a direct cause of disorder (as assumed by Freud).

− The psychodynamic approach is not based on scientific research. Freud's theoretical views emerged from his interactions with clients in the therapeutic situation. This provided a weak form of evidence because what Freud's patients said in therapy was often influenced by his biases and preconceptions. Freud's observations were largely based on a rather narrow sample of people: white, middle-class, Victorian Viennese women. That limits the extent to which we can generalise his ideas to other types of patient.

− The psychodynamic approach is limited because it ignores genetic factors involved in the development of mental disorder.

− Many of Freud's key concepts (e.g. id, ego, superego, fixation, Oedipus complex) are imprecise, making it hard to assess their usefulness.

Section Summary

- The psychodynamic approach was based on the assumption that mental disorders have their origins in psychological factors.
- According to Freud there are three levels of the mind: conscious; preconscious; and unconscious.
- The mind is divided into three parts: the id (motivational forces), the ego (the cognitive system), and the superego (conscience).
- The ego devotes much of its time to trying to resolve conflicts between the id and the superego. It protects itself by using various defence mechanisms including repression, denial, displacement, projection, and intellectualisation.
- According to Freud's theory of personality development, there are five psychosexual stages: oral; anal; phallic; latency; and genital.
- Fixation occurs if a child experiences severe problems or excessive pleasure at any psychosexual stage. Adults experiencing great difficulties show regression back to a stage at which they have previously fixated and can be associated with mental disorder.
- Freud founded developmental psychology, put forward one of the first systematic personality theories, and proposed the first systematic approach to abnormality focused on psychological factors.
- Freud's notion that the unconscious mind is important has been supported by most of the evidence.
- Freud's approach was unscientific and most of his theoretical ideas are hard to test experimentally.
- Freud's observations were based on a narrow sample of people (mostly middle-class, Victorian Viennese women).

HUMANISTIC PSYCHOLOGY

The humanistic approach to psychology was developed mainly by Carl Rogers and Abraham Maslow in the United States during the 1950s. According to Cartwright (1979, pp. 5–6), humanist psychology "is concerned with topics that are meaningful to human beings, focusing especially upon subjective experience and the unique unpredictable events in individual human lives".

Humanist psychologists focus on personal responsibility, free will, and the individual's striving for personal growth and fulfilment. In studying these topics, humanistic psychologists rely heavily on **phenomenology**, which involves reporting pure experience with no attempt to interpret it. According to Rogers (1951, p. 133), "This kind of personal, phenomenological type of study … is far more valuable than the traditional 'hard-head' empirical approach. This kind of study, often scorned by psychologists as being 'merely self-reports', actually gives the deepest insight into what the experience has meant." This strong statement is somewhat anti-scientific and rejects the use of the experimental method.

Humanistic psychology has an obvious appeal. In our everyday lives, we often try to understand someone else's personality by asking them about their experiences. This is not very different from the approach favoured by humanistic psychologists. We will initially consider Maslow's contribution and then that of Rogers. This is done because they focused on somewhat different (although related) issues. Note, however, that Maslow and Rogers agreed on nearly all their major assumptions, and so between them they represent the humanistic approach very clearly.

KEY TERMS

Phenomenology: a technique involving the direct reporting of experience.

Free will: the notion that we are free to make our own decisions.

Free will

There has been a very long-lasting controversy concerning the factors responsible for our behaviour. Believers in determinism argue people's actions are totally determined by the external and internal forces operating on them. In contrast, those believing in **free will** claim individuals *choose* their own behaviour.

Humanistic psychologists are strong believers in free will. They argue individuals exercise choice in their behaviour and deny that people's behaviour is at the mercy of outside forces. They claim that regarding human behaviour as being determined by external forces is "de-humanising" and incorrect.

Rogers developed a form of therapy (client-centred or person-centred) based on the assumption that the client has free will. The therapist is called a "facilitator" precisely because his/her role is to make it easier for clients to exercise free will so as to maximise the rewardingness of their lives. This form of therapy is discussed in detail later.

The issues involved in deciding whether humans possess free will are complex. Most people believe they have free will but this does not prove their belief is correct. The humanistic psychologists' claim that we are free to behave as we wish is an exaggeration. In fact, our behaviour is influenced by heredity, past experience, and the present environment.

Maslow's hierarchy of needs (including self-actualisation)

Abraham Maslow argued that Freud was too limited and negative. According to Maslow (1954, p. 5), "Freud supplied us the sick half of psychology, and we must now fill it out with the healthy half."

Maslow (1954) claimed that most theories of human motivation had focused on basic physiological needs or our needs to reduce and avoid pain. He argued motivation is actually much broader. He put forward a **hierarchy of needs**. Physiological needs (such as those for food and water) are at the bottom of the hierarchy. Next come security and safety needs (such as curiosity and the need for understanding) and aesthetic (artistic) needs. Finally, at the top of the hierarchy there is the need for **self-actualisation** (achieving the most we are capable of). Maslow argued the higher needs will emerge only when the lower needs are more or less satisfied.

All the needs towards the bottom of the hierarchy are regarded as deficiency needs. This is because they are designed to reduce inadequacies or deficiencies. In contrast, needs towards the top of the hierarchy (e.g. self-actualisation) represent growth motivation and are designed to produce personal growth. Self-actualisation was described in the following way by Maslow (1954): "A musician must make music, an artist must paint, a poet must write, if he is to be ultimately at peace with himself. What a man be, he must be. This need we may call self-actualisation."

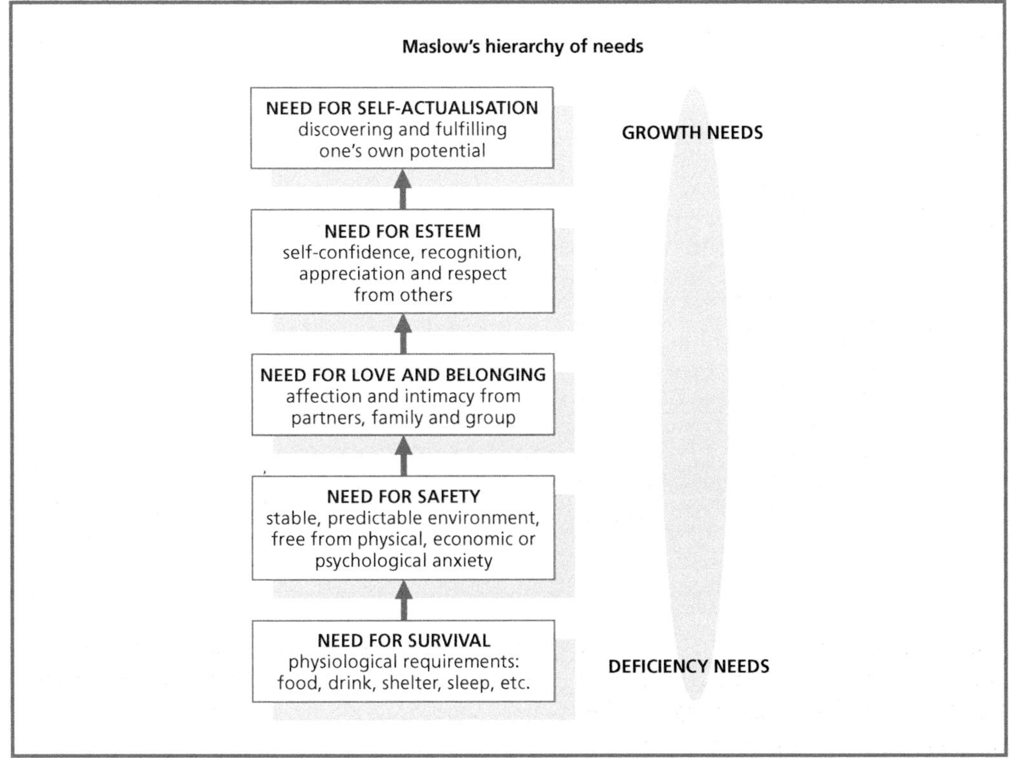

KEY TERMS

Hierarchy of needs: the notion that humans have several needs ranging from basic physiological needs at the bottom of the hierarchy to self-actualisation at the top.

Self-actualisation: at the top of Maslow's hierarchy of needs, it is the need to make the fullest possible use of our abilities and skills.

Maslow characterised Einstein as a famous individual who demonstrated "self-actualisation"— including characteristics such as self-acceptance, resistance to cultural influences, empathy, and creativeness.

Self-actualised individuals have an acceptance of themselves, spontaneity, the need for privacy, resistance to cultural influences, deep interpersonal relations, creativeness, and a philosophical sense of humour. Maslow identified Abraham Lincoln and Albert Einstein as famous examples of self-actualised individuals.

Maslow's theory is more complex than sometimes appreciated. He argued that most individuals work upwards through the hierarchy of needs, but accepted that is *not* always the case. Some individuals have to satisfy their need for self-esteem before they can satisfy their need for love. Maslow also accepted we do not have to satisfy our physiological or safety needs totally before addressing higher-level needs.

Maslow (1962) studied self-actualisation by focusing on **peak experiences**. Such experiences are characterised by acceptance of the world as it is and by feelings of joy, wonder, and awe. Maslow found (as he had expected) that self-actualised individuals reported more peak experiences than other people.

Findings

Since deficiency needs typically need to be satisfied before individuals can focus on growth needs, it should be harder to satisfy growth needs than deficiency ones. Maslow (1970) estimated that Americans satisfy 85% of their physiological needs, 70% of their safety needs, 50% of their belongingness and love needs, 40% of their self-esteem needs, but only 10% of their self-actualisation needs. However, these estimates were based on very limited data and so should not be taken too seriously.

Maslow predicted that higher-level needs can only be satisfied provided the need immediately below it has been satisfied. Taormina and Gao (2013) asked adults to complete a questionnaire designed to assess the complete hierarchy of needs and found support for Maslow's prediction. They also found (in line with Maslow's theory) that individuals with high life satisfaction had the highest levels of satisfaction of needs at all five levels of the hierarchy.

Aronoff (1967) found that when individuals had their security and esteem needs met they were more likely to choose a less predictable and more challenging job such as fishing.

According to Maslow, children whose deficiency needs (e.g. access to health and dental care) are satisfied should show more satisfaction of growth needs (e.g. academic achievement) than those whose deficiency needs are not satisfied. Noltemeyer et al. (2012) obtained findings supporting this prediction. However, their evidence was only *correlational*—perhaps children with access to health care are generally more intelligent and/or have more parental support than those who do not.

Further support for Maslow's theory was provided by Aronoff (1967). He compared fishermen and cane cutters in the British West Indies. Fishermen worked alone and generally earned more than cane cutters working in groups. Cane cutting was a more secure job because the rewards fluctuated much less than for fishermen and because cane cutters were paid even when sick. As predicted by Maslow's theory, individuals whose security and esteem needs were met were more likely to choose the challenging and responsible job of fisherman.

Mathes et al. (1982) found individuals reporting more peak experiences were more likely than those reporting few such experiences to emphasise higher-level values (e.g. beauty; truth; justice). They were also less likely to focus on lower-level deficiency values (e.g. taking from others rather than giving). These findings fit Maslow's theory.

Maslow claimed peak experiences can produce long-lasting beneficial changes. Support for this claim was reported by Roepke (2013). Many people indicated that peak experiences led to deeper spirituality, increased meaning in life, enhanced self-esteem, and improved relationships. However, Maslow was wrong in at least one respect. He suggested that *all* peak experiences are positive. In fact, some peak experiences are negative and occur in threatening circumstances (Wilson & Spencer, 1990).

KEY TERM

Peak experiences: states of euphoria in which there is complete acceptance of the world as it is.

EVALUATION

- ⊕ Maslow's theory is more comprehensive than previous theories of motivation and personality.
- ⊕ Maslow emphasised the more positive and uplifting aspects of human motivation whereas previous theorists (e.g. Freud) focused more on the negative side of human nature.
- ⊖ It is very hard to carry out experimental research into the theory, in part because Maslow favoured an anti-scientific approach. He emphasised the value of phenomenology, which closely resembles introspection and is open to all the same criticisms (see earlier in the chapter).
- ⊖ Maslow's account of the development of self-actualisation de-emphasised the role of environmental factors (e.g. schooling; supportive parents; training).
- ⊖ Maslow focused on the positive value of high self-esteem and personal achievement. This approach is more relevant to individualistic cultures (e.g. UK; USA) in which the emphasis is on personal responsibility than collectivistic ones (e.g. China) in which the emphasis is on co-operation and working for the benefit of the group (Kitayama & Markus, 1994).
- ⊖ Maslow was too optimistic in his assumption that everyone has the potential to become a self-actualiser. The fact that the average British person spends 25 hours a week slumped in front of a television set suggests there are many people whose motivation for personal growth is not enormous!

Focus on the self

According to Rogers (1951), the concept of "self" is of central importance to an understanding of human personality. An individual's self-concept is mainly conscious. It consists of our thoughts and feelings about ourselves as individuals and in relation to others. The importance Rogers attached to the concept of "self" can be seen in this quotation:

> *Below the level of the problem situation about which the individual is complaining ... lies one central search ... at the bottom each person is asking, "Who am I, really? How can I get in touch with this real self, underlying all my surface behaviour? How can I become myself" (Rogers, 1967, p. 108).*

There are *three* aspects of the self-concept within Rogers' theory:

1. **Self-worth**: this is self-esteem and concerns what we think about ourselves.
2. **Self-image**: this is how we see ourselves (e.g. as a good or bad person).
3. **Ideal self**: the self-concept an individual would most like to have.

Distinguishing between our *current* self-concept (represented by self-worth and self-image) and our *desired* self-concept (represented by the ideal self) is important. Theoretically, it is important to work out the discrepancy between them. One way of doing so is by using the **Q-sort method**. With this method, the person being assessed is presented with a pile of cards, each containing a statement of personal relevance (e.g. "I am a friendly person"; "I am tense most of the time"). The person initially decides which statements best describe his/her own self, which statements are the next best in their descriptive power, and so on right down to the least descriptive ones. After that, precisely the same procedure is followed with respect to the individual's ideal self. Finally, the investigator calculates the discrepancy between the two categorisations.

KEY TERMS

Self-worth: this is our self-esteem and relates to our feelings of self-worth.

Self-image: this is how we see ourselves; our self-image can be positive (e.g. good person; friendly person) or negative (e.g. bad person; unfriendly person).

Ideal self: the self-concept that is most desired by an individual.

Q-sort method: a test to assess the self-concept and the ideal self; it involves sorting descriptive statements on cards.

Congruence

Rogers emphasised the importance of **congruence**, by which he meant a lack of conflict between an individual's perceived self and their experience and behaviour. We try to preserve congruence in our everyday lives: "Most of the ways of behaving which are adopted by the organism are those which are consistent with the concept of the self" (Rogers, 1967, p. 487).

What happens if we experience incongruence (e.g. behaving aggressively even though we regard ourselves as gentle)? According to Rogers, incongruence often creates anxiety, and can cause us to respond defensively. Two key defensive processes are denial and distortion. Denial involves refusing to accept at the conscious level that the experience happened. Distortion, which occurs more often than denial, involves misremembering the experience to make it consistent with the perceived self (e.g. "I didn't really behave aggressively at all").

Role of conditions of worth

? Can you think of any barriers that would prevent a person from attaining his or her "ideal self"? Are any of them related to "conditions of worth"?

According to Rogers, parents should give their children unconditional positive regard to promote healthy development. Children receive **unconditional positive regard** when they are fully accepted by their parents regardless of how they behave. Such children have no need to deny or distort their experiences to achieve congruence. In contrast, some parents impose **conditions of worth** on their children, meaning the children must behave in certain ways to be accepted by their parents. This can easily produce incongruence. Suppose the parents require politeness at all times from their children for them to be regarded positively. That creates incongruence when the children are rude.

Findings

Rogers' approach was rather anti-scientific and so there is relatively little evidence for or against his theoretical approach. However, we will briefly discuss two studies. Gough et al. (1978) used the Q-sort method to identify air force officers having a large discrepancy between their self-concept and their ideal self, and those having only a small discrepancy. According to Rogers, those with a small discrepancy should have better adjusted psychologically. When all the air force officers were rated by other people, those with a small discrepancy were perceived as being efficient, co-operative, and outgoing. In contrast, those with a large discrepancy were perceived as unfriendly, awkward, and confused.

According to Rogers, the self-concept of well-adjusted individuals is coherent and integrated. This assumption was studied by Donahue et al. (1993). Participants indicated the extent to which their feelings and behaviour were similar across various social roles (e.g. daughter, student, friend). Well-adjusted individuals (i.e. high self-esteem, non-anxious, not depressed) typically had an integrated self in that they perceived themselves as being essentially the same

KEY TERMS

Congruence: a lack of conflict between an individual's self-concept and his/her experience of life.

Unconditional positive regard: accepting someone else fully regardless of his/her behaviour.

Conditions of worth: setting conditions that need to be satisfied in order to accept someone else fully.

person across their social roles. In contrast, poorly adjusted individuals with low self-esteem differed greatly across their social roles. Thus, the findings supported Rogers.

Influence on counselling psychology

There are similarities between counselling psychology and clinical psychology because the central focus of both is to provide effective treatment for psychologically maladjusted individuals. However, **counselling psychology** is typically used to treat less seriously disturbed individuals than **clinical psychology**.

The main approach to counselling psychology stemming from the humanistic approach is client-centred therapy (later re-named person-centred therapy). It was proposed by Rogers. Rogers summarised the essence of his approach as follows (cited in Kirschenbaum, 1979, p. 89):

> *It is the client who knows what hurts, what direction to go, what problems are crucial, what experiences have been deeply buried. It began to occur to me that unless I had a need to demonstrate my own cleverness and learning I would do better to rely upon the client for the direction of movement in the process.*

The main approach to counselling psychology stemming from the humanistic approach is person-centred therapy, which allows clients to become self-actualised by thinking about themselves in an honest and accepting way.

According to Rogers, the main goals of therapy are to allow clients to develop a sense of personal agency and to become self-actualised by thinking about themselves in an honest and accepting way. These goals are achieved by the therapist displaying three qualities:

1. *Unconditional positive regard*: the therapist is consistently supportive.
2. *Genuineness*: the therapist is spontaneous and open.
3. *Empathy*: the therapist has a good understanding of the client's feelings and concerns.

Rogers' therapeutic approach can usefully be described as non-directive—the client determines the direction in which therapy proceeds rather than the therapist. Non-directive therapy can be contrasted with directive therapy in which the therapist dictates what happens as is the case, for example, with psychoanalysis.

Rogers' approach to therapy has had enormous influence—the great majority of therapists working in counselling psychology adopt a non-directive approach owing much to his pioneering efforts. However, the impact of person-centred therapy has been much less within clinical psychology. This makes sense because person-centred therapy is of little value in treating serious mental disorders (Rudolph et al., 1980).

Why has person-centred therapy been so influential within counselling psychology? A central reason is because it is of proven effectiveness. Grave et al. (1990) compared person-centred therapy with three forms of behaviour therapy in clients having mainly interpersonal problems. All four forms of treatment were moderately and comparably effective. The clients who did best with person-centred therapy had relatively high levels of social skills and assertiveness.

Orlinsky et al. (1994) reviewed studies that had considered the effects on therapy of the three key characteristics Rogers claimed therapists should display: genuineness; unconditional personal regard; and empathy. All these characteristics were positively related to client recovery but the effects were sometimes rather small.

As indicated already, contemporary counselling psychology is strongly influenced by Rogers' person-centred therapy. The main change over the years has been an increase in **eclecticism**—an approach in which therapists use various techniques selected from different types of therapy rather than a single therapeutic approach. Nowadays, counselling psychologists often combine the humanistic approach with elements of other forms of therapy (mostly cognitive therapy and behaviour therapy).

KEY TERMS

Counselling psychology: an approach to therapy typically used in the treatment of individuals who are only moderately disturbed.

Clinical psychology: an approach to therapy typically used in the treatment of individuals who are seriously disturbed and suffer from one or more mental disorders.

Eclecticism: the use of a range of different forms of treatment by therapists.

EVALUATION

- (+) Rogers was concerned with issues of major concern to people, such as making their self-concept resemble their ideal self more closely.
- (+) Rogers' humanistic approach led him to develop client-centred (or person-centred) therapy which has proved of moderate effectiveness.
- (+) Even though Rogers proposed his form of therapy over 60 years ago, it remains very influential within counselling psychology.
- (+) The humanistic approach strongly influenced the dramatic rise of positive psychology, which focuses on "such issues as what enables happiness ... how optimism and hope affect health, ... and how talent and creativity come to fruition" (Seligman & Csikszentmihalyi, 2000, p. 5).
- (−) "It is difficult to evaluate Rogers' theory, since it is more of a philosophical view of the person than a formal, concrete psychological theory" (Cooper, 1998, p. 22). It is also hard to submit Rogers' theoretical ideas to rigorous scientific test.
- (−) Rogers' great reliance on phenomenology meant he did not explore unconscious processes in detail.
- (−) Rogers' approach is limited. Adult personality is partly determined by childhood experiences and partly by genetic factors, but these influences on adult personality were largely ignored by Rogers.
- (−) The humanistic approach (and person-centred therapy) "emphasised the self and encouraged a self-centredness that played down concerns for collective well-being" (Seligman & Csikszentmihalyi, 2000, p. 7).
- (−) The entire humanistic approach is excessively optimistic. At the risk of over-simplification, it is assumed by humanistic psychologists that people are "naturally" good and so all they have to do is "to be true to themselves". If only that were true!

Section Summary

- Humanistic psychologists such as Rogers and Maslow focused on personal responsibility, free will, and the individual's striving for personal growth and fulfilment.
- Humanistic psychologists rely heavily on phenomenology and mostly adopt a rather anti-scientific approach.
- Maslow put forward a theory of motivation based on a hierarchy of needs. Physiological needs are at the bottom of the hierarchy and the need for self-actualisation is at the top. The higher needs emerge only when the lower ones are satisfied. Self-actualised individuals have more peak experiences than other people.
- Maslow's emphasis on the value of high self-esteem and self-actualisation is more relevant to individualistic cultures than collectivistic ones.
- Rogers argued there are three aspects to the self-concept: self-worth, self-image, and ideal self. Individuals with a small discrepancy between their self-concept and their ideal self are often better adjusted psychologically.
- Rogers emphasised the importance of congruence between an individual's perceived self and his/her experience and behaviour. Incongruence often creates anxiety and can lead to denial and distortion.
- Rogers' client-centred therapy (later re-named person-centred therapy) has been very influential within counselling psychology. This therapeutic approach focuses on the

client becoming self-actualised. This is facilitated if the therapist displays unconditional positive regard, genuineness, and empathy. This approach has been reasonably effective.
- Rogers' approach encourages self-centredness (sometimes at the expense of concern for others) and de-emphasises unconscious processes and the role of childhood experiences and genetic factors in determining adult personality.
- The entire humanistic approach is excessively optimistic about human nature.

COMPARISON OF APPROACHES

In the course of this chapter, we have discussed five major approaches to understanding behaviour. In this section, we will compare these five approaches. Each approach was designed to focus on rather different aspects of human behaviour and so the theoretical assumptions (and relevant evidence) vary across approaches. As a consequence, each approach ignores several aspects of behaviour and so provides a somewhat limited account. However, each approach has made a significant contribution to our understanding of behaviour.

Our comparison of the five approaches will be based on the Table. I will consider the various features one by one to clarify the information contained in the Table. Note that there are some connections among the features. For example, an approach in which most of the research is on non-human species is unlikely to attach great importance to consciousness. The reason is that we cannot study consciousness in other species, and indeed most of them may lack consciousness altogether.

Main focus + aspects de-emphasised

Psychology is concerned with understanding human (and animal) behaviour. This is a vast undertaking and so we should not be surprised that each approach focuses on some aspects of psychology at the expense of others. For example, learning approaches focus mostly on simple rather than complex learning. We can see one reason why this is the case if we consider operant conditioning. When learning is simple, the relevant responses (e.g. lever presses) are easy to measure. In contrast, what happens when someone spends 30 minutes solving a very complex problem cannot readily be reduced to the production of one or more responses.

Learning approaches also focus on motivation. For example, Skinner found (unsurprisingly) that rats were far more inclined to press a lever for food reward or reinforcement when they were hungry than when they were not.

The learning approach de-emphasises or ignores huge areas within psychology. Consider, for example, a sample of the topics of major importance within cognitive psychology: attention, perception, learning, memory, reading, speech perception, speaking, writing, decision making,

Which psychological approach would you use to account for this behaviour?

SUMMARY: FIVE APPROACHES

Feature	Learning	Cognitive	Biological	Psychodynamic	Humanistic
Main focus	Simple learning + motivation	Mental processes (e.g. attention; rehearsal) and structures (e.g. schemas)	Genetic factors + physiology + neurochemistry + evolution	Mental disorders + development + personality + motivation	Psychological well-being + counselling + motivation
Aspects de-emphasised	Complex learning; genetics; personality; cognitive processes + structures	Genetics; personality; motivation	Mental processes + structures; some environmental influences	Normal individuals; genetic factors; positive emotions; neurochemistry	Non-conscious processes; genetics; neurochemistry; development
Species	Human + other	Human only	Human + other	Human only	Human only
Preferred method	Experiments	Experiments	Twin studies + experiments	Case studies (some experiments)	Phenomenology
Scientific?	Yes	Yes	Yes	No?	No
Relevant data	Behaviour	Behaviour + brain imaging computer models	Concordance rates + physiological + neurochemical measures	Patients' reports	Verbal reports
Consciousness?	No/Yes	Yes	Yes?	Yes	Yes
Non-conscious processes?	Yes	Yes	No?	Yes	No

problem solving, and the development of expertise. Practically none of these topics (except learning) has been studied in depth within the learning approach.

Skinner argued the environment has a major influence on most behaviour. This focus on *external* factors led him to de-emphasise the importance of *internal* factors in determining behaviour. The role of internal factors can be seen in much of our behaviour. For example, if you set yourself the internal goal of doing well in AS Psychology, this will often influence your behaviour more than immediate environmental rewards available.

The cognitive approach focuses on mental processes (e.g. attention; perception; thinking) and on mental structures (e.g. schemas; long-term memory). Its scope is much greater than that of learning approaches. Indeed, since these mental processes are of importance and relevance in nearly all situations, the cognitive approach has become increasingly important in several other areas of psychology including abnormal psychology (see Chapter 8), social psychology, and developmental psychology.

What is de-emphasised within cognitive psychology? Most cognitive psychologists have ignored the role of genetic factors in behaviour and biological factors generally. More surprisingly, they have de-emphasised the importance of individual differences even though there are very large individual differences in cognitive ability and in performance on complex cognitive tasks. However, cognitive psychologists started to focus more on individual differences in recent years.

Cognitive psychology also de-emphasises long-term planning and goals. The great majority of research in cognitive psychology takes place in the laboratory and involves experimental sessions of no more than 30–40 minutes. It is not possible to shed much light on long-term goals with such research.

The main focus of the biological approach is broad and very different to that of the other theoretical approaches. As we have seen, the biological approach focuses on genetic factors influencing individual differences in behaviour. In addition, it emphasises the importance of evolutionary processes in understanding behaviour. Finally, and most importantly, it considers the precise role of physiological and neurochemical processes that intervene between stimulus and response.

What is de-emphasised within the biological approach? There has traditionally been little focus on mental processes such as those studied by cognitive psychologists. Related to this, advocates of the biological approach often de-emphasise how internal physiological processes depend on the precise way in which individuals interpret the current situation.

The psychodynamic approach is very broad in focus. This approach is mainly associated with the understanding and treatment of mental disorders. In addition, however, Freud proposed the first systematic theories within developmental and personality psychology. Without a shadow of a doubt, Freud expanded the scope of psychology to a far greater extent than any other psychologist.

What aspects of psychology were de-emphasised by Freud? He largely ignored positive emotions in favour of negative ones such as anxiety and depression. He devoted little attention to biological factors such as genetic factors and internal physiological and neurochemical processes. Finally, and perhaps most importantly, most of his theorising de-emphasised the psychological processes found in normal, healthy individuals.

The humanistic approach focused mostly on motivation ranging from basic needs to self-actualisation and on psychological well-being. Thus, the emphasis was very much on the positive emotions and how to achieve them.

What aspects of psychology were de-emphasised by the humanistic psychologists? They virtually ignored biological factors of all kinds and paid relatively little attention to developmental issues (i.e. the influence of childhood experiences on adult personality). They had only limited interest in cognitive processes and structures (e.g. the nature of the self).

Species

The cognitive, psychodynamic, and humanistic approaches all focus exclusively (or almost so) on understanding human behaviour. The slight exception is the cognitive approach, since some research has investigated mental processes in various non-human species. It is understandable these approaches should focus on humans given that we are far more interested in understanding other humans than in explaining the behaviour of non-human species. Another factor is that the psychodynamic and humanistic approaches rely heavily on people's reports about themselves and the reasons why they behave as they do. For obvious reasons, we cannot do this with any other species.

Why do the learning approaches and the biological approach both focus on non-human species as well as on humans? In the case of learning approaches, the emphasis was on simple learning. Since virtually all species are capable of simple learning, it made sense for advocates of learning approaches to consider non-human as well as human learning.

In the case of the biological approach, the focus on non-human species is understandable from the perspective of the theory of evolution. Since the human species evolved out of non-human species, there are important similarities across species in terms of physiology, neurochemistry, and genetic transmission from one generation to the next.

The biological approach focuses on non-human species as well as humans, because there are important similarities in terms of physiology, neurochemistry and genetics.

Preferred method + science

Several different methods have been used to study and understand human behaviour. The experimental method, in which the experimenter manipulates the situation to observe its effects, is the method generally most likely to produce important and valid findings. Researchers using the cognitive or learning approaches typically make use of the experimental method and study behaviour under laboratory conditions.

Most research carried out within the biological approach makes use of the experimental method. However, the biological approach also makes use of several different methods. For example, those working within the biological approach sometimes carry out twin studies using identical and fraternal twins. Twin studies are important because they tell us whether or not genetic factors are involved in the development of various mental disorders. However, they do not involve the experimental method because the experimenter does not control or manipulate anything.

The humanistic approach is the one most opposed to the experimental method. Humanistic psychologists' preferred method involves phenomenology (the direct reporting of experience) and they are often opposed to the experimental method because they regard it as artificial and limited. The psychodynamic approach is similar in that it does not involve the use of the experimental method (although that is less true now than it was in the days of Freud). Their preferred method is the case study, in which patients describe and interpret their life experiences with the assistance of the therapist.

? **Which of the approaches to psychology is the most scientific?**

Which of the five approaches adopt a scientific approach to understanding human behaviour? Since the experimental method represents the most scientific approach available to psychologists, it follows that the learning, cognitive, and biological approaches all adopt a scientific approach. In contrast, the psychodynamic and humanistic approaches rarely make use of the experimental method. As a result, they must be regarded as unscientific or at least as less scientific than the other three approaches. Some ideas within the psychodynamic and humanistic approaches have been submitted to scientific test, but those initially advocating these approaches did not themselves carry out any scientific research.

Part of the reason for the above differences between the five approaches is that they have addressed different issues. Psychodynamic theorists are concerned in part with the impact of experiences from many years ago (e.g. traumatic childhood events) on an individual's current life and humanistic psychologists are interested in the individual's striving to self-actualise and move towards his/her ideal self. Issues such as these are very difficult (or impossible) to study under scientific laboratory conditions. More specifically, remember that use of the experimental method involves manipulating some independent variable and observing its effects on behaviour (the dependent variable). Researchers cannot manipulate adults' childhood experiences nor can they manipulate the lengthy processes involved in the slow progress towards self-actualisation in the laboratory.

Relevant data

There are several forms of data we can collect when confronted by the complex task of understanding human behaviour. As we saw earlier in the chapter, it was generally believed from the time of the ancient Greeks until comparatively recently that introspection was the best (and perhaps the only) relevant method. The humanistic and psychodynamic approaches have continued this tradition.

Historically, the learning approach was based on the assumption that behavioural measures are objective and of great usefulness, whereas introspection provides subjective data lacking validity. However, the learning approach has developed over the years. For example, Bandura's social learning theory developed into a more cognitive approach in which he recognised the importance of mediational processes.

As we saw earlier in the chapter, the cognitive approach has greatly expanded in scope in recent decades. For many years, cognitive psychology relied heavily on behavioural data. Nowadays, in contrast, it also regards patterns of brain activity and the timing of brain activity as very relevant data. Finally, there is increasing interest in the data provided by computer models based on the assumption that computer models that successfully mimic human behaviour may shed light on the processes shown by humans when performing a given task.

Finally, there is the biological approach. Concordance rates are typically used as relevant data in twin studies. In addition, numerous physiological and neurochemical measures are regarded as relevant data. Thus, the relevant data within the biological approach differ substantially from the relevant data in any other approach.

Consciousness + non-conscious processes

The five approaches differ with respect to the importance they attach to consciousness and the role of non-conscious processes in human behaviour. At one extreme, humanistic psychologists strongly emphasise the importance of conscious experience. They acknowledge the existence of unconscious forces. However, they adopt the optimistic viewpoint that we can use our conscious capacity to develop as human beings in defiance of such forces.

There is a marked contrast here with the psychodynamic approach. Freud attached much less importance than humanistic psychologists to the power of consciousness. Indeed, he believed that much of the time we are essentially at the mercy of processes occurring within the unconscious. The psychodynamic approach regards unconscious processes as more important than any of the other four approaches.

Most early theorists within the learning approach did not think it was necessary to take account of consciousness in their theorising. They did not focus explicitly on unconscious processes but nevertheless believed that much learning occurred in a fairly "automatic" way without the intervention of conscious processes. We must not exaggerate, however—Bandura with his social learning approach has emphasised the importance of conscious processes for several decades.

Theorists within the cognitive approach increasingly accept that unconscious processes have major influences on human cognition and on behaviour. In addition, however, they mostly accept the importance of conscious processes although there are disputes about the extent to which such processes directly influence behaviour.

Finally, the biological approach has not traditionally been especially concerned about the distinction between conscious and unconscious processes. The kinds of research they carry out studying detailed physiological processes typically do not shed much light on either type of process. However, research using the electroencephalogram (EEG) has shed light on different states of consciousness (see Chapter 6 on Biopsychology).

Conclusions

The five approaches to psychology discussed in this chapter differ substantially in several ways from each other. It is natural to wonder which is the best. However, that is not a very fruitful question. Each approach was designed to address different issues about human and/or animal behaviour. As a result, the approaches differ with respect to their main focus, their preferred methods and techniques, what is regarded as relevant data, and their key assumptions.

The main conclusion we should come to is that all five approaches have made a valuable contribution to our understanding of human behaviour. However, it is generally the case in psychology that more progress is made over time by scientific approaches than by those that are non-scientific or anti-scientific. For example, the cognitive approach (which is fully scientific) has made substantial progress over the past 60 years. It is less clear that the same can be said for the humanistic approach (which is often anti-scientific).

EXAM HINT

In the exam, you might be asked to write a short evaluation of one approach, or to give two limitations of one approach. Alternatively, you might be asked to outline and evaluate one or more approaches in a longer essay question. Comparing approaches systematically can help you to evaluate them individually as well. If you are evaluating an individual approach, it is perfectly acceptable to contrast its strengths or weaknesses with another approach, as long as you do not allow your focus to drift from the approach in hand. For example, you might highlight the relative strength of the behavioural approach by pointing out that it has a stronger scientific basis than the psychodynamic and humanist approaches.

ACTIVITY: Comparing approaches

Draw up a summary table including the five approaches along one side, and the key comparisons along the other. These are:

- Main focus and aspects de-emphasised
- Species studied
- Preferred method and science
- Relevant data
- Consciousness and non-conscious processes

Section Summary

- The five approaches to psychology vary widely in terms of their main focus and the aspects of psychology that are de-emphasised. This is understandable given the history of each approach.
- The cognitive, psychodynamic, and humanistic approaches focus almost exclusively on understanding human behaviour. In contrast, the learning approaches and the biological approach focus on non-human species as well as on humans.
- Researchers within the cognitive and learning approaches typically use the experimental method and are fully scientific and the same is true of most research carried out within the biological approach. The humanistic approach is opposed to the experimental method and to science, and the same is true to a lesser extent of the psychodynamic approach.
- Traditionally, the learning approach regarded behavioural measures as the main relevant data but there is now more acceptance of cognitive measures. The cognitive approach regards brain imaging and behavioural data as relevant. The biological approach regards numerous physiological and neurochemical measures as relevant. Finally, the psychodynamic and humanistic approaches rely heavily on introspection.
- Humanistic psychologists emphasise conscious processes and experience, whereas psychodynamic psychologists emphasise unconscious processes. Researchers within the cognitive approach mostly accept the importance of conscious and unconscious processes. The distinction between conscious and unconscious processes is less important within the learning and biological approaches.

Further Reading

- The approaches discussed in this chapter are covered in greater depth by M. Jarvis (2000) *Theoretical approaches in psychology* (London: Routledge).
- An interesting perspective on the early history of scientific psychology is provided by T. H. Leahey (1992) The mythical revolutions of American psychology. *American Psychologist*, *47*, 308–318.
- The cognitive approach to psychology is discussed at length in M. W. Eysenck (2012) *Fundamentals of cognition (2nd Edn)* (Hove: Psychology Press).
- The biological approach to psychology is discussed at length by J. Ward (2010) *The student's guide to cognitive neuroscience (2nd Edn)* (Hove, UK: Psychology Press).

Revision Questions

1. Freud proposed that the personality is made up of three elements which interact.

   a. Describe two features of the ego. (4 marks)

   b. Describe two features of the id. (4 marks)

2. Psychologists often try to understand issues involved in cognitive processing by linking the way we think to the way a computer functions.

   In one study involving reaction times, a participant stated that he felt that he was being asked to do too many things at the same time. His reaction times were slower in the multi-tasking condition than in the single task condition.

   Briefly suggest how his response might help psychologists understand human cognitive processing. (4 marks)

3. "I would like to train my dog to jump through a hoop" suggested a new dog owner to an animal psychologist. "How should I set about it?"

   "I should use a token economy system" suggested the psychologist.

   Explain which type of conditioning a token economy is based on. (2 marks)

4. James timed how long it would take his pet rat to learn its way through a maze with a reward of food pellets at the end. His findings were as follows:

   Attempt 1 16 sec

   Attempt 2 12 sec

   Attempt 3 11 sec

   Attempt 4 8 sec

   Attempt 5 4 sec

   Calculate the mean time that the rat took to work through the maze. Show your working. (1 mark)

5. How much faster was the speed of the rat's final attempt than its first attempt?

   1. 4 times as fast as the first attempt
   2. 3 times as fast as the first attempt
   3. 2 times as fast as the first attempt (1 mark)

6. Two psychologists wanted to account for why little Susan always sucked her thumb when she needed to go to the dentist for a check-up.

   A behaviourist argued that she had seen her elder brother do the same just before his check-ups. However, a psychoanalyst suggested she was regressing to the oral stage in her development.

   a. Outline what is meant by social learning theory and explain how social learning might account for the behaviour described above. (6 marks)

   b. Discuss two limitations of the psychodynamic explanation given above. (6 marks)

What you need to know

The AS-level specification covers this topic as part of the Approaches in Psychology section, and you will only need to cover the first four subjects on the list below (Divisions of the nervous system, Structure and function of sensory, relay and motor neurons, Function of the endocrine system, and Fight or flight response). This will be examined in Paper 2 of the exam.

If you are studying A-level, you will need to cover everything in this chapter. Biopsychology will be examined in Paper 2 of the exam.

Biopsychology

6

Biopsychology is concerned with the ways in which biological factors influence mental processes, emotions, and behaviour. There are close links between psychology and biology, and biopsychology involves exploring those links in detail. In this section, we will focus on some of the key aspects of biopsychology.

DIVISIONS OF THE NERVOUS SYSTEM: CENTRAL AND PERIPHERAL (SOMATIC AND AUTONOMIC)

The nervous system contains all the neurons in the body. As we will see, the various parts of the nervous system are specialised for different functions. The nervous system is made up of between 15 and 20 billion neurons (nerve cells) and a much larger number of **glia** (small cells fulfilling various functions). The nervous system is divided into two main sub-systems:

- **Central nervous system**: this consists of the brain and the spinal cord; it is protected by bone and fluid circulating around it.
- **Peripheral nervous system**: this consists of all the other nerve cells in the body; it is divided into the somatic nervous system and the autonomic nervous system.

KEY TERMS

Glia: small cells in the nervous system that fulfil various functions (e.g. absorbing chemicals released by neurons; removing waste material from dead neurons).

Central nervous system: the brain and spinal cord.

Peripheral nervous system: it consists of all the nerve cells in the body not located within the central nervous system; it consists of the somatic nervous system and the autonomic nervous system.

Central nervous system

We will have much more to say about the brain later in this chapter (see also discussion in Chapter 5). In view of the importance of the brain, it is not surprising it is the most protected part of the body. Both the brain and the spinal cord are encased in bone and covered in protective membranes. In addition, there is the blood–brain barrier. This is a protective mechanism permitting blood to flow freely to the brain but ensuring that most substances in the bloodstream do not reach the brain tissue.

The brain is divided into three main regions: hindbrain; midbrain; and forebrain. These terms refer to their locations in the embryo's nervous system and do not indicate clearly the relative position of the different brain regions in an adult. We will briefly consider each of these regions.

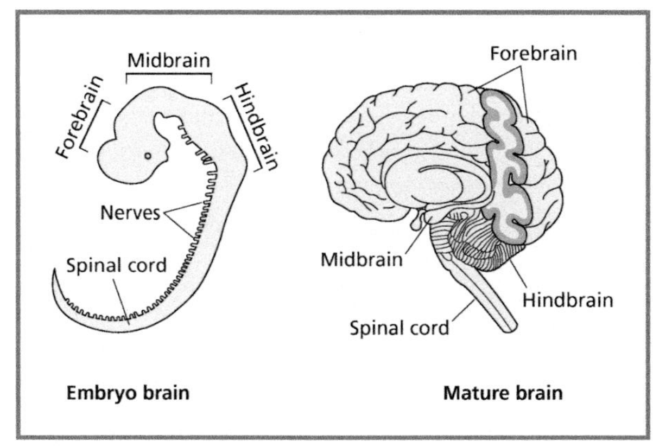

Hindbrain

The hindbrain is at the back of the brain. It consists of the medulla, the pons, and the cerebellum. The medulla is located immediately behind the spinal cord. It is involved in the control of crucial functions such as breathing, vomiting, salivation, and the regulation of the cardiovascular system. The pons is in front of the medulla and the two structures together form the **reticular formation**. This is involved in controlling levels of arousal. Finally, there is the cerebellum, which is a large structure within the hindbrain. It is involved in the control of balance and movement.

Midbrain

The midbrain is divided into the tectum or roof and the tegmentum, which is the middle part of the midbrain. The tectum consists of areas that are used as routes for sensory information. The tegmentum contains parts of the reticular formation (other parts lie within the hindbrain). It also contains the **substantia nigra**. Damage to this structure can lead to depletion of dopaminergic cells and the onset of Parkinson's disease, a disease that is characterised by progressively impaired motor control.

Forebrain

This is easily the largest and the most important division of the human brain. The outer layer of the forebrain is the cerebral cortex. About 90% of the human cerebral cortex is neocortex (literally, new cortex). It is deeply furrowed or grooved. The ridges between these furrows are known as gyri. Far and away the largest furrow is the longitudinal fissure running between the cerebral hemispheres. The two hemispheres are almost separate from each other but are connected directly by a bridge known as the corpus callosum. In sum, the cerebral cortex is a continuous sheet resembling a scrunched-up blanket stuffed into a box (David Carey, personal communication).

Two of the most obvious features of each hemisphere are the central sulcus and the lateral (or Sylvian) fissure ("fissure" means" "furrow"). These features help to define the four lobes or areas of each hemisphere: the frontal, parietal, temporal, and occipital lobes.

Important parts of the forebrain are underneath the cerebral cortex. Two series of interconnected structures in this part of the brain are the limbic system and the basal ganglia motor system. The **limbic system** consists of various structures including the amygdala, the septum, the hippocampus, and the hypothalamus. The main functions of the limbic system are to regulate several kinds of motivated behaviour including eating, aggression, avoidance behaviour, and sexual behaviour and associated emotions such as anger and anxiety. The basal ganglia assist in the production of voluntary motor responses.

The thalamus and the hypothalamus are two important structures. The hypothalamus (discussed in detail later) is much smaller than the thalamus and is situated below it. The hypothalamus is involved in the control of several functions such as body temperature, hunger, and thirst. It is also involved in the control of sexual behaviour. Finally, the hypothalamus plays an important role in the control of the endocrine (hormone) system.

What about the **thalamus**? It acts as a relay station passing signals on to higher brain centres. For example, the medial geniculate nucleus receives signals from the inner ear and sends them to the primary auditory cortex. In similar fashion, the lateral geniculate nucleus receives information from the eye and sends it to the primary visual cortex and the ventral posterior nucleus receives somatosensory (bodily sensation) information and sends it to the primary somatosensory cortex (discussed later).

Spinal cord

The spinal cord is a thin structure going from the base of the brain all the way down to the coccyx bone at the lower end of the back. It is protected by 24 vertebrae or bony segments running from the neck to the lower back regions. The spinal cord consists of an inner area of grey matter and an outer area of white matter. White matter consists of myelinated or sheathed axons whereas grey matter consists of cell bodies and unmyelinated axons. The spinal cord contains 31 pairs of spinal nerves, with each nerve dividing into two roots as it approaches the spinal cord. The dorsal root at the back contains sensory neurons that assist

KEY TERMS

Reticular formation: a part of the brain concerned with arousal, the regulation of sleep, and the control of breathing.

Substantia nigra: a structure in the midbrain; damage to this structure can play a role in the onset of Parkinson's disease.

Limbic system: this part of the forebrain consists of various structures (e.g. hypothalamus; hippocampus; amygdala) involved in emotion and motivation.

Thalamus: part of the forebrain and involved in several functions including wakefulness and sleep.

in the transmission of sensory signals to the brain. The ventral root at the front contains motor neurons that are involved in the transmission of motor signals to skeletal muscles and to internal organs (e.g. stomach; heart).

Peripheral nervous system

As mentioned already, the peripheral nervous system divides into two parts: the somatic nervous system and the autonomic nervous system. The somatic nervous system is concerned with interactions with the *external* environment, whereas the autonomic nervous system is concerned with the body's *internal* environment.

The **somatic nervous system** consists in part of nerves carrying signals from the eyes, ears, skeletal muscles, and the skin to the central nervous system (see Figure). It also consists of nerves carrying signals from the central nervous system to the skeletal muscles, skin, and so on.

The **autonomic nervous system** controls the involuntary movement of non-skeletal muscles. The organs within the control of the autonomic nervous system include the heart, lungs, eyes, stomach, and the blood vessels of the internal organs. The autonomic nervous system is divided into the sympathetic nervous system and the parasympathetic nervous system (see Figure).

The **sympathetic nervous system** is called into play in situations needing arousal and energy. It produces increased heart rate, reduced activity within the stomach, pupil dilation or expansion, and relaxation of the bronchi of the lungs. These changes prepare us for fight or flight (discussed in detail later).

The **parasympathetic nervous system** is involved when the body tries to save energy. The effects of activity in the parasympathetic nervous system are the *opposite* to those of activity in the sympathetic nervous system. The parasympathetic nervous system produces decreased heart rate, increased activity within the stomach, pupil contraction, and constriction of the bronchi of the lungs.

The sympathetic nervous system and the parasympathetic nervous system are both important. For example, consider someone with excessive activity of the sympathetic nervous system but very little activity of the parasympathetic nervous system. He/she would probably be a highly stressed individual who found life very demanding.

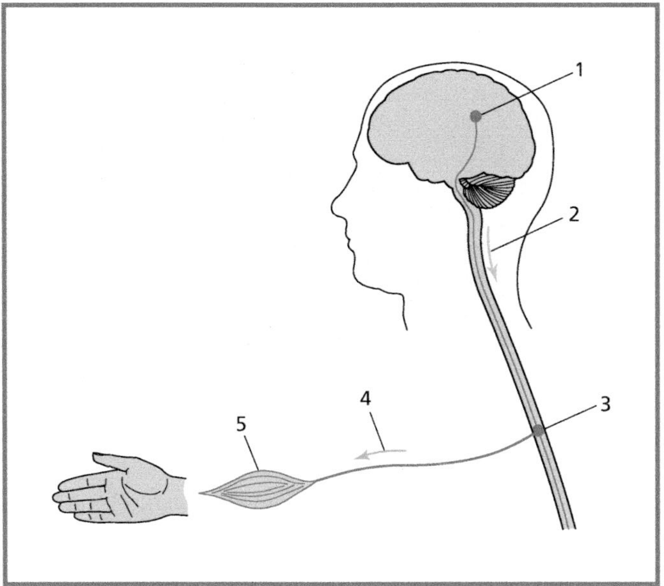

The somatic nervous system: What happens when you decide to move your fingers. (1) The decision arises in the brain; (2) is transmitted via the spinal cord; (3) transfers to another nerve (or series of nerves); (4) the instruction is transmitted to the skeletal muscles; (5) the muscles contract or relax, moving the fingers.

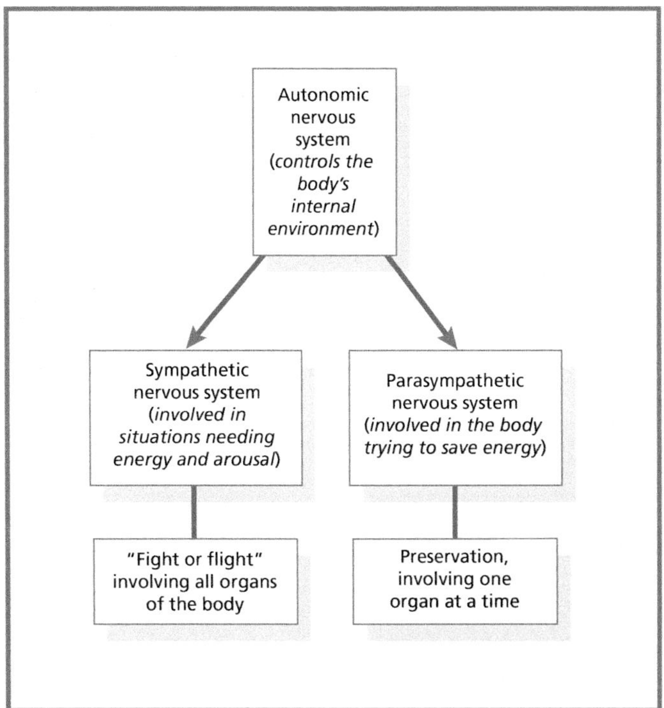

KEY TERMS

Somatic nervous system: the part of the peripheral nervous system that controls the voluntary movements of skeletal muscles and hence the limbs.

Autonomic nervous system: the part of the peripheral nervous system that controls the involuntary movement of non-skeletal muscles; it is divided into the sympathetic nervous system and the parasympathetic nervous system.

Sympathetic nervous system: the part of the autonomic nervous system that produces arousal and energy (e.g. an increased heart rate).

Parasympathetic nervous system: the part of the autonomic nervous system that is involved in reducing arousal and conserving energy (e.g. by reducing heart rate).

Activities of the autonomic nervous system

Sympathetic branch	Parasympathetic branch
Increased heart rate	Decreased heart rate
Reduced activity within the stomach	Increased activity within the stomach
Saliva production is inhibited (mouth feels dry)	Saliva production increased to aid digestion
Pupil dilation or expansion	Pupil contraction
Relaxation of the bronchi of the lungs	Constriction of the bronchi of the lungs
Glucose is released	Glucose is stored

Section Summary

- The central nervous system consists of the brain and spinal cord.
- The brain is divided into three parts: the hindbrain, the midbrain, and forebrain.
- The hindbrain is involved in the control of breathing and arousal. The midbrain is also involved in the control of arousal. The forebrain consists of the cerebral cortex which resembles a scrunched-up blanket and is involved in nearly all cognitive processes. Other parts of the forebrain are involved in the control of motivation and emotion.
- The peripheral nervous system consists of the somatic and autonomic nervous systems. The somatic nervous system carries signals from the eyes, ears, skeletal muscles, and skin to the central nervous system.
- The autonomic nervous system controls the involuntary movement of non-skeletal muscles. It is divided into the sympathetic nervous system (used in situations requiring arousal and energy) and the parasympathetic nervous system (producing opposite effects to those of the sympathetic nervous system).

STRUCTURE AND FUNCTION OF SENSORY, RELAY, AND MOTOR NEURONS

KEY TERMS

Neuron: cells that are specialised to conduct electrical impulses.

Soma: a cell body containing a nucleus.

Dendrites: parts of the neuron that conduct nerve impulses towards the soma or cell body.

Axon: a part of the neuron that conducts nerve impulses away from the cell body or soma.

Sensory neurons: neurons within the peripheral nervous system that respond to stimulation by sensory receptors and send signals towards the brain and spinal cord.

We will start by considering general properties of neurons. After that, we will focus on differences among different types of neurons (i.e. sensory, relay, and motor). **Neurons** are cells specialised for transmitting electrical impulses. They form the basic units of the nervous system. There are various kinds of neurons but most possess the same basic underlying structure (see Figure):

- A cell body or **soma** which contains a nucleus. It is in the soma that most of the metabolic work of each neuron occurs.
- At one end of the cell body are **dendrites**, which receive input from other neurons and conduct nerve impulses towards the soma.
- At the other end of the cell body is the **axon**, which conducts nerve impulses away from the soma and towards other neurons.

The average neuron sends impulses to approximately 1,000 other neurons. In order to understand the nature of these neurons bear in mind neurons can carry a message in only *one* direction. It is important to distinguish among sensory, relay, and motor neurons:

Sensory neurons: these neurons respond to a given type of stimulation (e.g. a particular wavelength of light) in sensory receptors and send signals to the spinal cord and brain. There are sensory neurons for all sense modalities (e.g. vision; hearing; smell; taste; touch). Sensory neurons are located in the peripheral nervous system. They are also known as afferent neurons because they carry signals *towards* the brain and spinal cord.

Sensory neurons receive information from sensory receptors. This information enters through the dendrites, passes to the cell body, and then is sent through the axon to the **axon terminals**. Most sensory neurons have long dendrites but relatively short axons.

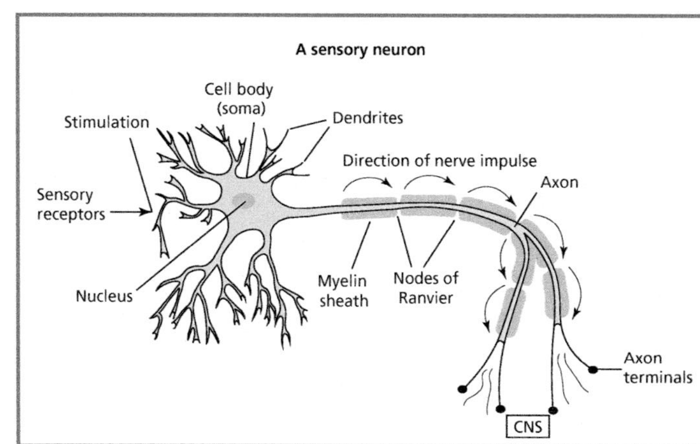

Motor neurons: these neurons within the peripheral nervous system transmit signals from the brain and spinal cord to effectors (muscles or glands). They are also known as efferent neurons because they carry signals *away from* the central nervous system.

Information enters motor neurons through the dendrites; it is then passed on to the cell, from where it proceeds through the axon until it reaches the axon terminals. The axon terminals are called motor end plates if the motor neuron connects with a muscle. The dendrites are usually short whereas the axons are long.

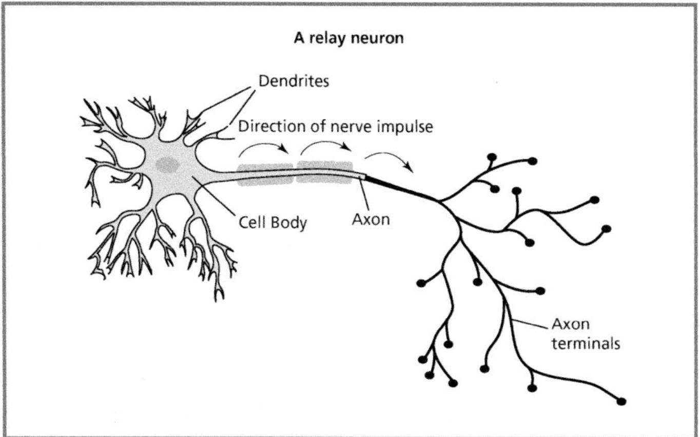

Relay neurons: these neurons form connections between other neurons. All the neurons in the central nervous system (including the brain) are relay neurons. These neurons (also called interneurons) are neither sensory nor motor; they receive signals from sensory neurons or other relay neurons and send signals to motor neurons or other relay neurons. There are more than 100 billion relay neurons in the body, which is more than the number of sensory or motor neurons. This is so because of the complexity of integrating sensory and motor processes and the diversity of processes occurring in the brain and spinal cord.

Information enters relay neurons through the dendrites from where it proceeds to the cell body. After that, information proceeds along the axon to the axon terminals. Relay neurons typically have short dendrites and axons and have many axon terminals.

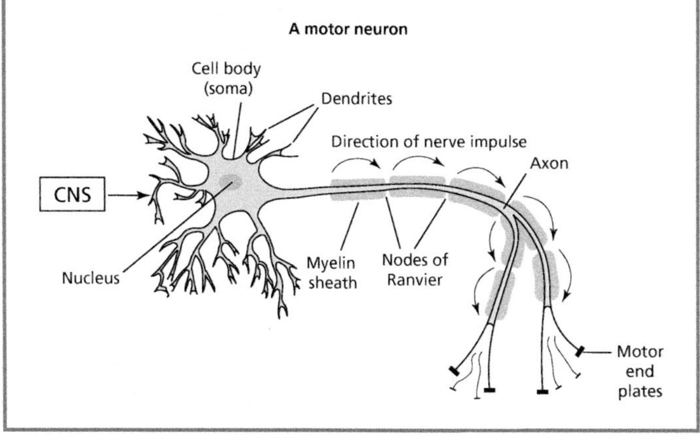

Synaptic transmission

Synapses are the very small gaps between adjacent neurons. When neurons fire, they release chemicals or **neurotransmitters** which cross the synapses and affect the receptors on the adjacent neurons. These neurotransmitters increase or decrease the membrane potential of the adjacent neuron. The membrane

KEY TERMS

Axon terminals: these are found at the end of an axon; they allow electrical impulses to pass from one neuron to the next.

Motor neurons: neurons within the peripheral nervous system that send signals away from the central nervous system to the muscles and glands.

Relay neurons: neurons within the central nervous system that receive input from sensory neurons or other relay neurons and send impulses to motor neurons or other relay neurons.

Synapses: the extremely small junctions between adjacent neurons where nerve impulses are relayed.

Neurotransmitters: chemicals that cross synapses and affect the receptors on adjacent neurons.

EXAM HINT

In the exam you may be asked to label a diagram of localised functions in the brain. Alternatively you may be asked to label a diagram of a sensory, relay or motor neuron or synapse. Make sure you revise the structures and can spell them correctly.

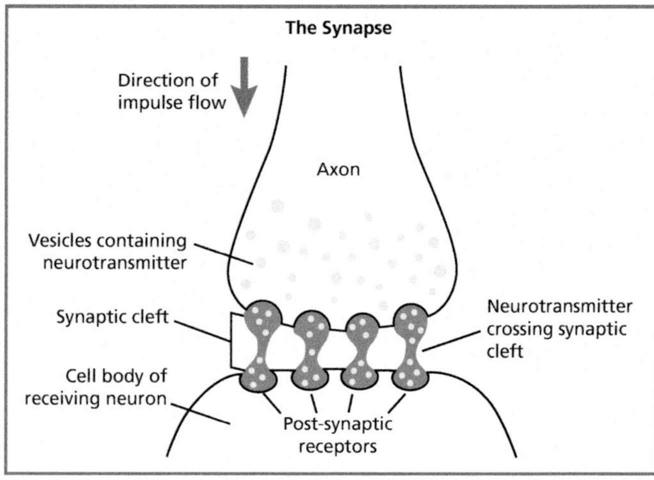

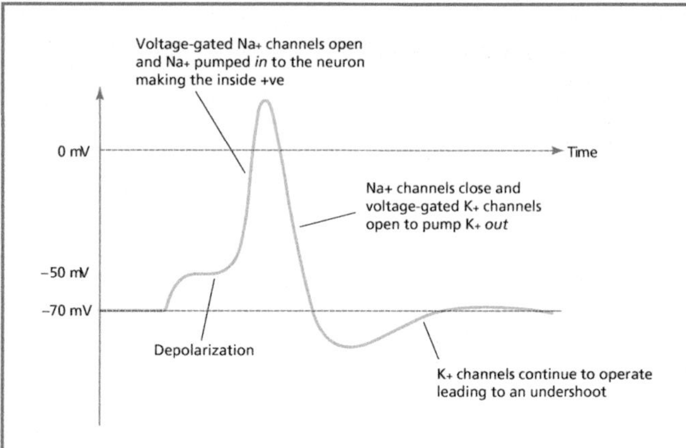

The action potential consists of a number of phases.

potential is the difference in electrical charge between the inside and outside of a neuron; its **resting potential** is about −70 mV (millivolts)—the potential inside the neuron is 70 mV less than outside it.

So far we have been talking as if the receptor area of each neuron has only a single synapse. In fact, there are generally thousands of synapses associated with the receptor area of each neuron. What determines whether or not any given neuron fires? If its membrane potential is reduced to −65 mV or less, then the neuron fires. This consists of an **action potential** which is generated at the axon hillock. It is a brief chemical event lasting about 1 ms and it reverses the membrane potential from −70 mV to about 40 mV.

In most synapses, the site of neurotransmitter release from one neuron is very close to the site of neurotransmitter reception at another neuron. Many neurons release only one neurotransmitter but some release two or more. Neurotransmitters initiate reactions in the postsynaptic neuron by binding to its receptors. Most neurotransmitters can bind to various types of receptors (e.g. serotonin has at least 10 types of receptors) and the nature of the receptor response varies across types. We can think of neurotransmitters as keys and of receptors as locks: there has to be a fit between the two for anything to happen.

Excitation and inhibition

Any given neuron may have as many as 15,000 connections with other neurons. What determines whether it fires (generates an action potential)? Let's consider the processes occurring during an action potential in more detail. Initially, the sodium and potassium channels open. This causes sodium **ions** to enter the neuron followed closely by potassium ions being driven out of the neuron. After 1 ms, the sodium ion channels close followed by the potassium channels. The closure of these channels causes the action potential to come to an end.

Neurotransmitters are of vital importance in determining whether a given neuron produces an action potential. Some neurotransmitters are excitatory. These neurotransmitters cause sodium ions to flow into the cell. Within the central nervous system, glutamate is the main excitatory neurotransmitter.

Other neurotransmitters are inhibitory. These neurotransmitters cause potassium channels to open in the post-synaptic neuron which can cause potassium ions to flow out of the cell. This makes the membrane potential more negative. GABA (gamma-aminobutyric acid) is the main inhibitory neurotransmitter in the central nervous system.

Any given neuron will typically be subject to excitatory and inhibitory influences from several neurotransmitters at any given moment. If the overall or net effect of these influences is inhibitory, this *reduces* the likelihood the neuron will generate an action potential. In contrast, if the overall or net effect of these influences is excitatory, this *increases* the likelihood the neuron will generate an action potential.

KEY TERMS

Resting potential: the condition in which the neuron is not firing when the electrical charge inside it is about −70mV.

Action potential: a brief electrical and chemical firing that allows nerve impulses to travel along an axon.

Ions: particles that are either positively or negatively charged.

Section Summary

- Neurons are specialised for transmitting electrical impulses; they form the basic units of the nervous system.
- Sensory neurons receive information from sensory receptors and carry signals towards the brain and spinal cord.
- Motor neurons transmit signals from the brain and spinal cord to effectors (muscles or glands).

- All the neurons in the central nervous system are relay neurons; they receive signals from sensory neurons or other relay neurons and send signals to motor neurons or other relay neurons.
- Synapses are the very small gaps that exist between adjacent neurons. When neurons fire, they release chemicals or neurotransmitters which cross the synapses and affect the receptors on the adjacent neurons.
- Any given neuron is typically subject to excitatory and inhibitory influences from several neurotransmitters at any given moment.

FUNCTION OF THE ENDOCRINE SYSTEM: GLANDS AND HORMONES

So far we have focused mainly on the nervous system and it is now time to consider the endocrine system. We will shortly be discussing the details of functioning within the endocrine system. First, however, we will consider the main differences between the two systems (Westen, 1996, p. 84):

> *Whereas the nervous system relies on electrochemical transmission of impulses to transmit messages between cells, the endocrine system provides another method of intercellular communication that is far more global, that is, not limited to connections between a relatively small number of individual cells. The difference . . . is analogous to the difference between word of mouth and mass media (which can communicate information to hundreds of millions of people at once). The endocrine system "broadcasts" its signals by releasing hormones into the bloodstream.*

The **endocrine system** consists of various ductless glands. Glands are organs of the body producing a substance (e.g. hormones; sweat) needed elsewhere in the body. The glands within the endocrine system include the following: pituitary gland; thyroid gland; adrenal gland; pancreas; and the gonads.

As indicated already, the endocrine system is *not* part of the nervous system. However, there are numerous interactions between the endocrine and the peripheral nervous system. More specifically, the endocrine glands secrete or release hormones (from the Greek "hormon" meaning to excite). They are ductless glands because they secrete hormones *directly* into the bloodstream rather than via a tube or passage. **Hormones** are chemical substances released into the bloodstream and they are so important they have been described as the "messengers of life". Dozens of hormones have been identified and additional ones are still being discovered.

Hormones can have dramatic effects on our behaviour and emotions, especially stress. Most hormones are slow acting because they are carried around the body fairly slowly by the bloodstream. The effects of hormones last for some time but typically diminish as the situation becomes less stressful.

KEY TERMS

Endocrine system: a system consisting of a number of ductless glands located throughout the body; this system produces the body's chemical messengers called hormones.

Hormones: chemical substances that are produced by one tissue before proceeding via the bloodstream to another tissue.

Nervous system
- Consists of nerve cells
- Acts by transmitting nerve impulses
- Acts rapidly
- Direct control
- Specific localised effects of neurotransmitters
- Short-lived effects

Endocrine system
- Consists of ductless glands
- Acts by release of hormones
- Acts slowly
- Indirect control
- Hormones spread around the body
- Hormones remain in the blood for some time

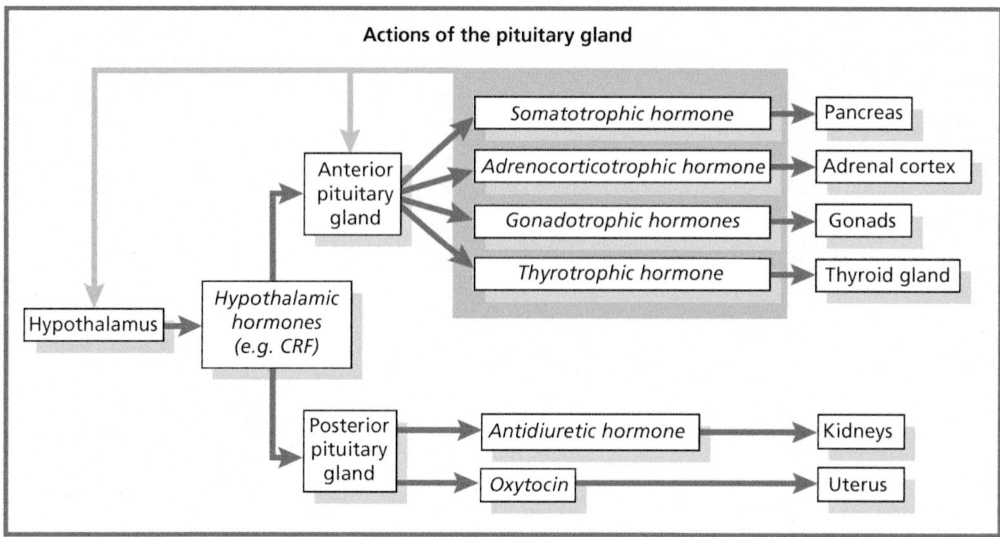

The parts of the endocrine system are distributed in various areas of the body. However, most of the endocrine system is controlled by the **hypothalamus**, a small structure at the base of the brain. There are direct connections between the hypothalamus and the anterior pituitary gland. Hypothalamic hormones (e.g. corticotropin-releasing factor) stimulate the anterior pituitary gland to secrete its hormones. After that, the hormones secreted by the anterior pituitary gland control the functioning of the other endocrine glands (see Figure). However, it is not simply the case that the hypothalamus controls the anterior pituitary gland which in turn controls the other endocrine glands. In addition, there is a negative feedback system: increases in hormone levels are detected by the pituitary gland leading to a decrease in the release of the hormones it controls.

Types of endocrine glands

Here are brief descriptions of the main types of endocrine glands. First, the pituitary gland is often referred to as the "master gland" of the body. The anterior pituitary gland synthesises several hormones with their release being controlled by the hypothalamus. These hormones include the following: growth hormone; prolactin, which controls the secretions of the mammary glands; adrenocorticotropic hormone (ACTH) which controls the secretions of the adrenal cortex; follicle-stimulating hormone and luteinising hormone which control the secretions of the gonads (sex glands: testes and ovaries); and thyroid-stimulating hormone which controls secretions of the thyroid gland.

Stress response

There is general agreement that stress involves an immediate shock response followed by a countershock response. The first or shock response depends mainly on the sympathetic adrenal medullary (SAM) system (see Figure). It is involved in the fight or flight response and is discussed in detail shortly. As we will see, the endocrine system is heavily involved in the SAM system's functioning.

The second or countershock response involves the hypothalamic–pituitary–adrenocoretical (HPA) axis (see Figure). As we will see, the endocrine system also has a major involvement in the functioning of the HPA axis. The two systems do *not* operate in total independence of each other—they often interact when we are coping with a stressful situation. In what follows, we will consider the two systems in turn with an emphasis on the role of the endocrine system.

KEY TERM

Hypothalamus: a small structure in the forebrain that is of relevance to eating, drinking, sexual activity, and temperature regulation.

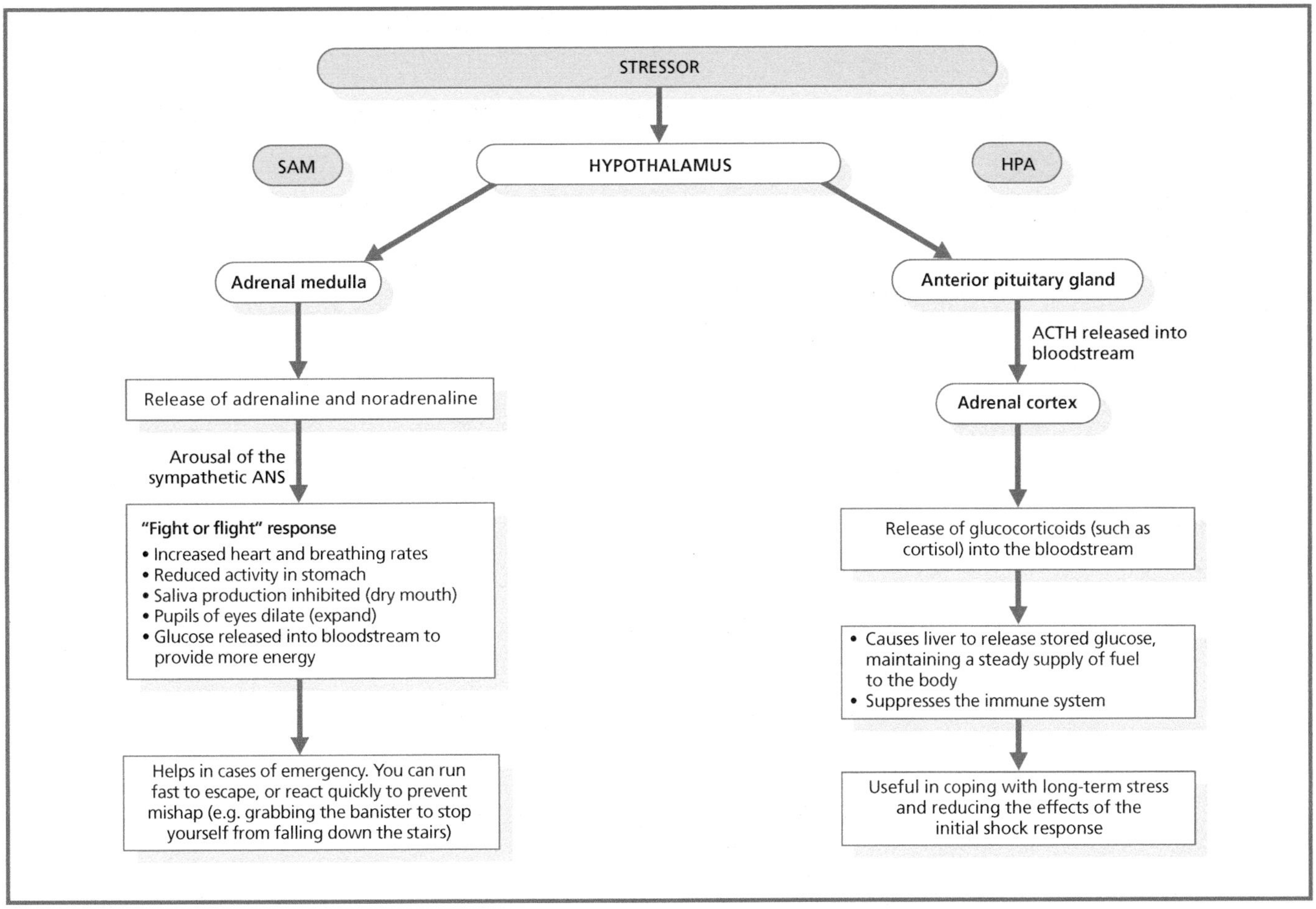

STRESSOR

↓

HYPOTHALAMUS

SAM

Adrenal medulla

↓

Release of adrenaline and noradrenaline

↓ Arousal of the sympathetic ANS

"Fight or flight" response

- Increased heart and breathing rates
- Reduced activity in stomach
- Saliva production inhibited (dry mouth)
- Pupils of eyes dilate (expand)
- Glucose released into bloodstream to provide more energy

↓

Helps in cases of emergency. You can run fast to escape, or react quickly to prevent mishap (e.g. grabbing the banister to stop yourself from falling down the stairs)

HPA

Anterior pituitary gland

↓ ACTH released into bloodstream

Adrenal cortex

↓

Release of glucocorticoids (such as cortisol) into the bloodstream

↓

- Causes liver to release stored glucose, maintaining a steady supply of fuel to the body
- Suppresses the immune system

↓

Useful in coping with long-term stress and reducing the effects of the initial shock response

FIGHT OR FLIGHT RESPONSE INCLUDING THE ROLE OF ADRENALINE

Imagine you are in a situation posing a real danger to your physical survival. If we go back hundreds or thousands of years, humans were often put in such situations when in the presence of a wild animal or an aggressive member of another tribe. What is the optimal way for our body to respond in such circumstances? What we need is for our body to become very aroused so we can respond with vigorous physical activity. This is likely to be effective. If the wild animal or tribesman is fairly small and not especially threatening, fight is the appropriate response. If the wild animal or tribesman is large and threatening, flight probably makes more sense.

The key point is that being ready for vigorous activity is very useful regardless of whether we decide fight or flight is more appropriate. It is for that reason that the aroused stress response is often called the fight or flight response.

The stress response is important for survival. An animal that does not feel stress when being pursued by a predator is not likely to survive because it does not become mobilised to respond.

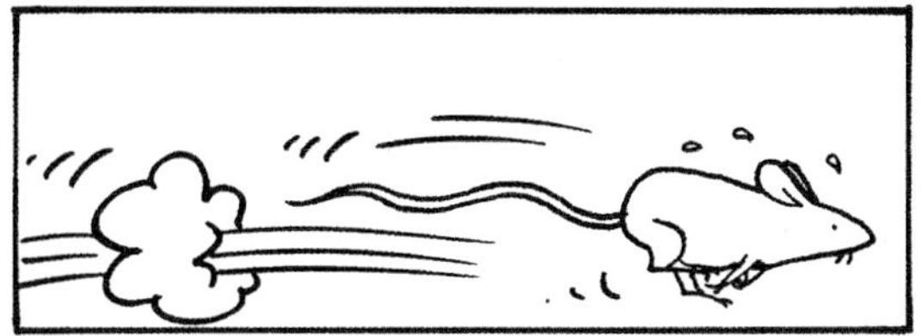

The bodily response to some stress rapidly involves the sympathomedullary pathway or **sympathetic adrenal medullary (SAM) system** (see Figure). There are several stages within the SAM system. First, activation within the hypothalamus leads to messages from the brainstem being sent to the **adrenal medulla**. The adrenal medulla is the inner part of the **adrenal glands** close to the kidneys. The adrenal glands are an important part of the endocrine system.

Second, the adrenal medulla secretes (releases) the hormones **adrenaline** and noradrenaline (Americans call these epinephrine and norepinephrine, respectively). Third, release of the hormones adrenaline (epinephrine) and noradrenaline (norepinephrine) leads to increased arousal of the sympathetic nervous system and reduced activity within the parasympathetic nervous system. These changes prepare us for fight or flight.

More specifically, there are the following effects: an increase in energy, increased alertness, increased blood flow to the muscles, increased heart and respiration rate, reduced activity in the digestive system, and increased release of clotting factors into the bloodstream to reduce blood loss in the event of injury. Adrenaline and noradrenaline increase the output of the heart which can cause an increase in blood pressure. These various changes involve the sympathetic nervous system. The sympathetic nervous system typically operates fairly automatically—stressors cause our heart rate to increase, energy levels to increase, and blood pressure to increase without any conscious control.

How can we explain individual differences in SAM system activity? Several factors are at work but here we will simply consider genetic ones. Frigerio et al. (2009) studied the stress response in infants. Individual differences in SAM activity under stress were associated with specific genetic factors.

? How are adrenaline and noradrenaline related to stress?

? Can you think of some situations in which the "fight or flight" response might be activated?

KEY TERMS

Sympathetic adrenal medullary (SAM) system: the source of the immediate stress response, also known as fight or flight, where the hypothalamus activates the autonomic nervous system, which in turn activates the adrenal medulla, producing the release of the stress hormones adrenaline and noradrenaline.

Adrenal medulla: the inner part of the adrenal glands; it is involved in the stress response by releasing the hormones adrenaline and noradrenaline.

Adrenal glands: the endocrine glands that are located adjacent to (and covering) the upper part of the kidneys.

Adrenaline: one of the hormones (along with noradrenaline) produced by the adrenal glands; it increases arousal by activating the sympathetic nervous system and reducing activity in the parasympathetic nervous system.

ACTIVITY: Measuring the fight or flight response

Heart rate is one measure that increases in the fight or flight response, and this is easy to monitor by taking the pulse. This can be done manually or by using a pulse monitor, something psychology and biology departments often have in their equipment. This type of data is ratio data and does not depend on opinion, and so it is empirical. The equipment would enable you to measure accurately, and you could record your data methodically, for example by using a simple table.

You could do an experiment on willing participants aged 16 or over, measuring their pulse rate when they are sitting relaxed, and then doing this again when they are in a slightly stressful situation, such as doing a set of puzzles or a simple computer game with a time deadline to create mild stress. Of course, for obvious reasons as well as the BPS Ethical Guidelines, they must not be stressed more than they would be in any normal everyday situation. If you set up this experiment in a special room, a classroom for instance, it would be a laboratory experiment. But if you did it in the participant's own home it would be a field experiment. Each of these situations has strengths and weaknesses, and you could consider, on balance, which situation would give you the most scientific results.

Tend and befriend

Most early research on the stress response was limited in that approximately 85% of the participants were male. Taylor et al. (2000) argued there are important differences between men and women in their reactions to stress. Men are much more likely than women to respond to a stressful situation with a fight or flight response. In contrast, women generally respond to stressful situations with a tend and befriend response. Thus, women respond to stressors by protecting and looking after their children (the tend response) and by actively seeking social support from others (the befriend response).

How can we explain this gender difference? Taylor et al. (2000) emphasised the role of oxytocin, a hormone secreted by men and women as part of the stress response. **Oxytocin** (which has been called the "cuddle hormone") makes individuals less anxious and more sociable and is associated with the tend and befriend response. Of direct relevance here, the effects of oxytocin are reduced by male sex hormones but increased by the female hormone, oestrogen.

There is support for the various assumptions of Taylor et al. (2000). Cardoso et al. (2013) studied individuals in a negative mood produced by the stressful experience of social rejection. Their key finding was that the administration of oxytocin increased the participants' trust in others which would presumably have increased the likelihood they would have sought social support. Luckow et al. (1998) reviewed 26 studies on gender differences in seeking and using social support. Women sought social support significantly more than men in 25 of these studies.

Women are more likely to use the "tend-and-befriend" response to stress than the "fight or flight" response more often used by men.

EVALUATION

- (+) Activity in the sympathomedullary pathway forms an important part of the stress response to dangerous situations. The SAM system has proved of enormous benefit to the survival of the human species because it prepares us for fight or flight.
- (+) The SAM system shows clearly the importance of the endocrine system—hormones secreted by the adrenal glands permit rapid and widespread activation of the body in the presence of danger or threat.
- (−) Activation of the SAM system is not only associated with physical danger. For example, we have elevated levels of adrenaline and noradrenaline when we concentrate hard on a task.

Hypothalamic–pituitary–adrenocortical (HPA) axis

We now turn to the hypothalamic–pituitary–adrenocortical (HPA) axis, which plays an important part in minimising any damage that might have been caused by excessive activity within the SAM system. As indicated already, activity in the HPA axis is initiated by (and in large measure controlled by) the hypothalamus. The HPA axis takes longer than the SAM system to be activated in stressful situations.

The crucial role the endocrine system plays within the hypothalamic–pituitary–adrenocortical (HPA) axis is indicated by the words used to describe it. As we have already seen, the pituitary gland is the most important gland within the endocrine system. The adrenal gland is also of major importance to the endocrine system. These two glands (and the hormones they release) all form part of the endocrine system.

How does the hypothalamus influence the HPA axis? First, the hypothalamus produces hormones (e.g. corticotropin-releasing factor or CRF) that stimulate the pituitary gland. This gland is the size of a pea and is below the hypothalamus.

Second, when the pituitary gland is activated by the hypothalamus, it releases several hormones. The most important **is adrenocorticotropic hormone (ACTH)** which stimulates the **adrenal cortex**. The adrenal cortex is the outermost layer of the adrenal glands. ACTH is strongly involved in the HPA axis stress response.

EXAM HINT

You could be asked specifically about the role of adrenaline in the fight or flight response. Make sure that you can outline the sympathetic adrenal medullary system that releases adrenaline and can identify all of the physiological changes that adrenaline produces.

KEY TERMS

Oxytocin: this hormone promotes feelings of well-being by increasing sociability and reducing anxiety.

Adrenocorticotrophic hormone (ACTH): a hormone secreted by the pituitary gland that stimulates the adrenal cortex and the secretion of various hormones including cortisol.

Adrenal cortex: the outermost part of the adrenal glands; it triggers the release of various hormones including cortisol during the stress response.

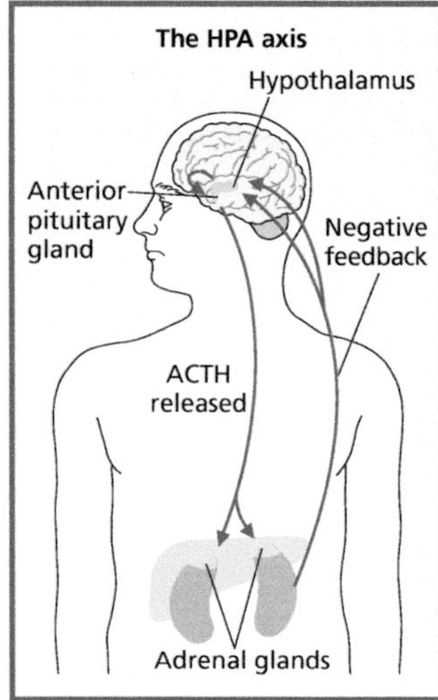

Third, ACTH in the adrenal cortex leads to the release of various **glucocorticoids**, which are hormones that influence **glucose** metabolism. The key glucocorticoid with respect to stress is cortisol. **Cortisol** is called the "stress hormone" because excess amounts are found in the urine of individuals experiencing stress.

How can we explain individual differences in HPA axis activity in response to stress? First, genetic factors are important. Mormede et al. (2011) discussed twin studies in which identical twins had much more similar HPA axis activity than fraternal twins.

Second, there are interesting gender differences. Male and female participants were exposed to achievement stressors (complex tasks) and to social rejection (being excluded from a conversation) (Stroud et al., 2002). Only males showed increased cortisol levels after exposure to achievement stressors and only females had increased cortisol after social rejection. These sex differences are consistent with stereotyped notions about men being more concerned than women about achievement whereas women are more concerned about social acceptance. However, these stereotypes have become increasingly less accurate reflections of the motivations of men and women in recent years.

? It is normal to have a fight or flight response reaction to a stressor—what change(s) have you noticed in your own body when faced with a stressful situation, such as a test or exam, or being told off? Could you feel your heart beating stronger, your breathing speeding up, or your muscles tensing?

Effects of activity in the HPA axis

- Good effect: Cortisol is important for coping with long-term stress, because it maintains a steady supply of fuel. More energy is available because of increased glucose levels.
- Good effect: The secretion of cortisol and other glucocorticoids has various useful functions:
  - The glucocorticoids help to conserve glucose for neural tissue.
  - The glucocorticoids elevate or stabilise blood glucose concentrations.
  - The glucocorticoids mobilise protein reserves.
  - The glucocorticoids conserve salts and water.
- Good effect: Cortisol is important in reversing some of the body's initial response to stress, thus putting bodily systems into a balanced state (Gevirtz, 2000).
- Bad effect: "The blood still has elevated levels of glucose (for energy) and some hormones (including adrenaline and the pituitary hormone ACTH), and the body continues to use its resources at an accelerating rate. Essentially, the organism remains on red alert" (Westen, 1996, p. 427).
- Bad effect: The anti-inflammatory action of glucocorticoids slows wound healing.
- Bad effect: Glucocorticoids suppress the immune system, which has the task of protecting the body against intruders such as viruses and bacteria. When immune responses are low, we are more likely to develop a disease (Kiecolt-Glaser et al., 1984, 1995).

KEY TERMS

Glucocorticoids: steroid hormones (e.g. cortisol) released from the adrenal cortex when the body is stressed.

Glucose: a form of sugar that is one of the main sources of energy for the brain.

Cortisol: a hormone produced by the adrenal gland that elevates blood sugar and is important in digestion, especially at times of stress.

EVALUATION

The HPA system is of value in reducing some of the negative impact of the SAM system response to stress. We can see this by considering individuals without adrenal glands who cannot produce the normal amounts of glucocorticoids. When exposed to a stressor, they must be given additional quantities of glucocorticoids to survive (Tyrell & Baxter, 1981). However, the beneficial effects of HPA activity are achieved at considerable cost and it cannot continue indefinitely at an elevated level of activity. If the adrenal cortex stops producing glucocorticoids, this eliminates the individual's ability to maintain blood glucose concentrations at the appropriate level.

I have discussed the SAM and HPA systems mostly as if they were entirely different and separate. This is not entirely correct. As Evans (1998, p. 60) pointed out, "At the level of the central nervous system, the crucially important SAM and HPA systems can be considered as one complex: they are as it were the lower limbs of one body."

Sex glands: Gonads

As mentioned earlier, hormones secreted by the pituitary gland stimulate the gonads (sex glands) which leads to the secretion of sex hormones from the sex glands. Two main classes of sex hormones are released by the gonads (testes in men; ovaries in women): androgens and oestrogens. **Androgens** are sex hormones present in greater amounts in males than in females; the most common androgen is testosterone. **Oestrogens** are sex hormones present in greater amounts in females than males; the most common oestrogen is oestradiol.

As a result, androgens are sometimes described as "male hormones" and oestrogens as "female hormones". This is misleading given that males and females produce both types of hormones. However, the level of androgens is 10 times higher in men than women, whereas the level of oestrogens is 10 times higher in women than men.

A very interesting (but controversial!) issue is the extent to which differences in behaviour between boys/men and girls/women reflect the workings of the endocrine system. Here we will briefly consider two topics within this area: (1) sex-typed behaviour; and (2) physical aggression.

Sex-typed behaviour

Boys tend to play with "boy" toys (e.g. diggers, trucks, guns) whereas girls tend to play with "girl" toys (e.g. dolls; kitchens)—this is known as sex-typed behaviour. Is sex-typed behaviour due to social and cultural factors or does it depend in part on biological differences? The latter might involve differences in sex hormones produced within the endocrine system—testosterone is present in greater amounts in male than female foetuses at 6 weeks of age, whereas the opposite is the case for oestrogens.

Important evidence has been obtained from individuals with **congenital adrenal hyperplasia**, a genetic disease in which the foetus is exposed to high levels of male sex hormones. Girls with this condition have a *conflict* between their social experiences (i.e. being treated as a girl) and their early high exposure to male sex hormones. In principle, this allows us to see whether sex hormones influence sex-typed behaviour.

Berenbaum and Beltry (2011) reviewed the evidence concerning girls with congenital adrenal hyperplasia. Their behaviour is influenced by their exposure to male sex hormones. For example, they play more than other girls with boys' toys and less with girls' toys. When they grow up, women with congenital adrenal hyperplasia are more likely than other women to choose male-dominant professions (30% vs 13%). They are also are more likely to enjoy rough sports (74% vs 50%) and to have a non-heterosexual orientation (19% vs 2%).

The obvious explanation for the above findings is the prenatal exposure to male sex hormones. An alternative explanation is that the parents of girls with congenital adrenal hyperplasia encourage them to have male-type interests and behaviour. The evidence does *not* support this explanation. Pasterski et al. (2005) found the parents encouraged their daughters to play with girls' toys. Indeed, they provided more positive feedback than parents of normal girls when their daughters played with girls' toys.

KEY TERMS

Androgens: sex hormones (e.g. testosterone) present in larger quantities in males than females.

Oestrogens: sex hormones (e.g. oestradiol) present in larger quantities in females than males.

Congenital adrenal hyperplasia: an inherited disorder of the adrenal gland causing the levels of male sex hormones in foetuses of both sexes to be unusually high.

Boys and girls tend to prefer different toys—is this nature or nurture?

Aggression

There are several reasons why males exhibit more physical aggression than females. For example, males are stronger and heavier than females, there may be social and cultural factors at work, and so on. Another possible reason is that high levels of male sex hormones such as testosterone are associated with physical aggression.

Research focusing on the possible role of the endocrine system in explaining sex differences in physical aggression was reported by Cohen-Kettenis and van Goozen (1997). They studied transsexuals undergoing hormone treatment in order to change sex. Female-to-male transsexuals were given high dosages of testosterone whereas male-to-female transsexuals were given female hormones and deprived of male hormones. Female-to-male transsexuals showed *increased* aggression during hormone treatment, whereas male-to-female transsexuals had *lowered* aggression levels.

Why does testosterone lead to increased aggression? Mehta and Beer (2009) exposed participants to social provocation. As expected, individuals with high levels of testosterone responded more aggressively to this provocation. Of most interest, testosterone led to reduced activity in brain areas associated with impulse control and self-regulation. Thus, testosterone reduces the tendency to inhibit aggressive behaviour when angry.

Conclusions

Most research has shown only that there is an *association* between the amount of any given sex hormone and sex-typed behaviour or aggression. Such evidence is insufficient to make causal inferences—for example, aggressive behaviour may increase the production of testosterone rather than testosterone helping to trigger aggression.

The research discussed above largely gets round that problem because the level of male sex hormones was manipulated or occurred prior to birth. However, the research involved very rare conditions (transsexuality; congenital adrenal hyperplasia). There are grounds for concern as to whether such findings will generalise to the population at large.

EVALUATION

The endocrine system plays a vital role in influencing our emotions, response to stress, and behaviour. Some of the clearest evidence of the importance of hormones within the endocrine system can be seen by considering what happens if the levels of various hormones become deficient or excessive. For example, consider individuals with abnormal levels of thyroid release. Those with excessive levels are very anxious and agitated. In contrast, individuals with low levels of thyroid release are often depressed and show evidence of cognitive impairments.

There are several other negative consequences of abnormal hormone levels but we will consider only two more. Some individuals with excessive release of glucocorticoids by the adrenal cortex suffer from Cushing's syndrome. This syndrome is characterised by depression and fatigue. Parathyroid deficiency can cause the build-up of a calcium deposit in the basal ganglia which in turn leads to symptoms resembling those found in schizophrenia. Thus, adequate or excessive levels of hormones can produce diverse behavioural and physiological disorders.

In spite of the importance of the endocrine system, we must remember it is influenced by many other factors. For example, individual differences in how we interpret various threatening situations help to determine the intensity and duration of the stress response within the endocrine system. Thus, the cognitive system plays a role in influencing the endocrine system.

Another point is that activity in the SAM system is not only associated with stress. For example, we have elevated levels of adrenaline and noradrenaline when we are concentrating hard on a task. There is also the issue of how we perceive our internal physiological state. Sometimes we perceive heightened activity in the SAM system as indicating we are stressed but sometimes we interpret it as meaning we are excited or stimulated.

Section Summary

- The endocrine system consists of various ductless glands. These glands secrete or release hormones into the bloodstream which are then spread around the body.
- Most of the endocrine system is controlled by the hypothalamus. There are direct connections between the hypothalamus and the anterior pituitary gland which is often described as the body's "master gland".
- The endocrine system has a major involvement in the immediate shock response and in the countershock response that follows it.
- Stress almost immediately produces the fight or flight response: the body becomes very aroused so that it can respond with vigorous physical activity (whether fight or flight).
- The fight or flight response involves the sympathetic adrenal medullary (SAM) system; the adrenal glands and adrenaline are both vitally involved in the activation of this system.
- There is evidence the fight or flight response to stress is more common among men whereas the tend and befriend response is more common among women. The tend and befriend response is influenced by oxytocin (the so-called "cuddle hormone").
- The hypothalamic–pituitary–adrenocortical (HPA) axis plays an important role in minimising any damage that might have been caused by excessive activity within the SAM system in response to stress.
- The HPA axis involves the hypothalamus producing hormones that stimulate the pituitary gland which in turn releases several hormones including ACTH.
- ACTH leads to the release of various hormones including cortisol, which is called the "stress hormone".
- The beneficial effects of HPA activity are achieved at considerable cost and it cannot continue indefinitely at an elevated level of activity.
- Hormones released by the pituitary gland stimulate the gonads (sex glands) leading to the secretion of sex hormones. Androgens are sex hormones present in greater amounts in males than females whereas oestrogens are present in greater amounts in females.
- Girls with congenital adrenal hyperplasia (a genetic disease in which the foetus is exposed to high levels of male sex hormones) are more likely than other girls to play with boys' toys and to choose male-dominant professions in adult life. These findings suggest that male sex hormones can influence sex-typed behaviour.
- Individuals given high dosages of male sex hormones tend to become more aggressive, suggesting that aggressive behaviour depends in part on hormonal factors.

LOCALISATION OF FUNCTION IN THE BRAIN

As is discussed in Chapter 5, the brain or cerebral cortex is divided into four lobes (structurally distinct areas): the frontal lobes; the parietal lobes; the temporal lobes; and the occipital lobes (see Figure on page 195 [Chapter 5]).

Our focus here is on localisation within the brain of some major functions. The brain is enormously complex and several different approaches have been taken to describing brain areas. One of the most popular is based on the work of Korbinian Brodmann (1868–1918), who produced a map of the brain consisting of what are known as Brodmann areas (see Figure). We will often refer to Brodmann areas (abbreviated as BA).

We can obtain an approximate sense of the localisation of brain functions with reference to the figure on page 240, with the front of the brain to the left. It provides a useful summary that we will make use of throughout this section.

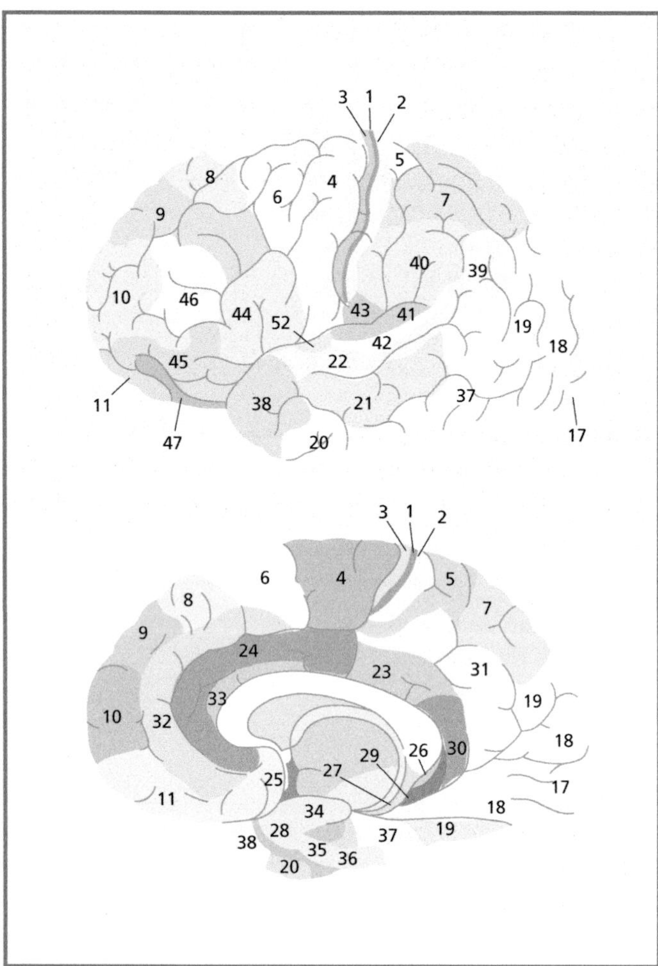

The Brodmann areas of the brain.

Before we proceed, it is important to emphasise that our focus will be on the brain areas most associated with various kinds of processing (e.g. visual; auditory). Other brain areas are very often involved. For example, consider visual processing which is typically associated with the occipital lobes at the back of the brain. Gaillard et al. (2009) carried out a study in which words were flashed briefly. In one condition, the words could be seen consciously by the participants but in another condition a visual mask was used to prevent conscious visual perception.

What Gaillard et al. (2009) found was that the occipital area of the brain was activated in both conditions indicating there was always some visual processing. However, there was far more activation in the frontal lobes when the words could be seen than when they could not. Thus, visual perception typically involves the frontal lobes as well as the occipital area. In similar fashion, conscious auditory perception generally involves activation in the prefrontal cortex (at the front of the frontal lobes) as well as within the auditory centre.

In sum, we will be discussing various centres (e.g. motor; visual; auditory) because there are areas within the brain relatively specialised for certain types of processing. In addition, however, there are other brain areas (especially the frontal lobes) involved in numerous kinds of processing. For example, an area at the front of the brain (the dorsolateral prefrontal cortex) is typically activated when someone has conscious awareness of motor intentions, visual processing, auditory processing, language processing, and so on.

Motor centre

The motor centre is the region within the cerebral cortex involved in the planning, control, and carrying out of voluntary movements. It is located within the frontal lobes.

There are several distinguishable areas within the motor centre. First, there is the **primary motor cortex** (with the motor centre shown in the figure on the left). The primary motor cortex is in Brodmann's area (BA) 4 and it controls movement in numerous parts of the body. This area in the left hemisphere is specialised for controlling movements of the right side of the body whereas this area in the right hemisphere controls movements of the left side of the body. Thus, damage to the primary motor cortex in one hemisphere often leads to movement problems on the other side of the body.

We need finer movement control in some parts of the body (e.g. hands) than in other parts of the body (e.g. trunk) (see Figure on page 241). As a consequence, larger areas within the primary motor cortex are devoted to body parts requiring fine control.

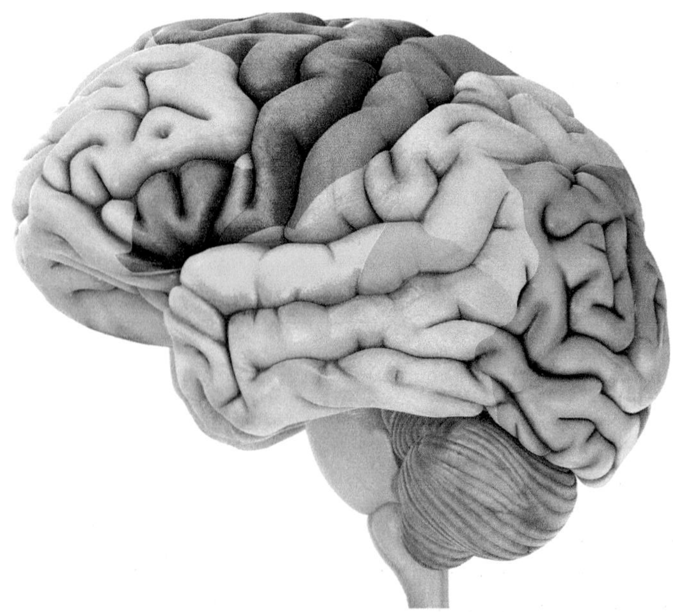

An illustration of the human brain showing Broca's area (purple), the motor centre (red), the somatosensory centre (orange), the visual centre (blue), Wernicke's area (green), and the auditory centre (yellow).

KEY TERM

Primary motor cortex: this brain area is responsible for the production of voluntary body movements.

Immediately in front of the primary motor cortex is the **premotor cortex**. It is located in BA 6 within the motor centre. This area is responsible for some aspects of motor control including movement preparation and the sensory guidance of movement. An important area within the premotor cortex is the **supplementary motor area (SMA)**. This area is involved in producing well-learned motor sequences such as playing a familiar tune on the piano.

Ward (2010, p. 158) summarised some of the differences between the supplementary motor area (SMA) and the rest of the premotor cortex as follows: "If the SMA is important for implementing internally generated actions, the [remaining] premotor region is more important for producing movements based on external contingencies (e.g. 'pull a handle if the light is blue, rotate it if it is red')."

Finally, note that areas over and above those discussed here are also involved in planning and executing our actions. One such area lies within the somatosensory centre (discussed shortly) and involves our perception of the position of our limbs in space. In addition, the fact that far more of the cortex is devoted to some body parts (e.g. the hands) than to others has great relevance for understanding why our touch sensitivity is greater in some body areas than others.

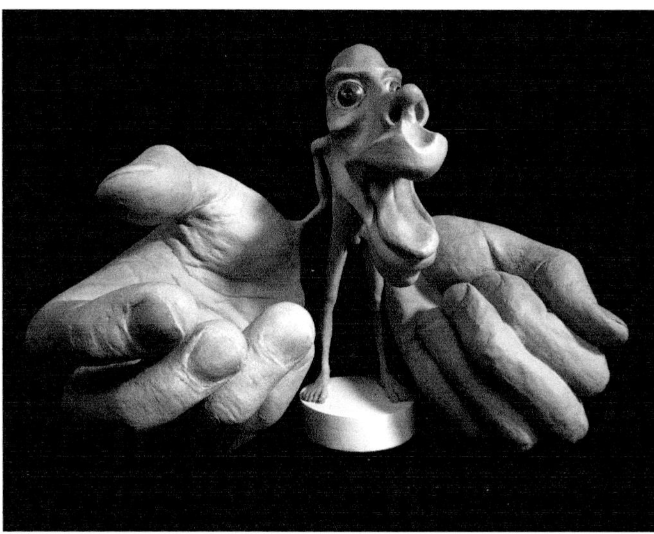

Motor homunculus model. Parts of the body are sized according to how much space the brain gives to controlling the movement of that part of the body.

Somatosensory centre

Somatosensation is "a cluster of perceptual processes that relate to the skin and body, and include touch, pain, thermal sensation and limb position" (Ward, 2010, p. 154). The term **proprioception** is used to refer to our awareness of the position of our limbs in space. In view of the variety of its functions, you won't be surprised to discover that the somatosensory centre is complex in its organisation and processing. For example, we commonly regard touch as a relatively straightforward sense modality. In fact, however, touch depends on several modalities including skin stretch, vibration, pressure, and temperature. As a result, psychologists sometimes refer to the "somatic senses" rather than to touch.

We can distinguish between a primary somatosensory area and a secondary somatosensory area (both within the somatosensory centre in the figure on page 240). The primary somatosensory area consists of a long thin strip of cortex that goes from ear to ear across the head. It is located in the parietal lobe and is in Brodmann area (BA) 3.

The primary somatosensory area is involved in processing and encoding sensory inputs from the skin and body in terms of their type and intensity. The secondary somatosensory area (also in the parietal lobe) is located in BA 40 and BA 43. Compared to the primary somatosensory area or cortex, it is involved in more complex processes such as sensorimotor integration and the integration of information from both sides of the body. Thus, processing in the primary somatosensory area is more basic than that in the secondary somatosensory area and is less affected by attention.

Visual centre

The first point that needs to be made about the visual centre in the brain is that far more of the brain is devoted to visual processing than to processing in any other sense modality. Most visual processing occurs within the occipital lobes located at the back of the brain (see the visual centre in the figure on page 240). Initial visual processing occurs in the primary visual area (located in BA 17). This is then followed by more detailed processing in the adjacent secondary visual area (located in BA 18). The primary and secondary visual areas are activated at an early stage of visual processing and they are involved in fairly basic processing of shape and colour.

There is a complexity about visual processing that should be mentioned here. What happens is that information from the left half of each retina (coming from the right visual field) goes to

KEY TERMS

Premotor cortex: this brain area is used to prepare for movement and to link body actions with environmental objects.

Supplementary motor area (SMA): this brain area is used in planning movement sequences (especially well-learned ones) and in co-ordinating movements involving both sides of the body.

Somatosensation: several perceptual processes based on information received from the skin and body.

Proprioception: our knowledge concerning the location in space of our limbs.

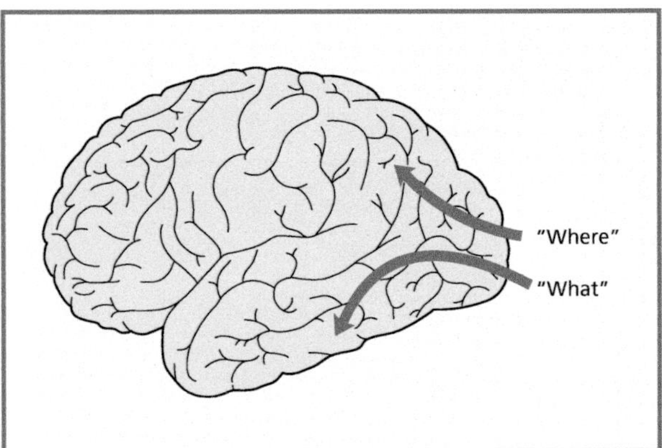

After early visual processing there are two visual pathways: The "what", or ventral, pathway that proceeds to the temporal lobe, and the "where" or "how" pathway (also known as the dorsal pathway) that proceeds to the posterior parietal cortex.

the left hemisphere, whereas information from the right half of each retina (coming from the left visual field) goes to the right hemisphere.

Several other brain areas after the primary and secondary visual areas are involved in visual processing. What is of most importance is that there are basically *two* visual pathways (the primary and secondary visual areas are not shown but are at the extreme left of the figure on page 240). First, there is the "what" or ventral (towards the bottom) pathway that proceeds to the temporal lobe. This pathway is of crucial importance to object recognition (deciding what object we are looking at). More specifically, this pathway is involved in fairly detailed processing of objects in the environment and it typically leads to conscious awareness of the visual environment.

Second, there is the "where" or "how" pathway (also known as the dorsal [towards the top] pathway) that proceeds to the posterior parietal cortex. This pathway is involved in processing movement and is used for visually guided action and for grasping an object. It operates faster than the "what" or ventral pathway and is often not associated with conscious awareness. For example, if a car is approaching you rapidly as you cross the road, you might well jump out of the way before you realise consciously that a car is close by.

Auditory centre

Several regions in the brain are involved in processing auditory stimuli such as speech and music. We can distinguish between primary auditory cortex and secondary auditory cortex (both within the auditory centre in the figure on page 240). **Primary auditory cortex** (sometimes known as the core region) is situated in the upper part of the temporal lobes. It is located primarily within BA 41. Destruction of this area in one hemisphere leads to some hearing loss but destruction of this area in both hemispheres produces much greater hearing loss.

Primary auditory cortex is surrounded by what used to be called secondary auditory cortex but is now more often referred to as the belt and **parabelt regions**. The **belt region** includes parts of BA 42, and the parabelt region occupies part of BA 22.

In general terms, primary auditory cortex is involved in processing simple features of the acoustic input such as loudness, tempo, and pitch. In contrast, the belt region and the parabelt region are involved in more complex auditory processing that includes integrating the information from different features of the acoustic input. It should be noted that the belt region has connections to the parabelt and primary auditory areas whereas the parabelt has direct connections to the belt but *not* to primary auditory cortex.

Language centre

Humans possess several different language skills of which the most important involve reading, speech comprehension, speech, and writing. As a consequence, numerous brain areas are involved in language and so there is no single language centre. More specifically, the visual centre is involved in reading, the auditory centre in speech comprehension, and the motor centre in writing and speaking. In fact, what actually happens is more complex than that. Hauk et al. (2004) presented participants with verbs such as "lick", "pick", and "kick". This was only a reading task, but the verbs nevertheless led to activation of relevant parts of primary motor cortex (e.g. *lick* activated areas associated with tongue movements).

The areas most commonly associated with the language centre are Broca's area (BA 44 and BA 45) and Wernicke's area (BA 22; some also include parts of BA 39 and BA 40) (both areas are shown in the figure on page 240). Since both areas are shortly discussed in detail, here we will simply identify the key features of these areas. Broca's area is involved in speech production—individuals who have damage to this area typically speak very little or produce laboured speech. In contrast, Wernicke's area is involved in comprehension—individuals with damage to this area typically have poor speech comprehension and also often produce almost meaningless speech.

It is important to note that several other areas are strongly associated with language. Berwick et al. (2013) discussed research on the language centre. In addition to Broca's area

KEY TERMS

Primary auditory cortex: the main area within the brain for receiving auditory input.

Parabelt region: this forms part of what used to be called secondary auditory cortex; it is connected to the belt region but not primary auditory areas.

Belt region: this forms part of what was previously called secondary auditory cortex; it is connected to the parabelt region and primary auditory areas.

and Wernicke's area, they reported evidence that all the following areas are also involved in language: BA 21, BA 37, BA 38, BA 41, BA 42, and BA 47! We should perhaps not be surprised that this is the case given that language is of fundamental importance to our everyday lives and involves several somewhat separate skills. In the absence of language, we would find it very difficult to communicate with other people or to understand what they want to communicate to us.

Hemispheric lateralisation

Most of the brain areas and centres we have discussed so far are represented in the right and left hemispheres of the brain. In most cases, that means the various forms of processing (e.g. visual; auditory) occur approximately equally in both hemispheres. However, that is by no means always the case. **Hemispheric lateralisation** means that one hemisphere or the other is specialised for certain processes. Some of the strongest evidence for hemispheric lateralisation comes from a consideration of handedness. Approximately 10% of the world's population is left-handed with approximately 80–85% being right-handed—a few people are ambidextrous and others have no strong dominance for either hand. This means the motor centre in the left hemisphere plays a dominant role with most people (the right side of the body is controlled by the left hemisphere)

Other strong evidence for hemispheric lateralisation has been found with respect to language. Two of the key areas involved in language processing (Broca's and Wernicke's areas) are located in the left hemisphere with 95% of right-handed individuals and approximately 70% of left-handed ones. These findings mean that the left hemisphere can be regarded as the *dominant* hemisphere for language.

Brain-damaged individuals sometimes have difficulty in understanding arithmetic; this condition is known as **dyscalculia**. Individuals with dyscalculia typically have damage to the parietal lobe and this damage more often involves the left hemisphere than the right one. Why is this? Fairly precise numerical operations depend more on the left than the right hemisphere whereas the right hemisphere is more involved in less precise operations (e.g. estimating the quantity of fruit in a basket).

What about the right hemisphere? There is accumulating evidence from studies on the structure and function of the brain that some aspects of visual and spatial attention are localised in the right hemisphere and this sometimes includes facial perception (Hervé et al., 2013). It has been argued that these functions are localised in the right hemisphere because the left hemisphere is typically more involved in major functions such as language and motor control and so has reduced capacity for other functions. However, the extent of spatial lateralisation is no greater in individuals who are right-handed than in those who are left-handed which suggests that is *not* the correct explanation.

We will consider research on split brain patients in a little while. These patients have lost the connections between the two hemispheres. As we will see, the functions of their left and right hemispheres are reasonably consistent with the findings discussed in this section.

The notion that some functions are centred in one hemisphere should not be interpreted in too literal a way. For example, Pulsifer et al. (2004) found that young children who had **hemispherectomy** (destruction of one entire hemisphere) were able to adjust and mostly showed only rather small impairments of cognitive functioning with increasing periods of time after hemispherectomy. These findings are indicative of considerable brain plasticity in young children (an issue discussed more fully shortly).

Finally, note that it is sometimes said that the left hemisphere is logical or analytical whereas the right hemisphere is creative. That is (at best!) an enormous oversimplification. What is actually the case is that both hemispheres typically work in *combination* to achieve most cognitive tasks and so we should not exaggerate the partial independence of functioning they sometimes show.

Broca's and Wernicke's areas

We possess numerous complex language abilities including the ability to understand spoken and written language and to produce spoken and written language. Numerous patients with brain damage have **aphasia**, which involves severe language disorder.

KEY TERMS

Dyscalculia: severe problems with arithmetic often due to brain damage.

Hemispherectomy: destruction of the whole of one hemisphere of the brain.

Aphasia: a disorder of language caused by brain damage.

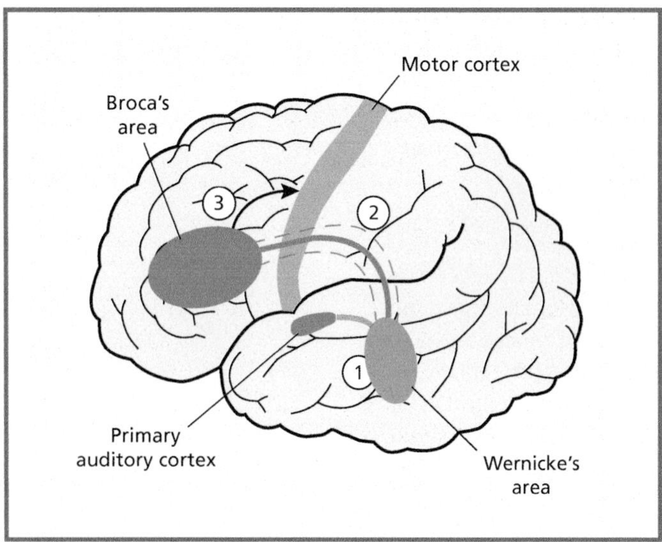

Broca's area and Wernicke's area. When someone speaks a word, activation goes from Wernicke's area (1) through the arcuate fasciculus (2) to Broca's area (3).

Some of the earliest (and most important) research attempting to locate the brain areas involved in some of these language abilities was carried out in the nineteenth century by Paul Broca (1824–1880). He discovered that the destruction of a small area of the brain (called "Broca's area" in his honour; BA 44 and BA 45) made a patient unable to speak. This area is located in the inferior part of the left frontal lobe. However, the patient's understanding of spoken language seemed to be essentially intact.

Subsequent research confirmed that, in nearly all right-handed individuals, Broca's area was located in the left hemisphere. Many patients with damage to Broca's area can speak but their speech is slow and lacking in fluency. Such patients are said to have **Broca's aphasia**.

Carl Wernicke (1848–1905) identified a very different form of language impairment caused by brain damage. He discovered that brain damage to the left temporal lobe (called "Wernicke's area"; BA 22, and perhaps parts of BA 39 and BA 40) caused a severe impairment in the understanding of speech rather than in the articulation of speech. Note, however, that patients with damage to Wernicke's area typically have problems in speech production—they produce fluent and apparently grammatical speech often lacking meaning. Such patients have **Wernicke's aphasia**.

Broca's area and Wernicke's area are both shown in the figure on page 240. When someone speaks a word, activation goes from Wernicke's area (1) through the arcuate fasciculus (2) to Broca's area (3). Thus, language processing often involves Broca's area *and* Wernicke's area.

The traditional view is oversimplified and indeed inaccurate in various ways. Consider, for example, a study by De Bleser (1988) on six very clear cases of Wernicke's aphasia and seven very clear cases of Broca's aphasia. Brain scans allowed the patients to be put into three groups: (1) damage to frontal areas including Broca's area; (2) damage to temporoparietal areas including Wernicke's area; and (3) large lesions including both Broca's and Wernicke's areas.

Four of the six patients with Wernicke's aphasia had damage only to Wernicke's area but the other two had damage in Broca's area as well as Wernicke's area. Of the seven patients with Broca's aphasia, four had damage to Broca's area but the others had damage to Wernicke's area.

Willmes and Poeck (1993) also used brain scans. They found 90% of patients with Wernicke's aphasia had brain damage in Wernicke's area. However, only 48% of patients with damage in Wernicke's area had Wernicke's aphasia!

EVALUATION

How can we make sense of the various findings concerning Broca's area and Wernicke's area? The distinction between Broca's aphasia involving Broca's area and Wernicke's aphasia involving Wernicke's area is approximately correct. However, there are three problems with this traditional view:

1. There are individual differences in the precise brain areas involved in any given language function. Thus, for example, Broca's area is of more importance in causing Broca's aphasia in some brain-damaged patients than in others.
2. Language processing in the brain involves several complex *networks* and so no language function (e.g. comprehension; speech production) involves only a *single* small brain region.
3. Patients exhibit a bewildering variety of symptoms of language impairment. As a result, describing patients as having Broca's aphasia or Wernicke's aphasia is far too neat and tidy.

KEY TERMS

Broca's aphasia: a form of language disorder involving damage to Broca's area producing slow speech lacking fluency.

Wernicke's aphasia: a form of language disorder involving damage to Wernicke's area producing impaired language comprehension and fluent but often meaningless speech.

Split brain research

There are many patients who have few connections between the two brain hemispheres following surgery (see Figure). In most of these patients, the corpus callosum (bridge) between the two hemispheres was cut surgically to contain epileptic seizures within one hemisphere. This structure is a collection of 250 million axons connecting sites in one hemisphere with sites in the other. For obvious reasons, such patients are generally referred to as **split brain patients**.

It is easy to imagine that split brain patients have great difficulty in functioning effectively in everyday life. This is *not* typically the case because such patients typically ensure environmental information reaches both hemispheres by moving their eyes around. However, the situation is very different under laboratory conditions when visual stimuli are presented briefly to only one hemisphere so the information is not available to the other hemisphere.

One of the major controversies concerning split brain patients is whether they have two consciousnesses, one in each hemisphere. Roger Sperry (1913–1994), who won the Nobel Prize for his research on split brain patients, claimed these patients have two consciousnesses. In contrast, Gazzaniga (2013) argued that they have only a single dominant conscious system known as the interpreter based in the left hemisphere. The interpreter "tries to make sense out of the many independent functions we have going on at any one time" (Gazzaniga, 2013, p. 13). One reason for arguing that consciousness is represented primarily or exclusively in the left hemisphere is because language is typically based in that hemisphere.

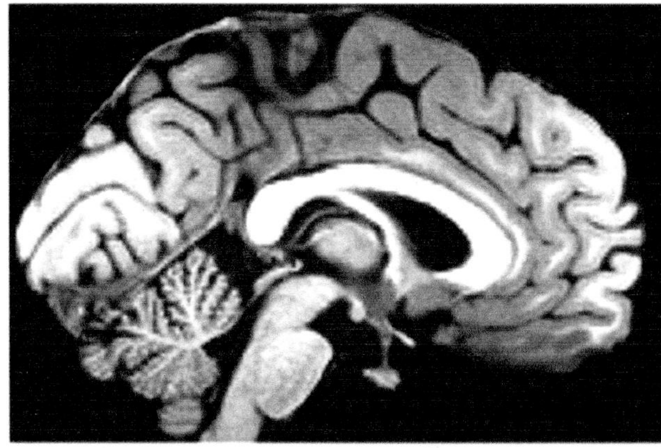

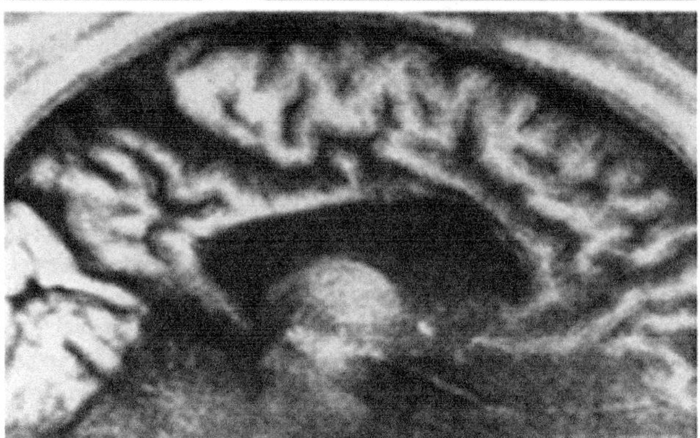

A normal brain (top) and that of a split-brain patient (bottom). The normal brain shows an intact corpus callosum whereas the bottom image shows its total absence. From Gazzaniga (2013). Republished with permission of Annual Reviews.

Findings

Evidence that the left hemisphere acts as an interpreter was reported by Gazzaniga (2013). A split brain patient, Paul S., was presented with a chicken claw to his left hemisphere and a snow scene to his right hemisphere. When asked to select relevant pictures from an array, he chose a picture of a chicken with his right hand (connected to the left hemisphere) and he chose a shovel with his left hand (connected to the right hemisphere).

The above findings may suggest Paul S. had a separate consciousness in each hemisphere. However, here is how he explained his choices: "Oh, that's simple. The chicken claw goes with the chicken, and you need a shovel to clean out the chicken shed" (Gazzaniga, 2013, p. 124). Thus, Paul's left hemisphere was *interpreting* behaviour initiated by the right hemisphere and there was no clear evidence the right hemisphere was contributing much to the interpretation.

If split brain patients have two streams of consciousness, we might expect *disagreements* between the two hemispheres. Such disagreements have occasionally been reported. Mark (1996, p. 191) discussed a patient having speech in both hemispheres: "She mentioned that she did not have feelings in her left hand. When I echoed the statement, she said that she was not numb, and then the torrent of alternating 'Yes!' and 'No!' replies ensued, followed by a despairing 'I don't know!'."

Even though there is suggestive evidence of two consciousnesses in a few patients, most of the evidence is consistent with the notion of a single dominant consciousness in the left hemisphere. Of particular importance, no split brain patients have ever reported feeling that their experience of themselves changed dramatically as a result of surgery or that two selves now inhabited their body (Gazzaniga, 2013).

As would be expected on the basis of our earlier discussion of hemispheric lateralisation, the two brain hemispheres of split brain patients differ in their processing. When stimuli are presented to the left hemisphere, patients can name, compare, and describe them. In contrast, when the same stimuli are presented to the right hemisphere, patients often fail to provide any verbal response or say there might have been some vague event. This is as expected given that language is typically centred in the left hemisphere.

KEY TERM

Split brain patients: individuals in whom the direct links between the hemispheres have been severed.

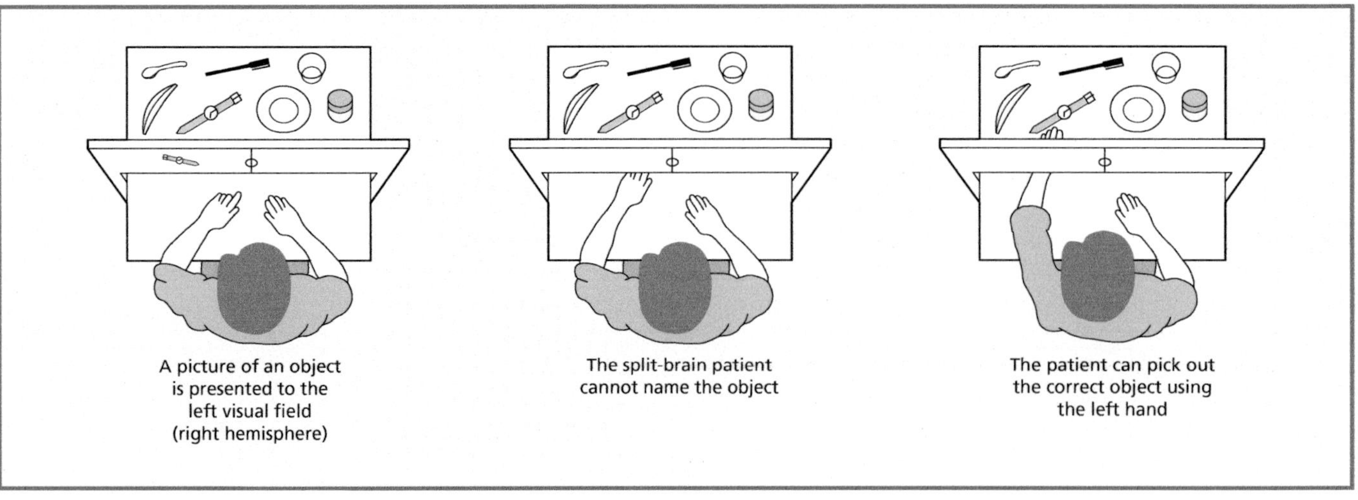

A picture of an object is presented to the left visual field (right hemisphere)

The split-brain patient cannot name the object

The patient can pick out the correct object using the left hand

The right hemisphere of split brain patients outperforms the left on tasks involving visual or touch perception of complex shapes, manipulations of geometric patterns, and judgements involving hand explorations of shapes. It is also better than the left hemisphere at face recognition. These findings suggest that the right hemisphere is specialised for many aspects of visual and spatial processing which is consistent with findings on hemispheric lateralisation in healthy individuals.

Conclusions

The findings from split brain patients provide striking evidence that there are important differences between the two brain hemispheres in terms of the types of processing at which they are most efficient. In general terms, the left hemisphere specialises in language-related activities whereas the right hemisphere specialises in visual and spatial processing. While such findings are important, we need to be aware that there are limitations in terms of how much findings from split brain patients tell us about processing in healthy individuals. In healthy individuals, there are extensive *interactions* between the two hemispheres and so their verbal and visual processing is co-ordinated in ways that cannot be achieved by split brain patients under controlled laboratory conditions.

Plasticity and functional recovery of the brain after trauma

So far in this chapter we have focused mostly on *stable* and relatively unchanging aspects of brain organisation. In reality, however, the brain should be regarded in more *dynamic* terms—it is always changing whether as a consequence of learning or when recovering from trauma (e.g. a stroke). In this section, we will provide some examples of these changes within the brain.

Plasticity

One of the important features of the brain is its **plasticity**, which refers to "changes in structure and function of the brain that affect behaviour and that are related to experience of training" (Herholz & Zatorre, 2012, p. 486). Note that the extent of brain plasticity varies as a function of age—in general, the brains of young children exhibit more plasticity than those of adults.

Some of the clearest evidence for plasticity has been found in individuals who develop expertise in a given area. For example, research has been carried out on London taxi drivers. In order to obtain a licence to drive black cabs, they have to acquire "The Knowledge". This consists of detailed knowledge of the 25,000 streets within six miles of Charing Cross and of the locations of thousands of hospitals, tube stations, and so on.

KEY TERM

Plasticity: changes in neural function and structure within the brain due to experience.

The hippocampus is of central importance in most learning. As a result, we might expect that the 3 years or so it takes to acquire The Knowledge would have a direct effect on the hippocampus. Supporting evidence was reported by Woollett et al. (2009). Experienced London taxi drivers had a greater volume of grey matter in the posterior hippocampus than novice drivers. Woollett et al. also found that older full-time taxi drivers had greater grey matter volume in this area than those who had retired.

Hyde et al. (2009) studied the effects of 15 months of instrumental musical training in 6-year-old children. There were significant increases in voxel size (a voxel is a small cube of brain tissue) in two areas directly involved in the development of musical expertise: the primary motor area and the primary auditory area or cortex. In addition, those with the greatest brain changes showed the greatest improvement in musical skills. Zatorre (2013) reviewed research on the effects of musical training on the brain and found they were greater among children and young adults than older adults.

In sum, the brain (especially in children) exhibits much plasticity during the development of expertise. Note, however, that some studies have failed to show definitely that practice caused changes in brain structure. For example, it could be the case that London taxi drivers have an enlarged hippocampus *before* they acquire The Knowledge.

Recovery from trauma

What happens when the brain suffers trauma whether due to some external factor (e.g. a car crash) or to a disease of the brain? The short answer is that the individual concerned often seems to show dramatic recovery of cognitive functioning. One of the most remarkable cases was reported by Lorber (1981). He studied a man with hydrocephalus (known non-technically as "water on the brain"). Hydrocephalus had caused the man's cerebral cortex to be crushed outwards towards the skull. Lorber estimated that the man's brain weighed only about 10% of that of healthy individuals. In spite of that, the man had an IQ of 126 (considerably above average) and obtained a university degree.

The above case (which apparently showed an amazing ability to recover from trauma) helped to establish the urban myth that we only use 10% of our brains in everyday life. In fact, it is more likely that hydrocephalus caused the brain to become compacted rather than destroyed (Rolls, 2010). Even so, it shows that the brain can show remarkable adaptability.

We turn now to the effects of strokes on cognition. In general, strokes have a less damaging effect on cognition when they occur in infancy or childhood rather than adulthood (Ward, 2010). Consider, for example, a study by Ballantyne et al. (2008) on children who had suffered a stroke around the time of birth. These children performed below the level of healthy controls on cognitive and language tasks. However, their cognitive and language skills developed at about the same rate, thus indicating much plasticity. You will remember the striking findings reported by Pulsifer et al. (2004)—they found that young children who had an entire hemisphere destroyed nevertheless managed to acquire a wide range of cognitive skills.

Ballantyne et al. (2008) reported evidence that there is more plasticity in infancy and childhood than in adulthood. The effects of strokes on adults depend on the brain hemisphere in which the stroke occurs and on the extent of the brain damage—language is more affected if the stroke is in the left hemisphere than in the right one and there is more cognitive impairment when a larger brain area is damaged. In contrast, neither the hemisphere in which the stroke occurred nor the extent of the brain damage influenced cognitive or language development in children who had a stroke around the time of birth.

Why doesn't brain damage to the left hemisphere in infants or young children cause severe delays in language learning? Studies using functional magnetic resonance imaging (fMRI) indicate that what happens is that language processing occurs primarily in the *right* hemisphere in such cases (e.g. Liegeois et al., 2004).

Conclusions

There is evidence from studies on the development of expertise and on recovery from trauma (e.g. stroke) that the brain possesses considerable plasticity. This plasticity is greater in infants and young children than in adults. Such plasticity is obviously advantageous—without it, young children with severe damage to the left hemisphere would be unable to develop language at all.

Section Summary

- Major brain functions typically involve several brain areas but it is generally possible to identify a centre that is relatively specialised for any given function.
- The motor centre is involved in the planning, control, and executing of voluntary movements; it is located in BA 4 and BA 6 and the left hemisphere controls movements of the right side of the body and vice versa.
- The somatosensory centre is involved in processes relating to touch, pain, limb position, and the sensation of warmth. It is located in BA 3, BA 40, and BA 43.
- Early processing within the visual centre occurs in BA 17 and BA 18. After that, there are two visual processing pathways: the what pathway deals with object recognition and proceeds to the temporal lobe; the where or how pathway deals with visually guided action and proceeds to the posterior parietal cortex.
- The auditory centre is located in BA 41 and parts of BA 42 and BA 22; primary auditory cortex is involved in basic auditory processing whereas the belt and parabelt regions are involved in more complex processing.
- The language centre is typically located mostly in the left hemisphere; key parts of this centre are Broca's area (BA 44 and BA 45) involved in speech production and Wernicke's area (BA 22) involved in language comprehension. Several others areas (e.g. BA 21, BA 37, BA 38) are also much involved in language processing.
- There is evidence for hemispheric lateralisation for some functions. The left hemisphere is generally dominant for language, handedness, and precise numerical calculations. In contrast, the right hemisphere is often dominant for aspects of visual and spatial attention including facial perception. In spite of the evidence for hemispheric lateralisation, young children show plasticity (e.g. they can acquire language even when their left hemisphere has been destroyed).
- The identification of Broca's area with speech production and Wernicke's area with comprehension is oversimplified. Some patients with damage to these areas do not have the predicted language impairments. In addition, some patients with language impairments associated with damage to Broca's or Wernicke's area do have brain damage in those areas.
- Split brain patients have one dominant consciousness (typically in the left hemisphere) and little or no consciousness in the other hemisphere. The left hemisphere of these patients is much superior to the right hemisphere on language tasks; in contrast, the right hemisphere is sometimes superior on tasks involving visual or touch perception.
- There is much evidence of brain plasticity. Individuals who develop expertise (e.g. taxi drivers; musicians) often have increased brain volume in those brain areas central to their expertise; such plasticity is greater in young children than in adults.
- One way of studying plasticity is to focus on recovery from trauma. Strokes in infancy or childhood have a less marked effect on cognitive abilities than strokes occurring in adulthood. Young children who have a stroke in the left hemisphere often manage to shift language processing successfully to the right hemisphere.

WAYS OF STUDYING THE BRAIN

Technological advances mean we have numerous exciting ways of obtaining detailed information about the brain's structure and functioning (see Chapter 5). In principle, we can work out *where* and *when* specific processes occur in the brain. This allows us to determine the order different brain areas become active when someone performs a task. It also allows us to find out whether two tasks involve the same brain areas in the same way or whether there are important differences.

At the most basic level, the many techniques available for studying the brain vary in the precision with which they identify the brain areas active when a task is performed (*spatial resolution*) and the time course of such activation (*temporal resolution*). High spatial and temporal resolutions are advantageous if a very detailed account of brain functioning is required. In contrast, low temporal resolution can be more useful if a general overview of brain activity is required.

Researchers have many techniques available for studying brain activity (Eysenck & Keane, 2015). Here we will be discussing a few of the most important techniques. For reasons that will be discussed shortly, functional magnetic resonance imaging (fMRI) and event-related potentials (ERPs) are two of the most-used techniques. In addition, the **electroencephalogram (EEG)** is of major historical importance.

Finally, we will be considering one of the earliest ways of studying the brain: post-mortem examination. Until comparatively recently, this was one of the few approaches available to psychologists who wanted to understand the role played by various brain areas in behaviour.

Functional magnetic resonance imaging (fMRI)

Magnetic resonance imaging (MRI) involves the use of an MRI scanner containing a very large magnet weighing up to 11 tons surrounding the participant. These changes are then interpreted by a computer and turned into a precise three-dimensional picture. MRI scans can be obtained from various angles but tell us only about brain *structure* rather than its *functions*.

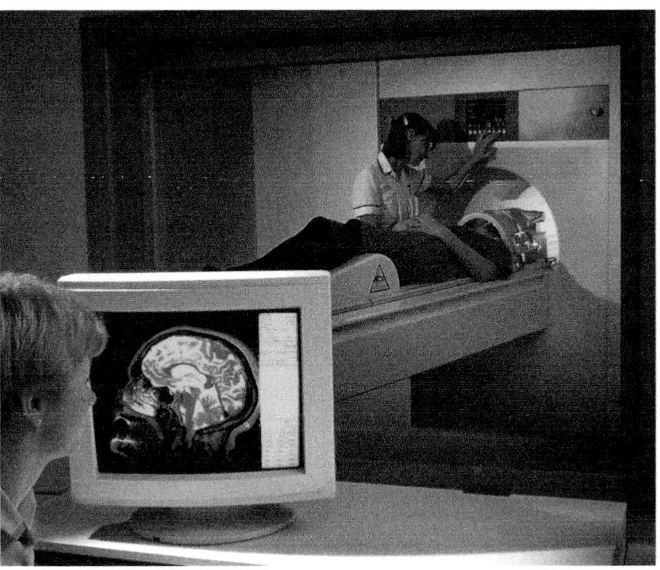

Functional magnetic resonance imaging (fMRI) scans have become an important source of data in psychology.

Researchers are generally more interested in brain functions than brain structure. Happily, MRI technology can provide functional information in the form of **functional magnetic resonance imaging (fMRI)**. What is measured in fMRI is based on assessing brain areas in which there is an accumulation of oxygenated red blood cells suggestive of activity. Technically, this is the BOLD (blood oxygen-level-dependent contrast) signal. Changes in the BOLD signal produced by increased neural activity take some time, so the temporal resolution of fMRI is about 2 or 3 seconds. However, its spatial resolution is very good (approximately 1 mm). Since its temporal and spatial resolutions are both much better than positron emission tomography (PET), fMRI has superseded PET.

It is important to note that the brain is constantly active. As a result, what typically happens in an experiment using fMRI is that brain activation while participants are passive or performing a control task is *subtracted* from their brain activation while performing an experimental task.

Findings

Several theories of obsessive–compulsive disorder (OCD) have emphasised the notion that there are important differences in brain functioning between OCD patients and healthy controls. One of the most influential of such theories starts with the assumption that there is an excitatory pathway in the brain which is influenced by an inhibitory pathway (see Chapter 7).

In OCD patients, the excitatory pathway is activated more easily than in healthy individuals whereas the inhibitory pathway has reduced effectiveness and so is less able to reduce activation within the excitatory pathway. As a consequence, patients with OCD have much greater activation in the excitatory pathway and this in turn produces excessive concerns about danger, harm, and hygiene.

How can we obtain evidence to support this influential theory? Much of it comes from fMRI studies. Menzies et al. (2008) carried out a meta-analysis of numerous fMRI studies. In many of these studies, attempts were made to provoke symptoms of OCD. As predicted, they reported that there was generally greater activity in the excitatory pathway among OCD patients

KEY TERMS

Electroencephalogram (EEG): the graphical representation of the brain's electrical activity recorded by multiple scalp electrodes.

Functional magnetic resonance imaging (fMRI): a brain-imaging technique based on imaging blood oxygenation using an MRI scanner; it has very good spatial resolution and reasonable temporal resolution.

than healthy controls. They also found that there was reduced activity in the inhibitory pathway in OCD patients compared with controls.

Another example of the value of fMRI can be seen with reference to the theoretical assumption that there are at least three types of long-term memory: episodic memory; semantic memory; and procedural memory (see Chapter 3). That assumption has proved somewhat controversial.

If the above assumption is correct, we would expect that different brain areas would be activated depending on the type of memory task in which participants were engaged. Most of the evidence supports this prediction (Henke, 2010; Eysenck & Keane, 2015). In general terms, the hippocampus is more strongly activated on episodic memory tasks than on semantic or procedural memory tasks. In contrast, the anterior temporal lobe is more activated on semantic memory tasks than episodic or procedural memory tasks and the basal ganglia are most activated on procedural memory tasks. These fMRI findings strongly support the notion that we should distinguish among three types of long-term memory.

Finally, note that other examples of the value of fMRI in resolving theoretical controversies are discussed in Chapter 5.

EVALUATION

fMRI has proved an extremely valuable technique for understanding brain functioning. It provides an accurate description of brain activation throughout the entire brain. It has played an important role in resolving several theoretical controversies. More generally, fMRI provides a rich source of information that increases our ability to understand the meaning or significance of participants' behaviour.

What are the limitations of fMRI? First, consider the fact that its temporal resolution is about 2 or 3 seconds. People can perform many cognitive operations over that kind of time period and so it is often very hard to relate the obtained pattern of brain activation to specific cognitive processes. Second, fMRI only shows an association or correlation between patterns of brain activation and behaviour. The brain activation may not be necessary for performance but may instead be irrelevant (e.g. reflecting unnecessary monitoring of performance or attending to non-task stimuli). Third, there are constraints on the responses participants can be asked to produce because even small movements can distort the BOLD signal. Fourth, fMRI provides only an indirect measure of underlying neural activity.

Electroencephalogram (EEG)

The electroencephalogram (EEG) is based on recordings of electrical brain activity measured at the surface of the scalp from multiple electrodes over periods of time that are typically 20–40 minutes long. Very small changes in electrical activity within the brain are picked up by scalp electrodes and can be seen on a computer screen.

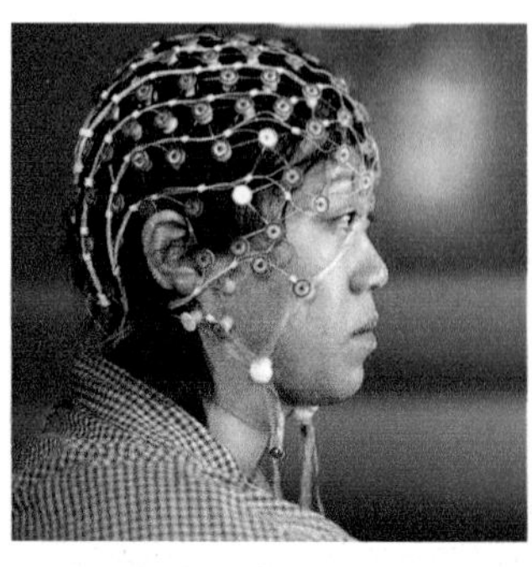

An EEG measures electrical activity in the brain by means of electrodes placed across the scalp.

EEG has reasonably good temporal resolution but its spatial resolution is poor because the electrodes on the scalp are some distance away from the brain itself.

EEG waves are typically classified according to their frequency, amplitude, and shape and account is also taken of where on the scalp the waves were recorded. In practice, the emphasis is typically on EEG waveform frequency (Hertz, Hz). More specifically, the following categories are often used:

- Alpha waves: 8–15 Hz per second: associated with relaxed alertness.
- Beta waves: more than 13 Hz per second: associated with active thinking, high alertness, and anxiety.
- Theta waves: 3.5–7.5 Hz per second: associated with drowsiness.
- Delta waves: 3 Hz or less per second: associated with slow-wave sleep.

Awake adults typically have waveform frequencies of 8 Hz or more. However, reduced frequencies (theta and delta waves) are found in sleep (discussed below).

The EEG is especially useful when we are interested in assessing someone's current state of arousal or awareness. Thus, for example, researchers have used EEG during sleep, during meditation, and in individuals in a vegetative state in which there is little or no conscious awareness.

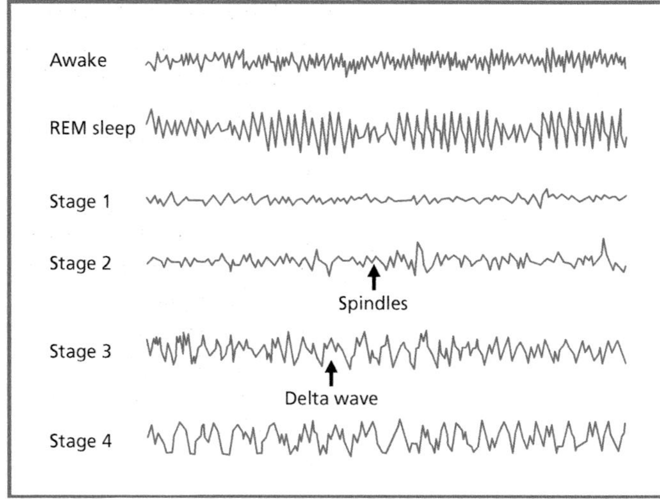

An EEG trace showing the different stages of sleep. From Bentley (2000).

Findings

One of the most successful uses of EEG was to identify the five major stages of sleep (discussed further later in the chapter). In essence, the EEG was recorded throughout sleep and showed large changes associated with different sleep stages. Relaxation when awake involves alpha waves, whereas the early sleep Stages 1 and 2 involve theta waves. The subsequent deeper sleep of Stages 3 and 4 involve delta waves, and finally REM sleep (Stage 5) involves rapid eye movement (REM) sleep and low voltage waves. Stages 1–4 are collectively said to involve slow-wave sleep because the EEG waves are slower than during wakefulness. As is discussed later, REM sleep is associated with dreaming but individuals woken up from REM sleep by no means always report that they had just been dreaming.

Individuals who engage in meditation typically report that it produces a sense of calm peacefulness and relaxation. We can check the validity of these reports by using EEG under meditation and under ordinary control conditions. Cahn and Polich (2006) carried out a meta-analysis (see page 302 [key term definition]) of studies using EEG during meditation. The typical finding was that various forms of meditation (e.g. mindfulness) were associated with a reduction in alpha waves and an increase in theta waves. This change is indicative of increased relaxation with meditation. In addition, as expected, the beneficial effects of meditation on EEG activity tend to increase with practice.

Finally, we consider patients in a **vegetative state** in which there is "wakefulness without conscious awareness". Cruse et al. (2011) tested the ability of 16 vegetative state patients to respond to two commands ("squeeze your right hand"; "squeeze your toes") while using EEG. Three of these patients responded to these commands with activation in the hand and toe motor areas respectively—indeed, their EEG records were very similar to those of healthy controls.

The above findings are more impressive than they initially seem. Successful task performance requires sustained attention, language comprehension (of the task instructions), working memory (to remember which task to perform), and response selection (between the two tasks). Until recently, it was thought that vegetative state patients could not engage in any of these cognitive processes. Thus, use of the EEG revealed that some vegetative state patients possess cognitive abilities that are not reflected in their behaviour.

EVALUATION

The electroencephalogram (EEG) is very useful for assessing states of arousal and consciousness. It proved especially valuable in identifying the main stages of sleep. In addition, EEG has shed light on the states of consciousness associated with meditation and has shown that behavioural measures sometimes fail to identify awareness in patients in the vegetative state.

What are the limitations of EEG? First, EEG is relatively insensitive because the electrodes are some distance away from the brain and so provide a rather indirect assessment of brain activity. Second, EEG has poor spatial resolution and so cannot provide accurate information about the locations of brain activity. Third, EEG is of little or no use in many situations—for example, we could not use EEG to study the processes involved in the performance of a cognitive task.

KEY TERM

Vegetative state: a condition produced by brain damage in which there is limited wakefulness but an apparent lack of awareness and purposeful behaviour.

Event-related potentials (ERPs)

What happens with event-related potentials (ERPs) is that the same stimulus (or very similar ones) are presented repeatedly and the EEG is averaged over numerous trials to produce a single waveform. This method produces **event-related potentials (ERPs)** from EEG recordings and allows us to distinguish genuine effects of stimulation from background brain activity.

ERPs have poor spatial resolution but their temporal resolution is excellent. Indeed, they can often indicate when a given process occurred to within a few milliseconds. The ERP waveform consists of a series of positive (P) and negative (N) peaks, each described with reference to the time in milliseconds after stimulus presentation. Thus, for example, the P200 is a positive wave peaking at about 200 ms.

ERPs provide very detailed information about the time course of brain activity. A behavioural measure (e.g. reaction time) typically provides only a *single* measure of time on each trial, whereas ERPs provide a *continuous* measure. However, ERPs do not indicate with precision which brain regions are most involved in processing, in part because skull and brain tissue distort the brain's electrical fields.

Findings

We will consider two examples of the usefulness of ERPs. First, we focus on patients suffering from obsessive–compulsive disorder (OCD; see Chapter 7), a condition involving intrusive thoughts (obsessions) and compensatory behaviours (compulsions). It seems likely that OCD patients are excessively responsive to their own errors and ERPs can be used to test this hypothesis. Precisely this was done by Endrass et al. (2014). OCD patients and healthy controls performed a task that generated a reasonable number of errors and the most important measure was an aspect of the ERP known as **error-related negativity (ERN)**—this is a negative wave occurring approximately 80–150 ms after an error has been committed. The key finding was that the ERN was significantly greater in OCD patients than in healthy controls. This supports the notion that OCD patients monitor their own errors to a greater extent than healthy controls.

Our second example concerns the ways in which our perception of speech is influenced by context. Everyone agrees that speech perception is influenced by context but there has been a theoretical controversy concerning *when* in speech perception this happens. The traditional view is that contextual information is processed *after* information concerning the meaning of the words within a sentence whereas a more recent view is that contextual information influences speech perception much earlier.

This controversy has been addressed by focusing on the N400 component of the ERP (a negative wave peaking at 400 ms)—a large N400 indicates that the individual has detected a mismatch between the meaning of the word currently being processed and its context. Nieuwland and van Berkum (2006) assessed the N400 in a study in which participants listened to stories such as the following:

> *A woman saw a dancing peanut who had a big smile on his face. The peanut was singing about a girl he had just met. And judging from the song, the peanut was totally crazy about her. The woman thought it was really cute to see the peanut singing and dancing like that. The peanut was salted/in love, and by the sound of it, this was definitely mutual.*

Some listeners heard "salted" near the end of the story whereas others heard "in love". The key finding was that the N400 was greater for "salted" than for "in love" even though "salted" was more appropriate in terms of word meanings. The large N400 to "salted" indicates that context can have a very rapid impact on speech processing—the fact that peanuts cannot be in love caused little or no conflict in the participants given the background context.

KEY TERMS

Event-related potentials (ERPs): the pattern of electroencephalogram (EEG) activity obtained by averaging the brain responses to the same stimulus (or similar stimuli) presented repeatedly.

Error-related negativity: a negative deflection in the ERP that occurs about 80–150 ms after an individual has made a behavioural error.

EVALUATION

Event-related potentials (ERPs) provide extremely useful information about the precise timing of brain processes. For example, it is hard using behavioural measures to work out precisely when contextual information influences speech perception. Much light has been shed on this issue by focusing on the N400 component of the ERP. ERPs can also clarify clinical issues such as the sensitivity to errors of OCD patients.

What are the limitations of ERPs as a way of studying the brain? First, ERPs are mainly of value when stimuli are simple and the task involves basic processes triggered by task stimuli. We cannot study most complex forms of cognition (e.g. problem solving) with ERPs because they involve several different processes spread over a long period of time.

Second, the fact that ERPs have poor spatial resolution means that we cannot use them to establish the precise brain regions associated with the performance of any given task.

Third, the use of ERPs involves *averaging* the EEG over numerous trials. Such averaging is not appropriate if participants exhibit significant learning and so the underlying processes and performance change over trials.

Post-mortem examinations

Most of the numerous exciting techniques for studying the brain were invented within the past 30–40 years. How did psychologists manage to study the brain in the era before these techniques existed? One of the most important approaches involved the use of post-mortem examinations. "Post-mortem" means "after death" and so this approach consists of examining in detail the brain of someone who has died.

In what follows we will discuss two convincing examples of the value of post-mortem examinations. First, we focus on the role of the brain in the mental disorder of schizophrenia. Second, we consider the brain's role in amnesia.

Findings

Schizophrenia is a serious mental disorder in which there is a partial loss of reality, hallucinations, and delusions. Twin studies indicate that genetic factors are important suggesting that insights into the origins and development of schizophrenia may be found by examining the brain post-mortem. Harrison (2000) reviewed research on post-mortem studies on schizophrenia. This research provided strong evidence that there are structural abnormalities in the brains of schizophrenic patients. More specifically, schizophrenics on average have a 25–40% enlargement of the lateral and third ventricles (cavities) in the forebrain, 4% smaller volume of the cortex than healthy controls, 5% smaller medial temporal lobe volume, and reduced cerebral asymmetries. In addition, the post-mortem evidence indicates that schizophrenics have alterations in various transmitter systems (e.g. dopamine; serotonin).

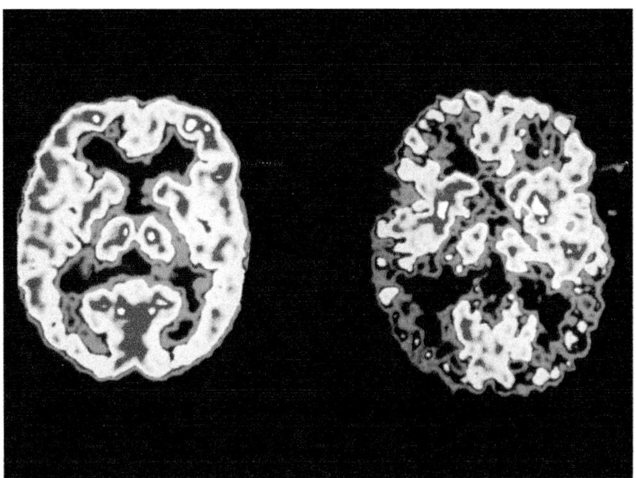

PET scans of a normal (left) and schizophrenic human brain.

As you may be thinking, it is no easy matter to *interpret* the above brain differences between schizophrenics and healthy controls. There are various reasons for this. First, some of these abnormalities (e.g. reduced cortical volume) are also found in several other disorders.

Second, a central issue is that the evidence we have is basically correlational in nature. In other words, we find that certain abnormalities in brain structure are *associated* with schizophrenia. This might be the case because these brain abnormalities play a role in causing schizophrenia. Alternatively, having schizophrenia may lead to brain abnormalities. Other possibilities are that changes occurring around the time of death create brain abnormalities in schizophrenics or the drugs taken by schizophrenics may influence brain structure.

Third, some of the abnormalities may simply be irrelevant to schizophrenia. How do we work out which are relevant and which are irrelevant?

Some of the earliest memory research towards the end of the nineteenth century involved amnesic patients with severe problems in long-term memory who had Korsakoff's syndrome. Korsakoff's syndrome mostly occurs as a result of chronic alcohol abuse. Post-mortem examinations have revealed that most patients with Korsakoff's syndrome have damage to the thalamus and the mammillary bodies (Kopelman et al., 2009). This damage occurs because chronic alcoholism causes thiamin deficiency.

The above findings would seem to suggest the mammillary bodies and thalamus play a key role in long-term memory. However, research using other patients and other techniques (e.g. fMRI) indicated that the hippocampus is of central importance in producing long-term memories. For example, the most famous amnesic patient of all time (HM; see Chapter 3) was found in post-mortem examination to have extensive damage to the hippocampus (Annese et al., 2014).

Since Korsakoff patients generally do not have damage to the hippocampus, how can we explain their amnesia? What happens in healthy individuals is that memories are formed in the hippocampus and are then subsequently stored in the frontal cortex. This does *not* happen in Korsakoff patients because damage to the mammillary bodies and thalamus prevents the memories formed in the hippocampus from reaching the frontal cortex.

EVALUATION

Post-mortem examinations can be very useful because they permit the brain to be studied in a very detailed and precise way. For example, we now have a comprehensive knowledge of the several brain abnormalities associated with schizophrenia. Post-mortem examinations are of less value than in the past because there are various methods (e.g. MRI) for assessing brain structure in detail in living individuals.

What are the limitations of post-mortem examinations? First, there are often problems of interpretation. The discovery that there is an association between a given disorder and certain brain abnormalities is typically insufficient evidence to conclude that the brain abnormalities helped to produce the disorder.

Second, some brain abnormalities detected on post-mortem examination may be due to changes occurring around the time of death or, in the case of mental disorders, effects produced by prolonged drug therapy.

Third, the findings of post-mortem examinations can be misleading. Post-mortem examinations of amnesic patients with Korsakoff's syndrome suggested that the mammillary bodies and the thalamus were of major importance in long-term memory. In fact, the hippocampus is the most important brain structure and damage to the mammillary bodies and thalamus prevents long-term memories being stored in the frontal cortex but does not prevent them being formed in the first place.

Section Summary

- Techniques for studying the brain vary in terms of spatial and temporal resolution.
- Functional magnetic resonance imaging (fMRI) has very good spatial resolution but poor temporal resolution. Research using fMRI has obtained evidence indicating differences in brain pathways between OCD patients and healthy controls.
- The theoretical assumption that there are three types of long-term memory (episodic; semantic; and procedural) has been supported by fMRI studies.
- fMRI is limited because it only shows an association between patterns of brain activation and behaviour.
- The EEG has proved useful in identifying several stages of sleep, in examining the effects of meditation on brain states, and in assessing cognitive processes in patients in a vegetative state.

- The EEG is limited because it has poor spatial resolution and it cannot be used to study complex processing sequences.
- Event-related potentials (ERPs) have poor spatial resolution but excellent temporal resolution.
- ERPs have revealed that OCD patients monitor their own errors more than healthy controls. They have also shown that context is taken into account very rapidly in speech perception.
- ERPs are limited in that they cannot be used to study complex cognitive processes and their poor spatial resolution means we cannot use ERPs to establish the precise brain regions involved in any given task.
- Post-mortem examinations permit a systematic and detailed analysis of the brain and any abnormalities in it.
- Post-mortem examinations have revealed several differences between the brains of schizophrenic patients and healthy individuals. Such examinations have also helped to shed light on the underlying brain mechanisms responsible for amnesia.
- Post-mortem examinations are limited because they provide information about brain structure rather than brain processes. It is often hard to interpret the evidence from post-mortem examinations (e.g. whether brain abnormalities played a role in causing a disorder or whether the disorder helped to cause the brain abnormalities).

BIOLOGICAL RHYTHMS

There are numerous biological rhythms that influence our physiological function and our behaviour. Here we will focus on some of the most important of these biological rhythms.

EXAM HINT

The A-level specification requires you to know about biological rhythms including circadian, infradian, and ultradian rhythms. All three are specified so make sure you revise examples of all three types and can explain the differences between them.

Circadian, infradian, and ultradian rhythms

Many biological rhythms possessed by human beings repeat themselves every 24 hours or so. As a result, they are known as **circadian rhythms** (from two Latin words meaning "about" and "day"). It is important to emphasise that there are approximately 100 different biological circadian rhythms. For example, temperature in humans varies over the course of the 24-hour day, reaching a peak of about 37.4°C in the late afternoon and a low point of about 36.5°C in the early hours of the morning. A key circadian rhythm for humans (and most other species) is the **sleep–wake cycle** (discussed in detail later).

There are also **infradian rhythms** which involve repeating cycles lasting more than a day. A well-known example of an infradian rhythm in humans is the menstrual cycle which typically lasts about 29 days (discussed shortly). Another example is seasonal affective disorder.

Finally, there are **ultradian rhythms** which involve cycles lasting less than a day. A good example of an ultradian rhythm is to be found within sleep. There is a characteristic sleep cycle lasting about 90 minutes and most sleepers work through a number of sleep cycles every night (discussed shortly). Another example is appetite.

KEY TERMS

Circadian rhythms: biological rhythms that repeat every 24 hours approximately.

Sleep–wake cycle: the pattern of alternating sleep and wakefulness; in humans it consists of approximately 8 hours of nocturnal sleep and 16 hours of daytime wakefulness.

Infradian rhythms: biological rhythms with a cycle of more than 1 day.

Ultradian rhythms: biological rhythms with a cycle of less than 1 day but more than 1 hour.

Infradian rhythms

There are several infradian rhythms (rhythms having a cycle of more than one day). We will concentrate on two of the most important ones: the menstrual cycle and seasonal affective disorder. We will start with the menstrual cycle, the key features of which are as follows:

- *Follicular phase*: follicle-stimulating hormone causes ovarian follicles to grow around egg cells or ova followed by the ovarian follicles releasing oestrogens (sex hormones).

- *Ovulation phase*: oestrogens lead to increased release of luteinising hormone (LH) and follicle-stimulating hormone (FSH) from the anterior pituitary causing a ruptured follicle to release its ovum.
- *Luteal phase*: the ruptured follicle releases progesterone so preparing the lining of the uterus for the implantation of a fertilised ovum or egg.
- *Pre-menstrual and menstrual phases*: the ovum or egg moves into the fallopian tube; if unfertilised, progesterone and oestradiol levels decrease.

The menstrual cycle depends mostly on internal processes and mechanisms. However, there is evidence that external or environmental factors can exert some influence over it. For example, women living in close proximity to each other sometimes show menstrual synchrony, i.e. go through the various stages of the menstrual cycle at about the same time. It is not entirely clear how this comes about. However, Stern and McClintock (1998) carried out an interesting (if rather unsavoury) study in which women had the sweat of other women applied to their upper lip. This led to menstrual synchrony suggesting that the effect depends at least in part on **pheromones** (chemicals released by one individual that influence someone else).

? Can you think of any evolutionary advantages for synchronised menstrual cycles?

There is also evidence that male sweat can influence the menstrual cycle. Preti et al. (2003) investigated the underlying mechanisms in a study in which female participants were exposed to male sweat. Their key finding was that male sweat speeded up the following pulse of luteinising hormone—this is a key hormone in determining the phases of the menstrual cycle.

Some individuals suffer from **seasonal affective disorder**, in which the great majority of sufferers experience severe symptoms of depression during the winter months. This disorder is related to seasonal variations in the production of melatonin (a hormone associated with increased sleepiness; discussed shortly). Melatonin is produced primarily at night and so more is produced during the dark winter months. As would be expected, seasonal affective disorder is more common in northern latitudes where the winter days are especially short. Terman (1988) found that nearly 10% of those living in New Hampshire (a northern part of the United States) suffered from seasonal affective disorder compared to only 2% of those living in the southern state of Florida.

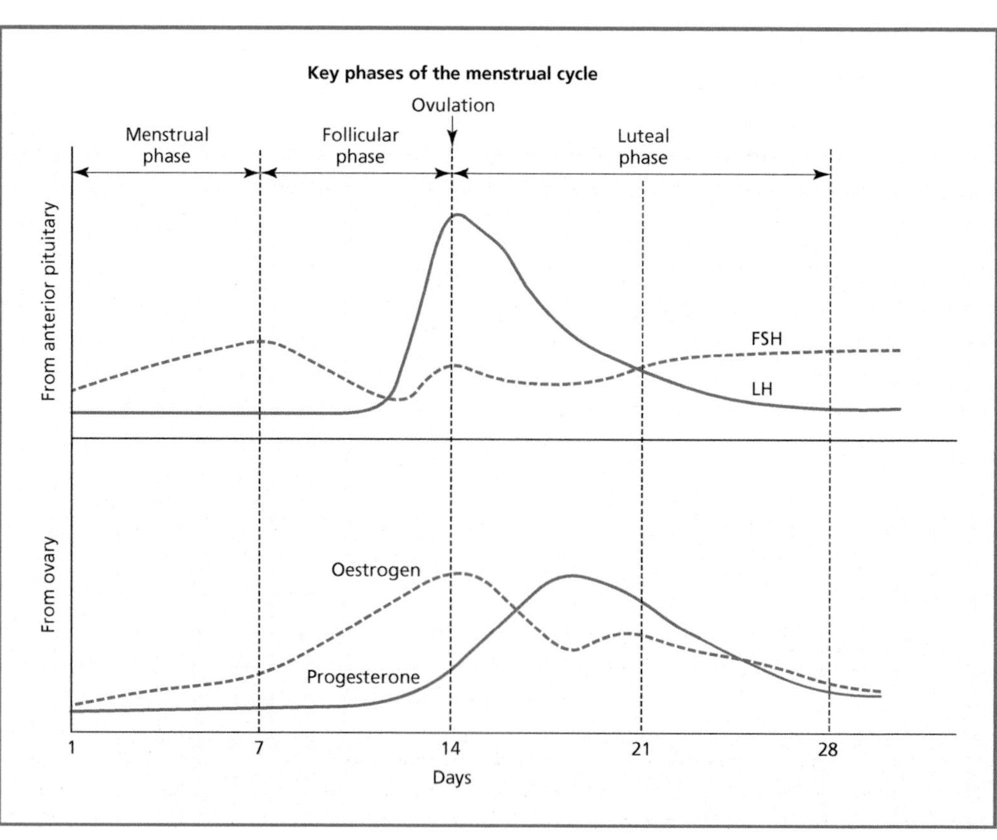

KEY TERMS

Pheromones: chemicals released by one individual that have an effect on another individual.

Seasonal affective disorder: a disorder that nearly always involves the sufferer experiencing severe depression during the winter months only.

Phototherapy is recommended for the treatment of seasonal affective disorder. This involves exposing sufferers to about 2 hours of intense light shortly after they wake up in the morning. This has been found to reduce or even eliminate depression (Lam et al., 2000).

Seasonal affective disorder can be treated by receiving phototherapy from a light box.

Conclusions

External factors play a role in both examples of infradian rhythms we have considered. We might imagine that the menstrual cycle would be determined almost entirely by internal factors (e.g. naturally occurring hormonal changes throughout the cycle). In fact, however, the existence of menstrual synchrony and the impact of male sweat on the menstrual cycle show this is *not* the case. Seasonal affective disorder clearly depends on the external environment, especially the number of hours of daylight. This interpretation is strengthened by the finding that phototherapy can reduce or eliminate the disorder.

Ultradian rhythms

There are many ultradian rhythms (rhythms that are repeated with a cycle of under 24 hours but more than 1 hour). Examples include urination, bowel activity, and appetite. One of the most important ultradian rhythms is the sleep cycle which will be the main focus in this section.

Much of our understanding of the sleep cycle depends on data obtained through use of the electroencephalogram (EEG; discussed earlier). Other useful physiological measures include eye movement data obtained from an electro-oculogram (EOG) and muscle movement data obtained from an electromyogram (EMG).

Research using the above measures has indicated that there are five different stages of sleep:

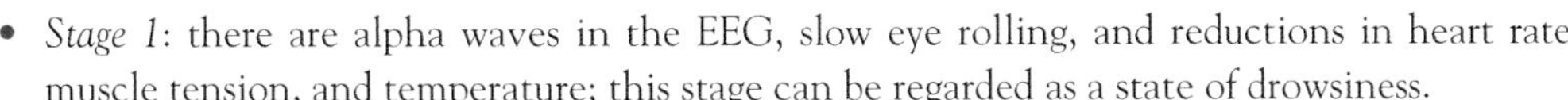

- *Stage 1*: there are alpha waves in the EEG, slow eye rolling, and reductions in heart rate, muscle tension, and temperature; this stage can be regarded as a state of drowsiness.
- *Stage 2*: the EEG waves become slower and larger but with short bursts of high-frequency sleep spindles; there is little activity in the EOG.
- *Stage 3*: The EOG and EMG records are similar to Stage 2 but there are many long, slow delta waves with some sleep spindles; this is a deeper stage of sleep than either of the first two stages.
- *Stage 4*: there is a majority of the long, slow delta waves present in smaller amounts than in the previous stage, and very little activity in the EOG or the EMG; this is a deeper stage of sleep than any of the first three stages.
- *Stage 5*: rapid eye movement or REM sleep, in which there are rapid eye movements and a very low level of EMG activity, while the EEG record is like that of Stage 1 (small amplitude fast EEG waves). REM sleep has been called paradoxical sleep because it is harder to awaken someone from REM sleep than from any other stage even though the EEG indicates the brain is very active.

After the sleeper has worked through the first four stages of progressively deeper sleep, he/she reverses the process. Stage 4 sleep is followed by Stage 3 and then by Stage 2. However, Stage 2 is followed by REM sleep (Stage 5). After REM sleep, the sleeper starts another sleep cycle working his/her way through Stages 2 3, and 4, followed by Stage 3, then Stage 2, and then REM sleep again. A complete sleep cycle lasts about 90 minutes and most sleepers complete five ultradian cycles during a normal night's sleep. The proportion of the time spent in

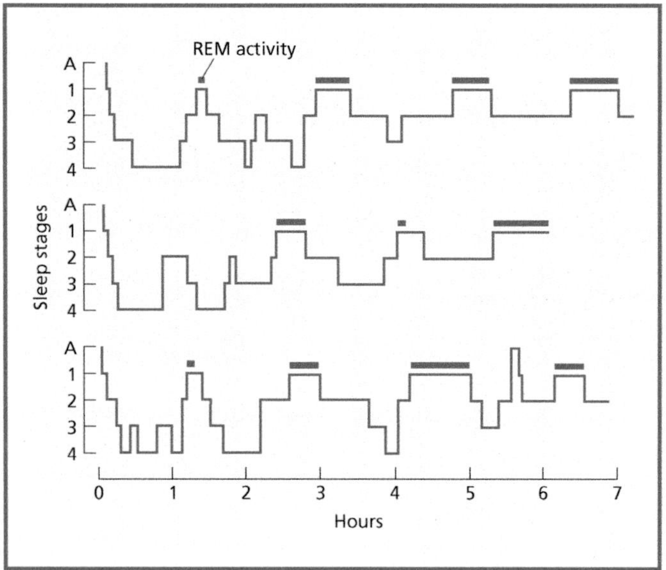

Cyclic variations in EEG during three typical nights' sleep. Note the increased REM activity as the night progresses, and reduced Stage 4 sleep.

REM sleep *increases* from one cycle to the next whereas that spent in Stage 4 sleep *decreases*.

It has often been claimed that dreaming occurs almost exclusively during REM sleep. That is *not* correct. Solms (2000, p. 618) reviewed the evidence and came to the following conclusion: "As many as 50 per cent of awakenings from non-REM sleep elicit dream reports, and 20 per cent of these are indistinguishable by any criterion from REM reports."

Does the sleep cycle always operate in the same way? The short answer is, "No". Randy Gardner, a 17-year-old student, remained awake for 264 hours or 11 days in 1964. He experienced various problems such as disorganised speech, and blurred vision, but otherwise coped with his massive sleep loss remarkably well. After his ordeal, Randy Gardner slept for 15 hours. However, over several nights after the end of his sleep deprivation, Randy recovered only 25% of the sleep he had missed. Of most interest here, he recovered almost 70% of Stage 4 deep sleep and 50% of REM sleep, with very small recovery percentages for the other stages of sleep. These findings indicate that there is *flexibility* in terms of the length of time devoted to each stage of sleep within the sleep cycle. They also indicate that stage 4 and REM sleep are of special importance.

? What are the drawbacks of using case studies to collect evidence?

Another example of an ultradian rhythm is appetite with most people eating two or more meals every day. The factors associated with appetite are numerous but we will just very briefly discuss a few. At the risk of oversimplification, the neurotransmitter neuropeptide Y and corticotropin-releasing hormone both play important roles. In essence, neuropeptide Y stimulates appetite and increases feeding behaviour. In contrast, corticotropin-releasing hormone inhibits appetite and reduces feeding behaviour. Amounts of neuropeptide Y and corticotropin-releasing hormone vary during the course of the day due to several internal and external factors and so play a significant role in producing an ultradian rhythm for appetite.

EXAM HINT

Sleep is an ultradian rhythm so you can use this section to answer questions on biological rhythms in general as well as questions on the role of endogenous pacemakers and exogenous zeitgebers.

Sleep–wake cycle

The 24-hour sleep–wake cycle is of particular importance to humans and is associated with other circadian rhythms. For example, as we have seen, body temperature is at its highest about halfway through the waking day (early to late afternoon) and at its lowest halfway through the sleeping part of the day (about three in the morning). Why is the sleep–wake cycle 24 hours long? Perhaps it is strongly influenced by **exogenous zeitgebers**. Exogenous factors are those originating outside the body and zeitgeber is a German word meaning "time giver". Thus exogenous zeitgebers are *external* events that have an impact on the sleep–wake cycle. The most obvious exogenous zeitgeber is the light–dark cycle and the fact that each dawn follows almost exactly 24 hours after the preceding one.

Another possible explanation for the sleep–wake cycle is that it depends on **endogenous pacemakers**. Endogenous factors are *internal* factors and pacemakers are biological mechanisms or "clocks" that influence the sleep–wake cycle. As we will see shortly, circadian rhythms (including the sleep–wake cycle) depend heavily on endogenous pacemakers.

KEY TERMS

Exogenous zeitgebers: external events that partially determine biological rhythms.

Endogenous pacemakers: internal biological mechanisms that influence the sleep-wake cycle.

Findings

How can we decide whether the sleep–wake cycle depends mainly on exogenous or external zeitgebers or on endogenous or internal pacemakers? One approach is to study individuals removed from the normal light/dark cycle (e.g. by being kept in the dark). Michel Siffre spent 7 months in a dark cave. At first, there was no very clear pattern in his sleep–wake cycle. Later on, however, he developed a sleep–wake cycle of about 25 hours rather than the standard one of 24 hours (Green, 1994). Wever (1979) discussed studies on individuals who spent weeks or months in a bunker or isolation suite. Most settled down to a sleep–wake cycle of about 25 hours.

CASE STUDY: Michel Siffre

Michel Siffre was studied for 7 months in 1972, when he volunteered to live underground in caves out of any contact with daylight and without any other clues about what time of day it was, such as a watch, clocks, or TV. He was safe and well fed, and the caves were warm and dry. He was always monitored via computers and video cameras, he had a 24-hour phone link to the surface, and he was well catered for in mind and body with books and exercise equipment. In this isolated environment, he quickly settled into a regular cycle of sleeping and waking. The surprise was that this cycle was of almost 25 hours, not 24! It was a very regular 24.9-hour rhythm, so that each "day" he was waking up nearly an hour later. The effect of this was that by the end of his months underground he had "lost" a considerable number of days and thought he had been underground for much less time than had actually passed.

The above evidence suggests there is an endogenous pacemaker having a cycle of about 25 hours. This is somewhat odd because it is unclear why we would have an endogenous rhythm discrepant from what we typically experience. In fact, however, there is a significant limitation in these studies. There was relatively little control over the participants' behaviour and they were able to control their own lighting conditions. Czeisler et al. (1999) compared what happened with this traditional approach (known as the free-running paradigm) with the forced desynchrony paradigm in which artificial 20- or 28-hour days were imposed on the participants (i.e. they did not control the lighting conditions). There was evidence for a 25-hour circadian rhythm in temperature with the free-running paradigm. However, the temperature circadian rhythm averaged 24 hours and 10 minutes with both the 20- and 28-hour days. Thus, the endogenous pacemaker has a period of 24 hours but this can be lengthened in artificial environments.

? What problems does this pose for shift workers?

The free-running paradigm led to overestimation of the duration of the endogenous pacemaker because participants could switch the lights on whenever they wanted. This matters because light is an exogenous zeitgeber that strongly influences the sleep–wake cycle. You probably wake up earlier in the summer than in the winter which provides some evidence you are responsive to the zeitgeber of light. Convincing evidence that light is an important zeitgeber was shown by Czeisler et al. (1989). When participants were exposed to bright light in the early morning there was an advance in the circadian temperature rhythm. In contrast, there was a delay in the circadian temperature rhythm when bright light was presented in the late evening.

KEY TERM

Suprachiasmatic nucleus (SCN): the structure within the hypothalamus that is involved in controlling various circadian rhythms including the sleep–wake cycle.

More evidence of the importance of light in determining circadian rhythms was reported by Flynn-Evans et al. (2014). They found 24% of the blind women in their sample had delayed or advanced circadian rhythms and a further 39% had abnormalities in their circadian rhythms.

In sum, there is an endogenous pacemaker (described in detail shortly) with a 24-hour cycle which is generally appropriate given that we all experience a 24-hour day. In addition, the endogenous pacemaker has the *flexibility* that it can be reset when required (e.g. after flying across several time zones). Without this flexibility, we would find ourselves falling asleep in the middle of the afternoon throughout a 2-week holiday on the west coast of America! Of course, as you may have discovered to your cost, it can take a few days for your sleep–wake cycle to adjust fully.

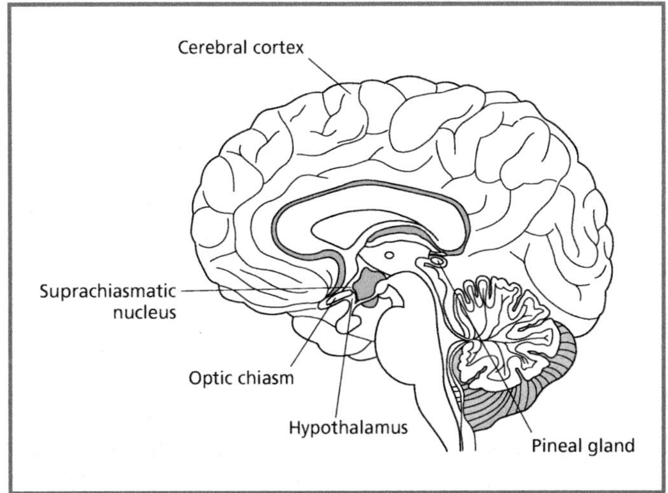

The endogenous mechanisms involved in regulating bodily rhythms.

Endogenous pacemakers

Endogenous pacemakers in humans involve complex biological systems. However, the **suprachiasmatic nucleus (SCN),** which is located within the hypothalamus, is an internal mechanism of special importance in influencing the sleep–wake cycle. We know the superchiasmatic nucleus (there are actually two nuclei very close together) forms the main circadian clock. For example, while damage to the SCN does not reduce how much of their time mammals spend sleeping, it does eliminate the normal

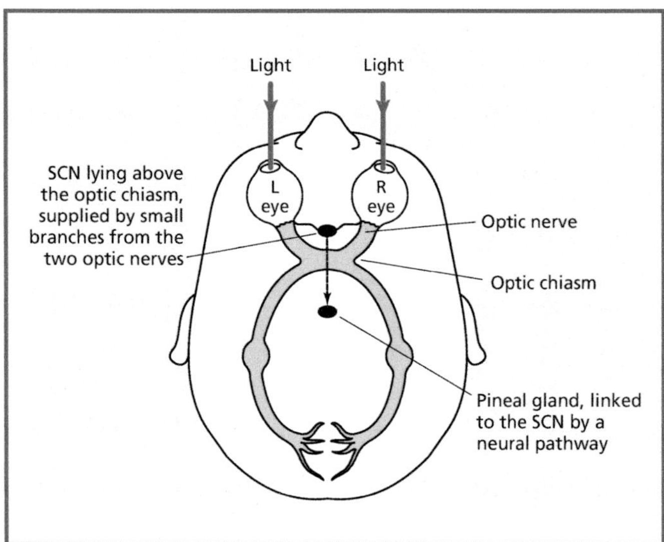

The visual pathway in the brain showing the connection to the suprachiasmatic nucleus (SCN) and onwards to the pineal gland.

sleep–wake cycle. Additional evidence comes from studies in which the SCN is isolated surgically from the rest of the brain. Even in these extreme circumstances, the SCN still exhibits circadian cycles of electrical and biochemical activity (Groos & Hendricks, 1982).

Compelling evidence that the SCN controls the sleep–wake cycle was provided by Ralph et al. (1990). They transplanted the suprachiasmatic nuclei from the foetuses of hamsters belonging to a strain having a 2-hour sleep–wake cycle into adult hamsters from a strain having a sleep–wake cycle lasting 25 hours. These adult hamsters rapidly adopted a 20-hour sleep–wake cycle.

According to Wickens (2000), a brain area has to possess three characteristics to fulfil the function of a circadian pacemaker. First, it should possess its own intrinsic rhythm. Second, it should receive visual information from the eyes to permit resetting of circadian rhythms in response to changing patterns of light and dark. Third, it should have output to other brain areas involved in circadian behaviour (e.g. the sleep–wake cycle).

So far we have considered the SCN only with respect to the first characteristic. With respect to the second characteristic, the SCN is very close to the optic chiasma which is where the nerve fibres from each eye cross to the other side of the brain. There is a pathway that branches off from the optic nerve and projects to the SCN. When this pathway was cut in hamsters they could not reset their circadian clock even though they could still see (Rusak, 1977).

Does the SCN possess the third characteristic of a circadian pacemaker? The SCN has connections with the pituitary gland and other areas of the hypothalamus. However, its most important projection is to the pineal gland (an endocrine gland) via the superior cervical ganglion. What happens is that darkness causes the superior cervical ganglion to release noradrenaline into pineal cells which is followed by the transformation of serotonin into melatonin.

Activity in the SCN leads to the release of the hormone **melatonin** from the pineal gland with more melatonin being released when light levels are low. Melatonin causes individuals to feel sleepier. It influences the brainstem mechanisms involved in sleep regulation and so plays a part in controlling the timing of sleep and waking periods. Individuals with a tumour in the pineal gland reducing melatonin secretion often find it very hard to get to sleep (Haimov & Lavie, 1996). People flying across several time zones often take melatonin because it makes them feel sleepy 2 hours afterwards (Haimov & Lavie, 1996).

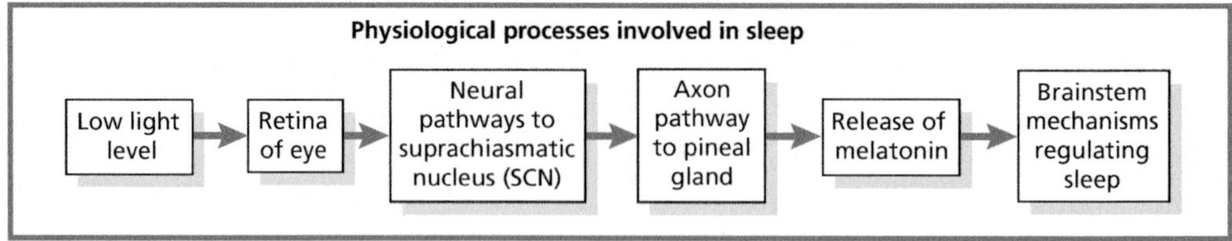

KEY RESEARCH STUDY

Shochat et al: Melatonin and the sleep–wake cycle

Convincing evidence of the key role played by melatonin in the sleep–wake cycle was reported by Shochat, Luboshitzky, and Lavie (1997). Participants spent 29 hours between 7 a.m. one day and noon the following day in a sleep laboratory. Throughout that time they spent 7 minutes in every 20 lying down in bed in a darkened room trying to sleep. Shochat et al. measured the levels of melatonin by taking blood samples up to three times an hour during the 29-hour session. The key finding was as follows: "We demonstrated a close and precise temporal relationship between the circadian rhythms of sleep propensity [the tendency to sleep] and melatonin; the nocturnal [night] onset of melatonin secretion consistently precedes the nocturnal sleep gate [period of greatest sleep propensity] by 100–120 min" (p. R367).

What are the limitations of Shochat et al.'s approach?

KEY TERM

Melatonin: a hormone that influences the onset of sleep.

Evaluation
Shochat et al.'s results were important in demonstrating that melatonin plays a role in sleep–wake cycles. However, it could be argued that trying to sleep in a laboratory situation is a task that does not have a great deal of ecological validity. The demand characteristics of the experiment and evaluation apprehension may have affected the participants, possibly even at a hormonal level. The sample used by Shochat et al. was also very small, consisting of only six male volunteers, and was not really representative. However, the study, like many others, provides a strong basis for future work.

The close relationship between increased melatonin and increased sleep propensity suggests (but does not prove) they are causally related. However, it has been found that individuals suffering from insomnia find it much easier to get to sleep when given melatonin 2 hours before bedtime.

We have seen that light and melatonin both influence the setting of the human circadian clock. What would happen if we manipulated *both* factors at the same time? Burke et al. (2013) addressed this issue. Participants were exposed to morning bright light and early evening administration of melatonin to advance the circadian clock. The effects on the circadian clock were greater than when only morning bright light or early evening melatonin was provided. Thus, these factors *combine* to reset the internal biological clock.

Can you think of anyone whose melatonin cycle differs from the norm?

Relationship between endogenous pacemakers and exogenous zeitgebers

We have seen that there is an endogenous pacemaker centred on the suprachiasmatic nucleus but also involving the pineal gland and the release of melatonin. In addition, there is compelling evidence for the importance of exogenous zeitgebers (especially those relating to light and darkness).

What is the relationship between these two determinants of the sleep–wake cycle? The key lies in the notion of **entrainment**—this involves the internal biological clock being adjusted to match environmental events or zeitgebers. Entrainment is very desirable. If the internal biological clock or endogenous pacemaker were totally inflexible, we would cope very poorly when travelling a long way east or west of where we live. In fact, our internal circadian clock possesses reasonable flexibility because it is responsive to environmental changes such as those occurring when we fly eastwards or westwards. In sum, endogenous pacemakers typically provide stability in the sleep–wake cycle and exogenous zeitgebers provide the means for adjusting this cycle when the environment changes in significant ways.

EXAM HINT

If you are asked to outline and evaluate or discuss one or more rhythms, you can describe how endogenous pacemakers and exogenous zeitgebers work together to regulate the rhythm and then discuss the research evidence for these processes.

Section Summary

- There are numerous biological rhythms, many of which fall into the categories of circadian, infradian, and ultradian.
- The menstrual cycle and seasonal affective disorder are both examples of infradian rhythms. Most women have a reasonably stable menstrual cycle of 29 days or so, but menstrual synchrony sometimes develops when several women live in close proximity.

KEY TERM

Entrainment: a process in which the internal clock or pacemaker is adjusted or changed by external zeitgebers.

Seasonal affective disorder depends on the number of hours of daylight and can be reduced by phototherapy.
- The sleep cycle, which consists of five successive stages, is a good example of an ultradian rhythm. It is generally fairly stable at about 90 minutes. However, the sleep cycle can be influenced by various factors (e.g. sleep deprivation). Appetite is another ultradian rhythm. It is influenced by numerous factors among which are neuropeptide Y (which stimulates appetite) and corticotropin-releasing hormone (which inhibits appetite).
- The sleep–wake cycle is a good example of a circadian rhythm. It is strongly influenced by an internal clock or pacemaker. However, this internal clock can be adjusted by external factors (zeitgebers) of which the most important is the light–dark cycle. Thus, the sleep–wake cycle exhibits flexibility when the environmental conditions alter.
- The suprachiasmatic nucleus (SCN) is the single most important part of the internal system that provides an endogenous pacemaker.
- Activity in the SCN leads to the release of the hormone melatonin which increases sleepiness.

Further Reading

- The functions of different brain areas are discussed in detail by J. Ward (2010) *The student's guide to cognitive neuroscience (2nd Edn)* (Hove, UK: Psychology Press).
- There is thorough coverage of most topics in biopsychology by J.P.J. Pinel (2014) *Biopsychology (8th Edn)* (Harlow: Pearson).
- James Kalat has also produced a textbook providing comprehensive coverage of biopsychology: J.W. Kalat (2012) *Biological psychology (11th Edn)* (Belmont, CA: Wadsworth Cengage).
- All the main biological rhythms are discussed in a reader-friendly way in W.J. Koukkari & R.B. Sothern (2006) *Introducing biological rhythms* (Berlin: Springer).

Revision Questions

The examination questions aim to sample the material in this whole chapter. For advice on how to answer such questions refer to Chapter 1, "How Can I Do Well in the Exam?".

1. a. Outline **two** functions of the pituitary gland. (3 + 3 marks)

   b. Outline the functions of Broca's area and Wernicke's area in the brain. (3 + 3 marks)
2. Explain what research on split-brain patients has shown about the interaction of the left and right hemispheres of the brain. (8 marks)
3. Outline and evaluate the use of two brain scanning techniques in psychological research. (8 marks)
4. Discuss the role of endogenous pacemakers and exogenous zeitgebers in the sleep–wake cycle. (16 marks)

EXAM HINT

Some examination questions require you to apply your knowledge. They start with a "stem" describing a scenario. Whilst you probably have not seen the scenario before, if you have revised everything you will have the knowledge needed to answer the question. Just remember to apply your knowledge. You might briefly outline a theory or research study but then must use this to explain the scenario.

What you need to know

The specifications for AS and A-level year 1 are the same for this topic, so you will need to cover everything in this chapter.

Psychopathology will be examined in Paper 2 of the AS exam and Paper 1 of the A-level exam.

Psychopathology 7

This chapter explores an extremely important area within psychology—psychopathology. **Psychopathology** is the scientific study of mental disorders including their classification and their underlying causes; it is also known as abnormal psychology.

What is **abnormality**? If clinicians are to treat patients with mental disorders, they need to distinguish between normal and abnormal behaviour. However, first they must define abnormality. Mental disorder has been likened to physical illness—for example, having a cold is an abnormal and undesirable state. We will consider that definition a little later.

Why do some people have mental disorders and others don't? Are mental disorders "caught" in the same way you catch a cold, or do they depend on genetic factors and/or personality? We will explore mental abnormality and its potential undesirability in this chapter.

Most definitions of abnormality and our explanations for mental disorder are based on Western beliefs. In recent years, however, there has been a growing recognition that it is very important to consider cultural and sub-cultural differences. We will be discussing these issues.

Later in the chapter, we will discuss three common and important mental disorders: phobias, depression, and obsessive–compulsive disorder (OCD). We will focus on their various characteristics or symptoms. After that, we consider how these disorders can be explained and, most importantly, how they can be treated.

DEFINITIONS OF ABNORMALITY

What is abnormality? The term "abnormal" can be defined as "deviating from what is normal or usual". What, then, is meant by the term "normal"? Conforming to a standard of some sort is one answer to that question. But how do we establish the standard? Several approaches will be considered here—all have something in their favour:

1. The standard can be defined in social terms—what is considered socially acceptable or deviant.
2. We might use the notion of "adequate functioning"—being able to cope reasonably well with the demands of daily life.

KEY TERMS

Psychopathology: the scientific study of mental illness or mental disorders including their classification and identification of the causes of mental disorders.

Abnormality: an undesirable state producing severe impairment in a person's social and personal functioning, often causing anguish. Abnormal behaviour deviates from statistical or social norms, causes distress to the individual or others, and is seen as a failure to function adequately.

Abnormal behaviour...?

...Not when rescuing a cat!

3. We could argue that normality represents what is common or typical in the population and that abnormality therefore represents what is uncommon or statistically infrequent.
4. There is the concept of **ideal mental health**—a state of contentment we all strive to achieve. If an individual's mental health deviates considerably from the ideal, we might describe it as abnormal.

Deviation from social norms

One important way of defining abnormality is based on the *impact* of an individual's behaviour on others. According to this approach, people behaving in a socially deviant and apparently incomprehensible way (especially if it upsets or distresses others) should be regarded as abnormal.

Social norms are the standards of behaviour regarded as acceptable within a given society. These standards of behaviour are expressed in rules. Some rules are explicit (e.g. "You must not steal goods belonging to other people"), whereas others are implicit (e.g. "Don't talk negatively about your friends"). Explicit and implicit rules both vary from culture to culture and over time within a given culture.

The social norms approach allows us to account for desirability of a pattern of behaviour, both for the individual and for society as a whole. **Deviation from social norms** is regarded as abnormal and undesirable. Many people labelled as clinically abnormal often behave in a socially deviant way. For example, anti-social personality disorder describes individuals who lack a conscience and behave aggressively towards others because they experience little or no guilt. Consider also the Case Studies described on the following pages.

The social norms approach to abnormality does not work well within certain groups in which the norms to which they adhere are very unusual. For example, consider the Heaven's Gate American religious group based in San Diego, California. The leader of this group was Marshall Applewhite, and he persuaded his followers that the planet Earth was about to be wiped clean and that their only chance of survival was to leave it immediately. This could be accomplished by committing mass suicide in order to reach a spacecraft following the comet Hale-Bopp.

In March 1997, Marshall Applewhite persuaded 38 out of the 39 other members of the group to commit mass suicide and he himself also committed suicide. The members of Heaven's Gate clearly conformed to the group's social norms. However, it is equally clear that their behaviour with its bizarre beliefs and willingness to commit suicide was very abnormal.

Marshall Applewhite, leader of the "Heaven's Gate" mass suicide in California in 1997.

EVALUATION

(+) The behaviour of most individuals diagnosed as having a mental disorder deviates from social norms. Consider, for example, two disorders discussed later in the chapter: social phobia and major depressive disorder. Social phobics have a great fear of social situations and so very often do their utmost to avoid such situations. Patients with major depressive disorder derive little enjoyment from most activities and so often become disengaged from many aspects of everyday life.

(+) Cultural context is important. For example, Kwakiutl Indians engage in a special ceremony in which they burn valuable blankets to cast shame on their rivals. If someone in our society deliberately set fire to his/her most valuable possessions, they would be regarded as very odd or mentally ill (Gleitman, 1986). Thus, whether any given form of behaviour is regarded as abnormal depends on that culture's prevailing norms.

(−) Conformity to social norms can be abnormal. A concrete example of this is the Heaven's Gate group discussed earlier.

(−) Social deviancy (failure to conform to social norms) is not necessarily a bad thing. Some people are socially deviant because they have chosen a non-conformist lifestyle and/or because their behaviour is motivated by high principles. Eccentrics

KEY TERMS

Ideal mental health: a state of contentment that we all strive to achieve.

Social norms: the explicit and implicit rules that specify what forms of behaviour, beliefs, and attitudes are acceptable within a given society.

Deviation from social norms: behaviour that does not follow accepted social patterns or unwritten social rules. Such violation is considered abnormal. These norms vary from culture to culture and from era to era.

deliberately ignore many social norms. However, most eccentrics are happy and are less prone to mental illness than other people (Weeks & James, 1995). Consider also "deviants" in Nazi Germany who risked their lives to help the Jews.

- The social deviance approach attaches too much importance to behaviour and de-emphasises what is going on *inside* individuals. For example, consider someone with major depressive disorder. They may try very hard to ensure their behaviour in public conforms to social norms even though they have a mental disorder and are suffering much internal distress. According to the social deviance approach, such individuals aren't abnormal.
- The concept of social deviancy is related to moral codes or standards, subjectively defined by a society, and these vary with prevailing social attitudes. For example, until the latter part of the twentieth century in Britain it was regarded as unacceptable for an unmarried woman to have a child. In the nineteenth century, single women who became pregnant were seen as social deviants and some were even locked up in psychiatric institutions.
- What is regarded as socially acceptable in many cultures is strongly influenced by political considerations. In Russia throughout much of the twentieth century, individuals who disagreed with the communist government were called dissidents. Their attitudes were seen as symptoms of mental derangement and they were confined in mental hospitals. Using social deviancy to establish a standard allows serious abuses of human rights to occur. Szasz (1960) suggested the concept of mental illness is a myth used by the state as a means of control. It is certainly open to such abuse.

? In what ways are you abnormal?

Moral codes

The subjective judgements we make when deciding whether or not a particular form of behaviour is normal are derived from the moral codes or standards we have observed in the behaviour of significant others. We never become entirely independent in our moral thinking. Even as adults our thinking about morality often refers to a collective understanding of the right way to behave in a given situation. Someone deviating from this may be perceived as "mad" or "bad".

KEY TERM

Failure to function adequately: a model of abnormality based on an inability to cope with day-to-day life caused by psychological distress or discomfort.

The fact that social deviance should be rejected as the only criterion of abnormality doesn't mean it is entirely irrelevant. After all, people derive much of their pleasure in life from their interactions with other people. As a result, most people find it important for a contented existence to avoid behaving in socially deviant ways that bemuse or upset others.

Failure to function adequately

Another way of defining abnormality is as a **failure to function adequately**. Most individuals seeking help from a clinical psychologist or psychiatrist suffer from a sense of psychological distress or discomfort due to their inability to cope with their work and/or personal lives (Pomerantz, 2014). This recognition of not functioning adequately could act as a standard of abnormality.

In most societies there are *expectations* about how people should live their lives and how they should contribute to the social groups around them. When an individual can't meet these obligations, then we (and usually they) feel they aren't functioning adequately. Rosenhan and Seligman (1989) suggested that the concept of distress and failure to function adequately can be extended to include a number of behaviours.

Camping in the middle of London may ordinarily be considered an abnormal behaviour in our society, but it is acceptable to those involved in a protest.

According to Rosenhan and Seligman (1989), we can identify *seven* abnormal characteristics. Each on its own may not cause a problem. However, when several are present, they are symptomatic of abnormality. We should think in terms of *degrees* of normality and abnormality rather than whether a behaviour or person is abnormal. Here are Rosenhan and Seligman's seven features:

- *Suffering*. Most abnormal individuals report they are suffering, and so this is a key feature of abnormality. However, nearly all normal individuals grieve when a loved one dies, and some abnormal individuals (e.g. psychopaths or those with anti-social personality disorder) treat other people very badly *without* suffering themselves.
- *Maladaptiveness*. Maladaptive behaviour prevents an individual from achieving major life goals (e.g. enjoying good relationships; working effectively). Most abnormal behaviour is maladaptive in this sense. However, maladaptive behaviour can also be due to deficient knowledge or skills.
- *Vividness and unconventionality of behaviour*. The ways abnormal individuals behave in various situations differ substantially from how most people behave. However, the same is true of non-conformists and eccentrics.
- *Unpredictability and loss of control*. Abnormal individuals' behaviour is often very variable and uncontrolled, and is also inappropriate. However, most people sometimes behave like this (e.g. after binge drinking).
- *Irrationality and incomprehensibility*. A common feature of abnormal behaviour is that it isn't clear why anyone would choose to behave in that way. However, we might simply not know the reasons for it.
- *Observer discomfort*. Those who see the unspoken rules of social behaviour being broken by others often experience some discomfort. However, observer discomfort may reflect cultural differences in behaviour and style rather than abnormality.
- *Violation of moral and ideal standards*. Behaviour may be judged abnormal when it violates established moral standards. However, the majority of people may fail to maintain those standards, which may be outdated or imposed by minority religious or political leaders. For example, various common sexual practices are illegal in parts of the United States.

CASE STUDY: **Sarah, a case of agoraphobia with panic disorder**

Sarah, a woman in her mid-thirties, was shopping for bargains in a crowded department store during the January sales. Without warning and without knowing why, she suddenly felt anxious and dizzy. She worried she was about to faint or have a heart attack. She dropped her shopping and rushed straight home. As she neared home, she noticed her feelings of panic lessened.

A few days later she went shopping again. On entering the store, she became increasingly anxious. After a few minutes, she had become so anxious that a shopkeeper took her to a first aid room. Once there, her feelings of panic became worse and she grew particularly embarrassed at the attention she was attracting.

After this she avoided going to the large store again. She even started to worry when going into smaller shops because she thought she might have another panic attack, and this worry turned into intense anxiety.

Eventually she stopped shopping altogether, asking her husband to do it for her.

Over the next few months, Sarah had panic attacks in more and more places. She became progressively more anxious the further away from her house she got. She tried to avoid places where she might have a panic attack but, as the months passed, this restricted her activities. Some days she found it impossible to leave the house. She felt her marriage was becoming strained and that her husband resented her dependence on him.

Sarah's behaviour was abnormal in many of the ways described in the text. It was socially deviant and interfered with her ability to function adequately, both from her own point of view and from that of her husband. She did not have many of the signs of mental healthiness, and suffered from the mental disorder of agoraphobia with panic disorder.

(Adapted from J.D. Stirling & J.S.E. Hellewell, 1999, *Psychopathology*. London: Routledge.)

A problem with Rosenhan and Seligman's features is that most involve subjective judgements. For example, behaviour causing severe discomfort to one observer may have no effect on another. Behaviour violating one person's moral standards may be consistent with another person's moral standards. Another problem is that some features apply to people who are nonconformists or simply have their own idiosyncratic style. However, there are no clear objective measures of abnormality.

ACTIVITY: The seven features of abnormality

Imagine a continuum from extremely abnormal behaviour at one end to normality at the other. At what point does our behaviour become unacceptable? Bearing in mind Rosenhan and Seligman's definitions, consider the experiences described below. For each one describe what would be acceptable behaviour and what would be abnormal. For example, what kind of expression of grief would go beyond the bounds of normality?

Suffering: Grief at the loss of a loved one.
Maladaptiveness: Disregard for one's own safety, e.g. taking part in extreme sports.
Vividness and unconventionality: Tattooing or body piercing.
Unpredictability and loss of control: Losing one's temper.
Irrationality and incomprehensibility: Remaining friendly towards someone who is hostile.
Observer discomfort: Laughing at inappropriate times, e.g. when someone is describing a sad event.
Violation of moral and ideal standards: Removing one's clothes to sunbathe on the beach.

- Are the criteria we use influenced by our cultural and personal backgrounds?
- Try to think of other examples for each standard.

EVALUATION

+ An argument in favour of the notion that abnormality can be defined as a failure to function adequately is that it is an important criterion with respect to many mental disorders. For example, consider depression and anxiety. Millions of people experience severe depression and/or anxiety some of the time. However, a key difference between those diagnosed with depression or anxiety as a mental disorder and the rest of the population is that the former find their depression and/or anxiety is seriously interfering with their everyday lives (e.g. work; relationships; social activities).

+ There are reasons why individuals decide to seek treatment for a mental disorder. However, perhaps the single most important reason is because they are finding it hard or impossible to function adequately day by day.

+ It is often fairly easy to assess the level of functioning by assessing the consequences of inadequate functioning (e.g. absenteeism from work; inadequate work performance; absence of friends; lack of non-work interests). However, value judgments are still often needed to decide the adequacy/inadequacy of functioning.

− A major limitation of this approach is that it is very *imprecise*. Abnormality is defined as a failure to function adequately and yet it isn't possible to define the key terms clearly. Inadequate functioning is a matter of degree, and it is entirely arbitrary to draw a dividing line between adequate and inadequate functioning.

− The "failure to function" approach assumes individuals who aren't functioning adequately are behaving abnormally. This assumption doesn't take sufficient account of *situational context*. For example, it is usually regarded as abnormal for someone to spend several weeks or months in a state of deep depression. However, that is a normal reaction if you are grieving because someone very close to you has just died.

− The approach doesn't take fully into account the fact that notions of abnormality vary within any given culture at different periods in history. For example, how homosexuality is regarded within American culture has altered over successive editions of DSM (*Diagnostic and Statistical Manual of Mental Disorders*). This is the system used by clinicians to classify mental illness in America. In DSM-II, published in 1968, homosexuality was classified as a sexual deviation. In DSM-III, published in 1980, homosexuality was no longer categorised as a mental disorder and that has remained the case in all subsequent updates of DSM (the current version is DSM-5).

- Another problem with this approach is that not all people who experience mental disorder are aware of their failure to function. For example, individuals suffering from schizophrenia often deny they have a problem (see the case study below). However, it is distressing to others, who may be able to judge the individual isn't functioning adequately and seek help on his/her behalf.

- The assumption that individuals who are functioning adequately aren't abnormal isn't entirely correct. Consider the English doctor Harold Shipman, who was responsible for the deaths of over 200 of his patients. In spite of his appalling crimes, Shipman functioned adequately enough to escape detection for many, many years. Even when his crimes were discovered, the police were surprised how quiet and dull Shipman appeared to be.

CASE STUDY: Simon, a boy with acute schizophrenia

Simon lived at home with his parents. Over some months his parents had become increasingly concerned about his behaviour. He had grown reclusive, spending a lot of time in his room, and had lost contact with his friends. His parents feared he might be taking drugs. They called the doctor when they found he had scratched the words "good" and "evil" on his arms. The GP was also concerned and contacted a psychiatrist who visited Simon at home. Simon at first pretended to be out. After some negotiation, he agreed to let the psychiatrist in. Initially, Simon was very suspicious and denied there was a problem. Eventually, he told the psychiatrist he was very worried about all the evil in the world, and had discovered he could tell whether people were good or evil just by looking at them. He described receiving messages from the radio and TV.

The psychiatrist was concerned when Simon said he left the house at night to look for evil people, believing it was his duty to fight them. The psychiatrist found Simon's bedroom was painted black and the curtains were taped shut. The walls were covered with crucifixes and mystical symbols, and Simon slept with a large knife near his bed in case he was confronted by evil people.

Simon was asked if he was willing to be admitted to a local hospital. He refused, saying he did not need help. However, the psychiatrist was so worried about the risks to Simon or others that he arranged for Simon to be admitted under the Mental Health Act. For the first few weeks in hospital, Simon continued to claim he was not ill and did not need treatment. Drug therapy resulted in significant improvements and he eventually returned home, continuing with his medication.

(Adapted from J.D. Stirling & J.S.E. Hellewell, 1999, *Psychopathology.* London: Routledge.)

We also need to consider psychopaths. Psychopathy is a mental disorder characterised by superficial charm, frequent lying, and a lack of concern for others. Many psychopaths commit violent crimes and are imprisoned, whereas others lead successful lives and even become business leaders. How can some psychopaths apparently function adequately in spite of having a mental disorder? Gao and Raine (2010) argued that such psychopaths are highly intelligent and so can achieve their goals by non-violent methods.

Police handout photograph of Dr Harold Shipman.

Statistical infrequency

We could approach the definition of abnormality in an indirect way by starting with normality. What is normal? One way of defining normality is in terms of **statistical frequency**—we could argue that what is common is also normal.

This approach makes some sense. Much of the behaviour exhibited by individuals diagnosed with a mental disorder is statistically infrequent in the population. For example, some patients

KEY TERM

Statistical frequency: behaviours that are statistically rare or deviate from the average/statistical norm are classified as abnormal.

with obsessive–compulsive disorder wash their hands hundreds of times a day and some schizophrenics claim to hear voices even when no-one is speaking.

The notion of statistical infrequency in relation to abnormality is of some importance. However, it doesn't allow us to identify *what* behaviours require treatment. In other words, it overlooks *desirability*. For example, an individual having an IQ (intelligence quotient) in excess of 130 is statistically unusual in that only 2% of the population have IQs that high. However, most people would be delighted to discover they had such a high IQ rather than being worried that they were abnormal!

In similar fashion, individuals who have very non-anxious personalities that are statistically very infrequent would not be regarded as abnormal. Indeed, having a non-anxious personality is probably fairly desirable.

Another problem with the statistical approach is deciding by how much someone's behaviour must deviate from the norm or average before it should be considered abnormal. Statistical definitions rely on an arbitrary cut-off point. For example, does someone need to be more depressed than 90% of the population, 95% of the population, or 99% of the population in order to be regarded as abnormal? It is impossible to provide a clear answer to such a question.

A further problem with statistical definitions is that they may not apply to people living in different times. Large changes over time were reported by Twenge et al. (2010). They compared the scores of American college students on the Minnesota Multiphasic Personality Inventory (MMPI) over the decades between 1938 and 2007. The MMPI assesses psychiatric symptoms, and Twenge et al.'s findings revealed a substantial increase in such symptoms over the decades. They concluded as follows: "Five times as many now score above common cutoffs for psychopathology" (p. 145).

How do Twenge et al.'s (2010) findings relate to the usefulness of statistical infrequency as a criterion for abnormality? The findings suggest there has been a marked increase in abnormality over the past 60 years or so. In contrast, someone favouring the statistical infrequency approach would argue that only, say, the 5% of the population with the greatest number of psychiatric symptoms are abnormal. That would mean the cut-off point between normality and abnormality would have to shift considerably over the decades to maintain that figure of 5% abnormality. I don't think many people would think that is a sensible way to proceed!

According to the statistical approach, how abnormal any symptom or behaviour is depends on its infrequency. Thus, *hylophobia* (fear or phobia about forests or wood), which is very rare, is regarded as a strong sign of abnormality. In contrast, contemplating suicide (which is less rare) is regarded as less indicative of abnormality. This makes no sense. What is omitted from the statistical approach is any assessment of the *severity* of symptoms as well as their infrequency.

In sum, the statistical infrequency approach has very little to recommend it. It is true that behaviour typically regarded as abnormal is generally relatively rare in the population. However, it would be absurd to argue that statistical infrequency should be the only criterion for abnormality. Statistically infrequent thoughts and behaviour can be desirable rather than undesirable. If we focus only on thoughts and behaviour generally regarded as undesirable, we can't identify those that are more and less serious or indicative of abnormality purely on the basis of their statistical infrequency.

EXAM HINT

You need to be able to write a paragraph to describe each definition of abnormality and evaluate each definition with two well explained points—strengths and/or weaknesses.

- *Deviation from social norms*: Remember these are culturally relevant and era dependent. Use examples to illustrate these points.
- *Failure to function adequately*: Be able to include some (not necessarily all) of Rosenhan and Seligman's criteria for failure to function, e.g. personal distress, observer discomfort, and maladaptiveness. Two or three well explained criteria, carefully evaluated, would be fine.
- *Statistical infrequency*: Remember that some personal qualities (e.g. very high intelligence; great courage) are statistically infrequent but are nevertheless highly desirable and by no means abnormal. Use examples to illustrate your description and your evaluation.
- *Deviation from ideal mental health*: Consider Jahoda's criteria for ideal mental health, e.g. positive self-attitudes, autonomy, and perception of reality. Two or three well-explained and evaluated criteria would be about right.

Deviation from ideal mental health

If we take the view that abnormality is related to the lack of a "contented existence", then we might seek a definition in terms of deviation from ideal mental health. This was the view taken by **humanistic psychologists** such as Carl Rogers and Abraham Maslow (see Chapter 5). They both felt **self-actualisation** (fulfilment of one's potential) was a key standard and goal for human endeavour. Very few people are fully self-actualised, so don't worry if you are only partially fulfilling your potential!

Rogers (1951) was the founder of **client-centred therapy**. This has played a major role in the development of counselling. Rogers believed maladjustment or abnormal development occurred when a child received only conditional love from his/her parents. What this means is that the child only receives love from his/her parents if the child behaves in certain ways. The resulting conflict between the self-concept and the ideal self means that the individual will try to be someone else to receive the love he/she wants.

Healthy psychological development occurs through receiving *unconditional* positive regard from significant others (i.e. love is given regardless of the child's behaviour). This leads to high **self-esteem** and self-acceptance. It frees the individual from seeking social approval and enables him/her to seek self-actualisation.

Maslow (1954) was interested in the factors driving or motivating individuals. He claimed we seek first to have our basic needs satisfied (e.g. hunger; safety). After that, people are driven by "higher" motives such as love, belonging, and knowledge. The highest motive of all is to seek self-actualisation (see diagram on page 209).

Humanists wanted to define the ultimate goals of human behaviour. Normal people would strive for these goals, and abnormality results from a failure to achieve them.

Jahoda (1958) argued that the concepts of abnormality and normality were useless because their definition varies as a function of the group or culture we are considering. She suggested it was preferable to identify the criteria for positive mental health and then look at the frequency of their distribution in any population. Jahoda tried to identify common concepts used when describing mental health. She argued there are six categories **clinicians** typically relate to mental health:

1. *Self-attitudes*. High self-esteem and a strong sense of identity are related to mental health.
2. *Personal growth*. The extent of an individual's actual growth, development, or self-actualisation is important.
3. *Integration*. This is a "synthesising psychological function" that integrates or combines the above two concepts. It can be assessed by the individual's ability to cope with stressful situations.
4. *Autonomy*. This is the degree to which an individual is independent of social influences. We must be careful here, because ignoring social influences can be a sign of mental illness!
5. *Perception of reality*. This is a prime factor in mental health. Individuals with good mental health don't need to distort their perception of reality, and they exhibit empathy and social sensitivity.
6. *Environmental mastery*. The extent to which an individual is successful and well-adapted, including the ability to love, adequacy at work and at play, good interpersonal relations, efficiency in meeting situational requirements, capacity for adaptation and adjustment, and efficient problem solving. Most of us don't succeed in all these areas!

Jahoda's approach seeks to identify the characteristics people need to be mentally or psychologically healthy rather than identifying the problems. As a result, the six categories she identified could be translated into useful therapeutic aims (treatment goals).

KEY TERMS

Humanistic psychology: an approach to psychology that focuses on higher motivation, self-development, and on each individual as unique.

Self-actualisation: fulfilling one's potential in the broadest sense.

Client-centred therapy: a form of humanistic therapy introduced by Rogers and designed to increase the client's self-esteem and reduce incongruence between self and ideal self.

Self-esteem: the feelings that an individual has about himself or herself.

Clinician (or clinical psychologist): a person who works in clinical psychology, concerned with the diagnosis and treatment of abnormal behaviour.

We all want to be mentally healthy, but should we all want to be totally "normal"?

EVALUATION

- (+) The ideal mental health approach has the advantage of focusing on positive characteristics—on health rather than illness.

- (+) This approach identifies six categories of mental health and so it is unusually comprehensive in scope. The categories (e.g. personal growth; accurate perception of reality; environmental mastery) seem of direct relevance to mental health (at least within Western cultures).

- (−) Any set of values is inevitably linked to a given culture and historical period. Many psychologists (e.g. Oyserman et al., 2002) distinguish between individualistic cultures and collectivistic ones. Individualistic cultures (e.g. the United Kingdom; the United States) emphasise independence and personal control. In contrast, collectivistic cultures (e.g. China; Japan) focus on interdependence and considering oneself as a member of a group.

  Jahoda's list of mentally healthy behaviours such as self-attitudes, autonomy, and personal growth makes more sense in individualistic cultures than collectivistic ones. For example, Heine et al. (1999) discussed research in which European-Canadian and Japanese students ranked 20 traits in terms of how much they ideally would like to possess them. European-Canadians rated self-confidence as the trait they would *most* like to possess, whereas the Japanese rated it as the trait they would *least* like to possess.

- (−) The vague criteria for ideal mental health are hard to measure. For example, how can we rate positive interpersonal relations or self-acceptance?

- (−) The "healthy behaviours" identified by Jahoda are ideals. Very few people ever achieve them, so many (or even most) of us could be classified as abnormal. However, it could be argued that abnormality involves a substantial falling short on most of the criteria for ideal mental health. That raises the tricky issue of how much of a falling short is required for behaviour to be regarded as abnormal.

- (−) Humans are social animals and so having close personal relationships with other people is of central importance to ideal mental health. Jahoda refers to this under environmental mastery, but still de-emphasises its importance.

- (−) There seems to be an implicit assumption that any given individual's mental health remains fairly constant over time. However, that is probably the exception. Most people have a period of reduced mental health after someone close to them dies, and an important failure is generally followed by reduced self-esteem.

- (−) Eccentrics often focus obsessively on their work and/or hobbies, and many aren't very interested in the opinions or company of others. Thus, they would seem to fall short of ideal mental health. In spite of that, as we saw earlier, eccentrics tend to be happier than other people. This suggests most have good mental health.

- (−) Jahoda's approach may not provide useful criteria for identifying abnormality. A psychological scale that measures psychological concepts (e.g. a person's level of self-esteem) can't provide an objective measurement.

EXAM HINT

If an exam question asks you to outline **two or more** definitions of abnormality then do not feel you have to cover all four of them. You may end up providing breadth but insufficient detail. If a question says "two or more" then you can receive full marks just covering two.

General issues

Here we consider some important general issues with all four approaches we have discussed above.

Cultural relativism

A fundamental limitation with all the definitions of abnormality we have examined is that they are culturally specific. The notion of **cultural relativism** means value judgments are *relative* to individual cultural contexts. As a result, we can't make *absolute* statements about what is normal and abnormal in human behaviour. For example, in the fifth edition of the Diagnostic and Statistical Manual of Mental Disorders (DSM-5; American Psychiatric Association, 2013), it states, "Ideas that appear to be delusional in one culture (e.g. witchcraft) may be commonly held in another" (p. 103).

Consider **culture-bound syndromes** (patterns of abnormal behaviour typically found only in a single culture). For example, *dhat syndrome* is a culture-bound syndrome found among males of the Indian subcontinent. Sufferers have multiple somatic complaints, and blame their physical and mental exhaustion on the presence of semen in their urine. The origins of this lie in the Hindu belief that semen is produced in the blood, and that the loss of semen will result in illness. Chadda and Ahuja (1990) examined patients with *dhat* and concluded they were suffering from neurotic depression or anxiety neurosis. Thus, a single underlying disorder (e.g. depression) may be expressed in different ways across cultures.

There are many other culture-bound syndromes, and we will briefly mention two more here. *Koro* involves extreme anxiety that the penis or nipples will recede into the body and possibly cause death. It is found in south and east Africa. Finally, there is *amok* (originally identified in Malaysia), which involves brooding followed by a violent outburst.

The importance of cultural context can be seen if we go back to Rosenhan and Seligman's seven features of abnormality (1989; see page 269). Many of those features refer to behaviour defined by the social norms or expectations of the culture. That is certainly true of vividness and unconventionality of behaviour; irrationality and incomprehensibility; and observer discomfort. In other words, abnormality has a somewhat different meaning across cultures. For example, hallucinations are considered normal in certain situations in some societies, but in the West they are seen as a manifestation of a mental disorder.

Finally, it is important to strike the right balance. Some features identified by Rosenhan and Seligman may be universal indicators of undesirable behaviour for the individual concerned and those around them. Examples include a refusal to eat, chronic depression, a fear of going outdoors, and anti-social behaviour. Thus, there are some universal indicators of abnormality, even though most behavioural signs of abnormality are culture-specific.

EXAM HINT

Culture bias works well for all four definitions. Use examples of social norms changing across cultures and examples of how the criteria for failure to function, statistical infrequency, and ideal mental health can be viewed differently across cultures to make sure your answer is DETAILED and FOCUSED on the definition specified in the question.

DSM-5

How do psychiatrists and clinical psychologists diagnose mental disorders (abnormal conditions)? They often use the *Diagnostic and Statistical Manual of Mental Disorders* (DSM), which contains over 200 disorders. The current version of DSM is DSM-5 (American Psychiatric Association, 2013). According to this version, a mental disorder (abnormal condition) is "a syndrome characterised by clinically significant disturbance in an individual's cognition, emotion regulation, or behaviour that reflects a dysfunction in the psychological, biological, or developmental processes underlying mental functioning. Mental disorders are usually associated with significant distress in social, occupational, or other important activities. An expectable or culturally approved response to a common stressor or loss, such as the death of a loved one, is not a mental disorder. Socially deviant behaviour (e.g. political, religious, or sexual) and conflicts that are primarily between the individual and society are not mental disorders unless the deviance or conflict results from a dysfunction in the individual, as described above."

KEY TERMS

Cultural relativism: the view that to understand and judge another culture it must be viewed from within that culture, and not from the perspective of the observer's own culture.

Culture-bound syndromes: patterns of abnormal behaviour found in one or a small number of cultures.

Labels and symptoms

Imagine you are in a situation where you have been wrongly diagnosed as suffering from a mental disorder such as schizophrenia. How would you react? Would you be incredulous? Furious? Tearful? Shocked and withdrawn? How could all those emotions be interpreted by those people whose job it is to assess your mental condition?

How does the definition of mental disorder within DSM-5 relate to the four approaches we have discussed? The adequate functioning approach is represented in that there is an emphasis on ability to cope with social, occupational, and other important activities. The social norms approach is relevant to the part of the definition indicating that responding to stress or loss in a culturally approved way is not indicative of abnormality. However, the definition goes on to indicate that there are many cases in which failure to conform to social norms does not indicate abnormality. Dysfunction in the processes underlying mental functioning is of some relevance to the ideal mental health approach. Finally, there is little in the DSM-5 definition of mental disorder of relevance to the statistical infrequency approach.

Conclusions

"Abnormality" is an imprecise concept. Abnormal behaviour can take different forms and involve different features. Moreover, no *single* feature can always be relied on to distinguish between normal and abnormal behaviour. As Lilienfeld and Marino (1995, p. 416) pointed out, "abnormality" is like many other concepts in that it has "unclear boundaries and an absence of defining features".

We could adopt a *multi-criterion approach* to defining abnormality combining the four approaches we have discussed. Suppose we were trying to decide whether a given individual was abnormal. If they failed to function adequately, their behaviour deviated in several ways from social norms and was mostly statistically infrequent, and their mental health deviated considerably from the ideal, we would probably be very confident they were abnormal.

On the other hand, suppose their behaviour didn't deviate from social norms but their mental health deviated very much from the ideal. That would suggest they were experiencing inner distress but were somehow managing to behave normally. In contrast, an approximation to ideal mental health combined with behaviour deviating from social norms and being statistically infrequent might indicate that the individual is an eccentric who is perfectly content but doesn't care about the impact of their behaviour on other people.

In sum, there are degrees of abnormality. Abnormality can manifest in terms of behaviour and/or in terms of inner distress. If we use all four approaches to defining abnormality, we can obtain a clearer idea of the ways someone is and is not abnormal. Even then, there is no sharp distinction between normality and abnormality. Pomerantz (2014) focused on the way in which major depressive disorder (discussed later) is defined in DSM-5. An important criterion is that the individual has experienced at least five out of nine symptoms for at least 2 weeks. That means an individual who has experienced seven symptoms for only 10 days does not have the disorder—it is clearly an arbitrary matter to identify the former individual as abnormal but not the latter one!

Section Summary

Deviation from social norms

- This is one way of defining abnormality. Social groups have norms of what is considered to be socially acceptable behaviour. Deviation from them is abnormal and undesirable.
- This approach has been criticised as follows:
  - Deviation from social norms depends on subjective moral standards and can be influenced by political considerations.

  - The same behaviour may deviate from the social norms of some cultures but not others.
  - Eccentrics deviate from social norms but are typically happy and well-adjusted.
  - The definition ignores the role of social context. In some cases (e.g. Nazi Germany) it may be desirable to be socially deviant.
  - This approach focuses too much on people's behaviour and not enough on their internal states.

Failure to function adequately

- This approach suggests that abnormality can be defined in terms of an inability to function adequately in day-to-day life and social interactions.
- An absence of distress and the ability to function are standards of normal behaviour.
- This approach has the benefit of taking the individual's experience into account. However, it has been criticised as follows:
  - How do we determine whether a person is functioning adequately?
  - Not all those with mental disorders are aware of their own distress or dysfunction.
  - The definition raises concerns about cultural bias and subjectivity as judgements by others on their behalf may be biased.
  - Rosenhan and Seligman have extended the "failure to function" model to cover seven features associated with abnormality, but these also rely on making subjective judgements.
  - Inadequate functioning may reflect the situational context rather than mental disorder.
  - Some individuals (e.g. Harold Shipman; psychopaths) may appear to function adequately in spite of being abnormal in important ways.

Statistical infrequency

- It is probably true that much of the behaviour exhibited by individuals with a mental disorder is statistically infrequent in the population.
- This approach is based on the notion that what is common is normal and what is rare or statistically infrequent is abnormal.
- Some characteristics that are rare (e.g. very high intelligence; a very non-anxious personality) are nevertheless desirable.
- Another criticism is that it is unclear by how much someone's behaviour must deviate from the normal before it should be considered abnormal.
- When deciding whether someone has a mental disorder we need to focus on the severity of their symptoms as well as on their infrequency.

Deviation from ideal mental health

- Another approach suggests abnormality can be defined in terms of deviation from ideal mental health.
- Humanistic psychologists consider the factors that may be important for normal development such as unconditional positive regard. They also see self-actualisation as an ultimate goal.
- This approach has been criticised as follows:
  - It is based on abstract and culturally relative ideals (e.g. personal growth) not shared by collectivistic societies. There are cultural variations in how to identify psychological health.
  - There have been changes in what is regarded as ideal mental health throughout history.
  - Unlike physical health, it is difficult to measure psychological health.
  - Nearly everyone's mental health deviates from the ideal, but we can't identify the point at which this is indicative of abnormality.

General issues

- Cultural relativism is a problem in all three of the approaches described. The definitions inevitably refer to some subjective, culturally determined set of values.
- However, there are also cultural universals—behaviours such as anti-social behaviour or chronic depression are universally viewed as abnormal and undesirable.
- The resolution may lie in using a combined approach that focuses on which features are more likely to be associated with abnormality. This is suggested by the definition of a mental disorder in DSM-5, which incorporates elements of several different definitions.
- Abnormality has "unclear boundaries and an absence of defining features".

BEHAVIOURAL, EMOTIONAL, AND COGNITIVE CHARACTERISTICS OF PHOBIAS, DEPRESSION, AND OBSESSIVE–COMPULSIVE DISORDER (OCD)

Most mental disorders have a wide range of symptoms associated with them. In this section, we focus on behavioural, emotional, and cognitive characteristics or symptoms associated with three common mental disorders: phobias; depression; and obsessive–compulsive disorder (OCD). Note that the three types of symptoms are all highly *interdependent*—having a given symptom may at least in part cause another symptom. For example, someone who is depressed often experiences very negative emotional states. These emotional states may lead him/her to avoid the company of other people (behavioural symptom).

Characteristics of phobias

Phobias involve a high level of fear of some object or situation with the level of fear being so strong that the object or situation is avoided whenever possible. Indeed, the main characteristic the phobias have in common is avoidance of the feared stimuli or situations. There are three main categories of phobia: specific phobia; social phobia (often called social anxiety disorder); and agoraphobia. Social phobia and agoraphobia are both serious disorders because they involve avoiding social situations and public places, respectively. In contrast, specific phobia often involves avoidance of certain creatures (e.g. spiders) which typically has a less disruptive effect on the patient's everyday life.

Social phobia

Social phobia (social anxiety disorder) involves extreme concern about one's own behaviour in social situations and about others' reactions. About 8% of people suffer from social phobia in any given year and 70% of them are female.

Halgin and Whitbourne (1997, p. 215) described a sufferer from social phobia:

> *Ted is a 19-year-old college student who reports that he is terrified at the prospect of speaking in class. His anxiety about this matter is so intense that he has enrolled in very large lecture classes, where he sits at the back of the room ... Sometimes he rushes from the classroom and frantically runs back to the dormitory.*

Here are diagnostic criteria for social phobia from DSM-5 (2013):

- A persistent fear of one or more social or performance situations in which the individual is exposed to unfamiliar people or possible scrutiny by others. The individual fears he/she will show anxiety symptoms that will be embarrassing and humiliating.

KEY TERM

Social phobia: a disorder in which the individual has excessive fear of social situations and often avoids them.

- Exposure to the feared situation nearly always provokes anxiety.
- This fear is unreasonable or excessive.
- The feared situations are avoided or endured with intense anxiety and distress.
- The avoidance, anxious participation, or distress in the feared situations interferes with the person's normal routine, occupational functioning, or social activities or there is marked distress about having the phobia.

Specific phobia

Specific phobia involves strong and irrational fear of some specific object or situation. Fears of spiders or snakes are especially common forms of specific phobia but there are actually hundreds of different specific phobias. The main forms of specific phobia include the following: animal type; natural environment type (e.g. fear of heights; fear of water); blood–injection–injury type; and situational type (e.g. fear of lifts or enclosed spaces). Approximately 10% of people in Western cultures develop specific phobia at some point in their lives and specific phobias are twice as common in women as in men. Since specific phobia is generally not a very serious condition, almost 90% of individuals with a specific phobia don't seek treatment for it.

Here is an account from a patient with spider phobia (Melville, 1978, p. 44):

> *Seeing a spider makes me rigid with fear, hot, trembling, and dizzy. I have occasionally vomited and once fainted in order to escape from the situation. These symptoms last three or four days after seeing a spider. Realistic pictures can cause the same effect, especially if I inadvertently place my hand on one.*

According to DSM-5 (2013), here are major diagnostic criteria for specific phobia:

- Marked and persistent fear of a specific object or situation.
- Exposure to the phobic stimulus nearly always produces a rapid anxiety response.
- Fear of the phobic object or situation is excessive.
- The phobic stimulus is either avoided or responded to with great anxiety.
- The phobic reactions interfere significantly with the individual's working or social life, or he/she is very distressed about the phobia.

Agoraphobia

Agoraphobia is an anxiety disorder in which there is great fear of open, public, or enclosed spaces. This fear can be so great that agoraphobics are often reluctant to leave the safety of their own homes. Agoraphobia is often found with panic disorder and so many agoraphobics try to avoid open or public places from which escape would be hard if they were to experience a panic attack. Thus, they are frightened of what might happen to them in public places rather than the public places themselves. However, agoraphobia and panic disorder are regarded as separate disorders in DSM-5 (2013) because many patients with agoraphobia do *not* also have panic disorder. About 75% of those suffering from agoraphobia are female.

? Can you suggest reasons why more women are agoraphobic than men?

Here are major diagnostic criteria for agoraphobia based on DSM-IV (1994) and DSM-5 (2013):

- Persistent fear or anxiety in two or more agoraphobia situations (e.g. using public transport; being in an open space; being in a crowd; being in an enclosed space) from which escape might be difficult or embarrassing.
- Exposure to agoraphobia situations nearly always produces severe fear or anxiety.
- Fear of the agoraphobia situations is excessive.
- Avoidance of the agoraphobia situation, needing a companion, or endurance of the situation with extreme distress.
- Significant distress or problems with social situations, work, or other areas of life.

KEY TERMS

Specific phobia: a strong and irrational fear of a given object (e.g. snake; spider) that is often avoided.

Agoraphobia: excessive fear of being in open, public, or enclosed spaces leading to avoidance of such spaces.

CASE STUDY: Lynn, an agoraphobic for 8 years

Friday 19th December

Today has been the biggest challenge. I woke up and immediately felt anxious. Too much time in bed and too much time to think have caused this. From 7 a.m. all I could think about was "I need to go out, I haven't been out in 2 days, what if I can't do it again". I sat and thought about it, and thought about it and thought about it. In the end I was so worked up that I could feel the panic attack getting closer. I ran to my bedroom and got dressed and went out. I knew if I just faced the problem instead of sitting thinking about it, I would feel much better. It worked. I went out and walked my usual route and felt fine. I enjoyed it actually even though it was freezing and pouring with rain. I ended up back in bed after this. Still not well at all and while suffering from the cold it is probably not a great idea to walk in the rain. But mentally I feel far better.

Saturday 20th December

Arrrghhh maybe that walk was a bad idea. I. AM. SO. ILL!!! There is no hope of me leaving my bed today. But I can rest easy and not obsess about not getting out again. I also have the added joy of looking after my three nephews tonight. I can barely look after myself right now.

Sunday 21st December

I feel sooo much better! Got up and took two of the boys out for a walk. We were out for quite a while. On returning home I learned my dad was heading out to do some Christmas shopping. I quickly jumped in the car with him and asked him to take me for a spin. I haven't been in the car since Tuesday so I wanted to prove to myself that I can still do it. We went around the usual route and then for some reason my dad took a wrong turn. Well of course the panic hit me immediately. I shouted that he would need to find somewhere to turn. The panic really does come over me in waves. One minute I felt it rise from my tummy to my head and then it would go down again. I think if I can mentally talk myself through this I will be ok but when taking the wrong turn my head just went "NO NO NO".

How does Lynn's account tie in with what you know about agoraphobia?
http://www.livingwithagoraphobia.blogspot.com/

Categories of symptoms or characteristics

As we have seen, the symptoms or characteristics of the three major forms of phobia are similar. How do these characteristics divide up into the emotional, behavioural, and cognitive categories? We will start with the emotional characteristics of the phobias. Social phobia, specific phobia, and agoraphobia are all characterised by severe fear or anxiety of the phobic object or situation and this can become distress in the presence of the phobic object or situation. This fear or anxiety is excessive and it is also persistent (lasting for at least 6 months).

Next there are the behavioural characteristics or symptoms. The most obvious behavioural characteristic is avoidance—phobic individuals very often avoid phobic objects or situations. This avoidance behaviour is important partly because the great majority of healthy individuals would *not* exhibit such behaviour when exposed to those objects or situations. The avoidance behaviour shown by phobic individuals often has far-reaching effects on their behaviour in everyday life. For example, it can disrupt their normal routine, their ability to work effectively and hold down a job, and their ability to have a full and enjoyable social life. In the case of social phobics, they are less likely than healthy individuals to be married and their earnings are typically lower.

Finally, there are the cognitive characteristics or symptoms. The fear or anxiety experienced by phobics with respect to the phobic object or situation is excessive or unreasonable. This suggests that their cognitive system misinterprets these objects or situations as being more threatening than is objectively the case. The cognitive system is also probably involved when phobics experience anxiety some time before encountering phobic objects or situations. For example, a social phobic may become anxious about attending a party several hours later because he/she is thinking and forming images of the embarrassing experiences they might have at the party.

How do the emotional, behavioural, and cognitive characteristics interact in the phobias? The emotional characteristics (fear, anxiety, distress) undoubtedly play a major role in triggering the behavioural characteristics (avoidance, disruptions to everyday life). In other words, the disruptive effects of avoidance behaviour on phobics' lives occur because they are trying to prevent or reduce severe fear or anxiety from occurring. So far as the cognitive characteristics are concerned, phobics' tendency to exaggerate the threateningness of phobic objects and situations increases the fear and anxiety associated with them.

Characteristics of depression

Most people have experienced mild depression. Even though mild depression is a long way from the intensity of depression found in patients, it is a miserable experience. Someone suffering from mild depression feels sad and pessimistic, has low self-esteem, and lacks motivation. We can see what is involved in depression by considering the thoughts of Martha Manning (1995), a therapist suffering from depression:

> *The house is deserted. I search for things to do. It is all I can do just to empty the dishwasher and sweep the floor. Then I lie on the couch and stare into space, vacant and deadened. I have a haircut appointment that I am already dreading, even though it's three hours away. How will I keep up a conversation with my effusive hairdresser? It will be a monumental effort just to move my lips into a smile. My face is simultaneously waxy and frozen. The muscles have gone on strike.*

? Why do you think depression is more common in women?

There is a large sex difference in depression—in most cultures and at most ages, women are twice as likely as men to suffer from depression. Approximately 7–8% of people suffer from depression in any given year meaning that 120 million people worldwide have depression.

Major depressive disorder

The most important disorder involving depression is major depressive disorder. According to DSM-5 (Diagnostic and Statistical Manual, fifth edition; 2013), the diagnosis of **major depressive disorder** involves the following criteria:

- Depressed mood or a loss of interest or pleasure in daily activities for more than 2 weeks.
- Specific symptoms, at least five of which must be present nearly every day for at least 2 weeks:

  1. Depressed mood or irritable most of the day.
  2. Decreased interest or pleasure in most activities most of the time.
  3. Significant weight change (5%) or change in appetite.
  4. Change in sleep: insomnia or excessive sleep.
  5. Change in activity: agitation or slowing down.
  6. Fatigue or loss of energy.
  7. Guilt/worthlessness: feelings of worthlessness or excessive guilt.
  8. Concentration: impaired ability to think or concentrate.
  9. Suicidality: thoughts of death or suicide.

- Impaired function with respect to social, occupational, or educational areas of life.

Other disorders involving depression

DSM-5 contains other depressive disorders. One is premenstrual dysphoric disorder. Many of the symptoms of this disorder resemble those for major depressive disorder. Common symptoms include irritability, breast pain, and bloating, and these symptoms must be related to the menstrual cycle.

Another depressive disorder is bipolar disorder. **Bipolar disorder** involves many of the symptoms of major depressive disorder (e.g. five of the nine specific symptoms listed for major depressive disorder) plus manic episodes. Symptoms associated with manic episodes include significant distress, inflated self-esteem, increased talkativeness, distractibility, increased activity, and decreased need for sleep. There are only about one-sixth as many cases of bipolar disorder as major depressive disorder in any given year and it is much harder to treat it.

KEY TERMS

Major depressive disorder: a mental disorder characterised by symptoms such as depressed mood, tiredness, and lack of interest and pleasure in various activities.

Bipolar disorder: a mental disorder involving a mixture of depressive and manic episodes.

Categories of symptoms or characteristics

As you can see, the symptoms of major depressive disorder are diverse. We will consider how these symptoms divide up into cognitive, behavioural, and emotional characteristics. First, we consider the cognitive characteristics or symptoms. These include thoughts of being worthless, thoughts of suicide, an impaired ability to think, and poor concentration. Second, we consider the emotional characteristics or symptoms which are of central importance in depression. Emotional symptoms include depressed mood, irritability, reduced pleasure in most activities, and feelings of guilt. These emotional symptoms relate to negative mood states or to an absence of positive mood states (e.g. reduced pleasure). Third, there are several behavioural symptoms. Depressed individuals show changes in behavioural activity levels (up or down), changes in eating behaviour (weight going up or down), a general reduction in normal activities associated with fatigue and reduced pleasure in such activities, and less effective behaviour in the social, job, and educational areas.

How are the cognitive, behavioural, and emotional characteristics or symptoms related to each other? Being depressed often makes individuals less inclined to become actively involved in the activities most people enjoy. Thus, the emotional characteristics of depression can lead to a general *disengagement* from everyday life (behavioural characteristics). However, this works both ways. When someone is disengaged from everyday life (behavioural characteristics), this can lead to negative emotional states. Thus, emotional factors can influence behaviour and behaviour can influence emotion.

? In what ways might a person's thoughts about themselves influence the way they react in a particular situation?

It is likely that thoughts of being worthless and thoughts of suicide (cognitive characteristics) can increase negative mood states (emotional characteristics). It is also likely that negative mood states can trigger negative memories which in turn increase negative mood states. Thus, cognitive factors can influence emotional factors and vice versa.

If someone is disengaged from life's activities (behavioural characteristics) this may increase thoughts of worthlessness (cognitive characteristics). This could also operate in the opposite direction—if someone has thoughts of being worthless, this may inhibit them from being actively involved in life (behavioural characteristics). Thus, behavioural factors may influence cognitive factors and vice versa.

CASE STUDY: Virginia Woolf

The author Virginia Woolf, who committed suicide in 1941 at the age of 59, was plagued by an intermittent form of depression. This affliction appears to have been bipolar depression, but was accompanied by extreme physical symptoms and psychotic delusions. In her biography of Woolf, Hermione Lee (1997) unravels the series of treatments administered to Woolf between 1895, when she experienced her first breakdown, and the 1930s. Later, Woolf's husband Leonard made detailed notes on her breakdowns (Lee, 1997, pp. 78–179):

In the manic stage she was extremely excited; the mind raced; she talked volubly and, at the height of the attack, incoherently; she had delusions and heard voices ... During the depressive stage all her thoughts and emotions were the exact opposite ... she was in the depths of melancholia and despair; she scarcely spoke; refused to eat; refused to believe that she was ill and insisted that her condition was due to her own guilt.

During the period from 1890 to 1930, Woolf consulted more than 12 different doctors, but the treatments barely altered during this time. They tended to consist of milk and meat diets to redress her weight loss; rest to alleviate her agitation; sleep and fresh air to help her regain her energy. Lithium had not yet been discovered as a treatment for manic depression. Instead, bromide, veronal, and chloral, most of which are sedatives, were prescribed. Lee points out that there is great uncertainty about the neuropsychiatric effects of some of these drugs, and Woolf's manic episodes may well have been the result of taking these chemicals.

Characteristics of obsessive–compulsive disorder (OCD)

Obsessive–compulsive disorder (OCD) is a serious disorder. What are the main symptoms associated with obsessive–compulsive disorder (OCD)? Unsurprisingly, the main symptoms can be divided up into obsessions and compulsions. Obsessions are persistent thoughts, impulses, or images that keep intruding into an individual's consciousness. Common obsessions relate to contamination, safety, doubting one's memory, and the need for order. In contrast, compulsions are rigid, repetitive actions individuals feel compelled to perform to reduce their anxiety level.

KEY TERM

Obsessive–compulsive disorder: a mental disorder involving recurrent intrusive thoughts (obsessions) and repetitive behaviours (compulsions) produced in response to obsessions.

An indication that an individual is suffering from obsessive compulsive disorder is the presence of repetitive behaviours that the individual feels compelled to perform as a means of reducing or avoiding distress; such as excessive hand washing.

There are substantial individual differences. Wilner et al. (1976) found that 69% of OCD patients had both obsessions and compulsions, 25% had obsessions only, and 6% had compulsions only.

Here is an account (Kraines, 1948, p. 183) of a woman with the disorder who:

> *complained of having "terrible thoughts." When she thought of her boyfriend she wished he were dead; when her mother went down the stairs, she "wished she'd fall and break her neck"; when her sister spoke of going to the beach with her infant daughter, the patient "hoped they would both drown." These thoughts "make me hysterical. I love them; why should I wish such terrible things to happen? It drives me wild, makes me feel I'm crazy and don't belong to society; maybe it's best for me to end it all than to go on thinking such terrible things about those I love."*

OCD is a severe condition with a lifetime incidence of 2.5% (Rachman, 2004). In a study by Torres et al. (2006), OCD was associated with more serious social and occupational impairment than other anxiety disorders. Even more disturbingly, about 25% of OCD patients had tried to commit suicide at some point. Men and women are equally likely to suffer from OCD, and it generally starts in late adolescence or adulthood.

According to DSM-5 (Diagnostic and Statistical Manual, fifth edition; 2013), the diagnosis of OCD requires the following symptoms to be present:

1. Obsessions: recurrent and persistent thoughts, urges, or images that are experienced as intrusive and unwanted and that cause marked anxiety and distress.
2. Obsessions: the individual tries to suppress or ignore obsessional thoughts, impulses or images or to neutralise them with some other thought or action.
3. Compulsions: repetitive behaviours (e.g. hand washing; checking) or mental acts (e.g. counting; repeating words silently) in response to an obsession.
4. Compulsions: the behaviours or mental acts are designed to prevent or reduce distress or prevent some dreaded event or situation; these behaviours or mental acts cannot realistically prevent dreaded events or situations and they are clearly excessive.

Common obsessions

- Fears about being contaminated by dirt, germs, or chemicals
- Fears of causing the house to flood, something to catch fire, or being burgled
- Aggressive thoughts about physically harming a loved one
- Anxieties about things being exactly right or symmetrical
- Intrusive thoughts or urges about sex
- Excessive doubts about one's own religious beliefs or morals
- An unfounded need to ask, tell, or confess

Common compulsions

- Cleaning: spending hours washing and scrubbing hands or cleaning household surfaces
- Checking: repeatedly checking and rechecking whether lights and appliances are switched or turned off, or unplugged
- Counting: spending hours counting meaningless strings of numbers
- Arranging: needing objects such as towels, cutlery, ornaments, or furniture placed in a certain way
- Repeating: speaking words or sentences again and again
- Completing: performing a task in a precise order repeatedly, until it is done perfectly (and if interrupted, often needing to start all over again from the beginning)
- Hoarding: collecting objects that are useless

Let's consider the nature of obsessions and compulsions in more detail. Obsessions are thoughts or images that are intrusive and feel foreign or alien to the person experiencing them. These obsessions can involve wishes (e.g. that an enemy would die), images (e.g. of disturbing sexual activities), impulses (e.g. desire to attack one's boss), ideas (e.g. that one's illegal actions will be discovered), or doubts (e.g. that a crucial decision was wrong). Akhtar et al. (1975) found most obsessions fell into five categories. The most frequent one was concerned with dirt and contamination, followed by aggression, orderliness of inanimate objects, sex, and religion.

Compulsions are actions performed repetitively because the patient believes there may be dire consequences if he/she doesn't perform them. These repetitive actions often take the form of compulsive rituals in which the same set of actions is performed in exactly the same way on every occasion. Cleaning compulsions (e.g. constant washing of the hands) and checking compulsions (e.g. endless checking that the front door is locked or the oven is turned off) are very common forms of compulsions. Indeed, Akhtar et al. (1975) found these were the two most common types of compulsions.

Most patients with OCD experience both obsessions and compulsions. One reason for this is because compulsive behaviour is often produced to reduce the anxiety associated with their obsessions. For example, someone who has obsessional thoughts about contamination may deal with them by engaging in elaborate cleaning rituals. Patients with OCD find their obsessions cause high levels of anxiety. In addition, patients' anxiety levels increase if they try to inhibit their obsessions or compulsions.

ACTIVITY

Most people can recall an occasion when they have felt compelled to return home to check that the gas has been turned off or the front door locked. Today, more people than ever before buy disinfecting products to combat germs. These are behaviours that can be taken to extremes in obsessive–complusive disorder.

How might you distinguish between behaviours that apply to most people sometimes, and behaviours that are symptomatic of obsessive–compulsive disorder?

Categories of symptoms or characteristics

We can categorise the symptoms of OCD into cognitive, behavioural, and emotional characteristics. There are several cognitive characteristics or symptoms associated with OCD mostly relating to obsessions rather than compulsions. More specifically, the obsessions found in OCD patients consist of intrusive, recurrent, and persistent thoughts, urges or images. These intrusive thoughts differ from excessive worries about real-life problems and patients with OCD generally recognise they are a product of his/her own mind. In other words, OCD patients have a major problem more because of their own thoughts than because of difficulties or events occurring in their lives.

Is there any common thread to the very diverse thoughts of OCD patients? OCD is a "what if" disorder (Rasmussen & Eisen, 1991). Patients with the disorder spend much of their time worrying that something terrible will happen. In the words of Rasmussen and Eisen (1991, p. 37), "The very fact that it is within the realm of possibility, however unlikely, that I will stab my baby, or poison my child, is enough to terrify me so that I can think of nothing else no matter how hard I try."

Other cognitive characteristics or symptoms relate to the ways in which OCD patients attempt to cope with their obsessional thoughts. They sometimes use thoughts to suppress or neutralise their obsessional thoughts.

The behavioural characteristics of OCD relate primarily to compulsions. OCD patients believe they can neutralise their obsessional thoughts with appropriate actions. More generally, compulsions consist of repetitive actions intended to prevent or reduce distress. These actions are excessive—they can't realistically prevent dreaded events from occurring and are observed only rarely in healthy individuals.

The emotional characteristics of OCD relate mostly to the marked anxiety and distress that is caused by the patient's obsessional thoughts. These thoughts cause distress in part because they are recurrent and persistent and the patient finds it very hard to control them.

How do the cognitive, behavioural, and emotional characteristics interact? In essence, what happens is that the patient has obsessional thoughts (cognitive characteristics). These obsessional thoughts cause anxiety and distress (emotional characteristics). In turn, the anxiety and distress caused by obsessional thoughts lead to various compulsions (behavioural characteristics) designed to prevent or reduce distress. Thus, there is a sequence running from obsessional thoughts through anxiety and distress to compulsive behaviour. Salkovskis (1996, p. 121) suggested that cognitive factors might be even more important than suggested so far: "OCD patients show a number of characteristic thinking errors linked to their obsessional difficulties. Probably the most typical and important is the idea that 'Any influence over outcome = responsibility for outcome'." In other words, OCD patients perceive there to be unusually close links between thinking and acting.

Section Summary

- There are three main categories of phobia: specific phobia; social phobia; and agoraphobia.
- All types of phobia are characterised by excessive fear or anxiety of the phobic object or situation, by behavioural avoidance of the phobic object or situation, and cognitive misinterpreting of how threatening the phobic object is.
- The emotional characteristics of phobias play a major role in triggering the behavioural avoidance.
- The most common mental disorder involving depression is major depressive disorder. There is also bipolar disorder, which involves many of the symptoms of major depressive disorder plus manic episodes.
- The symptoms of major depressive disorder include cognitive characteristics (thoughts of being worthless; thoughts of suicide), emotional characteristics (depressed mood; reduced pleasure; irritability), and behavioural characteristics (reduction in normal activities; changes in eating behaviour; ineffective behaviour).
- In depression, the emotional characteristics lead to disengagement from everyday life and disengagement leads to negative emotions. Negative thoughts help to cause negative emotions and vice versa.
- In obsessive–compulsive disorder (OCD), obsessions are persistent thoughts or impulses and compulsions are rigid, repetitive actions.
- In OCD, obsessional thoughts lead to anxiety and distress, leading to compulsive behaviour.

BEHAVIOURAL APPROACH TO EXPLAINING AND TREATING PHOBIAS

In this section we will be focusing on the behavioural approach to the phobias (specific phobia, social phobia, and agoraphobia). Our coverage is divided into two sub-sections. First, we consider how the behavioural approach tries to explain the phobias. Second, we focus on how the behavioural approach has been used to treat the phobias.

EXAM HINT

You need to know the behavioural, emotional, and cognitive characteristics of phobias but you should only use this material in the exam if it has been asked for in a question. Do not include them if the question asks you to consider the explanations of phobias because simply describing the characteristics is not part of the explanations.

Explaining phobias

As discussed earlier, there are three major categories of phobia: specific phobia; social phobia; and agoraphobia. If we are to treat phobias effectively, it is important to explain *why* phobias arise in the first place. Our main emphasis will be on the behavioural approach to explaining phobias. However, we will also consider briefly other approaches—this will allow us to identify factors involved in the development of phobias *not* considered within the behavioural approach.

Behavioural approach

According to many of those favouring behavioural explanations, phobic fears are acquired by classical conditioning. Classical conditioning is a form of learning first shown by Ivan Pavlov (see Chapter 5). In essence, a neutral or conditioned stimulus (e.g. a tone) is paired repeatedly with a second or unconditioned stimulus (e.g. presentation of food). After a while, the natural or unconditioned response to the second or unconditioned stimulus (e.g. salivation) comes to be made to the neutral stimulus when presented on its own. This learned response is the conditioned response. According to the behavioural account, what happens in the development of a phobia is that the conditioned or phobic stimulus (e.g. dog; social situation) is associated with a painful or aversive unconditioned stimulus creating fear (e.g. being attacked by a dog; being exposed to public humiliation).

? Can a conditioning account explain the relative frequency of different phobias?

According to the above account, phobic individuals would be much more likely than other people to have had a frightening experience with the phobic object. There is support for this prediction. Barlow and Durand (1995) reported that 50% of individuals with specific phobia for driving remembered a traumatic experience while driving (e.g. a car accident) as having caused the phobia. Hackmann et al. (2000) found 96% of social phobics remembered some socially traumatic experience that had happened to them (often in adolescence). Thorpe and Burns (1983) carried out a study on agoraphobics, 70% of whom reported an anxiety-provoking event apparently triggering the disorder. However, in only 55% of these patients was the event consistent with an explanation of agoraphobia based on conditioning.

Other evidence is less supportive of the conditioning account. Only 2% of water-phobic children claimed to have had a direct conditioning experience involving water (Menzies & Clarke, 1993). DiNardo et al. (1988) found 50% of dog phobics had become very anxious during an encounter with a dog, which apparently supports conditioning theory. However, 50% of healthy controls without dog phobia had also had an anxious encounter with a dog! Thus, dog phobia doesn't seem to depend on having had a frightening encounter with a dog.

? How might one explain why only some individuals go on to develop a phobia after a fearful experience?

KEY RESEARCH STUDY

Watson and Rayner (1920): Little Albert

John B. Watson and Rosalie Rayner (1920) showed in a classic study that emotions could be classically conditioned like any other response. Their participant was an 11-month-old boy called "Little Albert", who was reared almost from birth in a hospital. Watson and Rayner found initially that objects such as a white rat, a rabbit, and white cotton wool didn't trigger any fear response. In other words, they could all be regarded as neutral stimuli.

Watson and Rayner then induced a fear response (unconditioned response) by striking a steel bar with a hammer (unconditioned stimulus). This startled Albert and made him cry. After that, they gave him a white rat to play with. As he reached to touch it, they struck the bar to make him frightened. They repeated this three times, and did the same 1 week later. After that, when they showed the rat to Albert he began to cry, rolled over, and started to crawl away quickly. Classical conditioning had occurred, because the previously neutral or conditioned stimulus (i.e. the rat) produced a conditioned fear response. The suggestion is that Albert had developed a phobia for the rat.

Watson and Rayner found that now the sight of any white and furry object (e.g. a white fur coat; a Father Christmas beard) provoked a fear response. This is called **generalisation**—Albert had learned to generalise his fear of the white rat to other similar objects. They

continued over

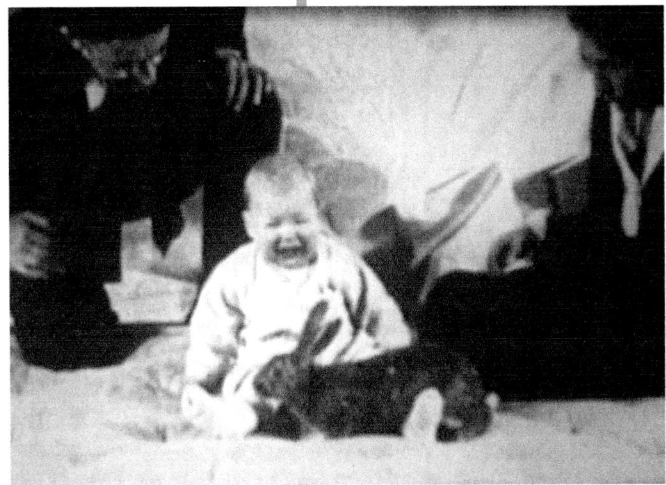

Watson and Rayner demonstrated that fears could be learned through classical conditioning using "Little Albert".

KEY TERM

Generalisation: in classical conditioning, the tendency to transfer a response from one stimulus to another that is quite similar.

intended to "re-condition" Albert to eliminate these fearful reactions. However, he was taken away from the hospital before this could happen.

Evaluation

This study is limited in several ways. First, the researchers used only one participant and so we can't draw any general conclusions especially since Little Albert was not a very representative infant—he was "stolid and unemotional". Second, deliberately reducing a child to tears and leaving him frightened of many innocuous objects is highly dubious ethically. Third, it is not clear that Little Albert developed strong fear responses. For example, the researchers reported the following after several days of conditioning: "Fear reaction slight … allowed the rat to crawl towards him without withdrawing." Fourth, it has proved hard to repeat the findings on Little Albert (Davison et al., 2004). One reason for this is probably the very limited and unscientific nature of the study. For example, Little Albert showed little or no fear during conditioning when he sucked his thumb. As Rolls (2010) pointed out, Watson and Rayner dealt with this problem by continually pulling his thumb out of his mouth!

Two-process model

An important conditioning account of phobias was put forward by Mowrer (1947) in his two-process model. The first stage involves classical conditioning (e.g. linking the white rat and the loud noise; see Chapter 5). The second stage involves operant conditioning. What happens here is that avoidance of the phobic stimulus reduces fear and fear reduction is reinforcing or rewarding. As a result, patients generally avoid phobic stimuli.

Let's expand on the processes involved in the acquisition of phobias. First, a link between the phobic stimulus and the unconditioned stimulus (e.g. loud noise) is formed via classical conditioning. In similar fashion, someone who suffers from social phobia has learned to associate social situations (conditioned stimulus) with extreme fear (unconditioned stimulus). Classical conditioning is greatest when the unconditioned stimulus follows almost immediately after the conditioned or phobic stimulus. As a result of classical conditioning, the phobic stimulus elicits a strong fear reaction.

Second, avoidance of the conditioned or phobic stimulus reduces anxiety or fear via operant conditioning. The process involved is known as **negative reinforcement**—this occurs when a given form of behaviour becomes more frequent when it causes an aversive or unpleasant stimulus to be avoided. For example, social phobics find it negatively reinforcing to avoid social situations because their avoidance behaviour is rewarded by fear reduction. Negative reinforcement is most effective when the behaviour (e.g. an avoidance response) is followed rapidly by fear reduction.

There is much support for Mowrer's two-process model. For example, consider a study by Solomon and Wynne (1953). Dogs were placed in a two-compartment apparatus. A change in the lighting (conditioned stimulus) acted as a warning that a strong electric shock (unconditioned stimulus) would shortly be presented. The dogs could avoid shock by jumping into the other compartment. Most dogs received a few shocks early in the experiment. After that, however, they generally avoided shocks and it can be argued this avoidance behaviour was reinforced or rewarded by reducing the dogs' fear.

? Why might this experiment be considered unethical today?

Maia (2010) identified limitations with the two-process model. First, if the dogs in a situation like that of Solomon and Wynne (1953) experience dozens of trials without receiving any electric shocks at all, this should reduce their anxiety level so much that the avoidance response would eventually be extinguished. However, this did *not* happen—the dogs continued to jump from one compartment to the other for hundreds of trials. Second, and related to the first point, the dogs often jumped from one compartment to the other faster and faster over hundreds of trials without any electric shocks. This finding that avoidance responses become *stronger* as fear *decreases* is inconsistent with predictions from Mowrer's model.

KEY TERM

Negative reinforcement: a form of operant conditioning in which a response (e.g. avoidance) is strengthened by being followed by prevention or removal of the aversive or phobic stimulus.

ACTIVITY: The behavioural model and phobias

Try to think of examples of situations that might cause the following phobias. Use the two-process model to explain how each phobia might have developed over repeated exposures to similar situations:

- Claustrophobia (fear of enclosed spaces)
- Agoraphobia (fear of open spaces)
- Arachnophobia (fear of spiders).

Are there any problems with this approach? What are the weaknesses of the behavioural model as an explanation for mental disorders?

Modelling

Conditioning accounts typically emphasise the notion that phobias are acquired when an individual has *direct* experience with the phobic object. Bandura (e.g. 1977a; see Chapter 5) argued that modelling or observational learning (which involves *indirect* experience) is very important. According to this perspective, specific phobias could result purely from modelling or observational learning.

Relevant evidence was reported by Merckelbach et al. (1996) in a study of girls with spider phobia. When asked about the onset of their phobia, 41% of the girls identified a conditioning event as having caused it. A further 18% identified their spider phobia as being due to observing fearful reactions to spiders by one of their parents. The children's reports were largely supported by their parents' recollections.

Dunne and Askew (2013) carried out an experimental study in which children saw pictures of three species of Australian animals. Reported fear for the animals was greater when seen with a model expressing fear than with no model. This finding shows fear of animals can be created through modelling.

EXAM HINT

Do think about the fact that there are several sub-classes of phobias. This means that you probably need more than one explanation to cover all phobias.

Other approaches to explaining phobias

There are several approaches other than the behavioural one for explaining phobias. Here we will focus on the biological and cognitive approaches.

? What are the limitations of twin and family studies of phobic disorders?

Biological approach

Much research on biological factors associated with phobias has focused on possible genetic factors. Of particular importance are twin studies. Monozygotic or identical twins share 100% of their genes whereas dizygotic or fraternal twins share only 50%. The crucial measure is the **concordance rate**—the chance one twin has a given disorder given that the other twin has it. If genetic factors are important, the concordance rate will be higher for identical than for fraternal twins.

Most evidence indicates genetic factors play a significant role in the development of all phobias. For example, Van Houtem et al. (2013) carried out a meta-analysis of twin studies on specific phobias and found that genetic factors were of moderate importance. Loken et al. (2014) found in a large-scale study that genetic factors were important for specific phobia, social phobia, and agoraphobia.

It is puzzling that people rarely develop specific phobias for potentially dangerous objects invented only recently such as cars. However, millions of people in Western cultures have spider or snake phobia even though they may have very rarely seen any spiders or snakes! Seligman (1970) put forward a biological explanation—he argued we are naturally fearful of objects that posed a threat to our survival during our evolutionary history. Seligman used the term preparedness to refer to our tendency to develop fears more easily to some objects than others because of our evolutionary past. This approach is important. However, we can't explain phobias such as *cherophobia* (fear of gaiety) or *triskaidekaphobia* (fear of the number 13) in evolutionary terms.

EXAM HINT

Note that the evidence for genetic factors comes mainly from twin and family studies. However, you should also consider the evolutionary explanations of preparedness as evidence for a genetic basis.

KEY TERM

Concordance rate: the probability within twin pairs that one twin has a given disorder or condition given that the other twin has it; typically calculated for identical and twin pairs.

ACTIVITY: Are you ready?

You can test the suggestion that we are born biologically prepared to fear certain animals.

You will need to draw up a list of 20 animals, ones that you feel people think are truly harmful, e.g. a tiger, and ones that you think are harmless, e.g. a worm. Then you can ask your sample to rate each animal on a kind of Likert scale: 1 = not really frightening, 2 = quite frightening, 3 = extremely frightening.

Collate your findings and ask yourself, "Do the findings support the idea that humans are born with a readiness to fear animals that are genuinely a threat to us?"

Cognitive approach

According to advocates of the cognitive approach, phobics have irrational and dysfunctional beliefs causing them to experience fear when exposed to phobic stimuli and/or situations. More specifically, phobics have an **interpretive bias**—they interpret ambiguous stimuli and situations in much more threatening ways than other people.

How does this interpretive bias arise? It is assumed it arises because of previous negative experiences involving the phobic stimuli (an assumption shared with the behavioural approach). However, there is an important difference. Those favouring the cognitive approach argue that numerous kinds of negative experiences play a role in producing phobias. In contrast, those favouring the behavioural approach claim that only negative experiences allowing for classical conditioning (i.e. the conditioned stimulus is followed shortly by the unconditioned stimulus) or modelling are of crucial importance.

The evidence suggests that patients with phobias have experienced more negative life events and experiences than healthy controls during their lives and that many of these events and experiences do not involve classical conditioning or modelling. Magee (1999) discovered that unpredictable and uncontrollable events causing physical harm (e.g. life-threatening accidents; a natural disaster) had been experienced by more agoraphobics than healthy controls. Social phobics were more likely than healthy controls to have experienced sexual assault by a relative or verbal aggression between parents. Finally, more specific phobics than healthy controls had experienced somewhat predictable but hard-to-control childhood experiences (e.g. chronic parental violence).

? What are the limitations of the cognitive approach?

The development of social phobia may be triggered if children feel unloved (rejecting parents) or if they have little control over their social lives (overprotective parents). Supporting evidence was reported by Lieb et al. (2000, p. 862): "Higher parental overprotection and higher parental rejection were significantly associated with increased rates of social phobia in offspring."

An important limitation of the cognitive approach is with respect to the causality issue—does interpretive bias help to trigger phobias or is it simply that having a phobia leads to interpretive bias for the phobic stimuli? If the latter is correct, then interpretive bias may play little role in the development of phobias. As we will see later, there is little convincing evidence that interpretive bias helps to cause phobias.

EXAM HINT

When evaluating one approach, you can contrast it with alternative explanations in order to evaluate it. But be careful not to deviate into describing these alternatives. You must consistently contrast the strengths and weaknesses of the approach you are evaluating with the strengths and weaknesses of the alternative approaches.

EVALUATION OF BEHAVIOURAL EXPLANATIONS OF PHOBIAS

- (+) There is evidence that phobias can be acquired through classical conditioning or through modelling.
- (+) As predicted, many phobics remember a specific experience that could have involved classical conditioning and that might have triggered the phobia.
- (+) The assumption within the two-process model that avoidance behaviour in phobic individuals is reinforced or rewarded by fear reduction provides a fairly convincing explanation.
- (−) It has proved hard to obtain strong support for the behavioural approach in the laboratory. As Rachman (2004, p. 82) concluded, "It is possible to produce conditioned fear responses in humans under laboratory conditions, but the responses tend to be weak, transient, and incomplete."
- (−) Phobic patients often cannot remember any experience that might have caused their phobia involving classical conditioning or modelling.

KEY TERM

Interpretive bias: the tendency to interpret ambiguous stimuli or situations in significantly more threatening ways than most other people.

- The fact that phobias are much more common for certain objects (e.g. snakes; spiders) than for others (e.g. cars) is hard to explain within the behavioural approach.
- Behavioural explanations leave much that is important out of account. Examples include genetic factors, life events, and cognitive factors.

What are the practical applications of theories of phobic disorders?

Treating phobias

According to behaviour therapists, what is key in the treatment of phobias is to eliminate patients' avoidance of their phobic stimuli and situations. This is often hard to do because patients find their avoidance behaviour is rewarding. For example, when a social phobic decides to avoid a social situation or an individual with a specific phobia decides to avoid an encounter with his/her phobic object, there is an almost immediate reduction in fear or anxiety. This reduction in fear is rewarding—it is like the relief we experience when we discover that some threatening event isn't actually going to happen.

Behavioural approach to treating phobias

The behavioural approach has led to the development of various forms of treatment for phobias. Here we will focus on two of the most important: systematic desensitisation and flooding or exposure therapy.

Systematic desensitisation

Systematic desensitisation is one of the main techniques within **behaviour therapy**. It is historically important because it was one of the first such techniques to be developed. It was introduced by Joseph Wolpe (1958, 1969) to treat individuals suffering from phobias involving excessive fear of certain stimuli (e.g. snakes; spiders).

What is involved in systematic desensitisation? The first stage is to provide clients with relaxation training in which they learn how to engage in deep muscle relaxation. Second, clients construct a fear hierarchy with the therapist's assistance. A **fear hierarchy** consists of a list of situations or objects producing fear in the client, starting with those causing only a small amount of fear and moving on to those causing increasingly great levels of fear. For example, the first item on the list of a snake-phobic person might be a small, harmless snake 50 feet away, with subsequent items featuring larger and more dangerous snakes closer to the client.

Third, clients learn how to use their relaxation techniques while imagining the objects or situations they fear, starting with those at the bottom of the fear hierarchy. The therapist describes the object or situation, and the client tries to form a clear image of it. The client often engages in covert desensitisation during therapy sessions and places himself/ herself in progressively more frightening real-life situations between sessions. An alternative approach is to present the actual object or situation itself (in vivo desensitisation).

When the client can imagine the less feared items in the fear hierarchy without experiencing fear, he/she moves on to the next items. Eventually, the client can confront the most feared object or situation in the fear hierarchy without fear, at which point he/she is regarded as cured.

KEY TERMS

Systematic desensitisation: a form of behaviour therapy in which the fear response to phobic stimuli is replaced by a different response (e.g. muscle relaxation).

Behaviour therapy: an approach to treatment using basic learning techniques to change maladaptive behaviour patterns into more appropriate ones.

Fear hierarchy: a list of feared situations or objects, starting with those creating only small amounts of fear and moving on to those creating large amounts of fear; used in the treatment of phobias.

ACTIVITY: Fear hierarchies

Try constructing a fear hierarchy, like the one below (see Figure), for a person with a fear of heights.

Systematic desensitisation puts demands on the expertise of the therapist. For example, it is essential to the success of systematic desensitisation that the therapist identifies the reasons for the client's anxiety. Consider someone who is very fearful of social situations. This fear may be totally irrational or it may occur because the individual concerned lacks social skills. If the latter is the case, then training in social skills is required in addition to systematic desensitisation.

Fear of dogs

If an individual has a fear of dogs, systematic desensitisation could be used to overcome this. The client might have learned their fear in the following way:

- Child is bitten by dog. Unpleasant bite (US) → fear (UR).
- Dog (NS) paired with US, becomes CS → fear (now CR).

This can be overcome by associating the dog with a new response—relaxation.

- Dog (CS) → fear (CR).
- Dog paired with new UCS (relaxation) → pleasant feelings (CR).

Why does systematic desensitisation work?

As we will see shortly, systematic desensitisation is a moderately effective form of treatment for phobia. How does it work? Several answers have been proposed. Wolpe (1958) argued that individuals learn through a process of conditioning to associate certain specific stimuli (e.g. snakes) with fear. The individual learns to produce a response *incompatible* with fear or anxiety (e.g. deep muscle relaxation) in the presence of the fear-evoking stimulus.

Wolpe used the term **reciprocal inhibition** to refer to the process of inhibiting anxiety by substituting a competing response. If relaxation is going to successfully inhibit the client's anxiety or fear, the amount of anxiety triggered by imagining the phobic stimulus must not be too great. That explains why systematic desensitisation starts with stimuli creating only a small amount of anxiety.

Wilson and Davison (1971) suggested a simpler explanation. According to them, the crucial process is one of **extinction**, which occurs when a response that is repeatedly produced in a given situation in the absence of reinforcement loses its strength (see Chapter 5). More specifically, imagining the phobic stimulus produces the anxiety response but there are no adverse consequences (e.g. being bitten by a snake). This lack of consequences eventually leads

KEY TERMS

Reciprocal inhibition: the process of inhibiting anxiety by substituting a competing response.

Extinction: elimination of a conditioned response when the conditioned stimulus is not followed by the unconditioned stimulus or a response is not followed by a reward.

to a reduction in the strength of the anxiety response. According to this explanation, *all* that matters is repeated non-reinforced exposure to the phobic stimulus.

There is a crucial difference in prediction between the reciprocal inhibition and extinction accounts—according to the former, deep muscle relaxation is essential, whereas it is almost irrelevant according to the latter.

? What are the two main explanations for how systematic desensitisation works in treating phobias?

Findings: Effectiveness

Choy et al. (2007) reviewed research on the effectiveness of systematic desensitisation in the treatment of phobias. Systematic desensitisation was generally moderately effective in reducing anxiety levels. However, its effects on avoidance of the feared object or situation were less consistent. For example, Rosen et al. (1976) found in a study on animal phobia that clients treated with systematic desensitisation were as likely as controls to continue to avoid the feared animals.

Four studies have assessed the long-term effects of systematic desensitisation by carrying out a follow-up several months after the end of treatment. According to Choy et al. (2007), the treatment gains (decreased anxiety and avoidance) present at the end of treatment were maintained at follow-up. For example, Denholtz et al. (1978) found 60% of clients treated for flying phobia continued to fly during the 3½-year follow-up period.

Does systematic desensitisation work because of reciprocal inhibition (with muscle relaxation inhibiting the anxiety response) or because of extinction (non-reinforced exposure to the feared stimulus)? The most direct approach to answering this question is to compare systematic desensitisation with and without relaxation. Levin and Gross (1985) reviewed the relevant literature. The picture was confused. In 10 studies, systematic desensitisation without relaxation was as effective as desensitisation with relaxation. However, there were 15 studies in which relaxation contributed to the success of systematic desensitisation!

McGlynn et al. (1981) shed light on the apparently inconsistent findings. They pointed out that extinction occurs only slowly over time. Thus, there would be very little extinction of anxiety if clients spent only a short period of time imagining each item in the fear hierarchy and if there were only a few treatment sessions. In such circumstances, any beneficial effects of systematic desensitisation would depend on relaxation and reciprocal inhibition. As they predicted, relaxation was generally important in treatment when there was little opportunity for extinction to occur. In contrast, effective treatment depended increasingly on extinction when each item was imagined for a long period of time and there were many treatment sessions.

EXAM HINT

Exam questions may ask you how you would use systematic desensitisation in a particular case, for example fear of flying or of going to the dentist. Don't be put off by this—it could make answering the question quite interesting. Just remember that in all cases the hierarchy is suggested by the client (not the therapist) and regardless of what the phobia is, they start at a low level of fear and progress upwards. It shouldn't be too difficult to give an example of what the lowest level and the highest level might be (e.g. looking at an airplane/flying in one; driving past the dentist/having some dental treatment).

Appropriateness

Systematic desensitisation can be regarded as an appropriate form of treatment for phobias for various reasons. First, it has a solid theoretical foundation based on the notion that through conditioning patients could learn to replace the anxiety response to feared stimuli with a relaxation response. Second, reducing or eliminating avoidance behaviour is of great importance in treating phobias and systematic desensitisation focuses directly on reducing avoidance. Third, and related to the second point, reducing avoidance behaviour is highly desirable because such behaviour restricts phobics' social and working lives.

There are some reasons for doubting the appropriateness of systematic desensitisation in the treatment of phobia. First, it is not altogether clear that relaxation is a necessary ingredient in order to produce symptom reduction. Second, systematic desensitisation doesn't address all the relevant factors. For example, individuals with social phobia often have limited social skills and low self-confidence, neither of which is treated by systematic desensitisation. Third, systematic desensitisation is generally less effective than flooding (see below). There are clearly doubts about the appropriateness of a form of therapy that is inferior to other methods of treatment.

EXAM HINT

Remember to assess the appropriateness of treatments by considering the following:

- How effective the treatment is across different symptoms
- The patient's level of functioning
- The effect of the treatment on relapse rates
- The patients' motivation to use the treatment versus drop-out rate
- If the action of the treatment is fully understood
- Ethical issues.

EVALUATION

- (+) Systematic desensitisation was one of the first techniques developed within behaviour therapy. It played a role in the subsequent development of related techniques such as flooding and virtual reality flooding (see below).
- (+) It is based on solid theoretical grounds, namely, the notion that through conditioning individuals can learn to replace the anxiety response to feared stimuli with a relaxation response.
- (+) The basic ingredients of systematic desensitisation (muscle relaxation; fear hierarchy; association of phobic stimuli with relaxation responses) can easily be manipulated to see whether each one is important in successful treatment.
- (+) Systematic desensitisation is of proven effectiveness. In the great majority of studies, individuals treated with systematic desensitisation improved more than those receiving no treatment (Choy et al., 2007).
- (+) Systematic desensitisation poses few ethical issues. The use of a fear hierarchy and deep muscle relaxation are designed to ensure that clients don't experience very unpleasant levels of anxiety.
- (−) Many phobias (e.g. snake phobia; spider phobia) treated by systematic desensitisation are relatively trivial in that they don't have the crippling effects on everyday life of other mental disorders (e.g. depression). However, systematic desensitisation has been used successfully to treat social phobia (excessive fear of social situations), and social phobia can severely disrupt people's lives.
- (−) As we will see shortly, most evidence (e.g. Choy et al., 2007) indicates that flooding or exposure therapy is more effective than systematic desensitisation in the treatment of phobias. This helps to explain why there has been a large reduction in the use of systematic desensitisation over the years (McGlynn et al., 2004).
- (−) There is a lack of clarity about precisely *why* systematic desensitisation is effective. However, Wolpe probably exaggerated the importance of muscle relaxation. Muscle relaxation often adds nothing to the effectiveness of systematic desensitisation. As we will see, flooding is effective without making any use of muscle relaxation.
- (−) There are various doubts about the appropriateness of systematic desensitisation in the treatment of phobia.

EXAM HINT

Compare the effectiveness of the different types of therapies, for example research suggests that flooding is more effective than systematic desensitisation for social phobia—but this may be due to cognitive changes that are typically not considered in relation to flooding.

Flooding

Flooding is a form of behaviour therapy resembling desensitisation. In **flooding**, phobic individuals are exposed to the object or situation they fear for lengthy periods of time until their anxiety level has reduced substantially. A crucial difference between flooding and systematic desensitisation is that the patient is exposed from the outset to the most feared phobic object or situation.

In recent years, flooding has been developed into virtual reality flooding, in which a computer program produces a virtual environment simulating the phobic situation. The patient typically has a head-mounted display that allows for visual and auditory input. Note that the flooding technique is often described as exposure therapy.

In flooding, individuals are exposed to the source of their anxiety for a prolonged period until their fear subsides.

KEY TERM

Flooding: a form of therapy in which patients are exposed to the object or situation they fear for lengthy periods of time until their anxiety level has reduced substantially; more often called exposure therapy.

Findings: Effectiveness

Flooding provides maximal scope for extinction to occur but does *not* involve muscle relaxation. If extinction is the crucial process in curing phobias, flooding, or exposure therapy, should be very effective. However, if muscle relaxation is essential, then flooding shouldn't be effective. In fact, flooding is consistently effective. For example, single-session flooding has proved very successful in treating specific phobia. Kaplan and Tolin (2011) reported that 65% of patients with specific phobia given a single session of flooding showed no symptoms of specific phobia 4 years later.

Most research has found that traditional flooding or exposure therapy and virtual reality flooding produce similar success rates. For example, Opris et al. (2012) found virtual reality flooding was as effective as various other forms of treatment for conditions including flying phobia, spider phobia, social phobia, and agoraphobia. Anderson et al. (2013) found that virtual reality flooding and traditional flooding were equally effective in the treatment of social phobia. Traditional flooding and virtual reality flooding are both often more effective than systematic desensitisation (Choy et al., 2007).

There has been a large increase in virtual reality flooding or exposure therapy in recent years. One reason for its increased use is that patients can easily be exposed to a wide range of situations. In the study by Anderson et al. (2013) on social phobia, for example, patients in the virtual reality condition were exposed to a virtual small group (about five people), a virtual classroom (about 35 people), and a virtual auditorium (more than 100 people). In every case, the therapist could program the computer to make the audience appear interested, bored, supportive, hostile, or distracted. It would clearly be much more difficult and expensive to expose patients to all of these situations in real-life situations.

Limitations with the flooding technique are discussed shortly. For now we will mention a single significant problem—prolonged exposure to feared stimuli can create intense levels of anxiety, and so the drop-out rate is sometimes rather high.

CASE STUDY: Acrophobia—Fear of Heights

Acrophobics have an overpowering fear of heights, a phobic fear that produces intense anxiety, panic attacks, and sends heart rate and blood pressure sky high. Traditionally, therapy has been based on the usual approaches—psychodynamic, behavioural, cognitive, bio-medical, and so on. However, a novel and highly successful new technique, virtual reality (VR), has been developed in California by Lamson. Sixty participants were recruited from advertisements and were assigned randomly to either the experimental (VR) or the control (drugs) group. Each participant set themselves a target to be reached after a week's therapy, and over 90% of the VR group achieved theirs.

The VR group wore headsets that took them into a café with an open terrace. During the 50-minute therapy session the participant had to "walk" across the terrace and over a plank that led to a bridge set in a hilly scene. Lamson monitored participants' blood pressure and heart rate, and found that the fear response did subside during the 50-minute session. This therapy is a development of flooding, but avoids the extreme anxiety of confronting the phobic stimulus in reality. It also avoids the risks, such as side effects, of even successful drug therapy. Perhaps one of the strengths of VR therapy is that it gives the clients confidence; they have been successful in the virtual world so this encourages them to be optimistic about success in the real world. As Lamson says, "within 3 months the woman who could barely start up a step ladder was on the roof cleaning the gutters".

Why is flooding effective?

It is often assumed that phobic patients have learned to associate the phobic stimulus or situation with a negative outcome (extreme fear) through classical conditioning. For example, a social phobic may associate social situation with extreme fear because of an earlier experience in which he/she experienced public humiliation.

What seems odd is that social phobics often continue to have exaggerated expectations of danger in social situations for many years thereafter. Why don't they learn that social situations are much less dangerous than they assume? The answer is that most phobics (whether they have social phobia, specific phobia, or agoraphobia) make use of **safety behaviours**—these are actions designed to reduce the fear or anxiety they associate with phobic situations. The main safety behaviour social phobics use is avoidance of social situations. Such avoidance has

KEY TERM

Safety behaviours: actions taken by phobic individuals to reduce their fear/anxiety level and prevent feared consequences.

EXAM HINT

Compare the effectiveness of the different types of therapies, for example research suggests that the traditional flooding and virtual reality flooding are more effective than systematic desensitisation but then an enhanced form of cognitive therapy has been found to be more effective than flooding for social phobia.

the severe disadvantage that it prevents them from learning that social situations are generally pleasurable and non-threatening. Flooding prevents social phobics from avoiding dreaded social situations and so allows them to learn that such situations are innocuous. This learning produces extinction of the fear response.

So far we have only discussed *active* avoidance—the phobic patient physically distances himself/herself from the phobic object or situation. However, there is more to avoidance than that. For example, social phobics when in a social situation will often use subtle safety behaviours (e.g. avoiding eye contact; saying very little). These safety behaviours are forms of *passive* avoidance designed to reduce anxiety (Abramowitz, 2013). However, they have the disadvantage that they make it harder for social phobics to learn that social situations are not dangerous. In essence, social phobics may think to themselves, "The only reason I am not experiencing extreme fear in this social situation is because I am making myself inconspicuous."

Traditional flooding or exposure therapy focused on preventing active avoidance and did not involve trying to prevent passive avoidance. However, it follows from what has been said so far that this form of therapy should be more effective when attempts are made to prevent passive as well as active avoidance. There is much evidence that this is the case—therapy that involves preventing the subtle safety behaviours associated with passive avoidance has proved more successful in the treatment of social phobia than therapy that does not (Clark et al., 2006; Wells et al., 1995). The same is true for agoraphobia and specific phobia (Telch et al., 2014).

Most accounts of the reasons for the effectiveness of flooding don't focus on the possibility that *cognitive* changes may be important. As we saw earlier, phobics have an interpretive bias—they greatly exaggerate the threat posed by the phobic object or situation. It is entirely possible that one reason why flooding is effective is that it produces a substantial reduction in phobics' interpretive bias. Evidence that cognitive changes are important (even though flooding does not directly involve trying to produce such changes) was reported by Vögele et al. (2010). Flooding to treat agoraphobia and social phobia was more effective when patients' thoughts changed during treatment so they perceived themselves as having more control over the phobic situation. There is evidence for all phobias that cognitive change partly explains the effectiveness of flooding (Telch et al., 2014).

Appropriateness

The reasons why flooding is an appropriate form of therapy for phobias are similar to those for systematic desensitisation. First, it is based on the theoretical foundation that exposure to phobic stimuli should produce extinction or habituation of the fear response. Second, flooding is explicitly designed to reduce avoidance behaviour which is a necessary ingredient for successful treatment. Third, flooding is as effective as (or more effective than) other forms of treatment for phobia and this makes it an appropriate treatment to use.

? To what extent should practical concerns take precedence over ethical issues?

In what ways is flooding an inappropriate form of treatment for phobia? First, it fails to consider cognitive factors and the limited social skills often found in social phobics. Second, the high levels of anxiety produced by flooding raise ethical issues. Third, the high anxiety produced by flooding often causes the drop-out rate to be rather high.

EVALUATION

- ⊕ Flooding or exposure therapy has been shown consistently to be an effective form of treatment for phobia. It is generally even more effective than systematic desensitisation.
- ⊕ There is reasonable support for the notion that flooding is effective because it extinguishes the fear response.
- ⊕ It is important in treatment to reduce phobics' avoidance behaviour and flooding focuses directly on reducing such behaviour.
- ⊖ Flooding in its traditional form does not take account of safety behaviours associated with passive avoidance and this limits its effectiveness.

- Explanations for the effectiveness of flooding typically ignore cognitive change even though there is increasing evidence that such change is important (Telch et al., 2014; Vögele et al., 2010).
- Flooding deliberately creates high levels of anxiety and this can upset patients so much they drop out of treatment.
- Flooding raises ethical issues concerning acceptable levels of suffering by patients.

Section Summary

Explaining phobias

- According to the behavioural approach, phobic fears are acquired by classical conditioning with the phobic stimulus becoming associated with a painful or aversive stimulus causing fear.
- There is mixed support for the prediction that phobic individuals should typically have had one or more frightening experiences with the phobic object.
- According to the two-process model, the first stage of the acquisition of phobias involves classical conditioning. The second stage involves operant conditioning—avoidance of the phobic stimulus reduces fear and fear reduction is rewarding.
- Conditioning accounts emphasise the notion that phobias are acquired through direct experience with the phobic object; however, modelling or observational learning (involving indirect experience) is also important.
- Factors involved in the acquisition of phobias not included within the behavioural approach are as follows: genetic factors; evolutionary preparedness; and interpretive bias.

Treating phobias

- Systematic desensitisation is one of the main forms of treatment used by behaviour therapists. It involves replacing the fear response to phobic stimuli with a different response (e.g. muscle relaxation).
- Systematic desensitisation is moderately effective. There has been some controversy as to whether its beneficial effects depend on extinction of the fear response to the phobic object.
- Flooding is a form of behaviour therapy in which (in contrast to systematic desensitisation) the patient is exposed from the outset to the most feared phobic object.
- Flooding or exposure therapy has proved to be an effective form of treatment for phobia because it extinguishes the fear response.
- The success of flooding often depends in part on cognitive change.
- There are ethical issues with flooding because it creates high levels of anxiety.

COGNITIVE APPROACH TO EXPLAINING AND TREATING DEPRESSION

In this section, we focus on the cognitive approach to explaining and treating depression. For convenience, we will start with a discussion of how the cognitive approach explains depression. This is followed by a discussion of how depression is treated within the cognitive approach.

Explaining depression: Cognitive approach

Several therapists have put forward similar cognitive approaches to explaining the factors responsible for depression. Here we will focus on two of the well-known approaches: those of Albert Ellis and Aaron Beck.

Ellis' ABC model

Albert Ellis (1962) was the first therapist to adopt the cognitive approach with his rational emotive therapy (subsequently relabelled rational emotional behaviour therapy). He argued that anxiety and depression occur as the final stage in a three-point sequence (see Figure). According to his ABC model, depression does *not* occur as a direct result of unpleasant events but rather is produced by the irrational thoughts triggered by unpleasant events.

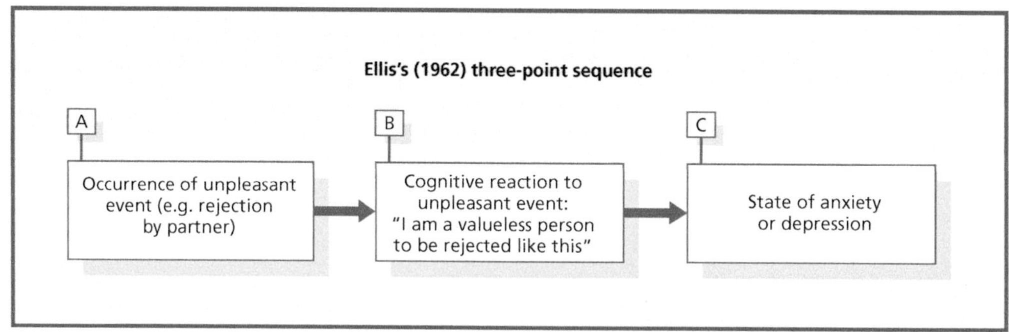

More specifically, an unpleasant event occurs at point A (adversity). At point B (beliefs), the individual puts his/her own interpretation on this unpleasant event. If the interpretation is negative or self-defeating, the individual experiences depression (or anxiety) at point C (consequences). However, if the individual interprets the unpleasant event in a positive or realistic way, this greatly reduces the amount of depression (or anxiety) experienced.

Ellis developed his ABC model into an ABCDEF model. He argued that individuals who are depressed should create a point D. This is a dispute belief system allowing them to interpret life's events in ways avoiding emotional distress (discussed in detail later). We can see the essence of this dispute belief system in this quotation from Ellis (1978):

> *If he [the client] wants to be minimally disturbable and maximally sane, he'd better substitute for all his absolutistic "It's terrible's" two other words which he does not parrot or give lip-service to but which he incisively thinks through and accepts—namely, "Too bad!" or "Tough shit!"*

Once the individual has successfully disputed his negative beliefs at point D, he/she can replace them with healthier and more positive ones. Point E involves the creation of effective or helpful beliefs. Finally, when the individual has done that, he/she should feel much better and be able to behave as he/she chooses. Point F involves functional emotions and behaviour.

According to Ellis, what is fundamental to explaining depression is that depressed individuals interpret unpleasant events in excessively negative or threatening ways (at point B). This causes depression and makes it hard for the individual to respond actively and appropriately to the unpleasant event. This emphasis suggests that the ABC model is very cognitive. In fact, the model *is* cognitive, but it is not *only* cognitive. As Ellis (2003) pointed out:

> *Rational emotive behaviour therapy assumes that human thinking, emotion, and action are not really separate or disparate processes... Much of what we call emotion is nothing more nor less than a certain kind—a biased, prejudiced, or strongly evaluate kind—of thought.*

Ellis' ABC model provides only a sketchy account of some factors that might explain the existence of depression. For example, suppose we assume that Ellis is correct in arguing that depression is associated with negative and self-defeating interpretations of unpleasant events. It is very hard to know whether these negative interpretations cause depression or whether depression causes negative interpretations. It could also be argued that Ellis' approach is descriptive rather than explanatory—for example, we aren't told precisely *why* some individuals produce negative interpretations of unpleasant events in the first place. Finally, it can be argued that Ellis de-emphasises the relevance of an individual's circumstances—if someone is confronting major problems (e.g. chronic ill health; divorce; job loss), it may be very hard for them to create positive, healthy beliefs.

Beck's negative triad

Aaron Beck agrees with Albert Ellis that depression can be explained from the cognitive perspective. According to him, maladaptive forms of thinking in depressed patients often involve automatic thoughts and over-generalisation. **Automatic thoughts** (e.g. "I always make a mess of things") are triggered effortlessly when depressed individuals experience failure. **Over-generalisation** involves drawing very general negative conclusions from specific evidence (e.g. failing to obtain one job is taken to mean the depressed person will never find a job again). Many (or most) of the automatic thoughts of depressed individuals involve over-generalisation.

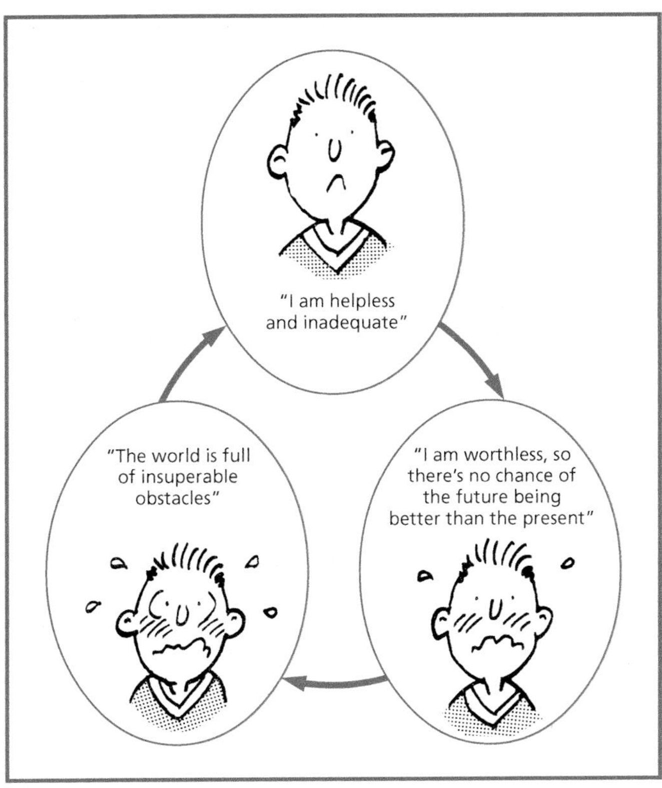

Most of the negative thoughts experienced by depressed individuals depend on cognitive schemas. A **cognitive schema** is "a well-organised cognitive structure of stored information and memories that forms the basis of core beliefs about self and others" (Beck & Dozois, 2011). Beck and Clark (1988) described depressive schemas (mental representations) consisting of organised negative information stored in long-term memory. According to Beck and Clark (p. 26):

> *The schematic organisation of the clinically depressed individual is dominated by an overwhelming negativity. A negative cognitive trait is evident in the depressed person's view of the self, world, and future ... As a result of these negative maladaptive schemas, the depressed person views himself [sic!] as inadequate, deprived and worthless, the world as presenting insurmountable obstacles, and the future as utterly bleak and hopeless.*

? Think of an occasion when you felt helpless or worthless. Could you try to re-interpret the occasion in a more positive way?

The cognitive schemas of depressed individuals are extremely important. They influence *what* they attend to in the environment, *how* they interpret it, and *what* information they retrieve from long-term memory. For example, depressed individuals exhibit **memory bias**, meaning that they tend more than healthy individuals to retrieve negative and unpleasant memories from long-term memory.

Beck (1976) used the term **cognitive triad** to refer to the unrealistic negative thoughts of depressed patients in the three areas of themselves, the world, and the future. Depressed individuals regard themselves as helpless, worthless, and inadequate. They interpret events in the world in an unrealistically negative and defeatist way, and they see the world as posing obstacles that can't be handled. Finally, they see the future as totally hopeless because their worthlessness will prevent their situation improving. Note that the thinking of depressed individuals exhibits over-generalisation in all three areas. There is convincing evidence that depressed individuals typically have negative views about themselves, the world, and the future (i.e. the cognitive triad) (Comer, 2009).

KEY TERMS

Automatic thoughts: negative thoughts or ideas that seem to arise spontaneously in the minds of depressed individuals.

Over-generalisation: the error of assuming that a single negative experience indicates that numerous similar experiences will occur in future (e.g. a single failure indicates that the individual will always fail).

Cognitive schema: organised information stored in long-term memory and used by individuals to form interpretations of themselves and the world in which they live.

Memory bias: the retrieval of relatively more negative or unpleasant information than positive or neutral information from long-term memory.

Cognitive triad: the depressed person's negative views of the self, the world, and the future.

Two further points need to be made about the cognitive triad. First, Beck argued that the cognitive triad is *not* found in individuals suffering from other mental disorders. For example, phobics have an inflated sense of danger in specific, avoidable situations and patients with OCD have exaggerated concerns about safety and the value of rituals in warding off perceived threats. In other words, Beck believed that the precise negative schemas of patients depend on the particular mental disorder from which they are suffering.

Second, we have seen that the cognitive triad is concerned with depressed individuals' very negative thoughts in the areas of themselves, the world, and the future. What should be added is that depressed individuals often show a remarkable lack of *positive* thoughts in any of these areas. For example, they refuse to accept that they possess several worthwhile qualities and characteristics that appear obvious to everyone else.

Beck and Dozois (2011) developed the cognitive approach. They argued that maladaptive cognitive schemas develop early in life. However, these schemas typically remain dormant and don't cause symptoms until they are activated by external events (e.g. difficult life problems). When activated, they cause the depressed individual to have negative views and interpretations about themselves, the world, and the future.

ACTIVITY: How do you feel?

It's your birthday and friends have arranged a get-together, but just before you go out to meet you get an e-mail from your closest friend saying he or she won't be there. No "sorry", no explanation, just a full stop.

	Irrational/negative	Rational/positive
Thoughts	S/he has sent a very offhand e-mail, why is s/he being so unpleasant?	Maybe s/he has had a bad day at work, or broken up with a friend, or had a row
Emotions	Hurt, upset, feeling not respected or liked, feeling rejected as a friend	Disappointed, don't understand, but hope to meet up very soon to sort this and be friends again and have fun
Behaviour	Be too cool to notice her/him next time you meet, act like you are just an acquaintance	Call her/his mobile and be nice, arrange to meet for a chat and a laugh

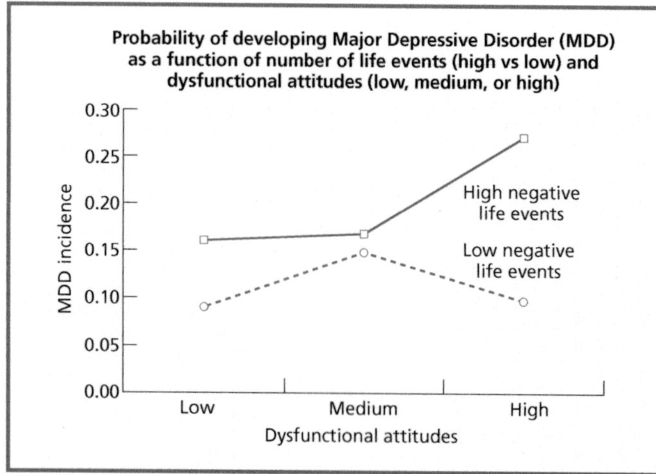

Adapted from Lewinsohn, Joiner, and Rohde (2001).

Causality

The crucial issue is whether the distorted and unrealistic thoughts of clients with depression actually played a part in the development of the disorder. Perhaps clients only start having these unrealistic thoughts *after* having developed depression. If so, this is a real problem—it would mean distorted thoughts have nothing to do with causing mental disorders!

Evidence that negative thinking can be involved in the development of major depressive disorder was obtained by Lewinsohn et al. (2001). They measured negative thinking (e.g. "My life is wasted unless I am a success") in adolescents not having a major depressive disorder at the outset of the study. One year later, Lewinsohn et al. assessed the negative life events experienced by the participants over the 12-month period and also assessed whether they were suffering from major depressive disorder. Those who had experienced many negative life events had an increased likelihood of developing major depressive disorder only if they were initially high in negative attitudes. Since these negative attitudes were assessed *before* the onset of depression, they seem to be a risk factor for developing that disorder when exposed to stressful life events.

More evidence that unrealistic thoughts may occur *before* a disorder develops and may play a part in its occurrence was reported by Evans et al. (2005), who assessed negative or dysfunctional self-beliefs in women in the 18th week of pregnancy. Women with the highest scores for negative self-beliefs were 60% more likely to become depressed subsequently than those with the lowest scores. Negative self-beliefs predicted the onset of depression 3 years later, which is strong evidence that negative or dysfunctional beliefs can play a role in causing depression.

In sum, there is much evidence that depressed individuals have the kinds of negative schemas and thoughts ascribed to them by Beck. One complex issue is whether Beck's approach is really explanatory. He provides good *descriptions* of how depressed individuals think but this is not the same as *explaining* why they have these negative thoughts. Another issue is whether depressed individuals' negative thoughts are all exaggerated. For example, it may well be realistic for someone who is unemployed, divorced, and unwell to have negative thoughts about the future.

Other approaches to explaining depression

There are several other approaches to explaining depression. Here we will focus on the biological and social approaches.

Biological approach

The biological approach assumes that genetic factors influence the development of depression. We can test this assumption with twin studies using monozygotic or identical twins and dizygotic or fraternal twins. If one twin has depression, what is the probability the other twin has the same disorder? This is the concordance rate. If genetic factors are important, the concordance rate should be higher for identical twins.

? What are the limitations of twin studies of depression?

McGuffin et al. (1996) found the concordance rate for major depressive disorder was 46% for identical twins compared to 20% for fraternal twins. With bipolar disorder, the concordance rate was 40% for identical twins compared to between 5% and 10% for fraternal twins, siblings, and other close relatives (Craddock & Jones, 1999). In the population at large, 7% are diagnosed with major depressive disorder and 1% with bipolar disorder, and ALL figures for identical and fraternal twins are much higher.

The above findings suggest genetic factors are involved in both types of depression (especially bipolar depression). However, some of the higher concordance rate for identical twins may reflect environmental rather than genetic influences—perhaps the identical twin pairs experienced more similar childhood environments than the fraternal twins.

Social factors

Depressed individuals often experience an above-average number of stressful life events before the onset of depression. Brown and Harris (1978) found 61% of depressed women had experienced at least one very stressful life event in the preceding 8 months compared to 19% of non-depressed women. However, life events were much more likely to play a role in triggering depression among women lacking an intimate friendship.

One limitation with most life-event studies is that the information is obtained several months afterwards, and so there may be problems in memory. Second, the causality is often unclear. For example, marital separation may cause depression, but depression can play an important role in causing marital separation.

Major depression is twice as common in women in most countries. Why is this? Women are poorer than men, have lower status jobs, have less adequate housing, and face more discrimination, all of which are associated with depression. Kendler et al. (1993) found that women reported significantly more negative life events than men in the past year in several areas of life (e.g. marital problems; financial problems; interpersonal difficulties).

EVALUATION

- ⊕ The cognitive approach to explaining depression has become very influential in recent years; this is reflected in the increase in cognitive therapy and cognitive behaviour therapy.
- ⊕ Distorted and irrational beliefs seem to be of central importance in depression. The cognitive triad is typically found in depressed patients but not in those with other mental disorders.
- ⊕ Distorted beliefs may play a part in the development of depression (Lewinsohn et al., 2001; Evans et al., 2005).
- ⊕ Of major importance in cognitive behaviour therapy is the attempt to eliminate the biased and distorted beliefs of individuals with mental disorders. The fact that cognitive behaviour therapy is at least as effective as other forms of therapy suggests that an emphasis on distorted beliefs is justified (discussed later).
- ⊖ We need more research to determine whether distorted beliefs help to cause the disorder (as predicted by the cognitive approach) or whether they are merely a *consequence* of having depression. More generally, it is not very clear *why* individuals develop negative thoughts and beliefs in the first place.
- ⊖ Related to the above point, the cognitive approach isn't very explanatory. As Davison and Neale (1996, p. 46) pointed out, "That a depressed person has a negative schema [organised knowledge] tells us that the person thinks gloomy thoughts. But everyone knows that such a pattern of thinking is actually part of the diagnosis of depression."
- ⊖ Little attention is paid to the role of social factors relating to life events and gender in the cognitive approach to depression.
- ⊖ The cognitive approach to depression is limited in that genetic factors are ignored.

Cognitive behaviour therapy for treating depression

Several forms of therapy based on the cognitive approach have been used to treat depression. Two of the most important of such forms of treatment for treating depression are both based on the notion that optimal treatment for depression involves cognitive and behavioural aspects. Beck's (1976, 2005) approach is often called cognitive behaviour therapy whereas Ellis' (1962, 2003) similar approach is called rational emotive behaviour therapy. Note that most approaches have increased their focus on behavioural interventions over the years—Beck's approach was originally called cognitive therapy and Ellis' was previously called rational emotive therapy.

The forms of therapy advocated by Ellis and by Beck have sufficient differences that it makes sense to discuss them separately. However, it is assumed within both therapeutic approaches that successfully challenging the patient's irrational thoughts is of crucial importance if recovery is to occur.

Rational emotive behaviour therapy

According to Ellis, we need to focus on the depressed individual's beliefs to understand why he/she is depressed. Beliefs are thoughts having an emotional component (conviction) and a factual component (validity or truth). Beliefs can be rational or irrational. Individuals who develop major depressive disorder (or an anxiety disorder) possess various **irrational beliefs**, that is, beliefs that are false or incorrect.

KEY TERM

Irrational beliefs: emotionally-laden thoughts that are false or incorrect; in depressed individuals, these beliefs are mostly inflexible and extreme.

The core irrational beliefs of depressed individuals are typically inflexible, dogmatic, and extreme and contain words such as "must", "should", "have to", and "need to". These irrational beliefs involve demandingness or absolutism in major areas of life such as love, approval, success, and achievement. Ellis argued that there are three major musts:

1. I must do well and be approved of by other people or else I am worthless.
2. Everyone must do "the right thing" or else they deserve to be punished.
3. My life must be easy with a minimum of discomfort or inconvenience.

Each of the above irrational beliefs has many other beliefs associated with it. Major must (1) is related to beliefs such as "I must be competent and successful" and "I need someone to love me". Major must (2) is related to beliefs such as "Everyone should treat me fairly and considerately" and "Other people must never criticise me". Major must (3) is related to beliefs such as "Things must turn out the way I want them to" and "It must be easy for me to change anything I don't like".

There are serious emotional consequences for depressed individuals when the life they experience falls short of their irrational beliefs. In such circumstances, depressed individuals often respond with awfulisation—they use words such as "awful", "catastrophe", "disaster", and "horrible" to describe their situation. They also tend to describe themselves in very negative terms, using words such as "useless", "idiot", loser", and "stupid".

We can contrast the irrational beliefs of depressed individuals with the rational beliefs of healthy individuals. Rational beliefs are flexible and express *preferences*—we would prefer it if most people liked us and we succeeded all the time, but we don't regard it as the end of the world if these things don't happen.

The main focus of rational emotive behaviour therapy is on challenging patients' irrational thoughts and beliefs. What happens initially is that the therapist challenges the patient's thoughts and beliefs. However, the emphasis is on training the patient to challenge and dispute his/her own irrational thoughts and beliefs. Here are some of the main ways in which a patient's irrational thoughts can be challenged successfully:

1. Scientific or empirical dispute: this involves asking, "Where is the evidence/proof that this thought or belief is true?"
2. Functional dispute: this involves asking, "Is my irrational belief making things worse or better for me?"
3. Logical dispute: this involves asking, "Does this belief square with common sense?"

When the depressed person's irrational thoughts have been challenged successfully, he/she needs to replace them with rational thoughts. Such thoughts are much more positive than irrational thoughts, they are much more flexible, and they lack the absolutistic nature of irrational thoughts. It is also important for depressed individuals to change their negative unhelpful emotions into healthy, self-helping ones. Finally, it is important for them to change their behaviour—for example, depressed individuals who believe the future is bleak and they are worthless individuals will lack the *motivation* to engage effectively with everyday life. In other words, successful therapy involves changing cognitions (beliefs), emotions, and behaviour if there is to be full recovery from depression.

Beck's cognitive behaviour therapy

In general terms, Beck's therapeutic approach to treating depression is based on three main hypotheses (Beck & Dozois, 2011):

? Why has cognitive behavioural therapy become such a popular therapeutic treatment for many mental disorders?

1. The access hypothesis: if individuals receive appropriate training, they can become aware of the content of their own thinking.
2. The mediation hypothesis: how individuals think about and interpret life's events influences their emotions and behaviour.
3. The change hypothesis: individuals can recover from depression by intentionally modifying their cognitive and behavioural reactions to life's events.

Beck (1976) argued that therapy for depression should involve uncovering and challenging the negative and unrealistic beliefs of depressed clients. As discussed earlier, of central importance here is the cognitive triad—negative thoughts depressed individuals have about themselves, about the world, and about the future.

Beck's cognitive behaviour therapy involves collaborative empiricism, guided discovery, and Socratic dialogue, all of which are designed to challenge the patient's irrational thoughts. Collaborative empiricism involves the therapist and the patient agreeing on the nature of the problem and the goals for therapy. Thoughts are treated as hypotheses rather than as facts. The benefit of doing this is that it means that the patient's thoughts can be tested to see whether they are valid.

CASE STUDY: Cognitive behavioural therapy

Here is a concrete example of cognitive behavioural therapy (Clark, 1996) involving a 40-year-old man with panic disorder (a disorder involving frequent panic attacks). The client tried to protect himself against having a heart attack during panic attacks by taking paracetamol and by breathing deeply. The hypothesis that this was what prevented him from having a heart attack was tested by the therapist and the client alternately sprinting and jogging around a football pitch. In addition, the client was given the homework of taking strenuous daily exercise without trying to control his breathing. The client rapidly accepted that his problem centred on his own mistaken beliefs.

Guided discovery is then used to allow patients to test their thinking through their own observations and experiments (as one does with hypotheses). Here are two examples. A depressed patient who argues people are always avoiding him/her can be asked to keep a diary of specific occasions on which this happens. It is very likely that it happens much less often than the patient imagines. A woman whose long-term relationship ended recently may claim that she'll never be happy again. This is tested by having her keep track of her emotional state as she resumes socialising with her friends.

Socratic dialogue is a form of guided discovery. It involves the therapist asking the patient a series of questions to make it easier for the patient to discover new ways of challenging their maladaptive thoughts. Beck et al. (1993, p. 103) stated that Socratic questions "should be phrased in such a way that they stimulate thought and increase awareness, rather than requiring a correct answer".

Suppose we have a depressed patient who argues she is dislikeable. Possible Socratic questions are as follows: "What evidence suggests that is the case?"; "Have you met anyone who did seem to like you?"; "Do you have any qualities you regard as likeable?"

One of the goals of the above techniques is to modify the patient's core beliefs and schemas. Another goal is to teach patients "how to become scientific investigators of their own thinking—to treat thoughts as hypotheses rather than as facts and to put these thoughts to the test" (Beck & Dozois, 2011, p. 400).

In sum, there are many similarities between Beck's approach and that of Ellis. However, there is a difference in emphasis with respect to the techniques used to challenge patients' irrational thoughts. Ellis' approach tends to involve more direct confrontation and argument with the patient, whereas Beck's approach focuses more on a joint patient–therapist discussion of the patient's ideas.

KEY TERM

Meta-analysis: a form of analysis in which the data from several related studies are combined to obtain an overall estimate.

Effectiveness

We will initially consider the effectiveness of Beck's form of therapy because it has been the focus of much more research than Ellis' rational emotive behaviour therapy. Braun et al. (2013) compared the effectiveness of Beck's form of therapy with several other psychological treatments for depression in a **meta-analysis** (see Chapter 8). They focused on the extent of recovery at the end of treatment and also at follow-up some time later. In essence, all the psychological forms of therapy they considered were moderately effective and there were very few differences in effectiveness among them.

Drug therapy is often used to treat depression. The most used drugs are the serotonin re-uptake inhibitors (SSRIs) such as Prozac (discussed in the section on OCD). It is of importance to decide whether cognitive behaviour therapy or drug therapy is the more effective form of treatment. DeRubeis et al. (2005) compared cognitive therapy with drug therapy involving SSRIs in patients with major depressive disorder. Approximately 58% of the patients in each group showed considerable improvement as a result of treatment.

Hollon et al. (2005) studied those depressed patients responding to treatment in the DeRubeis et al. (2005) study for 12 months after the end of treatment. Of those withdrawn from cognitive therapy, 31% suffered a relapse, as did 76% of those withdrawn from drug therapy. What do these findings mean? They suggest that drug therapy is mostly a palliative treatment that suppresses the symptoms of depression without changing the underlying processes. In contrast, cognitive therapy is mostly a curative treatment because it reduces or eliminates the processes causing depression.

Craighead and Dunlop (2014) carried out meta-analyses to work out whether psychotherapies such as cognitive behaviour therapy are more effective when used on their own or in combination with drug therapy. For long-lasting depression, combined treatment was generally more effective. These findings suggest that drug therapy can make a contribution to recovery over and above that of cognitive behaviour therapy.

How effective is rational emotive behaviour therapy? David et al. (2008) addressed this issue in a study in which they compared the effectiveness of rational emotive behaviour therapy, Beck's cognitive therapy, and drug therapy. All three forms of therapy were comparably effective at the end of treatment. At 6-month follow-up, however, there was some evidence that rational emotive behaviour therapy was more effective than the other two forms of therapy.

Appropriateness

There are several ways in which cognitive behaviour therapy is an appropriate form of treatment for depression. First, it is based on solid theoretical foundations provided by our understanding of the ways in which depression affects cognition and behaviour. Second, since many (or most) of the symptoms of depressed patients are basically cognitive, it seems entirely appropriate for therapy to have as its central focus the changing of their negative and irrational attitudes into ones that are more positive and realistic. Third, it is also appropriate for cognitive behaviour therapy to focus on changing behaviour because of the limited and disengaged behaviour often displayed by depressed patients. Fourth, cognitive behaviour therapy can be regarded as more appropriate than drug therapy given that its beneficial effects are more lasting.

In what ways is cognitive behaviour therapy an inappropriate form of treatment for depression? First, it is important to consider precisely why depressed patients have negative beliefs about themselves, the world, and the future. If (as is often the case) those beliefs are based on realistic concerns then it seems inappropriate for therapy to de-emphasise those concerns. Second, the central problems experienced by depressed patients often revolve around personal relationships (especially close ones). Such relationships are often not considered sufficiently within cognitive behaviour therapy. Third, cognitive behaviour therapy is inappropriate in that a significant proportion of patients who have recovered subsequently suffer a relapse. The limited nature of cognitive behaviour therapy is shown by the finding that the relapse rate is lower when it is combined with drug therapy.

EVALUATION

- ➕ Cognitive behaviour therapy has established itself over the past 40 years as one of the most common and effective forms of treatment for depression.
- ➕ Cognitive behaviour therapy and rational emotive behaviour therapy have both benefitted from their increased focus on behaviour.
- ➕ There is substantial evidence that depressed individuals possess numerous irrational beliefs that produce severe emotional states.
- ➕ It has proved therapeutically effective to challenge the irrational thoughts of depressed individuals.
- ➕ The beneficial effects of cognitive behaviour therapy when used with depressed patients are longer lasting than those of drug therapy (Hollon et al., 2005). This is so because cognitive behavioural therapy is designed to cure depression whereas drug therapy focuses on reducing the symptoms.
- ➖ The emphasis in therapy is on challenging thoughts and beliefs of which the individual patient is consciously aware. However, unconscious processes probably play an important role in the development and maintenance of depression.
- ➖ Those who advocate cognitive behaviour therapy to treat depression exaggerate the importance of cognitive processes. Many clients develop more rational and less distorted ways of thinking about important issues with no beneficial changes in their maladaptive behaviour. In addition, many beliefs of depressed patients simply reflect the reality of their difficult everyday lives, rather than being distortions of that reality!
- ➖ Cognitive behaviour therapy de-emphasises factors regarded as important in other forms of therapy. For example, little attention is paid to physiological or biological processes, and the emphasis is on current problems rather than traumatic childhood experiences (as in psychoanalysis).
- ➖ Patients with depression are very concerned about their emotional state. Cognitive behaviour therapy with its emphasis on hypothesis testing can seem too "cold" and "rational" to emotionally disturbed patients (James Walsh, pers. com).
- ➖ Cognitive behaviour therapy often involves a complex mixture of cognitive and behavioural ingredients. As a result, it can be hard to determine precisely *which* ingredients are most responsible for the success of treatment.
- ➖ There can be ethical issues concerning the desirability of telling patients the problem lies within them rather than reality.

Section Summary

Explaining depression: Cognitive approach

- Ellis was the first therapist to adopt a cognitive approach to depression with his rational emotive therapy. According to his ABC model, individuals interpret adversity (point A) in line with their beliefs (point B) which determines the emotional consequences (point C). With depressed individuals, negative beliefs and interpretations at point B help to cause depression at point C.
- In Ellis' extended ABCDEF, D is the dispute belief system, E involves effective or helpful beliefs, and F involves functional emotions and behaviour.

- Beck argued that negative cognitive schemas cause depressed individuals to have negative and unrealistic thoughts that involve much over-generalisation. The most important of such thoughts are found in the cognitive triad—negative thoughts with respect to oneself, the world, and the future.
- It is crucially important whether negative thoughts help to produce depression or whether such thoughts are only a consequence of having depression. There is limited support for the former viewpoint.
- Other, non-cognitive factors associated with the development of depression are genetic factors, life events, and gender.

Cognitive behaviour therapy for treating depression

- Ellis' rational emotive behaviour therapy focuses on depressed individuals' irrational beliefs which are absolutist and inflexible.
- Patients challenge their irrational thoughts in various ways: scientific or empirical dispute; functional dispute; and logical dispute.
- When patients' irrational thoughts have been challenged successfully, they are replaced by healthier rational thoughts which are positive and flexible.
- Successful rational emotive behaviour therapy involves changing emotions and behaviour as well as cognitions.
- Beck's cognitive behaviour therapy involves using collaborative empiricism, guided discovery, and Socratic dialogue to challenge patients' irrational thoughts. Thoughts are treated as hypotheses and their validity then tested.
- Beck's form of cognitive behaviour therapy is at least as effective as other forms of therapy for depression and its beneficial effects are longer lasting than those of drug therapy.
- Rational emotive behaviour therapy seems to be comparably effective to Beck's cognitive behaviour therapy.
- Limitations of the therapies advocated by Ellis and by Beck include:
  - the de-emphasis on the very difficult problems that many depressed individuals have to contend with;
  - the de-emphasis on unconscious processes;
  - the exaggerated focus on cognitive processes which can seem too cold and rational to patients;
  - the complexity of cognitive behaviour therapy makes it hard to determine precisely which components are most responsible for the success of treatment.

BIOLOGICAL APPROACH TO EXPLAINING AND TREATING OBSESSIVE–COMPULSIVE DISORDER (OCD)

In this section, we will consider the biological approach to explaining and treating obsessive–compulsive disorder (OCD). We start with a discussion of the biological approach's explanation of OCD, followed by a focus on how OCD is treated within the biological approach.

Explaining OCD: Biological approach

There are several aspects to the biological approach to understanding OCD. For convenience, we will divide up our coverage into genetic, neural, and evolutionary explanations.

Genetic explanations

Twin studies have been carried out to decide whether genetic factors are important in the development of OCD. As discussed earlier, twin studies involve comparisons between identical and fraternal twins. Identical twins share 100% of their genes whereas fraternal twins share only 50%. The most important measure is the concordance rate—if one twin has OCD, what is the probability that the other twin also has it? If genetic factors are important, the concordance rate will be higher for identical twins than for fraternal twins.

Carey and Gottesman (1981) found identical twins showed a concordance rate of 87% for obsessive symptoms and features compared to 47% in fraternal twins. That difference suggests that genetic factors are moderately important. Van Grootheest et al. (2005) reviewed twin studies on obsessive–compulsive disorder. *All* the studies reported higher concordance rates for identical than for fraternal twins, and the overall conclusion was that there is a moderate genetic influence on the development of obsessive–compulsive disorder. However, the concordance rates for identical twins were well short of 100%, indicating that environmental factors are of major importance.

ACTIVITY: Twin studies and genetics

Twin studies are done to investigate how much of a behaviour is genetic as opposed to environmental; i.e. nature rather than nurture. One twin study of individuals with obsessive–compulsive disorder showed an 87% concordance rate for identical twins and a 47% rate for fraternal twins.

It would be a good exercise to make a poster showing how and why identical and fraternal twins differ genetically, including the difference in shared genes.

You could also incorporate the concordance rates for obsessive–compulsive disorder and explain what the significance of the difference in rates tells us. This would not only make these facts clear to you, they would, if presented clearly and well, be an asset to the class.

Family studies provide additional support for the importance of genetic factors. For example, Nestadt et al. (2000) found the lifetime incidence of obsessive–compulsive disorder was higher in the relatives of obsessive–compulsive disorder patients (11.7%) than in the relatives of healthy controls (2.7%).

If genetic factors are important in the development of OCD, cultural factors may be unimportant. Fontenelle et al. (2004) compared patients with OCD in Brazil, North America, Latin America, Europe, Africa, and Asia. There was generally an early onset of the disorder in nearly all cultures, and most patients in all cultures had a mixture of obsessions and compulsions. However, more patients had aggressive obsessions in Brazil than elsewhere, and there were many religious obsessions in the Middle East. Fontenelle et al. (2004, p. 403) concluded that, "The core features of OCD [obsessive–compulsive disorder] are probably relatively independent of cultural variations."

Evaluation

? What type of environmental factors do you think may play a role in obsessive–compulsive disorders?

Twin and family studies have consistently found evidence that genetic factors are of importance. However, environmental factors are very important for various reasons. First, one reason why the concordance rate is higher for identical than for fraternal twins may be because the environments in which identical twins are brought up tends to be more similar than those in which fraternal twins are brought up.

Second, environmental factors probably also play a role in explaining why the incidence of OCD is higher among the relatives of patients than among the relatives of healthy controls. Close contact with a relative suffering from OCD may be very stressful and the stress thus created may increase the chances of developing the disorder.

Third, if genetic factors were all-important in the development of OCD, then the concordance rate for identical twins should theoretically be 100%. The actual figure is consistently far lower than that (generally about 50–60%), indicating that environmental factors are important.

Neural explanations

Several neural explanations of OCD have been proposed. We will briefly consider the following types of explanations: (1) brain dysfunction; (2) serotonin deficiency.

Brain dysfunction

It is often argued that there are differences in brain anatomy and functioning between OCD patients and healthy controls. The brain areas involved include the orbitofrontal cortex (which is close to the eyes), the anterior cingulate, the caudate nucleus, the striatum (just below the cerebral cortex), and the thalamus. There is an excitatory direct pathway (the orbitofrontal–subcortical pathway) which is associated with an inhibitory indirect pathway.

In healthy individuals, the excitatory direct pathway is influenced by the indirect pathway's inhibitory function. In OCD patients, in contrast, the excitatory direct pathway is activated more readily than in healthy individuals and there is reduced effectiveness of the inhibitory indirect pathway. As a result, there is excessive activation of the direct pathway. This leads to exaggerated concerns about danger, harm, or hygiene and thus to compulsions designed to neutralise the perceived threat.

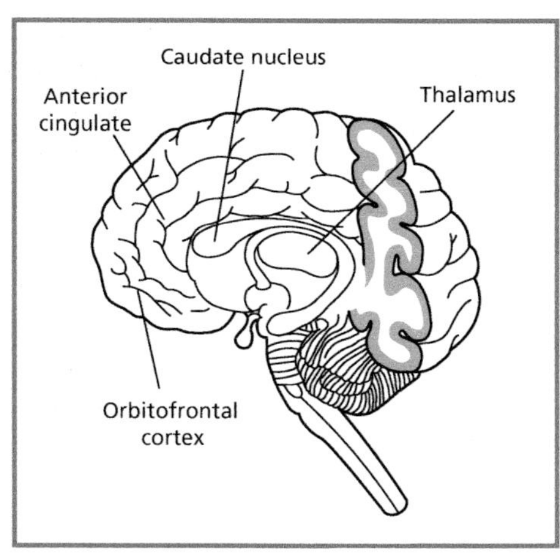

What evidence supports this theory? Much of it comes from neuroimaging studies (Pauls et al., 2014). It has been found repeatedly that OCD patients have unusually high activation within the orbitofrontal cortex. In addition, several studies have obtained excessive activity in the caudate nucleus. Furthermore, the anterior cingulate (involved in conflict resolution) is also more activated in OCD patients than in healthy controls.

Could you use this knowledge to diagnose OCD? How reliable would the diagnosis be?

More evidence supporting the theory comes from brain-damaged patients. Obsessive–compulsive symptoms often seem to increase or decrease when the orbital region and/or the caudate nucleus are damaged through either illness or accident. Comer (2009) discussed the case of an obsessive–compulsive patient who shot himself in the head in an attempt to commit suicide. Even though he survived, there was extensive damage to brain areas such as orbital region and the caudate nucleus. After his injury, the patient reported a dramatic reduction in his symptoms.

Finally, there have been some studies involving surgery to parts of the brain circuitry associated with OCD. In many cases, this has led to a reduction in some of the symptoms of OCD.

Evaluation

There is strong evidence (especially from neuroimaging studies) indicating that certain brain circuits are associated with OCD. It is plausible that excessive activation can cause obsessional thoughts and lead to compulsive behaviour. The theory is also supported by findings from surgical cases and brain-damaged individuals.

What are the limitations of research on brain circuitry in OCD? First, what we have with neuroimaging studies is an *association* between elevated activity in certain brain areas and OCD. Since it is only an association, it doesn't show that those brain areas play a role in *causing* obsessive–compulsive disorder. It is very possible that having obsessive–compulsive symptoms leads to increased brain activity in areas concerned with thinking and action. However, it can be argued that surgical cases provide somewhat stronger evidence that certain brain circuits are directly involved in OCD.

Second, the hypothesis doesn't provide a comprehensive account of the origins of OCD. For example, as we will see shortly, environmental factors (e.g. life events) are important in producing obsessive–compulsive disorder. However, it is unclear how they might influence brain activity.

Serotonin deficiency

Serotonin is a neurotransmitter (chemical that transmits electrical impulses across neurons). According to the serotonin hypothesis, OCD patients have deficient levels of serotonin or deficient serotonin metabolism. On the face of it, this hypothesis is supported by studies using drug therapy to treat OCD (discussed later). In essence, some of the most effective drugs for OCD (e.g. selective serotonin re-uptake inhibitors or SSRIs) increase serotonin levels which is exactly what would be predicted on the serotonin hypothesis. It should be noted at this point that OCD patients also often have abnormal levels of the transmitter dopamine so we should not focus too much just on serotonin.

Studies in which serotonin levels in obsessive disorder patients have been assessed have typically found no differences between them and healthy controls. As Rachman (2004, p. 75)

KEY TERM

Serotonin: a neurotransmitter that influences emotional states.

concluded, "There is no evidence that patients with OCD have more or less serotonin than non-patients, or more or less serotonin than patients with other forms of anxiety disorder." In addition, there is no evidence that patients with relatively low levels of serotonin respond better to drug therapy than patients whose serotonin levels are higher. Even if there were an association between OCD and low serotonin levels, that wouldn't prove that low serotonin levels help to cause OCD—the causality might go in the other direction.

It is likely that serotonin plays some role in OCD. However, it is clearly a substantial oversimplification to argue that OCD patients have low levels of serotonin which are increased in a neat and tidy fashion by drugs. Further problems with the serotonin hypothesis are discussed later in the section on drug therapy for OCD.

Evolutionary explanations

? Can you think of some ways OCD may be adaptive?

In principle, there is an almost infinite list of obsessions and compulsions from which patients with OCD might suffer. In practice, however, most of their compulsions revolve around washing and checking. Why is this the case? Throughout most of human history, many (or even most) people died prematurely because they lived in unhygienic conditions that led to disease. Accordingly, it was totally adaptive for individuals to be very concerned with hygiene issues and to wash themselves thoroughly several times a day. Historically, too, most human beings until fairly recently lived in potentially dangerous environments with little protection from wild animals or adverse climate. As a result, it was sensible for them to check carefully that everything in their environment was in order.

Szechtman and Woody (2004) argued that most obsessional thoughts and images and most compulsions revolve around the idea of security or safety. We have a security motivation system to detect potential dangers and prevent them turning into emergencies. This system has an "easy-to-turn-on, hard-to-turn-off quality". This makes evolutionary sense, "because repeated false alarms are much less costly than even a single failure to prepare for upcoming danger". What distinguishes patients with OCD from healthy individuals is that they find it much harder to turn off their security motivation system.

The notion of a security motivation system helps to explain why most obsessions and compulsions are associated with issues of security and safety that were extremely important in our evolutionary past. Recent evidence supporting this theory is discussed in Chapter 5.

ACTIVITY: Evolution and obsessive–compulsive disorder

Evolutionary explanations for the persistence of obsessive–compulsive disorder down the generations is based on the concept that the obsessions and compulsions could have been adaptive, though perhaps in a milder form. You could make this clear by constructing a PowerPoint presentation with the obsession and compulsion as the frame title and the adaptive function of this as the text box. You would need to research as many obsessions and compulsions as you can, using internet sources—online archives from newspapers such as the tabloids can also be useful here.

Then you need to think of a possible adaptive value to our hunter–gatherer ancestors, and you could also discuss these possibilities with your classmates. If you do make the presentation then you have the opportunity to use colour and graphics to attract attention and enhance what you are communicating.

Other explanations of OCD

We have seen the biological approach to explaining OCD has proved successful in many ways. However, several other approaches are also of value and we will discuss three of them briefly: the cognitive, behavioural, and social.

Cognitive approach

From a cognitive perspective, it has been argued that an inflated sense of personal responsibility plays a major role in producing the obsessions and compulsions of OCD patients. Salkovskis (1991, pp. 13–14) suggested the behaviour patterns of these patients "reflect an attempt to prevent themselves from being responsible for adverse consequences that might arise from not acting on the content of the thought (prevention of harm through, for example, washing and checking)". The existence of compulsive rituals makes it hard for OCD patients to realise their obsessions and dysfunctional thoughts about danger are incorrect.

Where does this inflated sense of personal responsibility come from? Numerous factors are involved. However, women who are pregnant or who have recently given birth have enormous responsibility for their child's well-being. According to Salkovskis' approach, we might expect pregnant women to show an increase in obsessive–compulsive symptoms. Neziroglu et al. (1992) found 39% of female obsessive–compulsive disorder patients with children reported an onset of the disorder during pregnancy.

What are the limitations of the cognitive approach? First, there is an *association* between an exaggerated sense of personal responsibility and OCD. This association does not show an exaggerated sense of personal responsibility helps to cause the OCD—the causality may be the other way around or exaggerated personal responsibility may be irrelevant to the development of OCD. Second, it is odd that an excessive sense of personal responsibility predominantly leads to washing and checking rather than other forms of behaviour.

Behavioural approach

The behavioural approach to explaining OCD involves a two-stage process. First, fear in OCD patients is triggered by stimuli (e.g. unwashed hands; obsessional thoughts) that are very unlikely to cause real harm. Second, these patients manage to reduce their level of fear by compulsive rituals (e.g. hand washing), and this behaviour is reinforced or rewarded by fear reduction.

This explanation is reminiscent of Mowrer's two-process model that was designed to explain the development of phobias (discussed earlier in the chapter). According to his model, neutral stimuli become associated with threatening thoughts or experiences through classical conditioning, and this leads to the development of anxiety. For example, shaking hands may become associated with the anxiety-provoking notion of contamination for someone with obsessive–compulsive disorder. Second, the individual discovers that the anxiety thus created can be reduced substantially by washing his/her hands.

Hodgson and Rachman (1977) obtained support for the above explanation. Patients with obsessive–compulsive disorder were exposed to situations triggering their obsessions (e.g. shaking hands if they had an obsession about contamination). As predicted, this produced a high level of anxiety. However, more importantly, when the patients performed their compulsive rituals (e.g. hand washing) when exposed to such situations, their level of anxiety rapidly decreased.

In sum, this approach is valuable in its emphasis on the fear-reducing function of compulsions and rituals. However, it fails to explain why so many of OCD patients' rituals relate to washing and checking rather than other possible ritualised forms of behaviour. In addition, the approach does not provide a clear account of how the rituals exhibited by OCD patients originated in the first place.

Social approach: Life events

Life events play a role in the development of obsessive–compulsive disorder. Khanna et al. (1988) discovered that patients with OCD had experienced significantly more negative life events than healthy controls in the 6 months prior to the onset of the disorder. Most of these events were undesirable and uncontrolled events in the areas of health and bereavement.

> ? If one of your relatives has suffered from a mental disorder, what reasons are there for you not to worry that you may also develop the same disorder?

There is also evidence that exposure to traumatic life events at some point in life is associated with obsessive–compulsive disorder. For example, Saunders et al. (1992) found those who had experienced childhood sexual abuse were about five times more likely than non-abused individuals to develop OCD.

The above studies simply show an association between life events and obsessive–compulsive disorder. An association does *not* prove there is a causal relationship—it isn't necessarily the case that the life events helped to cause the disorder, and alternative explanations are possible. For example, individuals who are very anxious and stressed a few months before developing OCD may through their own behaviour help to create life events (e.g. losing their job or marital separation). Another potential problem with life-event data is that the information is generally obtained retrospectively several months or even years after the events in question and so may involve memory distortions.

CASE STUDY: OCD

Mike was a "normal" teenager who went to school and college, although he says he always felt shy and rather anxious. What was he anxious about? He worried that he'd forgotten to shut the front door firmly so it locked when he left the house, and that he would lose his door key. He was anxious about how others perceived him, what they thought of him, anxious about being laughed at or mocked in other ways. This doesn't sound abnormal—most adolescents, and many adults, have anxieties like these. But Mike then found he could control his anxiety for a while by performing repetitive behaviours. When he entered a room Mike would have to touch each wall, tapping it seven times, and he would need to do this discreetly so it was not noticed. He also had to wash his hands frequently, even if they seemed not dirty; and he'd need to soap and then rinse them vigorously seven times. He had to tap the light switches in any room he was in, and there were numerous other little behaviours that he would need to do to feel calmer and safe. However, this feeling of calmness, the lessening of his anxieties, would only last for a finite time and then he would feel the anxiety start to increase in him again.

When Mike got to 19 years old he started to think more positively about himself and decided he needed to be back in charge of his behaviour, not ruled by anxieties and fears. He had some CBT (cognitive behavioural therapy) sessions, which supported him in questioning the logic of his obsessions and the usefulness of his compulsions. Mike did realise his behaviour was personally unhelpful as well as unrealistic, and was able, gradually, to stop the compulsive actions without being overcome by his fears.

He describes his freeing himself from OCD as a long and difficult struggle, but in his twenties he is a quiet person, working successfully in IT and enjoying life, although he says he is still a worrier!

Mike could have a personality that predisposes him to being anxious, but what might have triggered everyday anxiety into becoming a disorder?

EVALUATION OF THE BIOLOGICAL APPROACH

- (+) There is strong evidence from twin and family studies that genetic factors play an important role in the development of OCD.
- (+) A substantial amount of research (much involving neuroimaging) has identified a brain circuit involving the orbitofrontal cortex, the anterior cingulate, the caudate nucleus, the striatum, and the thalamus. This brain circuit is often more activated in OCD patients than in healthy controls, and so it may help to explain OCD.
- (+) The biological approach can explain the finding that most compulsions relate to washing and checking in evolutionary terms. For example, evolution may have led to the development of a security motivation system that is overactive in OCD patients.
- (−) Most research on an overactive brain circuit in OCD has failed to establish causality—does an overactive brain circuit lead to OCD or does OCD lead to an overactive brain circuit?
- (−) The origins of an overactive brain circuit in OCD have not been identified.
- (−) It appears that many OCD patients have an inflated sense of personal responsibility but the biological approach doesn't provide an explanation of this.
- (−) The important notion that OCD patients exhibit compulsive behaviour in an attempt to reduce the fear created by their obsessions is de-emphasised within the biological approach.
- (−) The biological approach de-emphasises the role played by negative life events in leading to OCD.

Biological approach to treating OCD

It is worth emphasising at the outset that treatments for OCD have improved greatly over the years. As Lack (2012, p. 86) pointed out, "Over the past three decades, obsessive–compulsive disorder (OCD) has moved from an almost untreatable, life-long psychiatric disorder to a highly manageable one." Drug therapy (easily the most used form of biological therapy) has played an important role in this success story. Of most relevance to the development of drug therapy for OCD is the serotonin hypothesis (discussed earlier), according to which OCD patients have deficient levels of the neurotransmitter serotonin or alternatively deficient serotonin metabolism.

? What is the natural function of serotonin?

Drug therapy

The most common drugs used in the treatment of OCD are selective serotonin re-uptake inhibitors (SSRIs). Neurotransmitters are chemicals that are released by one neuron and then take up by other neurons. Neurotransmitters that aren't taken up by other neurons are taken up by the same neurons that released them in the first place. This process is called "re-uptake". In essence, SSRIs inhibit the re-uptake of serotonin which means that more serotonin is available to be taken up by other neurons. The end result is that there is an increased concentration of serotonin. If a deficiency of serotonin is associated with the development and maintenance of OCD, it is reasonable to expect that drugs correcting that deficiency should prove effective in treatment of that condition. Several SSRIs have been developed including fluvoxamine, fluoxetine (Prozac), sertraline, and paroxetine.

SSRIs were preceded by other drugs such as serotonin re-uptake inhibitors (SRIs) that were less selective in their action (SSRIs have most of their effect on serotonin). The most effective of the SRIs is clomipramine. This is noteworthy because this drug has greater effects on the neurotransmitter serotonin than do the other SRIs.

As discussed earlier in the chapter, the role of serotonin in OCD is more complex than the above account suggests. Indeed, the two key assumptions that have been made about SRIs and SSRIs (and the reasons why they are effective) are oversimplified. First, patients with OCD generally don't have low serotonin levels (Rachman, 2004). However, it is possible that various brain structures in obsessive–compulsives show increased sensitivity to serotonin.

Second, while SSRIs initially seem to increase serotonin levels, that isn't the case when the drugs are taken over a relatively long period of time. Dolberg et al. (1996) found that over time the effects of SSRIs on serotonin receptors actually produced a functional *decrease* in the availability of serotonin.

Effectiveness

According to the traditional view, we might expect SRIs and SSRIs to be effective early in treatment (when they increase serotonin levels) but should become less so when they no longer increase serotonin levels sometime later on. In fact, precisely the *opposite* pattern has been found. Dougherty et al. (2002) found SSRIs sometimes produced an increase in the symptoms of obsessive–compulsive disorder early in treatment. After 6 weeks or more, however, SSRIs began to be effective at reducing symptoms.

Eddy et al. (2004) considered the effectiveness of various classes of drugs (including SSRIs and SRIs) and cognitive behaviour therapy in an extensive review. The findings were reasonably clear-cut:

1. The SSRIs and SRIs were more effective than other drugs in terms of improvement from pre- to post-treatment with the most effective drug of all being the SRI clomipramine.
2. Different forms of cognitive and cognitive behaviour therapy were effective in treating OCD. However, the overall effectiveness of the SRIs and SSRIs tended to be somewhat greater.
3. There was evidence that combined treatments (i.e. drugs + cognitive behaviour therapy) were more effective than either treatment on its own. One of the reasons why combined treatments are effective is because they are often associated with a reduced drop-out rate (Hill & Beamish, 2007).

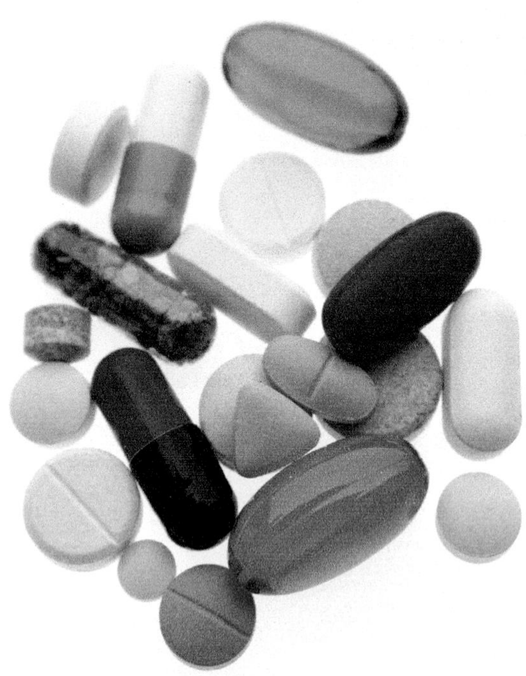

What is the optimal form of drug therapy given the different strengths and limitations of the various drugs available? One recommended approach (Schruers et al., 2005) is to start for 10–12 weeks with an SSRI. If that drug isn't effective, then switch for the following 10–12 weeks to a different SSRI. If that also proves ineffective, then switch for the final 10–12 weeks to clomipramine.

Bloch et al. (2006) reviewed studies on OCD patients who showed no recovery after 3 months of drug therapy with SSRIs. It was found that switching them to antipsychotic drugs had beneficial effects. However, only one-third of the patients showed reduced symptoms with antipsychotic drugs following failure with SSRIs.

Limitations

So far we have focused mostly on short-term effects of drug therapy. However, it is obviously important to consider the long-term effects of drug therapy (especially after the drugs are no longer being administered). How effective is drug therapy for obsessive–compulsive disorder in the long term? Hollon et al. (2006) pointed out that treatments can be effective in two different senses. Some effective treatments are *palliative*—they suppress the symptoms of a disorder while applied but don't focus on the processes producing the disorder. Other effective treatments are *curative*—they reduce or eliminate the symptoms of a disorder AND the underlying processes.

Drug therapy is effective in treating OCD, particularly when combined with cognitive behavioural therapy. However, they are palliative rather than curative, so relapse rates are high when drugs aren't administered any longer.

The available evidence suggests drug therapy for OCD is palliative rather than curative. Simpson et al. (2004) compared groups of patients with OCD administered behaviour therapy or drug therapy (the SRI clomipramine) who responded successfully to treatment. During the 12 weeks following the end of active treatment, 45% of the patients who had received clomipramine relapsed back into the disorder compared to only 12% of those who had received exposure and response prevention. Thus, the beneficial effects of drug therapy often don't last for long after treatment has ceased.

We saw earlier that the SRI clomipramine is one of the most successful drugs in the treatment of OCD. However, there are three problems with this drug. First, patients taking it are more likely than those taking the SSRIs to drop out of the study because of its side effects. These side effects include dry mouth, drowsiness, sedation, and sweating. Second, only a minority of patients were willing to take clomipramine over a 1-year period. Third, clomipramine can pose dangers when it is taken by patients who have heart problems or who are at risk of attempting suicide.

Drop-out is also a real problem with the SSRIs. Abramowitz et al. (2009) reviewed several studies and found that the drop-out rate varied between 24% and 89%.

Appropriateness

There are various reasons for arguing that drug therapy for OCD is appropriate. First, it has proved effective in reducing anxiety levels and reducing many of the symptoms of OCD. Second, it is reasonably appropriate theoretically given that there is evidence that OCD is associated with complex abnormalities of serotonin function. Third, drug therapy seems to be appropriate when used in combination with cognitive behaviour therapy because it reduces anxiety levels sufficiently that the drop-out rate is reduced.

? **What are some risks associated with taking SRIs and SSRIs?**

In what ways is drug therapy inappropriate in the treatment of OCD? First, while it reduces the symptoms during drug therapy it often fails to produce continuing benefits thereafter. That means that it doesn't have much effect on the underlying mechanisms responsible for OCD. Second, drug therapy using SRIs and SSRIs is inappropriate in that we lack detailed information concerning their effects on the brain. Third, the appropriateness of drug therapy for obsessive–compulsive disorder is reduced by the fact that many patients drop out of treatment because of side effects (e.g. dry mouth; drowsiness). Fourth, there are some types of patients (e.g. those with heart problems or in danger of committing suicide) for whom drug therapy is totally inappropriate.

EVALUATION

- (+) SRIs and SSRIs have both been found to be as effective as (or more effective than) psychological forms of treatment such as cognitive behaviour therapy for OCD.
- (+) Part of the problem with OCD is biochemical and so drug therapy is in principle an appropriate form of treatment since it produces biochemical changes.
- (+) Drug therapy has often proved especially effective when used in combination with cognitive behaviour therapy.
- (−) Drug therapy doesn't have much effect on the underlying mechanisms responsible for OCD. As a result, drug therapy reduces the symptoms of the disorder while patients take drugs but often fails to produce benefits that continue afterwards.
- (−) We don't know in detail *why* SRIs and SSRIs are successful in reducing obsessional and compulsive symptoms.
- (−) There is typically a fairly high drop-out rate with drug therapy and patients complain of drug-related symptoms such as dry mouth or drowsiness.
- (−) Drug therapy is wholly inappropriate for some types of patients (e.g. those with heart problems or in danger of committing suicide).
- (−) McHugh et al. (2013) found in a review that 75% of patients preferred psychological treatment to drug treatment. This is important because the evidence indicates that treatment tends to be effective when patients receive their preferred form of treatment (McHugh et al., 2013).

EXAM HINT

In the examination you might be asked to interpret some research findings about the effectiveness of different treatments for a psychopathological disorder, presented in a table or on a graph. In this case, your knowledge of research methods and data analysis is more important than your knowledge of the different treatments. Make sure that your answer responds to the data presented, which might differ from what you have learned from the findings of specific studies discussed in this book.

Section Summary

Explaining OCD: Biological approach

- Twin and family studies have provided convincing evidence that genetic factors are important in the development of OCD.
- There are differences in brain functioning between patients with OCD and healthy controls. More specifically, OCD patients have excessive activation of an excitatory pathway and reduced effectiveness of an inhibitory indirect pathway. These differences may or may not be causally relevant to OCD.
- According to the serotonin hypothesis, OCD patients have deficient levels of serotonin or deficient serotonin metabolism. This is certainly no more than partially correct.
- According to the evolutionary approach, humans have a security motivation system to detect potential dangers because such a system was essential during the evolution of humans. OCD patients find it harder than healthy individuals to turn off their security motivation system.
- There are several other explanations of OCD: OCD patients have an inflated sense of personal responsibility; compulsions reduce the anxiety associated with obsessions; and life events help to trigger OCD.

Biological Approach to Treating OCD

- The most common drugs used in treating OCD are SRIs and SSRIs, both of which increase the availability of serotonin. However, these drugs typically fail to increase serotonin availability when administered over a fairly long period of time.
- SRIs and SSRIs have been found to be at least as effective as cognitive behaviour therapy in the treatment of OCD in the short term. Combined treatments with drugs + cognitive behaviour therapy have sometimes proved most effective.

- Drug therapy seems to be palliative rather than curative as is shown by disappointingly high relapse rates when drugs aren't administered any longer.
- Drugs have various side effects including dry mouth and drowsiness and can't be taken by patients with heart problems or danger of committing suicide.
- There is a fairly high drop-out rate with drug therapy.
- Most patients prefer psychological treatment to drug treatment. This matters because patients generally show more recovery if given their preferred form of treatment

EXAM HINT

It is quite common for questions in the psychopathology section of the exam to be based on a short scenario. Whilst you probably have not seen the scenario before, if you have revised everything you will have the knowledge needed to answer the question. Just remember to apply your psychological knowledge to explain the case study. You might be asked to identify the cognitive, emotional, or behavioural characteristics of the disorder or explain possible causes or treatments. You will gain marks for outlining appropriate concepts from an approach and for applying this knowledge to the case study. You will also gain marks for writing something that is coherent (i.e. it makes sense) and that uses key terms from the approach in an appropriate way, so do make sure that you learn the terminology in this chapter and in the approaches chapter.

Further Reading

- There are several excellent and thorough textbooks on abnormal psychology. The main issues within abnormal psychology are discussed in an accessible and reader-friendly way in A.M. Pomerantz (2014) *Clinical psychology: Science, practice, and culture (3rd Edn)* (Thousand Oaks, CA: Sage). Chapter 7 provides an excellent discussion of the complex issue of defining abnormality.
- A second textbook that can be recommended because of its focus on the main issues in abnormal psychology is V.M. Durand and D.H. Barlow (2013) *Essentials of abnormal psychology (6th Edn)* (Belmont, CA: Thomson/Cengage).

Revision Questions

1. Which of the following is not a definition of abnormality (1 mark)

   Failure to function adequately

   Adopting a behaviour that will cause offence

   Statistical infrequency

   Deviation from ideal mental health.

2. a. Outline two definitions of abnormality. (3 +3 marks)

   b. Explain one limitation of each of the definitions answered in (a.). (2+2 marks)

3. a. Outline the main characteristics of phobias. (6 marks)

   b. Explain what is involved in flooding. (3 marks)

4. "I have hated birds for as long as I can remember—if I see a bird outside I could not go out" sighed Ahmed about his bird phobia.

   Describe how it may be possible to treat Ahmed using the technique known as "systematic desensitisation". (6 marks)

5. Describe and evaluate the cognitive approach to explaining depression. (12 marks)
6. Describe and evaluate the use of drug therapy to treat OCD. (12 marks)

What you need to know

The specifications for AS level and for A-level year 1 include all of the sections listed below. However, the A-level specification includes some sub-sections that you are not required to learn at AS level. It may help to familiarise yourself with the specification so you are clear on what you need to revise. To help you, there are some notes in the margins throughout this chapter, indicating material that isn't covered at AS level.

Research Methods will be examined in Paper 2 of the AS exam and Paper 1 of the A-level exam.

Research Methods

8

In a sense, we are all "armchair psychologists"—everyone has opinions about human behaviour. Psychologists don't just present theories about why people behave as they do, but they also seek to support or challenge these theories with **research**—systematic study of a problem—including experiments, interviews, and case studies. Throughout this book we rely on such evidence as a means of analysing theories. In this chapter we will consider the different methods used to conduct research, as well as other important features of the research process.

RESEARCH METHODS

Like any other **science**, psychology is concerned with theories and data. All sciences share one fundamental feature: they aim to discover facts about the world using systematic and objective methods of investigation. The research process starts with casual observations about one feature of the world, for example, that people imitate the violence they see on television or that there are concerns about how the Nazis so easily made ordinary people obey them (see page 61). These observations collectively form a **theory** (a general explanation or account of certain findings or data). For example, someone might put forward a theory claiming that genetic factors play a role in all mental disorders.

Theories invariably produce a number of further expectations, which can be stated as a **research hypothesis**—a formal and unambiguous statement about what you believe to be true. Here is an example of a hypothesis: Obsessive–compulsive disorder is a condition that depends in part on genetic factors (see page 305). A hypothesis is stated with the purpose of trying to prove or disprove it. And that is why scientists conduct research—to prove or disprove their hypotheses. If it is disproved, the theory has to be adjusted, and a new hypothesis produced, and tested, and so on. This process is shown in the Figure on page 318.

What is the relationship between theories and hypotheses? Theories provide rather *general* accounts of a range of findings. The various assumptions built into a theory will typically generate several hypotheses—thus, hypotheses are *specific* predictions that follow from some theory.

Psychologists spend a lot of their time collecting data to test various hypotheses. In addition to **laboratory experiments**, they use many different methods of investigation, each of which can provide useful information about human behaviour.

EXAM HINT

Understanding research methods is at the heart of psychology. Your knowledge of research methods is tested in every paper at AS and A Level. Questions on research methods will be included throughout the different topics that you have studied. There will also be a section dedicated to research methods on paper 2. Across the qualification as a whole, 25–30% of the available marks will test your knowledge of research methods. Around a third of the research methods marks (10% of the total) will test your mathematical data analysis skills.

KEY TERMS

Research: the process of gaining knowledge and understanding via either theory or empirical data collection.

Science: a branch of knowledge conducted on objective principles. It is both an activity and an organised body of knowledge.

Theory: a general explanation of a set of findings. It is used to produce an experimental hypothesis.

Research hypothesis: a statement put forward at the beginning of a study stating what you expect to happen, generated by a theory.

Laboratory experiment: an experiment conducted in a laboratory setting or other contrived setting away from the participants' normal environments. The experimenter manipulates some aspect of the environment to observe its effects on the participants' behaviour.

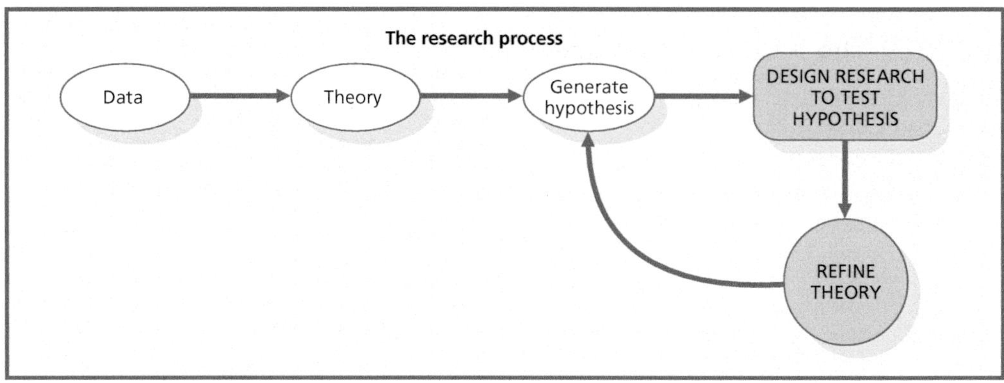

When a researcher has decided which hypothesis he/she wants to test, the next crucial issue is to decide *which* research method is the one that is most appropriate. It may seem natural to ask which of the various research methods (discussed below) is the best. This question is too simple: a given research method may be the best way to test certain hypotheses but may be much less suitable for testing other hypotheses. In what follows, we will consider the advantages and limitations of each research method in turn.

EXPERIMENTAL METHOD: LABORATORY EXPERIMENTS

There are various experimental methods including laboratory, field, and natural experiments. Most studies using experimental methods are laboratory experiments. This method is not the only scientific method, but it is the most scientific because it is highly objective and systematic. As we will see, experimental methods have the great advantage of permitting us to work out cause-and-effect relationships. We will start by focusing mostly on laboratory experiments, and then consider the three main types of experiments using experimental methods.

A variable is something that varies! How long you sleep each night is a variable, whereas the number of days in a week is a fixed quantity.

Dependent and independent variables

In order to understand what is involved in the experimental method, we will consider a concrete example. Put yourself in the position of the British psychologist Alan Baddeley (1966), who thought acoustic coding was important in short-term memory, with people tending to confuse similar-sounding words when they tried to recall them in the right order. This led him to test the following hypothesis: More errors will be made in recalling acoustically similar word lists in the correct order than in recalling acoustically dissimilar word lists (see page 78).

In order to test this hypothesis, Baddeley compared the numbers of errors in short-term memory with lists of words that were acoustically similar (e.g. man, cap, can, cab, mad, mat, map) and others that were acoustically dissimilar (e.g. pit, few, cow, pen, sup, bar, day). This hypothesis refers to two **variables**—whether the list words were acoustically similar or dissimilar and the performance of the people learning the lists (errors made).

The variable directly manipulated by the experimenter is called the **independent variable (IV)** (i.e. acoustic similarity vs dissimilarity). The other variable, the one affected by the IV, is called the **dependent variable (DV)** (i.e. how many errors are made on each type of list). (It is called *dependent* because it depends on something the experimenter controls.) The DV is some aspect of behaviour that is going to be measured or assessed, to decide whether or not the IV caused a change in behaviour.

KEY TERMS

Variables: things that vary or change.

Independent variable (IV): some aspect of the research situation that is manipulated by the researcher in order to observe whether a change occurs in another variable.

Dependent variable (DV): an aspect of the participant's behaviour that is measured in the study.

ACTIVITY: The experimental process

To apply what you have learnt about the experimental process, refer to one of the experiments on short-term memory processing (e.g. Baddeley, 1966; Jacobs, 1887; Peterson & Peterson, 1959) and work out the IV and DV.

The experimental process can be summarised thus:

- Experimenter acts on IV
- Changes in IV lead to changes in DV
- Changes in DV measured by experimenter

Experimental control

We come now to the most important principle of the experimental method: control. The IV is manipulated and the DV is free to vary. However, all other variables *must* be *controlled*, i.e. kept constant, so we can assume the only variable causing any subsequent change in the DV *must* be the IV. In our example, we would control all aspects of the situation (extraneous variables) other than acoustic similarity by making sure both types of word lists had words of the same length, frequency of occurrence in the language, and so on. Other factors we may need to control when using the experimental method are always using the same room for the experiment, keeping the temperature the same, and having the same lighting.

? What are the main obstacles to replication in research using human participants?

Extraneous variables

Variables that are *not* controlled may become **extraneous variables**. Such variables are not of interest to the researcher, but may get in the way of the link between the independent and dependent variable. For example, suppose we were interested in seeing whether people's ability to learn was impaired when the learning occurred under loud noise rather than no noise. Suppose we tested different participants at different times of day ranging between early morning and late evening. Time of day would be an extraneous variable because it is likely to affect the dependent variable (learning performance). This problem could be dealt with by running all participants at approximately the same time of day or ensuring that participants in the loud noise and no noise conditions were tested on average at the same time of day.

Confounding variables

It is of major importance when designing an experiment to avoid having any confounding variables. Confounding variables are variables that influence the dependent variable that are mistakenly manipulated along with the independent variable.

Let's consider a concrete example. Suppose we predicted that our participants would make more errors when recalling lists consisting of acoustically similar words than when recalling lists consisting of acoustically dissimilar words. Suppose also that the words used in the acoustically similar lists were much longer words than those used in the acoustically dissimilar lists. We wouldn't know whether the higher number of errors with acoustically similar lists than acoustically dissimilar lists was due to the independent variable (acoustic similarity vs dissimilarity) or the extraneous variable of word length (confounding variable). The presence of any extraneous variables is really serious, because they prevent us from being able to interpret our findings.

How do we avoid confounding variables? This can be done by carefully ensuring that any potential confounding variables are controlled. In terms of our example, there are two main possibilities. First, we could ensure that all words in both types of lists had the same word length so word length couldn't possibly explain any differences in learning. Second, we could vary word length randomly but make sure that on average word length was comparable with the two types of list. It is generally fairly easy to eliminate confounding variables when their presence is detected.

KEY TERM

Extraneous variables: variables other than the independent variable that are not controlled and may affect the dependent variable (measure of behaviour) and so prevent us from interpreting our findings.

Operationalisation of variables

Psychologists carry out studies to test hypotheses such as "Social pressure produces conformity" or "The orders of an authority figure produce obedience". However, there is no agreement on the best way to measure psychological concepts or variables such as "social pressure",

What might be an operational definition of fatigue, or hunger?

It might be said that the operational definition of "intelligence" is "that which is measured by intelligence tests". What is the main weakness of this definition?

"conformity", "authority figure", or "obedience". The most common approach is to make use of **operationalisation**—defining each variable of interest in terms of the operations taken to measure it. Such a definition is termed an operational definition.

Operational definitions can be used to operationalise independent variables (e.g. social pressure) and dependent variables (e.g. conformity). Consider Asch's research on conformity (see Chapter 2). He defined the independent variable of "social pressure" as the number of confederates unknown to the participants involved in making the same incorrect judgement on crucial trials. He defined the dependent variable of "conformity" as the percentage of trials on which the participants' public judgements on crucial trials agreed with the rest of the group even though their judgements were incorrect. Note that Asch could have defined "social pressure" as the number of friends or members of the participants' ingroup present and he could have defined "conformity" as participants' private judgements

Operationalisation is often used when researchers want to assess the effects of intelligence or personality on certain aspects of behaviour. For example, intelligence is generally operationalised by assuming that a given intelligence test provides an adequate measure of intelligence. In fact, however, it is improbable that any single test can capture all the richness of intelligence.

EVALUATION

Operationalisation generally provides a clear and fairly objective definition of most variables. For example, it is possible to provide operational definitions for a complex independent variable such as social pressure. In the absence of operationalisation, it would simply be impossible to carry out research on most topics in psychology.

There are various weaknesses associated with the use of operational definitions. First, operational definitions are circular and arbitrary. For example, conformity can be measured in several different ways and it is not obvious which measure is the "best".

Second, an operational definition typically covers only *part* of the meaning of the variable or concept. For example, conformity can reveal itself in terms of how participants feel about themselves as well as their responses on a task.

Third, we need to worry when the findings using one operational definition are very different from those using a different operational definition of the same variable. Such a difference indicates something is wrong, but it may be hard to discover exactly *what* is wrong.

Participants and settings

Proper use of the experimental method requires careful consideration of how participants are allocated to the various conditions. Suppose we found that participants learning in a quiet setting performed better than those learning in a noisy setting, but, by mistake, all the most intelligent participants were in the quiet condition and the least intelligent ones in the noise condition. We then wouldn't know whether the good performance in the quiet condition was due to quiet or to the cleverness of the participants. The main way of guarding against this possibility is by means of **randomisation**, in which participants are allocated at random. That helps to ensure there are no systematic differences between the participants in the various conditions.

Numerous studies are carried out using students as participants. This raises the issue of whether students are *representative* of society as a whole. For example, students tend to be more intelligent and much younger than most people. However, they are representative in the sense that about half of all students are male and half are female.

KEY TERMS

Operationalisation: defining all variables in such a way that it is easy to measure them.

Randomisation: the allocation of participants to conditions on a random basis, i.e. totally unbiased distribution.

Strengths of the experimental method applied to laboratory experiments

The greatest strength of the experimental method is that it allows us to establish causal (or cause-and-effect) relationships. The independent variable in an experiment is often regarded as a cause, and the dependent variable is the effect. We assume that, if *y* (e.g. many errors in recall) follows *x* (e.g. acoustically similar word list), then it is reasonable to infer that *x* caused *y*.

However, findings from studies based on the experimental method do *not* necessarily establish causality. Consider an imaginary study carried out in a hot country. Half the participants sleep in bedrooms with the windows open, and the other half sleep in bedrooms with the windows closed. More of those sleeping in bedrooms with the windows open catch malaria. Having the window open or closed is *relevant* to catching the disease, but it tells us nothing direct about the major causal factor in malaria (infected mosquitoes).

The other major strength of the experimental method is known as **replicability**. If an experiment has been carefully controlled, other researchers should be able to repeat or replicate the findings.

Note: Replicability is not on the AS-level specification.

Another strength of the experimental method is that it possesses high **internal validity**. That means that the experiment is valid in terms of the context in which in which it is carried out.

Replication is important to confirm an experimental result. If the result is "real", it should be possible to obtain the same result when you repeat the experiment. However, if it was a fluke, it isn't likely to be repeatable. Therefore, it is highly desirable in research to replicate a study using precisely the same techniques and conditions. If the conditions aren't the same, it could explain why the results differ. This may allow us to make sense of the inconsistent findings from studies following up on Hofling et al.'s (1966) study on nurses obeying doctors when they shouldn't (see page 41).

Then there is the issue of objectivity. The experimental method applied to laboratory experiments is more objective than other methods. However, total objectivity is impossible since the experimenter's interests, values, and judgements will always have some influence, and the control of all extraneous variables is impossible. Nevertheless, the experimental method offers the best chance of objectivity.

Limitations of the experimental method applied to laboratory experiments

The experimental method applied to laboratory experiments often lacks **ecological validity**, which is the extent to which experimental findings are applicable to everyday settings. The problem here was expressed in exaggerated terms by Heather (1976). He claimed the only thing learned from laboratory experiments is how people behave in laboratory experiments! One of the criteria for useful research is that it possesses high **external validity**, i.e. it has validity outside the research situation itself. Many laboratory experiments, because they lack ecological validity, also lack external validity.

ACTIVITY: Experiments

Construct a brief outline for each of the following:

- An experiment that should show high internal validity
- An experiment that will be unlikely to show high internal validity
- A experiment that is unlikely to show high external validity.

KEY TERMS

Replicability: the ability to repeat the methods used in a study and achieve the same findings.

Internal validity: the validity of an experiment in terms of the context in which it is carried out; concerns events within the experiment.

Ecological validity: the extent to which research findings can be generalised to naturally occurring situations.

External validity: the validity of an experiment outside the research situation itself; the extent to which the findings of a research study are applicable to other situations, especially "everyday" situations.

Mundane realism and experimental realism

Carlsmith et al. (1976) drew a distinction between **mundane realism** and **experimental realism** (see Chapter 6). Experimental realism (where participants are fooled that an artificial set-up is real) may be more important than mundane realism (where an artificial situation closely resembles a real-life situation) in producing findings that generalise to real-life situations. In practice, laboratory experiments often lack mundane realism *and* experimental realism.

? In what way have you altered your own natural behaviour when you were aware of being observed? Was this because you thought other people expected you to behave in a certain way or was there some other reason?

ACTIVITY: Mundane realism

Asch's famous line-matching experiment had experimental realism (see page 22). Discuss with a partner or in a small group how you could adapt the experiment to increase its mundane realism, and produce a list of your recommendations.

Other limitations of the experimental method applied to laboratory experiments are demand characteristics (the features of an experiment "inviting" participants to behave in certain predictable ways) and investigator effects (the investigator's expectations influence participants' behaviour). These issues are discussed at length later in the chapter.

A LABORATORY EXPERIMENT: Eyewitness testimony (see Chapter 3)

Loftus has run a large number of laboratory experiments looking at the factual accuracy of eyewitnesses' memory. Several of these involved participants looking at slides or film of car crashes. In one such experiment there were two conditions. Some participants were asked if they had seen any broken glass after the accident whereas others were asked if they had seen the broken glass. The only difference between the two groups was the wording, "any" or "the", with the latter suggesting the glass was there, thus being a leading question.

This type of experiment has been criticised as having low ecological validity and low mundane realism. Can you explain why this was a *laboratory* experiment, and exactly why it has those criticisms?

Laboratory experiments

Strengths:

- Establish cause-and-effect relationships
  - Allow the researcher to control the independent variable and the situation in which participants are tested
- Allow for replication
- Permit good control of extraneous and confounding variables
  - Good internal validity
  - Permit problems with demand characteristics and investigator effects to be reduced by the single-blind and double-blind technique, respectively (discussed later)

Limitations:

- Artificial
- Participants know they are being observed (demand characteristics)
  - Evaluation apprehension
  - Investigator effects (triggered by his/her expectations)
- Low mundane and experimental realism
- Lack ecological validity
  - Low in external validity

KEY TERMS

Mundane realism: the use of an artificial situation that closely resembles a natural situation.

Experimental realism: the use of an artificial situation in which participants become so involved they are fooled into thinking the set-up is real rather than artificial.

ACTIVITY: Laboratory experiments

To apply what you have learnt, find a study to illustrate each of the strengths and limitations of laboratory experiments (e.g. Asch's 1951, 1956 experiment has been replicated many times, thus showing it is reliable).

Field Experiments

Field experiments are carried out in natural settings such as in the street, in a school, or at work. Some field experiments (e.g. Hofling et al., 1966) have focused on obedience to authority (see page 41). Another example is a study by Shotland and Straw (1976). They arranged for a man and a woman to stage an argument and a fight close to several bystanders. In one condition, the woman screamed, "I don't know you!" In a second condition, she screamed, "I don't know why I ever married you!" When the bystanders thought the fight involved strangers, 65% of them intervened, against only 19% when they thought it involved a married couple. Thus, the experiment showed people were less likely to lend a helping hand when it was a "lovers' quarrel" than when it was not.

Field experiments, like laboratory experiments, involve direct control of the independent variable by the experimenter and also direct allocation of participants to conditions. Thus, causal relationships can be determined (provided the experiment is carried out carefully and extraneous variables are avoided!). Field experiments are also reasonably well controlled, which means they can be replicated.

Strengths of field experiments

What are the strengths of field experiments? First, the behaviour of the participants is often more *typical* of their normal behaviour and less artificial than in laboratory experiments. In other words, field experiments tend to have high ecological validity.

Second, it is often possible to establish cause-and-effect relations. This is the case because the researcher is able to control the independent variable.

Third, there is a low risk of problems with demand characteristics. This advantage stems from the participants' lack of awareness that their behaviour is being assessed by the researcher.

Limitations of field experiments

What are the limitations of field experiments? First, it is hard to eliminate extraneous variables in the field, because the researcher has much less control over the situation than under laboratory conditions. This can be a serious weakness that prevents the researcher from establishing cause-and-effect relations.

A FIELD EXPERIMENT: **Prejudice**

A study in 2001 found that people were less likely to help gays and lesbians compared to heterosexuals. Researchers telephoned over 200 British men and women at home and said it was a wrong number, but asked if the participant would make a call on to the caller's partner. This partner was of course a confederate, and was either same-sex or opposite-sex, to give the impression of a gay/lesbian or heterosexual partnership. The apparently heterosexual callers were most likely to receive the requested help, and the apparently gay men the least likely, with the apparently lesbian women in between.

Can you think what extraneous variables might have had an effect here in producing these findings?

KEY TERM

Field experiment: a study in which the experimental method is used in a more naturalistic situation.

Second, it is often hard (or impossible) to ensure participants are allocated at *random* to the various conditions. Consider, for example, the study by Shotland and Straw (1976; discussed above) in which bystanders were less likely to lend a helping hand when apparently witnessing a "lovers' quarrel" because it just happened that the bystanders in that condition generally had less helpful personalities.

Third, it is hard to obtain large amounts of very detailed information from participants. Field experiments are limited in this way because (1) it is generally not possible to introduce bulky equipment into a natural setting, and (2) the participants in a field experiment are likely to realise they are taking part in an experiment if attempts are made to obtain a lot of information from them.

Fourth, field experiments pose ethical issues. Most field experiments don't lend themselves to obtaining *informed consent* from the participants. For example, the study by Shotland and Straw (1976) would have been meaningless if the participants had been asked beforehand to give their consent to witnessing a staged quarrel! In addition, it isn't possible to offer the **right to withdraw**—participants who don't know they are taking part in an experiment can't be given the right to withdraw from it!

KEY TERMS

Right to withdraw: the basic right of participants in a research study to stop their involvement at any point, and to withdraw their results if they wish to do so.

Natural experiment: a type of experiment where use is made of some naturally occurring variable(s).

Field experiments

Strengths:

- Behaviour of participants more typical than in a laboratory experiment, high ecological validity
  - High external validity
- Establish cause-and-effect relationships
- Participants not aware they are being observed so low risk of demand characteristics

Limitations:

- Ethical issues, such as a lack of voluntary informed consent or right to withdraw
  - Low internal validity
- Typically, only partial control of the situation
  - Non-random assignment of participants to conditions
  - Only limited data can be obtained from each participant

ACTIVITY: Field experiments

To apply your knowledge of field experiments, describe a field study and clearly identify its advantages and limitations (e.g. Hofling et al., 1966).

Natural Experiments

Another form of experimental method involves using a naturally occurring event for research purposes. Such **natural experiments** don't qualify as genuine experiments. Use of the experimental method requires that the independent variable is *manipulated* by the experimenter.

Adams and Adams (1984) designed a natural experiment around the eruption of the Mount St Helens volcano in which they assessed the effects of stress on the population of a small town threatened by the eruption.

An example of a natural experiment is a study reported by Charlton (1998). It was based on the introduction of television to the island of St Helena, and was designed to see whether television causes violence. Its inhabitants received television for the first time in 1995 (the naturally occurring event), but there was no evidence of any negative effects on the children.

Another example of a natural experiment is one by Adams and Adams (1984) following the eruption of the Mount St Helens volcano in Northwest America in 1980. As the volcanic eruption had been predicted, Adams and Adams could assess the inhabitants of the small town of Othello before and after it happened. There was a 50% increase in mental health appointments, a 198% increase in stress-aggravated illness, and a 235% increase in diagnoses of mental illness after the eruption compared to beforehand.

A third example of a natural experiment is the study by Hodges and Tizard (1989; see page 151–152) on the long-term effects of privation in children taken into care when very young. Some of the children were adopted whereas others returned to their natural home. The decision about whether each child should be adopted or restored to his/her home was the naturally occurring event outside the control of the researchers. Contrary to what might have been expected, the adopted children on average showed better emotional adjustment than the restored children.

> ? What might be the practical uses of results such as those from the Mount St Helens study?

A NATURAL EXPERIMENT: Exam stress

So do you think exams are stressful? How would we test this? A natural experiment could ask for student volunteers to give blood samples 8 weeks before exams and again after the first exam. Analysis would give levels of the stress hormones adrenaline, noradrenaline, and cortisol.

- What would you expect to see happen? Can you write this as a hypothesis?
- Can you identify the IV, the variable that was changing naturally (because this would be a natural experiment)?
- And what would be the DV, the variable that the research team measured?

Strengths of natural experiments

What are the strengths of natural experiments? First, the participants in natural experiments are often not aware they are taking part in an experiment (even though they often know their behaviour is being observed), so they behave fairly naturally.

Second, natural experiments allow us to study the effects on behaviour of independent variables it would be unethical for the experimenter to manipulate. For example, consider the study by Hodges and Tizard (1989). No ethical committee would have allowed children to be taken into care and then either adopted or restored to their natural home to satisfy the researchers' requirements. It would also have been unethical for an experimenter to deliberately expose people to a very stressful situation like the Mount St Helens volcanic eruption.

Third, natural experiments are generally high in ecological validity. This is the case because natural experiments involve observing behaviour under real-life conditions. Thus, they tend also to be high in external validity.

> ? Natural experiments are such a good way of doing research, so why are so few actually done?

Limitations of natural experiments

What are the limitations of natural experiments? First, the participants aren't assigned at random to conditions. As a result, observed differences in behaviour between groups may be due to differences in the types of participants in the groups rather than to the effects of the independent variable. For example, in the study by Hodges and Tizard (1989; Chapter 3), the children who were adopted were *initially* better adjusted than the children who were restored to their natural home. Thus, the finding that the adopted children subsequently showed better emotional adjustment than the restored children may be due to their personality or early experiences rather than to the fact that they were adopted.

Second, the researcher doesn't have control over the situation. As a result, there may be extraneous variables that make it hard or impossible to decide whether the natural event was responsible for the findings. For example, the introduction of television into St Helena may have coincided with other changes in that society that helped to prevent television from having negative effects on the children.

Third, and linked to the second point, the lack of control over the situation often means that it isn't possible to establish cause-and-effect relations.

Natural experiments

Strengths	Limitations
• Participants behave naturally • Investigate the effects of independent variables that it would be unethical to manipulate • High in ecological validity — High in external validity	• IV not directly manipulated • Participants not allocated at random to conditions • Difficult to identify what aspects of the independent variable have caused the effects on behaviour • Not possible to establish cause and effect — Low in internal validity

Quasi-experiments

Quasi-experiments often resemble proper laboratory or field experiments (*quasi* means almost). However, there is one important difference—the experimenter does not directly manipulate the independent variable. That means there is a resemblance between quasi-experiments and natural experiments. However, the two differ in that quasi-experiments are typically carefully planned whereas natural experiments are not.

Numerous quasi-experiments have been carried out over the years. For example, suppose we want to compare the performance of men and women on some task or explore the differences in behaviour between extraverts and introverts. The experimenter can't randomly assign participants to the male or female group nor can he/she use random allocation when forming the extraverted and introverted groups.

The fact that the experimenter can't randomly allocate participants to conditions means we can't establish causality with quasi-experiments. Suppose, for example, that we find that women perform some task better than men. There are various possible interpretations of such a finding—it could be a genuine gender difference, it might be that the female participants are more intelligent than the male ones, or it might be that the task is of more interest to women than to men.

Quasi-experiments

Strengths

- Allow for replication
  - Reasonable control of extraneous variables
  - High in external validity

Limitations

- IV not directly manipulated
- Participants not allocated at random to conditions
- Not possible to establish cause and effect
- Low in internal validity

CORRELATIONS

? When would one have to use a correlational design?

KEY TERMS

Quasi-experiments: research that is similar to an experiment but certain key features are lacking, such as the direct manipulation of the independent variable by the experimenter and random allocation of participants to conditions.

Co-variables: the variables involved in a correlational study that may vary together (co-vary).

Correlation: an association that is found between two variables.

The essence of the correlational approach is that it involves the assessment of the relationship between two variables (known as **co-variables**) obtained from the same individuals. For example, we could test the hypothesis that watching violence on television leads to aggressive behaviour by obtaining information from a number of people about: (1) the amount of violent television they watched (one variable), and (2) the extent to which they behaved aggressively in various situations (second variable).

If the above hypothesis is correct, those who have seen the most violence on television would tend to be the most aggressive. In other words, this study would be looking for a **correlation**, or association, between watching violent programmes and being aggressive. The closer the link between them, the greater would be the correlation or association.

Another example based on the correlational approach is the finding that the more serious life events (e.g. divorce; illness) an individual has experienced the more likely they are to develop depression (Chapter 7, page 299). It is possible that life events help to cause depression but it is also possible that individuals who are somewhat depressed anyway may experience more life events due to their depressed state.

The two examples we have discussed both involve focusing on positive correlations. In a positive correlation, as scores on one variable increase so do scores on the other variable. There are also negative correlations. With negative correlations as scores on one variable increase, scores on the other variable decrease.

There is more on the presentation of correlational information in the section on scattergrams (see page 378). There you can see examples of positive and negative correlations.

A CORRELATIONAL ANALYSIS: **Television violence and aggressive behaviour**

Positive correlations between hours of television violence watched and actual aggressive behaviour for children and adolescents are shown by the majority of correlational analyses on this topic. Such research has been done in many countries including Poland, the UK, Finland, Australia, and the USA. But does this mean that watching violence on TV actually causes people to become more hostile in their behaviour? One important point is that correlations cannot be used to infer cause and effect, because they merely show a link that may, or may not, be causal. For example, it is possible that people who are naturally more aggressive prefer to watch violent programmes, as they find them more enjoyable, more exciting. And another point in this research area is that although studying in a wide range of countries seems to have allowed for cultural relativism, in fact, these are all Western industrialised types of culture and so there may be cross-cultural differences that have not been demonstrated.

How do correlational studies differ from experiments?

There are several major differences between correlational studies and experiments. First, and most importantly, in experiments the researcher manipulates an independent variable to observe its effect on a dependent variable (e.g. aspect of behaviour). In contrast, in correlational studies we basically obtain two dependent variables from each participant.

Second, it follows from the first point that we can't establish causality—if the two dependent variables correlate, we don't know the direction of causality or even whether there is any causal link at all between them.

Third, in most correlational studies, there is no attempt to assess the behaviour of the participants under controlled conditions. Instead, the participants' behaviour is assessed using questionnaires or other measures not obtained under laboratory conditions.

Fourth, we can study a wider range of variables with correlational studies than with experiments. For example, we can't manipulate the number of life events experienced by a given participant under laboratory conditions but we can assess it via questionnaire in a correlational study.

Strengths of correlational studies

What are the strengths of correlational methods? First, correlational methods allow us to see there is a relationship between two variables. This doesn't *prove* that one variable is causing the other, but is a very useful starting point for further research.

Second, many hypotheses can't be examined directly by means of experimental designs. For example, the hypothesis that life events cause various physical diseases can't be tested by forcing some people to experience lots of negative events! All we can do is examine correlations or associations between the number and severity of negative life events and the probability of suffering from various diseases.

Third, we can obtain large amounts of data on a number of variables in a correlational study much more rapidly and efficiently than using experimental designs. For example, **questionnaires** permit researchers to study the associations between aggressive behaviour and numerous activities (such as watching violent films in the cinema, reading violent books, being frustrated at work or at home).

Fourth, correlational research *can* produce reasonably definite information about causal relationships if there is *no* association between the two co-variables. For example, if there were

KEY TERM

Questionnaire: a survey requiring written answers.

no association at all between serious life events and depression, this would suggest that depression is *not* caused by serious life events.

Fifth, **correlational analysis** is used in prediction. If you find that two variables are correlated, you can predict one from another. It is also a useful method when manipulation of variables is impossible.

Limitations of correlational studies

What are the limitations of correlational studies? First, and most importantly, correlational designs make it hard (or impossible) to establish cause and effect. In our first example, the existence of an association between the amount of television violence watched and aggressive behaviour would be consistent with the hypothesis that watching violent programmes can *cause* aggressive behaviour. However, it could equally be that aggressive individuals may choose to watch more violent programmes than those who are less aggressive, in other words the causality operates in the other direction. Or there is a third variable accounting for the association between watching violent programmes and aggressive behaviour, e.g. people in disadvantaged families may watch more television and their deprived circumstances may also cause them to behave aggressively. If that were the case, then the number of violent television programmes watched might have no direct effect at all on aggressive behaviour.

Correlation or causation?

Second, and linked to the first point, researchers don't control or manipulate any aspect of the situation with correlational studies. This is the main reason why it is so hard to interpret the findings that emerge from such studies.

Third, correlations are limited in what they tell us about the relationship between two variables. More specifically, they assess linear relationships in which there is a simple linear (straight) relationship between two variables. In the real world, however, there are often more complex relationships but these aren't identified by correlations. For example, consider the relationship between weight and physical health. Physical health is relatively poor among those who are severely underweight or overweight and highest in those of intermediate weight. This inverted-U or curvilinear relationship between weight and physical health can't be assessed using simple correlations.

Correlational studies

Strengths

- Allow us to see that there is a relationship between two variables
- Allow study of hypotheses that cannot be examined directly
- More data on more variables can be collected more quickly than in an experimental set-up
- Problems of interpretation are reduced when no association is found

Limitations

- Cause and effect cannot be established
- Interpretation of results is difficult
- Direction of causality is uncertain
- Variables other than the one of interest may be operating

KEY TERM

Correlational analysis: testing a hypothesis using an association that is found between two variables.

ACTIVITY: Correlational studies

To apply what you have learnt, consider a correlational study that looks at the relationship between life events and depression. With reference to this study identify the strengths and limitations as outlined above.

OBSERVATIONAL TECHNIQUES

Behaviour is observed in virtually every psychological study. For example, in Milgram's (1963; see Chapter 2) research on obedience to authority, a film record was made of the participants' behaviour so their emotional states could be observed. However, we will consider studies in which **observational techniques** are of central importance.

There are several observational techniques (Coolican, 2004). Researchers wishing to carry out an observational study have to make various decisions concerning precisely how they are going to do this. Here are the main contrasts between types of observational study:

1. **Controlled observation vs naturalistic observation**: the researcher exercises control over the environment in which the observations are made with controlled observation. In contrast, the naturalistic observation involves observation of participants in natural situations without any direct intervention from the researcher/observer.
2. **Covert vs overt observation**: the participants are unaware they are being watched and their behaviour recorded with covert observation. In contrast, they are aware of being watched with overt observation.
3. **Participant vs non-participant observation**: with participant observation, the observer is directly involved in the interactions of the participants, who are typically group members. In contrast, the observer is *not* directly involved in group activities and interactions with other participants with non-participant observation.

What are the limitations of covert vs overt observation? The main limitation with participants knowing they are being observed (overt observation) is that this knowledge may very well influence their behaviour. For example, Zegoib et al. (1975) found that mothers who knew they were observed interacted more with their children and behaved more warmly towards them than did mothers who didn't know. The main limitation with participants not knowing they are being observed (covert observation) is that it is regarded as unethical for participants not to give full informed consent to their involvement in a study.

Controlled observation

Many studies (especially in developmental psychology) involve controlled observations using situations subject to at least some experimental control. For example, Ainsworth and Bell (1970; see Chapter 4) carried out a laboratory study in which infants were observed as they responded to a carefully organised sequence of events involving the mother/caregiver leaving the infant and returning. These observations were used to categorise the infants' behaviour in terms of attachment style.

Strengths of controlled observations

What are the advantages of controlled observations? First, controlled observations are often used in the context of a laboratory experiment. In principle, this can provide the positive features of the experimental method (e.g. possibility to infer cause-and-effect relationships) together with detailed observational information.

Second, if the situation is well controlled, there is less risk of unwanted extraneous variables influencing participants' behaviour than is the case with naturalistic or participant observations. This is important because it increases the researcher's ability to interpret his/her findings.

Third, richer and more complete information is often obtained from studies using controlled observations than from conventional experimental studies in which participants are only required to produce limited responses.

Limitations of controlled observations

The method of controlled observations has various limitations. First, carrying out studies in artificial situations (e.g. laboratories) can influence the participants' behaviour. This may be especially the case with young children who can become anxious in a strange environment.

KEY TERMS

Observational techniques: those research techniques that involve observing behaviour, covertly or openly or as a participant in the activity.

Controlled observations: observations in which the researcher exercises control over some aspects of the environment in which the observations are made.

Naturalistic observation: unobtrusive observations from a study conducted in a natural setting.

Covert observation: the participants are not aware they are being watched and their behaviour recorded by the observer.

Overt observation: the participants are aware they are being watched and their behaviour recorded by the observer.

Participant observation: observations in natural situations where the observer interacts directly with the participants.

Non-participant observation: observations in natural situations where the observer does not interact directly with the participants.

Second, the artificiality of the situation may make it hard to generalise the findings to more natural situations. In other words, the research may lack ecological validity.

Third, there can be problems with controlled observations when participants know their behaviour is being observed. These problems include investigator effects (due to experimenter expectations) and demand characteristics (due to participant expectations).

A CONTROLLED OBSERVATION: **Attachment and cuddly toys**

Toddlers' attachment to their cuddly toys was investigated in an observational study. Their mothers were asked about each child's favourite toys. Then, with their mothers nearby, the toddlers were assessed under varying levels of situational stressfulness, and the preferred toys in each situation were noted. As expected, the children's preference for familiar toys increased as the stressfulness of their situation increased.

What do you think of the ethics of such experiments? What precautions would you take to make sure the participants were always well looked after?

Naturalistic observation

Naturalistic observation involves methods designed to examine behaviour in natural situations *without* the experimenter interfering. This approach was developed by ethologists such as Lorenz. They studied non-human species in their natural habitat and discovered much about the animals' behaviour.

An example of the use of naturalistic observation in human research is an attachment study by Anderson (1972). He observed children in a London park and noticed it was very unusual to see a child under the age of 3 wandering more than 200 feet from his/her mother before returning.

Naturalistic observation was also used by Schaffer and Emerson (1964), who carried out a **longitudinal** observational study on children (see page 118–119). They found children differed considerably in their attachment behaviour. However, most children develop fairly strong attachments to one or more adults during early childhood.

? What advantages might be gained by observing children in a naturalistic environment rather than in a laboratory?

A NATURALISTIC OBSERVATION: **Social behaviour**

A lot of research puts people into unusual settings or situations where we cannot be sure we are seeing real-life behaviour. This is a justification for doing naturalistic observations, seeing natural everyday behaviour. It is also a strategy for some very sensitive research areas. For example, social behaviours of preschool children who have a history of abuse can be observed and compared with those of children with no such history. The results of these observations of children at play have shown that the abused children made fewer social interactions, were more withdrawn, and when they did interact they used more negative behaviours such as aggression, compared to the other group.

How would you decide what counted as negative behaviours, as aggression? How would you set up your behavioural categories so that you could use several observers yet have reliable data?

What factors or issues might cause difficulties in observing people like this?

KEY TERMS

Longitudinal: over an extended period of time, especially with reference to studies.

Evaluation apprehension: concern felt by research participants that their performance is being judged.

Strengths of naturalistic observations

Here are the main strengths of naturalistic observations. First, if the participants are unaware that they are being observed, this method provides a way of observing people behaving naturally. This removes problems from demand characteristics (guessing what the experiment is about) or **evaluation apprehension** (seeking the approval of the researcher).

Second, many studies based on naturalistic observations provide richer and fuller information than typical laboratory experiments. For example, Schaffer and Emerson's (1964) naturalistic observations on attachment behaviour in children can be compared with Ainsworth and Bell's (1970) structural observation research (see Chapter 4). Schaffer and Emerson's approach allowed them to show that young children often form multiple important attachments, an important finding not considered by Ainsworth and Bell.

Third, the fact that people's behaviour is being observed in real-life situations means that it is likely that the findings will have ecological validity.

Fourth, it is sometimes possible to use naturalistic observation when other methods can't be used (when participants can't be disrupted at work). Naturalistic observation may work better than other methods with children and non-human animals.

? How can an experiment tell us more about "why" a behaviour has occurred than an observational study can?

Limitations of naturalistic observations

Here are the most important limitations of naturalistic observations. First, the experimenter has essentially no control over the situation. This means there may be extraneous variables involved, which makes it very hard (or impossible) to decide what caused the participants to behave as they did. Second, the participants are often aware they are being observed and so their behaviour isn't natural. Note, however, that this is also true of most other kinds of research.

Third, there can be problems of replication with studies using naturalistic observation. For example, consider naturalistic observations carried out in schools. There are enormous differences among schools, and this is likely to produce large differences in observational data across schools.

Fourth, naturalistic observations pose ethical issues if the participants don't realise their behaviour is being observed (**undisclosed observation**). This can happen if one-way mirrors are used or participants are observed in public places and voluntary informed consent isn't obtained.

Naturalistic observation, for example, observing children's behaviour in a playground, can provide more extensive information than a laboratory study. However, the participants' behaviour may alter if they are aware that they are being observed.

ACTIVITY: Naturalistic observation

This could be done in small groups. People often assume that boys' play is rougher than girls' play. This is a casual observation, but you could devise a hypothesis from it, then operationalise this. How would you do your observations, and how would you ensure inter-observer reliability (agreement among observers)? What behavioural categories would you use? What might be problems in doing this naturalistic observation? One person should act as the recorder and make a list of what the group says, and this could then be shared with other groups.

Participant observation

The extent of the observer's participation in the participants' activities can vary enormously. At one extreme, the observer may not disclose his/her research role in order to be accepted as a fully-fledged member of the group. At the other extreme, the observer may fully disclose his/her role and act primarily as an observer in his/her dealing with the group.

KEY TERM

Undisclosed observation: an observational study where the participants have not been informed that it is taking place.

We will discuss very briefly two studies involving participant observations. Whyte (1943) joined an Italian street gang in Chicago, and became a participant observer. He didn't indicate he was a researcher, but simply said he was writing a book about the area. The problem he encountered in interpreting his observations was that his presence in the gang influenced their behaviour. One gang member expressed this point as follows: "You've slowed me down plenty since you've been down here. Now, when I do something, I have to think what Bill Whyte would want me to know about it and how I can explain it."

Try to fit in as a member of the group and remain detached as an observer.

Festinger et al. (1956) became participant observers by joining a religious sect that believed the world was about to come to an end. When the world didn't end on the day the sect members thought it would, their leader argued they had saved the world through their faith. The participant observers didn't reveal to the sect members that they were researchers and the sect members didn't suspect anything.

A PARTICIPANT OBSERVATION: **Football**

Football fans—are they supporters or are they hooligans? Much of what is reported in the media might suggest the latter, but when Marsh (Marsh et al., 1996) joined supporters' clubs and attended games to do his participant observations he found that there was a clear social order among the fans, and an understood set of social norms about what behaviours were and were not acceptable. For example, aggressive chants and gestures were acceptable, but actual violent contact was not. These findings did not apply to a minority who attended games not for the actual football but for opportunities to fight, but Marsh focused on the vast majority of genuine supporters.

Do you think it is ethically acceptable to join an organisation in order to observe people without their consent? Why do some researchers do this, and what problems might arise if consent was sought?

Strengths of participant observations

Here are some of the main advantages of participant observations. First, studies involving such observations are generally high in ecological validity because groups are observed in real-life settings. Second, some studies using participant observations (e.g. Whyte's, 1943, study of an Italian street gang) are long-lasting, which helps to ensure that detailed and rich information is obtained.

Third, in studies such as those of Whyte (1943) and Festinger et al. (1956), it would have been extremely difficult for useful research to have been carried out by researchers who didn't join the street gang or the religious sect, respectively.

Fourth, it is often easy to interpret the participants' behaviour because it has been observed over long periods of time in various situations. The direct involvement of the researchers in the group means that they are likely to develop a deep understanding of the motives and behaviour of those being observed.

? What ethical issues would you flag up for participant observation research? And what issue of validity could there be?

? Sometimes it is not possible to write field notes as events are happening. What does memory research tell us about the usefulness and accuracy of notes written after the event?

Limitations of participant observations

There are various limitations with the use of participant observations. First, there are ethical problems about researchers deceiving the members of groups in order to join them. There is an obvious failure to obtain fully informed consent from group members.

Second, the presence of a participant observer can change and distort the behaviour of group members. This is shown in the quotation above from Whyte's (1943) study. This is an example of an investigator effect.

Third, there can be real problems concerning the accuracy and objectivity of the reports produced by participant observers. Participant observers who have not disclosed their research role generally write down what happened sometime after any given event so as not to arouse suspicion. In addition, if participant observers become involved with the group they are observing, this may bias their reports.

Non-participant observation

What are the strengths of non-participant observation, in which the researcher/observer is not directly involved in the participants' interactions? First, it can have high ecological validity provided that the study is carried out under naturalistic conditions. Second, it has the advantage over participant observation that the genuine participants' behaviour will not be affected by the researcher, thus avoiding investigator effects. Third, it also has the advantage over participant observation that the researcher's observations are less likely to be distorted because they are more detached from the group being observed.

What are the limitations of non-participant observation? First, it is typically harder for the researcher to make detailed observations of a group over a long period of time if he/she is somewhat detached from it than is the case with participant observation. Second, another disadvantage of non-participant observation compared to participant observation is that the observer's detachment may mean he/she finds it difficult to interpret the group's behaviour adequately. Third, the real participants may become suspicious if they realise that they are being watched over long periods of time by the observer.

SELF-REPORT TECHNIQUES INCLUDING INTERVIEW AND QUESTIONNAIRE

Non-psychologists often think the best way to understand others' behaviour is by asking them about it. This can be done in various ways including the use of interview and questionnaire techniques. Of course, much of value can be learned in this way, but there are two major problems with **self-report techniques**:

1. Most people want to create a favourable opinion of themselves and this may lead them to distort their answers to personal questions.
2. Many people don't understand themselves very well, and so their self-reports may not be very informative.

Interview techniques

Interviews come in many different shapes and sizes. They differ in terms of the amount of structure built into the interview and the types of questions asked. **Structured interviews** are those in which the interviewer asks the same questions to all interviewees and also exerts some control over the types of answers interviewees produce (e.g. short answers vs detailed answers). In contrast, **unstructured interviews** involve little control from the interviewer—the questions vary from interviewee to interviewee and the interviewee is relatively free to say whatever he/she wants.

Interviews do not have to be totally structured or unstructured. In fact, many interviews are semi-structured. What that means is that all interviewees are asked similar (but not identical) questions, with the precise choice of questions being partly determined by the answers given by the interviewee.

? Have you ever been interviewed while out shopping? How would you classify this interview style?

ACTIVITY: Interview technique

Divide the class into small groups and ask each group to prepare one kind of interview technique. They should present a short demonstration to the class. Which ones worked best? What problems arose? Which would be the best ways to collect data?

KEY TERMS

Self-report techniques: participants provide their own account of themselves, usually by means of questionnaires, surveys, or interviews.

Interview: a verbal research method in which the participant answers a series of questions.

Structured interview: all interviewees are asked the same questions in the same order and the interviewee is required to produce certain types of answers (e.g. short vs detailed).

Unstructured interview: the questions asked by the interviewer and the order in which they are asked vary from interviewee to interviewee; in addition, the interviewee chooses how to answer each question.

Strengths of interviews

The precise strengths of interviews depend on the type of interview. Unstructured interviews can produce very rich and personal information from the person being interviewed. It could be argued that this is often the case when therapists interview clients to assess their experiences and emotions. Most experimental studies focus on a very narrow aspect of behaviour, but unstructured interviews can range over a large number of topics within a manageable period of time.

Structured interviews can *compare* the responses of different interviewees, all of whom have been asked the same questions. Another advantage is good *reliability*, in that two different interviewers are likely to obtain similar responses from an interviewee when they ask exactly the same questions in the same order. In addition, there is a reasonable chance of being able to replicate the findings in another study. Finally, it is usually fairly easy to analyse the data obtained from structured interviews because the data tend to be in numerical form.

Limitations of interviews

Unstructured interviews have a problem with the unsystematic variation of information obtained from different interviewees, making the data hard to analyse. Another weakness is that what the interviewee says is determined in a complex way by the *interaction* between him/her and the interviewer. For example, the gender, age, and personality of the interviewer may influence the course of the interview, making it hard to work out which of the interviewee's contributions are affected by the interviewer. Such influences are known as **interviewer bias**. Finally, the fact that the information obtained from interviewees is influenced by the interviewer means that the data obtained can be regarded as unreliable.

In structured interviews, what the interviewee says may be somewhat constrained and artificial because of the high level of structure built into the interview. Interviewees may find this off-putting, and it may lead them to give short, formal answers. In addition, there is none of the flexibility associated with unstructured interviews. That can be a major limitation. Suppose, for example, the interviewee says something dramatic and unexpected in answer to a question. The interviewer might feel it important to ask more questions about the interviewee's answer but he/she is prevented by the requirement to use a fixed set of questions. Finally, the fact that the interviewer asks different questions to each interviewee makes it hard to *compare* the responses provided by different interviewees.

? How would research results be affected by the possibility that people might decide to give the socially acceptable response to statements such as "Smacking children is an appropriate form of punishment"?

Three weaknesses are common to both types of interview (with the first two also being common to most questionnaires). First, there is the issue of **social desirability bias** due to the fact that most people want to convey a positive impression of themselves. For example, people are much more willing to admit they are unhappy when filling in a questionnaire anonymously than when being interviewed (Eysenck, 1990).

Second, we can only extract information of which the interviewee is consciously aware. This is a significant weakness, because people are often unaware of the reasons why they behave in certain ways (Nisbett & Wilson, 1977).

Third, many interviewers lack some of the skills necessary to conduct interviews successfully. Good interviewers can make an interview seem natural, are sensitive to non-verbal cues, and have well-developed listening skills (Coolican, 2004).

AN INTERVIEW: Gender stereotypes

We are all familiar with gender stereotypes, but when do we start learning this type of social norm? One study showed that 5-year-old children in the USA already have well-established gender stereotypes. These children were read short stories in which the main character was described by "masculine" adjectives (e.g. tough, forceful) or "female" ones (e.g. emotional, excitable). Then each child was interviewed and asked about whether the characters were male or female. Almost all of the children were clear which sex the character belonged to.

If you were going to replicate this study what would you do as a pilot study, and why would you be doing one?

KEY TERMS

Interviewer bias: the effects of an interviewer's expectations on the responses made by an interviewee.

Social desirability bias: the tendency to describe oneself in a more positive and socially desirable way than is actually the case.

Questionnaire techniques

What happens with use of questionnaire techniques is that participants are given a set of questions together with instructions about how to record their answers. In principle, questionnaires can be used to explore an almost endless range of issues. In practice, however, most questionnaires focus on an individual's personality or his/her attitudes and beliefs.

The types of items found in questionnaires can vary considerably. At one extreme, there are closed questions which require respondents to select from a small number of choices (e.g.

"Yes" or "No"). At the other extreme, there are open questions which give respondents great flexibility in their responses.

Most questionnaires use closed items. Such items are easier to score and tend to produce more reliable or consistent data. However, open items have their own advantages. For example, they are more realistic, in that in everyday life we can generally answer questions in our own way, and they produce richer information than closed questions.

As is discussed later in the chapter, it is harder to produce good questionnaires than might be imagined. Coolican (2004) identifies the following common mistakes that plague questionnaire construction:

- *Complexity:* the item is difficult to understand.
- *Ambiguity:* the item can be interpreted in more than one way.
- *Double-barrelled items:* the item effectively contains two questions but the respondent must give an overall "Yes" or "No" response. For example, "Global warming is definitely happening and huge resources should be put into doing something about it."
- *Leading questions:* the item contains within it the implication that a certain response is expected. For example, "Don't you think that this government is discredited?"

? Think back to what you learned about eyewitness testimony. How might Loftus' work relate to researching by asking questions? What would researchers have to be very careful about in forming questions for the interview?

Strengths of questionnaires

One of the main strengths of questionnaires is that large amounts of data can be collected rapidly at relatively little cost.

Second, we can explore almost any aspect of personality and any attitudes or beliefs using questionnaires. Thus, questionnaire techniques are very versatile.

Third, many questionnaires have high reliability or consistency and reasonable validity. For example, there is a fairly strong relationship between people's attitudes towards major political parties and their actual voting behaviour (Franzoi, 1996). High reliability is more common with closed questions than with open ones.

Fourth, open items have the advantage that they can be a rich source of information about the interviewee. Such items allow the interviewee to answer questions in their preferred way.

Limitations of questionnaires

Questionnaires possess various weaknesses. First, people may be inclined to pretend that their personalities and their attitudes are more desirable than they actually are—social desirability bias.

Second, people may lack conscious awareness of their true personality and attitudes. You must have met people who have little or no idea of the impact they have on others.

Third, many questionnaires are poorly constructed and so lack reliability or consistency and validity. Problems of reliability are especially likely with open-ended items. It is also hard with open-ended items to make coherent sense of the very diverse answers provided by different participants.

People adjust what they say to fit the circumstances.

A QUESTIONNAIRE: Different smells

We know that even though our sense of smell isn't good scents still are important, especially when they trigger memories. One research study looked at memories of a visit to the Jorvik Viking Centre in York where different smells, e.g. of a fish market, are part of the experience. Participants had visited the centre some years before, and were given the questionnaire about that experience with or without a selection of bottled smells from the centre. The findings showed much better recall with the smells than without them, supporting the idea that these smells acted as memory cues.

How do you think you would find participants for this sort of investigation? What are the strengths and limitations of your chosen sampling method?

Fourth, the use of fixed-choice or closed questions is rather artificial. People often find it hard to answer a complex question with "yes" or "no". The limited data obtained from such questions can mean that relatively little is discovered about an individual's personality or beliefs.

Fifth, participants may need to have high literacy skills to understand the precise meaning of the items on a questionnaire.

Interviews and questionnaires

Strengths:

- Unstructured interviews can be more revealing
- Structured interviews permit comparison between interviewees and facilitate replication
- Questionnaires allow for collection of large amounts of data

Limitations:

- Interviewer bias
- Social desirability bias
- People don't always know what they think
- Good interviewing requires skill

Section Summary

Research methods

- Much research is scientific. The scientific method involves:
  - making observations;
  - formulating theories that generate hypotheses;
  - testing the hypotheses by designing research, then collecting data, and finally revising the theory in line with the new data.

Experimental method: Laboratory experiments

- The key principle of the experimental method is that an independent variable is manipulated (with all extraneous and confounding variables controlled) to observe its effect on a dependent variable.
- Operationalisation of variables involves defining the independent and dependent variables in terms of the operations taken to measure them.
- Participants should be randomly allocated to conditions to ensure there are no systematic differences between participants in the various conditions.
- Use of the experimental method often (but by no means always) allows us to infer causality, and it aims to be replicable.
- Laboratory experiments often lack ecological validity and are low in external validity. They can be artificial.

Field experiments

- Field experiments are carried out in natural settings (e.g. in the street; in a school; at work).
- Strengths of field experiments:
  - Field experiments are less artificial than laboratory experiments.
  - They suffer less from factors such as demand characteristics and evaluation apprehension.
- Limitations of field experiments:
  - They are less controlled.
  - They create ethical problems in terms of lack of informed consent.

Natural experiments

- Natural experiments resemble experiments but involve some naturally occurring independent variable rather than an independent variable under the control of the researcher.
- Strengths of natural experiments:
  - One advantage of natural experiments is that participants are unaware they are taking part in an experiment, which prevents demand characteristics.
  - Natural experiments also permit the study of variables that couldn't ethically be manipulated by an experimenter.
- Limitations of natural experiments:
  - These include problems of interpreting the findings due to a lack of randomisation.
  - There is also an ethical concern about taking advantage of people at a time of possible high stress.
  - The presence of extraneous variables limits the ability to interpret the findings and it is hard to show cause-and-effect relations.

Quasi-experiments

- Quasi-experiments resemble natural experiments in that there is no direct control over the independent variable.
- Quasi-experiments differ from natural experiments in that the research involves more planning than is possible with natural experiments. In addition, quasi-experiments often look at the effects of personal characteristics (e.g. gender; personality) on behaviour.

Correlations

- Strengths of correlational analysis:
  - Many issues can only be studied by assessing correlations or associations between variables.
  - Correlational studies determine the extent that co-variables vary together, and offer the possibility of obtaining large amounts of data very rapidly.
- Limitations of correlational analysis:
  - Investigations using correlational analysis are less useful than experimental designs, because they don't permit inferences about causality.
  - Variables other than the one of interest may explain positive and negative correlations.

Observational techniques

- It is important in observational studies to use unambiguous behavioural categories for recording participants' behaviour.
- There is an important distinction between controlled and naturalistic observation—the former involves the researcher controlling the situation whereas the latter involves observation in natural situations with no direct intervention from the researcher.
- Participants' behaviour is more natural if they are unaware of being observed (covert observation) than if they know they are being observed (overt observation), but this raises ethical issues due to lack of informed consent.

- Strengths of controlled observations are:
  - Use of the experimental method sometimes permits inferences about cause and effect.
  - There is a reduced risk of extraneous variables compared to other types of observational study.
- Limitations of controlled observation are:
  - Use of artificial situations can reduce generalisability.
  - There can be investigator effects and demand characteristics.
- Naturalistic observation occurs in natural situations without any interference from the researcher. Strengths of naturalistic observation are:
  - They provide a way of observing people behaving naturally.
  - They provide rich and full information about behaviour.
- Limitations of naturalistic observations are:
  - The researcher has no control over the situation.
  - There can be problems of replication.
- Participant observation occurs in natural situations with the observer being more or less actively involved whereas in non-participant observation the observer is not actively involved. Advantages of participant observations are:
  - There is flexibility in terms of the observer's involvement.
  - Participant observation is the most effective way of studying the behaviour of certain groups (e.g. street gangs).
- Limitations of participant observations are:
  - The presence of the participant observer distorts the behaviour of the group members.
  - The reports produced by participant observers are sometimes inaccurate and lacking in objectivity.
- Non-participant observation is where the observer is not directly involved in the activities of the group being observed. Strengths of non-participant observation are:
  - Findings are unlikely to be distorted because the observer is somewhat detached from those being observed and there are no investigator effects.
- Limitations of non-participant observation are that the researcher may be too detached to understand fully the behaviour of those being observed and it can be hard for a researcher to observe a group over a long period of time without attracting attention and suspicion.

Self-report techniques

- There are several types of interview ranging from the unstructured to the fully structured.
- Unstructured interviews:
  - These are responsive to the personality, interests, and motivations of the interviewee and so tend to produce full information.
  - However, the data obtained tend to be unreliable.
- Structured interviews:
  - Structured interviews permit comparisons among interviewees, and they tend to be fairly reliable.
  - However, what the interviewee says can be constrained and artificial, and the data tend to be more quantitative.
- Questionnaire techniques involve presenting respondents with a set of closed or open questions or items.
- Closed questions are more reliable but open ones are more realistic.
- Strengths of questionnaires:
  - They are inexpensive and involve the rapid collection of much data.
  - Many questionnaires have good reliability and reasonable validity.
- Limitations of questionnaires:
  - Questionnaires can produce problems due to social desirability bias, and those completing questionnaires can only provide information of which they are consciously aware.
- Questionnaire techniques are mostly used in correlational studies, and so causal inferences cannot be drawn.

SCIENTIFIC PROCESSES

In order to carry out a study successfully, care and attention must be devoted to each stage in its design and implementation. This section is concerned with these issues. We will focus mainly on *experimental designs,* although many of the same issues also apply to non-experimental designs. As we will see, several decisions need to be made when designing an experimental study.

Common sense recommends a quiet rather than a noisy place for study—but to test the hypothesis that noise interferes with learning requires an experimental design.

Aims and hypotheses

The first step when designing a study is to decide on the **aims** and **hypotheses** of the study. The aims are usually more *general* than the hypotheses. They help to explain the reasons for the investigator deciding to test some specific hypothesis or hypotheses. Thus, the aims tell us *why* a given study is being carried out, whereas the hypotheses tell us *what* the study is designed to test. Typically, researchers start with the aims and then translate those aims into specific hypotheses.

As an example, suppose we had the aim of discovering which components of the working memory system are involved in playing chess (see Chapter 3). We could test this by having chess players select moves while at the same time performing another task involving the central executive, the visuo-spatial sketchpad, or the phonological loop. The hypotheses might be more specific than the aim: Hypothesis 1: The quality of chess moves will be impaired by a second task involving the central executive; Hypothesis 2: The quality of chess moves will be impaired by a second task involved involving the visuo-spatial sketchpad. It might also be hypothesised that a second task involving the phonological loop would not impair the quality of chess moves.

? In what way are research aims and hypotheses different?

Hypotheses

Experimental hypothesis

Most experimental research using the experimental method starts with someone thinking of an **experimental hypothesis** so they are clear about what they aim to prove or disprove. The experimental hypothesis is a prediction (or forecast) of what the researcher thinks will happen to the dependent variable when the independent variable changes. For example, "Loud noise will have an effect on people's ability to learn the information in a chapter of an introductory psychology textbook".

We have just seen that we talk about an experimental hypothesis in the context of a proper experiment. However, there is a more general term (**alternative hypothesis**) that can be used to refer to all hypotheses that aren't null hypotheses (discussed later). Thus, every experimental hypothesis is also an alternative hypothesis, but *not* every alternative hypothesis is also an experimental hypothesis. For example, we might carry out a correlational study, and form the hypothesis that the number of life events a person has experienced will correlate with the level of depression (see Chapter 6). That is an alternative hypothesis but *not* an experimental hypothesis.

There are two types of experimental or alternative hypothesis: directional and non-directional. A **directional hypothesis** predicts the *nature* of the effect of the independent variable on the dependent variable, e.g. "Loud noise will reduce people's ability to learn the information contained in the chapter of a textbook". Thus, such hypotheses predict not only that the independent variable will affect the dependent variable but also spell out precisely the *direction* of that effect.

In contrast, a **non-directional hypothesis** predicts the independent variable will have an effect on the dependent variable, but the *direction* of the effect is not specified, e.g. "Loud noise

KEY TERMS

Aims: the purpose of a research study.

Hypothesis: a statement of what you believe to be true.

Experimental hypothesis: the hypothesis written prior to conducting an experiment, which usually specifies the independent and dependent variables.

Alternative hypothesis: any hypothesis (including an experimental hypothesis) that isn't a null hypothesis.

Directional hypothesis: a prediction that there will be a difference or correlation between two variables and a statement of the direction of this difference.

Non-directional hypothesis: a prediction that there will be a difference between two variables but the direction of that difference is not predicted.

will have an effect on people's ability to learn the information contained in the chapter of a textbook". This latter hypothesis allows for the possibility that loud noise might actually improve learning, perhaps by making people more alert.

So, a directional hypothesis states the predicted direction in which the independent variable will influence the dependent variable (i.e. increase or decrease). In contrast, a non-directional hypothesis just predicts a change—but not its direction.

ACTIVITY: Devising hypotheses

Devise suitable experimental hypotheses for the following:

- An investigator considers the effect of noise on students' ability to concentrate and complete a word-grid. One group only is subjected to the noise in the form of a distractor, i.e. a television programme.
- An investigator explores the view that there might be a link between the amount of television children watch and their behaviour at school.

Participants and settings

Proper use of the experimental method requires careful consideration of how participants are allocated to the various conditions. Suppose we found that participants learning in a quiet setting performed better than those learning in a noisy setting, but, by mistake, all the most intelligent participants were in the quiet condition and the least intelligent ones in the noise condition. We then wouldn't know whether the good performance in the quiet condition was due to quiet or the cleverness of the participants. The main way of guarding against this possibility is by means of randomisation, in which participants are allocated at random. That helps to ensure that there are no systematic differences between the participants in the various conditions.

Numerous studies are carried out using students as participants, raising the issue of whether students are representative of society as a whole. For example, students tend to be more intelligent and much younger than most people. However, they are representative in the sense that about half of all students are male and half are female.

Variables

Experimental hypotheses predict that some aspect of the situation (e.g. the presence of loud noise) will have an effect on the participants' behaviour (e.g. their learning of the information in the chapter). The experimental hypothesis refers to an independent variable (IV) (the aspect of the experimental situation manipulated by the experimenter), for example, the presence versus absence of loud noise. The hypothesis also refers to a dependent variable (DV) (an aspect of the participants' behaviour measured or assessed by the experiment), for example, measuring learning.

ACTIVITY: Generating a hypothesis

1. Generate a hypothesis for each of these questions:
   - What are "football hooligans" really like?
   - Do children play differently at different ages?
   - What are the effects of caffeine on attention and concentration?
2. Identify the independent variable (IV) and dependent variable (DV) from each hypothesis.
3. Identify whether your hypotheses are directional or non-directional.

In a nutshell, experimental hypotheses predict that a given independent variable will have some specified effect on a given dependent variable.

ACTIVITY: Independent and dependent variables

In order to confirm that you do understand what independent (IV) and dependent (DV) variables are, try identifying them in the following examples.

Remember:

- The DV depends on the IV.
- The IV is manipulated by the experimenter or varies naturally.
- The DV is the one we measure.

1. Long-term separation affects emotional development more than short-term separation. (The two variables are length of separation and emotional development.)
2. Participants conform more when the model is someone they respect. (The two variables are extent of conformity and degree of respect for the model.)
3. Participants remember more words before lunch than after lunch. (The two variables are number of words remembered and whether the test is before or after lunch.)
4. Boys are better than girls at throwing a ball. (The two variables are gender and ability to throw a ball.)
5. Physical attractiveness makes a person more likeable. (The two variables are the attractiveness of a person's photograph and whether they are rated as more or less likeable.)

See page 392 for the answers.

Sampling

Studies in psychology rarely involve more than about 100 participants. However, researchers generally want their findings to apply to a much larger group of people. In technical terms, the participants selected for a study form a **sample** taken from some larger **population** (called the target or sample population) consisting of all the members of the group from which the sample has been drawn.

Two major problems can arise with sampling techniques. First, there may be bias. Second, it may not be possible to generalise from the sample to the population. Both of these problems are discussed below.

ACTIVITY: Target populations

Identify an appropriate target population for each project below. You would select your research sample from this population.

- To discover whether there are enough youth facilities in your community.
- To discover whether cats like dried or tinned cat food.
- To discover whether children aged between 5 and 11 watch too much violent television.
- To discover the causes of anxiety experienced by participants in research studies.

Bias and generalisation

When we carry out a study, we want the findings obtained from our sample to be true of the population from which they were drawn. In order to achieve this, we need a **representative sample**, i.e. participants who are representative or typical of the population in question. Only if we have a representative sample can we *generalise* from the behaviour of our sample to the target population in general.

Many studies have non-representative samples. For example, the participants in many published studies in psychology are undergraduate university students, who are clearly not representative of society in age or intelligence. However, researchers who carry out such studies

KEY TERMS

Sample: a part of a population selected such that it is considered to be representative of the population as a whole.

Population: the total number of cases about which a specific statement can be made. This in itself may be unrepresentative.

Representative sample: the notion that the sample is representative of the whole population from which it is drawn.

often draw very general conclusions about people in general. Such studies are said to have bias. **Bias** means that some individuals in the population (i.e. students) are much more likely to be included in the sample than should happen on the basis of their frequency in the population.

There is also the issue of **generalisation** which is the extent to which the findings researchers obtain from a sample can be applied to the population. In this case, researchers can at best generalise their findings from a student sample to the student population and certainly cannot assume their findings apply to non-students in the population. Note that bias and generalisation are linked—if a sample is biased, we can't validly generalise the findings. Note also that we can't generalise our findings beyond the population from which the sample is drawn even if the sample isn't biased.

Another illustration of bias and problems with generalisation comes from the fact that the overwhelming majority of psychological research has been on people from Western, Educated, Industrialized, Rich, and Democratic (WEIRD) societies (Henrich et al., 2010). Detailed figures were provided by Arnett (2008), who considered leading psychological research. Of the participants, 96% were from WEIRD societies (68% from the United States alone). Thus, most research is not remotely representative of the world's population as a whole and so we can't assume that findings from WEIRD societies are applicable to non-WEIRD societies.

Ideally, psychological experiments should select a random sample of the population, although true randomness can be hard to achieve.

Random sampling

The best way of obtaining a representative sample from a population (e.g. students) is to use **random sampling**. The essence of random sampling is that each and every member of the population has an equal probability of being selected for a given study or experiment.

Why is it so desirable for sampling to be random? In essence, the goal of sampling is to ensure that the sample of participants selected is as representative as possible of the population from which they are sampled. Suppose the population consists of all 500 students at a sixth form college. This could be done by picking students' names out of a hat, or by assigning a number to everyone in the population from which the sample is to be selected. After that, a computer or random number tables could be used to generate a series of random numbers to select the sample.

The main advantage of random sampling is that it provides us with an unbiased sample. It also allows us to generalise from the sample to the population. However, as we will see shortly, it is easier said than done to achieve a truly random sample.

If we wanted to have a representative sample of the entire adult population, we could apply one of the methods of random selection just described to the electoral roll. However, even that would be an imperfect procedure—several groups of people including children and young people, homeless people, illegal immigrants, and prisoners aren't listed.

KEY TERMS

Bias: some people have a greater or lesser chance of being selected than they should be, given their frequency in the population.

Generalisation: the extent to which the findings obtained from a given sample apply to a much larger population.

Random sampling: selecting participants on some random basis (e.g. picking numbers out of a hat). Every member of the population has an equal chance of being selected.

ACTIVITY: Sampling

Find a study to illustrate volunteer sampling and another one to illustrate opportunity sampling. (Clue: most of the studies you have covered used a volunteer sample, whereas some of the studies have used opportunity samples.)

EVALUATION OF RANDOM SAMPLING

It is very hard for an experimenter to obtain a random sample for the following reasons:

1. It may not be possible to identify all of the members of the larger population from which the sample is to be selected.

2. It may not be possible to contact all those who have been selected randomly to appear in the sample—they may have moved house, or be away on holiday. You would end up with a sample that is definitely not random.
3. Some of those selected to be in the sample are likely to refuse to take part. This might not matter if those who agree to take part in research are very similar to those who don't. However, as is discussed below, volunteers typically differ in various ways from non-volunteers.
4. It is typically impossible to achieve a random sample with natural experiments or field experiments.

However, random sampling can be regarded as the "gold standard". If we are able to achieve random sampling, this should eliminate the problem of bias.

Systematic sampling

An alternative to random sampling is what is known as **systematic sampling**. This involves selecting participants systematically from a population (e.g. by selecting every tenth or hundredth person). This is less effective than random sampling, because it can't be claimed that every member of the population is equally likely to be selected. This departure from random sampling means that some bias is typically introduced into the sample. As mentioned already, having a biased sample limits our ability to generalise the findings to the population. As is discussed later, it is easier said than done to persuade all those selected by systematic sampling to be included in the study—we can't force reluctant individuals to take part.

Systematic sampling is not as effective as random sampling but it does help to overcome the biases of the researcher. If we select every hundredth name on the list, we avoid missing names that we cannot pronounce, or do not like the look of, for whatever reason.

Stratified sampling

Suppose we wanted to assess young children's attitudes to sport in a small junior school with 200 children between the ages of 5 and 11. Since attitudes to sport are likely to change as a function of age, we need to make sure that each age is properly represented. We can do this by regarding each year group as a layer or stratum. **Stratified sampling** involves taking full account of the numbers in each layer or stratum. We can do this by making use of the following formula:

Sample size for any given layer = Total sample size/population size × layer size

Let's consider a concrete example. Suppose there are 20 children in year 3 and our total sample size = 50. The number of children from year 3 to be included in our sample is as follows:

$50/200 \times 20 = 5.$

Stratified sampling is most effective when the children to be included in each layer are chosen by random sampling. When this is done, stratified sampling can be free of bias. There may be issues of generalisation depending on whether or not the junior school we have selected is representative of junior schools in general. One of the implications of stratified sampling is that we often can't use it straightforwardly. In the example above, we knew precisely how many children were in each layer or stratum. In other kinds of study, we might lack this precise information and so stratified sampling couldn't be implemented fully.

Opportunity sampling

Random sampling is often expensive and time-consuming. As a result, many researchers use **opportunity sampling**. This involves selecting participants on the basis of their availability. Opportunity sampling is often used by students carrying out experiments, and it is also very common in natural experiments.

? Psychology students often use other psychology students as the participants in their research. What problems are likely to arise, for example, in terms of evaluation apprehension and demand characteristics?

KEY TERMS

Systematic sampling: a modified version of random sampling in which the participants are selected in a quasi-random way (e.g. every 100th name from a population list).

Stratified sampling: this involves selecting a sample from several layers or strata in proportion to the size of the layer.

Opportunity sampling: participants are selected because they are available, not because they are representative of a population.

EVALUATION OF OPPORTUNITY SAMPLING

Opportunity sampling is the easiest method to use. However, it has the severe weakness that the participants may be very unrepresentative. For example, students who are friends of the student carrying out a study may be more likely to take part than students who are not. It is often hard to know whether the use of an opportunity sample has distorted the results.

Opportunity sampling gives the illusion of being drawn from a large population. However, it is generally drawn from a very small sample, such as people who shop in the town centre on a weekday. Thus, the sample depends on who is available at the time and thus is almost bound to introduce bias which may be severe. Strictly speaking, we could at best generalise our findings to people who shop in the town centre on a weekday. The implication is that we should avoid opportunity sampling unless there is no realistic alternative.

Volunteer sampling

In practice, research in psychology typically involves **volunteer sampling**. That is, the participants in a study (whether initially selected via random or opportunity sampling) nearly always consist of volunteers who have agreed to take part. It would be unethical to try to force anyone to become a participant in any given study. As a result, researchers have to accept that many of those invited to participate in a study will refuse.

Do volunteer samples differ in important ways from a random sample? If so, we have **volunteer bias**. Volunteers tend to be more sensitive to demand characteristics (cues used by participants to work out what a study is about), and are also more likely to comply with those demand characteristics. Marcus and Schutz (2005) found volunteers were more agreeable, open to experience, and extraverted than non-volunteers.

Volunteer bias is especially likely when researchers are trying to recruit participants for a study on a sensitive topic. Strassberg and Lowe (1995) found several differences between volunteers and non-volunteers for several studies on human sexuality. The volunteers had had more sexual experience, had less sexual guilt, and reported a more positive attitude towards sexuality.

Many field experiments are free of volunteer bias because the participants haven't chosen to take part. However, that can introduce ethical issues given that they might have decided not to take part if given the opportunity.

KEY TERMS

Volunteer sampling: choosing research participants who have volunteered, e.g. by replying to an advertisement. Volunteer samples may not be representative of the general population, which means the research may not be generalisable.

Volunteer bias: any systematic differences between volunteers and non-volunteers.

Sample size

An important issue relating to sampling is the total number of participants to be included in the sample. What is the ideal number of participants in each condition? That is like asking how long is a piece of string (i.e. there is no definite answer). However, here are some relevant factors:

- It is generally expensive and time-consuming to use large samples.
- If we use very small samples (fewer than 10 participants in each condition), this reduces the chances of obtaining a statistically significant effect.
- Sampling bias is likely to be greater with small samples than large ones.
- The size of the sample population matters. If a relatively small sample is drawn from a large and diverse population (e.g. the entire population of the UK), it is very likely to be biased.

If there is a golden rule that applies to deciding on sample size, this is it:

The smaller the likely effect being studied, the larger the sample size needed to demonstrate it.

Consider the total number of participants to be included...

Experimental Designs

The second step in the research process is to identify an appropriate design. We will consider experimental design in this section. If we wish to compare two groups with respect to a given independent variable, they must not differ in any other important way. Imagine an experiment in which we wanted to test the hypothesis that loud noise impairs learning. Suppose all the least able participants in a learning experiment received the loud noise, and all the most able ones received no noise. We wouldn't know whether it was the loud noise or the low ability level that was more responsible for poor learning performance. How should we select our participants so as to avoid this problem? There are *three* main methods.

1. **Independent groups design**. Each participant is selected for only one group (e.g. no noise or loud noise), most commonly by randomisation. This could involve using a random process such as tossing a coin to allocate one of two conditions for all participants, or you could let all participants draw slips of paper numbered 1 and 2 from a hat. This **random allocation** means that in most cases the participants in the two groups end up equivalent in ability, age, and so on. An example of a study using an independent groups design is the study by Loftus and Palmer (1974; see page 104) on eyewitness testimony. Each group was asked a different question concerning the speed of the cars involved in the accident.
2. **Matched pairs design**. Each participant is selected for only one group, but the participants in the two groups are matched for some relevant factor or factors (e.g. ability, sex, age). In our example, using information about the participants' ability would ensure that the two groups were matched in terms of range of ability. More generally, when we use the matched pairs design, we need to ask ourselves what individual characteristics are likely to influence performance (i.e. the dependent variable). In the example, we might argue that participants' hearing ability is a relevant factor—those with the most acute hearing might find the loud noise more off-putting than those with less good hearing. Accordingly, we could match our two groups for hearing ability. This type of design is used fairly infrequently—it is usually assumed that random allocation within the independent groups design is appropriate as well as less time consuming than using the matched pairs design.
3. **Repeated measures design**. Each participant appears in both groups, so there are exactly the same participants in each group. In our example, this would mean that each participant learns the chapter in the loud noise condition and also in the no-noise condition. We don't need to worry about the participants in one group being cleverer than those in the other group because the *same* people appear in both groups! An example of a study using a repeated measures design is the one by Peterson and Peterson (1959; see pages 75–76) on short-term forgetting at various retention intervals, in which all participants were tested at all retention intervals.

KEY TERMS

Independent groups design: a research design in which each participant is in one condition only. Each separate group of participants experiences different levels of the IV. Sometimes referred to as an unrelated or between-subjects design.

Random allocation: placing participants in different experimental conditions using random methods to ensure no differences between the groups.

Matched pairs design: a research design that matches participants on a one-to-one basis rather than as a whole group.

Repeated measures design: a research design in which the same participants appear in both or all groups or conditions.

ACTIVITY: Research designs

For each of the three designs mentioned (independent group design, matched pairs design, and repeated measures design), try to find at least one study that illustrates the design. With the study you have chosen for repeated measures design, identify the measures that were taken to prevent order effects and explain how counterbalancing was achieved. Note that relatively few studies used the matched pairs design—why do think that is the case?

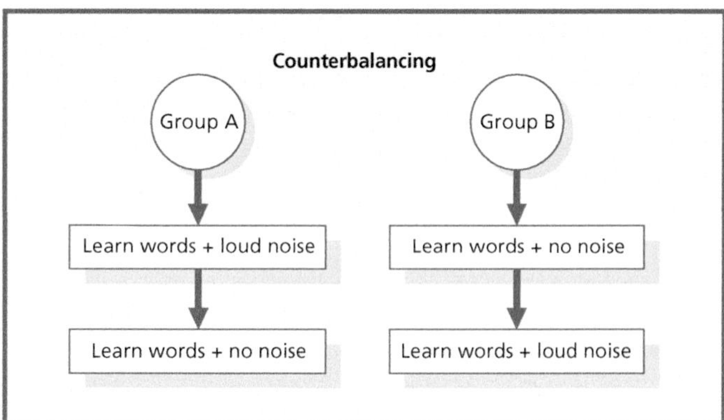

Counterbalancing

The main problem with using the repeated measures design is there may be order effects. Participants may perform better when they appear in the second group because they have gained useful information about the experiment or about the task, or less well because of tiredness or boredom. It would be hard to use the repeated measures design in our example—participants are almost certain to show better learning of the chapter the second time they read it regardless of whether they are exposed to loud noise.

There is a way around the problem of order effects based on **counterbalancing**. Half the participants learn the chapter first in loud noise and then in no noise, whereas the other half learn the chapter first in no noise and then in loud noise. In that way, any order effects should be balanced out.

Experimental and control groups

In some experiments, one group is used to provide baseline information. In our example, one group receives the **experimental treatment** (noise) whereas the other receives nothing (no noise). This latter group serves as the **control group**. Their behaviour informs us about how people behave when they aren't exposed to the experimental treatment so we can make comparisons. The group who have the noise are called the **experimental group**.

If a repeated measures design is used, then we have two different conditions: a control condition and an experimental condition.

Advantages and weaknesses of different research designs

Advantages of the independent groups design are that there are no order effects, and no participants are lost between trials. In addition, it can be used when a repeated measures design is inappropriate (e.g. when looking at gender differences). Finally, only one set of stimulus materials is required because each participant only appears in one condition. This design is typically the only one that can feasibly be used in most field experiments because participants would become suspicious if exposed to a given staged situation on two occasions.

Weaknesses of the independent groups design include the fact that there may be important **individual differences** between participants to start with (to minimise this there should be randomisation). In addition, you need more participants than with a repeated measures design.

The matched pairs design controls for some individual differences between participants and can be used when a repeated measures design is inappropriate. However, it is fairly difficult (and expensive!) to match participants in pairs. In addition, you need a large pool of participants from whom to select (more than with a repeated measures design).

Advantages of the repeated measures design are that it controls for *all* individual differences and it requires fewer

KEY TERMS

Counterbalancing: used with repeated measures design to overcome the problems of practice and order effects, and involves ensuring that each condition is equally likely to be used first and second by participants.

Experimental treatment: the alteration of the independent variable.

Control group: the group of participants who receive no treatment and act as a comparison to the experimental group to study any effects of the treatment.

Experimental group: the group receiving the experimental treatment.

Individual differences: the characteristics that vary from one individual to another; intelligence and personality are major ways in which individuals differ.

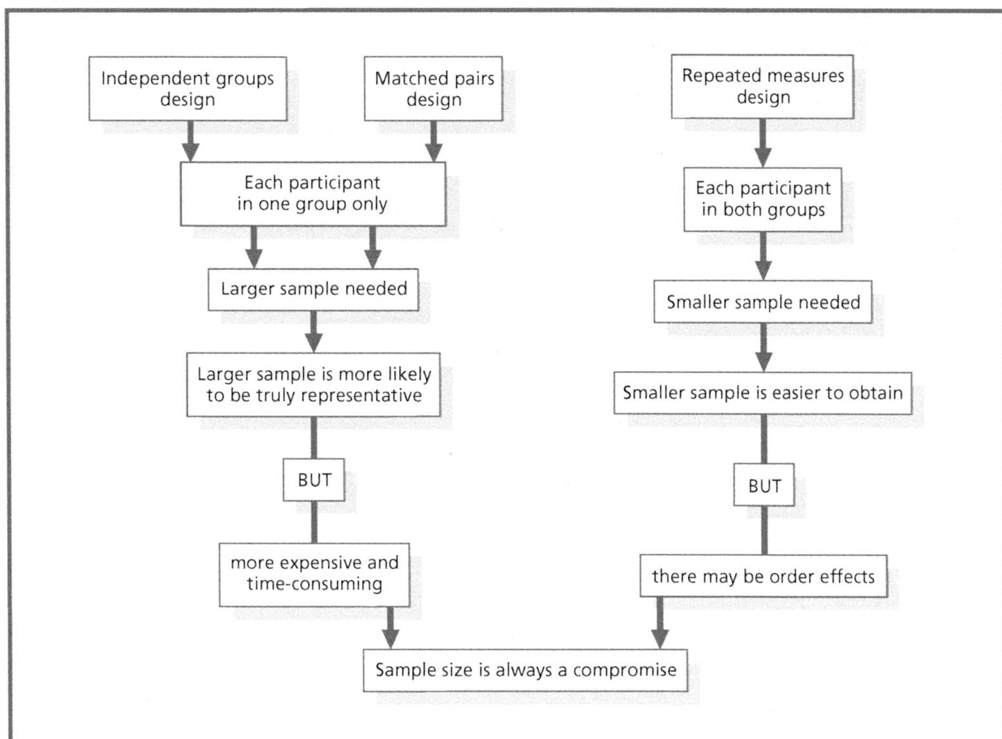

EXAM HINT

When exam questions say "Identify the experimental design used in this study", students often fail to give an answer because they can't remember what "experimental design" means—or they muddle up experimental designs with research methods. This question means "Did the study use an independent groups design, repeated measures, or matched pairs?". Try to think of a mnemonic to help you to remember these experimental designs. For example, you could create an acrostic—a sentence where each word begins with the first letter of the words you are trying to remember, such as "Richard of York Gave Battle in Vain" to remember the colours of the rainbow: Red, Orange, Yellow, Green, Blue, Indigo, Violet.

participants than the other designs. The weaknesses are that it can't be used in studies in which participation in one condition has large effects on responses in the other, or in which participants are likely to guess the purpose of the study, thus introducing problems with demand characteristics. There are also general problems with order effects, although counterbalancing can reduce them.

Control: Random allocation, counterbalancing, randomisation, and standardisation

Of crucial importance in experimentation (regardless of the research design used) is for the experimenter/researcher to control all the important aspects of the situation and the participants so that findings can be obtained that are free of bias and that can be generalised. Here we will briefly review key factors involved in ensuring that that is the case. First, as we saw earlier, it is very important that participants are randomly allocated to conditions. If that can be done, it prevents bias from occurring. The process of randomly allocating participants to conditions is known as randomisation. Another key factor associated with experimenter control is counterbalancing—the reasons why this is so important have been discussed already.

? If an experimenter used different wording in the instructions to different participants, how might this affect the results of the study?

There is a final factor that is very important—standardisation. **Standardisation** means that all participants are treated in the same way and that the same procedures are followed for all of them. Of course, there are differences due to manipulation of the independent variable but everything else should be the same for all participants. One of the most important aspects of standardisation is using the same instructions with all participants. One way of achieving this is to write the instructions down and have the experimenter or the participants read them. Standardisation can also reduce investigator effects (discussed earlier). For example, it is "natural" for the experimenter to like some participants more than others but it is his/her responsibility to act as far as possible in precisely the same way towards all of them.

Why is standardisation so important? Remember that the essence of experiments is to ensure that any differences between groups are due to the impact of the independent variable on the dependent variable rather than any other factor. This goal can only be achieved provided that standardised procedures are used because any differences in the way in which different participants are treated or the instructions they receive may influence the findings.

KEY TERM

Standardisation: the process of ensuring that the procedures, treatment of the participants, and the wording of instructions are all the same for all participants.

Pilot studies

An important consideration in designing good studies is to try out your planned procedures in a small-scale trial run called a **pilot study**. Such a preliminary study is a "dress rehearsal" ahead of the experiment itself. The aims of carrying out a pilot study typically include the following:

- At the most general level, pilot studies make it possible to check out standardised procedures and general design before investing time and money in the major study.
- Pilot studies provide a way of checking the details of the experiment are appropriate. For example, suppose you want your participants to learn a list of 15 words presented in categories or randomly. Your hypothesis is that learning will be better when the words are presented in their categories rather than randomly. If you present the words very rapidly, participants may not have enough time to learn the words. However, if you present the words very slowly, the participants may learn nearly all the words even in the condition with random presentation. A pilot study allows you to select a presentation time that produces an effect of presenting the words in categories or randomly.
- A pilot study may indicate that participants don't understand precisely what they are expected to do. For example, there may be ambiguity about some of the instructions or about some of the items on a questionnaire they have to fill in. Carrying out a pilot study can eliminate such ambiguities.
- Pilot studies can be very useful when researchers want to decide between two possible ways of carrying out their study. For example, Wilson et al. (1998) were unsure whether to use telephone or face-to-face interviews in a study on health care. The pilot study suggested they would obtain a more representative sample (and that more people would agree to participate) if they used telephone interviews.
- When carrying out research, it is important to have enough participants to obtain significant findings. However, it is wasteful of time and resources to use far more participants than is needed to achieve the purposes of the study. A pilot study can often shed light on the appropriate number of participants to include in the main study.

EXAM HINT

You might be asked to explain *what* a pilot study is—but you are more likely to be asked *how* you would do it in a particular study or *why* you would do it. If you are asked how or why make sure you do answer this question, rather than explaining what it is. And also remember to contextualise your answer to make your answer specific to the study you are discussing by including particular details of, for example, the participants and the materials to be used.

Demand characteristics and investigator effects

The findings from any given study can be distorted for several reasons. As Coolican (2004, p. 93) pointed out, "The necessary social interaction that must occur between experimenter and participant makes the psychological experiment different in kind from those in the natural sciences." Distorted findings can occur because participants have mistaken views concerning what is expected of them or because the investigator's or experimenter's expectations influence participants' behaviour. We will consider both of these possibilities in turn. Both demand characteristics and investigator effects are limitations of the experimental method (see earlier discussion).

? Why do you think volunteers are more likely than non-volunteers to be sensitive to the demand characteristics of a study?

Demand characteristics

An important reason why laboratory experiments are more artificial than other research methods is because the participants in laboratory experiments know their behaviour is being observed. One consequence of being observed is that the participants are often responsive to what are known as demand characteristics. **Demand characteristics** are those aspects of a study used by participants to try to work out what is expected of them. These characteristics can then lead participants to behave in certain ways. According to Orne (1962), participants are influenced by demand characteristics because they try to comply with what they perceive to be the demands of the situation.

Young et al. (2007) obtained evidence of strong demand characteristics in a study on the experience of motion sickness in a virtual environment. They assessed motion sickness via questionnaire. This questionnaire was given only after the participants had been in the virtual environment or before and afterwards. Reports of motion sickness after being in the virtual environment were much greater when the questionnaire had also been administered beforehand. Participants given the questionnaire beforehand were alerted to the demand characteristic that

KEY TERMS

Pilot study: a smaller, preliminary study that makes it possible to check out standardised procedures and general design before investing time and money in the major study.

Demand characteristics: features of an experiment that help participants to work out what is expected of them, and lead them to behave in certain predictable ways.

the study concerned the experience of motion sickness—it was almost as if taking the questionnaire beforehand made the participants sick!

Demand characteristics may help to explain why Milgram (1963, 1974) found higher levels of obedience in his experiments at Yale University than in a run-down office building (65% and 48%, respectively) (see page 38). Demand characteristics were also probably involved in Zimbardo's Stanford prison experiment, where the prison-like environment suggested that certain forms of behaviour were expected (see pages 31–32).

? Is honesty the best policy? Would demand characteristics be reduced if both participants and experimenters knew the true aims of the experiment?

Reducing demand characteristics

Information about the demand characteristics in any given experimental setting can be obtained by asking participants afterwards to describe what they felt the experiment was about. The experimenter can then take steps to ensure the results of future experiments aren't adversely affected by demand characteristics.

Some problems with demand characteristics can be reduced by the **single-blind technique**, in which the participants aren't informed of the condition in which they have been placed. Instead, they are usually given a false account of the purpose of the experiment so they won't seek cues about the nature of the research. However, this raises ethical issues, because full informed consent can't be obtained in such circumstances.

Investigator effects

The ideal investigator/experimenter is someone who behaves in exactly the same mildly positive way with every participant, and who doesn't allow his/her expectations and experimental hypotheses to influence the conduct of a study. In reality, however, the expectations and personality characteristics of the investigator/experimenter often have an effect on the participants' behaviour. These are **investigator effects**.

An important investigator effect is **experimenter expectancy**, in which the expectations of the investigator/experimenter have a systematic effect on participants' performance. Rosenthal (1966) showed the effects of experimenter expectancy in a study of flatworms. Participants recruited as experimenters recorded twice as many movements in the flatworms they had been told would be "highly active" than the ones they had been told would be "inactive".

The way in which experimenters behave and talk may influence the behavior of the participant.

The most famous example of an investigator/experimenter effect was reported by Rosenthal and Jacobson (1968). They arranged for teachers to "overhear" that certain randomly selected children were expected to make late gains in academic development. What happened was that these children did actually make greater gains than non-selected children. This was described as the **Pygmalion effect**, in which individuals can perform surprisingly well because others expect them to.

Investigator effects also seem to have been involved in the Stanford prison experiment (see Chapter 2). The main researcher (Philip Zimbardo) was centrally involved in the study and indicated to the mock guards how he expected them to behave.

How does the Pygmalion effect occur? Rosenthal (2003) argued that four factors are involved:

1. *Climate:* teachers behave more warmly towards students for whom they have high expectations.
2. *Input:* teachers teach more material to students of whom they expect much.
3. *Output:* teachers ask their "special" students for answers more often than other students.
4. *Feedback:* teachers give more detailed feedback to "special" students.

KEY TERMS

Single-blind technique: a procedure in which participants are not informed which condition they are in.

Investigator effects: the effects of an investigator's expectations on participants' responses.

Experimenter expectancy: the systematic effects that an experimenter's expectations have on the performance of the participants.

Pygmalion effect: an effect in which individuals perform surprisingly well because others expect them to; it is a kind of self-fulfilling effect in which others' expectations turn into reality.

ACTIVITY: The researcher and participant relationship

This section offers various ways in which the relationship between the researcher and participant can affect the outcome of the research.

To investigate this, select suitable studies to illustrate the following issues: demand characteristics, evaluation apprehension, and investigator effects. For example, in Bowlby's (1944) study of juvenile thieves, he diagnosed the affectionless psychopaths himself and it might have been his own expectations that influenced his decisions.

EXAM HINT

You may be asked to describe one way that investigator effects might threaten the validity of your study. Consider one of the following:

- Researcher bias when setting the research question (formulation).
- In the carrying out of research (e.g. giving away the demand characteristics and the research expectancy effect).
- In the analysis of the results (manipulation of data).
- In the interpretation of results.

Reducing investigator effects

How can we minimise investigator effects? One approach is to use the **double-blind technique**, in which neither the investigator working with the participants nor the participants know the research hypothesis being tested. The double-blind technique reduces the possibility of investigator bias, but is often too expensive and impractical to use. However, as more and more studies involve participants interacting with computers rather than human investigators/experimenters, the incidence of investigator effects is less than it used to be. In addition, data are increasingly stored directly in computers, making it harder to misrecord the information obtained from participants.

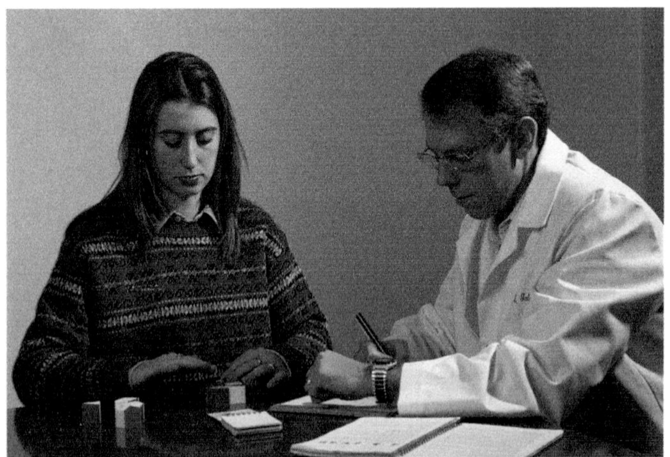

Participants in psychological experiments usually try to perform the task set by the experimenter as well as they can in order to gain his or her approval.

Evaluation apprehension

Another consequence of participants in laboratory experiments knowing they are observed is evaluation apprehension, a term used by Rosenberg (1965). The basic idea is that many people are anxious about being observed by the experimenter and want him/her to evaluate them favourably. This may lead them to behave in ways they wouldn't normally.

Observational Design

Earlier in the chapter we discussed various observational techniques used in psychological research. An issue of central importance in observational research is the following: how can observers avoid being *overloaded* in their attempts to record their observations of others' behaviour? Here we will discuss two major approaches all of which involve the researcher recording only a small fraction of all the behaviour observed. Before doing this, it should be mentioned that researchers increasingly make video recordings in their observational studies. That has the substantial advantage that they can go back to the video repeatedly to make sure that they haven't missed any behaviour of interest to them.

First, there is **time sampling**, where observations are made only during certain time intervals (e.g. the first 10 minutes of each hour). There are two main approaches that can be taken with time sampling: the time intervals can be chosen systematically or randomly. If the time intervals are selected systematically, this has the limitation that the findings will probably not generalise to time intervals other than the one selected. For example, consider an observational study taking place in a junior school. It is decided to observe the amount of fidgeting shown by the students between 2:30 and 3:00pm every day. If (as seems likely) young children get tired and fidget more as the school day wears on, the researchers might obtain an exaggerated view of how much fidgeting is occurring on average.

If the time intervals are selected randomly, this has the advantage that the researcher would be able to generalise his/her findings because there would be no bias in terms of the time intervals sampled. Observing fidgeting among school children at several different randomly chosen time intervals would give us a better idea of the general amount of the fidgeting they

KEY TERMS

Double-blind technique: a procedure where neither the participant nor the investigator knows the condition to which the participant has been assigned; it reduces experimenter effects.

Time sampling: a technique used in observational studies. Observations are only made during specified time periods (e.g. the first 10 minutes of each hour).

exhibited than would be provided by the systematic approach. One disadvantage with random selection of time intervals is that it is often not feasible to use this approach. For example, teachers in a school may be unwilling to put up with the possible disruption to lessons throughout the day that would occur with the random approach.

In general, time sampling has the advantage that the researcher knows the extent to which his/her findings generalise. However, time sampling can be ineffective if the event of interest to the researcher occurs only infrequently or unpredictably. The reason is that this event will often not occur during the time intervals during which observations are being made and so will be missed.

Second, there is **event sampling**. This focuses only on actions or events of particular interest to the researcher. For example, suppose the researcher is interested in observing how much fighting occurs in a junior school. Since this is (hopefully!) a fairly rare event, it would make sense to use event sampling rather than time sampling. However, event sampling can be demanding of time and effort—it may be necessary to observe an individual or group continuously over several hours or days if the event is likely to occur at unpredictable times.

Behavioural categories

It is important for researchers to develop precise and unambiguous categories. After that, they need to ensure observers are trained in the use of those categories to produce high reliability or consistency of measurement. Reliability can be assessed by correlating the observational records of two or more observers, producing a measure of inter-observer reliability.

One reason why it is important to ensure the categories used are very clear is because of the dangers of observer bias. **Observer bias** occurs when an observer's record of what he/she has observed is distorted by his/her expectations. For example, the same behaviour displayed by a boy and a girl might be more likely to be categorised as aggressive when produced by a boy because of stereotypes about male aggression.

The most common answer to the above issues is that observers should use a set of behavioural categories (e.g. smiles; raises a fist; walks away), recording the frequency with which each of these types of behaviour is exhibited by each participant.

Naturalistic observations are observations made under natural or real-life conditions. It is important with such observations that observers should be unaware of the hypothesis or hypotheses being tested. Why is that? If observers know the hypothesis, they may see what they expect to see rather than what is actually happening—this is observer bias

Development and use of categories

Various steps are involved in the development and use of behavioural categories. First, the researchers need to define the behavioural categories to be used in the study. Decisions about which behavioural categories to use depend in part on the specific hypotheses the researcher wants to test. For example, if the researcher wants to test the hypothesis that boys are more aggressive than girls, it obviously makes sense to focus on behavioural categories relevant to verbal and non-verbal forms of aggression. The development of appropriate categories can be facilitated if the researcher spends some time observing boys and girls to see the various forms of aggressive behaviour they display.

Second, the researcher needs to decide whether the behavioural categories should be based on simple recording or on interpretation. For example, an observer may *record* that the participant has moved forwards or may *interpret* that movement as an aggressive action. In either case, what is important is that every behavioural category is unambiguously defined.

In practice, most behavioural categories used in research contain at least some interpretation. For example, Bales (1950) developed the interaction process analysis, which allows observers to categorise the interactions of group members. The observers record inferred meanings for the forms of behaviour shown by members of a group (e.g. "offers suggestion" or "gives information"). Categories based on simple recording are sometimes easier to use (e.g. it isn't hard to decide whether someone is moving forwards) than those based on interpretation. However, behavioural categories based on interpretation are more meaningful and of more theoretical interest.

? Imagine that you are going to conduct an observation of children in a playgroup with two other researchers. To what extent do you think that you will all record the same behaviours? How might you cope with any disagreements?

KEY TERMS

Event sampling: a technique for collecting data in an observational study. The observer focuses only on specified events.

Observer bias: distorted interpretations of participants' behaviour; often based on the observer's expectations.

Note: Inter-observer reliability is not on the AS-level specification.

Third, when the behavioural categories have been decided on, the next step is to ensure observers are properly trained in their use. It is of real importance to show that different observers use the behavioural categories in the same way. The issue here is that of reliability or consistency of measurement. Reliability can be assessed by asking two or more observers to produce observational records at the same time. When these records are correlated, we have a measure of **inter-observer reliability** (sometimes known as *inter-rater* or *inter-judge reliability*).

Reliability of measurement is very important. However, even if a system of behavioural categories is reliable, that doesn't prove it is valid in the sense of assessing what we want to assess. Validity can be shown by relating observers' records to other kinds of evidence. For example, Pepler and Craig (1995) had observers rate the aggressiveness of children's interactions using various behavioural categories. The children identified by observers as the most aggressive tended to be those rated as most aggressive by teachers, thus showing evidence for validity in the observers' records.

Design of interviews and questionnaire construction

In this section we focus on appropriate ways of designing interviews. We start by considering interview design and then move on to questionnaire design.

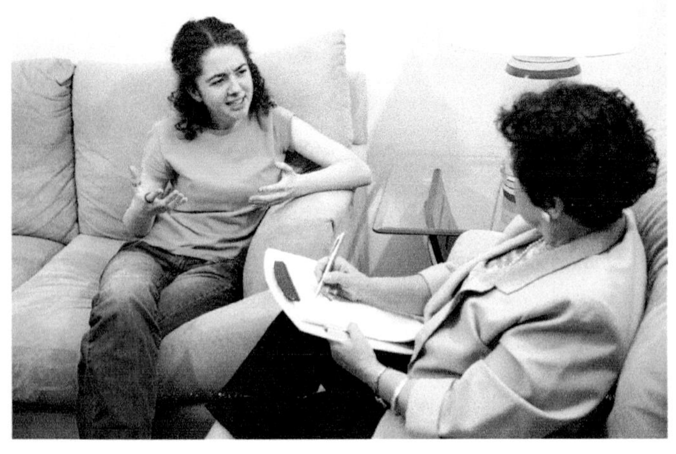

There are various types of interviews used for psychological experimentation, from unstructured interviews to fully structured designs that have a standard set of questions with restricted-choice answers.

Interview design

As we saw earlier in the chapter, interviews vary in the amount of structure they possess. At one extreme, there are unstructured or non-directive interviews, in which the interviewer allows the person being interviewed to discuss almost anything he/she wants. At the other extreme, there is the fully structured interview. In this type of interview, a standard set of questions is asked in the same fixed order to all interviewees, who are constrained in their possible answers to each question.

There is not much difference between a fully structured interview and a questionnaire. There are also many kinds of interviews between these two extremes—they possess some structure but lack the inflexibility of fully structured interviews.

Another difference between types of interviews concerns the nature of the questions asked. We can distinguish between closed and open questions. Closed questions require one of a small number of possible answers; example: "Do you approve of the government?" In contrast, open questions allow the interviewee considerable scope as to his/her answer; example: "What do you think about the government?" Open questions are associated with unstructured interviews and closed questions with structured interviews.

Selecting interview and question types

How should a researcher decide which type of interview and question to choose? Unstructured interviews and open questions would be suitable in the following circumstances:

- The researcher wants to obtain a lot of rich and personal information from each interviewee.
- The researcher wants to maximise the chances the interviewees will feel involved in the interview.
- The researcher wants to obtain a general impression of the interviewees' views rather than very specific and detailed information.
- It is not of central importance to compare the responses of different interviewees.
- The interviewer or interviewers are well trained to cope with the requirements of conducting unstructured interviews.

KEY TERM

Inter-observer reliability: the extent to which there is agreement between the behavioural ratings of two observers.

Structured interviews and closed questions would be suitable in the following circumstances:

- The researcher wants to obtain information that is easy to analyse.
- The researcher wants to obtain reliable data and to compare directly the answers given by different interviewees.
- The researcher has clear ideas concerning the questions he/she wants interviewees to answer.
- The interviewer(s) have limited training but can cope with the requirements of asking closed questions in a standard order.

Interviewer's characteristics

An important issue when designing an interview is to consider various characteristics of the interviewer or interviewers. Their gender, ethnicity, age, and personal qualities can all affect the interviewees' answers. For example, Wilson et al. (2002) found Californian Latino men interviewed by women reported fewer sexual partners than men interviewed by men. In addition, men were more likely to report sex with prostitutes to an older interviewer.

The views or expectations of the interviewer may bias the responses given by interviewees—this is known as interviewer bias. Interviewer bias can be minimised by instructing interviewers to remain non-evaluative and fairly neutral regardless of whether they personally agree or disagree with what an interviewee is saying.

Questionnaire design

Questionnaires are used for many purposes (e.g. to assess personality; to assess attitudes), and how a questionnaire is designed needs to reflect fully the purpose for which it is being designed. However, some general considerations underlying questionnaire design are discussed in the box.

How can you decide how good any given questionnaire is? Three key characteristics of a good questionnaire are standardisation, reliability, and validity (reliability and validity are discussed more fully later in the chapter). **Standardised tests** are ones that have been administered to a large representative sample so an individual's score can be compared against that of others. For example, a score of 26 out of 60 on an attitude scale measuring prejudice doesn't mean much on its own—it only becomes meaningful when we know what percentage of people score more and less than 26 on that scale.

Questionnaire construction

The first step is to generate as many ideas as possible relevant to the questionnaire. Then discard those ideas of little relevance, working on the basis (Dyer, 1995, p.114) that: "It is better to ask carefully designed and quite detailed questions about a few precisely defined issues than the same number on a very wide range of topics."

Closed and open questions

There is an important distinction between closed and open questions. **Closed questions** invite the respondent to select from various possible answers (e.g. yes or no; yes, unsure, or no; putting different answers in rank order). In contrast, **open questions** allow respondents to answer in whatever way they prefer.

What are the advantages and limitations of these two approaches? Most questionnaires use closed questions, because the answers are easy to score and to analyse and don't require any complex interpretations from the person scoring the answers. As a result, questionnaires that use closed questions typically have reasonable reliability and validity. Reliability concerns the consistency of measurement—for example, reliability is high if individuals answer questionnaire items in the same way when tested on two occasions separated by a week or month. Validity is the extent to which a test measures what it is supposed to be measuring.

Closed questions where the answer options are very restricted (e.g. requiring "yes" or "no" answers) have two limitations. First, they often provide very limited information

KEY TERMS

Standardised tests: tests on which an individual's score can be evaluated against those of a large representative sample.

Closed questions: questions where the answer has to be selected from a limited set of options.

Open questions: questions where the respondent can answer freely without being constrained by a predetermined set of options.

(e.g. Are you happy? Yes or no?). In addition, they can be misleading because respondents may find it very hard to decide whether the more accurate answer is yes or no. These limitations are often largely overcome by using what are known as Likert-type scales (discussed further shortly) providing a range of different possible answers. Here is an example:

I am a happy person

Strongly agree Agree Don't know Disagree Strongly disagree

There is a slight limitation with such closed questions—where exactly is the dividing line between agree and strongly agree or between disagree and strongly disagree?

Open questions have the advantage that they provide much fuller and richer information from the respondents. Respondents often prefer open questions because they are free to express their opinions on an issue fully and without the constraints associated with closed questions. However, questionnaires containing open questions have the serious limitation that it is much harder to analyse the findings from such questions because the respondents' answers are typically very diverse. This makes it difficult to score those answers and so questionnaires with open questions typically have fairly low reliability and validity. If two researchers consider a respondent's answers to open questions they often differ substantially in their interpretations of those answers. In essence, the use of open questions can be useful at an early stage of investigation to obtain a sense of what issues people feel are important. The insights so obtained can then be used to develop a questionnaire containing closed questions.

An issue that is very relevant to all questionnaires whether they used open or closed questions is that of social desirability bias (discussed earlier). In essence, social desirability bias is the tendency for respondents to provide answers that are socially desirable even if untrue. For example, if you ask someone the question, "Are you a good person?" it is obvious that the socially desirable answer is "Yes" even if that is not true! Accordingly, it is important when designing open or closed questions to try to avoid emotionally loaded questions where there is only one desirable answer.

Ambiguity and bias

Questions that are ambiguous or are likely to be interpreted in various ways should be avoided. Questions that are very long or complicated should also be avoided, because they are likely to be misunderstood. Emotive questions should be avoided because they make people defensive and result in answers that are not true. Finally, biased questions should be avoided. Here is an example of a biased question: "In view of the superiority of Britain, why should we consider further political integration with the rest of Europe?"

Attitude scale construction

One of the most common ways to construct an attitude scale is to use the Likert procedure. Initially various statements are collected together, and participants indicate their level of agreement on a 5-point scale running from "strongly disagree" at one end to "strongly agree" at the other end. For positive statements (e.g. "Most Hollywood stars are outstanding actors"), strongly disagree is scored as 1 and strongly agree as 5, with intermediate points being scored 2, 3, or 4.

For negative statements (e.g. "Most Hollywood stars are not outstanding actors"), the scoring is reversed so that strongly disagree is scored as 5 and strongly agree as 1.

Question styles: A survey on chocolate

Closed question: Do you like chocolate? (tick one)

YES NO NOT SURE

Open question: Why do you like or dislike chocolate?

Ambiguous question: Is chocolate likely to do you more harm than a diet that consists mainly of junk food?

Biased question: Plain chocolate is a more sophisticated taste than milk chocolate. Which type do you prefer?

ACTIVITY: Construct your own questionnaire

1. Select an area of study from the work you are doing in class.
2. Research the topic to gain ideas about the possible questions to ask.
3. Develop sub-topics to investigate. It may be best to generate questions with a group of people because more varied ideas are produced (brainstorming). Each group member should put forward ideas that are received uncritically by the group. Later, the group can select the best questions.
4. Write the questions. It may help to include some irrelevant "filler" questions to mislead the respondent as to the main purpose of the survey.
5. Decide on a sequence for the questions. It is best to start with easy ones.
6. Write standardised instructions, which must include guidance regarding respondents' ethical rights.
7. Conduct a pilot run and redraft your questionnaire in response to areas of confusion or difficulty.
8. After you have conducted your questionnaire, analyse the results using descriptive data (see next section, "Data Handling and Analysis").
9. Debrief participants and advise them of your findings.

Note: Reliability and validity are not on the AS-level specification.

Reliability and validity

As mentioned earlier, **reliability** refers to the extent to which a given questionnaire provides consistent findings. For example, if individuals who appear prejudiced on a questionnaire on one day don't appear prejudiced when re-tested on the same questionnaire the following day, the questionnaire is unreliable and of little use. The most common way of assessing reliability is the **test–retest** technique—numerous people are given the same questionnaire on two occasions and the scores are then correlated. If the correlation is high, it means the questionnaire is reliable.

EXAM HINT

Remember the difference between reliability and validity.

- Reliability—CONSISTENCY
- Internal reliability—TRUTH
- External validity—GENERALISABILITY

If you are assessing research in a long-answer question do try to improve the quality of your evaluation by assessing reliability and validity.

Validity refers to the extent to which a questionnaire is measuring what it is supposed to be measuring. Validity is a very important issue with respect to questionnaires and other tests (e.g. intelligence tests). There are several kinds of validity:

First, there is face validity. **Face validity** is a very simple form of validity. It involves inspecting the items within a test to see whether they appear to be relevant to what the test is claimed to measure. For example, suppose a test is supposed to measure trait anxiety (a personality dimension relating to susceptibility to **anxiety**). The test would have good face validity if it contained items referring to worries about the future, tension, and feelings of unease.

Second, there is concurrent validity. **Concurrent validity** involves comparing or correlating the scores on a test with a previous test that is valid or with some relevant external criterion. For example, consider again a test designed to measure trait anxiety. A relevant external criterion might be the scores on the test obtained by patients with anxiety disorders. If the test genuinely assessed susceptibility to anxiety, we would expect anxious patients to have much higher scores than healthy individuals.

Third, there is predictive validity. **Predictive validity** refers to the extent to which scores on a given test predict future scores on a test or other criterion. For example, we could see whether trait anxiety scores obtained at one point in time predict who will develop an anxiety disorder subsequently or whether they predict scores on another test of trait anxiety known to be valid. Predictive validity is overall the most important type of validity.

KEY TERMS

Reliability: the extent to which a test produces consistent findings.

Test–retest: a technique used to establish reliability, by giving the same test to participants on two separate occasions to see if their scores remain relatively similar.

Validity: the extent to which a test is measuring what it is intended to measure.

Face validity: this involves deciding whether a test measures what it is supposed to measure by considering the items within it.

Anxiety: a normal emotion similar to nervousness, worry, or apprehension, but if excessive it can interfere with everyday life and might then be judged an anxiety disorder.

Concurrent validity: deciding whether a test measures what it is claimed to measure by relating the scores on the test to some other test or criterion.

Predictive validity: assessing whether a test is measuring what it is claimed to measure by seeing whether scores on the test predict some *future* performance (e.g. on a related test).

Ethics

Ethics are a set of moral principles used to guide human behaviour. There are few (if any) absolutes in ethics. However, any society or group of people develops ethics to determine what is right or wrong for that group. The need for ethical control leads to the establishment of a set of rules or **ethical guidelines** to judge the acceptability of behaviour.

The British Psychological Society (BPS) is the major organisation for professional psychologists in the United Kingdom. In 1990, the BPS published its Ethical Principles for Conducting Research with Human Participants. The key to carrying out research in an ethical way was expressed as follows: "The investigation should be considered from the standpoint of all participants; foreseeable threats to their psychological well-being, health, values, and dignity should be eliminated." Thus, every effort should be made to ensure participants do not experience pain, stress, or distress.

This code has been adapted by professional bodies all over the world. Within Britain, the British Psychological Society (BPS) issued a code of ethics (2006; updated slightly in 2009; revised in 2014) that should be followed by anyone involved in psychological research (see below). Thus, the role of the British Psychological Society's code of ethics is to provide comprehensive guidelines as to the requirements of ethical research that help to determine whether an experimenter's proposed research is acceptable or whether it breaches one or more ethical principles.

Below, I discuss the essential features of the BPS code of ethics followed by a consideration of ethical issues in the design and conduct of psychological studies. Before that, however, I will briefly consider why most ethical guidelines (including those of the BPS) have only limited force. Someone who infringes the BPS code of ethics has not necessarily committed a crime, although they may be barred from the British Psychological Society. In extreme cases, of course, researchers who flagrantly ignore ethical principles have occasionally committed crimes.

? Why do you think views about the kinds of research that are ethically acceptable have changed over the years?

There are other drawbacks. First, the establishment of a set of ethical guidelines enshrines its principles and may close off discussions about better solutions to a given ethical dilemma. Second, the code makes it seem the guidelines are ethical "truths". In fact, however, such guidelines are constantly reviewed, in part because of changing social attitudes. Third, ethical codes may take personal responsibility away from the individual researcher. It may even invite individuals to find loopholes and "play the system".

The BPS code of human research ethics (2014) can be found at: www.bps.org.uk/sites/default/files/documents/code_of_human_research_ethics.pdf. The previous BPS code of ethics (2009) can be found at http://www.bps.org.uk

BPS code of ethics (2014)

The BPS code of ethics (2006, 2009, revised 2014) applies to all psychologists and not simply those involved in research, and so is also relevant to clinical and occupational psychologists. The code contains numerous standards and guidelines, and we will consider only the main ones here. Its role is to provide valuable guidance to researchers to help to ensure all psychological research is entirely ethical. Any research not consistent with the BPS code of ethics is likely to be unethical or at least ill-judged.

The BPS code of ethics (2014) is based on four major ethical principles:

Respect for the autonomy, privacy, and dignity of individuals and communities

The essence of this principle is expressed in the following terms in the current BPS code of human research ethics: "Rights to privacy, self-determination, personal liberty and natural justice are of particular importance to psychologists, and they have a responsibility to protect and promote those rights in their research activities. As such, psychologists have a responsibility to develop and follow procedures for valid consent, confidentiality, anonymity, fair treatment and due process" (2014, p. 8).

KEY TERMS

Ethics: a set of moral principles used to guide human behaviour.

Ethical guidelines: written codes of conduct and practice to guide and aid psychologists in planning and running research studies to an approved standard, and dealing with any issues that may arise.

Scientific integrity

According to the BPS code of ethics (2014, pp. 8–9): "Research should be designed, reviewed and conducted in a way that ensures its quality, integrity and contribution to the development of knowledge and understanding ... Quality relates primarily to the scientific design of the research and the consideration of potential risks of harm and protocols for addressing such difficulties."

Social responsibility

According to the BPS code of human research ethics (2014, p. 10): "A shared collective duty for the welfare of human and nonhuman beings, both within the societies in which psychology researchers live and work, and beyond them, must be acknowledged by those conducting the research ... psychologists should acknowledge the evolution of social structures in relation to societal needs and be respectful of such structures."

Maximising benefit and minimising harm

According to the BPS code of ethics (2014, p. 11): "Psychologists should consider all research from the standpoint of the research participants, and any other persons, groups or communities who may be potentially affected by the research, with the aim of avoiding potential risks to psychological well-being, mental health, personal values, the invasion of privacy or dignity ... When risks arise as an unavoidable and integral element of the research, robust risk assessment and management protocols should be developed and complied with. Normally, the risk of harm should be no greater than that encountered in ordinary life."

Specific ethical issues

The BPS code of ethics (2009, 2014) elaborates on specific ethical issues researchers must take full account of. Here we will briefly discuss a few of them.

Risk

Researchers need to take particular care when research involves more than minimal risk. Examples include the use of vulnerable groups (e.g. young children), potentially sensitive topics (e.g. participants' sexual behaviour), research involving deception, and research that might produce stress or humiliation.

Valid or informed consent

According to the BPS code of ethics (2014, p. 15), "Researchers should ensure that every person from whom data are gathered ... consents freely to the process on the basis of adequate information. They should be able, during the data gathering phase, freely to withdraw or modify their consent and to ask for the destruction of all or part of the data that they have contributed." This issue is discussed further later.

Confidentiality

The BPS code of ethics (2014, p. 22) states: "Participants in psychological research have a right to expect that information they provide will be treated confidentially and, if published, will not be identifiable as theirs. In the event that confidentiality and/or anonymity cannot be guaranteed, the participant must be warned of this in advance of agreeing to participate."

Deception

The essence of an ethical approach to deception in psychological research is as follows (BPS code of ethics, 2014, p. 24): "All psychologists should seek to supply as full information as possible to those taking part in their research, recognising that providing all of that information at the start of a person's participation may not be possible for methodological reasons. If the reaction of participants when deception is revealed later ... is likely to lead to discomfort, anger or objections from the participants then the deception is inappropriate." Issues relating to deception are discussed further shortly.

Debriefing

The previous version of the BPS code of ethics had this to say about the importance of debriefing:

i. "Debrief research participants at the conclusion of their participation, in order to inform them of the outcomes and nature of the research, to identify any unforeseen harm, discomfort of misconceptions, and in order to arrange for assistance as needed" (2009, p. 20).
ii. "Take particular care when discussing outcomes with research participants, as seemingly evaluative statements may carry unintended weight" (2009, p. 20).

The 2014 version states that, "When the research data gathering is completed ... it is important to provide an appropriate debriefing for participants. In some circumstances, the verbal description of the nature of the investigation will not be sufficient to eliminate all possibility of harmful after-effects" (p. 26).

? Without ethical guidelines, how difficult would it be to express misgivings about questionable research methods?

Ethical issues in the design and conduct of psychological research

The issue of ethics is critical to psychological research. The experimenter in most psychological research is in a more powerful position than the participants, and it is essential to ensure participants aren't exploited or persuaded to behave in ways they don't want to. In addition, a professional group of people is one that "polices" itself and therefore these ethical standards are a key feature of the professionalism of psychology.

Subjects or participants?

Until recently members of the public taking part in psychology experiments were called "subjects". This reflected the view that they were only passively involved in the research process (they did what the researcher told them) and it emphasised the power of the researcher (as the person in authority). The subject in a psychological experiment was in a rather vulnerable and exploitable position. Kelman (1972, p. 993) pointed out, "most ethical problems arising in social research can be traced to the subject's power deficiency". It follows that steps must be taken to ensure the participant is *not* placed in a powerless and vulnerable position. This is the task of an ethical code.

As a consequence of this insight it has become the practice to refer to such individuals as participants rather than subjects. The change in terminology allows for a more humane respect for those participating in experiments.

Cost–benefit analysis

Ethics are determined in part by a balance between means and ends, or a **cost–benefit analysis**. Certain things are less acceptable than others. However, if the ultimate end is for the good of humankind, we may feel it is ethically justified. For example, most people believe it is more acceptable to cause suffering to animals to find a cure for some serious human illness than to develop a new cosmetic.

Diener and Crandall (1978) argued there are various drawbacks with the cost–benefit approach. First, it is hard (if not impossible) to predict costs and benefits prior to conducting a study.

Second, even after the study has been completed, it is still hard to assess costs and benefits accurately. This is partly because it depends on *who* is making the judgements. A participant may judge the costs differently from the researcher, and benefits may be judged differently in years to come.

Third, cost–benefit analyses tend to ignore the important rights of individuals in favour of practical considerations of possible usefulness of the findings.

There are probably more major ethical issues associated with designing and conducting research in psychology than any other scientific discipline. Why is this? First, all psychological experiments involve the study of living creatures. The rights of these participants to be treated in a caring and respectful way can easily be infringed by an unprincipled experimenter.

KEY TERM

Cost–benefit analysis: a comparison between the costs of something and the related benefits, in order to decide on a course of action.

Second, the findings of psychological research may reveal unpleasant or unacceptable facts about human nature, or about certain groups within society. No matter how morally upright the experimenter may be, there is always the danger that extreme political organisations will use research findings to further their political aims. Such research is often described as "socially sensitive", and psychologists have a responsibility to consider carefully the uses to which their findings may be put.

Third, these political aims may include social control. The techniques discovered in psychological research may be exploited by dictators or others seeking to exert unjustifiable influence on society or to inflame people's prejudices.

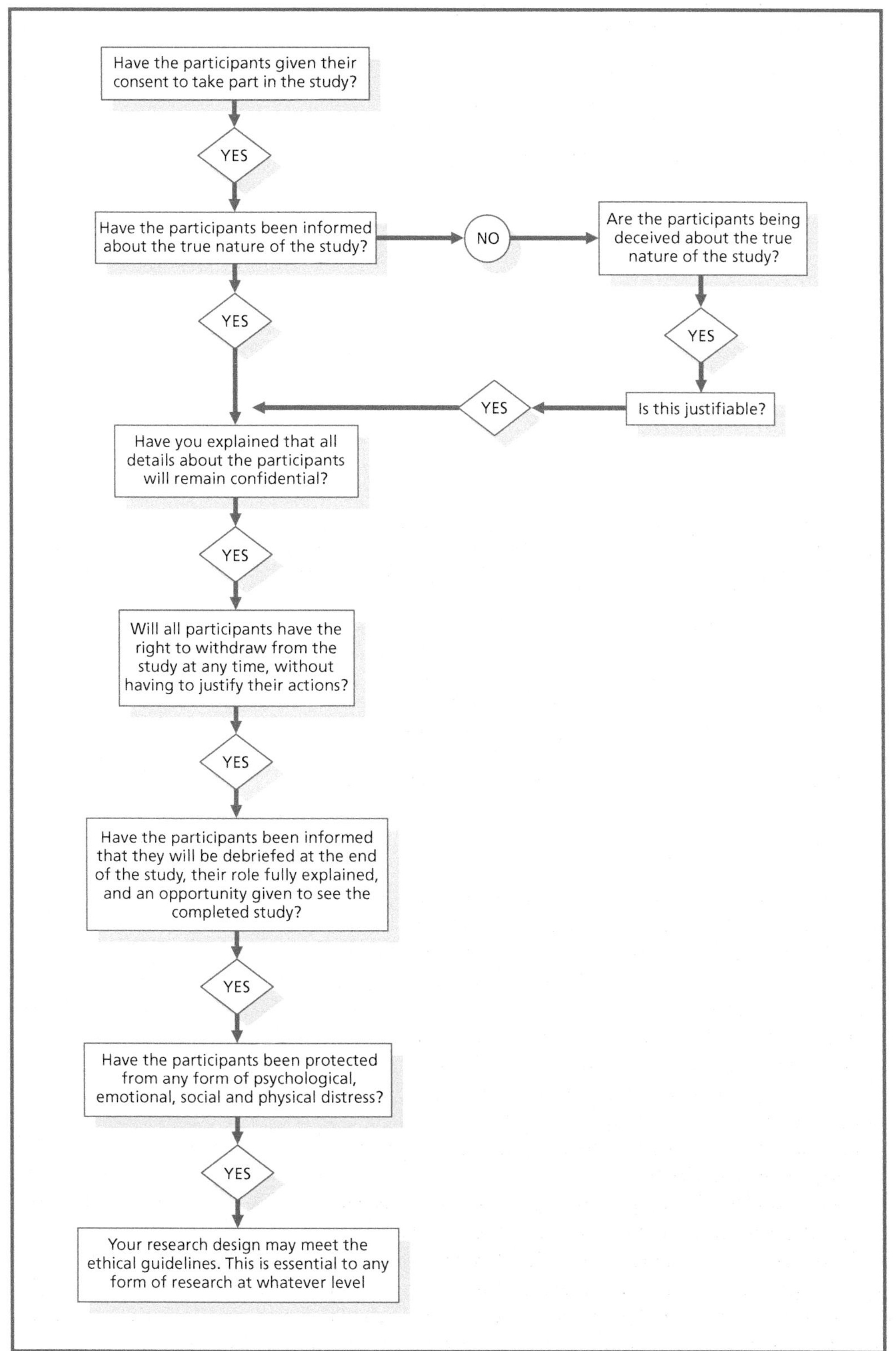

This flow chart shows ethical decisions to be taken by researchers designing a psychological study.

Use of deception

Honesty is a fundamental moral and ethical principle, and anyone agreeing to take part in psychological research naturally expects to be given full information beforehand. However, **deception** is sometimes necessary. A well-known example of research necessarily involving deception is that of Asch (1951, 1956; see Chapter 2) on conformity. If the participants had been told the experiment was designed to study conformity to group pressure, and that all the other participants were confederates of the experimenter, this important research would have been pointless.

Deception is certainly widespread. Menges (1973) considered about 1000 experimental studies carried out in the United States. Full information about what was going to happen was provided in only 3% of cases. However, full informed consent is far more common nowadays than it was over 40 years ago.

? How would you feel if you found out you were deliberately deceived as a participant in a research study? Would you be willing to take part in another study after knowing this?

When is deception justified? First, the less potentially damaging the consequences of the deception, the more acceptable it is. Second, it is easier to justify the use of deception in studies that are important scientifically. Third, deception is more justifiable when there are no alternative, deception-free ways of studying an issue.

How can we deal with the deception issue?

One way of avoiding the ethical problems associated with deception is the use of **role-playing experiments**. Zimbardo's Stanford prison experiment (see Chapter 2) is an example of such an experiment—the participants played the role of prison guards and prisoners over a period of several days. In role-playing experiments, the participants are not deceived (e.g. they know it isn't a real prison), but try to behave as if they didn't know the true state of affairs. This approach can eliminate many of the ethical problems with deception studies.

Debriefing is an important method for dealing with deception and other ethical issues. At the end of the study, participants should be told the actual nature and purpose of the research, and asked not to tell future participants. In addition, debriefing typically involves providing information about the experimental findings and offering participants the opportunity to have their results excluded from the study if they wish.

Debriefing can reduce any distress caused by the experimenter. According to Aronson (1988), participants should leave the research situation in "a frame of mind that is at least as sound as it was when they entered". This is *not* always the case after debriefing. Suppose you had been fully obedient in a Milgram-type experiment on obedience to authority (see Chapter 2). You might feel guilty you had allowed yourself to give what might have been fatal electric shocks to someone with a heart condition.

Informed consent

As we have seen, it is the right of participants (wherever possible) to provide voluntary **informed consent**. This means several things: being informed about what will be required; being informed about the purpose of the research; being informed of their rights (e.g. the right to confidentiality, the right to leave the research at any time); and finally giving their consent. It is important

KEY TERMS

Deception: in research ethics, deception refers to deliberately misleading participants, which was accepted in the past. Currently the view is that deception should be avoided wherever possible, as it could lead to psychological harm or a negative view of psychological research.

Role-playing experiments: studies in which participants are asked to imagine how they would behave in certain situations.

Debriefing: attempts by the experimenter at the end of a study to provide detailed information for the participants about the study and to reduce any distress they might have felt.

Informed consent: relates to an ethical guideline which advises that participants should understand what they are agreeing to take part in. They should be aware of what the research involves, and their own part in this.

for researchers designing psychological studies to try hard to ensure participants provide informed consent. However, there are many situations where this is not possible:

When setting up observational research it is important to consider whether the participants would normally expect to be observed by strangers in the situation. For example, making observations of the people in this picture would be acceptable, but observing them in a changing room would not.

- Children or participants who have impairments limiting their understanding and/or communication. In such cases, the informed consent of an adult is sought.
- When deception is a necessary part of the research design as in Asch's or Milgram's research. Role-playing experiments can be used to provide informed consent, but such experiments have serious limitations.
- In field experiments when participants aren't aware they are taking part in a piece of psychological research. An example is the study by Shotland and Straw (1976) in which participants witnessed a staged quarrel between two people.
- There is an issue as to whether truly informed consent is possible. How easy is it for non-psychologists to understand *fully* what is expected of them? Prior to participation, would the "teacher" in Milgram's research have anticipated how he/she would feel when giving shocks?

ACTIVITY: Field experiments and ethics

Find a partner and toss a coin to see who is going to support doing field experiments and who is going to oppose them on ethical grounds. Then give yourselves 5 minutes to write an argument supporting your view of why these experiments are, or are not, ethically all right. Exchange your written comments, and discuss what each of you has said.

Another way to obtain consent

One way of obtaining consent is to ask the opinion of members of the population from which the research participants are drawn. This is what Milgram did, and it is called seeking **presumptive consent**. The problem with presumptive consent is that the actual participants may find the experiment less acceptable than the non-participants whose opinions were sought beforehand.

Right to withhold data

Another means of offering informed consent is to do it afterwards. When the experiment is over, during debriefing, participants should be offered the chance to withhold their data. In essence, this gives them the same power as if they had refused to take part. However, participants exercising their right to withhold data may nevertheless have had experiences during the experiment they wouldn't have agreed to if they had realised beforehand what was going to happen.

Minimising harm

We have seen that the BPS code of ethics (2014) emphasises the need to minimise harm. "Harm" can mean various things. It includes both physical and psychological damage. As that code of ethics points out, the key test of whether a participant has been harmed to an unethical extent is to ask whether the risk of harm was greater than in everyday life.

Physical harm

We might include excessive anxiety as physical harm because the results can be physically evident. If you consider the description of some of Milgram's participants (see Chapter 6), it is clear they experienced physical as well as psychological harm—some had seizures, and many perspired and bit their lips. Stress is a psychological state but has a physical basis (see Chapter 6).

KEY TERM

Presumptive consent: a substitute for voluntary informed consent, it is presumed that if one set of people regard an experimental procedure as acceptable this applies to all people, including the experimental participants whose consent has not been obtained.

Watson and Rayner claimed that their experiment with Little Albert (see Chapter 7) was ethical because the psychological harm inflicted was no greater than what he might experience in real life. Is this acceptable?

Psychological harm

Psychological harm is harder to measure, and many studies infringe psychological "safety". Many of Milgram's participants would have felt disappointed with their own apparent willingness to obey unjust authority, which may have led to psychological harm (e.g. reduced self-esteem).

We can also consider **confidentiality** and the **right to privacy** as forms of **protection of participants from psychological harm**. Confidentiality means that no information (especially sensitive information) about any given participant should be revealed by the experimenter to anyone else. Right to privacy is a matter of concern when conducting observational research. It wouldn't be appropriate, for example, to observe a person's behaviour in their bedroom without their permission. However, it would be acceptable to observe people in a public place (e.g. a park) where public scrutiny is expected.

Dealing with ethical issues in research

We have seen the BPS code of ethics provides an excellent set of ethical principles. Any researcher who carefully and meticulously follows all aspects of this code of ethics is unlikely to encounter ethical problems when conducting a psychological study. However, there are potential ethical issues arising from individual differences among participants. Consider, for example, a participant who has paranoid symptoms making him/her exceptionally sensitive to others' imagined negative views. Such a person in the Asch situation might suffer far more than most people and it may be hard to anticipate this reaction.

In practice, most ethical issues arising during the course of a psychological study occur because (as we have seen) it is not always possible to adhere to every single recommendation in the code of ethics. Examples include studies in which it is impossible to obtain informed consent or where deception is essential.

How should researchers deal with ethical issues that may arise in spite of their best efforts? First, they need to have robust procedures in place that will allow them to detect as soon as possible that their psychological study has ethical problems. Pilot studies can play a vital role here, alerting researchers of ethical issues at a very early stage of the research. The withdrawal of several participants from a study might also indicate that it poses ethical issues. Debriefing is also very important. Remember that debriefing involves the experimenter at the end of the study providing detailed information about the study to participants.

Second, if it becomes apparent that some participants have experienced distress during the course of the study, there are various possible courses of action for the researcher:

1. The debriefing provides an opportunity to try to reduce or eliminate participants' distress and to arrange for expert assistance if that seems required.
2. Future participants can be explicitly warned that they may experience negative reactions during the study based on the researcher's experience with previous participants.
3. Nearly all institutions (e.g. universities; research centres) that are involved in psychological research have an ethics committee. When ethical issues arise, the researcher can refer these issues to the relevant ethics committee so that it can decide what course of action is appropriate.
4. Suppose it turns out (as in our earlier example concerning the Asch situation) that only rare individuals suffering from paranoia experience large amounts of distress. One possibility would be to assess subsequent participants' paranoia level to exclude anyone who might experience undue distress.
5. If the ethical issues arising in the course of a psychological study are serious and cannot be dealt with by any of the above courses of action, the researcher may have no ethical option other than to abandon the study.

In sum, responsible researchers are constantly vigilant during a psychological study to ensure that none of the participants are experiencing distress or psychological harm of any kind. As and when they become aware that there are such problems, they should rapidly adopt one of the courses of action described above to resolve the problem or stop the study.

KEY TERMS

Confidentiality: the requirement for ethical research that information provided by participants in research is not made available to other people.

Right to privacy: the requirement for ethical research that no participants are observed in situations that would be considered private.

Protection of participants from psychological harm: an ethical guideline saying that participants should be protected from psychological harm, such as distress, ridicule, or loss of self-esteem. Any risks involved in the research should be no greater than those in the participants' own lives. Debriefing can be used to counter any concern over psychological harm.

ACTIVITY: Ethical issues in research methods

In groups of three, design a summary table to illustrate the ethical issues involved in laboratory, field, and natural experiments, with each group member taking one type of experiment then reporting back to the group.

Role of peer review

How do psychologists find out about the research that has been carried out around the world? In essence, the findings of psychological research are published in professional journals most of which are peer-reviewed. **Peer review** means that the quality or value of a research manuscript is evaluated by other researchers who are typically experts in the area of the research. The purpose is generally to decide whether the research being evaluated is of sufficient quality to merit publication in a given professional research journal. The process of peer review is important—with the leading journals in psychology, approximately 85% of the manuscripts submitted are rejected!

The main advantage of peer review is that the quality of research is judged by those best placed to evaluate it. Indeed, it is hard (or impossible) to think of a superior method to ensure that the best research is published in the top journals. For this reason, peer review is used by virtually all the leading journals everywhere in the world. Another advantage of peer review is that many research manuscripts are accepted by a journal subject to revision. What typically happens is that the research manuscript is improved as a result of the researchers revising it to take account of the suggestions and criticisms of the expert reviewers.

What are the disadvantages of peer review? First, the evaluation of research manuscripts is a somewhat imprecise and subjective process. On average, there is only modest agreement on the quality of a research manuscript by two or three expert reviewers. On occasion, research manuscripts of mine have been rated as excellent by one reviewer but as poor by another!

Second, peer reviewers are sometimes excessively sceptical about new and original findings. For example, back in the early 1960s it was generally agreed that classical conditioning occurred slowly. However, Garcia discovered with taste aversion that rats showed classical conditioning in only one trial. This makes evolutionary sense because rats that took a long time to develop taste aversion would probably not survive. In spite of the great importance of Garcia's discovery, his research was turned down by several leading journals because expert reviewers were unwilling to accept his findings.

Implications of psychological research for the economy

Psychological research of many kinds has produced substantial benefits for the economy. Here I will focus on two areas that have produced especially striking benefits—clinical psychology and health psychology.

Approximately 75 million Europeans suffer from anxiety and/or depression in any given year. Apart from the cost in human misery, there are very large financial costs as well. The total annual cost of mental disorders within Europe is estimated at about £220 billion when account is taken of lost workdays and productivity loss. Research in clinical psychology (including meta-analyses designed to compare the effectiveness of different forms of therapy) has been very effective in making these costs much lower than they would otherwise have been. We can't put a precise figure on it but it is probable that the benefits of the development of increasingly effective treatments has produced costs savings running into billions or tens of billions of pounds.

KEY TERM

Peer review: the process of evaluating the quality of someone's research by other researchers; this is typically done to decide whether the research should be published in a professional journal.

The number of people in England and Wales dying from heart disease was 68,000 fewer in the year 2000 than 1981 (Ünal et al., 2005). This reduction produced a total gain of about 925,415 life years. There are two main ways we might explain this reduction: (1) medical advances (e.g. use of statins; new surgical interventions); (2) lifestyle changes (e.g. reductions in smoking). You may be surprised to learn that Ünal et al. found that 79% of the gain in life years was due to lifestyle changes and only 21% to medical interventions!

What is the relevance of the above findings to psychology? Lifestyle changes involve changing behaviour and the experts in devising ways of changing behaviour are psychologists. More specifically, many health psychologists focus on interventions to produce beneficial lifestyle changes. Viswesvaran and Schmidt (1992) reviewed 633 smoking cessation studies. The annual success rate achieved by health psychologists was 30% with multi-component packages compared to only 6% for smokers receiving no treatment. If all 10 million smokers in the UK received multi-component smoking cessation packages from health psychologists, this could produce a gain of 24 *million* life years!

Section Summary

Aims and hypotheses

- The first stage in designing a study is to decide on its aims and hypotheses.
- Aims tell us *why* and hypotheses tell us *what*.
- The experimental/alternative hypothesis:
  - may be directional or one-tailed, or non-directional or two-tailed.
- The experimental or alternative hypothesis predicts some effect of the independent variable on the dependent variable.

Sampling

- The participants selected for a study represent a sample from some target population. They should form a representative sample and be selected to avoid sampling bias.
- Two issues with sampling are bias and generalisation. Bias means some individuals in the population are more likely to be included in the sample than others. Generalisation refers to the extent to which the findings from any given sample can be applied to a population.
- Random sampling: This is the best approach but is hard to achieve in practice because of problems in identifying whole populations, finding all participants, and obtaining responses from them.
- Systematic sampling is a modified version of random sampling in which participants are selected in a quasi-random fashion. Stratified sampling involves random sampling applied to several layers or strata in the population.
- Opportunity sampling: This is the easiest (but least satisfactory) method. The problem is that the sample is likely to be very unrepresentative.
- Volunteer sampling: In practice, researchers nearly always have to rely on volunteers. Volunteers often differ in important ways from non-volunteers. They tend to be more likely to comply with demand characteristics and to be more open and agreeable.
- The number of participants in each condition or group should depend on the likely size of the effect(s) being studied.

Experimental designs

- There are three main types of experimental design:

1. Independent groups design, in which there may be an experimental and a control group.
2. Matched pairs design.
3. Repeated measures design, in which there may an experimental and a control condition.

- With an independent groups design, random allocation is generally used to assign participants to groups. The aim is to ensure that both groups are equivalent.
- Matched pairs design use: the participants in the two groups are matched for some relevant factor(s).
- Repeated measures design compensates for any participant variation because the participants in both conditions are the same. However, there is the problem of order effects, which may be overcome by using counterbalancing.
- An advantage of the independent groups design is that there are no order effects and it can be used when a repeated measures design is inappropriate.
- The matching pairs design controls for some individual differences between participants (an advantage over the independent groups design). However, this design is more difficult and expensive to use and so is used much less in practice.

Control

- The experimenter needs to control all the important aspects of the situation and the participants so that findings are free of bias and can be generalised.
- Factors that help to achieve experimenter control are random allocation, standardisation of procedures, randomisation, and counterbalancing.

Pilot studies

- Pilot studies allow researchers to check out standardised procedures and general design with relatively little effort.
- Pilot studies help to ensure that participants understand clearly what is expected of them.
- Pilot studies can assist researchers to decide between various ways of carrying out a study.
- Pilot studies can help researchers to decide how many participants will be needed in the study itself.

Demand characteristics and investigator effects

- Demand characteristics involve the participants responding on the basis of their beliefs about the research hypothesis or hypotheses.
- Demand characteristics can be minimised by using a single-blind experimental design.
- Investigator effects include experimenter expectancy, as in the study by Rosenthal and Jacobson (1968) on teachers' expectations about children's ability. The Pygmalion effect they observed seems to depend on climate, input, output, and feedback.
- One way of overcoming investigator effects is to use a double-blind technique. Another approach is have participants interact with computers rather than a human experimenter.

Observational design

- Observational studies can involve time sampling with observations being made only during certain time intervals. It is easier to generalise findings if the time intervals are chosen randomly rather than systematically. Time sampling has the disadvantage that rare events may be missed.
- Observational studies can involve event sampling in which certain actions or events of special interest to the experimenter are recorded. This approach can be very demanding of time and effort.
- There are several stages in developing behavioural categories for studies using naturalistic observations:

1. Relevant categories need to be identified.
2. Categories based on recording or interpretation need to be produced.
3. Observers need training in use of the categories to enhance reliability.
4. Behavioural categories must produce reliable measurement.

Design of interviews and questionnaire construction

- Interviews vary in terms of structure and type of question (closed vs open).
- Unstructured interviews and open questions are suitable when:
  - the researcher wants rich, personal information;
  - the researcher doesn't intend to compare responses across interviewees;
  - the interviewers have been fully trained.
- Structured interviews and closed questions are suitable when:
  - the researcher wants data that are easy to analyse;
  - the researcher wants reliable data;
  - the researcher knows what information he/she wants from interviewees.
- Interviewer characteristics such as age, gender, and ethnicity can all influence interviewees' responses. There is also the issue of interviewer bias.
- Questionnaire design requires choosing between open and closed questions and avoiding ambiguity and bias. Open questions allow respondents to answer freely whereas closed questions require respondents to select their answer from a limited set of options.
- Open questions provide rich data but typically have poor reliability and the answers are hard to interpret. Closed questions produce data that are easy to analyse and that mostly have good reliability and reasonable validity. Most questionnaires in common use make use of closed questions.
- Questionnaires should be standardised on large representative groups so any individual's score can be interpreted.
- Questionnaires should be reliable in the sense of providing consistent measurement. This can be assessed by the test–retest technique.
- Questionnaires should be valid in that they measure what they are supposed to be measuring. There are various forms of validity: face validity; concurrent validity; and predictive validity.

Ethics

- The BPS issued a code of ethics in 2006 (revised in 2009 and 2014).
- It is based on four principles: respect; competence; responsibility; and integrity.
- Researchers need to maintain confidentiality, obtain informed consent, protect participants from harm, and avoid deception.
- Researchers should inform participants that they can withdraw from the study at any point and may decline to answer any questions.
- Participants should be debriefed at the end of their participation.

Ethical issues in design and conduct of psychological studies

- Researchers often use a cost–benefit analysis when deciding whether a study is ethical. However, it is often hard to predict costs and benefits in advance.
- Researchers should strive to avoid deception, but this isn't always possible. Debriefing can reduce the negative effects of deception.
- It is very important for researchers to have participants' voluntary informed consent. When this isn't feasible, it is possible to use presumptive consent and participants can be offered the right to withhold their data.
- Researchers must protect participants from physical and psychological harm.

Dealing with ethical issues in research

- Most ethical issues in ongoing research arise because it is not always possible to adhere to every single recommendation in the code of ethics.
- Researchers should use various means (e.g. pilot studies; debriefing) to discover ethical issues as soon as possible in the research.
- There are several courses of action a researcher can take when his/her research is clearly causing distress to the participants. These include warning participants of potential negative reactions during the study, consulting the local ethics committee,

not selecting as participants individuals especially susceptible to distress, and abandoning the study.

Peer review process

- Peer review involves research manuscripts being evaluated by expert researchers to decide whether they should be published in a given journal.
- Peer review is superior to any other method for determining the quality of research. However, it has limited reliability and experts are sometimes too sceptical of new and unexpected findings.

Implications of psychological research for the economy

- Research that has facilitated the development of increasingly effective psychological therapies for mental disorders has produced very large economic benefits.
- Health psychologists have devised various techniques to produce beneficial lifestyle changes and these changes have produce substantial increases in longevity.

DATA HANDLING AND ANALYSIS

So far in this chapter our focus has been on the most important kinds of research methods including the experimental method, observational techniques, self-report techniques, and correlations. We have also discussed the major scientific processes that are involved in the design and carrying out of research. What happens when we have collected data from all of our participants? The next (and final) stage is to make coherent sense of these data. In this section, we will be focusing on many of the ways in which researchers handle and analyse data.

Quantitative and qualitative data

The data obtained from a study may or may or may not be in numerical or quantitative form, i.e. in the form of numbers. Even if the data aren't in quantitative form, we can still carry out *qualitative* analyses based on the experiences of the individual participants. There is a major distinction here between quantitative data and qualitative data. **Quantitative data** are data in the form of numbers or scores. Such data have the advantage that we can combine the scores from different participants and can analyse group data in several different ways.

Note: Case studies are in the A-level specification but not the AS one.

Most laboratory research in psychology involves the collection of quantitative data. Indeed, the great majority of research studies discussed in this book involve quantitative data. For example, consider the very influential research by Asch on conformity (see Chapter 2). Asch focused mostly on critical trials on which all members of the group other than the actual participant produced the same wrong answer when judging lines. Asch calculated the number (or percentage) of critical trials on which he/she conformed to the wrong judgments of other group members.

In contrast, **qualitative data** are not in the form of numbers; they generally take the form of verbal reports of various kinds. For example, we can easily obtain qualitative data from people's everyday speech, from their writings, from television programmes, and from case studies. The emphasis in qualitative research is on the stated experiences of the participants and on the meanings they attach to themselves, to other people, and to the environment.

What determines whether researchers decide to collect quantitative or qualitative data? Researchers who want to obtain very rich and complex information from a single individual (or a small number of individuals) will typically collect qualitative data. For example, consider case studies. A **case study** is the detailed study of a given individual. Sigmund Freud conducted several case studies in which during psychoanalysis he asked patients to discuss in great detail their lives and fears. The intention was to achieve a deep understanding of the patient's underlying problems.

KEY TERMS

Quantitative data: data in the form of scores or numbers (e.g. on a scale running from 1 to 7).

Qualitative data: data in the form of categories (e.g. has fun watching movies; has fun watching TV) or more complex narrative accounts.

Case study: the detailed study of a single individual (or a few individuals); it typically involves qualitative data.

ACTIVITY: Qualitative and quantitative data

List all of the research methods covered in the first section of this chapter and, for each of them, say how they might produce qualitative and quantitative data

Collection techniques

We can see clearly the distinction between quantitative and qualitative data if we consider interviews and questionnaires. As discussed earlier, we can distinguish between closed and open questions. Closed questions are ones requiring the respondent to select an answer from a limited number of options, whereas open questions provide the respondent with great flexibility in terms of the answer he/she gives. Here is an example of a closed question that readily provides quantitative data:

I am a contented person
Strongly agree Agree Don't know Disagree Strongly disagree

We could score this as follows: strongly agree = 1; agree = 2; don't know = 3; disagree = 4; and strongly disagree = 5.

Here is an example of an open question: In what ways are you a contented person and in what ways are you a discontented person? The respondent might produce 200–300 words in response to such a question.

There are many studies in which we can collect various kinds of quantitative data. For example, consider a study by Bahrick et al. (1975) on people's long-term memory for those they had been at school with. He obtained four different types of quantitative data from them: free recall of their schoolmates; photo recognition memory; name recognition; and matching of names and photos.

The most common way of collecting quantitative data is based on the number of correct responses produced. However, it is also possible to use other data collection techniques. For example, we can measure reaction time—Bahrick et al. (1975) could have assessed how long it took their participants to produce each correct response.

It is increasingly common for experiments to involve the use of computers. In many cases, quantitative data are collected automatically by the computer and thus don't need to be recorded by the researcher.

We turn now to qualitative data. Qualitative data are very often obtained when researchers report a case study. The data are often presented in the form of direct quotations from the participant. For example, Griffiths (1993) chronicled one teenage boy's descent into pathological gambling and his subsequent recovery. Most of the data were collected in separate interviews with "David" and his mother. Here is part of what David had to say:

? Many of the data in Griffiths' (1993) study were retrospective. How do you feel this may have affected the results?

I always got the feeling of being "high" or "stoned" ... Although winning money was the first thing that attracted me to playing fruit machines, this gradually converted to light, sounds and excitement ... I was always very upset about losing all my money and I returned many times to try to win back my losses ... The only time I found it possible to think about giving up was after leaving the arcade at closing time and [vowing] never to return ... Whenever I felt depressed (which was practically all the time) or rejected, the urge to play machines became even bigger.

KEY TERM

Discourse analysis: a qualitative method involving the analysis of meanings expressed in various forms of language (e.g. speeches; writings). The emphasis is often on effects of social context on language use.

An important approach involving qualitative data is **discourse analysis**, which focuses on language and "assumes people use language to construct the world as they see it, and according to context and interests" (Coolican, 2004, p. 240). Its main emphasis is on meaning (i.e. what the speaker or writer is trying to say), and the key underlying assumption is that how we use language is greatly affected by the social context.

Gilbert and Mulkay (1984) carried out an interesting study on discourse analysis. They presented accounts of scientists' research in their writings and when they were being interviewed. It was clear the scientists appeared much more confident about the meaning of their findings when being interviewed.

ACTIVITY: Investigating conformity quantitatively and qualitatively

One way to investigate conformity is to stand near a traffic light and observe how many cars go through the red light, i.e. the drivers do not conform to our traffic regulations. The results of such a study would involve a frequency count of the number of people who did this. You could distinguish between male and female drivers, and people who are on their own or with passengers.

A qualitative approach would be to interview individuals about their driving habits and consider the reasons given as to why people do not always conform to traffic signals.

Which approach would provide "better" or more useful information?

EVALUATION OF QUALITATIVE DATA AND TECHNIQUES

- (+) Qualitative data offer the prospect of understanding people as rounded individuals in a social context, and the approach can be broader than the quantitative one.
- (+) Second, qualitative techniques can suggest interesting hypotheses that could be tested in subsequent research. For example, Griffiths' (1993) study on the teenage gambler David suggested that depression was responsible in part for him starting to gamble and then continuing to do so.
- (+) Third, qualitative research such as the study by Ainsworth and Bell (1970) on children's attachment (see pages 140–141) can successfully reduce very complex forms of behaviour to a manageable number of meaningful categories.
- (+) Fourth, content analysis and discourse analysis have shown convincingly that how we talk or write are influenced by the immediate social context.
- (−) Qualitative data have the substantial disadvantage that we typically can't use such data to compare different groups or to generalise our findings.
- (−) A limitation of the qualitative approach is that there is social desirability bias—the tendency for people to present themselves in the best possible light.
- (−) The qualitative data may come from a very unrepresentative sample. For example, David may not be representative of pathological gamblers.
- (−) If the researcher accumulates a huge amount of material (e.g. in a case study), he/she can easily show bias by emphasising only those bits fitting his/her favoured hypothesis. The researcher can also show bias in his/her choice of categories or the contexts from which qualitative data are obtained.
- (−) Qualitative analysis isn't very useful in several areas of psychology (e.g. memory). For example, it wouldn't have made much sense if Peterson and Peterson (1959; see pages 75–76) in their study of short-term memory had described their findings in qualitative terms!

Note: Content analysis and coding are not on the AS-level specification.

Converting qualitative measures into quantitative data

So far we have implied that there is a rigid distinction between studies in which quantitative data are collected and those in which qualitative data are collected. That is by no means the case. As we are about to see, it is often possible within the confines of a qualitative study to convert qualitative measures into quantitative data.

We will show how this is done with reference to content analysis. According to Colman (2001, p. 162), **content analysis** can be defined as techniques "for the systematic and objective description and classification of ... written or spoken verbal communications". These communications can include articles published in newspapers, speeches made by politicians on radio and television, books, and popular music.

Our focus will be on two studies. First, Cumberbatch (1990) used content analysis in a study of advertisements on British television and found only about 25% of the women in these advertisements seemed to be over 30 years old, compared to about 75% of men. On the face of it (perhaps literally!), this reflects sexist bias. In these advertisements, there were twice as many men as women, but 89% of voice-overs (especially those communicating expert/official information) involved men. The use of categories (e.g. under 30 years old; over 30 years old) allowed Cumberbatch to convert qualitative measures into quantitative data.

Second, Lau and Russell (1980) tested the hypothesis that players and coaches would explain wins and defeats in very different ways. They assumed wins would be explained by *internal* factors (e.g. "Our players were better than theirs"), whereas defeats would be explained by *external* factors (e.g. "We had no luck with the referee"). The qualitative data were obtained by searching through newspaper articles reporting on 33 major sporting events and categorising the comments of players and coaches.

What stages did the above researchers go through to convert qualitative measures into quantitative data? First, they started with general hypotheses. Cumberbatch (1990) hypothesised there would be evidence of sexism in television advertisements. In Lau and Russell's (1980) study, it was predicted that those on the winning side in sporting events would explain their success in terms of internal factors whereas those on the losing side would favour external factors.

Second, the researchers identified *categories* of theoretical relevance into which the qualitative measures could be placed. For example, Cumberbatch used categories of "below 30" and "above 30", predicting that a sexist approach would lead to far more women than men being young. There can be difficulties here—for example, do you agree the appropriate definition of young is "under the age of 30"?

Third, it is desirable to have two or more judges or coders assign the information into categories to ensure it is done in a reliable or consistent way. For example, consider the study by Lau and Russell (1980). Here is what was said by the member of a losing baseball team: "I think we've hit the ball all right. But I think we're unlucky." That is clearly identifying an external factor as causing the defeat. Here is what was said by the manager of a winning baseball team: "Piniella has done it all." This identifies an internal factor (the high ability of one of his players) as causing the victory.

Lau and Russell (1980) had two coders decide whether each statement reflected internal or external factors. There was an 88% agreement, and nearly all the discrepancies were resolved by discussion. Ideally, the coders or judges should not know the researcher's hypotheses or the identities of those providing the material to minimise the chances of distortion in the coding.

Fourth, the use of categories allowed the researchers to convert qualitative measures into quantitative data. For example, Lau and Russell (1980) converted their qualitative data into the following percentages: when they won, players and coaches made 80.3% internal attributions and only 19.7% external attributions. However, when they lost they made 52.8% internal attributions and 47.2% external attributions. These quantitative data were then analysed statistically and supported their hypothesis.

In sum, it is often possible to convert qualitative measures into quantitative data. First, the qualitative measures are converted into categories. Second, this category information is then used to test the researcher's hypothesis or hypotheses.

KEY TERM

Content analysis: a qualitative research method involving the analysis of behaviours or the written or spoken word into pre-set categories, a processing known as coding.

An investigator might study attitudes towards A-level psychology by carrying out interviews with several A-level students. One of the categories into which their statements are then placed might be "negative attitudes towards statistics". A consideration of the various statements in this category might reveal numerous reasons why A-level psychology students dislike statistics!

Primary and secondary data including meta-analysis

What typically happens in research is that the researcher collects data in a psychological study and he/she then analyses them to test the hypotheses that motivated the study in the first place. Such data are called **primary data**—they are data collected directly by the researcher specifically for the purpose of addressing the hypotheses of interest to him/her.

The great majority of data from research studies discussed in this book are primary data. For example, Asch was interested in the effects of social influence on conformity (see Chapter 2), and so he collected primary data in the form of the number of critical trials on which each participant conformed (responded in agreement with the unanimous incorrect judgements of the other group members). Another example is the study by Peterson and Peterson (1959) on forgetting in short-term memory (see Chapter 3). They directly assessed short-term memory at several different retention intervals.

In contrast, **secondary data** are typically data collected by someone other than the researcher before his/her study took place and for a purpose that differs from that of the researcher. In other words, secondary data are data that are being re-used.

We can see the difference between primary and second data if we consider research that has been carried out into environmental and genetic determinants of intelligence. What sometimes happens is that the researcher collects data on intelligence (IQ) directly from identical and fraternal twins—these are primary data. He/she also has access to official records of the socioeconomic status of the twins—these are secondary data. When the data are combined for purposes of statistical analysis, it turns out that environmental factors determine individual differences in intelligence much more among twins of low socioeconomic status than those of high status (e.g. Turkheimer et al., 2003).

What are the advantages and disadvantages of each type of data? Primary data have the advantages that they are directly relevant to the researcher's hypotheses and that they are obtained under his/her control and supervision. In sum, primary data address targeted issues. Primary data have the disadvantages that they are often costly and time-consuming to obtain and can involve considerable effort on the researcher's part. In contrast, secondary data have the advantages of being inexpensive and not time-consuming because they have previously been collected. The disadvantages of secondary data are that it is often hard to assess their quality given that the researcher had nothing to do with their collection and the data may be of only limited value to the researcher's purposes.

Glass (1976) argued that it is often very valuable to go beyond the usual research strategy of collecting and analysing primary data. He argued that researchers should think of carrying out secondary analyses. He defined secondary analysis as "the re-analysis of data for the purpose of answering the original research questions with better statistical techniques, or answering new questions with old data" (Glass, 1976, p. 3).

What is probably the most important (and increasingly popular) form of secondary analysis is meta-analysis. Glass (1976, p. 3) defined **meta-analysis** as "the analysis of analyses. I use it to refer to the statistical analysis of a large collection of analysis results from individual studies for the purpose of integrating the findings."

Why is meta-analysis useful? The most important reason is that any single study typically produces limited findings that may be biased because of the nature of the sample, the precise method used to test the hypothesis or hypotheses, and measures used to assess the dependent variable, and so on. On the assumption that the biases found in any given study are unlikely

KEY TERMS

Primary data: the data that are collected directly by the researcher during the course of a study to test his/her hypotheses.

Secondary data: data that are used by a researcher even though they were collected by someone else and with a different purpose in mind.

Meta-analysis: a form of statistical analysis based on combining the findings from numerous studies on a given issue.

to be found in most other studies on the same topic, meta-analysis provides in principle a way of "washing out" these biases and obtaining an accurate overall assessment of what is happening. At the simplest level, meta-analysis has the advantage of being based on substantially more data than any of the individual studies within the meta-analysis and this increases the likelihood of obtaining accurate findings.

Findings

Meta-analysis can be used to answer many questions. For example, it is especially useful when it comes to comparing the effectiveness of different forms of therapy for mental disorders. Craighead and Dunlop (2014) addressed the issue of whether cognitive behaviour therapy for depression was more effective when provided on its own or in combination with drug therapy. They showed in a meta-analysis that combined treatment was generally more effective.

Smith et al. (1980) used meta-analysis to analyse the findings from 475 diverse studies in which the effectiveness of several forms of therapy in treating mental disorders was compared. Overall, they discovered that, "Different types of psychotherapy (verbal or behavioural, psychodynamic, client-centred, or systematic desensitisation) do not produce different types or degrees of benefit." More specifically, they found that on average patients receiving any systematic form of psychotherapy were better off than 80% of untreated controls in terms of recovery.

Smith et al. (1980) also obtained several other more specific findings. First, the effectiveness of therapy did not depend on its length. Second, some forms of therapy were especially effective with certain disorders. For example, cognitive therapy and cognitive behaviour therapy were most effective with specific phobias, fear, and anxiety, whereas client-centred therapy worked best with patients having low self-esteem. Second, any form of therapy was more effective when provided by therapists who believed in it. Note that most of these findings couldn't have been obtained from any single study on its own—it was only when numerous studies were compared that these findings emerged.

EVALUATION

- ⊕ Secondary data can provide additional useful information over and above that provided by primary data.
- ⊕ Meta-analysis has the great advantage over analyses based on a single study in that it often provides a coherent overall picture of the pattern of findings on a given topic
- ⊕ Meta-analysis is well suited to providing answers to many important questions such as whether a given form of therapy is effective for a given mental disorder.
- ⊕ Most meta-analyses answer fairly straightforward questions such as, "Is treatment x for major depression more or less effective than treatment y?" However, many meta-analyses have been more ambitious than that (e.g. Smith et al., 1980).
- ⊖ The "Apples and Oranges" problem: studies that aren't very similar to each other may nevertheless be included within a single meta-analysis (Sharpe, 1997). This problem can be reduced by having fairly strict criteria to determine which studies are included in any given meta-analysis.
- ⊖ The "File Drawer" problem: it is generally harder for researchers to publish studies with non-significant findings. Since meta-analyses often ignore unpublished findings, the studies included may not be representative of all the studies on a given topic (Sharpe, 1997). This problem can be reduced by asking researchers in the area of the meta-analysis to supply all their relevant unpublished data.

 The "Garbage in–Garbage out" problem: many psychologists carrying out meta-analyses include all the relevant studies they can find. This means that very poor and inadequate studies are included along with high-quality ones.

Descriptive statistics

Suppose we have carried out an experiment on the effects of noise on learning with three groups of nine participants each. One group was exposed to very loud noise, another to moderately loud noise, and the third was not exposed to any noise. What they had learned from a book chapter was assessed by giving them various questions, producing a score between 0 and 20.

What is to be done with the **raw scores**? There are two key types of measures that can be taken whenever we have a set of scores from participants in a given condition: **measures of central tendency**, and **measures of dispersion**.

Mean

Scores	Number of scores	
1	1	
2	2	
4	3	
5	4	
7	5	
9	6	
9	7	
9	8	
17	9	
63	9	Total
63 ÷	9	= 7

Measures of central tendency

Measures of central tendency describe how the data cluster together around a central point. They provide some indication of the size of average or typical scores. There are three main measures of central tendency: the mean, the median, and the mode.

Mean

The **mean** in each group or condition is calculated by adding up all the scores in a given condition, and then dividing by the number of participants in that condition. Suppose the scores of the nine participants in the no-noise condition are as follows: 1, 2, 4, 5, 7, 9, 9, 9, 17. The mean is given by the total (63), divided by the number of participants (9) giving 7 (see box).

One of the advantages of the mean is that we can rapidly estimate the mean score for a very large number of participants if we have information about the total overall score. For example, suppose we know that the total overall score is somewhere between 15,000 and 17,000 and that there were between 900 and 1,100 participants. We assume the total overall score is 16,000 and that there were 1,000; this gives us an estimated mean of 16 which is unlikely to be far removed from the true figure.

The mean height of these children is 113cm. Stating the mean is one way of describing the data (in this case height).

The mean takes *all* the scores into account, making it a **sensitive** measure of central tendency. This is especially the case if the scores resemble the **normal distribution**, which

KEY TERMS

Raw scores: the data before they have been summarised in some way.

Measures of central tendency: ways of representing the mid-point of a set of data such as the mean, median, and mode.

Measures of dispersion: ways of expressing the spread of the data such as the range or standard deviation.

Mean: an average worked out by dividing the total of participants' scores by the number of participants.

Sensitive: in the context of statistics, "sensitive" means more precise, able to reflect small differences or changes.

Normal distribution: a bell-shaped distribution in which most of the scores are close to the mean. This characteristic shape is produced when measuring many psychological and biological variables, such as IQ and height.

An unexpected breakdown would cause the mean lap time to be very misleading.

is a bell-shaped distribution in which most scores cluster fairly close to the mean (discussed fully later—see Figure).

However, the mean can be very misleading if the distribution differs markedly from normal and there are one or two extreme scores in one direction. Suppose eight people complete one lap of a track in go-karts. For seven of them, the times taken (in seconds) are as follows: 25, 27, 28, 29, 34, 39, and 42. The eighth person's go-kart breaks down, and so the driver has to push it around the track, taking 288 seconds to complete the lap. The resulting overall mean of 64 seconds (see box) is clearly misleading, because no-one took even close to 64 seconds to complete one lap.

In sum, the mean has the advantage of being very sensitive in the sense that it takes account of all the scores. Its main weakness is that it becomes very misleading if there are a few extreme scores.

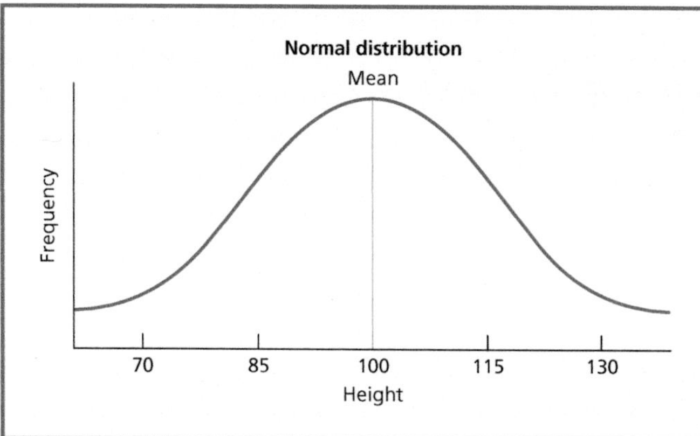

This is a normal distribution. It could represent the height of people in your class or the x-axis could be the "life-time" of a light bulb, given in weeks. Most of the scores will be clustered around the mean. The further away from the mean you get, the fewer cases there are.

Median

Another way of describing the general level of performance in each condition is the **median**. If there is an *odd* number of scores, the median is simply the middle score, having an equal number of scores higher and lower than it. In the example with nine scores in the no-noise condition, the median is 7 (see box).

Matters are slightly more complex if there is an *even* number of scores. In that case, we take the two central values and work out their mean. For example, suppose we have the following scores in size order: 2, 5, 5, 7, 8, 9. The two central values are 5 and 7, and so the median is $(5 + 7)/2 = 6$.

The main advantage of the median is that it is unaffected by a few extreme scores, because it focuses only on scores in the middle of the distribution. In the case of our go-kart data, the median would be 31.5, a more accurate "average" in this case than the mean. The median also has the advantage that it is easier to work out than the mean.

The main limitation of the median is that it ignores most of the scores, and so it is often less sensitive than the mean. It is also not always *representative* of the scores obtained, especially if there are only a few scores. Suppose we had five scores: 1, 1, 8, 25, 29. The median for these scores is 8, but that conveys a misleading impression.

Example of a misleading mean

Scores
25
27
28
29
34
39
42
288
512 ÷ 8 = 64

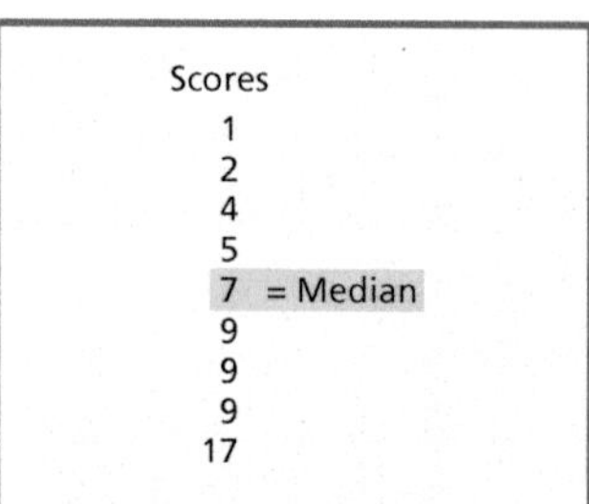

KEY TERM

Median: the middle score out of all the participants' scores.

Mode

The final measure of central tendency is the **mode**. This is simply the most frequently occurring score. In the no-noise condition example, this is 9 (see box).

The mode is unaffected by one or two extreme scores, and is the easiest measure of central tendency to work out. It can be worked out even when some of the extreme scores are not known.

Scores	
1	
2	
4	
5	
7	
9	
9	= Mode
9	
17	

The mode is useful where other measures of central tendency are meaningless, for example when calculating the number of children in the average family. It would be unusual to have 0.4 or 0.6 of a child!

However, its limitations generally outweigh these advantages. The greatest limitation is that the mode tends to be unreliable. For example, suppose we have the following scores: 4, 4, 6, 7, 8, 8, 12, 12, 12. The mode of these scores is 12. If just one score changed (a 12 becoming a 4), the mode would change to 4! Also, information about the exact values of the scores obtained is ignored in working out the mode. This makes it a less sensitive measure than the mean.

A final consideration is that it is possible for there to be more than one mode. In the case of the following scores 4, 4, 4, 4, 5, 6, 6, 8, 8, 8, 8 there are two modes (4 and 8) and the scores are therefore called **bimodal**. And some sets of data have no mode, as in our go-kart data.

EVALUATION

Mean

1. Advantages: The mean is typically more sensitive and accurate than the median or the mode. It has the advantage over the mode that it takes account of all the scores. When the scores form a normal distribution, the mean plays a major role in estimating population values (discussed later).

2. Limitations: The sensitivity of the mean means that it can easily be distorted if there are a few very discrepant scores. Another limitation is that it produces odd values like the average family having 2.2 children.

Median

1. Advantages: The median is not affected by extreme or discrepant scores. It is easier to calculate than the mean (unless there are several tied scores). It can still be used even when the value of some extreme scores is unknown.

2. Limitations: It can't be used to estimate population values. It can be misleading when there are only a few scores (e.g. 7, 8, 9, 148, 172—the median is 9!)

Mode

1. Advantages: The mode provides the most frequent or typical value within a set of scores. It is unaffected by extreme or discrepant scores. It can be assessed even when some scores at not known. It can be more informative than the mean when all scores are in whole numbers (e.g. the mode for family size is 2).

2. Limitations: The mode can't be used to estimate population values. It is of little or no use when there are two or more modes in a data set (e.g. 5, 5, 7, 9, 9).

KEY TERMS

Mode: the most frequently occurring score among participants' scores in a given condition.

Bimodal: a distribution with two modes.

Measures of dispersion

In addition to having an estimate of central tendency, it is also useful to work out measures of dispersion, such as the range and standard deviation. These measures indicate the extent to which the scores cluster around the average or are spread out. In other words, measures of dispersion indicate how much *variability* there is in the data.

The range

The simplest measure of disperson is the **range**, which can be defined as the difference between the highest and the lowest score in any condition. In the case of the following numbers: 4, 5, 5, 7, 9, 9, 9, 17, the range is calculated as follows: highest number minus lowest number, or 17 − 4 = 13.

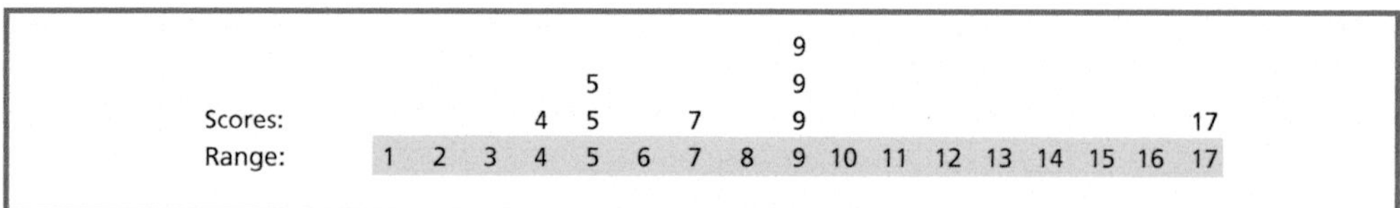

In fact, it is preferable to calculate the range slightly differently (Coolican, 1994). The revised formula (when we are dealing with whole numbers) is as follows: (highest score − lowest score) + 1, i.e. (17 − 4) + 1 = 14. This formula is preferable because it takes account of the fact that the scores were rounded to whole numbers. In our sample data, a score of 17 stands for all values between 16.5 and 17.5, and a score of 4 represents a value between 3.5 and 4.5. If we take the range as the interval between the highest possible value (17.5) and the lowest possible value (3.5), this gives us a range of 14, which is precisely the figure produced by the formula.

What has been said so far about the range applies only to whole numbers. Suppose that we measure the time taken to perform a task to the nearest tenth of a second, with the fastest time being 21.3 seconds and the slowest time being 36.8 seconds. The figure of 21.3 represents a value between 21.25 and 21.35, and 36.8 represents a value between 36.75 and 36.85. As a result, the range is 36.85 − 21.25, which is 15.6 seconds, whereas 36.8 − 21.3 = 15.5.

The range is easy to calculate and takes full account of extreme values. However, it can be greatly influenced by one score that is very different from all of the others. In the example above, the inclusion of the participant scoring 17 increases the range from 9 to 17. It is preferable to use the standard deviation (discussed next) rather than the range where there is an extreme or outlying score.

There is another problem with the range as applied to the example above—it ignores all but two of the scores, and so provides an inadequate measure of the general spread or dispersion of the scores around the mean or median.

Standard deviation

The most generally useful measure of dispersion is the **standard deviation**. It is harder to calculate than the range, but generally provides a more accurate measure of the spread of scores. However, many calculators allow the standard deviation to be worked out rapidly and effortlessly. To calculate the standard deviation manually, follow these steps (also illustrated in the worked example in the box):

1. Work out the mean of the sample. This is given by the total of all of the participants' scores $\Sigma x = 130$ (the symbol Σ means "the sum of") divided by the number of participants ($N = 13$). Thus, the mean ($\bar{x}$) is 10.
2. Subtract the mean in turn from each score ($x - \bar{x}$). The calculations are shown in the fourth column.
3. Square each of the scores in the fourth column $(x - \bar{x})^2$.

KEY TERMS

Range: the difference between the highest and lowest score in any condition.

Standard deviation: a measure of the spread of the scores around the mean. It takes account of every measurement and can be used to estimate population values.

4. Work out the total of all the squared scores, $\Sigma(x - \bar{x})^2$. This comes to 136.
5. Divide by one less than the number of participants, $N - 1 = 12$. This gives us 136 divided by 12, which equals 11.33. This is known as the **variance** (s^2), which is in squared units.
6. Use a calculator to take the square root of the variance. This produces a figure of 3.37. This is the standard deviation (*SD*).

This method is used when we want to estimate the standard deviation of the population. If we want merely to describe the spread of scores in our sample, then the fifth step is to divide the result of the fourth step by *N*. Where data are normally distributed, about two-thirds of the scores in a sample should lie within one standard deviation of the mean. This is shown in the graph on the right.

In our example, the mean of the sample is 10.0, one standard deviation above the mean will be 13.366 and one standard deviation below the mean will be 6.634. Eight out of the thirteen scores lie between these two values, which is 61.5%, which is only slightly below the expected percentage.

The standard deviation takes account of *all* the scores. As a result, it provides a sensitive measure of dispersion. It also has the advantage that it describes the spread of scores in a normal (or bell-shaped) distribution with great precision. For example, we know that 68.26% of the scores in a normal distribution will be within one standard deviation above or below the mean, 95.44% of the scores will be within two standard deviations above or below the mean, and 99.73% scores will be within three standard deviations.

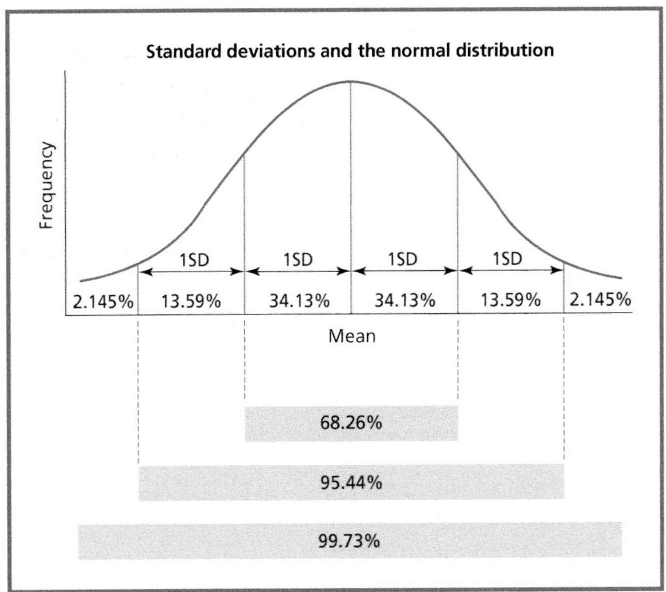

Two-thirds of a normally distributed population (or 68.26%) are located within one standard deviation of the mean, 95.44% fall within two standard deviations, and 99.73% fall within three standard deviations.

EVALUATION

- ⊕ The standard deviation can be used to estimate population values when there is a normal distribution (e.g. 68% of scores within a population will lie within one standard deviation of the mean).
- ⊕ It takes account of all the scores.
- ⊕ It provides a sensitive measure of dispersion.
- ⊖ It is distorted by extreme values.
- ⊖ It can't be used to estimate population values when the overall distribution is not normal or bell-shaped.

Standard deviation: A worked example

Participant	Score (x)	Mean ($\bar{x}$)	Deviation ($x - \bar{x}$)	Deviation^2 ($(x - \bar{x})^2$)
1	13	10	3	9
2	6	10	−4	16
3	10	10	0	0
4	15	10	5	25
5	10	10	0	0
6	15	10	5	25
7	5	10	−5	25
8	9	10	−1	1
9	10	10	0	0
10	13	10	3	9
11	6	10	−4	16
12	11	10	1	1
13	7	10	−3	9
13	130	10	$\Sigma(x - \bar{x})^2 = 136$	

Total of scores (Σx) = 130
Number of participants (N) = 13

Mean $(\bar{x}) = \frac{\Sigma x}{N} = \frac{130}{13} = 10$

Σ means "the sum of"

Variance $(s^2) = \frac{136}{13 - 1} = 11.33$

$\bar{x}$ is the symbol for the mean

Standard deviation (SD) = $\sqrt{11.3} = 3.37$

Calculation of percentages

Suppose we administer a test to 283 girls and 170 boys. Among the girls, 144 pass the test and among the boys 63 pass the test. Which gender has performed better? We can answer this question

KEY TERM

Variance: the extent of variation of the scores around the mean.

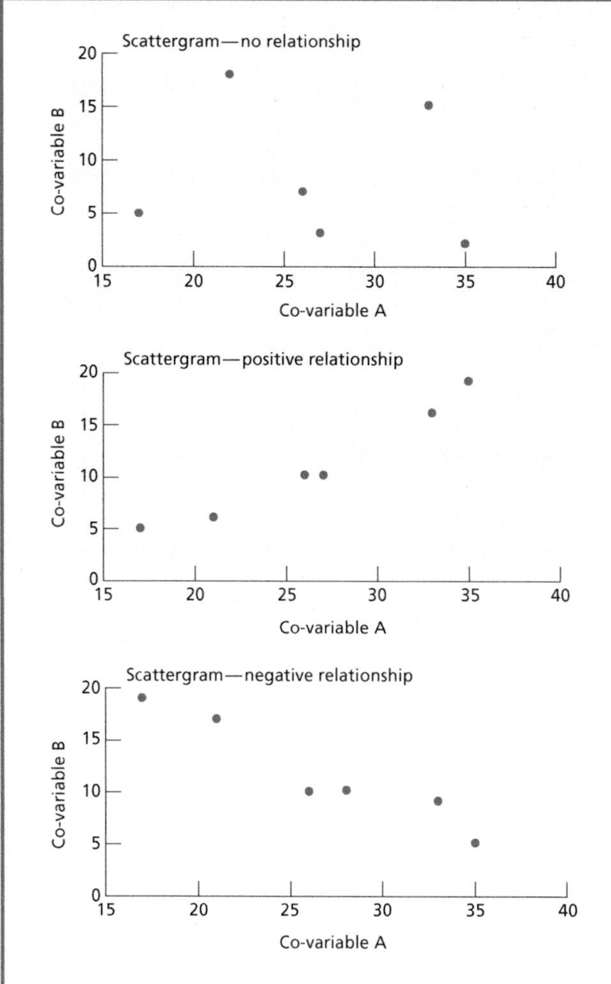

by working out the **percentage** of girls and of boys passing the test. What percentage of girls passed the test. We calculate this as follows:

$$\frac{144}{283} \times 100 = 50.9\%$$

In similar fashion, the percentage of boys passing the test is calculated as follows:

$$\frac{63}{170} \times 100 = 37.1\%$$

Thus, the girls have performed better than the boys! Their percentage success rate was greater than that of the boys.

Finally, we will use some of the above data to calculate another percentage. What percentage of the students tested were female? There were 283 girls in a total of 283 + 170 = 453 students tested. The calculation is as follows:

$$\frac{283}{453} \times 100 = 62.5$$

Positive, negative and zero correlations

We can use correlations in numerous situations. We need to have information concerning the same two variables from each participant. In a study on children, for example, we might have information about how much violent television they have watched (variable A) and how aggressive they are (variable B). We could use a correlation to see whether children who watch the most violent television tend to be the most aggressive. Here we would predict a **positive correlation**—this happens when two variables (sometimes known as co-variables) increase together.

Alternatively, we could correlate amount of concern about global warming (variable A) with frequency of flying (variable B). Here we might predict a **negative correlation**. This happens when there is an inverse or negative relationship between two variables (co-variables)—as one increases so the other decreases.

There is a third possibility. If there is no systematic relationship between two co-variables, that would indicate there is a **zero correlation**.

KEY TERMS

Percentage: number or ratio expressed as a fraction of 100.

Positive correlation: when two co-variables increase at the same time.

Negative correlation: as one co-variable increases the other decreases; they still vary in a constant relationship.

Zero correlation: when there is no systematic relationship between two co-variables.

Scatter diagram: two-dimensional representation of all the participants' scores in a correlational study.

Scatter diagram

When we have two measures of behaviour from each member of a single group of participants (called co-variables), we can present the data in a **scatter diagram** (also known as a scattergram). This is a two-dimensional representation of all the participants' scores in a correlational study. We use a dot for each participant indicating where he/she falls on the two dimensions.

If there a zero correlation (no correlation), then the dots should not form a pattern. Instead, they should appear to be distributed at random. Have a look at the top scatter diagram in the Figure. This shows a zero correlation.

You have just seen one example of a scatter diagram. Now it is your turn to produce your own scatter diagram based on the following data:

Participant	Variable A	Variable B
1	17	5
2	21	6
3	26	11
4	22	11
5	33	17
6	35	20

What does your scatter diagram (or scattergram) look like? It should resemble the second scatter diagram shown in the Figure. As you can see, the dots form a pattern going from the bottom left of the scattergraph to the top right. In other words, dots further to the right are mostly higher than those on the left. The closer the dots come to forming a straight line, the stronger the positive correlation. The example shows a positive correlation.

If there is a negative correlation between the two variables, the dots will form a pattern going from the top left to the bottom right. In other words, dots further to the right are mostly lower than those on the left. Again, the closer the dots come to forming a straight line, the stronger the negative correlation. The third scatter diagram shown in the Figure is an example of a negative correlation or relationship.

One of the main advantages of scattergrams or scatter diagrams is that they make it fairly easy for us to estimate the results of calculations. As we have seen, if the dots mostly go from bottom left to top right, then we can estimate that there is a fairly strong positive correlation. In contrast, if the dots mostly go from top left to bottom right, there is a fairly strong negative correlation. Finally, if there is no obvious pattern to the dots, this suggests that there is either no correlation (zero correlation) or a very small one.

We can assess the extent to which two co-variables are correlated using the **correlation coefficient**. A coefficient is a number expressing the degree to which two things are related. If two variables are perfectly correlated, the coefficient is 1.0. Perfect positive correlation is +1.0, and perfect negative correlation is –1.0. Of course, perfect correlation is rare. A correlation coefficient of –0.75 would reflect a strong inverse or negative relationship between two variables. A correlation of –0.85 would suggest an even stronger inverse relationship.

Note: Analysis and interpretation of correlation, including correlation coefficients are not on the AS-level specification.

A correlation coefficient of –0.25 or +0.25 would suggest a weak relationship between the two variables. A zero correlation coefficient (0.0) indicates a complete lack of relationship. It is possible to calculate the correlation coefficient between co-variables using a statistical test.

It is relevant at this point to discuss the issues of significant figures. **Significant figures** are the number of digits carrying meaning in any reported finding. Consider, for example, a correlation of +0.756. The initial zero does not carry meaning—practically all correlation coefficients start with 0. Therefore, a correlation of +0.758 has three significant figures. Is is better to report the correlation coefficient as +0.758 or as +0.76? There are two considerations here. First, if you report it as +0.758 that implies that you know what the *fourth* significant figure is—for example, if you knew that the fourth significant figure was 7 (i.e. we have +0.7587) than this would convert to +0.759 to three significant figures. Most of the time, it would be incorrect to assume that the actual coefficient correlation can be calculated with such precision and so it would be preferable to use only two significant figures (i.e. +0.76).

Second, the number of participants is important. If you have a limited number of participants you cannot claim to have such information to justify reporting correlation coefficients to three significant figures. In contrast, if you had data from thousands of participants, then it would be appropriate to report your correlation coefficients to at least three significant figures. Note that most people have a tendency to report findings to more statistical figures than is warranted!

How can we interpret correlational data? A correlation coefficient (even a very strong one) only indicates an *association* between two variables, it does NOT show one variable causes the other. For example, suppose we find that children who watch much violent television are more aggressive. This may be because watching violent television causes aggressive behaviour, or it might be that naturally aggressive children choose to watch violent television programmes. We simply don't know which interpretation is preferable from correlational data alone.

In similar fashion, finding that concern about global warming correlates negatively with amount of flying only indicates a negative association between those two variables. It may be that those most concerned about global warming deliberately avoid flying. However, there are many other possibilities. Perhaps relatively poor people are the ones most concerned about global warming, and they don't fly much because they can't afford it. We can't choose between these interpretations purely on the basis of one negative correlation.

KEY TERMS

Correlation coefficient: a number that expresses the extent to which two variables are related or vary together.

Significant figures: the number of digits in a reported finding that carry meaning.

Distributions: Normal and skewed

It was discovered a long time ago that there is often a normal or bell-shaped distribution when we consider individual differences. In other words, when we plot the frequency of different values, we find the greatest frequencies in the middle of the distribution and the smallest frequencies at the low and high extremes. This is at least approximately a normal distribution with individuals' height, length of their index finger, IQ, and so on. Here are some of the main characteristics of a normal distribution:

1. The curve is completely specified by the mean and the standard deviation.
2. The curve is symmetrical about the mid-point of the horizontal axis.
3. This mid-point is the point at which the mean, median, and mode all fall.
4. There are fewer and fewer values as we move away from the mid-point of the distribution but the tail ends of the distribution never reach the horizontal axis.
5. Within a normal distribution, 68% of the scores are within one standard deviation of the mean, 95% within two standard deviations, and 99.7% within three standard deviations.
6. In the real world, we often find approximations to the normal distribution. However, there are nearly always minor deviations from a perfectly normal distribution.

We can see some of the advantages of the normal distribution if we consider individual differences in intelligence, usually assessed in terms of **intelligence quotient (IQ)**. Since IQ is normally distributed, we can easily make sense of any given individual's IQ. For example, suppose someone has an IQ of 115. He/she is one standard deviation above the mean of the population and so is more intelligent than 84% of the population. Suppose we want to know what IQ is required to be more intelligent than 70% of the population. Statisticians can rapidly work out that an IQ of about 108 would be required.

Skewed distributions are ones which deviate substantially from the characteristics of the normal distribution. More specifically, skewed distributions are lop-sided—their peak frequency is *not* in the middle of the distribution but rather is off to one side. In addition, there is a pronounced tail in the distribution on the side of the peak where over 50% of the values are to be found. There are two types of skewed distribution:

1. **Negatively skewed distribution**: Most of the values are to the left of the peak frequency and the mean is lower than the median, which in turn is lower than the mode. This type of distribution is often found when a task or test is rather easy and so most participants obtain high scores.
2. **Positively skewed distribution**: Most of the values are to the right of the peak frequency. The mean is higher than the median which in turn is higher than the mode. This type of distribution is often found when a task is very difficult and so most participants obtain low scores.

What are the main characteristics of skewed distributions?

1. The curve differs substantially from that of the normal distribution and so it is not completely specified by the mean and standard deviation.
2. The curve is asymmetrical in shape with most values lying above (positively skewed distribution) or below (negatively skewed distribution) the peak frequency.

KEY TERMS

Intelligence quotient (IQ): a measure of general intelligence with a population mean of 100 and a standard deviation of approximately 15.

Skewed distributions: distributions that differ substantially in shape from the normal distribution.

Negatively skewed distribution: most of the scores are to the left of the peak frequency and the mode is higher than the mean.

Positively skewed distribution: most of the scores are to the right of the peak frequency and the mode is lower than the mean.

3. The mean, median, and mode all fall at different points on the curve.
4. Negatively skewed distributions often occur because of a "ceiling effect" meaning that the task is very easy; positively skewed distributions often occur because of a "floor effect" meaning the task is very difficult.

Quantitative data: Presentation, display, and construction

Measures of central tendency and of range are ways of summarising data. Perhaps it is even more helpful to use visual displays to summarise information and get a feel for what it means. Note that I said *summarise*—there is no advantage in producing a visual display that simply shows the data for each participant! If information is presented in a graph, this may make it easier for people to understand what has been found, compared to simply presenting information about the central tendency and dispersion. Note that there is a discussion of scattergrams (or scatter diagrams) and how to construct them earlier in the chapter.

Suppose we ask 25 male athletes to run 400 metres as rapidly as possible, and record their times (in seconds). Having worked out a table of frequencies (see the boxed example below), there are several ways to present these data.

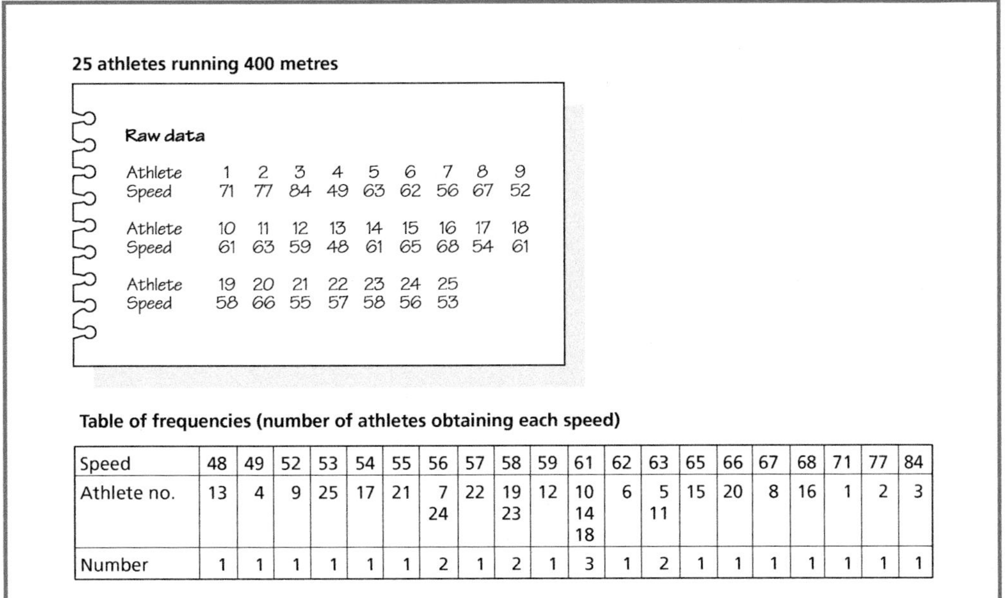

25 athletes running 400 metres

Raw data

Athlete	1	2	3	4	5	6	7	8	9
Speed	71	77	84	49	63	62	56	67	52

Athlete	10	11	12	13	14	15	16	17	18
Speed	61	63	59	48	61	65	68	54	61

Athlete	19	20	21	22	23	24	25
Speed	58	66	55	57	58	56	53

Table of frequencies (number of athletes obtaining each speed)

Speed	48	49	52	53	54	55	56	57	58	59	61	62	63	65	66	67	68	71	77	84
Athlete no.	13	4	9	25	17	21	7 24	22	19 23	12	10 14 18	6	5 11	15	20	8	16	1	2	3
Number	1	1	1	1	1	1	2	1	2	1	3	1	2	1	1	1	1	1	1	1

Note: Histograms are not on the AS-level specification.

KEY TERMS

Histogram: a graph in which the frequencies of scores in each category are represented by a vertical column; data on the y-axis must be continuous with a true zero.

Class intervals: categories into which scores can be divided to summarise frequencies.

Histogram

In a **histogram** (see Figure), the scores are indicated on the horizontal axis and the frequencies are shown on the vertical axis. How do we set about constructing a histogram? First, you have to divide the data into categories or **class intervals** of the same width. These class intervals need to be chosen so that they are not too broad because that would mean there would be very few class intervals and so much information would be lost. The class intervals should also not be too narrow—that would mean that some of the class intervals were empty. However, *all* class intervals must be represented even if there are no scores in them.

Second, note that the histogram in the Figure has categories such as 50–54 and 55–59. What that means precisely is that the class interval 50–54 consists of the frequency of all scores between 49.5 and 54.5 and the class interval 55–59 contains all scores

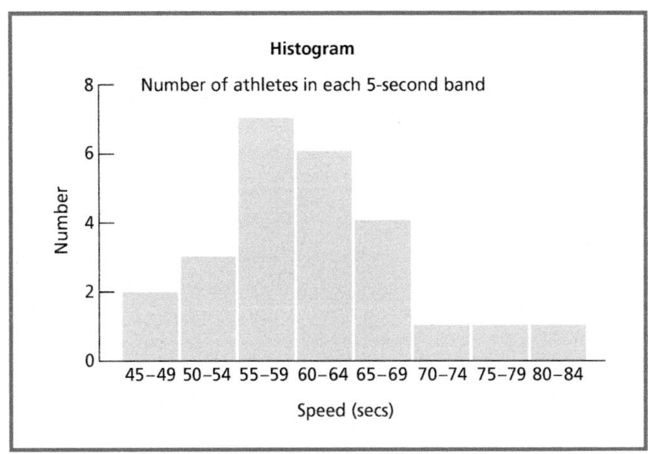

A histogram provides a means of summarising the data.

KEY TERM

Bar chart: like a histogram, a representation of frequency data, but the categories do not have to be continuous; used for nominal data.

between 54.5 and 59.5. What is often done is to label each class interval with a number representing the mid-point of that category (e.g. 52.0, 57.0).

Third, you construct the histogram with the columns varying in height in accordance with the corresponding frequencies. Note that there shouldn't be any gap between adjacent columns.

How can we interpret the histogram shown in the Figure? It shows clearly that most of the athletes ran 400 metres between about 55 and 69 seconds with relatively few athletes taking less or more time than that. It also indicates that there is a tail on the distribution on the right side with one athlete taking over 80 seconds.

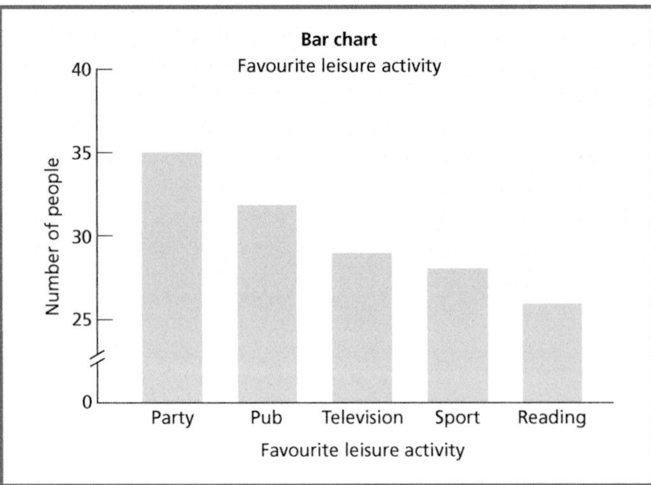

A bar chart makes it easy to compare the popularity of different leisure activities. We can see at a glance that going to a party was the most popular leisure activity, whereas reading a good book was the least popular. The data in this chart are in nominal categories.

Bar charts

Bar charts are often used when the data are in categories rather than in numbers. The categories are shown along the horizontal axis, and the frequencies are indicated on the vertical axis, as in a histogram. The categories in bar charts cannot be ordered numerically in a meaningful way, but in ascending (or descending) order of popularity. Various kinds of information can be represented in bar charts including frequencies, sample means, or percentages. The rectangles in a **bar chart** should *not* touch each other. Bar charts are often called bar graphs. Note, however, that bar charts or graphs can be displayed so that frequencies are indicated on the horizontal axis—this can make it easier to see precisely how the various categories differ in frequency.

The scale on the vertical axis of a bar chart normally starts at zero, although it is sometimes convenient for presentational purposes to have it start at some higher value. If so, it should be made clear in the bar chart that the lower part of the vertical scale is missing. The columns in a bar chart often represent frequencies, but they can also represent means or percentages for different groups (Coolican, 2004).

There is an example of a bar chart in the Figure. It shows the frequencies of different favourite leisure activities. As you can see, it is organised for convenience so that the category with the largest frequency is on the left and the one with the smallest frequency is on the right. Sometimes this will not be appropriate. For example, if you had a bar chart displaying frequencies of some category in children aged 4, 5, and 6, it would make sense to have 4-year-olds at the left followed by 5-year-olds and 6-year-olds.

How can we interpret the bar chart shown in the Figure? We can see immediately that parties and going to the pub are the favourites with reading being much less favoured.

We could present the data from the above study in other forms. The actual numbers of each favourite leisure activity are as follows: party: 35 participants; pub: 32 participants; television: 29 participants; sport: 28 participants; and reading: 26 participants. Thus, the total number of participants was 150 and we could work out the percentage favouring each activity. To do this, we take each score in turn and divide it by 150 then multiply it by 100. This gives us the following percentages to one place of decimals: party (23.3%); pub (21.3%); television (19.3%); sport (18.7%); and reading (17.3%).

It is very easy to convert the above figures into fractions (parts of the whole). Thus, 35 ÷ 150 = .233, 32 ÷ 150 = .213, and so on. We could easily use these fractions to construct a pie chart (see Figure) showing the relative importance of the various favourite activities.

Reading 17.30%
Party 26.30%
Sport 18.70%
Pub 21.30%
Television 19.30%

A pie chart showing the relative importance of the various favourite activities.

If we knew the total number of participants (150) and the percentage of participants in any given category, we could work out how many participants were in that category. For example, we are told that 23.3% of the participants had parties as their favourite leisure activity. What we need to do is as follows: 23.3 × 1.50 = 35.05 (which rounds off to 35).

We can look at the data from the above study in yet another way. Suppose we argued that parties, the pub, and sport are all social activities whereas television and reading are non-social activities (don't worry if this categorisation doesn't sound right to you!). On that basis, 95 participants have a social favourite leisure activity and 55 have a non-social activity. We can express this as a **ratio** (the relative size of two classes that can be expressed as a proportion). The ratio of non-social to social favourite activities is 55:95. We can express this as a fraction $\frac{55}{95}$. This can be reduced down to $\frac{11}{19}$.

Graphs and charts should be clearly labelled and presented so that the reader can rapidly make sense of the information contained in them. It is also helpful to use squared paper when recording numbers and drawing graphs.

ACTIVITY: Qualitative and quantitative analysis

Ask each of the class or another group of people to answer two questions:

a. Does having a tan make a person look more attractive? Yes/no
b. Is it healthy and safe to stay out in the sun for as long as possible in the summer? Yes/no

Then count your answers and make two bar charts. Is this qualitative or quantitative analysis?

Do the two bar charts match or not? Why? Is this now qualitative or quantitative analysis?

Tables and calculation of means

If we want to provide a summary of our findings from a study, we don't have to produce a graph or visual display. Instead, we can produce a table summarising what has happened. Tables have the advantage that several different kinds of summary information can be included in a single table. They also have the advantage that precise figures (e.g. for group means) are provided, whereas it is often only possible to work out approximate figures when looking at graphs. However, tables have the disadvantage that they can be a little harder to interpret than a graph, and it can be harder to visualise what has been found.

Below we have the data from a study in which 6-year-olds and 9-year-olds learned and recalled a word list consisting of 20 words while being presented with loud noise or no noise. The scores indicate the number of words correctly recalled by each participant.

	6-year-olds		9-year-olds	
	Loud noise	**No noise**	**Loud noise**	**No noise**
	4	6	13	15
	8	9	9	10
	5	5	12	8
	10	12	7	8
	7	8	10	12
	7	10	9	16
		8	10	13
				13
Total:	41	58	70	95
No.	6	7	7	8
Mean:	6.8	8.3	10.0	11.9
Range:	7	8	7	9

KEY TERM

Ratio: the relative size of two classes; it can be expressed as a proportion.

Here is how we calculate the mean: we take the total in each condition and divide it by the number of participants in that condition: 41 divided by 6 = 6.8; 58 divided by 7 = 8.3.

Here is how we calculate the range: we use the formula (highest score − lowest score) + 1:

(10 – 4) + 1 = 7; (12 – 5) + 1 = 8.

Here is what our table will look like:

Table. Effects of loud noise and age on recall of a word list (maximum score = 20).

	6-year-olds		9-year-olds	
	Loud noise	**No noise**	**Loud noise**	**No noise**
No. of participants	6	7	7	8
Mean correct items	6.8	8.3	10.0	11.9
Range	7	8	7	9

How can we interpret these findings? They indicate that memory performance at both ages is better in the absence of loud noise and so loud noise impairs performance. We can see that the older children (9-year-olds) perform better than the younger children (6-year-olds). We can also see that there were relatively few participants in each condition and that the dispersion of the scores as assessed by the range was similar in all conditions.

We can also construct frequency tables. We can see how this is done with reference to our earlier example of 25 athletes running 400 metres. Here is what the table will look like:

Table. Frequency table showing the time taken by 25 male athletes to run 400 metres divided into 5-second class intervals.

Time taken (in sec.)	Frequency	Percentage
45–49	2	8
50–54	3	12
55–59	7	28
60–64	6	24
65–69	4	16
70–74	1	4
75–79	1	4
80–84	1	4

Inspection of the frequency table indicates that most of the athletes (68%) ran 400 metres in between 55 and 69 seconds. A few athletes took less time than that and a few others took more time than that.

Statistical tests of difference

In this section, we will be discussing statistical tests that allow us to decide whether the differences between two conditions or groups are statistically significant. Initially, we will consider some general principles that need to be taken into account. After that, we will proceed to the tests themselves.

When deciding which statistical test to use, it is important to consider aspects of the data. There are four types of data of increasing levels of precision:

- Nominal: the data consist of numbers of participants falling into various categories (e.g. extraverted; introverted).
- Ordinal: the data can be ordered from lowest to highest (e.g. the finishing position of athletes in a race).
- Interval: the data differ from ordinal data because the units of measurement are fixed throughout the range; for example, there is the same "distance" between a height of 1.82 metres and 1.70 metres as between 1.70 metres and 1.58 metres.
- Ratio: the data have the same characteristics as interval data but also have a meaningful zero point; for example, time measurements provide ratio data because the notion of zero time is meaningful and 10 seconds is twice as long as 5 seconds.

Note: Nominal, ordinal and interval levels of measurement are not on the AS-level specification.

Statistical tests can be divided into parametric tests and non-parametric tests. **Parametric tests** should only be used when the data obtained from a study satisfy various requirements: there should be interval or ratio data and the data should be normally distributed (i.e. in the shape of a bell-shaped curve). In contrast, **non-parametric tests** can nearly always be used even when the requirements of parametric tests are not satisfied.

As discussed earlier, there are three kinds of design that can be used when we are interested in deciding whether the differences between two conditions or groups are significant. First, there is the independent groups design in which each participant is allocated at random to one and only one condition. Second, there is the repeated measures design in which the same participants are used in both conditions. Third, there is the matched pairs design in which the participants in the two conditions are matched in terms of some variable (e.g. age; intelligence) that might be relevant to their performance.

If the independent groups design has been used, then the Mann-Whitney U test is likely to be an appropriate test to use. If the repeated measures or matched pairs design has been used, then the Wilcoxon matched pairs signed ranks test is likely to be appropriate. They are both non-parametric tests and so can be used with ordinal, interval, or ratio data and the data don't have to be normally distributed. We will also discuss the sign test which (like the Wilcoxon matched pairs signed ranks test) can be used when a repeated measures or matched pairs design has been used. The sign test can be used when the data are ordinal. If the data are interval or ratio, it would be more informative to use the Wilcoxon test.

Note: The concept of statistical significance is not on the AS-level specification.

General issues

Two more issues need to be considered before discussing how to use these two statistical tests. First, we use statistical tests to choose between the following:

- Experimental hypothesis (e.g. extensive training improves performance).
- **Null hypothesis,** which asserts there is no difference between conditions (e.g. extensive training has no effect on performance).

If the statistical test indicates there is only a small probability of the difference between conditions (e.g. extensive training vs no training) having occurred if the null hypothesis were true, we reject the null hypothesis in favour of the experimental hypothesis.

Why do we focus initially on the null hypothesis rather than the experimental hypothesis? The reason is that the experimental hypothesis is rather imprecise. It may state that extensive training improves performance but it doesn't indicate the *extent* of the improvement. This imprecision makes it hard to evaluate an experimental hypothesis directly. In contrast, a null hypothesis such as that extensive training has no effect on performance is precise and this precision allows us to use statistical tests to decide the probability that it is correct.

Psychologists generally use the 5% (.05) level of **statistical significance**. What this means is that the null hypothesis is rejected (and the experimental hypothesis accepted) if the probability that the results were due to chance is 5% or less. This is often expressed as $p < .05$ where p = the probability of the result if the null hypothesis is correct and < means less than. The key decision

KEY TERMS

Parametric tests: statistical tests that require interval or ratio data and normally distributed data.

Non-parametric tests: statistical tests that don't involve the requirements of parametric tests.

Null hypothesis: this hypothesis states that there will be no differences between the two conditions being compared (other than chance differences).

Statistical significance: the level at which the decision is made to reject the null hypothesis in favour of the experimental hypothesis.

is whether or not to reject the null hypothesis and that is why the .05 level of statistical significance is so important. However, our data sometimes indicate that the null hypothesis can be rejected at the 1% level ($p < .01$). What that means is that the probability that the results were due to chance is 1% or less.

Findings that are significant at the 1% level are clearly more impressive than those that are significant only at the 5% level. As a result, if an experimenter's findings are significant at the 1% and 5% levels, it is customary to use the 1% level when reporting their statistical significance.

Second, you may remember earlier in the chapter that we distinguished between directional and non-directional hypotheses. A directional hypothesis predicts the direction of the findings (e.g. extensive training enhances performance) whereas a non-directional hypothesis does not (e.g. the effect of extensive training on performance will differ from that of no training). If the researcher has used a directional hypothesis, it is appropriate to assess the findings using a one-tailed test. It is called a one-tailed test because the researcher is only interested in differences between the two conditions in one direction. In contrast, if the researcher has used a non-directional hypothesis, a two-tailed test should be used. It is called a two-tailed test because the researcher is unsure which condition will have the larger scores.

Mann-Whitney U test

This test is used when an independent groups design has been used and the data are ordinal, interval, or ratio. Suppose we have two conditions. In both conditions, participants have to fire arrows at a board and the score obtained is recorded. There are 10 participants in Condition A in which no training is provided before their performance is assessed. There are 12 participants in Condition B and they receive extensive training before their performance is assessed. There is a directional hypothesis: extensive training will improve performance and so a one-tailed test is appropriate. In other words, the scores in Condition B should be significantly higher than those in Condition A.

Mann-Whitney U test: A worked example

Experimental hypothesis: Extensive training improves performance
Null hypothesis: Training has no effect on performance

Participant	Condition A	Rank	Participant	Condition B	Rank
1	4	2	1	21	15
2	10	9	2	26	18
3	12	11	3	20	14
4	28	20	4	22	16
5	7	5	5	32	22
6	13	13	6	5	3
7	12	11	7	12	11
8	2	1	8	6	4
9	9	7.5	9	8	6
10	27	19	10	24	17
			11	29	21
			12	9	7.5

Smaller sample = Condition A

Sum of ranks in smaller sample (T) = 98.5

Number of participants in smaller sample (N_A) = 10

Number of participants in larger sample (N_B) = 12

Formula: $U = N_A N_B + \left(\frac{N_A(N_A + 1)}{2}\right) - T$

Example: $U = (10 \times 12) + \left(\frac{10(10 + 1)}{2}\right) - 98.5 = 76.5$

Formula for calculating U′: $U' = N_A N_B - U$

Example: $U' = (10 \times 12) - 76.5 = 43.5$

Comparing U and U′, U′ is the smaller value. The calculated value of U′ (43.5) is checked against the tabled value for a one-tailed test at 5%.

Table values

	$N_A = 10$
$N_B = 12$	34

Conclusion: As 43.5 is greater than 34, the null hypothesis should be retained—i.e., training has no effect on performance in this task.

The first step is to rank all the scores from both groups together with a rank of 1 being given to the smallest score, a rank of 2 to the second smallest score, and so on. If there are tied scores, then the mean of the ranks involved is given to each of the tied participants. For example, two participants were tied for the 7th and 8th ranks and so they both received a rank of 7.5.

The second step is to work out the sum of the ranks in the smaller sample which is Condition A in our example. This value is known as T and it is 98.5 in our example.

The third step is to calculate U from the formula in which N_A is the number of participants in the smaller sample and N_B is the number in the larger sample:

$$U = N_A N_B + \left(\frac{N_A(N_A + 1)}{2}\right) - T$$

The fourth step is to calculate U′ from the formula $U' = N_A N_B - U$.

The fifth step is to compare U and U′, selecting whichever is the smaller value provided the results are in the predicted direction. The smaller value (i.e. 43.5) is then looked up in Appendix Table 1. The observed value must be equal to (or smaller than) the tabled value in order to be significant. In this case, we have a one-tailed test because the experimental hypothesis stated that extensive training would improve performance and the statistical significance level is the standard $p < .05$ (5% level). With 10 participants in our first condition and 12 in our second condition, the table value for significance is 34. As our value of 43.5 is greater than 34, the conclusion is that we retain the null hypothesis.

Wilcoxon matched pairs signed ranks test

The Wilcoxon matched pairs signed ranks test can be used when a repeated measures or matched pairs design has been used and the data are at least ordinal. We will see how this test is calculated by using a worked example (see Figure). There were 12 participants in an experiment who were involved in both conditions. In Condition A they were presented with 20 words to learn in a situation with no noise; learning was followed 5 minutes later by a test of free recall in which they wrote down as many words as they could remember in any order. Condition B involved presenting 20 different words to learn in a situation of loud noise, again followed by a test of free recall. The experimenter predicted that free recall would be higher in the no-noise condition. Thus, there was a directional hypothesis and so a one-tailed test is appropriate.

The first step is to place all the data in a table in which each participant's two scores are in the same row. The second step is to subtract the Condition B score from the Condition A score for each participant to give the difference (d). The third step is to omit all participants whose two scores are the same, i.e. d = 0. The fourth step is to rank all the difference scores obtained in the second step from 1 for the smallest difference, 2 for the second smallest difference, and so on. For this purpose, ignore the + and − signs, thus taking the absolute size of the difference. The fifth step is to add up the sum of the positive ranks (50 in the example) and separately add up the sum of the negative ranks (5 in the example). The smaller of these values is T which in this case is 5. The sixth step is to work out the number of participants whose two scores are not the same. In the example, $N = 10$.

The obtained value of T must be the same as (or less than) the tabled value (see Appendix Table 2) for the results to be significant. The tabled value for a one-tailed test and $N = 10$ is 11 at the 5% ($p < .05$) level of statistical significance and it is 5 at the 1% level. Thus, the findings are significant at the 1% level ($p < .01$) on a one-tailed test. We can conclude that our directional hypothesis has been supported at that level.

Wilcoxon matched pairs signed ranks test: A worked example

Experimental hypothesis: Free recall is better when learning takes place in the absence of noise than in its presence

Null hypothesis: Free recall is not affected by whether or not noise is present during learning

Participant	Condition A *(no noise)*	Condition B *(loud noise)*	Difference (d) *(A – B)*	Rank
1	12	8	4	7.5
2	10	10	0	–
3	7	8	−1	2.5
4	12	11	1	2.5
5	8	3	5	9
6	10	10	0	–
7	13	7	6	10
8	8	9	−1	2.5
9	14	10	4	7.5
10	11	9	2	5
11	15	12	3	6
12	11	10	1	2.5

Sum of positive ranks (7.5 + 2.5 + 9 + 10 + 7.5 + 5 + 6 + 2.5) = 50

Sum of negative ranks (2.5 + 2.5) = 5

Smaller value (5) + T

Number of participants who scored differently in condition A and B (N) = 10

Question: For the results to be significant, the value of T must be the same as, or less than, the tabled value.

Table values

	5%	1%
N = 10	S = 1	5

Conclusion: In this experiment T is less than the tabled value at the 5% level and the same as the tabled value at the 1% level of significance, so the null hypothesis is rejected in favor of the experimental hypothesis.

Sign test

Remember that the sign test is used when we have a repeated measures or matched pairs design. It is most useful when the data are ordinal. It can also be used with interval or ratio data, but it is a relatively insensitive test and so with such data the Wilcoxon test would be preferable.

We will use the data from our worked example on the Wilcoxon test (see box). Remember that the prediction is that free recall will be higher in the no-noise condition than the loud-noise condition. We start by drawing up a table in which each participant's scores in Condition A and Condition B are recorded. Each participant whose score in Condition A is greater than his/her score in Condition B is given a plus sign (+) in the sign column and each participant whose score in Condition B is greater than his/her score in Condition A is given a minus sign (–) in the sign column. Each participant whose scores in both conditions are the same receives a 0 sign in the sign column; such participants are ignored in the subsequent calculations—they do not contribute to N (the number of paired scores) because they provide no evidence about effect direction.

Sign test: A worked example

Experimental hypothesis: Free recall is better when learning takes place in the absence of noise than in its presence

Null hypothesis: Free recall is not affected by whether or not noise is present during learning

Participant	Condition A *(no noise)*	Condition B *(loud noise)*	Sign
1	12	8	+
2	10	10	0
3	7	8	–
4	12	11	+
5	8	3	+
6	10	10	0
7	13	7	+
8	8	9	–
9	14	10	+
10	11	9	+
11	15	12	+
12	11	10	+

Number of + signs = 8
Number of – signs = 2
Number of 0 signs = 2

Number of participants with differing scores (N) = 8 + 2 = 10
Number of participants with less-frequent sign (S) = 2

Question: Is the value of S in this example the same as or lower than the tabled value for S?

Table values

	5%
N = 10	S = 1

Conclusion: In this experiment the value of S is higher than the tabled value when N = 10. The null hypothesis (that noise has no effect on learning and memory) cannot be rejected.

In the example, there are 8 plus signs, 2 minus signs, and 2 participants had the same score in both conditions. If we ignore the 2 participants with the same scores in both conditions, this gives us $N = 10$. Now all we need to do is to work out the number of these 10 participants having the less frequently occurring sign; this value is known as S. In our example, $S = 2$. We can then refer to Table 3 in the Appendix with $N = 10$ and $S = 2$ and the statistical significance is the standard 5% or $p < .05$. The tabled value for a one-tailed test (we have a directional hypothesis) is 1. Thus, our obtained S value of 2 isn't significant at the 5% level. We therefore conclude that we cannot reject the null hypothesis that noise has no effect on learning and memory.

How can it be that the same data can produce a significant finding using the Wilcoxon matched pairs signed ranks test but not on the sign test? The reason is that the sign test is insensitive (or lacking in power) because it takes no account of the *size* of each individual's difference in free recall in the two conditions. It is because this information is made use of in the Wilcoxon test that a significant result was obtained using that test.

Algebraic symbols

We have seen that the algebraic symbol < is used to indicate "less than". For example, if we discover using a statistical test that the probability of our obtained difference between two conditions on the null hypothesis is less than 5%, we would express this as follows: $p < .05$. In similar fashion, if the probability were less than 1%, we would express it as follows: $p < .01$. There is also an algebraic symbol that is used to indicate "much less than": this is <<. For example, we could indicate that the probability of our findings is much less than 1% by writing $p << .01$.

There are comparable algebraic symbols to indicate "more than" and "much more than". As you may have guessed, the symbol for "more than" is > and that for "much more than" is >>. Thus, for example, if our findings in a study failed to reach the 5% level of significance, we could express this as follows: $p > .05$. If the findings were a long way away from reaching the 5% level of significance we could express this as follows: $p >> .05$.

There are other algebraic symbols that are useful in psychology. The simplest of these is = which means "equal to". Thus, for example, $8 + 2 = 10$. Another symbol is ~ which means "approximately equal to". Finally, there is $\propto$ which means "proportional to" and refers to the relationship between two variables (e.g. $A \propto B$). Two variables are directly proportional if increases in one variable (A) are associated with increases in the other variable (B). For example, one variable might be "hours of television watched" and the other variable might be "aggressive behaviour". Two variables are inversely proportional if increases in one variable are associated with decreases in the other variable. For example, one variable might be "concerns about global warming" and the other variable might be "frequency of flying".

Section Summary

Quantitative and qualitative data

- Quantitative data are in the form of numbers or scores whereas qualitative are not in the form of numbers and often consist of verbal reports.
- Closed questions on interviews and questionnaires produce quantitative data whereas open questions produce qualitative data.
- Discourse analysis is a qualitative approach in which the meanings of language communications are analysed.
- Qualitative data can provide rich and detailed information about individuals, but have the disadvantage that we typically can't use such data to compare different groups or to generalise our findings.
- Content analysis is a qualitative technique in which qualitative data are assigned to pre-set categories; it is sometimes possible to convert such qualitative measures into quantitative data.

Primary and secondary data including meta-analysis

- Primary data are data collected directly by the researcher and designed to test the researcher's hypotheses.
- Secondary data are data used by the researcher even though they were collected by someone else beforehand and for a purpose different to that of the researcher.
- Meta-analysis is the most important form of secondary analysis; it involves combining the findings from numerous studies to address major issues.
- Meta-analyses have clarified the relative effectiveness of different forms of therapy for several different mental diseases.

- Problems with meta-analysis include the apples and oranges problem, the file drawer problem, and the garbage in–garbage out problem.

Descriptive statistics

- The three main measures of central tendency are the mean, median, and mode. The mean is typically more sensitive and accurate than the median or mode. However, it can easily be distorted if there are a few very discrepant scores.
- The median is not affected by extreme or discrepant scores. However, it can be misleading when there are only a few scores.
- The mode is very easy to calculate but it is of little or no use when there are two or more modes in a data set.
- The range and standard deviation are the main measures of dispersion. The range is distorted by one or two extreme scores or outliers and it ignores most of the scores. The standard deviation takes account of all the scores and is especially useful when the overall distribution is normal or bell-shaped.
- When we have scores on two variables from all participants, we can use correlations. Correlations are positive when the two variables increase together, negative when increases in one variable are associated with decreases in the other variable, and zero when there is no relationship between the two variables.
- Correlational data can be represented in a scatter diagram or scattergram.

Distributions: Normal and skewed

- A normal distribution is one that is completely specified by the mean and standard deviation. The normal distribution curve is symmetrical about the mid-point of the horizontal axis and this is the point at which the mean, median, and mode all fall. With a normal distribution, 68% of the scores lie within one standard deviation of the mean.
- Skewed distributions differ substantially from the characteristics of the normal distribution, notably with the distribution being asymmetrical.
- In negatively skewed distributions, most of the scores are to the left of the peak frequency and the mean is lower than the mode.
- In positively skewed distributions, most scores are to the right of the peak frequency and the mean is higher than the mode.

Quantitative data: Presentation, display, and construction

- We can construct a histogram from quantitative data by dividing the scores into categories or class intervals and then producing columns varying in height in accordance with the frequency of each category.
- Bar charts are often used when data are in categories rather than numbers. Each category is represented by a column indicating the frequency of that category.
- The information in bar charts can be converted into percentages, fractions, and ratios.
- We can use the findings from any given study to construct a table that summarises the data. For example, we can represent the frequencies of different scores by means of a frequency table.

Statistical tests of difference

- We can use parametric tests to compare scores in two conditions provided that the data are normally distributed; otherwise, we need to use non-parametric tests.
- We can use the Mann-Whitney U test when we have an independent groups design and a Wilcoxon matched pairs signed ranks test when we have a matched pairs or repeated measures design. Both these tests are non-parametric. The sign test (another non-parametric test) can also be used when we have a matched pairs or repeated measures design. However, it is less sensitive than the Wilcoxon test.
- We use a one-tailed test if the hypothesis is directional and a two-tailed test if it is non-directional.

- If the probability of obtaining by chance the difference we obtained between our two groups is less than 5% ($p < .05$), we reject the null hypothesis in favour of the experimental hypothesis. More striking findings may also be statistically significant at less than 1% level ($p < .01$).

You have reached the end of the chapter on research methods in psychology. Research is fundamental to the status of psychology as a scientific subject. It enables us to be more than "armchair psychologists". We should be able to provide systematic, reliable, and valid evidence for our views.

Further Reading

- A book that covers most research methods in a very accessible way is H. Coolican (2014) *Research methods and statistics in psychology (6th Edn)* (Hove, UK: Psychology Press).
- Another useful textbook is J.J. Foster and J. Parker (1995) *Carrying out investigations in psychology: Methods and statistics* (Leicester, UK: BPS Books).
- The various forms of non-experimental study and qualitative analysis are described in C. Dyer (2006) *Research in psychology: A practical guide to research methods and statistics* (Oxford: Blackwell).

EXAM HINT

- There are so many different types of research methods question that it really is a good idea to prepare for the different types of question as you work your way through the topic.
- PRACTISE, PRACTISE, PRACTISE—it's more important than with any of the other topics because unlike the other topics where you can know all the possible questions without looking at an exam paper, with this question you need to be familiar with the research summary that is part of the question.
- Contextualise—research methods questions often include the phrase "... in the context of this investigation", which means you must relate your answer to the study described in the question. For example, if you are asked to give a criticism don't generalise, but instead pick up on something specific from the summary in the question.

ACTIVITY: ANSWERS (FROM PAGE 341)

1. IV = length of separation, DV = emotional development.
2. IV = degree of respect for model, DV = degree of conformity.
3. IV = whether test is before or after lunch, DV = number of words recalled.
4. IV = gender, DV = ability to throw a ball.
5. IV = attractiveness, DV = rating for likeability.

Revision Questions

Some people argue that memory for images is better than memory for words. A psychologist tested this idea in an experiment. First, a pilot study was carried out. Then, 24 participants were randomly allocated to one of two conditions.

Condition A: there were 12 participants in this condition. All were placed in a room and given 10 minutes to look at 50 words and to try to remember the words. After 10 minutes they were told to write down as many words on the list as possible. Answers were collected by the psychologist after 15 minutes.

Condition B: there were 12 participants in this condition. The participants were given 10 minutes to look at 50 images of objects. After 10 minutes they were told to write down the names of as many objects as they could. Answers were collected by the psychologist after 15 minutes.

The psychologist counted the number of correctly recalled words in both conditions.

Table: Total number of ideas generated in Condition A (words) and in Condition B (images)

	Condition A	Condition B
1	18	19
2	17	25
3	28	28
4	33	29
5	14	36
6	18	42
7	18	44
8	28	40
9	29	39
10	32	36
11	30	40
12	28	42
Mean number of words recalled	24	35

1. a. Identify the experimental design used in this study. (1 mark)

   b. Outline one advantage of this experimental design. (2 marks)
2. Identify another experimental design that the experimenter could have used for this study. (1 mark)
3. a. Apart from random allocation of participants, suggest an extraneous variable that might have affected the results of this study. (1 mark)

   b. Explain how the impact of this extraneous variable on the findings could have been reduced. (3 marks)
4. Write a suitable hypothesis for the study. (3 marks)
5. Explain why the psychologist carried out a pilot study. (2 marks)
6. Explain how the psychologist could have used random allocation to assign the participants to the two conditions. (3 marks)
7. Calculate the range of scores in each condition. (2 marks)
8. Calculate the standard deviation of the participant scores in condition A. (12 marks)
9. Which is the most appropriate measure of distribution to use with the data from this experiment? Explain your answer. (4 marks)
10. Draw an appropriate graph to represent these findings. Give the graph an appropriate title and label the axes. (4 marks)

Note: Most of this section is only applicable to A-level. If you are studying AS level you only need to know about the Sign test.

RESEARCH METHODS: APPENDIX

In order to use the statistical tables on the following pages, you first need to decide whether:

1. Your data are in numerical form, in which case they are suitable for quantitative analysis; otherwise, use qualitative analysis.
2. You have obtained nominal, ordinal, interval, or ratio data.
3. Your data show a difference between the two conditions (the experimental hypothesis) or not (the null hypothesis).
4. You can use parametric tests (i.e. if data are interval or ratio, normally distributed, and the variances in the two conditions are similar); otherwise non-parametric tests can be used. Non-parametric tests can be used in nearly all cases, and it is the most useful of these that are described in this book.

Once you have obtained your results, you can construct a table of frequencies, and decide which type of chart or graph you wish to use in order to present your data graphically in the clearest way possible.

The next step to take is to analyse your data, as follows:

1. Calculate measures of central tendency: mean, median, and mode.
2. Calculate measures of dispersion: range, interquartile range, variation ratio, and standard deviation.

You will then need to apply further statistical analysis using the statistical tests described in Chapter 8. Please refer to the worked examples for each of these and follow the step-by-step instructions in the main text.

How to decide which test to use

The main purpose of these tests is to decide the probability of the null hypothesis being correct, and to evaluate its significance. Each test involves calculating your observed value from your results, and then looking up the critical value in a table of values, to see whether your value is greater than, equal to, or less than the critical value. Use the appropriate column or table, depending on (a) whether you used a one- or two-tailed test and (b) which level of significance or probability (p) you wish to check. If p is less than or equal to .05 or 5%, which is the standard probability of significance used by psychologists, the null hypothesis is rejected in favour of the experimental hypothesis. To see whether the findings are highly significant, look at whether the null hypothesis still holds true at $p = .01$, or 1%, or even $p = .001$, or .1%.

If your experimental hypothesis is directional (i.e. you predicted the direction of any effects), you need to use a one-tailed test; otherwise you have a non-directional hypothesis, in which case you need to use a two-tailed test.

If the design of your test of difference is independent, as long as the data are ordinal or interval, the Mann-Whitney U test can be used. If you have used a repeated measures or matched participants design, the sign test can be used, as long as the data are ordinal; or if the data are interval or ratio, the Wilcoxon matched pairs signed ranks test can be used. The latter is more sensitive than the sign test. The sign test provides us with a crude analysis, which is sufficient when data are ordinal, but when actual values are obtained (interval or ratio data) the Wilcoxon test will provide a more sophisticated analysis. Therefore, although it is possible to use the sign test for interval or ratio data, it would be best to limit its use to analysis of ordinal data.

If you manipulated the independent variable (some aspect of the situation), you need to use a test of difference (such as the Mann-Whitney U test, the sign test, or the Wilcoxon matched pairs signed ranks test); otherwise, you need to use a test of correlation (such as Spearman's rho test, as long as the data are ordinal, interval, or ratio) or a test of association (such as the chi-squared test, as long as the data are nominal).

How to use the tables

In the Mann-Whitney U test, use the smaller value of U and U′ to look up the critical value of U for a one- or two-tailed test, as appropriate, at .05, initially (bottom table, page 397). If the tabled value is equal to or less than your value at that level, the null hypothesis is retained; if it is greater than your value, it is rejected and your experimental hypothesis is proved.

In the sign test, look up the critical value of S for a one- or two-tailed test, as appropriate, for N, the number of participants with differing scores, at .05, initially. If the tabled value is equal to or less than your value at that level, the null hypothesis is retained; if it is greater than your value, it is rejected and your experimental hypothesis is proved.

In the Wilcoxon test, look up the critical value of T for a one- or two-tailed test, as appropriate, for N, the number of participants with differing scores, at .05, initially. If the tabled value is equal to or less than your value at that level, the null hypothesis is retained; if it is greater than your value, it is rejected and your experimental hypothesis is proved.

Tips

Remember that decisions based on statistical tests are open to error, but if you follow the standard procedures outlined in Chapter 8 the potential for errors can be minimised. Try to be as unbiased as possible, and try not to assume too much about the results in advance.

Ensure that you have not made errors of either Type I, which can be reduced by using a greater level of significance (e.g. $p = .01$, or 1%, or even $p = .001$, or .1%), or Type II, which can be reduced by using a lesser level of significance (e.g. $p = .10$, or 10%).

In the Mann-Whitney U test, remember that ties are possible—this reduces the accuracy, but has only a small effect unless there are several ties.

The tests described in Chapter 8 provide different levels of analysis, and they require a particular type of data. The following chart outlines the tests that can be used for different data types and experimental designs. Please note that this chart deals only with the statistical tests described in Chapter 8.

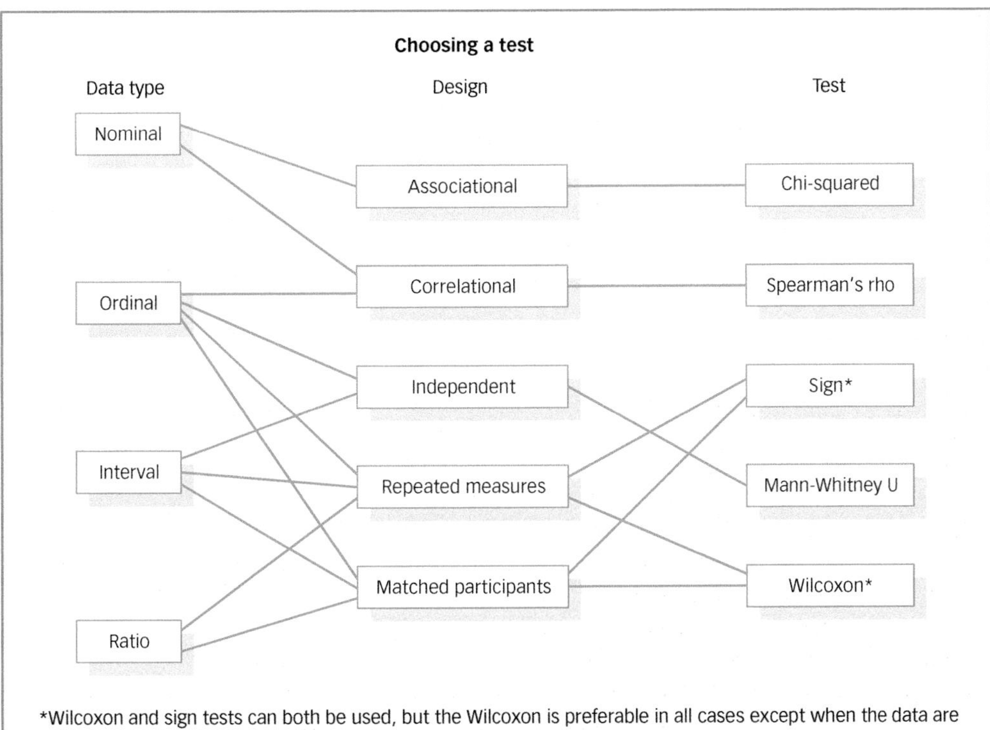

Table 1: Mann-Whitney U test

Critical values of U for a one-tailed test at .005; two-tailed test at .01*

	N_A																			
N_B	1	2	3	4	5	6	7	8	9	10	11	12	13	14	15	16	17	18	19	20
1	—	—	—	—	—	—	—	—	—	—	—	—	—	—	—	—	—	—	—	—
2	—	—	—	—	—	—	—	—	—	—	—	—	—	—	—	—	—	—	0	0
3	—	—	—	—	—	—	—	—	0	0	0	1	1	1	2	2	2	2	3	3
4	—	—	—	—	—	0	0	1	1	2	2	3	3	4	5	5	6	6	7	8
5	—	—	—	—	0	1	1	2	3	4	5	6	7	7	8	9	10	11	12	13
6	—	—	—	0	1	2	3	4	5	6	7	9	10	11	12	13	15	16	17	18
7	—	—	—	0	1	3	4	6	7	9	10	12	13	15	16	18	19	21	22	24
8	—	—	—	1	2	4	6	7	9	11	13	15	17	18	20	22	24	26	28	30
9	—	—	0	1	3	5	7	9	11	13	16	18	20	22	24	27	29	31	33	36
10	—	—	0	2	4	6	9	11	13	16	18	21	24	26	29	31	34	37	39	42
11	—	—	0	2	5	7	10	13	16	18	21	24	27	30	33	36	39	42	45	48
12	—	—	1	3	6	9	12	15	18	21	24	27	31	34	37	41	44	47	51	54
13	—	—	1	3	7	10	13	17	20	24	27	31	34	38	42	45	49	53	56	60
14	—	—	1	4	7	11	15	18	22	26	30	34	38	42	46	50	54	58	63	67
15	—	—	2	5	8	12	16	20	24	29	33	37	42	46	51	55	60	64	69	73
16	—	—	2	5	9	13	18	22	27	31	36	41	45	50	55	60	65	70	74	79
17	—	—	2	6	10	15	19	24	29	34	39	44	49	54	60	65	70	75	81	86
18	—	—	2	6	11	16	21	26	31	37	42	47	53	58	64	70	75	81	87	92
19	—	0	3	7	12	17	22	28	33	39	45	51	56	63	69	74	81	87	93	99
20	—	0	3	8	13	18	24	30	36	42	48	54	60	67	73	79	86	92	99	105

*Dashes in the body of the table indicate that no decision is possible at the stated level of significance.
For any N_A and N_B the observed value of U is significant at a given level of significance if it is *equal* to or *less* than the critical values shown.

Source: R. Runyon and A. Haber (1976). *Fundamentals of behavioural statistics* (3rd ed.). Reading, MA: McGraw Hill, Inc. With the kind permission of the publisher.

Critical values of U for a one-tailed test at .01; two-tailed test at .02*

	N_A																			
N_B	1	2	3	4	5	6	7	8	9	10	11	12	13	14	15	16	17	18	19	20
1	—	—	—	—	—	—	—	—	—	—	—	—	—	—	—	—	—	—	—	—
2	—	—	—	—	—	—	—	—	—	—	—	—	0	0	0	0	0	0	1	1
3	—	—	—	—	—	—	0	0	1	1	1	2	2	2	3	3	4	4	4	5
4	—	—	—	—	0	1	1	2	3	3	4	5	5	6	7	7	8	9	9	10
5	—	—	—	0	1	2	3	4	5	6	7	8	9	10	11	12	13	14	15	16
6	—	—	—	1	2	3	4	6	7	8	9	11	12	13	15	16	18	19	20	22
7	—	—	0	1	3	4	6	7	9	11	12	14	16	17	19	21	23	24	26	28
8	—	—	0	2	4	6	7	9	11	13	15	17	20	22	24	26	28	30	32	34
9	—	—	1	3	5	7	9	11	14	16	18	21	23	26	28	31	33	36	38	40
10	—	—	1	3	6	8	11	13	16	19	22	24	27	30	33	36	38	41	44	47
11	—	—	1	4	7	9	12	15	18	22	25	28	31	34	37	41	44	47	50	53
12	—	—	2	5	8	11	14	17	21	24	28	31	35	38	42	46	49	53	56	60
13	—	0	2	5	9	12	16	20	23	27	31	35	39	43	47	51	55	59	63	67
14	—	0	2	6	10	13	17	22	26	30	34	38	43	47	51	56	60	65	69	73
15	—	0	3	7	11	15	19	24	28	33	37	42	47	51	56	61	66	70	75	80
16	—	0	3	7	12	16	21	26	31	36	41	46	51	56	61	66	71	76	82	87
17	—	0	4	8	13	18	23	28	33	38	44	49	55	60	66	71	77	82	88	93
18	—	0	4	9	14	19	24	30	36	41	47	53	59	65	70	76	82	88	94	100
19	—	1	4	9	15	20	26	32	38	44	50	56	63	69	75	82	88	94	101	107
20	—	1	5	10	16	22	28	34	40	47	53	60	67	73	80	87	93	100	107	114

*Dashes in the body of the table indicate that no decision is possible at the stated level of significance.
For any N_A and N_B the observed value of U is significant at a given level of significance if it is *equal* to or *less* than the critical values shown.

Source: R. Runyon and A. Haber (1976). *Fundamentals of behavioural statistics* (3rd ed.). Reading, MA: McGraw Hill, Inc. With the kind permission of the publisher.

Critical values of U for a one-tailed test at .025; two-tailed test at .05*

	N_A																			
N_B	1	2	3	4	5	6	7	8	9	10	11	12	13	14	15	16	17	18	19	20
1	—	—	—	—	—	—	—	—	—	—	—	—	—	—	—	—	—	—	—	—
2	—	—	—	—	—	—	—	0	0	0	0	1	1	1	1	1	2	2	2	2
3	—	—	—	—	0	1	1	2	2	3	3	4	4	5	5	6	6	7	7	8
4	—	—	—	0	1	2	3	4	4	5	6	7	8	9	10	11	11	12	13	13
5	—	—	0	1	2	3	5	6	7	8	9	11	12	13	14	15	17	18	19	20
6	—	—	1	2	3	5	6	8	10	11	13	14	16	17	19	21	22	24	25	27
7	—	—	1	3	5	6	8	10	12	14	16	18	20	22	24	26	28	30	32	34
8	—	0	2	4	6	8	10	13	15	17	19	22	24	26	29	31	34	36	38	41
9	—	0	2	4	7	10	12	15	17	20	23	26	28	31	34	37	39	42	45	48
10	—	0	3	5	8	11	14	17	20	23	26	29	33	36	39	42	45	48	52	55
11	—	0	3	6	9	13	16	19	23	26	30	33	37	40	44	47	51	55	58	62
12	—	1	4	7	11	14	18	22	26	29	33	37	41	45	49	53	57	61	65	69
13	—	1	4	8	12	16	20	24	28	33	37	41	45	50	54	59	63	67	72	76
14	—	1	5	9	13	17	22	26	31	36	40	45	50	55	59	64	67	74	78	83
15	—	1	5	10	14	19	24	29	34	39	44	49	54	59	64	70	75	80	85	90
16	—	1	6	11	15	21	26	31	37	42	47	53	59	64	70	75	81	86	92	98
17	—	2	6	11	17	22	28	34	39	45	51	57	63	67	75	81	87	93	99	105
18	—	2	7	12	18	24	30	36	42	48	55	61	67	74	80	86	93	99	106	112
19	—	2	7	13	19	25	32	38	45	52	58	65	72	78	85	92	99	106	113	119
20	—	2	8	13	20	27	34	41	48	55	62	69	76	83	90	98	105	112	119	127

*Dashes in the body of the table indicate that no decision is possible at the stated level of significance.
For any N_A and N_B the observed value of U is significant at a given level of significance if it is *equal* to or *less* than the critical values shown.

Source: R. Runyon and A. Haber (1976). *Fundamentals of behavioural statistics* (3rd ed.). Reading, MA: McGraw Hill, Inc. With the kind permission of the publisher.

Critical values of U for a one-tailed test at .05; two-tailed test at .10*

	N_A																			
N_B	1	2	3	4	5	6	7	8	9	10	11	12	13	14	15	16	17	18	19	20
1	—	—	—	—	—	—	—	—	—	—	—	—	—	—	—	—	—	—	0	0
2	—	—	—	—	0	0	0	1	1	1	1	2	2	2	3	3	3	4	4	4
3	—	—	0	0	1	2	2	3	3	4	5	5	6	7	7	8	9	9	10	11
4	—	—	0	1	2	3	4	5	6	7	8	9	10	11	12	14	15	16	17	18
5	—	0	1	2	4	5	6	8	9	11	12	13	15	16	18	19	20	22	23	25
6	—	0	2	3	5	7	8	10	12	14	16	17	19	21	23	25	26	28	30	32
7	—	0	2	4	6	8	11	13	15	17	19	21	24	26	28	30	33	35	37	39
8	—	1	3	5	8	10	13	15	18	20	23	26	28	31	33	36	39	41	44	47
9	—	1	3	6	9	12	15	18	21	24	27	30	33	36	39	42	45	48	51	54
10	—	1	4	7	11	14	17	20	24	27	31	34	37	41	44	48	51	55	58	62
11	—	1	5	8	12	16	19	23	27	31	34	38	42	46	50	54	57	61	65	69
12	—	2	5	9	13	17	21	26	30	34	38	42	47	51	55	60	64	68	72	77
13	—	2	6	10	15	19	24	28	33	37	42	47	51	56	61	65	70	75	80	84
14	—	2	7	11	16	21	26	31	36	41	46	51	56	61	66	71	77	82	87	92
15	—	3	7	12	18	23	28	33	39	44	50	55	61	66	72	77	83	88	94	100
16	—	3	8	14	19	25	30	36	42	48	54	60	65	71	77	83	89	95	101	107
17	—	3	9	15	20	26	33	39	45	51	57	64	70	77	83	89	96	102	109	115
18	—	4	9	16	22	28	35	41	48	55	61	68	75	82	88	95	102	109	116	123
19	0	4	10	17	23	30	37	44	51	58	65	72	80	87	94	101	109	116	123	130
20	0	4	11	18	25	32	39	47	54	62	69	77	84	92	100	107	115	123	130	138

*Dashes in the body of the table indicate that no decision is possible at the stated level of significance.
For any N_A and N_B the observed value of U is significant at a given level of significance if it is *equal* to or *less* than the critical values shown.

Source: R. Runyon and A. Haber (1976). *Fundamentals of behavioural statistics* (3rd ed.). Reading, MA: McGraw Hill, Inc. With the kind permission of the publisher. Copyright © The McGraw-Hill Companies Inc.

Table 2: Wilcoxon signed ranks test

	Levels of significance			
	One-tailed test			
	.05	.025	.01	.001
	Two-tailed test			
Sample size	.1	.05	.02	.002
$N = 5$	$T \leqslant 0$			
6	2	0		
7	3	2	0	
8	5	3	1	
9	8	5	3	
10	11	8	5	0
11	13	10	7	1
12	17	13	9	2
13	21	17	12	4
14	25	21	15	6
15	30	25	19	8
16	35	29	23	11
17	41	34	27	14
18	47	40	32	18
19	53	46	37	21
20	60	52	43	26
21	67	58	49	30
22	75	65	55	35
23	83	73	62	40
24	91	81	69	45
25	100	89	76	51
26	110	98	84	58
27	119	107	92	64
28	130	116	101	71
29	141	125	111	78
30	151	137	120	86
31	163	147	130	94
32	175	159	140	103
33	187	170	151	112

Calculated T must be *equal* to or *less* than the tabled (critical) value for significance at the level shown.

Source: From R. Meddis (1975). *Statistical handbook for non-statisticians*. London: McGraw-Hill.

Table 3: Sign test

	Level of significance for one-tailed test				
	.05	.025	.01	.005	.0005
	Level of significance for two-tailed test				
N	.10	.05	.02	.01	.001
5	0	—	—	—	—
6	0	0	—	—	—
7	0	0	0	—	—
8	1	0	0	0	—
9	1	1	0	0	—
10	1	1	0	0	—
11	2	1	1	0	0
12	2	2	1	1	0
13	3	2	1	1	0
14	3	2	2	1	0
15	3	3	2	2	1
16	4	3	2	2	1
17	4	4	3	2	1
18	5	4	3	3	1
19	5	4	4	3	2
20	5	5	4	3	2
25	7	7	6	5	4
30	10	9	8	7	5
35	12	11	10	9	7

Calculated S must be *equal* to or *less* than the tabled (critical) value for significance at the level shown.

Source: F. Clegg (1983). *Simple statistics*. Cambridge, UK: Cambridge University Press. Reproduced by permission of Cambridge University Press.

Sample Questions

Paper 1: Introductory Topics in Psychology

A Social Influence
B Memory
C Attachment

Paper 2: Psychology in Context

A Approaches in Psychology
B Psychopathology
C Research Methods

Paper 1: Introductory Topics in Psychology

Section A

Social Influence

1. Which two of the following do not influence the rates of conformity to a majority? (2)

1. Face to face communication
2. Culture
3. Gender
4. Era
5. Age

2. In the 1952 film *12 Angry Men* a single juror amongst 12 believes that a young man (the defendant) is innocent of killing his own father and sets out to convince the rest of the jury.

Briefly explain how principles involved in social influence might have led the rest of the jury to come to change their views of the young man's innocence. (6)

3. Describe and evaluate two studies of obedience. (12)

Summary Questions

What is meant by normative social influence, and informational social influence?
Outline social impact theory.
How far does research support the claim that we conform to "fit in and be accepted by a group"?
What is experimental realism?
What is mundane realism?

What is meant by the term "validity"?
What is a field experiment?
Outline two factors that can produce independent behaviour.

Section B

Memory

4. Complete the following statement about short-term memory. Shade one box only. (1)

Increasing the capacity of short-term memory can take place through:

Chunking
Recognition
Delay

5. Complete the following statement about long-term memory. Shade one box only. (1)

Long-term memory can be improved by:

Active processing
Repression
Confabulation
Repetition

6.1 Read the item and then answer the questions below.

Participants in an experiment were given a list of words to remember. The participants were then divided into two groups. One group was asked to simply recall (standard recall condition) the list whilst the other group was asked to recall the list by trying to form a mental image of the words (imagery condition). All participants were then given an "accuracy score" (out of 20) (20 = full recall, 0 = no recall).

The results of the experiment are shown in Table 1.

Table 1: The median accuracy score for the standard recall condition and the imagery condition

	Standard recall condition	Imagery condition
Median	10	15

Sketch an appropriate graphical display to show the median accuracy scores in Table 1. (6)

1 mark for each of the following:

- Display as a bar chart
- Both axes labelled correctly
- Title, reference to IV and DV
- Appropriate scaling for y axis
- Bars are separate
- Bars are plotted reasonably correctly

6.2 The experiment used an independent groups design. Explain how this study could have been modified by using a matched pairs design. (4)

7. Identify and outline how anxiety might affect EWT. (4)

8. Outline and evaluate research into the effect of misleading information on the accuracy of EWT. (8)

Summary Questions

What is the peg-word system?
Outline what is meant by encoding specificity.
How can encoding specificity improve memory?
What are some problems associated with investigating eye witness testimony in a laboratory?
How might being in a state of anxiety affect EWT?
What problems are associated with getting information from children who witness crimes?
What questions might you ask a friend who has been mugged if you wanted to encourage accurate recall?

Section C

Attachment

9.1 In their meta-analytic study, van IJzendoorn and Kroonenberg (1988) analysed results of 32 separate studies investigating attachment styles. Which of the following countries had the highest proportion of anxious avoidant attachment styles? (1)

China
Israel
Germany
Netherlands

9.2 In the same study, which one of the following attachment types was found to be most common in all of the countries investigated? Shade one box only. (1)

Anxious–avoidant
Anxious–resistant
Disorganised
Secure

9.3 Which one of the following is not a feature of a securely attached child: (1)

Showing distress by crying when the mother leaves the child
Orienting behaviour in the presence of the mother
Child not easily comforted when the mother returns after separation
Strangers treated differently from the mother

9.4 Which one of the following statements is true? (1)

Cross-cultural studies of attachment only investigate the variation between cultures and not the variation within cultures
There was no difference in the variation within cultures compared to the variation between cultures
The variation between cultures was greater than the variation within cultures
The variation within cultures was greater than the variation between cultures

9.5 Outline two factors that affect a child's response to separation. (4)

10.1 "It's so interesting" commented Bejal, the mother of 2-year-old Priya, to members of her support group … "whenever I make a sound, baby Priya tries to make a similar one"

Outline two features of caregiver–infant interaction with reference to Bejal and Priya. (4)

10.2 Read the item and then answer the question that follows. (4)

"Studies of attachment often involve observation of interactions between mother and baby pairs where researchers note all behaviours as they occur."

Explain how such observational research might be refined through the use of behavioural categories.

11. When Julia was 6 months old she was taken away from her parents because they could no longer look after her because of their problems of drug dependency. She was taken into care but found it difficult to settle. She was adopted when she was 8 years old but did not develop a close relationship with her adoptive parents. "She has been aggressive towards her younger brother" commented her adoptive parents and "the school are always complaining about her work. She does not seem to get on with other people at all".

    Discuss Bowlby's maternal deprivation theory. Refer to the experience of Julia as part of your discussion. (12)

Summary Questions

Outline the behaviour of a child who is securely attached.
Outline two factors that affect a child's response to short-term separation.
Discuss how a child may recover from early institutionalisation.
Explain why some people are disobedient.
How can minority groups get others to accept their views?
How is it possible to use social psychological research findings inappropriately?

Paper 2: Psychology in Context

Section A

Approaches in Psychology

1. Complete the following sentence. Shade one box only. (1)

   Motor neurons carry information
   1. Away from the brain
   2. Both to and from the brain
   3. Towards the brain
   4. Within the brain

2. Complete the following sentence. Shade one box only. (1)

   The autonomic nervous system
   1. Comprises two sub-systems
   2. Connects the central nervous system and the senses
   3. Consists of the brain and spinal cord
   4. Controls involuntary responses

3. Freud proposed that the personality is made up of three elements which interact.
   Describe two features of the ego. (4)

4. Psychologists often try to understand issues involved in cognitive processing by linking the way we think to the way a computer functions.

   In one study involving reaction times, a participant stated that he felt that he was being asked to do too many things at the same time.
   Briefly suggest how his response might help psychologists understand human cognitive processing. (5)

5. "I would like to train my dog to jump through a hoop" suggested a new dog owner to an animal psychologist. "How should I set about it?"

   "I should use a token economy system", suggested the psychologist.
   Explain which type of conditioning a token economy is based on. (2)

..ould take my pet rat to learn its way through a maze with a reward of food pellets at the end:

Attempt 1	16 sec
Attempt 2	12 sec
Attempt 3	11 sec
Attempt 4	8 sec
Attempt 5	4 sec

Calculate the mean time that the rat took to work through the maze (show your working). (2)

7. The speed of the rat's final attempt was shorter by how many times than the first attempt made by the rat? (1)

1. 4 times as fast as the first attempt
2. 3 times as fast as the first attempt
3. 2 times as fast as the first attempt

8. Two psychologists wanted to account for why little Susan always sucked her thumb when she needed to go to the dentist to have her teeth looked at.

A behaviourist argued that she had seen her elder brother do the same just before he needed to be seen and a psychoanalyst suggested she was regressing to the oral stage in her development.

Outline what is meant by social learning theory and explain how social learning might account for the behaviour described. (6)

Discuss two limitations of social learning theory or psychodynamic psychology. (6)

Summary Questions

Distinguish between the genotype and the phenotype.
Describe the structure of personality according to Freud.
What is systematic desensitisation?
Describe what happens at synapses.
What is your understanding of humanistic psychology?
What is cognitive psychology?

Section B

Psychopathology

9.1 Which of the following is not a definition of abnormality? (1)

Failure to function adequately
Adopting a behaviour that will cause offence
Statistical infrequency
Deviation from ideal mental health

9.2 Which approach in the treatment of mental disorder might make use of "flooding"? (1)

Cognitive
Biological
Behavioural
Psychodynamic

10. The degree to which OCD is inherited is between 45% and 65% (based on the analysis of behaviour of over 400 pairs of twins).

Based on the above study, what are the likely causes of OCD? (4)

11. "I have hated birds for as long as I can remember—if I see a bird outside I could not go out" sighed Ahmed with bird phobia.

    Describe how it may be possible to treat Ahmed using the technique known as "systematic desensitisation". (6)

12. Outline and evaluate the cognitive approach in treating depression. (12)

Summary Questions

What is the aim of CBT?
What is flooding?
What is aversion therapy?
What did Freud have to say about dreams?
Give three defence mechanisms.
What is classical conditioning?
What are the obsessions and compulsions in OCD?

Section C

Research Methods

13. Some people argue that memory for images is better than memory for words. A psychologist tested this idea in an experiment. Twenty-four participants were randomly allocated to one of two conditions.

    Condition A: there were 12 participants in this condition. All were placed in a room and given 10 minutes to look at 50 words and to try to remember the words. After 10 minutes they were told to write down as many words on the list as possible. Answers were collected in by the psychologist at the end of the 15 minutes.

    Condition B: there were 12 participants in this condition. The participants were given 10 minutes to look at 50 images of objects. After 10 minutes they were told to write down the names of as many objects as they could. Answers were collected by the psychologist at the end of the 15 minutes.

    The psychologist counted the number of correctly recalled words in both conditions.

Table 2: Total number of ideas generated in Condition A (words) and in Condition B (images)

	Condition A	Condition B
1	18	19
2	17	25
3	28	28
4	33	29
5	14	36
6	18	42
7	18	44
8	28	40
9	29	39
10	32	36
11	30	40
12	28	42
Mean number of words recalled	24	35

13.1 Identify the experimental design used in this study and outline one advantage of this experimental design. (3)

13.2 Give another experimental design the experimenter might have considered using. (1)

13.3 Apart from random allocation of participants, suggest how the effect of one other extraneous variable could have been reduced. Justify your answer. (3)

13.4 Write a suitable hypothesis for the study. (3)

13.5 Why might the psychologist have organised a pilot study? (2)

13.6 What is the range of scores in each condition? (2)

13.7 What is the standard deviation of the participant scores in conditions A and B? Show your working. (4)

13.8 Explain how the psychologist could have used random allocation to assign the 24 participants to condition A and Condition B. (3)

13.9 How might the psychologist have further analysed the data using percentages? (2)

Summary Questions

What are the levels of data?
What is the mean, median, and mode?
What are the characteristics of a normal distribution?
What factors affect the choice of statistical test?
When would you use a Spearman's rho?
What are demand characteristics?
What is meant by peer review in research?

References

Abramowitz, J.S. (2013). The practice of exposure therapy: Relevance of cognitive-behavioural theory and extinction. *Behavior Therapy*, *44*, 548–558.

Abramowitz, J.S., Taylor, S., & McKay, D. (2009). Obsessive-compulsive disorder. *Lancet*, *374*, 491–499.

Abrams, D., Wetherell, M., Cochrane, S., Hogg, M.A., & Turner, J.C. (1990). Knowing what to think by knowing who you are: Self-categorisation and the nature of norm formation, conformity and group polarisation. *British Journal of Social Psychology*, *29*, 97–119.

Adams, P.R., & Adams, G.R. (1984). Mount Saint Helens's ashfall: Evidence for a disaster stress reaction. *American Psychologist*, *39*, 252–260.

Adorno, T.W., Frenkel-Brunswik, E., Levinson, D., & Sanford, R. (1950). *The authoritarian personality*. New York: Harper.

Ainsworth, M.D.S., & Bell, S.M. (1970). Attachment, exploration and separation: Illustrated by the behaviour of one-year-olds in a strange situation. *Child Development*, *41*, 49–67.

Ainsworth, M.D.S., Blehar, M.C., Waters, E., & Wall, S. (1978). *Patterns of attachment: A psychological study of the strange situation*. Hillsdale, NJ: Lawrence Erlbaum Associates Inc.

Akhtar, S., Wig, N.N., Varma, V.K., Pershad, D., & Verma, S.K. (1975). Phenomenological analysis of symptoms in obsessive-compulsive neurosis. *British Journal of Psychiatry*, *127*, 342–348.

Alexandrov, E.O., Cowan, P.A., & Cowan, C. (2005). Couple attachment and the quality of marital relationships: Method and concept in the validation of the new couple attachment interview and coding system. *Attachment & Human Development*, *7*, 123–152.

Allen, B.P., & Lindsay, D.S. (1998). Amalgamations of memories: Intrusion of information from one event into reports of another. *Applied Cognitive Psychology*, *12*, 277–285.

Allen, V.L., & Levine, J.M. (1971). Social support and conformity: The role of independent assessment of reality. *Journal of Experimental Social Psychology*, *7*, 48–58.

Altemeyer, B. (1981). *Right-wing authoritarianism*. Winnipeg: University of Manitoba Press.

American Psychiatric Association: Diagnostic and Statistical Manual of Mental Disorders, Fifth Edition (2013). Arlington, VA: American Psychiatric Association.

Anderson, J. (1972). Attachment out of doors. In N. Blurton-Jones (Ed.), *Ethological studies of child behaviour*. Cambridge, UK: Cambridge University Press.

Anderson, P.L., Price, M., Edwards, S.M., Obasaju, M.A., Schmertz, S.K., Zimand, E., et al. (2013). Virtual reality exposure therapy for social anxiety disorder: A randomised controlled trial. *Journal of Consulting and Clinical Psychology*, *81*, 751–760.

Anderson, S.W., Rizzo, M., Skaar, N., Stierman, L., Cavaco, S., Dawson, J., et al. (2007). Amnesia and driving. *Journal of Clinical and Experimental Neuropsychology*, *29*, 1–12.

Angoa-Perez, M., Kane, M.J., Briggs, D.I., Herrera-Mundo, N., Sykes, C.E., Francescutti, D.M., et al. (2014). Mice genetically depleted of brain serotonin do not display a depression-like behavioural phenotype. *ACS Chemical Neuroscience*, *5*, 908–919.

Annese, J., Schenker-Ahmed, N.M., Bartsch, H., Maechler, P., Sheh, C., Thomas, N., et al. (2014). *Nature Communications*, *5* (Article 3122).

Apicella, F., Chericoni, N., Costanzo, V., Baldini, S., Billeci, L., Cohen, D., et al. (2013). Reciprocity in interaction: A window on the first year of life in autism. *Autism Research and Treatment*, *2013*, Article ID 705895.

Arendt, H. (1963). *Eichmann in Jerusalem: A report on the banality of evil*. New York: Viking Press.

Arnett, J. (2008). The neglected 95%: Why American psychology needs to become less American. *American Psychologist*, *63*, 602–614.

Aronoff, J. (1967). *Psychological needs and cultural systems: A case study*. Princeton, NJ: Van Nostrand.

Aronson, E. (1988). *The social animal (5th Edn)*. New York: Freeman.

Asch, S.E. (1951). Effects of group pressure on the modification and distortion of judgements. In H. Guetzkow (Ed.), *Groups, leadership and men*. Pittsburgh, PA: Carnegie.

Asch, S.E. (1956). Studies of independence and conformity: A minority of one against a unanimous majority. *Psychological Monographs*, *70* (Whole no. 416).

Atkinson, R.C., & Shiffrin, R.M. (1968). Human memory: A proposed system and its control processes. In K.W. Spence & J.T. Spence (Eds), *The psychology of learning and motivation, Vol. 2*. London: Academic Press.

Avtgis, T.A. (1998). Locus of control and persuasion, social influence, and conformity: A meta-analytic review. *Psychological Reports*, *83*, 899–903.

Baddeley, A.D. (1966). The influence of acoustic and semantic similarity on long-term memory for word sequences. *Quarterly Journal of Experimental Psychology*, *18*, 302–309.

Baddeley, A.D. (2001). Is working memory still working? *American Psychologist*, *56*, 851–864.

Baddeley, A.D. (2012). Working memory: Theories, models, and controversies. *Annual Review of Psychology*, *63*, 1–29.

Baddeley, A.D., & Hitch, G.J. (1974). Working memory. In G.H. Bower (Ed.), *The psychology of learning and motivation, Vol. 8*. London: Academic Press.

Baddeley, A.D., Hitch, G.J., & Allen, R.J. (2009). Working memory and binding in sentence recall. *Journal of Memory and Language*, *61*, 438–456.

Baddeley, A.D., Thomson, N., & Buchanan, M. (1975). Word length and the structure of short-term memory. *Journal of Verbal Learning and Verbal Behavior, 14*, 575–589.

Bahrick, H.P., Bahrick, P.O., & Wittinger, R.P. (1975). Fifty years of memory for names and faces: A cross-sectional approach. *Journal of Experimental Psychology: General, 104*, 54–75.

Bahrick, H.P., Hall, L.K., & Da Costa, L.A. (2008). Fifty years of college grades: Accuracy and distortions. *Emotion, 8*, 13–22.

Bakermans-Kranenburg, M.J., van IJzendoorn, M.H., & Juffer, F. (2003). Less is more: Meta-analyses of sensitivity and attachment interventions in early childhood. *Psychological Bulletin, 129*, 195–215.

Baldwin, M.W., Keelan, J.P.R., Enns, V., & Koh-Rangarajoo, E. (1996). Social-cognitive conceptualisation of attachment working models: Availability and accessibility effects. *Journal of Personality and Social Psychology, 71*, 94–109.

Bales, R.F. (1950). *Interaction process analysis: A method for the study of small groups*. Reading, MA: Addison-Wesley.

Ballantyne, A. O., Spilkin, A. M., Hesselink, J., & Trauner, D. A. (2008). Plasticity in the developing brain: Intellectual, language and academic functions in children with ischaemic perinatal stroke. *Brain, 131*, 2975–2985.

Bandura, A. (1965). Influences of models' reinforcement contingencies on the acquisition of imitative responses. *Journal of Personality and Social Psychology, 1*, 589–593.

Bandura, A. (1969). Social-learning theory of identificatory processes. In D.A. Goslin (Ed.), *Handbook of socialisation theory and research*. New York: Rand McNally & Co.

Bandura, A. (1977a). *Social learning theory*. Englewood Cliffs, NJ: Prentice Hall.

Bandura, A. (1977b). Self-efficacy: Toward a unifying theory of behavioural change. *Psychological Review, 84*, 191–215.

Bandura, A. (1999). Social cognitive theory of personality. In L.A. Pervin & O.P. John (Eds), *Handbook of personality: Theory and research (2nd Edn)*. New York: Guilford Press.

Bandura, A., & Huston, A.C. (1961). Identification as a process of incidental learning. *Journal of Abnormal and Social Psychology, 63*, 311–318.

Banyard, P., & Hayes, N. (1994). *Psychology: Theory and application*. London: Chapman & Hall.

Barlow, D.H., & Durand, V.M. (1995). *Abnormal psychology: An integrative approach*. New York: Brooks/Cole.

Baron, R.S., VanDello, J., & Brunsman, B. (1996). The forgotten variable in conformity research: The impact of task importance on social influence. *Journal of Personality and Social Psychology, 71*, 915–927.

Barrett, H. (1997). How young children cope with separation: Toward a new conceptualisation. *British Journal of Medical Psychology, 70*, 339–358.

Barrett, L.F., & Russell, J.A. (1998). Independence and bipolarity in the structure of current affect. *Journal of Personality and Social Psychology, 74*, 967–984.

Bartlett, F.C. (1932). *Remembering: A study in experimental and social psychology*. Cambridge, UK: Cambridge University Press.

Bateson, P. (1979). How do sensitive periods arise and what are they for? *Animal Behavior, 27*, 470–486.

Bäuml, K.-H., & Kliegl, O. (2013). The critical role of retrieval processes in release from proactive interference. *Journal of Memory and Language, 68*, 39–53.

Beck, A.T. (1976). *Cognitive therapy of the emotional disorders*. New York: New American Library.

Beck, A.T. (2005). The current state of cognitive therapy: A 40-year retrospective. *Archives of General Psychiatry, 62*, 953–959.

Beck, A.T., & Clark, D.A. (1988). Anxiety and depression: An information processing perspective. *Anxiety Research, 1*, 23–36.

Beck, A.T., & Dozois, D.J.A. (2011). Cognitive therapy: Current status and future directions. *Annual Reviews of Medicine, 62*, 397–409.

Beck, A.T., Wright, F.D., Newman, C.F., & Liese, B.S. (1993). *Cognitive therapy of substance abuse*. New York: Guilford Press.

Beebe, B., Jaffe, J., Markese, S., Buck, K., Chen, H., Cohen, P., et al. (2010). The origins of 12-month attachment: A microanalysis of 4-month mother-infant interaction. *Attachment & Human Development, 12*, 3–141.

Beebe, B., & Steele, M. (2013). How does microanalysis of mother-infant communication inform maternal sensitivity and infant attachment? *Attachment & Human Development, 15*, 583–602.

Belsky, J., & Fearon, R.M.P. (2002). Early attachment security, subsequent maternal sensitivity, and later child development: Does continuity in development depend upon continuity of caregiving? *Attachment and Human Development, 4*, 361–387.

Belsky, J., Rovine, M., & Taylor, D.G. (1984). The Pennsylvania Infant and Family Development Project, III: The origins of individual differences in infant-mother attachment: Maternal and infant contributions. *Child Development, 55*, 718–728.

Bentley, E. (2000). *Awareness: Biorhythms, sleep and dreaming*. London: Routledge.

Benton, T.R., Ross, D.F., Bradshaw, E., Thomas, W.N., & Bradshaw, G.S. (2006). Eyewitness memory is still not common sense: Comparing jurors, judges and law enforcement to eyewitness experts. *Applied Cognitive Psychology, 20*, 115–129.

Berenbaum, S.A., & Beltry, A.M. (2011). Sexual differentiation of human behaviour: Effects of prenatal and pubertal organisational hormones. *Frontiers in Neuroendocrinology, 32*, 183–200.

Berman, M.G., Jonides, J., & Lewis, R.L. (2009). In search of decay in verbal short-term memory. *Journal of Experimental Psychology: Learning, Memory, and Cognition, 35*, 317–333.

Berwick, R.C., Friederici, A.D., Chomsky, N., & Bolhuis, J.J. (2013). Evolution, brain, and the nature of language. *Trends in Cognitive Sciences, 17*, 89–98.

Bickman, L. (1974). The effect of social status on the honesty of others. *Journal of Social Psychology, 85*, 87–92.

Binder, J.R., & Desai, R.H. (2011). The neurobiology of semantic memory. *Trends in Cognitive Sciences, 15*, 527–536.

Bjork, R.A., & Bjork, E. L. (1992). A new theory of disuse and an old theory of stimulus fluctuation. In A. Healy, S. Kosslyn, & R. Shiffrin (Eds), *From learning processes to cognitive processes: Essays in honor of William K. Estes, Vol. 2*, pp. 35–67. Hillsdale, NJ: Erlbaum.

Blass, T. (1991). Understanding behaviour in the Milgram obedience experiment: The role of personality, situations, and their interactions. *Journal of Personality and Social Psychology, 60*, 398–413.

Blass, T. (2012). A cross-cultural comparison of studies of obedience using the Milgram paradigm: A review. *Social and Personality Psychology Compass, 6*, 196–205.

Blass, T., & Schmitt, C. (2001). The nature of perceived authority in the Milgram paradigm: Two replications. *Current Psychology, 20*, 115–121.

Bloch, M., Landeros-Weisenberger, A., Kelmendi, B., Coric, V., Bracken, M., & Leckman, J. (2006). A systematic review: Antipsychotic augmentation with treatment refractory obsessive-compulsive disorder. *Molecular Psychiatry, 11*, 622–632.

Bokhorst, C.L., Bakermans-Kranenburg, M.J., Fearon, R.M.P., van IJzendoorn, M.H., & Schuengel, C. (2003). The importance of shared environment in mother–infant attachment security: A behavioural genetic study. *Child Development, 74*, 1769–1782.

Bond, R. (2005). Group size and conformity. *Group Processes and Intergroup Roles, 6*, 331–354.

Bond, R., & Smith, P.B. (1996). Culture and conformity: A meta-analysis of studies using Asch's line judgement task. *Psychological Bulletin, 119*, 111–137.

Boring, E.G. (1950). *A history of experimental psychology*. New York: Appleton-Century-Crofts.

Bothwell, R.K., Brigham, J.C., & Pigott, M.A. (1987). An exploratory study of personality differences in eyewitness memory. *Journal of Social Behavior and Personality, 2*, 335–343.

Bouchard, T.J., Lykken, D.T., McGue, M., Segal, N.L., & Tellegen, A. (1990). Sources of human psychological differences: The Minnesota study of twins reared apart. *Science, 250*, 223–228.

Bouchard, T.J., & McGue, M. (1981). Familial studies of intelligence: A review. *Science, 250*, 223–228.

Bouchard, T.J., & McGue, M. (2003). Genetic and environmental influences on human psychological differences. *Journal of Neurobiology, 54*, 4–45.

Bower, G.H., Black, J.B., & Turner, T.J. (1979). Scripts in memory for text. *Cognitive Psychology, 11*, 177–220.

Bowlby, J. (1944). Forty-four juvenile thieves: Their characters and home life. *International Journal of Psycho-Analysis, 25*, 19–52 and 107–127.

Bowlby, J. (1951). *Maternal care and mental health*. Geneva, Switzerland: World Health Organisation.

Bowlby, J. (1953). *Child care and the growth of love*. Harmondsworth, UK: Penguin.

Bowlby, J. (1969). *Attachment and love, Vol. 1: Attachment*. London: Hogarth.

Bowlby, J. (1973). *Attachment and loss: Vol. 1. Attachment*. New York: Basic Books.

Braun, S.R., Gregor, B., & Tran, U.S. (2013). Comparing bona fide psychotherapies of depression in adults with two meta-analytical approaches. *PLoS ONE*, 8 (Issue 6), e68135.

Breland, K., & Breland, M. (1961). The misbehavior of organisms. *American Psychologist, 16*, 681–684.

Bretherton, I., & Munholland, K.A. (2008). Internal working models in attachment relationships: Elaborating a central construct in attachment theory. In J. Cassidy & P.R. Shaver (Eds), *Handbook of attachment: Theory, research, and clinical application (2nd Edn)* (pp. 102–127). New York, NY: Guilford Press.

Brewer, K.R., & Wann, D.L. (1998). Observational learning effectiveness as a function of model characteristics: Investigating the importance of social power. *Social Behavior and Personality, 26*, 1–10.

British Psychological Society (2014). Code of ethics. http://www.bps.org.uk/sites/default/files/documents/code_of_ethics_and_conduct.pdf.

Brotheridge, C.M. (2006). The role of emotional intelligence and other individual difference variables in predicting emotional labour relative to situational demands. *Psicotherma, 18, suppl.*, 139–144.

Brotheridge, C.M., & Grandey, A.A. (2002). Emotional labour and burnout: Comparing two perspectives of "people work". *Journal of Vocational Behavior*, 60, 17–39.

Brown, G.W., & Harris, T. (1978). *Social origins of depression*. London: Tavistock.

Buehler, R., Griffin, D., & Ross, M. (1994). Exploring the "planning fallacy": Why people underestimate their task completion times. *Journal of Personality and Social Psychology*, 67, 366–381.

Burger, J. (2009). Replicating Milgram: Would people still obey today? *American Psychologist*, 64, 37–45.

Burger, J.M. (2011). Alive and well after all these years. *The Psychologist, 24*, 654–657.

Burke, T.M., Markwald, R.R., Chinoy, E.D., Snider, J.A., Bessman, S.C., Jung, C.M., & Wright, K.P. (2013). *Sleep*, 36, 1617–1624.

Bus, A.G., & van IJzendoorn, M.H. (1988). Attachment and early reading: A longitudinal study. *Journal of Genetic Psychology*, *149*(2), 199–210.

Bushman, B. J. (1988). The effects of apparel on compliance: A field experiment with a female authority figure. *Personality and Social Psychology Bulletin, 14*, 459–467.

Bushnell, I.W.R., Sai, F., & Mullin, J.T. (1989). Neonatal recognition of the mother's face. *British Journal of Developmental Psychology, 7*, 3–13.

Bystrova, K., Ivanova, V., Edhborg, M., Matthiesen, A.-S., Ransjö-Arvidson, A.B., Mukhamedrakhimov, R.M., et al. (2009). Early contact versus separation: Effects on mother-infant interaction one year later. *Birth*, 36, 97–109.

Cahn, B.R., & Polich, J. (2006). Meditation states and traits: EEG, ERP, and neuroimaging studies. *Psychological Bulletin, 132*, 180–211.

Campoy, G. (2011). Retroactive interference in short-term memory and the word-length. *Acta Psychologica*, 138, 135–142.

Campoy, G. (2012). Evidence for decay in verbal short-term memory: A commentary on Berman, Jonides, and Lewis (2009). *Journal of Experimental Psychology: Learning, Memory, and Cognition, 38*, 1129–1136.

Cardoso, C., Ellenbogen, M.A., Serravalle, L., & Linnen, A.-M. (2013). Stress-induced negative mood moderates the relation between oxytocin administration and trust: evidence for the tend-and-befriend response to stress? *Psychoneuroendocrinology*, 38, 2800–2804.

Carey, G., & Gottesman, I. (1981). Twin and family studies of anxiety: Phobic and obsessive disorders. In D.F. Klein & Rabkin (Eds), *Research and changing concepts*. New York, NY: Raven Press.

Carlsmith, H., Ellsworth, P., & Aronson, E. (1976). *Methods of research in social psychology*. Reading, MA: Addison-Wesley.

Carpenter, G. (1975). Mother's face and the newborn. In R. Lewin (Ed.), *Child alive*. London: Temple Smith.

Cartwright, D.S. (1979). *Theories and models of personality*. Dubuque, IO: Brown Company.

Caspi, A., Moffitt, T.E., Newman, D.L., & Silva, P.A. (1996). Behavioral observations at age 3 years predict adult psychiatric disorders: Longitudinal evidence from a birth cohort. *Archives of General Psychiatry*, 53, 1033–1039.

Centofanti, A.T., & Reece, J. (2006). The cognitive interview and its effect on misleading postevent information. *Psychology, Crime & Law, 12*, 669–683.

Chadda, R.K., & Ahuja, N. (1990). Dhat syndrome. A sex neurosis of the Indian subcontinent. *British Journal of Psychiatry, 156*, 577–579.

Charlton, A. (1998). TV violence has little impact on children, study finds. *The Times*, 12 January, p. 5.

Choy, Y., Fyer, A.J., & Lipsitz, J.D. (2007). Treatment of specific phobia in adults. *Clinical Psychology Review, 27*, 266–286.

Clark, D.M. (1996). Panic disorder: From theory to therapy. In P. Salkovskis (Ed.), *Frontiers of cognitive therapy*. New York: Guilford Press.

Clark, D.M., Ehlers, A., Hackmann, A., McManus, F., Fennell, M., Grey, N., et al. (2006). Cognitive therapy versus exposure and applied relaxation in social phobia: A randomised controlled trial. *Journal of Consulting and Clinical Psychology*, 74, 568–578.

Clark, R.D. (1994). The role of censorship in minority influence. *European Journal of Social Psychology, 24*, 331–338.

Cohen, N.J., & Squire, L.R. (1980). Preserved learning and retention of pattern analysing skills in amnesia: Dissociation of knowing how and knowing that. *Science, 210*, 207–210.

Cohen-Kettenis, P.T., & van Goozen, S.H.M. (1997). Sex reassignment of adolescent transsexuals: A follow-up study. *Journal of American Child Adolescent Psychiatry*, 36, 263–271.

Cohn, D.A., Silver, D.H., Cowan, C.P., Cowan, P.A., & Pearson, J.L. (1992). Working models of childhood attachment and couple relationships. *Journal of Family Issues, 13*, 432–449.

Colman, A.M. (2001). *A dictionary of psychology*. Oxford: Oxford University Press.

Colomb, C., & Ginet, M. (2012). The cognitive interview for use with adults: An empirical test of an alternative mnemonic and of a partial protocol. *Applied Cognitive Psychology, 26*, 35–47.

Comer, R.J. (2009). *Abnormal psychology (7th Edn)*. New York: Worth.

Conrad, R. (1964). Acoustic confusions in immediate memory. *British Journal of Psychology, 55*, 75–84.

Conway, A.R.A., Kane, M.J., & Engle, R.W. (2003). Working memory capacity and its relation to general intelligence. *Trends in Cognitive Sciences, 7*, 547–552.

Coolican, H. (1994). *Research methods and statistics in psychology (2nd Edn)*. London: Hodder & Stoughton.

Coolican, H. (1996). *Introduction to research methods and statistics in psychology*. London: Hodder & Stoughton.

Coolican, H. (2004). *Research methods and statistics in psychology (4th Edn)*. London: Hodder & Stoughton.

Cooper, C. (1998). *Individual differences*. London: Arnold.

Cooper, L.A., & Shepard, R.N. (1973). Chronometric studies of the rotation of mental images. In W.G. Chase (Ed.), *Visual information processing*. New York: Academic Press.

Cowan, N., Elliott, E.M., Saults, J.S., Morey, C.C., Mattox, S., Hismjatullina, A., & Conway, A.R.A. (2005). On the capacity of attention: Its estimation and its role in working memory and cognitive aptitudes. *Cognitive Psychology, 51*, 42–100.

Craddock, N., & Jones, I. (1999). Genetics of bipolar disorder. *Journal of Medical Genetics, 36*, 585–594.

Craighead, W.E., & Dunlop, B.W. (2014). Combination psychotherapy and antidepressant medication treatment for depression: For whom, when, and how. *Annual Review of Psychology, 65*, 267–300.

Cruse, D., Chennu, S., Chatelle, C., Bekinschtein, T.A., Fernandez-Espejo, D., Pickard, J.D., et al. (2011). Bedside detection of awareness in the vegetative state. *Lancet, 378*, 2088–2094.

Crutchfield, R.S. (1955). Conformity and character. *American Psychologist, 10*, 191–198.

Cumberbatch, G. (1990). *Television advertising and sex role stereotyping: A content analysis* (Working paper IV for the Broadcasting Standards Council). Communications Research Group, Aston University: Birmingham, UK.

Czeisler, C.A., Duffy, J.F., Shanahan, T.L., Brown, E.N., Mitchell, J.F., Rimmer, D.W., et al. (1999). Stability, precision, and near-24-hour period of the human circadian pacemaker. *Science, 284*, 2177–2181.

Czeisler, C.A., Kronauer, R.E., Allan, J.S., Duffy, J.F., Jewett, M.E., Brown, E.N., & Ronda, J.M. (1989). Bright light induction of strong (type 0) resetting of the human circadian pacemaker. *Science, 244*, 1328–1333.

Dalton, A.L., & Daneman, M. (2006). Social suggestibility to central and peripheral misinformation. *Memory, 14*, 486–501.

Dambrun, M., & Vatiné, E. (2010). Reopening the study of extreme social behaviour: Obedience to authority within an immersive video environment. *European Journal of Social Psychology, 40*, 760–773.

Daneman, M., & Carpenter, P.A. (1980). Individual differences in working memory and reading. *Journal of Verbal Learning and Verbal Behavior, 19*, 450–466.

Darwin, C. (1859). *The origin of species*. London: Macmillan.

Davey, G.C.L. (1983). An associative view of human classical conditioning. In G.C.L. Davey (Ed.), *Animal models of human behaviour: Conceptual, evolutionary, and neurobiological perspectives*. Chichester: Wiley.

David, B., & Turner, J.C. (1999). Studies in self-categorisation and minority conversion: The in-group minority in intragroup and intergroup contexts. *British Journal of Social Psychology, 38*, 115–134.

David, D., Szentagotai, A., Lupu, V., & Cosman, D. (2008). Rational emotive behaviour therapy, cognitive therapy, and medication in the treatment of major depressive disorder: A randomised clinical trial, posttreatment outcomes, and six-month follow-up. *Journal of Clinical Psychology, 64*, 728–746.

Davison, G.C., & Neale, J.M. (1996). *Abnormal psychology (rev. 6th Edn)*. New York: Wiley.

Davison, G., Neale, J.M., & Kring, A.M. (2004). *Abnormal psychology with cases*. Hoboken, NJ: John Wiley & Sons.

De Bleser, R. (1988). Localisation of aphasia: Science or fiction? In G. Denese, C. Semenza, & P. Bisiacchi (Eds.), *Perspectives on cognitive neuropsychology*. Hove, UK: Psychology Press.

Deffenbacher, K.A., Bornstein, B.H., Penrod, S.D., & McGorty, K. (2004). A meta-analytic review of the effects of high stress on eyewitness memory. *Law and Human Behavior, 28*, 687–706.

De Fulio, A., Donlin, W.D., Wong, C.J., & Silverman, K. (2009). Employment-based abstinence reinforcement as a maintenance intervention for the treatment of cocaine dependence: A randomized controlled trial. *Addiction, 104*, 1530–1538.

Denholtz, M.S., Hall, L.A., & Mann, E. (1978). Automated treatment for flight phobia: A 3½-year follow-up. *American Journal of Psychiatry, 135*, 1340–1343.

DeRubeis, R.J., Hollon, S.D., Amsterdam, J.D., Shelton, R.C., Young, P.R., Salomon, R.M., et al. (2005). Cognitive therapy vs. medications in the treatment of moderate to severe depression. *Archives of General Psychiatry, 62*, 409–416.

Deutsch, M., & Gerard, H.B. (1955). A study of normative and informational influence upon individual judgement. *Journal of Abnormal and Social Psychology, 51*, 629–636.

de Waal, F.B.M. (2002). Evolutionary psychology: The wheat and the chaff. *Current Directions in Psychological Science, 11*, 187–191.

Dewar, M.T., Cowan, N., & Della Sala, S. (2007). Forgetting due to retroactive interference: A fusion of Müller and Pizecker's (1900) early insights into everyday forgetting and recent research on retrograde amnesia. *Cortex, 43*, 616–634.

De Wolff, M.S., & van IJzendoorn, M.H. (1997). Sensitivity and attachment: A meta-analysis on parental antecedents of infant attachment. *Child Development, 68*, 571–591.

De Young, C.G., Peterson, J.B., & Higgins, D.M. (2002). Higher-order factors of the Big Five predict conformity: Are there neuroses of health? *Personality and Individual Differences, 33*, 533–552.

Diagnostic and Statistical Manual of Mental Disorders (DSM-5). (2013). New York: American Psychiatric Association.

Dickens, W.T., & Flynn, J.R. (2001). Heritability estimates versus large environmental effects: The IQ paradox resolved. *Psychological Review, 108*, 346–369.

Diener, E., & Crandall, R. (1978). *Ethics in social and behavioural research*. Chicago: The University of Chicago Press.

DiNardo, P.A., Guzy, L.T., Jenkins, J.A., Bak, R.M., Tomasi, S.F., & Copland, M. (1988). Aetiology and maintenance of dog fears. *Behaviour Research and Therapy, 26*, 241–244.

Dolberg, O.T., Iancu, I., Sasson, Y., & Zohar, J. (1996). The pathogenesis and treatment of obsessive-compulsive disorder. *Clinical Neuropharmacology, 19*, 129–147.

Dollard, J., & Miller, N.E. (1950). *Personality and psychotherapy*. New York: McGraw-Hill.

Domjan, M. (2005). Pavlovian conditioning: A functional perspective. *Annual Review of Psychology, 56*, 179–206.

Donahue, E.M., Robins, R.W., Roberts, B., & John, O.P. (1993). The divided self: Concurrent and longitudinal effects of psychological adjustment and self-concept differentiation. *Journal of Personality and Social Psychology*, 64, 834–846.

Dougherty, D.D., Rauch, S.L., & Jenike, M.A. (2002). Pharmacological treatments for obsessive-compulsive disorder. In P.E. Nathan & J.M. Gorman (Eds), *A guide to treatments that work (2nd Edn)*. New York: Oxford University Press.

Duncan, J., & Owen, A.M. (2000). Consistent response of the human frontal lobe to diverse cognitive demands. *Trends in Neurosciences*, 23, 475–483.

Dunne, G., & Askew, C. (2013). Vicarious learning and unlearning of fear in childhood via mother and stranger models. *Emotion*, 13, 974–980.

Dunst, C.J., & Kassow, D.Z. (2008). Caregiver sensitivity, contingent social responsiveness, and secure infant attachment. *Journal of Early and Intensive Behavior Intervention*, 5, 40–56.

Dyer, C. (1995). *Beginning research in psychology*. Oxford, UK: Blackwell.

Dykas, M.J., & Cassidy, J. (2011). Attachment and the processing of social information across the life span: Theory and evidence. *Psychological Bulletin*, 137, 39–46.

Eagly, A.H. (1978). Sex differences in influenceability. *Psychological Bulletin*, 85, 86–116.

Eagly, A.H., & Carli, L. (1981). Sex of researchers and sex-typed communications as determinants of sex differences in influenceability: A meta-analysis of social influence studies. *Psychological Bulletin*, 90, 1–20.

Eakin, D. K., Schreiber, T. A., & Sergent-Marshall, S. (2003). Misinformation effects in eyewitness memory: The presence and absence of memory impairment as a function of warning and misinformation accessibility. *Journal of Experimental Psychology: Learning, Memory, and Cognition*, 29, 813–825.

Easterbrook, J.A. (1959). The effect of emotion on cue utilisation and the organisation of behaviour. *Psychological Review*, 66, 183–201.

Ebbinghaus, H. (1885/1913). *Über das Gedächtnis* (Leipzig: Dunker) [translated by H. Ruyer & C.E. Bussenius]. New York: Teacher College, Columbus University.

Eddy, K.T., Dutra, L., Bradley, R., & Westen, D. (2004). A multidimensional meta-analysis of psychotherapy and pharmacotherapy for obsessive-compulsive disorder. *Clinical and Psychology Review*, 24, 1011–1030.

Ein-Dor, T., Mikuliner, M., Doron, G., & Shaver, P.R. (2010). The attachment paradox: How can so many of us (the insecure ones) have no adaptive advantages? *Perspectives on Psychological Science*, 5, 123–141.

Ein-Dor, T., & Perry, A. (2014). Full house of fears: Evidence that people high in attachment anxiety are more accurate in detecting deceit. *Journal of Personality*, 82, 83–92.

Elicker, J., England, M., & Sroufe, L.A. (1992). Predicting peer competence and peer relationships in childhood from early parent-child relationships. In R.D. Parke & G.W. Ladd (Eds), *Family-peer relationships: Modes of linkage*. Hillsdale, NJ: Lawrence Erlbaum Associates, Inc.

Ellis, A. (1962). *Reason and emotion in psychotherapy*. Secaucus, NJ: Prentice-Hall.

Ellis, A. (1978). The basic clinical theory of rational emotive therapy. In A. Ellis & R. Grieger (Eds), *Handbook of rational emotive therapy*. New York: Springer.

Ellis, A. (2003). Similarities and differences between rational emotive behaviour therapy and cognitive therapy. *Journal of Cognitive Psychotherapy*, 17, 225–240.

Endrass, T., Riesel, A., Kathmann, N., & Buchanan, U. (2014). Performance monitoring in obsessive-compulsive disorder and social anxiety disorder. *Journal of Abnormal Psychology*, 123, 705–714.

Ericsson, K.A., & Simon, H.A. (1980). Verbal reports as data. *Psychological Review*, 67, 215–251.

Evans, J., Heron, J., Lewis, G., Araya, R., & Wolke, D. (2005). Negative self-schemas and the onset of depression in women: Longitudinal study. *British Journal of Psychiatry*, 186, 302–307.

Evans, P. (1998). Stress and coping. In M. Pitts & K. Phillips (Eds), *The psychology of health (2nd Edn)*. London: Routledge.

Eysenck, M.W. (1990). *Happiness: Facts and myths*. Hove, UK: Psychology Press.

Eysenck, M.W. (1994). *Individual differences: Normal and abnormal*. Hove: Lawrence Erlbaum Associates.

Eysenck, M.W., & Keane, M.T. (2015). *Cognitive psychology: A student's handbook (7th Edn)*. Hove: Psychology Press.

Fawcett, J.M., Russell, E.J., Peace, K.A., & Christie, J. (2013). Of guns and geese: A meta-analytic review of the 'weapon focus' literature. *Psychology, Crime & Law*, 19, 35–66.

Fearon, R.P., Bakermans-Kranenburg, M., van IJzendoorn, M.H., Lapsley, A.-M., & Roisman, G.I. (2010). The significance of insecure attachment and disorganisation in the development of children's externalising behaviour: A meta-analytic study. *Child Development*, 81, 435–456.

Festinger, L., Riecken, H.W., & Schachter, S. (1956). *When prophecy fails*. Minneapolis: University of Minnesota Press.

Fisher, R.P., Geiselman, R.E., & Amador, M. (1990). A field test of the cognitive interview: Enhancing the recollections of actual victims and witnesses of crime. *Journal of Applied Psychology*, 74, 722–727.

Fisher, R.P., Geiselman, R.E., Raymond, D.S., Jurkevich, L.M., & Warhaftig, M.L. (1987). Enhancing enhanced eyewitness memory: Refining the cognitive interview. *Journal of Police Science and Administration*, 15, 291–297.

Flynn-Evans, E.E., Tabandeh, H., Skene, D.J., & Lockley, S.W. (2014). Circadian rhythm disorders and melatonin production in 127 blind women with and without light perception. *Journal of Biological Rhythms*, 29, 215–224.

Foerde, K., & Shohamy, D. (2011). The role of the basal ganglia in learning and memory: Insight from Parkinson's disease. *Neurobiology of Learning and Memory*, 96, 624–636.

Fontenelle, L.F., Mendlowicz, M.V., Marques, C., & Versiani, M. (2004). Trans-cultural aspects of obsessive-compulsive disorder: A description of a Brazilian sample and a systematic review of international clinical studies. *Journal of Psychiatric Research*, 38, 403–411.

Fox, N.A., Kimmerly, N.L., & Schafer, W.D. (1991). Attachment to mother/attachment to father: A meta-analysis. *Child Development*, 62, 210–225.

Fraley, R.C. (2002). Attachment stability from infancy to adulthood: Meta-analysis and dynamic modelling of developmental mechanisms. *Personality and Social Psychology Review*, 6, 123–151.

Fraley, R.C., Roisman, G.I., Booth-LaForce, C., Owen, M.T., & Holland, A.S. (2013). Interpersonal and genetic origins of adult attachment styles: A longitudinal study from infancy to early adulthood. *Journal of Personality and Social Psychology*, 104, 817–838.

Fraley, R.C., & Spieker, S.J. (2003). What are the differences between dimensional and categorical models of individual differences in attachment? Reply to Cassidy (2003), Cummings (2003), Sroufe (2003), and Waters and Beauchaine (2003). *Developmental Psychology*, 39, 423–429.

Franzoi, S.L. (1996). *Social psychology*. Madison, WI: Brown & Benchmark.

Freud, S. (1885/1950). The effects of cocaine on thought processes. In *Collected papers*, *Vol. V*. London: Hogarth (Original work published in 1885).

Frigerio, A., Ceppi, E., Rusconi, M., Giorda, R., Raggi, M.E., & Fearon, P. (2009). The role played by the interaction between genetic factors and attachment in the stress response. *Journal of Child Psychology and Psychiatry*, 50(12), 1513–1522.

Gabbert, F., Memon, A., & Allan, K. (2003). Memory conformity: Can eyewitnesses influence each other's memories for an event? *Applied Cognitive Psychology*, *17*, 533–543.

Gaillard, R., Dehaene, S., Adam, C., Clémenceau, S., Hasboun, D., Baulac, M., et al. (2009). Converging intracranial markers of conscious access. *PLoS Biology*, *7*, e1000061.

Galbally, M., Lewis, A.J., van IJzendoorn, M., & Permezel, M. (2011). The role of oxytocin in mother–infant relations: A systematic review of human studies. *Harvard Review of Psychiatry*, *19*, 1–14.

Gao, Y., & Raine, A. (2010). Successful and unsuccessful psychopaths: A neurobiological model. *Behavioral Science and Law*, *28*, 194–210.

García-Bajos, E., Migueles, M., & Aizpurua, A. (2012). Bias of script-driven processing on eyewitness memory in young and older adults. *Applied Cognitive Psychology*, *26*, 737–745.

Gardikiotis, A. (2011). Minority influence. *Social and Personality Psychology Compass*, *5/9*, 679–693.

Gathercole, S., & Baddeley, A.D. (1990). Phonological memory deficits in language-disordered children: Is there a causal connection? *Journal of Memory and Language*, *29*, 336–360.

Gauld, A., & Stephenson, G.M. (1967). Some experiments relating to Bartlett's theory of remembering. *British Journal of Psychology*, *58*, 39–50.

Gazzaniga, M.S. (2013). Shifting gears: Seeking new approaches for mind/brain mechanisms. *Annual Review of Psychology*, *64*, 1–20.

Geiselman, R.E., & Fisher, R.P. (1997). Ten years of cognitive interviewing. In D.G. Payne & F.G. Conrad (Eds), *Intersections in basic and applied memory research*. Mahwah, NJ: Lawrence Erlbaum Associates Inc.

Geiselman, R.E., Fisher, R.P., MacKinnon, D.P., & Holland, H.L. (1985). Eyewitness memory enhancement in police interview: Cognitive retrieval mnemonics versus hypnosis. *Journal of Applied Psychology*, *70*, 401–412.

George, C., Kaplan, N., & Main, M. (1984). *Adult Attachment Interview protocol*. Unpublished manuscript, University of California at Berkeley.

Geraerts, E., Schooler, J.W., Merckelbach, H., Jelicic, M., Hunter, B.J.A., & Ambadar Z. (2007). Corroborating continuous and discontinuous memories of childhood sexual abuse. *Psychological Science*, *18*, 564–568.

Gergely, G., Bekkering, H., & Kiraly, I. (2002). Rational imitation in preverbal infants. *Nature*, *415*, 755.

Gevirtz, R. (2000). Physiology of stress. In D. Kenney, J. Carlson, J. Sheppard, & F.J. McGuigan (Eds), *Stress and health: Research and clinical applications*. Sydney: Harwood Academic Publishers.

Gewirtz, J.L. (1991). Identification, attachment, and their developmental sequencing in a conditioning frame. In J.L. Gewirtz (Ed.), *Attachment and dependency* (pp. 213–229). Oxford: Winston.

Gilbert, G.N., & Mulkay, M. (1984). *Opening Pandora's box: A sociological analysis of scientists' discourse*. Cambridge, UK: Cambridge University Press.

Glanzer, M., & Cunitz, A.R. (1966). Two storage mechanisms in free recall. *Journal of Verbal Learning and Verbal Behavior*, 5, 351–360.

Glass, G.V. (1976). Primary, secondary, and meta-analysis of research. *Educational Researcher*, 5, 3–8.

Gleitman, H. (1986). *Psychology (2nd Edn)*. London: Norton.

Godden, D.R., & Baddeley, A.D. (1975). Context dependent memory in two natural environments: On land and under water. *British Journal of Psychology*, 66, 325–331.

Goh, W.D., & Lu, S.H.X. (2012). Testing the myth of encoding-retrieval match. *Memory & Cognition*, *40*, 28–39.

Goldfarb, W. (1947). Variations in adolescent adjustment of institutionally reared children. *American Journal of Orthopsychiatry*, *17*, 499–557.

Goodwin, K.A., Kukucka, J.P., & Hawks, I.M. (2013). Co-witness confidence, conformity, and eyewitness memory: An examination of normative and informational social influences. *Applied Cognitive Psychology*, *27*, 91–100.

Gough, H.G., Lazzari, R., & Fioravanti, M. (1978). Self versus ideal self: A comparison of five adjective check list indices. *Journal of Consulting and Clinical Psychology*, *46*, 1085–1091.

Grave, K., Caspar, F., & Ambuhl, H. (1990). Differentielle Psychotherapieforschung: Vier Therapieformen in Vergleich. *Zeitschrift für Klinische Psychologie*, *19*, 287–376.

Green, S. (1994). *Principles of biopsychology*. Hove, UK: Psychology Press.

Griffiths, M.D. (1993). Fruit machine addiction in adolescence: A case study. *Journal of Gambling Studies*, 9(4), 387–399.

Groos, G., & Hendricks, I. (1982). Circadian rhythms in electrical discharge of rat suprachiasmatic neurons recorded in vitro. *Neuroscience Letters*, *34*, 283–288.

Guiton, P. (1966). Early experience and sexual object choice in the brown leghorn. *Animal Behaviour*, *14*, 534–538.

Haas, K. (1966). Obedience: Submission to destructive orders as related to hostility. *Psychological Reports*, *19*, 32–34.

Hackmann, A., Clark, D.M., & McManus, F. (2000). Recurrent images and early memories in social phobia. *Behaviour Research and Therapy*, *38*, 601–610.

Haimov, I., & Lavie, P. (1996). Melatonin—a soporific hormone. *Current Directions in Psychological Science*, 5, 106–111.

Halgin, R.P., & Whitbourne, S.K. (1997). *Abnormal psychology: The human experience of psychological disorders (2nd Edn)*. New York: McGraw-Hill.

Haney, C., Banks, W.C., & Zimbardo, P.G. (1973). Interpersonal dynamics in a simulated prison. *International Journal of Criminology and Penology*, *1*, 69–97.

Haney, C., & Zimbardo, P.G. (2009). Persistent dispositionalism in interactionist clothing: Fundamental attribution error in explaining prison abuse. *Personality and Social Psychology Bulletin*, *35*, 807–814.

Hardt, O., Nader, K., & Nadel, L. (2013). Decay happens: The role of active forgetting in memory. *Trends in Cognitive Sciences*, *17*, 111–120.

Harlow, H.F. (1958). The nature of love. *American Psychologist*, *13*, 673–685.

Harlow, H.F. (1959). Love in infant monkeys. *Scientific American*, *200*, 68–74.

Harlow, H.F., & Harlow, M.K. (1962). Social deprivation in monkeys. *Scientific American*, *207*(5), 136–146.

Harlow, H.F., & Mears, C. (1979). *The human model: Primate perspectives*. Washington, DC: Winston.

Harrison, P.J. (2000). Postmortem studies in schizophrenia. *Dialogues in Clinical Neuroscience*, *2*, 349–357.

Harrist, A.W., & Waugh, R.M. (2002). Dyadic synchrony: Its structure and function in children's development. *Developmental Review*, *22*, 555–592.

Haslam, S.A., & Reicher, S.D. (2012). When prisoners take over the prison: A social psychology of resistance. *Personality and Social Psychology Review*, *16*, 154–179.

Hassin, R.R. (2013). Yes it can: On the functional abilities of the human unconscious. *Perspectives on Psychological Science*, 8, 195–207.

Hauk, O., Johnsrude, I., & Pulvermuller, F. (2004). Somatotopic representation of action words in human motor and premotor cortex. *Neuron, 41*, 301–307.

Hay, D.F., & Vespo, J.E. (1988). Social learning perspectives on the development of the mother–child relationship. In B. Birns & D.F. Hay (Eds), *The different faces of motherhood*. New York: Plenum Press.

Hazan, C., & Shaver, P.R. (1987). Romantic love conceptualised as an attachment process. *Journal of Personality and Social Psychology, 52*, 511–524.

Heather, N. (1976). *Radical perspectives in psychology*. London: Methuen.

Heine, S.J., Lehman, D.R., Markus, H.R., & Kitayama, S. (1999). Is there a universal need for positive self-regard? *Psychological Review, 106*, 766–794.

Henke, K. (2010). A model for memory systems based on processing modes rather than consciousness. *Nature Reviews Neuroscience, 11*, 523–532.

Henrich, J., Heine, S.J., & Norenzayan, A. (2010). The weirdest people in the world. *Behavioral and Brain Sciences, 33*, 61–83.

Herholz, S.C., & Zatorre, R.J. (2012). Musical training as a framework for brain plasticity, behaviour, function, and structure. *Neuron, 76*, 486–502.

Herve, P.Y., Zago, L., Petit, L., Mazoyer, B., & Tzourio-Mazoyer, N. (2013). Revisiting human hemispheric specialisation with neuroimaging. *Trends in Cognitive Sciences, 17*, 69–80.

Hess, E.H. (1958). Imprinting in animals. *Scientific American, 198*, 81–90.

Hill, N.R., & Beamish, P.M. (2007). Treatment outcomes for obsessive-compulsive disorder: A critical review. *Journal of Counseling and Development*, 85, 504–510.

Hinds, A.L., Woody, E.Z., Drandic, A., Schmidt, L.A., Van Ameringen, M., Coroneos, M., & Szechtman, H. (2010). The psychology of potential threat: Properties of the security motivation system. *Biological Psychology*, 85, 331–337.

Hinds, A.L., Woody, E.Z., Van Ameringen, M., Schmidt, L.A., & Szechtman, H. (2012). When too much is not enough: Obsessive-compulsive disorder as a pathology of stopping, rather than starting. *PloS ONE, 7* (Issue 1), e30586.

Hitch, G., & Baddeley, A.D. (1976). Verbal reasoning and working memory. *Quarterly Journal of Experimental Psychology, 28*, 603–621.

Hodges, B.H., & Geyer, A.L. (2006). A nonconformist account of the Asch experiments: Values, pragmatics, and moral dilemmas. *Personality and Social Psychology Review, 10*, 2–19.

Hodges, J., & Tizard, B. (1989). Social and family relationships of ex-institutional adolescents. *Journal of Child Psychology and Psychiatry, 30*, 77–97.

Hodgson, R., & Rachman, S. (1977). Obsessional compulsive complaints. *Behaviour Research and Therapy*, 15, 389–395.

Hofling, K.C., Brotzman, E., Dalrymple, S., Graves, N., & Pierce, C.M. (1966). An experimental study in the nurse–physician relationship. *Journal of Nervous and Mental Disorders, 143*, 171–180.

Hogg, M., & Vaughan, G. (2005). *Social Psychology (4th Edn)*. London: Prentice-Hall.

Holland, C.D. (1967). Sources of variance in the experimental investigation of behavioural disturbance. *Dissertation Abstracts International, 29*, 2802A (University Microfilm No. 69–2146).

Hollon, S.D., DeRubeis, R.J., Shelton, R.C., Amsterdam, J.D., Salomon, R.M., O'Reardon, J.P., et al. (2005). Prevention of relapse following cognitive therapy vs. medications in moderate to severe depression. *Archives of General Psychiatry, 62*, 417–422.

Hollon, S.D., Stewart, M.O., & Strunk, D. (2006). Enduring effects for cognitive behaviour therapy in the treatment of depression and anxiety. *Annual Review of Psychology, 57*, 285–315.

Horder, J., Matthews, P., & Waldmann, R. (2011). Placebo, Prozac and PloS: Significant lessons for psychopharmacology. *Journal of Psychopharmacology, 25*, 1277–1288.

Howes, C., Matheson, C.C., & Hamilton, C.E. (1994). Maternal, teacher, and child care correlates of children's relationships with peers. *Child Development, 65*(1), 264–273.

Hyde, K.L., Lerch, Norton, A., Forgeard, M., Winner, E., Evans, A.C., et al. (2009). Musical training shapes structural brain development. *Journal of Neuroscience, 29*, 3019–3025.

Ihlebaek, C., Lave, T., Eilertsen, D.E., & Magnussen, S. (2003). Memory for a staged criminal event witnessed live and on video. *Memory, 11*, 319–327.

Immelmann, K. (1972). Sexual and other long-term aspects of imprinting in birds and other species. In D.S. Lehrmann, R.A. Hinde, & E. Shaw (Eds), *Advances in the study of behaviour, Vol. 4*. New York: Academic Press.

Ioannides, A.A., Popescu, M., Otsuka, A., Bezerianos, A., & Liu, L. (2003). Magnetoencephalographic evidence of the interhemispheric asymmetry in echoic memory lifetime and its dependence on handedness and gender. *NeuroImage, 19*, 1061–1075.

Isabella, R.A., & Belsky, J. (1991). Interactional synchrony and the origins of infant-mother attachment: A replication study. *Child Development, 62*, 373–384.

Jacobs, J. (1887). Experiments on 'prehension'. *Mind, 12*, 75–79.

Jacobson, J.L., & Wille, D.E. (1986). The influence of attachment pattern on developmental changes in peer interaction from the toddler to the preschool period. *Child Development, 57*, 338–347.

Jacoby, L.L., Debner, J.A., & Hay, J.F. (2001). Proactive interference, accessibility bias, and process dissociations: Valid subjective reports of memory. *Journal of Experimental Psychology: Learning, Memory, and Cognition, 27*, 686–700.

Jahoda, M. (1958). *Current concepts of positive mental health*. New York: Basic Books.

Janis, I. (1972). *Victims of groupthink: A psychological study of foreign-policy decisions and fiascos*. Boston: Houghton-Mifflin.

Jarvis, M. (2000). *Theoretical approaches in psychology*. London: Routledge.

Johnson, M.K., Hastroudi, S., & Lindsay, D.S. (1993). Source monitoring. *Psychological Bulletin, 114*, 3–28.

Johnson, S.C., Dweck, C.S., & Chen, F.S. (2007). Evidence for infants' internal working models of attachment. *Psychological Science, 18*, 501–502.

Judge, T.A., Erez, A., Bono, J.E., & Thoresen, C.J. (2002). Are measures of self-esteem, neuroticism, locus of control, and generalised self-efficacy indicators of a common core construct? *Journal of Personality and Social Psychology*, 83, 693–710.

Kagan, J. (1984). *The nature of the child*. New York: Basic Books.

Kahneman, D. (2011). *Thinking, fast and slow*. London: Penguin.

Kahneman, D., & Tversky, A. (1979). Intuitive prediction: Biases and corrective procedures. *TIMS Studies in Management Science, 12*, 313–327.

Kan, I.P., Alexander, M.P., & Verfaellie, M. (2009). Contribution of prior semantic knowledge to new episodic learning in amnesia. *Journal of Cognitive Neuroscience, 21*, 938–944.

Kaplan, J.S., & Tolin, D.F. (2011). Exposure therapy for anxiety disorders. *Psychiatric Times, 28*, 33–37.

Kelman, H.C. (1958). Compliance, identification and internalisation: Three processes of attitude change. *Journal of Conflict Resolution, 2*, 51–60.

Kelman, H.C. (1972). The rights of the subject in social research: An analysis in terms of relative power and legitimacy. *American Psychologist, 27*, 989–1016.

Kelman, H.C., & Lawrence, L. (1972). Assignment of responsibility in the case of Lt. Calley: Preliminary report on a national survey. *Journal of Social Issues, 28*, 177–212.

Kendler, K.S., Kessler, R.C., Neale, M.C., Heath, A.C., & Eaves, L.J. (1993). The prediction of major depression in women – Toward an integrated aetiological model. *American Journal of Psychiatry, 150*, 1139–1148.

Kendler, K.S., Neale, M.C., Prescott, C.A., Kessler, R.C., Heath, A.C., Corey, L.A., & Eaves, L.J. (1996). Childhood parental loss and alcoholism in women: A causal analysis using a twin-family design. *Psychological Medicine, 26*, 79–95.

Kenealy, P.M. (1997). Mood-state-dependent retrieval: The effects of induced mood on memory reconsidered. *Quarterly Journal of Experimental Psychology, 50A*, 290–317.

Keppel, G., & Underwood, B.J. (1962). Proactive inhibition in short-term retention of single items. *Journal of Verbal Learning and Verbal Behavior, 1*, 153–161.

Khanna, S., Rafjendra, P.N., & Channabasavanna, S.M. (1988). Life events and onset of obsessive-compulsive disorder. *International Journal of Social Psychiatry, 34*, 305–309.

Kiecolt-Glaser, J.K., Garner, W., Speicher, C.E., Penn, G.M., Holliday, J., & Glaser, R. (1984). Psychosocial modifiers of immunocompetence in medical students. *Psychosomatic Medicine, 46*, 7–14.

Kiecolt-Glaser, J.K., Marucha, P.T., Malarkey, W.B., Mercado, A.M., & Glaser, R. (1995). Slowing of wound healing by psychological stress. *Lancet, 346*, 1194–1196.

Kim, H., & Markus, H.R. (1999). Uniqueness or deviance, harmony or conformity: A cultural analysis. *Journal of Personality and Social Psychology, 77*, 785–800.

Kirschenbaum, H. (1979). *On becoming Carl Rogers*. New York: Delacorte/Delta Press.

Kitayama, S., & Markus, H.R. (1994). *Emotion and culture: Empirical investigations of mutual influence*. Washington, DC: American Psychological Association.

Klauer, K.C., & Zhao, Z. (2004). Double dissociations in visual and spatial short-term memory. *Journal of Experimental Psychology: General, 133*, 355–381.

Klaus, M.H., & Kennell, J.H. (1976). *Parent–infant bonding*. St Louis: Mosby.

Koluchová, J. (1976). The further development of twins after severe and prolonged deprivation: A second report. *Journal of Child Psychology and Psychiatry, 17*, 181–188.

Koluchová, J. (1991). Severely deprived twins after twenty-two years' observation. *Studia Psychologica, 33*, 23–28.

Konkle, T., Brady, T.F., Alvarez, G.A., & Oliva, A. (2010). Conceptual distinctiveness supports detailed visual long-term memory for real-world objects. *Journal of Experimental Psychology: General, 139*, 558–578.

Kopelman, M.D., Thomson, A.D., Guerrini, I., & Marshall, E.J. (2009). The Korsakoff syndrome: Clinical aspects, psychology and treatment. *Alcohol and Alcoholism, 118*, 148–154.

Kosslyn, S.M. (1994). *Image and brain: The resolution of the imagery debate*. Cambridge, MA: MIT Press.

Kosslyn, S.M., & Thompson, W.L. (2003). When is early visual cortex activated during visual mental imagery? *Psychological Bulletin, 129*, 723–746.

Krackow, A., & Blass, T. (1995). When nurses obey or defy inappropriate physician orders: Attributional differences. *Journal of Social Behavior and Personality, 10*, 585–594.

Kraines, S.H. (1948). *The therapy of the neuroses and psychoses (3rd Edn)*. Philadelphia: Lea & Febiger.

Kringelbach, M.L., & Berridge, K.C. (2009). Towards a functional neuroanatomy of pleasure and happiness. *Trends in Cognitive Sciences*, 13, 479–487.

Kruglanski, A.W., Chen, X., Dechesne, M., Fishman, S., & Orehek, C. (2009). Fully committed: Suicide bombers' motivation and the quest for personal significance. *Political Psychology, 30*, 331–357.

Kruglanski, A.W., & Fishman, S. (2006). Terrorism between "syndrome" and "tool". *Current Directions in Psychological Science, 15*, 45–48.

Kumsta, R., Kreppner, J., Rutter, M., Beckett, C., Castle, J., Stevens, S., et al. (2010). Deprivation-specific psychological patterns. *Monographs of the Society for Research in Child Development, 75*, 48–78.

Kurosawa, K. (1993). The effects of self-consciousness and self-esteem on conformity to a majority. *Japanese Journal of Psychology*, 63, 379–387.

Lack, C.W. (2012). Obsessive-compulsive disorder: Evidence-based treatments and future directions for research. *World Journal of Psychiatry, 2*, 86–90.

Lam, R.W., Tam, E.M., Shiah, I.S., Yatham, L.N., & Zis, A.P. (2000). Effects of light therapy on suicidal ideation in patients with winter depression. *Journal of Clinical Psychology, 61*, 30–32.

Lamb, M.E. (1997). *The role of the father in child development (3rd Edn)*. New York: Wiley.

Lamson, R. (1997). *Virtual therapy: Prevention and treatment of psychiatric conditions in virtual reality environments*. Montreal: Polytechnic International Press.

Larsen, J.D., Baddeley, A.D., & Andrade, J. (2000). Phonological similarity and the irrelevant speech effect: Implications for models of short-term memory. *Memory, 8*, 145–157.

Lau, R., & Russell, D. (1980). Attributions in the sports pages. *Journal of Personality and Social Psychology, 39*, 29–38.

Leahey, T.H. (1992). The mythical revolutions of American psychology. *American Psychologist, 47*, 308–318.

Lee, H. (1997). *Virginia Woolf*. London: Vintage.

Lesar, T.S., Briceland, L., & Stein, D.S. (1997). Factors related to errors in medication prescribing. *Journal of the American Medical Association, 277*, 312–317.

Levin, R.B., & Gross, A.M. (1985). The role of relaxation in systematic desensitization. *Behavior Research and Therapies, 23*(2), 187–196.

Levine, J.M., Saxe, L., & Ranelli, C. (1975). Extreme dissent, conformity reduction and the bases of social influence. *Social Behavior and Personality*, 3, 117–126.

Levy, C.M., & Ransdell, S. (1995). Is writing as difficult as it seems? *Memory & Cognition, 23*, 767–779.

Lewinsohn, P.M., Joiner, T.E., & Rohde, P. (2001). Evaluation of cognitive diathesis-stress models in predicting major depressive disorder in adolescents. *Journal of Abnormal Psychology, 110*, 203–215.

Lieb, R., Wittchen, H.U., Hofler, M., Fuetsch, M., Stein, M.B., & Merikangas, K.R. (2000). Parental psychopathology, parenting styles, and the risk of social phobia in offspring – A prospective-longitudinal community study. *Archives of General Psychiatry, 57*, 859–866.

Liegeois, F., Connelly, A., Cross, J. H., Boyd, S. G., Gadian, D. G., Vargha-Khadem, F., & Baldeweg, T. (2004). Language reorganization in children with early-onset lesions of the left hemisphere: An fMRI study. *Brain, 127*, 1229–1236.

Lilienfeld, S.O., & Marino, L. (1995). Mental disorder as a Roschian concept: A critique of Wakefield's "harmful dysfunction" analysis. *Journal of Abnormal Psychology, 104*, 411–420.

Lippa, R.A., Collaer, M.L., & Peters, M. (2010). Sex differences in mental rotation and line angle judgments are positively associated with gender equality and economic development across 53 nations. *Archives of Sexual Behavior*, *39*, 990–997.

Locke, E.A. (1968). Toward a theory of task motivation and incentives. *Organizational Behavior and Human Performance*, *3*, 157–189.

Loehlin, J.C., & Nichols, R.C. (1976). *Heredity, environment, and personality: A study of 850 sets of twins*. Austin, TX: University of Texas Press.

Loftus, E. (1979). *Eyewitness testimony*. Cambridge, MA: Harvard University Press.

Loftus, E.F. (1992). When a lie becomes memory's truth: Memory distortion after exposure misinformation. *Current Directions in Psychological Science*, *1*, 121–123.

Loftus, E.F., Loftus, G.R., & Messo, J. (1987). Some facts about "weapons focus". *Law and Human Behavior*, *11*, 55–62.

Loftus, E.F., & Palmer, J.C. (1974). Reconstruction of automobile destruction: An example of the interaction between language and memory. *Journal of Verbal Learning and Verbal Behavior*, *13*, 585–589.

Loftus, E.F., & Zanni, G. (1975). Eyewitness testimony – Influence of wording of a question. *Bulletin of the Psychonomic Society*, *6*, 86–88.

Logie, R.H., Baddeley, A.D., Mane, A., Donchin, E., & Sheptak, R. (1989). Working memory and the analysis of a complex skill by secondary task methodology. *Acta Psychologica*, *71*, 53–87.

Loken, E.K., Hettema, J.M., Aggen, S.H., & Kendler, K.S. (2014). The structure of genetic and environmental risk factors for fears and phobias. *Psychological Medicine*, *44*, 2375–2394.

London, P., & Lim, H. (1964). Yielding reason to social pressure: Task complexity and expectation in conformity. *Journal of Personality*, *33*, 75–98.

Lorber, J. (1981). Is your brain really necessary? *Nursing Mirror*, *152*, 29–30.

Lorenz, K. (1935). Der Kumpan in der Umwelt des Vogels. Der Artgenosse als auslösendes Moment sozialer Verhaltnesweisen. *Journal für Ornithologie*, *83*, 137–215.

Lozoff, B. (1983). Birth and "bonding" in non-industrial societies. *Developmental Medicine and Child Neurology*, *25*, 595–600.

Lucas, T., Alexander, S., Firestone, I.J., & Baltes, B.B. (2006). Self-efficacy and independence from social influence: Discovery of an efficacy–difficulty effect. *Social Influence*, *1*, 58–80.

Lucassen, N., Tharner, A., IJzendoorn, M.H., Bakermans-Kranenburg, M.J., Volling, B.L., Verhulst, F.C., et al. (2011). The association between paternal sensitivity and infant-father security: A meta-analysis of three decades of research. *Journal of Family Psychology*, *25*, 986–992.

Luckow, A., Reifman, A., & McIntosh, D.N. (1998). *Gender differences in caring: A meta-analysis*. Paper presented at 106th Annual Convention of the American Psychological Association, San Francisco.

Ludeke, S.G., & Krueger, R.F. (2013). Authoritarianism as a personality trait: Evidence from a longitudinal behaviour genetic study. *Personality and Individual Differences*, *55*, 480–484.

Luria, A.R. (1968). *The mind of a mnemonist*. New York: Basic Books.

Lustig, C., Konkel, A., & Jacoby, L.L. (2004). Which route to recovery? Controlled retrieval and accessibility bias in retroactive interference. *Psychological Science*, *15*, 729–735.

Maass, A., & Clark, R.D. (1984). Hidden impact of minorities: Fifteen years of minority influence research. *Psychological Bulletin*, *95*, 428–450.

Maccoby, E.E. (1980). *Social development: Psychological growth and the parent–child relationship*. San Diego, CA: Harcourt Brace Jovanovich.

Magee, W.J. (1999). Effects of negative life experiences on phobia onset. *Social Psychiatry and Psychiatric Epidemiology*, *34*, 343–351.

Maia, T.V. (2010). Two-factor theory, the actor-critic model, and conditioned avoidance. *Learning & Behavior*, *38*, 50–67.

Main, M., & Solomon, J. (1986). Discovery of a disorganised disoriented attachment pattern. In T.B. Brazelton & M.W. Yogman (Eds), *Affective development in infancy*. Norwood, NJ: Ablex.

Main, M., & Weston, D.R. (1981). The quality of the toddler's relationship to mother and father: Related to conflict behaviour and the readiness to establish new relationships. *Child Development*, *52*, 932–940.

Manning, M. (1995). *Undercurrents: A life beneath the surface*. New York: HarperCollins.

Mannix, E., & Neale, M. (2005). What differences make a difference? The promise and reality of diverse teams in organisations. *Psychological Science in the Public Interest*, *6*, 31–55.

Mantell, D.M. (1974). *True Americanism: Green Berets and war resisters*. New York: Teachers College Press.

Marcus, B., & Schutz, A. (2005). Who are the people reluctant to participate in research? Personality correlates of four different types of non-response as inferred from self- and observer ratings. *Journal of Personality*, *73*, 959–984.

Marcus-Newhall, A., Pedersen, W.C., Carlson, M., & Miller, N. (2000). Displaced aggression is alive and well: A meta-analytic review. *Journal of Personality and Social Psychology*, *78*, 670–689.

Mares, M.-L., & Woodard, E. (2005). Positive effects of television on children's social interactions: A meta-analysis. *Media Psychology*, *7*, 301–322.

Mark, V. (1996). Conflicting communicative behaviour in a split-brain patient: Support for dual consciousness. In S. Hameroff, A. Kaszniak, & A. Scott (Eds), *Toward a science of consciousness: The first Tucson discussions and debates* (pp. 189–196). Cambridge, MA: MIT Press.

Marsh, P., Fox, K., Carnibella, G., McCann, J., & Marsh, J. (1996). *Football violence in Europe*. The Amsterdam Group. SIRC: Oxford.

Martin, R., Hewstone, M., & Martin, P.Y. (2003). Resistance to persuasive messages as a function of majority and minority status. *Journal of Experimental Social Psychology*, *39*, 585–593.

Maslow, A.H. (1954). *Motivation and personality*. New York: Harper.

Maslow, A.H. (1962). *Toward a psychology of being*. Princeton, NJ: Van Nostrand.

Maslow, A.H. (1970). *Toward a psychology of being (3rd Edn)*. New York: Van Nostrand.

Mathes, E.W., Zevon, M.A., Roter, P.M., & Joeger, S.M. (1982). Peak experience tendencies: Scale development and theory testing. *Journal of Humanistic Psychology*, *22*, 92–108.

Mathy, F., & Feldman, J. (2012). What's magic about magic numbers: Chunking and data compression in short-term memory. *Cognition*, *122*, 346–362.

McCarthy, G., & Maughan, B. (2010). Negative childhood experiences and adult love relationships: The role of internal working models of attachment. *Attachment & Human Development*, 12, 445–461.

McCartney, K., Harris, M.J., & Bernieri, F. (1990). Growing up and growing apart: A developmental meta-analysis of twins studies. *Psychological Bulletin*, *107*, 226–237.

McCourt, K., Bouchard, T.J., Lykken, D.T., Tellegen, A., & Keyes, M. (1999). Authoritarianism revisited: Genetic and environmental influences examined in twins reared apart and together. *Personality and Individual Differences*, *27*, 985–1014.

McGlynn, F.D., Mealiea, W.L., & Landau, D.L. (1981). The current status of systematic desensitisation. *Clinical Psychology Review*, *1*, 149–179.

McGlynn, F.D., Smitherman, T.A., & Gothard, K.D. (2004). Comment on the status of systematic desensitisation. *Behavior Modification*, 28, 194–205.

McGuffin, P., Katz, R., Watkins, S., & Ruthherford, J. (1996). A hospital-based twin register of the heritability of DSM-IV unipolar depression. *Archives of General Psychiatry, 53*, 129–136.

McHugh, R.K., Whitton, S.W., Peckham, A.D., Welge, J.A., & Otto, M.W. (2013). Patient preference for psychological vs. pharmacologic treatment of psychiatric disorders: A meta-analytic review. *Journal of Clinical Psychiatry, 74*, 595–602.

McVay, J.C., & Kane, M.J. (2012). Drifting from low to "D'oh!": Working memory capacity and mind wandering predict extreme reaction times and executive control errors. *Journal of Experimental Psychology: Learning, Memory, and Cognition, 38*, 525–549.

Meeus, W.H.J., & Raaijmakers, Q.A.W. (1995). Obedience in modern society: The Utrecht studies. *Journal of Social Issues, 51*(3), 155–175.

Mehta, P.H., & Beer, J. (2009). Neural mechanisms of the testosterone-aggression relation: The role of orbitofrontal cortex. *Journal of Cognitive Neuroscience, 22*, 2357–2368.

Melamed, D., & Savage, S.V. (2013). Status, numbers and influence. *Social Forces, 91*, 1085–1104.

Melville, J. (1978). *Phobias and obsessions*. New York: Penguin Books.

Memon, A., Meissner, C.A., & Fraser, J. (2010). The cognitive interview: A meta-analytic review and study space analysis of the past 25 years. *Psychology, Public Policy and Law, 16*, 340–372.

Mendonça, J.S., Cossette, L., Strayer, F.F., & Gravel, F. (2011). Mother-child and father-child interactional synchrony in dyadic and triadic interactions. *Sex Roles, 64*, 132–142.

Menges, R.J. (1973). Openness and honesty versus coercion and deception in psychological research. *American Psychologist, 28*, 1030–1034.

Menzies, L., Chamberlain, S.R., Laird, A.R., Thelen, S.M., Sahakian, B.J., & Bullmore, E.T. (2008). Integrating evidence from neuroimaging and neuropsychological studies of obsessive-compulsive disorder: The orbitofronto-striatal model revisited. *Neuroscience and Biobehavioral Reviews, 32*, 525–549.

Menzies, R.G., & Clarke, J.C. (1993). The aetiology of childhood water phobia. *Behaviour Research and Therapy*, 31, 499–501.

Merckelbach, H., Muris, P., & Schouten, E. (1996). Pathways to fear in spider phobic children. *Behaviour Research and Therapy, 34*, 935–938.

Milgram, S. (1963). Behavioural study of obedience. *Journal of Abnormal and Social Psychology, 67*, 371–378.

Milgram, S. (1965). Some conditions of obedience and disobedience to authority. *Human Relations, 18*, 57–76.

Milgram, S. (1974). *Obedience to authority: An experimental view*. New York: Harper & Row.

Miller, F.D. (1975). *An experimental study of obedience to authority of varying legitimacy*. Unpublished doctoral dissertation, Harvard University.

Miller, G.A. (1956). The magical number seven, plus or minus two: Some limits on our capacity for processing information. *Psychological Review, 63*, 81–97.

Misra, M., Guo, T., Bobb, S.C., & Kroll, J.F. (2012). When bilinguals choose a single word to speak: Electrophysiological evidence for inhibition of the native language. *Journal of Memory and Language, 67*, 224–237.

Miyake, A., Friedman, N.P., Emerson, M.J., Witzki, A.H., Howerter, A., & Wager, T. (2000). The unity and diversity of executive functions and their contributions to complex "frontal lobe" tasks: A latent variable analysis. *Cognitive Psychology, 41*, 49–100.

Monroney, L. (2008). Translating from a cult back into society. brahmakumaris.info/forum/viewtopic.php?f=11&t=2737.

Moore, B.R. (1973). The form of the auto-shaped response with food or water reinforcers. *Journal of the Experimental Analysis of Behavior, 20*, 163–181.

Mormede, P., Foury, A., Barat, P., Corcuff, J.-B., Terenina, E., Marissal-Arvy, N., et al. (2011). Molecular genetics of hypothalamic-pituitary-adrenal axis activity and function. *Annals of the New York Academy of Sciences, 1220*, 127–136.

Morris, P.E. (1979). Strategies for learning and recall. In M.M. Gruneberg & P.E. Morris (Eds), *Applied problems in memory*. London: Academic Press.

Moscovici, S. (1980). Toward a theory of conversion behaviour. In L. Berkowitz (Ed.), *Advances in experimental social psychology, Vol. 13*. New York: Academic Press.

Moscovici, S. (1985). Social influence and conformity. In G. Lindzey & E. Aronson (Eds), *Handbook of social psychology (3rd Edn)*. New York: Random House.

Moscovici, S., Lage, E., & Naffrenchoux, M. (1969). Influence of a consistent minority on the responses of a majority in a colour perception task. *Sociometry, 32*, 365–380.

Moscovici, S., & Nemeth, C. (1974). *Social psychology: Classic and contemporary integrations (7th Edn)*. Oxford: Rand McNally.

Mowrer, O.H. (1947). On the dual nature of learning: A reinterpretation of "conditioning" and "problem-solving". *Harvard Educational Review, 17*, 102– 148.

Mueller, S.T., Seymour, T.L., Kieras, D.E., & Meyer, D.E. (2003). Theoretical implications of articulatory duration, phonological similarity, and phonological complexity in verbal working memory. *Journal of Experimental Psychology: Learning, Memory & Cognition, 29*, 1353–1380.

Murphy, G.L. (2011). Models and concepts. In E.M. Pothos & A.J.Wills (Eds), *Formal approaches in categorisation* (pp. 299–312). Cambridge: Cambridge University Press.

Murray, L., & Trevarthen, C. (1985). Emotional regulation of interactions between two-month-olds and their mothers. In T. Field & N. Fox (Eds), *Social perception in infants* (pp. 177–197). Norwood, NJ: Ablex.

Nairne, J.S., Whiteman, H.L., & Kelley, M.R. (1999). Short-term forgetting of order under conditions of reduced interference. *Quarterly Journal of Experimental Psychology, 52A*, 241–251.

Nemeth, C. (2009). Minority influence theory. In P. Van Lange, A. Kruglanski, & T. Higgins (Eds), *Handbook of theories of social psychology*. New York: Sage.

Nemeth, C., Mayseless, O., Sherman, J., & Brown, Y. (1990). Exposure to dissent and recall of information. *Journal of Personality and Social Psychology*, 58, 429–437.

Nemeth, C., Swedlund, M., & Kanki, G. (1974). Patterning of the minority's responses and their influence on the majority. *European Journal of Social Psychology, 4*, 53–64.

Nemeth, C., & Wachtler, J. (1974). Creating perceptions of consistency and confidence – Necessary condition for minority influence. *Sociometry, 37*, 529–540.

Nestadt, G., Samuels, J., Riddle, M., Bienvenu, O.J., Liang, K.Y., LaBuda, M., et al. (2000). A family study of obsessive-compulsive disorder. *Archives of General Psychiatry, 57*, 358–363.

Newell, A., & Simon, H.A. (1972). *Human problem solving*. Englewood Cliffs, NJ: Prentice Hall.

Neziroglu, F.A., Anemone, R., & Yaryuratobias, J.A. (1992). Onset of obsessive-compulsive disorder in pregnancy. *American Journal of Psychiatry, 149*, 947–950.

NICHD Early Child Care Research Network (2000). Factors associated with fathers' caregiving activities and sensitivity with young children. *Journal of Family Psychology, 14*, 200–219.

Nicholson, I. (2011). "Torture at Yale": Experimental subjects, laboratory torment and the "rehabilitation" of Milgram's "Obedience to Authority". *Theory & Psychology, 21*, 737–761.

Nieuwland, M.S., & van Berkum, J.J.A. (2006). When peanuts fall in love: N400 evidence for the power of discourse. *Journal of Cognitive Neuroscience, 18*, 1098–1111.

Nisbett, R.E., & Wilson, T.D. (1977). Telling more than we can know: Verbal reports on mental processes. *Psychological Review, 84*, 231–259.

Noltemeyer, A., Bush, K., Patton, J., & Bergen, D. (2012). The relationship between deficiency needs and growth needs: An empirical investigation of Maslow's theory. *Child and Youth Services Review, 34*, 1862–1867.

O'Connor, T.G., Caspi, A., De Fries, J.C., & Plomin, R. (2000). Are associations between parental divorce and children's adjustment genetically mediated? An adoption study. *Developmental Psychology*, 36, 429–437.

Oh, S.H. (2013). Do collectivists conform more than individualists? Cross-cultural differences in compliance and internalization. *Social Behavior and Personality, 41*, 981–994.

Oliner, S.P., & Oliner, P.M. (1988). *The altruistic personality*. New York: Free Press.

Opris, D., Pintea, S., García-Palacios, Botella, C., Szamosközi, S., & David, D. (2012). Virtual reality exposure therapy in anxiety disorders: A quantitative meta-analysis. *Depression and Anxiety*, *29*, 85–93.

Orlinsky, D.E., Grave, K., & Parks, B.K. (1994). Process and outcome in psychotherapy – Noch Einmal. In A.E. Bergin & S.L. Garfield (Eds), *Handbook of psychotherapy and behaviour change (4th Edn)*. New York: Wiley.

Orne, M.T. (1962). On the social psychology of the psychological experiment: With particular reference to demand characteristics and their implications. *American Psychologist, 17*, 776–783.

Orne, M.T., & Holland, C.C. (1968). On the ecological validity of laboratory deceptions. *International Journal of Psychiatry*, 6(4), 282–293.

Oyserman, D., Coon, H.M., & Kemmelmeier, M. (2002). Rethinking individualism and collectivism: Evaluation of theoretical assumptions and meta-analyses. *Psychological Bulletin*, *128*, 3–72.

Paik, H., & Comstock, G. (1994). The effects of television violence on anti-social behaviour: A meta-analysis. *Communication Research, 21*, 516- 546.

Palmer, S. E. (1975). The effects of contextual scenes on the identification of objects. *Memory & Cognition*, 3, 519–526.

Papagno, C., Valentine, T., & Baddeley, A.D. (1991). Phonological short-term memory and foreign-language learning. *Journal of Memory & Language*, 30, 331–347.

Paquette, D. (2004). Theorising the father-child relationship: Mechanisms and developmental outcomes. *Human Development, 47*, 193–219.

Parke, R.D. (1981). *Fathers*. Cambridge, MA: Harvard University Press.

Pasiak, C. (2011). The effect of mother-child interactional synchrony: Implications for preschool aggression and social competence. *Electronic Theses and Dissertations, University of Windsor*. Paper 46.

Pasterski, M.E., Geffner, C., Brain, P., Hindmarsh, C., & Hines, M. (2005). Hormone-behaviour associations in early infancy. *Hormones and Behavior*, 56, 498–502.

Pauls, D.L., Abramovitch, A., Rauch, S.L., & Geller, D.A. (2014). Obsessive- compulsive disorder: An integrative genetic and neurobiological perspective. *Nature Reviews Neuroscience*, *15*, 410–424.

Pepler, D.J., & Craig, W.M. (1995). A peek behind the fence: Naturalistic observations of aggressive children with remote audiovisual recording. *Developmental Psychology*, *31*, 548–553.

Perfect, T.J., Wagstaff, G.F., Moore, D., Andrews, B., Cleveland, V., Newcombe, S., et al. (2008). How can we help witnesses to remember more? It's an (eyes) open and shut case. *Law and Human Behavior, 32*, 314–324.

Perrin, S., & Spencer, C. (1980). The Asch effect: A child of its time. *Bulletin of the British Psychological Society*, 33, 405–406.

Perry, G. (2012). *Behind the shock machine*. New York: New Press.

Peterson, L.R., & Peterson, M.J. (1959). Short-term retention of individual verbal items. *Journal of Experimental Psychology*, 58, 193–198.

Pickel, K.L. (2009). The weapon focus effect on memory for female versus male perpetrators. *Memory*, *17*, 664–678.

Pierce, T., & Lydon, J. (2001). Global and specific relational models in the experience of social interactions. *Journal of Personality and Social Psychology*, 80, 613–631.

Pietromonaco, P.R., & Feldman Barrett, L. (2000). The internal working models concept: What do we really know about the self in relation to others? *Review of General Psychology*, 4, 135–175.

Pinker, S. (1997). *How the mind works*. New York: Norton.

Pomerantz, A.M. (2014). *Clinical psychology: Science, practice, and culture (3rd Edn)*. Thousand Oaks, CA: Sage.

Popper, K.R. (1968). *The logic of scientific discovery*. London: Hutchinson.

Popple, A.V., & Levi, D.M. (2000). Guest editorial: Wundt versus Galton–Two approaches to gathering psychophysical measurements. *Perception*, 29, 379–381.

Posada, G., Gao, Y., Fang, W., Posada, R., Tascon, M., Scholmerich, A., et al. (1995). The secure-based phenomenon across cultures: Children's behaviour, mothers' preferences, and experts' concepts. *Monographs of the Society for Research in Child Development*, 60, 27–48.

Posner, M.I. (1969). Abstraction and the process of recognition. In J.T. Spence & G.H. Bower (Eds), *The psychology of learning and motivation: Advances in learning and motivation*, *Vol.* 3. New York: Academic Press.

Preti, G., Wysocki, C.J., Barnhart, K.T., Sondheier, S.J., & Leyden, J.J. (2003). Male axillary extracts contain pheromones that affect pulsatile secretion of luteinising hormone and mood in women recipients. *Biology of Reproduction*, 68, 2107–2113.

Prull, M.W., & Yockelson, M.B. (2013). Adult age-related differences in the misinformation effect for context-consistent and context-inconsistent objects. *Applied Cognitive Psychology, 27*, 384–395.

Pulsifer, M.B., Brandt, J., Salorio, C.F., Vining, E.P.G., Carson, B.S., & Freeman, J.M. (2004). The cognitive outcome of hemispherectomy in 71 children. *Epilepsia*, 45, 243–254.

Pylyshyn, Z.W. (2002). Mental imagery: In search of a theory. *Behavioral and Brain Sciences*, 25, 157–238.

Rachman, (2004). *Anxiety*. Hove, UK: Psychology Press.

Ralph, M.R., Foster, R.G., Davis, F.C., & Menaker, M. (1990). Transplanted suprachiasmatic nucleus determines circadian period. *Science*, *247*, 975–978.

Rank, S.G., & Jacobsen, C.K. (1977). Hospital nurses' compliance with medication overdose orders: A failure to replicate. *Journal of Health and Social Behaviour*, 18, 188–193.

Rasmussen, S.A., & Eisen, J.L. (1991). Epidemiology, clinical features and genetics of obsessive-compulsive disorder. In M.A. Jenike, L. Baer, & W.E. Minichiello (Eds), *Obsessive-compulsive disorder: Practical management*. Kirkland, WA: Hogrefe and Huber.

Reicher, S., & Haslam, S.A. (2006). Rethinking the psychology of tyranny: The BBC prison study. *British Journal of Social Psychology, 45*, 1–40.

Reicher, S.D., Haslam, S.A., & Smith, J.R. (2012a). Working toward the experimenter: Reconceptualising obedience within the Milgram paradigm as identification-based followership. *Perspectives on Psychological Science*, *7*, 315–324.

Reicher, S.D., Haslam, A., Spears, R., & Reynolds, K.J. (2012b). A social mind: The context of John Turner's work and its influence. *European Review of Social Psychology, 23*, 344–385.

Robbins, T.W., Anderson, E.J., Barker, D.R., Bradley, A.C., Fearnyhough, C., Henson, R., et al. (1996). Working memory in chess. *Memory & Cognition, 24*, 83–93.

Robertson, J., & Bowlby, J. (1952). Responses of young children to separation from their mothers. *Courier Centre International de l'Enfance, 2*, 131–142.

Robertson, J., & Robertson, J. (1971). Young children in brief separation. *Psychoanalytic Study of the Child, 26*, 264–315.

Roediger, H.L. III, & Karpicke, J.D. (2006). Test-enhanced learning: Taking memory tests improves long-term retention. *Psychological Science, 17*, 249–255.

Roepke, A.M. (2013). Gains without pains? Growth after positive events. *The Journal of Positive Psychology, 8*, 280–291.

Rogers, C.R. (1951). *Client-centred therapy*. Boston, MA: Houghton Mifflin.

Rogers, C.R. (1967). *On becoming a person*. London: Constable.

Roisman, G.I., & Fraley, R.C. (2008). A behaviour-genetic study of parenting quality, infant attachment security, and their covariation in a nationally representative sample. *Developmental Psychology, 44*, 831–839.

Rolls, G. (2010). *Classic case studies in psychology (2nd Edn)*. London: Hodder Education.

Rönnlund, M., Nyberg, L., Backman, L., & Nilsson, L.G. (2005). Stability, growth, and decline in adult life span development of declarative memory: Cross-sectional and longitudinal data from a population-based study. *Psychology and Aging, 20*, 3–18.

Roopnarine, J.L., Hooper, F.H., Ahmeduzzaman, M., & Pollack, B. (1993). Gentle play partners: Mother-child and father-child play in New Delhi, India. In K. Macdonald (Ed.), *Parent-child play: Description and implication* (pp. 287–304). Albany: State University of New York Press.

Rosch, E., Mervis, C.B., Gray, W.D., Johnson, D.M., & Boyes-Braem, P. (1976). Basic objects in natural categories. *Cognitive Psychology, 8*, 382–439.

Rosen, G.M., Glasgow, R.E., & Barrera, M., Jr. (1976). A controlled study to assess the clinical efficacy of totally self-administered systematic desensitization. *Journal of Consulting and Clinical Psychology, 44*, 208–217.

Rosenberg, M.J. (1965). When dissonance fails: On eliminating evaluation apprehension from attitude measurement. *Journal of Personality and Social Psychology, 1*, 28–42.

Rosenhan, D. (1969). Some origins of concern for others. In P. Mussen, J. Langer, & M. Covington (Eds), *Trends and issues in developmental psychology*. New York: Holt, Rinehart & Winston.

Rosenhan, D.L., & Seligman, M.E.P. (1989). *Abnormal psychology (2nd Edn)*. New York: Norton.

Rosenthal, R. (1966). *Experimenter effects in behavioural research*. New York: Appleton-Century-Crofts.

Rosenthal, R. (2003). Covert communication in laboratories, classrooms, and the truly real world. *Current Directions in Psychological Science, 12*, 151–154.

Rosenthal, R., & Jacobson, L. (1968). *Pygmalion in the classroom*. New York: Holt, Rinehart & Winston.

Rothbaum, F., Kakinuma, M., Nagaoka, R., & Azuma, H. (2007). Attachment and amae: Parent–child closeness in the United States and Japan. *Journal of Cross-Cultural Psychology, 38*, 465– 486.

Rothbaum, F., Pott, M., Azuma, H., & Weisz, J. (2000). The development of close relationships in Japan and the United States: Paths of symbiotic harmony and generative tension. *Child Development, 71*, 1121–1142.

Rotter, J.B. (1966). Generalised expectancies for internal versus external control of reinforcement. *Psychological Monographs, 80*, whole no. 609.

Roy, D.F. (1991). Improving recall by eyewitnesses through the cognitive interview: Practical applications and implications for the police service. *The Psychologist: Bulletin of the British Psychological Society, 4*, 398–400.

Rudolph, J., Langer, L., & Tausch, R. (1980). Demonstrations of the psychic results and conditions of person-centred individual psychotherapy. *Zeitschrift für Klinische Forschung und Praxis, 9*, 23–33.

Rusak, B. (1977). Involvement of the primary optic tracts in mediation of light efferents on hamster circadian rhythms. *Journal of Comparative Psychology, 118*, 165–172.

Rutter, M. (1972). *Maternal deprivation reassessed*. Harmondsworth, UK: Penguin.

Rutter, M. (1981). *Maternal deprivation reassessed (2nd Edn)*. Harmondsworth, UK: Penguin.

Rutter, M., & the ERA Study Team (1998). Developmental catch-up and deficit following adoption after severe early privation. *Journal of Child Psychology and Psychiatry, 39*, 465–476.

Rutter, M., Sonuga-Barke, E.J., & Castle, J. (2010). I. Investigating the impact of early institutional deprivation on development: Background and research strategy of the English and Romanian adoptees (ERA) study. *Monographs of the Society for Research in Child Development, 75*, 1–20.

Sabini, J., Siepman, M., & Stein, J. (2001). The really fundamental attribution error. *Psychological Inquiry, 12*, 1–15.

Sagi, A., van IJzendoorn, M.H., & Koren-Karie, N. (1991). Primary appraisal of the Strange Situation: A cross-cultural analysis of the pre-separation episodes. *Developmental Psychology, 27*, 587–596.

Salkovskis, P.M. (1991). The importance of behaviour in the maintenance of anxiety and panic: A cognitive account. *Behavioural Psychotherapy, 19*, 6–19.

Salkovskis, P.M. (1996). Cognitive-behavioural approaches to the understanding of obsessional problems. In R.M. Rapee (Ed.), *Current controversies in the anxiety disorders*. New York: Guilford Press.

Saunders, B.E., Villeponteaux, L.A., Lipovsky, J.A., Kilpatrick, D.G., & Veronen, L.J. (1992). Child sexual assault as a risk factor for mental disorders among women–A community survey. *Journal of Interpersonal Violence, 7*, 189–204.

Schacter, D.L., & Addis, D.R. (2007). The cognitive neuroscience of constructive memory: Remembering the past and imagining the future. *Philosophical Transactions of the Royal Society B: Biological Sciences, 362*, 773–786.

Schaefer, C., Coyne, J.C., & Lazarus, R.S. (1981). The health-related functions of social support. *Journal of Behavioral Medicine, 4*, 381–406.

Schaffer, H.R. (1977). *Mothering*. London: Fontana; Cambridge, Mass.: Harvard University Press.

Schaffer, H.R., & Emerson, P.E. (1964). The development of social attachments in infancy. *Monographs of the Society for Research on Child Development, 29(3)*, 1–77.

Schruers, K., Koning, K., Luemans, J., Haack, M.J., & Griez, E. (2005). Obsessive-compulsive disorder: A critical review of therapeutic perspectives. *Acta Psychiatrica Scandinavica, 111*, 261–271.

Schweppe, J., Grice, M., & Rummer, R. (2011). What models of verbal working memory can learn from phonological theory: Decomposing the phonological similarity effect. *Journal of Memory and Language, 64*, 256–269.

Seligman, M.E. (1970). On generality of laws of learning. *Psychological Review, 77*, 406–418.

Seligman, M.E.P., & Csikszentmihalyi, M. (2000). Positive psychology: An introduction. *American Psychologist, 55*, 5–14.

Seyranian, V., Atuel, H., & Crano, W.D. (2008). Dimensions of majority and minority groups. *Group Processes & Intergroup Relations, 11*, 21–37.

Shaffer, D.R. (1993). *Developmental psychology*. Pacific Grove, CA: Brooks/Cole.

Shallice, T., & Warrington, E.K. (1970). Independent functioning of verbal memory stores: A neuropsychological study. *Quarterly Journal of Experimental Psychology, 22*, 261–273.

Sharman, S.J., & Powell, M.B. (2012). A comparison of adult witnesses' suggestibility across various types of leading questions. *Applied Cognitive Psychology, 26*, 48–53.

Sharpe, D. (1997). Of apples and oranges, file drawers and garbage: Why validity issues in meta-analysis will not go away. *Clinical Psychology Review, 17*, 881–901.

Shaver, P.R., & Hazan, C. (1993). Adult romantic attachment: Theory and evidence. In D. Perlman & W. Jones (Eds), *Advances in personal relationships Vol. 4* (pp. 29–70). London: Kingsley.

Sherif, M. (1935). A study of some factors in perception. *Archives of Psychology, 27*, 187.

Shewmon, D.A., Holmes, G.L., & Byrne, P.A. (1999). Consciousness in congenitally decorticate children: Developmental vegetative state as self-fulfilling prophecy. *Developmental and Child Neurology, 41*, 364–374.

Shochat, T., Luboshitzky, R., & Lavie, P. (1997). Noctural melatonin onset is phase locked to the primary sleep gate. *American Journal of Physiology, 273*, R364–R370.

Shotland, R.L., & Straw, M.K. (1976). Bystander response to an assault: When a man attacks a woman. *Journal of Personality and Social Psychology, 34*, 990– 999.

Shute, R.E. (1975). The impact of peer pressure on the verbally expressed drug attitudes of male college students. *American Journal of Drug and Alcohol Abuse, 2*, 231–243.

Siebert, M., Markowitsch, H.J., & Bartel, P. (2003). Amygdala, affect and cognition: Evidence from 10 patients with Urbach-Wiethe disease. *Brain, 126*, 2627–2637.

Sigal, J.J., Rossignol, M., Perry, J.C., & Ouimet, M.C. (2003). Unwanted infants: Psychological and physical consequences of inadequate orphanage care 50 years later. *American Journal of Orthopsychiatry, 73*, 3–12.

Silke, A. (2003). Deindividuation, anonymity, and violence: Findings from Northern Ireland. *Journal of Social Psychology, 143*, 493–499.

Silverman, K., Robles, E., Mudric, T., Bigelow, G.E., & Stitzer, M.I. (2004). A randomised trial of long-term reinforcement of cocaine abstinence in methadone-maintained patients who inject drugs. *Journal of Consulting and Clinical Psychology, 72*, 839–854.

Simon, H.A. (1974). How big is a chunk? *Science, 183*, 483–488.

Simons, D.J., & Chabris, C.F. (2011). What people believe about how memory works: A representative survey of the US population. *Public Library of Science One, 6*, e22757.

Simpson, H.B., Liebowitz, M.R., Foa, E.B., Kozak, M.J., Schmidt, A.B., Rowan, V., et al. (2004). Post-treatment effects of exposure therapy and clomipramine in obsessive-compulsive disorder. *Depression and Anxiety, 19*, 225–233.

Skagerberg, E.M., & Wright, D.B. (2008). The prevalence of co-witnesses and co-witness discussions in real eyewitnesses. *Psychology, Crime & Law, 14*, 513–521.

Skinner, B.F. (1938). *The behaviour of organisms*. New York: Appleton-Century-Crofts.

Smith, E.E., & Jonides, J. (1997). Working memory: A view from neuroimaging. *Cognitive Psychology, 33*, 5–42.

Smith, E.R., & Mackie, D.M. (2000). *Social psychology (2nd Edn)*. Philadelphia: Psychology Press.

Smith, M.L., Glass, G.V., & Miller, T.I. (1980). *The benefits of psychotherapy*. Baltimore: John Hopkins Press.

Smith, P., & Bond, M.H. (1993). *Social psychology across cultures: Analysis and perspectives*. New York: Harvester Wheatsheaf.

Smyke, A.T., Koga, S.F., Johnson, D.E., Fox, N.A., Marshall, P.J., Nelson, C.A., et al. (2007). The caregiving context in institution-reared infants and toddlers in Romania. *Journal of Child Psychology and Psychiatry, 48*, 210–218.

Snyder, K.M., Ashitaka, Shimada, H., Ulrich, J.E., & Logan, G.D. (2014). What skilled typists don't know about the QWERTY keyboard. *Attention, Perception, & Psychophysics, 76*, 162–171.

Solms, M. (2000). Dreaming and REM sleep are controlled by different brain mechanisms. *Behavioral and Brain Sciences, 23*, 843–850.

Solomon, R.L., & Wynne, L.C. (1953). Traumatic avoidance learning: The outcomes of several extinction procedures with dogs. *Psychological Monographs, 67* (Whole No. 354).

Solso, R. (1995). *Cognitive psychology (4th Edn)*. Boston: Allyn & Bacon.

Spence, I., Yu, J.J., Feng, J., & Marshman, J. (2009). Women match men when learning a spatial skill. *Journal of Experimental Psychology: Learning, Memory, and Cognition*, 35(No. 4), 1097–1103.

Sperling, G. (1960). The information that is available in brief visual presentations. *Psychological Monographs, 74* (Whole No. 498), 1–29.

Spiers, H.J., Maguire, E.A., & Burgess, N. (2001). Hippocampal amnesia. *Neurocase, 7*, 357–382.

Spitz, R.A. (1945). Hospitalism: An inquiry into the genesis of psychiatric conditions in early childhood. *Psychoanalytic Study of the Child, 1*, 113–117.

Spitz, R.A., & Wolf, K.M. (1946). Anaclitic depression. *Psychoanalytic Study of the Child, 2*, 313–342.

Srivastava, M., Simakov, O., Chapman, J., Fahey, B., Gauthier, M.E.A., Mitros, T., et al. (2010). The Amphimedon queenslandica genome and the evolution of animal complexity. *Nature*, 466, 720–726.

Stams, G.J.M., Juffer, F., & van IJzendoorn, M.H. (2002). Maternal sensitivity, infant attachment, and temperament in early childhood predict adjustment in middle childhood: The case of adopted children and their biologically unrelated parents. *Developmental Psychology, 38*, 806–821.

Stern, K., & McClintock, M.K. (1998). Regulation of ovulation by human pheromones. *Nature, 392*, 177–179.

Sternberg, R.J. (1995). *In search of the human mind*. New York: Harcourt Brace.

Steyvers, M., & Hemmer, P. (2012). Reconstruction from memory in naturalistic environments. In B.H. Ross (Ed.), *The Psychology of Learning and Motivation*, 56, 126–144.

Strassberg, D.S., & Lowe, K. (1995). Volunteer bias in sexuality research. *Archives of Sexual Behavior, 24*, 369–382.

Stroud, L.R., Salovey, P., & Epel, E.S. (2002). Sex differences in stress responses: Social rejection versus achievement stress. *Biological Psychiatry*, 52, 318–327.

Stuss, D.T., & Alexander, M.P. (2007). Is there a dysexecutive syndrome? *Philosophical Transactions of the Royal Society B, 362*, 901–915.

Szasz, T.S. (1960). *The myth of mental illness*. London: Paladin.

Szechtman, H., & Woody, E. (2004). Obsessive-compulsive disorder as a disturbance of security motivation. *Psychological Review, 111*, 111–127.

Szewczyk-Sokolowski, M., Bost, K.K., & Wainwright, A.B. (2005). Attachment, temperament, and preschool children's peer acceptance. *Social Development, 14*, 379–397.

Tajfel, H., & Turner, J.C. (1979). An integrative theory of intergroup conflict. In W.G. Austin & S. Worchel (Eds), *The social psychology of intergroup relations* (pp. 33–47). Monterey, CA: Brooks/Cole.

Tanford, S., & Penrod, S. (1984). Social influence model: A formal integration of research on majority and minority influence processes. *Psychological Bulletin*, 95, 189–225.

Taormina, R.J., & Gao, J.H. (2013). Maslow and the motivation hierarchy: Measuring satisfaction of the needs. *American Journal of Psychology*, *126*, 155–177.

Tavris, C. (1974). The frozen world of the familiar stranger. *Psychology Today, June*, 71–80.

Taylor, S.E., Cousino-Klein, L., Lewisz, B.P., Grunewald, T.L., & Updegraff, J.A. (2000). Behavioural response to stress in females: Tend and befriend, not fight-or-flight. *Psychological Review, 107*, 411–429.

Telch, M.J., Cobb, A.R., & Lancaster, C.L. (2014). Exposure therapy. In P. Emmelkamp & T. Ehring (Eds), *The Wiley handbook of anxiety disorders*. Chichester: Wiley.

Terman, M. (1988). On the question of mechanism in phototherapy for seasonal affective disorder: Consideration of clinical efficacy and epidemiology. *Journal of Biological Rhythms*, 3, 155–172.

Tetlock, P.E., Peterson, R.S., McGuire, C., Chang, S., & Feld, P. (1992). Assessing political group dynamics: A test of the groupthink model. *Journal of Personality and Social Psychology*, 63, 403–425.

Thomas, L.K. (1998). *Multicultural aspects of attachment*. http://www.bereavement.demon.co.uk/lbn/attachment/lennox.html. [See also Thomas, L.K. (1995). Psychotherapy in the context of race and culture. In S. Fernando (Ed.), *Mental health in a multi-ethnic society*. London: Routledge.]

Thorndike, E.L. (1898). Animal intelligence: An experimental study of the associative processes in animals. *Psychological Review Monograph Supplements*, 2, No. 4 (Whole No. 8).

Thorndike, E.L. (1905). *The elements of psychology*. New York: A.G. Seiler.

Thorpe, G.L., & Burns, L.E. (1983). *The agoraphobic syndrome: Behavioural approaches to evaluation and treatment*. Wiley: Chichester.

Tilker, H.A. (1970). Socially responsible behaviour as a function of observer responsibility and video feedback. *Journal of Personality and Social Psychology*, *14*, 95–100.

Tollestrup, P.A., Turtle, J.W., & Yuille, J.C. (1994). Actual victims and witnesses to robbery and fraud: An archival analysis. In D.F. Ross, J.D. Read, & M.P. Toglia (Eds), *Adult eyewitness testimony: Current trends and developments*. New York: Wiley.

Tolman, E. C. (1932). *Purposive behaviour in animals and men*. New York: Century.

Tolman, E. C. (1948). Cognitive maps in rats and men. *Psychological Review*, 55, 189–208.

Torres, A.R., Prince, M.J., Bebbington, P.E., Bhugra, D., Brugha, T.S., Farrell, M., et al. (2006). Obsessive-compulsive disorder: Prevalence, comorbidity, impact, and help-seeking in the British National Psychiatric Morbidity Survey of 2000. *American Journal of Psychiatry*, *163*, 1978–1985.

Trevarthen, C. (1998). The concept and foundations of infant intersubjectivity. In S. Braten (Ed.), *Intersubjective communication and emotion in early ontogeny* (pp. 15–46). Cambridge: Cambridge University Press.

Tronick, E.Z., Morelli, G.A., & Ivey, P.K. (1992). The Efe forager infant and toddler's pattern of social relationships: Multiple and simultaneous. *Developmental Psychology*, 28, 568–577.

Tuckey, M.R., & Brewer, N. (2003a). How schemas affect eyewitness memory over repeated retrieval attempts. *Applied Cognitive Psychology*, 7, 785–800.

Tuckey, M.R., & Brewer, N. (2003b). The influence of schemas, stimulus ambiguity, and interview schedule on eyewitness memory over time. *Journal of Experimental Psychology: Applied*, 9, 101–118.

Tulving, E. (1979). Relation between encoding specificity and levels of processing. In L.S. Cermak & F.I.M. Craik (Eds), *Levels of processing in human memory*. Hillsdale, NJ: Lawrence Erlbaum Associates.

Tulving, E. (2002). Episodic memory: From mind to brain. *Annual Review of Psychology*, 53, 1–25.

Tulving, E., & Psotka, J. (1971). Retroactive inhibition in free recall: Inaccessibility of information available in the memory store. *Journal of Experimental Psychology*, 87, 116–124.

Turkheimer, E., Haley, A., Waldron, M., D'Onofrio, B., & Gottesman, I.I. (2003). Socio-economic status modifies heritability of IQ in young children. *Psychological Science*, *14*, 623–628.

Twenge, J.M., Gentile, B., DeWall, C.N., Ma. D., Lacefield, K., & Schultz, D.R. (2010). Birth cohort increases in psychopathology among young Americans, 1938–2007: A cross-sectional meta-analysis of the MMPI. *Clinical Psychology Review*, 30, 145–154.

Twenge, J.M., & Im, C. (2007). Changes in the need for social approval, 1958–2001. *Journal of Research in Personality*, *41*, 171–189.

Tyrell, J.B., & Baxter, J.D. (1981). Glucocorticoid therapy. In P. Felig, J.D. Baxter, A.E. Broadus, & L.A. Frohman (Eds), *Endocrinology and metabolism*. New York: McGraw-Hill.

Ünal, B., Critchley, J.A., Fiden, D., & Capewell, S. (2005). Life-years gained from modern cardiological treatments and population risk factor changes in England and Wales, 1981–2000. *American Journal of Public Health*, 95, 103–108.

Valentine, E.R. (1992). *Conceptual issues in psychology*. Hove: Psychology Press.

van Avermaet, E. (1996). Social influence in small groups. *Introduction to social psychology: A European perspective (2nd Edn)*. Oxford: Blackwell.

van Grootheest, D.S., Cath, D.C., Beekman, A.T., & Boomsma, D.I. (2005). Twin studies on obsessive-compulsive disorder: A review. *Twin Research and Human Genetics*, 8, 450–458.

Van Houtem, C.M.H.H., Laine, M.L., Boomsma, D.I., Ligthart, L., van Wijk, A.J., & De Jongh, A. (2013). A review and meta-analysis of the heritability of specific phobia subtypes and corresponding fears. *Journal of Anxiety Disorders*, 27, 379–388.

van IJzendoorn, M.H., & Kroonenberg, P.M. (1988). Cross-cultural patterns of attachment: A meta-analysis of the Strange Situation. *Child Development*, 59, 147–156.

van IJzendoorn, M.H., Schuengel, C., & Bakermans-Kranenburg, M.J. (1999). Disorganised attachment in early childhood: Meta-analysis of precursors, concomitants, and sequelae. *Development and Psychopathology*, *11*, 225–249.

Vaughn, B.E., & Waters, E. (1990). Attachment behaviour at home and in the laboratory: Q-sort observations and Strange Situation classifications of one-year-olds. *Child Development*, *61*, 1965–1973.

Vernet, J.-P., Vala, J., Amâncio, L., & Butera, F. (2009). Conscientisation of social cryptomnesia reduces hostile sexism and rejection of feminists. *Social Psychology*, 40, 129–132.

Viswesvaran, C., & Schmidt, F.L. (1992). A meta-analytic comparison of the effectiveness of smoking cessation methods. *Journal of Applied Psychology*, 77, 554–561.

Vogel, E.K., Woodman, G.E., & Luck, S.J. (2001). Storage of features, conjunctions, and objects in visual working memory. *Journal of Experimental Psychology: Human Perception and Performance*, 27, 92–114.

Vögele, C., Ehlers, A., Meyer, A.H., Frank, M., Hahlweg, K., & Margraf, J. (2010). Cognitive mediation of clinical improvement after intensive exposure therapy of agoraphobia and social phobia. *Depression and Anxiety, 27*, 294–301.

Vredeveldt, A., Hitch, G.J., & Baddeley, A.D. (2011). Eyeclosure helps memory by reducing cognitive load and enhancing visualization. *Memory & Cognition, 39*, 1253–1263.

Ward, J. (2010). *The student's guide to cognitive neuroscience (2nd Edn)*. Hove, UK: Psychology Press.

Wartner, U.G., Grossmann, K., Fremmer-Bombik, E., & Suess, G. (1994). Attachment patterns at age six in South Germany: Predictability from infancy and implications for preschool behaviour. *Child Development, 65*, 1014–1027.

Watson, J.B. (1913). Psychology as the behaviourist views it. *Psychological Review, 20*, 158–177.

Watson, J.B., & Rayner, R. (1920). Conditioned emotional reactions. *Journal of Experimental Psychology, 3*, 1–14.

Weeks, D., & James, J. (1995). *Eccentrics: A study of sanity and strangeness*. New York: Villiard.

Weinfield, N.S., Whaley, G.J.L., & Egeland, B. (2004). Continuity, discontinuity, and coherence in attachment from infancy to late adolescence: Sequelae of organisation and disorganisation. *Attachment and Human Development, 6*, 73–97.

Wells, A., Clark, D.M., Salkovskis, P., Ludgate, J., Hackmann, A., & Gelder, M. (1995). Social phobia: The role of in-situation safety behaviours in maintaining anxiety and negative beliefs. *Behavior Therapy, 26*, 153–161.

Westen, D. (1996). *Psychology: Mind, brain, and culture*. New York: Wiley.

Wever, R. (1979). *Circadian rhythms system of man: Results of experiments under temporal isolation*. New York: Springer.

Whyte, W.F. (1943). *Street corner society: The social structure of an Italian slum*. Chicago: University of Chicago Press.

Wickens, A. (2000). *Foundations of biopsychology*. Harlow, UK: Prentice Hall.

Wild, C., Davis, M.H., & Johnsrude, J.S. (2012). The perceptual clarity of speech modulates activity in primary auditory cortex: fMRI evidence of interactive processes in speech perception. *NeuroImage, 60*, 1490–1502.

Williams, J.M., & Warchal, J. (1981). The relationship between assertiveness, internal-external locus of control, and overt conformity. *Journal of Psychology, 109*, 93–96.

Willmes, K., & Poeck, K. (1993). To what extent can aphasic syndromes be localised? *Brain, 116*, 1527–1540.

Wilner, A., Reich, T., Robins, I., Fishman, R., & van Doren, T. (1976). Obsessive-compulsive neurosis. *Comprehensive Psychiatry, 17*, 527–539.

Wilson, G.T., & Davison, G.C. (1971). Processes of fear reduction in systematic desensitisation: Animal studies. *Psychological Bulletin, 76*, 1–14.

Wilson, K., Roe, B., & Wright, L. (1998). Telephone or face-to-face interviews? A decision made on the basis of a pilot study. *International Journal of Nursing Studies, 35*, 314–321.

Wilson, S., Brown, N., Mejia, C., & Lavori, P. (2002). Effects of interviewer characteristics on reported sexual behavior of California Latino couples. *Hispanic Journal of Behavioral Sciences, 24*(1), 38–62.

Wilson, S.R., & Spencer, R.C. (1990). Intense personal experiences–Subjective effects, interpretations, and after-effects. *Journal of Clinical Psychology, 46*, 565–573.

Wixted, J.T. (2004). The psychology and neuroscience of forgetting. *Annual Review of Psychology, 55*, 235–269.

Wolfson, A. (2005). "Trial to start for $200 million lawsuit over strip-search hoax", *Louisville Courier-Journal*, 2007-09-09. See http://www.usatoday.com/news/nation/2007-09-mcdonaldslawsuit_N.htm

Wolpe, J. (1958). *Psychotherapy by reciprocal inhibition*. Stanford, CA: Stanford University Press.

Wolpe, J. (1969). *The practice of behaviour therapy*. Oxford, UK: Pergamon Press.

Wood, W., Lundgren, S., Ouellette, J.A., Busceme, S., & Blackstone, T. (1994). Minority influence: A meta-analytic review of social influence processes. *Psychological Bulletin, 115*, 323–345.

Woodworth, R.S. (1938). *Experimental psychology*. London: Methuen.

Woollett, K., Spiers, H.J., & Maguire, E.A. (2009). Talent in the taxi: A model system for exploring expertise. *Philosophical Transactions of the Royal Society B: Biological Sciences, 364*, 1407–1416.

Wundt, W. (1874). *Grundzüge der Physiologischen Psychologie* [Principles of physiological psychology]. Leizpig: Engelmann.

Yegiyan, N.S., & Lang, A. (2010). Processing central and peripheral detail: How content arousal and emotional tone influence encoding. *Media Psychology, 13*, 77–79.

Young, S.D., Adelstein, B.D., & Ellis, S.R. (2007). Demand characteristics in assessing motion sickness in a virtual environment: Or does taking a motion sickness questionnaire make you sick? *IEEE Transactions on Visualization and Computer Graphics, 13*, 422–428.

Yuille, J.C., & Cutshall, J.L. (1986). A case study of eyewitness memory of a crime. *Journal of Applied Psychology, 71*, 291–301.

Zatorre, R.J. (2013). Predispositions and plasticity in music and speech learning: Neural correlates and implications. *Science, 342*, 585–589.

Zegoib, L.E., Arnold, S., & Forehand, R. (1975). An examination of observer effects in parent–child interactions. *Child Development, 46*, 509–512.

Zimbardo, P.G. (1971). The power and pathology of imprisonment. Congressional Record (Serial No. 15, 1971-10-25). Hearings before Subcommittee No. 3 of the Commitment on the Judiciary, House of Representatives, Ninety-Second Congress, *First Session on Corrections, Part II, Prisons, Prison Reform and Prisoner's Rights: California*. Washington, DC: U.S. Government Printing Office.

Zimbardo, P.G. (1989). *Quiet rage: The Stanford Prison Experiment video*. Stanford, CA: Stanford University.

Zimbardo, P.G. (2006). On rethinking the psychology of tyranny: The BBC prison study. *British Journal of Social Psychology, 45*, 47–53.

Illustration credits

Chapter 1

Page 4: MAKENBOLUO / Shutterstock.com; Page 13: lightpoet / Shutterstock.com.

Chapter 2

Page 19: Andrey Yurlov / Shutterstock.com; Page 22: JustASC / Shutterstock.com; Page 26: Debra James / Shutterstock.com; Page 32: Reproduced with permission of P.G. Zimbardo Inc.; Page 35: Image courtesy of the German Federal Archive; Page 36: From the film Obedience © 1968 by Stanley Milgram. Copyright © renewed 1991 by Alexandra Milgram and distributed by Penn State Media Sales. Permission granted by Alexandra Milgram; Page 41: Amawasri Pakdara / Shutterstock.com; Page 44: Konstantin Chagin / Shutterstock.com; Page 50: Image courtesy of the National Archives and Records Administration; Page 58: Photo by Warren K. Leffler; Page 63: © Everett Collection Historical / Alamy.

Chapter 3

Page 72: Rosli Othman / Shutterstock.com; Page 76: From Peterson and Peterson (1959). Copyright © American Psychological Association. Reproduced with permission; Page 77: Pressmaster / Shutterstock.com; Page 89: From Robbins et al. (1996). Copyright © 1996 by the Psychonomic Society, Inc. Reproduced with permission of Springer Science + Business Media; Page 89: Patryk Stanisz / Shutterstock.com; Page 91: From Klauer and Zhao (2004). Copyright © American Psychological Association. Reproduced with permission; Page 99: Antonio Guillem / Shutterstock.com; Page 103: Copyright © image100 / Corbis; Page 107: Copyright © Guy Cali / Corbis; Page 108: BruceParrott / Shutterstock.com; Page 111: © Jochen Tack / Alamy.

Chapter 4

Page 117: Shutterstock.com; Page 123: Liquorice Legs / Shutterstock.com; Page 126 Copyright © Science Photo Library; Page 128: Reproduced with kind permission of Harlow Primate Laboratory, University of Wisconsin; Page 132: Reproduced with kind permission of Harlow Primate Laboratory, University of Wisconsin; Page 133: Cristi Matei / Shutterstock.com; Pages 134 & 135: Photos courtesy of Michael W. Eysenck; Page 136: Shutterstock.com; Page 143: From Fraley and Spieker (2003). Copyright © American Psychological Association. Reproduced with permission; Page 149: Smailhodzic / Shutterstock.com; Page 154: Copyright © Bernard Bisson / Sygma / Corbis; Page 157: CandyBox Images / Shutterstock.com.

Chapter 5

Page 164: From http://psy.uniklinikum-leipzig.de/eng/geschi-e.htm; Page 169: © Bettmann / Corbis; Page 172: © Steve Allen / Brand X / Corbis; Page 175: homydesign / Shutterstock.com; Page 176: Reproduced with kind permission of Professor Albert Bandura; Page 179: lculig / Shutterstock.com; Page 182: Reprinted from Stevyers and Hemmer (2012), Copyright © 2012, with permission from Elsevier; Page 186: Shutterstock.com; Page 189: Science Photo Library; Page 192: Jan Kaliciak / Shutterstock.com; Page 193: Dolly / Shutterstock.com; Page 195: From Ward, J. (2010). *The student's guide to cognitive neuroscience, second edition* © 2010 Psychology Press; Page 198: Paul Matthew Photography / Shutterstock.com; Page 201: From http://en.wikipedia.org/wiki/File:Sigmund_Freud_LIFE.jpg; Page 210: From http://upload.wikimedia.org/wikipedia/commons/d/d3/Albert_Einstein_Head.jpg; Page 210: Shutterstock.com; Page 213: Adam Gregor / Shutterstock.com; Page 218: Norma Cornes / Shutterstock.com.

Chapter 6

Page 233: Paul Banton / Shutterstock.com; Page 235: Galina Barskaya / Shutterstock.com; Page 237 left and right>: Shutterstock.com; Page 240: Dorling Kindersley / Getty Images; Page 241: Natural History Museum, London / Science Photo Library; Page 245: From Gazzaniga, M.S. (2013). Shifting gears: Seeking new approaches for mind / brain mechanisms, *Annual Review of Psychology*, 64, 1–20. Republished with permission of Annual Reviews; Page 245: Geoff Tompkinson / Science Photo Library; Page 250: Courtesy University of Nottingham, Malaysia campus; Page 253: Copyright © Dr Robert Friedland / Science Photo Library; Page 257: Image Point Fr / Shutterstock.com.

Chapter 7

Page 266: © Reuters / Corbis; Page 267: godrick / Shutterstock.com; Page 270: © British News Service / Alamy; Page 282: Shutterstock.com; Page 285: Reproduced with the kind permission of Benjamin Harris, University of New Hampshire: Page 292: photobar / Shutterstock.com; Page 312: STILLFX / Shutterstock.com.

Chapter 8

Page 324: Courtesy USGS / Cascades Volcano Observatory; Page 331: Cristy / Shutterstock.com; Page 339: Robert Kneschke / Shutterstock.com; Page 342: Gemenacom / Shutterstock.com; Page 250: Copyright © Richard T. Nowitz / Corbis; Page 252: Lisa F. Young / Shutterstock.com; Page 361: Pavel L Photo and Video / Shutterstock.com; Page 373: sonya etchison / Shutterstock.com.

Appendix

Table 1: From Runyon, R. & Haber, A. (1976). *Fundamentals of behavioural statistics (3rd Edn)*. Reading, MA: McGraw Hill Inc. Reproduced with permission from McGraw Hill Inc.

Table 2: From Meddis, R. (1975). *Statistical handbook for non-statisticians*. London: McGraw-Hill, London. Reproduced with permission from McGraw Hill.

Table 3: From Clegg, F. (1983). *Simple statistics*. Cambridge: Cambridge University Press. Reproduced with permission from Cambridge University Press.

Cartoons by Sean Longcroft http://longcroft.net/

Index

Note: Page numbers for definitions of key terms are in **bold** type.